F. H. WILKERSON
69 BLAUVELT Rd.
NANUET — N.Y.

The Child in the Educative Process

McGraw-Hill Series in Education

HAROLD BENJAMIN, *Consulting Editor*

The Child in
the Educative Process

DANIEL A. PRESCOTT, Ed.D.

Director, Institute for Child Study
University of Maryland

McGRAW-HILL BOOK COMPANY, INC.

1957   New York   Toronto   London

THE CHILD IN THE EDUCATIVE PROCESS

IX
50770

To William T. Grant—

merchant, philanthropist, and friend

Preface

During the past sixteen years it has been my privilege to work directly with hundreds of small groups of teachers in their own schools. Each teacher in these groups was gathering information about some pupil in his class who interested him and presenting this information periodically to the group, and the group was working out ever-deepening interpretations of each child's motivations, behavior, adjustment problems, and developmental tasks. My role was that of consultant to each group, bringing them the scientific information they needed and guiding them in the processes they used in interpreting the data concerning each child.

These experiences have changed greatly my conceptions of the educative process and of the teacher's tasks in the classroom. They have forced me to accept the fact that children learn and cannot be "taught" in the usually accepted sense of that term. They have demonstrated the profound significance for individual children of the multitude of judgments which teachers must make every day as they interact with their pupils as individuals and in groups. They have shown me the tremendous complexity and interrelatedness of the factors which influence children's learning readinesses and perceptions and upon which the teacher's judgments must depend if they are to be sound judgments.

This book is an attempt to share with others some of the insights I have gained and a few samples of the experiences through which these insights came. It has four parts.

Part One shows that learning, development, and adjustment are individual matters which take place in a group context in which persons at home, other children at school, and the teacher all play important parts It demonstrates the extraordinary complexity of the teacher's task, sets forth a group of philosophical, social, and scientific assumptions upon which a sound understanding of the educative process must rest, and demonstrates the sensitiveness of the educative process to such matters as interpersonal relationships, mood and climate of the classroom, timing of disciplinary action, concept of self of individual children, and the management of emotional tensions. It concludes by describing the professional characteristics of the teacher who can be effective in carrying on the educative process in a room full of children.

Part Two analyzes the knowledge and skills a teacher must have to understand his pupils as individual, developing persons. It demonstrates various steps in a child-study program which staff members of the Institute for Child Study at the University of Maryland have found to be effective in developing these knowledges and skills in members of the educational profession. The case records are a way of sharing our experiences of children, too. They afford a sample of the cumulating experiences which gave rise to the ideas presented in Part One and so constitute a partial validation of these ideas. Each one of the hundreds of case studies that our consultants have participated in analyzing has turned out to be about a unique personality following his own idiomatic pattern of growth, learning, development, and adjustment.

It is precisely this uniqueness of individuals within a context of social alikeness that makes it necessary to apply scientific knowledge and the scientific method in making judgments about how to carry on the educative process. For uniqueness is the inevitable consequence of biological heredity, diverse innate patterns of growth, the unique accumulation of experiences that shape perceptions, qualitatively different emotional-adjustment problems, varying capacities and aptitudes, and the way each individual sees himself and his place in society and the universe.

But children and youth also seek to win belonging, to be like other people, and to see themselves as exemplifying what is most valued in their society and by those who love them. To stress either individual uniqueness or group standards without relating each to the other in a functional way is to distort the educative process and to prevent the healthy development of many children and youth. Hence the necessity for a careful understanding of each pupil as a person operating within a particular social setting. This sets a formidable professional task for every teacher. In this book I have tried to show how the appropriate use of scientific knowledge about human beings and of the scientific method of arriving at professional judgments can help school people accomplish this task.

Part Three contains a brief statement of a theoretical foundation for the explanation of human development, behavior, and adjustment which has proved usable and valuable to participants in our child-study program. No claim is made that this is the best, the only valid, or the only workable explanation of how individuals develop and of why they behave as they do. Probably none of our consultants working out of the Institute for Child Study would agree to all the statements in the form given. And as rapidly as new research findings become available, my own formulations change and will continue to change. This is the way of science.

School people need some such guiding and organizing formulation to permit them to analyze, understand, and guide the learning and behavior of their pupils. Without it, they become preoccupied with instructional content and materials and, in making judgments, leave out of consideration many factors that are potent in shaping readiness and behavior. A usable formulation simply has to include material from the biological, social, psychological, medical, and psychiatric sciences. I have tried to supply a usable formulation.

Part Four describes practical steps which various school systems are taking to implement the educative process as it was described in Part One. One of these steps is providing for the in-service professional growth of school personnel through participation in a systematic three-year program of child study. Frequently this is followed by "action research" through which the educational implications of new insights are discovered and applied. These implications cannot be stated for and used by school people who are not prepared to understand individual children in their group and social contexts.

I would not have anyone think that the ideas presented and the processes described in this book are uniquely the fruits of my own thinking and actions. From the early experimentation under the Commission on Teacher Education and at the University of Chicago, through the development and maturing of the child-study program at the Institute for Child Study at the University of Maryland, the work has been carried out by successive groups of cooperating persons. Ideas have been developed by the interaction of the members of these groups, and processes have been invented and tested in the same groups.

During these sixteen years, so many persons have been involved in the development of the ideas and processes described in this book that it is not possible to distinguish and acknowledge the specific contributions of many individuals. Dr. Caroline Tryon, Dr. Fritz Redl, and Miss Sally Kate Mims of the Greenville County, South Carolina, public schools were key persons in the initial experimentation. Dr. Madelaine Mershon, Miss Columbia Winn, and Dr. Virginia Hufstedler Love played vital roles during the second phase of our work, when we extended the experimentation into Texas, Louisiana, and Maryland. The Institute for Child Study was established at the University of Maryland in 1947, and it was here, through nine years of arduous group efforts by an exceptionally devoted staff, that the child-study program was matured operationally and tested by research. Every member of the Institute staff has made numerous and significant contributions. To each of them goes my admiration, my gratitude, and my acknowledgment of intellectual indebtedness.

Within two years of its establishment, the many tasks being undertaken by the Institute for Child Study became unreasonably heavy for its small initial staff. Fortunately, the Grant Foundation learned of our work, saw its immediate worth to members of the educational profession, appreciated its long-term value to the children and youth of the country, and came to our aid with a subvention. This help enabled us to add four persons to our staff immediately, to provide three or more generous fellowships a year for persons training to become consultants, and to employ a number of graduate assistants.

Now, in 1956–57, the Institute is carrying on a full program of graduate instruction leading to the master's and doctoral degrees. Well over forty thousand persons have completed three or more years of work in the child-study program for in-service teachers, and we are serving annually between four and five thousand members of the educational profession in ten states through our field program. We are also launching some long-term basic research in the field of human development and education. It is quite impossible adequately to express the appreciation of every staff member and fellow of the Institute and of the University administration for the generous support from the Grant Foundation that has made this rapid development possible. The subventions total more than $390,000 over a period of nine years, including generous help toward the preparation of this book.

All case records have been carefully disguised to prevent recognition of individuals and families. I am grateful to the teachers who gave permission for their materials to be used and regret that they must not be identified. I am grateful also to the publishers who have permitted quotation of copyright material. Acknowledgments are made in footnotes in each case.

I also wish to thank Dr. Madelaine Mershon, Dr. H. Gerthon Morgan, and Mrs. Annelise Boehmer Prescott for reading and constructively criticizing the manuscript.

This is not a book of final answers. It tells only what I feel I have learned through the years of exploring ways of making scientific knowledge about human beings available to and usable by members of the educational profession as they work with children. I hope that it will stimulate further and ever more fruitful action by others, designed gradually to change education from a completely empirical art to a social process that makes full use of scientific knowledge and of the scientific method. When this is accomplished, valuable human material no longer will be damaged accidentally or left undeveloped, but will be more adequately nurtured and stimulated by the educative process to full "self-realization" and socially responsible participation in the life of our nation.

DANIEL A. PRESCOTT

Contents

PART ONE

On the Educative Process

CHAPTER 1

The Teacher's Task

The Struggle for the Minds of Men

A world-wide battle is on to determine what kind of minds men shall have. It is now recognized that men's attitudes and behavior are not determined by instinct, but by what they have felt and learned through their accumulating experiences. For this reason, groups and governments are seeking to control the experiences of children and youth as a means of evoking the feelings, thoughts, and actions they desire.

There are those who want men's minds to be acquiescent to the voice of authority as to the meaning of life and the goals of action, subservient to the directives of a ruling group as to their day-to-day functioning, adjusted to hard work, privations, and suffering, yet eager to serve, to build, to die, if needful, for the achievement of goals they have had no part in formulating. Considerable success is being achieved by groups of this persuasion. Coerced by fear and hatred, limited in their access to information, overwhelmed by reiterated affirmations and slogans, encouraged by the direct experience of modest evidences of progress, deluded by falsehoods of tremendous magnitude, and stirred by a new sense of the power that lies in the weight of their numbers, men and women are developing the desired minds en masse. What these totalitarian peoples, armed with modern scientific knowledge and with technical skills for exploiting the material world, may do at the behest of their masters is a legitimate cause for anxiety.

There are others who want the minds of men to be curious, analytical, and questioning and their goals determined partially by themselves as individuals and partially by group processes in which all have an opportunity to participate. According to their view, loyalties are voluntarily accorded, not coerced, and codes of conduct are based upon an appreciative valuing of shared effort and mutual concern for one another's development and happiness. Desirable actions are conceived to be "self-actualizing" and at the same time nonexploitive, socially responsible, and socially

3

valuable. The goal of the envisioned society is to give every individual the maximum opportunity for self-realization through self-chosen and self-regulated participation in the life of the larger community of human beings—participation characterized by consideration of the feelings and interests of others and promotion of the common good as well as of the self-realizing goals. This is the democratic ideal, which seems to accord with the natural dynamic of living things to realize their potentials through group action.

Obviously the educative process by which an individual will learn to function in this kind of world is fundamentally different from that required under totalitarian systems. For human minds and behavior *can be controlled from without; or human minds can participate in shaping their own behavior and destiny.* But the two educative processes are mutually exclusive. If the individual is coerced and driven he will expect to coerce and drive others. But if the individual is encouraged by experience from his early days actively to discriminate for himself between behavior alternatives on the basis of valid information and social values, then this will seem to him to be the natural way to decide things. If he lives among individuals who value and are considerate of him and of others, as well as of themselves, then he will regard it as right and proper to value and to be considerate of others. In other words, each child gradually discovers his own "self-role" and "self-significance." But what he discovers is determined by what he experiences in his school, home, and community.

The Influence of Leaders

Kurt Lewin and his associates were among the first to investigate the effects of different leader roles upon the mentality and actions of individuals in groups and upon the "atmospheres" of groups.[1] They distinguished autocratic, laissez-faire, and democratic patterns of group leadership and group atmosphere and set up experimental situations in which each of these patterns was employed. Laissez-faire leadership resulted in the disorganization of the group. No worthwhile group activity ensued, and the individuals found little pleasure or value in what went on when they were together. Autocratic leadership, in contrast, proved quite effective in getting things done. But when the leader was absent, the members of the group did not hold to a plan of action, nor did they develop any effective alternative action. Rather, they turned against each other and began to hurt or humiliate individuals. In other words, without their leader,

---

[1] Lewin, K., Lippitt, R., and White, R. K. Patterns of Aggressive Behavior in Experimentally Created Social Climates. *J. Soc. Psychol.*, 1939, **10**, 271–299. Lippitt, R. An Experimental Study of the Effect of Democratic and Authoritarian Group Atmospheres. *Univ. of Iowa Stud. Child Welf.*, 1940, **16**, No. 3.

they were unhappy and frustrated at not moving ahead and took it out on each other. They had learned only to be dependent on the leader.

The groups under democratic leadership turned out quite differently. The leader had a real role as a catalyst, but the group actually planned, made decisions, and carried them out. When the leader was absent, the members of the group proved able to carry on with what they were doing, to formulate additional plans, and to realize these plans. They enjoyed what they did, and the morale remained excellent.

In a small way this experiment demonstrates how the minds of men are formed by their experiences. It implies that the ways in which teachers work with children in the classroom will help determine the kinds of people the children become.

THE INTERACTION OF TEACHERS AND PUPILS

H. H. Anderson and his associates [2] have carried on a very interesting and valuable series of investigations of the interaction between teachers and children in the classroom. Carefully trained observers noted and evaluated, on a time-sample basis, every interaction between the teacher and the group and between the teacher and every pupil in succession. Each interaction was evaluated as "dominative" or "socially integrative." Dominative interactions were contacts in which the child was directed to act or feel or think according to the teacher's wishes. Socially integrative interactions were contacts in which the teacher was permissive or, more often, facilitative of what the child himself was seeking to know, do, or feel. Anderson found that, although all teachers interact with individual children in both ways, most teacher contacts are dominative rather than facilitative. He also found that some teachers tend to be predominantly directive and dominating, whereas others tend to be predominantly permissive and facilitative.

But one of the most amazing and thought-provoking findings of Anderson's researches concerned the tremendous number of individual interactions per hour between the teacher and her pupils. For example, his observers spent ninety-six hours in the classroom of Teacher C and observed that during this period she averaged 321.8 contacts per hour with individual children. This meant 5.36 contacts per minute. Teacher D made

[2] Anderson, H. H., and Brewer, J. E. Effects of Teachers' Dominative and Integrative Contacts on Children's Classroom Behavior. *Appl. Psychol. Monogr.*, 1946, No. 8. Also, Dominative and Socially Integrative Behavior of Kindergarten Teachers. *Appl. Psychol. Monogr.*, 1945, No. 6. Anderson, H. H. The Measurement of Domination and of Socially Integrative Behavior in Teachers' Contacts with Children. *Child Developm.*, 1939, 10, 73–89. Also, Domination and Social Integration in the Behavior of Kindergarten Children and Teachers. *Genet. Psychol. Monogr.*, 1939, 21, 287–385.

even more contacts with her pupils. In the same amount of time she averaged 398.4 contacts per hour with individual children, or 6.64 contacts per minute.[3] In addition, there were contacts with the group as a whole. The groups Anderson studied ranged from the first through the sixth grades and included classes studying the full range of elementary school subjects. In all groups and in all subjects the number of contacts per minute was roughly comparable. At first these figures seem almost incredible, but they have been validated by very careful scientific procedures and are not open to question.

Teachers interact with children an enormous number of times every hour of the day, no matter what they are teaching or what the grade level may be. Furthermore, every one of these interactions is evaluative, requiring a judgment and a feeling about the situation. It is no wonder that teaching is so fatiguing. The wonder is that so many of the judgments teachers make are good judgments that promote the learning, development, and adjustment of children and youth.

The Significance of Teachers' Decisions

Is there really an educative process, or is there merely random learning by children in a sort of custodial institution that we call the school? If there is really an educative process, its moments of functional operation must be when teachers and pupils interact, when the pupils interact among themselves, and when the individual pupils feel and think and act as a result of these contacts.

During any single school day a teacher obviously must make hundreds of decisions—decisions about each individual pupil, about the class as a whole, and about each of the subgroups that children form among themselves or that the teacher forms for one purpose or another. These accumulating decisions create the conditions under which the pupils live and learn at school. For example, they determine the freedom or restriction of movement, of speech, of access to materials, of spontaneous inquiries or comments, of choice of experiences. They profoundly influence the kinds of relationships the children are able to establish and maintain with adults in the school and with each other in the classroom, on the playground, and everywhere about the school. These decisions often determine the actual learning experiences to which the children are exposed, the content upon which attention is focused, and the food for mental, social, and spiritual growth that is offered each child. They determine the aspects of life and the world with which the pupils are brought into contact, and they evoke or fail to evoke the various steps of the reasoning process and

[3] Anderson, H. H., Brewer, J. E., and Reed, M. F. Studies of Teachers' Classroom Personalities, III, *Appl. Psychol. Monogr.*, 1946, No. 11, p. 149.

encourage or discourage curiosity and imagination. They promote certain codes of conduct and imply the validity of certain attitudes and values for living in our times and in our society. These judgments permit some adjustment processes and mechanisms to operate and discourage others. They emphasize certain meanings as valid and condemn others as untrue and unacceptable. In short, *the multitudinous daily decisions made by teachers are the fundamental bases of the educative process in our schools.*

We rightly have a good deal of confidence in the ability of our teachers to make these professional decisions, for, in the main, the outcomes of the educative process are good. Yet teachers themselves often are much worried as to whether their decisions have been the best possible ones. They are acutely aware of momentary errors of judgment with every child and with every group. Sometimes they are disturbed by obvious long-term mistakes with certain individuals who become delinquent, maladjusted, or hopeless failures. To what extent and by what means can these decisions be improved? Can the sciences that study human beings give significant help to members of the teaching profession in the momentous struggle for the minds of men?

THE BASES OF CLASSROOM DECISIONS

Cultural Factors

Teachers make most of their classroom decisions in an extensive context of tradition, goals, pressures, and experience. For example, religious and philosophical assumptions—beliefs about the meaning and goals of life and about good and evil—profoundly affect every teacher's reactions to what each child does and says. These beliefs are a part of the social tradition which each teacher has internalized.

Teachers have internalized more than this, however. Each teacher carries the cultural background of his or her sex, region of the country, ethnic group, social class, and generation within the larger national and racial culture. This cultural background implies certain attitudes toward children, certain goals for children to accomplish and roles for them to play, certain approved methods of motivating and disciplining the children, and a certain expectancy regarding the teacher's own status and roles in the community.

Furthermore, these are times of very rapid social and cultural change not only in our own country but throughout the world. Every teacher must take a stand with regard to these controversial questions. If he cares, one way or the other, about the changes occurring in the world, he is sure to try to slow up or to speed up particular changes by his ways of dealing with the ideas and incidents that present themselves in the classroom.

Rigidity or tolerance, objectivity or partisanship, looking for facts or admitting only selected facts to consciousness are attitudes and mental habits that are characteristic of all human beings, including classroom teachers. It is obvious and inevitable that a teacher's religion, social philosophy, cultural background, philosophy of education, attitudes toward social controversies, and habits of thinking when dealing with debatable matters will influence his decisions in the classroom.

Professional Factors

Because teachers are members of a profession, a whole series of professional considerations enter into their classroom decisions. There is the course of study; there is knowledge of how the principal, the supervisor, the superintendent of schools, the school board, and one's fellow teachers want the class conducted and the subject matter presented. Many parents also express opinions and attitudes, and the children themselves show by word and act how they feel about school and what they wish it were like. These factors constitute additional pressures upon the teacher, which influence his judgments to a considerable degree.

Each teacher also carries with him memories of his own school days and unexpressed vows to try to be like certain teachers he once had and never to be like certain others. Then there are memories of ideas and attitudes expressed in professional courses or professional meetings, in professional books, in demonstration lessons, or in professional committees. These professional concepts and attitudes are a part of the mass of factors that influence the teacher's perception of classroom situations. Especially, there is the teacher's own background of responsible working experience in the classroom. Actual experience is very convincing. Certain things have worked, certain things have failed, others have stirred up crises, and still others have seemed too theoretical or nebulous ever to be really worth trying.

For all these reasons, current educational practice has a tremendous momentum. It tends to persist in its various methods and materials because these patterns have worked more-or-less well, have prevented disturbance, and have the sanction of tradition expressed through flesh-and-blood people. The professional factors that influence a teacher's classroom decisions and judgments, then, are pressures from the course of study and from a whole hierarchy of educational authorities and colleagues, professional training and study, and individual professional experience.

Scientific Factors

The teacher's classroom judgments are also influenced by another set of factors: his concepts of how children grow and learn, his knowledge of the circumstances that govern each child's life, his estimate of each child's motivation and needs, and his ideas of the structure and dynamics of the class group as a whole. Unfortunately, one finds great weaknesses in these areas.

Today there exists a large body of scientific knowledge about human growth, learning, emotions, and behavior, but most teachers obviously have had only limited access to it. Clinical psychologists and guidance experts have made clear the scope and nature of the information that a person must have about a particular child or youth in order to be able to understand him, but the cumulative records of most public school systems simply do not contain this information and teachers generally have not been trained to secure it. A valid interpretation of a child's motivation, needs, developmental tasks, and adjustment problems must be arrived at by using the scientific method of reasoning, which includes safeguards against invalid and inadequate data, biased conclusions, and oversimplified interpretations. However, most teachers have never been trained and habituated to use the scientific method of reasoning to the point where they are self-disciplined in these mental processes. For these reasons, mistaken interpretations of children's motivations and needs are constantly being made.

Teachers also have been misled, unintentionally, in their thinking about *groups* of children. They have been given so-called "homogeneous groups," and naturally enough they have concluded that the children in these groups were more or less alike and could all be taught and guided by the same techniques; but this has not proved to be true. More recently teachers have been taught to give sociometric tests and to make sociograms, only to discover that these valuable data alone do not afford them an understanding of the dynamics of the group or of the roles played by individuals in the group.

Perhaps the foregoing paragraphs explain why Anderson found teachers making many more dominative and directive interactions with children than facilitative and socially integrative ones. Lacking scientific knowledge, data about individuals and groups, and self-discipline in the scientific processes of diagnosis, teachers have not been able to understand their pupils. They have, therefore, very naturally fallen back upon their knowledge of subject matter, of classroom teaching methods, and of social and educational traditions, and upon their personal ideals as the bases of their decisions as to what to expect and demand of their pupils.

This book represents an effort to strengthen the third angle of the triangle of factors that are the bases for the teacher's decisions when interacting with his pupils, that is, when carrying on the educative process. It reports conclusions reached and describes procedures worked out through sixteen years of experimentation with ways of helping teachers to understand their pupils more adequately on the basis of the findings of scientific research.

CHILDREN AS THEY ARE

Theoretical discussions like that above communicate meaning only in a limited degree. They are bound to awaken widely different associations in the minds of different readers, many of them quite far afield from the ideas in the mind of the writer. Consequently, it is necessary repeatedly to come back to concrete situations and to operating motivations in order that we may all have the same considerations in mind with which to think. Accordingly, a series of anecdotes and materials about specific children in specific school situations follows. They have been selected almost at random from some case records made by teachers in the child-study program at the Institute for Child Study at the University of Maryland. They should be read with the following questions in mind: What *would I* have done or said if I had been the teacher in this situation? Why *should I* have done or said this in this situation? What would my reasons have been? Would the reasons that influenced my decision have been really adequate to justify this decision? What else would have helped me to be sure of my decision or to arrive at a better one?

THE CASE OF JANE

JANE, 12 years old, 6th grade

Nov. 29, 12:30 P.M.   The children were getting ready to go out on the playground. Jane waited and walked out with me. When we got to the playground Jane put both arms around me and rubbed her chin against me. I said, "Jane, why don't you play with the other children?" Jane answered, "I only like to play with Rolf, Billy, and Ann, or Wally and Francie." (All these children are her neighbors and all are under six years old.)

FEB. 4, 2:13 P.M.   I asked the "Singing Wheels" group to get into their circle. Some of the children said, "Jane won't come into our reading group." I asked Jane to get her book. She said, "I'll get my book but I won't read." She joined the group, but I didn't ask her to read because I was afraid she would refuse.

VALENTINE'S DAY, FEB. 14, 2:00 P.M.   Jane gave me a Valentine lollipop for my son. Some of the children brought in refreshments. Jane helped serve them quietly and efficiently. Jane wrote the following story today:

THE FRIENDLY VALENTINE

Once there was two valentines named friendly valentine and lonely valentine and they lived together. And friendly valentine when valentine day came around she was send to a little boy. And lonely valentine was send back to the factory. And friendly valentine was being shown to everybody while lonely valentine was threw in the back of the room. And there was another valentine with him and they made a pair and they said they wasn't going to be lonely anymore. And one night a little girl came to by a valentine and right a way she fell in love with them and her mother did to and they boght them and lonely valentine wasn't lonely anymore.

What would I have done on the playground on November 29 when Jane refused to play with her classmates and made an active show of affection toward me? When I ask this of myself I am forced to consider other questions: Should a teacher be concerned about a pupil's play life as well as with his classroom learning? Why should a twelve-year-old want to play only with six-year-olds? Or was this talk only an evasion, because Jane really wanted most to stay close to the teacher? Was Jane dodging feeling like a social outcast among her classmates? Or was she seeking attention or love from her teacher? Or were both factors operating?

The February 4 anecdote also is very thought-provoking. The teacher made Jane get her book and come to the group but made no response to Jane's defiant, "I'll get my book, but I won't read." If the teacher let Jane "get away" with this defiance and task avoidance, what would happen to class "discipline" and to discipline of Jane in particular? Or did the teacher sense that Jane had a genuine and adequate reason for not reading at that time? Did Jane get away with something, or was she incapable of responding in another way because of emotional factors in operation at this time? Did the teacher's action cause her to be involved functionally in the reading lesson? Perhaps she learned more by listening and following the others than she would have learned if a scene had been created over her defiance. Perhaps the situation helped Jane to feel accepted as a person by her teacher and as a group member by her classmates. If so, was this more important at that moment than disciplining her, making an example of her for the other children, or forcing her to attack the problem of improving her reading skills? What purposes or goals of education should guide a teacher in a situation like this? What depth of understanding of the child is needful to make a sound decision?

Finally, what is to be made of the Valentine's Day composition? It certainly reveals a shocking lack of language competency for a twelve-year-old girl in the sixth grade. Is this due to lack of intelligence on the child's part, or to laxness on the part of this and other teachers? Or is it due to still other factors? What should I know about this child in order to decide what to do about these terrible mistakes with language? Whatever would make a child choose a topic like this for a Valentine's Day composition? The title is "Friendly Valentine," but the story is really about Lonely Valentine. Everything finally came out all right for Lonely Valentine. Should this composition be treated as psychological projective material rather than as a class exercise in composition? Has Jane revealed a deep feeling of insecurity, a basic core of longing for love, in this writing? If so, what is the responsibility of the school, of the teacher specifically, toward Jane? How would I have dealt with Jane in the light of this composition?

For a conscientious person, such decisions as those Jane's teacher had to make about her from day to day must have been quite disturbing. How could one *know* with any satisfying certainty what would be the best thing for Jane?

THE CASE OF RODNEY

RODNEY, 14 years old, height 6 feet, 1 inch, weight 169 pounds, 10th Grade.

SEPT. 4   Today at 2:30 I was standing in the hall while classes were changing. Ted was asking me about the story we had read in literature. At that moment Rodney was approaching us; he passed slowly and commented to me as he went by, "Miss Neal, you'd better watch these older students who have returned to finish school; they'll do anything for a grade." By that time Rodney was in his room, but Ted had turned red in the face and replied, "That boy is as despicable as my brother Pete."

SEPT. 10   I was grading some papers tonight, and when I got to Rodney's paper I found that he had defined a matador as a "bull slinger."

SEPT. 12   The bell had rung for classes to reconvene after lunch. Three of the high school girls, Alice, Janet, and Norah, were ascending the steps. Rodney was following, and I was following Rodney. I did did not hear one sound from any of the group, but, as I watched, Rodney proceeded to flip Alice across the posterior. Immediately Alice yelled, "Rodney, don't ever let me see you do that again or I'll slap your face until it blisters." Rodney laughingly replied, "Oh, what did I do? Don't tell me you haven't had that happen before."

OCT. 14   The mountains encircling this area have been on fire for several days. At first no one seemed alarmed, but forest rangers could not combat the blazes, so they appealed for help. Employees of the different companies were fighting the fires. Then, today, Explorer Scouts were asked to help, and seven boys left my English class. Rodney alone remained with 14 girls. He, at this time, had his head on the desk. He raised it slightly when I asked, "Aren't you an Explorer Scout, Rodney?" and answered, "Yeah, but fighting fire is too much like work."

Nov. 8   Tonight was the Homecoming Game for us. It was really a hot contest, because it was being played between us and the neighboring school. We were behind 13 to 0.

I noticed a long, lanky fellow jump from the wall around the stands to the bench of the cheerleaders. It was Rodney. He grabbed the megaphone and yelled, "Give the old fight yell, and yell it."

Rodney kept the megaphone to his mouth and used the right arm in a beating time motion as he spelled:

F   I   G   H   T
F   I   G   H   T
F   I   G   H   T
Fight, Fight, Fight

At the end of the last "Fight" he gave forth with a big scream.

From here Rodney left for the concession stand, where I lost him in the crowd.

Nov. 10   It just dawned on me today when I saw Doris, one of the cheerleaders, that I would mention Rodney's cheer leading at the game.

So I said, "Doris, I believe Rodney would make you a good yell leader." Doris replied, rather unconcernedly, "Maybe he would; he's *too* lazy to play football."

The *too* was emphasized; so I decided not to press the issue any farther.

JAN. 16   Early this morning during our speech class, I suggested that we use some resources from our own community in lecturing to us about the importance of speech. Rodney was in the group, and he immediately asked, "Miss Neal, just whom would you suggest?"

I replied, "I think Mr. W would be able to give us some valuable information."

Rodney laughed and said, "Huh! He doesn't know as much as I do. He's supposed to have a degree in electrical engineering, and I know more about electricity now than he'll ever know."

"Let's not be so critical," I said.

Rodney still insisted, "That's not being critical; that's being truthful."

JAN. 20   Mrs. D is substituting for Mr. Q, who has entered the Air Corps. She came to me today and stated, "I have a problem, and I think maybe you can help me solve it."

I assured her that I'd try; so here was the problem: Mrs. D had given an exam in history, and all the children had made passing scores but Rodney and A. However, Mrs. D said the crisis arose when she found a note attached to Rodney's paper saying: "Mrs. D, you don't know how to give a test; I suggest you see Miss Neal for assistance."

I was embarrassed, but I immediately said, "To me that's a problem that only you and Rodney can solve."

Mrs. D finally decided that she didn't plan to be at school but a day or so and she thought she would ignore it.

FEB. 2   I was greeted in my first-period class this morning by Rodney.
He opened the door just slightly and said, "Miss Neal, may I speak to
you?" Without moving from my desk where I was checking the roll,
I said, "Yes, Rodney, come on in."

He added, "I'd rather speak to you privately."

I walked to the hallway and said, "What is it you want?"

Rodney began to comment, somewhat stumbling over his words,
"Miss Neal, I saw X School's debate coach yesterday, and I arranged
to go debate them tomorrow. I think we need the practice, don't
you?"

Although I was a bit astonished at his making the arrangements, I
added, "Yes, I do agree that you need some practice."

Rodney began to smile and said, "You aren't mad, are you, Miss
Neal?"

I smiled and said, "No."

Then quickly Rodney asked, "When can you meet with us de-
baters?"

I told him my best time would be after school. With this statement he left.

Rodney was very young for his grade and very large in size for his age.
Ted was back finishing school after his military service and consequently
was quite old for the grade. In the September 4 anecdote, was Rodney
expressing hostility or only trying to joke? Was he, in an immature way,
trying to attract attention from the teacher or from Ted? Or was he expressing a basic disrespect for and to Ted? Does the teacher have a role
in such a situation? Should or could she have tried to help Rodney in a
conference after such an episode? If so, what would she have said to him?

Were the September 10 and September 12 episodes merely adolescent
exuberance and fun making? Or were they evidence of "freshness," im-
pudence, and smart-aleckiness? Should they have been noticed or ignored? Should a teacher monitor and repress such spontaneous expressions
in youth?

Was Rodney afraid to go fire fighting on October 14? Did he lack civic
spirit? Has he as yet not learned to endure physical fatigue and discomfort
in order to carry out a worthwhile activity as a part of a group? If so,
does the school have a function in relation to such a character inadequacy? If I had been Rodney's teacher, would I have discussed this with
Rodney or not? If so, what would I have said?

Was Rodney's spontaneous cheer leading on November 8 a constructive
expression of school spirit or a bid for the limelight? Did Doris on November 10 express the attitude of most of his peers toward Rodney? Has
Rodney ever thought of this? Should the teacher be concerned about it?
Could anything constructive be done to help Rodney? By whom? Who
should initiate it?

Is it possible that Rodney does actually know more about electricity than Mr. W, who has a degree in electrical engineering? Such things sometimes happen, and in this case it might be true. If so, is Rodney right that Mr. W has nothing of significance to say to the group about the importance of public speaking? Supposing that Rodney does have as keen a sense of the importance of public speaking as Mr. W, should the latter still be brought in to address the class? Or should Rodney be substituted? If Rodney's ideas are better, but if, in the teacher's opinion, the class would not accept them, is there a way that Rodney could be prepared to make his own contribution to the group later?

The anecdote of January 20 is only one of a series in which Rodney criticized and humiliated his teachers or disturbed their work in class. In one case he was suspended for several days for walking out of a class after a verbal clash with the teacher. Actually, most of his criticisms were justified, but indiscreet, ill-timed, humiliating, and disruptive. Is he simply too smart for his school? Should he be sent instead to a private school that caters only to students with high IQs? Are his capacities being wasted and left undeveloped in this school? Or is he an insufferable egotist who needs to be taken down a peg? Does he need discipline, admonition, the challenge of more difficult tasks, placement only with gifted teachers, the friendship of wise adults, or more companionship with his father?

Miss Neal displayed great poise and wisdom on February 2 when Rodney announced that he had made a date for a practice debate with another school without consulting her. This might be regarded as intelligent initiative on his part or as a failure to understand his place in the social scheme of things. At any rate, the debating team won its regional competition and then progressed into the fourth round of the state debate tournament. Rodney achieved the highest rating in the state on discussion ability and won $10 and a gold pin. He was also elected president of the state high school speech association, made up of over five hundred speech contestants. Miss Neal said, "His acceptance speech was actually a work of art, from my viewpoint," and one of the girls on his team said, "Oh, Miss Neal, aren't you proud of Rodney? He's just the smartest and most handsome boy in the entire group!"

Does this mean that all is now well with Rodney? Or does it mean that Rodney is in more danger than ever of becoming maladjusted and a misfit? Will the less-gifted teachers simply have to suffer with this "big mind" for another two years, while he brings more and more honors to the school? Or have his teachers a special educational task to perform in getting him ready for college? He will be able to pass his college-entrance exams without help from any of them. Is that enough, or does the school have additional obligations and goals with regard to Rodney? It is very easy to say, "Yes, the school should teach him modesty so that

he can enjoy good relationships with his peers." But how would a teacher
go about helping Rodney toward this goal?

THE CASE OF CHESTER

CHESTER, 11 years old, 6th Grade.

Oct. 13   Today when we got into the room from lunch I missed
Chester. None of the children knew where he was. In about five minutes he came in to say that Miss T, the principal, wanted him to do a
job for her. When I asked him the nature of the job he was very
indefinite. I suspected something, so I said, "Let's find out what it is."
He hesitated, but went along. He had his head down when I looked
back.

The principal gave this account. Chester had stopped in her office
to see what she was doing and to chat. She had told him to go along
to his room, but he had stopped long enough to ask if she had a job
for him. She had told him, "Not at the present time." With that he
had left the office. When she finished telling me what had happened,
she turned to Chester to say, "When I need you for a job I will come
to your room to check with Miss C about the work."

On the way back to the classroom Chester walked down the hall
beside me as though he had done nothing. It hadn't seemed to register
with him that he had, for he chatted quite freely.

Oct. 17   The children in our district work in workbooks that are at
the grade level where they are placed, that are below this grade level,
or that are above it, according to the capacity of the individual. Chester
was working in fifth-grade arithmetic and spelling workbooks. He has
asked me several times to let him use sixth-grade workbooks, but I
have hesitated because I was not sure he was ready for them. Today
he approached me with a proposition. "Miss C, if you will let me try
sixth-grade workbooks, I will work hard. You help me with them here,
and Mother will help me with the fifth-grade ones at home." I looked
at him with a smile. He said, "Mother told me that she would." I
had read in the cumulative record that his mother helped him at home,
so I said, "All right, we will try." Then I asked, "How will you get
the books? Your fee money has been used for fifth-grade ones." He
answered, "I'll sell doughnuts to pay for them." (A local doughnut
company has worked out a plan whereby the children can buy doughnuts at wholesale price and sell them at retail and so make themselves
a profit.)

Nov. 19   Chester had played around all morning and had not done
his work (reading). When playtime came, I said, "Chester, you have
had your play. Now you must work while the others play." The children went to the playground, and on my way there I stopped by the
office. When I reached the playground, there was Chester playing
football as hard as any of them. I thought, "You are as slick as an
eel. You can be in one place, and before an eye can be batted you
are in another." I told him that he would have to go in. He kicked a
rock and muttered something. I just looked at him and waited. He
went behind a bush and threw down something. Again I waited and

soon he came out. I took his hand and started to the room with him. All the time he muttered. I went in with him, saw that he started work, and left. When we came in he had finished.

JAN. 12   Chester wrote this story today.

MY FAMILY

There are five of us. My brother, Bill, has blonde hair and blue eyes. He is nine years old and in the fourth grade. He isn't as old as I am but he is lots bigger. He is taller and weighs more. My sister's name is Sally. She is 13 years old and in the seventh grade. She has brown hair and blue eyes. Mother has brown hair and blue eyes. She is 33 years old and daddy is 33 too. He has red hair and blue eyes. My hair is red like his. He said that he was little like me when he was a boy. He said that when he did start to grow he really grew. Mother says that I may do like daddy did.

On October 13 Chester told his teacher a lie. At any rate, he said that the principal, Miss T, wanted him to do a job for her, when actually she had said no such thing. Was Chester trying to avoid something in his own classroom? Or did he need the psychological warmth that came to him through being with Miss T? Or did he simply want attention? Or was he testing the limits of what would be permitted by his teacher and the principal? What should Chester have felt as he walked down the hall with his teacher after being shown up? What would I as his teacher have wanted him to feel? What would I have wanted him to learn from the episode, and how would I have gone about getting it across to him? Should the school take a moralistic or a psychological view of this episode, or just ignore it, since he didn't get away with it? Or should one look for a deeper significance? Should it start the teacher thinking about Chester and trying to understand his motivation?

Would I have consented to let Chester start working in sixth-grade arithmetic and spelling workbooks before he had finished the fifth-grade ones, as he suggested on October 17? Should one have a rule about such things? Was he really interested in doing the work, or did he merely want to be working in the same books as some of his friends whom he admired? Or did he want to be able to report to his mother something that he thought would please her and win praise for himself? Did he want to prove to his teacher that he was more competent than she believed him to be? Or did he need to prove to himself that he could do this more advanced work? Was his motivation a combination of these desires? On what bases would I have decided what was best for him?

The November 19 episode showed how hard it was for Chester to get down to work on something that he could not do well, for reading was his weak subject. Without constant supervision and firmness Chester simply would not do his reading. What would I decide, then, was most developmental for Chester? Would I simply continue to check up on him, or would I punish him? Both have been tried. Must he be constantly supervised, or can he become self-activating once he gets pleasure from accomplishment, praise for progress, and free time to do more things that he actively wants to do? Or are there perhaps special reasons for his difficulties with reading that might be unearthed and dealt with?

Chester's composition on "My Family" affords some insights into things that are bothering him. It is completely descriptive except in two places, when he reveals his preoccupation with his own extremely small stature. His brother has outstripped him in growth, and this has set him to wondering about his own final size and adequacy. His dad is giving him some reassurance and hope. Are things like this important for a teacher to know? How would such knowledge influence the teacher's feelings towards Chester? How would they influence the decisions to be made about him in the classroom?

THE CASE OF JOHN

JOHN ANDERSON, 11 years old, 5th Grade.

SEPT. 24   John was late. . . .

SEPT. 25   John was late again. The boys overslept. . . .

OCT. 6   John returned to school after his absence on October 3 and the morning of October 6. . . .

OCT. 7   John came to school late. . . .

OCT. 10   The three teachers (regular teacher and two student teachers) were having a conference when, at approximately 3:20 P.M., John entered the room. We greeted him, and then I asked him what it was that he wanted.

"I don't want to see you about anything. I just didn't feel like going home yet. I thought I'd like to come back and sit awhile."

"You are welcome."

He walked around, looked at bulletin boards a few minutes, then he sat down. He made no effort to engage in any more conversation. Suddenly he rose, said good-by and left.

OCT. 14   During the social studies period John was absorbed in reading *All Sails Set* by Sperry. This is a story of clipper ships, and clipper ships are the particular things that John is especially interested in. During the group discussion, led by the group chairman, John did not participate. When he was asked by the chairman what information he had to share with the group, he refused to give any information. Near the end of the group's work for the day, John came over to me.

"Mrs. S, I would like to leave the group I am working in. I don't want to stay in this group."

"John, aren't you interested in sea transportation?"

"Oh yes, I am really interested. That book I am reading is great."

"Then what makes you stop wanting to work on clipper ships?"

"I don't want to stop. I'd just rather do my work alone."

"Is there any reason you have for preferring to work alone?"

"The children don't like me. They are mean to me. They say I smell."

FEB. 24 During social studies discussion this morning John seemed not to be listening at all. He made several contributions but each time his contribution had no bearing whatever on the topic under discussion. Finally Mr. S, the student teacher, said, "What's the matter, John? You don't seem to be listening very carefully today."

John gave a little laugh and answered, "I know. It's because I have worries today." . . . Mr. S went on with the lesson.

Later . . . I walked over and said, "John, what are you worried about?"

"I have lots of worries."

"What are they? Perhaps I can help with some of them."

"I lost my safety-patrol belt . . ."

"Is that your only worry?"

"No, I'm worried about my birthday."

"I wouldn't worry about birthdays. We all have them. . . ."

"Sunday is my birthday and I am wondering if I will have a party."

"Do you usually have a party on your birthday?"

"No. I've never had a party, but my mother says she will get me a present. Maybe I'll get a dog."

FEB. 25 ". . . I'm going to have a birthday party with my brother. His birthday is the 16th and so I have to wait to have a party with him."

"That will be nice. Will you have other boys in for the party?"

"Well, no, my father says we can't bring anyone in. You know— things at home [he hesitated]—well, we just can't bring anybody in."

MONDAY, MAR. 2 John was absent this morning. He came this afternoon—with no note of excuse. He handed me a brown paper bag.

"Well, I had a birthday party after all. My mother had ice cream and cake for me. I brought you a piece of my cake."

"Thank you. I am glad you had a nice birthday."

"Yes, I overslept this morning."

"Did you get your dog?"

"Oh no, but I had cake and ice cream. It was nice."

After he left I investigated the contents of the bag—a piece of coconut cake, not homemade. . . .

MAR. 3 . . . John was helping me put science equipment away. "I like to do things to help people," he said. . . .

. . . "That's fine," I said. "The birthday cake was very good. Coconut is one of my favorite cakes. It's so nice you had a nice birthday."

"It wasn't nice."

"But I thought you told me that you had ice cream and cake."

"No, I didn't even get any cake until my mother came home from work on Monday." Tears filled his eyes. "But my mother says we will have a party when it's my brother's birthday. A party for both of us."

With that he continued to put the science equipment away.

Tardiness and absence marked John's first six weeks in the fifth grade. The school had regulations regarding excuses. John sometimes had excuses, and sometimes he had none. Most often the excuse was, "I overslept because there was nobody at home to wake me. Then I had to get myself some breakfast." But this was not the formal written excuse from home that the school required. Such an excuse actually was unobtainable to John. How can a teacher deal with a situation like this? Is it a case for the truant officer? Or should John be reprimanded? Or should he be punished? Or should he be drawn toward the school by love and interesting activities?

On October 10, far from wanting to absent himself from school, John stayed at school beyond dismissal time. Was he avoiding something at home or something on the way home—a task at home, perhaps, or a fight on the way home? Or was he seeking something at school—to get help on some learning task, to get counsel on some problem, or to enjoy the warmth and reassurance that comes with talking with somebody who understands and accepts him? Should the motivation for this little visit be explored with the idea of uncovering a need to be met? Or should it just be passed by with no notice beyond a cordial greeting?

What would I decide if a pupil asked to leave a group that rejects him because they say he smells bad? Suppose my own nose told me that this was true. Could I decide what to say before I knew why he smells unpleasant? Is it running ears? Or no facilities for bathing at home? Is it unwashed, infected feet in unwashed socks? Or is it simply the pattern and standard of living of his social group? Is it neglect or rejection at home? Or is it a willful refusal to be clean as a symbolic rebellion against parental authority? How I should deal with the problem certainly would depend upon the combination of factors causing it. How could I get the necessary facts? Who could help me get the facts, and who could help me do something about it? Would a friendly visit with the mother at home help? Or should I simply write a note home about it? The decision about what to say to John and what to do is surely not an easy one. John, the other pupils, and my own situation would all have to be considered.

Then consider the sequence of anecdotes from February 23 through March 3, in which we get a small picture of the impact of his twelfth birthday upon John. A wrong decision about what to say to John and how to treat him at any one of a half-dozen times would have checked this flow of communication from him to his teacher, this development of a supporting intimate relationship between them. On February 24, Mr. S, the student teacher, made the initial wise judgment when he decided to go on with the lesson and neither to reprimand John for his inattention nor to explore publicly the nature of his worries. This left John without tension in relation to his teacher and, therefore, open to later approach. The teacher's approach put her on his side at once: "Perhaps I can help with some of them." Then her knowledge of psychology—specifically, her awareness that people usually are unable to reveal their deepest concerns immediately —prevented her from being deflected by John's anxiety at losing his safety-patrol belt. She made further communication easy for John.

> "Is that your only worry?"
> "No, I'm worried about my birthday."

Here again the teacher was wise in not forcing the issue and in giving John time to deal with any of his own emotions that might interfere with communication. Obviously the birthday stood for many things for John, just as birthdays do for all of us. Here the meaning was too intense for John to reveal the full dimensions of his feelings; hence he said, either because of convention or as a reflection of his longing and reverie, "I'm wondering if I'll have a party." He knew that he would not have a party, as his response to the teacher's next question revealed, "No, I've never had a party, but my mother says she'll get me a present. Maybe I'll get a dog." This was indeed intimate talk, close to the heart, possible only with somebody greatly to be trusted. There would be no party, but there might be a present, perhaps even a dog, a devoted companion.

This conversation must have set up a dozen questions in the teacher's mind, all of which she was wise enough not to pose at this time. Perhaps John's inattention in class had been caused by a reverie in which he was fancying himself for once the accepted center of a social event—a birthday party. Had the mother really promised a present? Or was the reverie concerned with an imaginary conversation with the mother in which she promised a present? Had John earlier asked to be permitted to have a dog and been refused or put off? Perhaps John's reverie had been a more searching one in which he had cast up an accounting of what it meant to be John rather than somebody else—no birthday parties, no presents, no dog—and had concluded, "I have *lots* of worries."

On February 25 John divulged an additional factor in his emotions, still within the context of his birthday reverie.

> "I am going to have a birthday party with my brother. His birthday is on the 16th and so I have to wait to have a party with him."

Was the brother the favored child? Had he had parties in the past? Must John always play second fiddle while the real recognition went to his brother? Or was this, too, only a mirage, a dream of what might have been said or planned? Knowingly or unwittingly, the teacher punctured this dream: "Will you have other boys in for the party?"

> "Well, no, my father says we can't bring anyone in. You know— things at home [he hesitated]—well, we just can't bring anybody in."

And with that the conversation stopped, but not John's feelings. Soon he walked away to watch a ball game. Who knows the hopes, the eager waiting, the keen disappointments, the unexpressed anguish and self-questioning of the next four days? Or who knows why John was absent on Monday morning, the day after his birthday? Or why he came Monday afternoon, armed to meet his teacher friend?

> "Well, I had a birthday party after all. My mother had ice cream and cake for me. I brought you a piece of my cake."

John's hurt was so deep that even his best friend had to be kept in the dark, had to be given tangible evidence that he was loved and had a meaningful, significant place at home, at least with his mother; hence the cake in the brown paper bag. Or was this part of acting out a reverie of what might have been in order to get a part of the feeling of the pleasure it would be to describe a party to one's teacher friend? Whatever the motivation, the teacher was momentarily fooled, as he intended she should be, and hence asked another indiscreet question:

> "Did you get your dog?"
> "Oh no, but I had cake and ice cream. It was nice."

Defense was followed by flight, for John immediately withdrew, while the teacher investigated the contents of the bag and established the fact that the cake had not been made at home as a loving ritual honoring the memory of John's coming.

But the relationship between John and his teacher was a very solid one, and he could not long endure a false note in it. Besides, he needed the reassuring warmth of contact with this accepting friend and the catharsis of expressing some of the emotion dammed up in him. Therefore, on March 3 he joined the teacher in helping to put away the science equipment and, before he knew it, found himself saying, "I like to do things to help people." This is indeed true, for elsewhere the record tells how John spent long hours shining shoes in order to give the money to his mother to help her out. The teacher naturally took this opportunity to imply that he had given her pleasure, too, by sharing his birthday cake and then said, "It's so nice that you had a nice birthday." This was too much for John, and he had to confess that the whole story was a fabrication. Tears filled his eyes, and his teacher understood how alone he was, how deep was his need for love and for somebody to believe in him and be nice to him.

This teacher's interest in John and the wisdom with which she decided when to speak and what to say had lowered bars between her and John and permitted him to communicate many of his feelings to her. Her subsequent genuine acceptance of him as a person told him that she valued him and enabled him to derive strength and reassurance from personal conversations, indeed from just being with her. As a result, John's teacher acquired the understanding described above. Was not this good both for the teacher and for John? Did not this warmth based on understanding and acceptance make it easier for John to learn and pleasanter for him to come to school? Did it not increase the probability that the teacher would make wise decisions about him from day to day in the classroom?

The Complex Responsibilities of Teaching

The preceding vignettes of children in the classroom and of children interacting with their teachers may seem to imply that the teachers' task is impossibly complex and bewildering. One must remember that the teachers who wrote these anecdotes were working every day with thirty to forty other children in addition to Jane, Rodney, Chester, or John. The job of getting to know all these children well enough to react to them with a sensitive understanding of what they need and with insightful wisdom about how to help them may seem quite impossible. Indeed it is impossible, unless provision is made for it, unless the teachers are carefully trained to do it, and unless systematic plans are made for accumulating information about children and for incorporating it into functional cumulative records. But it is far from impossible; on the contrary, it is perfectly feasible if the people who direct the education of teachers and the operation of schools provide for it.

Many teachers, after a year or two in our child-study program, have felt overwhelmed by the immensity and significance of the professional tasks and opportunities that they discover are theirs. A few have even drawn back from their dawning vision of opportunities for service, afraid to let themselves accept the responsibilities that the profession carries for deeply discerning persons. But there have not been many who preferred to remain pedagogical artisans—devotees of lesson plans and teaching techniques alone, helpful as these are. Most teachers wish to be professionals rather than craftsmen and are willing to devote years to the study and labor that will increase their assurance of making sound judgments when interacting with their Janes and Rodneys, their Chesters and Johns.

If there are faults, or rather inadequacies, in some of our teachers, they are the result of inadequate and inappropriate training rather than of lack of devotion to the task or to limitations of capacity. Anyone who has worked directly with hundreds and thousands of teachers is sure to have been moved with admiration at most teachers' willingness to work hard to help their pupils and at their tremendous sense of responsibility. If some are confused, it is because of leadership characterized by clichés and "inspirational" admonitions, because of lack of opportunity to participate in clear-cut philosophical analysis, and because of superficial application of available scientific knowledge.

The Child-study Program

The child-study program is no panacea for all our professional ills. It cannot transform poorly prepared teachers into highly competent professional persons in ten easy lessons. It is a very limited service based upon sixteen years of experimental efforts to help teachers understand children as individuals in their own classrooms. For the first five years of its existence, experimentation was carried on for the Commission on Teacher Education of the American Council on Education, with financial assistance from the General Education Board. The next three years were devoted to pioneering attempts to apply what we had learned during the life of the Commission, working out of the University of Chicago under the committee on field service of the department of education. During the nine years terminating in September, 1956, work was carried on under the aegis of the Institute for Child Study of the University of Maryland with the aid of subventions from the Grant Foundation. The details of the procedures that have proved to be of most help to teachers in service will be described later in this volume. Here it is appropriate only to describe briefly some of the needs of teachers that have been impressively demonstrated during the past sixteen years and to affirm faith, engendered by these sixteen years of intimate work with them, in the capactiy and motivation of teachers to become true professionals.

Insuring Sound Judgments

Earlier in this chapter attention was called to the hundreds of judgments a teacher makes every day when interacting with a class and with individual pupils. It was pointed out that these multitudinous decisions determine the freedom or restriction of movement, of speech, of access to materials, of spontaneous inquiries or comments, and of choice of experiences by the pupil. They influence the relationships the child is able to establish and maintain with the teacher, with other adults in the school, and with other children. They determine the actual learning experiences to which the child is exposed. They evoke or fail to evoke the higher mental functions of reasoning, appreciation of beauty, and creative imagination; they promote certain codes of conduct. They permit the child to use certain adjustment mechanisms and discourage or punish others. In other words, these daily decisions by the teacher are the fundamental bases of the educative process in our schools as it is experienced by particular children.

Obviously the judgments must vary from child to child and from situation to situation. We, therefore, have been continually alert, during our long period of experimental work with teachers, to discern the factors that lie behind good judgments. In a sense we have been asking ourselves, "What really accounts for the wise judgments of the master teachers we know?" And we have learned much from these master teachers both about what is necessary and about what is practical.

We now feel that really sound professional decisions by a teacher must rest upon the five following factors:

1. A set of clear-cut convictions about the meaning and purpose of education, a group of basic assumptions about what schools are for—in other words, a deeply felt philosophy of education.

2. A valid knowledge of the scientific principles that explain how children grow and develop—how they learn and become the persons they become, and why they behave as they do at the various developmental levels.

3. A valid understanding of each child's picture of himself and of his world. With this comes an understanding of each child's motivations, developmental tasks, and adjustment problems.

4. A knowledge of the structure and dynamics of each class as a group, because the children in it will function together throughout the year and because the structure and dynamics of the group influence the motivation and behavior of individual children and of the teacher.

5. A thoroughgoing knowledge of the subject matter that the school is offering to the children and of the materials and methods (experiences) by which children most readily gain access to this content, discover its relationship to themselves and their lives, and then develop a functional mastery of it.

The remainder of this book will present a point of view on each of the first four of these factors. It also will describe *how* we have helped teachers to increase their knowledge of explanatory scientific principles, to study the structure and dynamics of class groups, to gain a valid knowledge of each child's picture of himself in his own private world, and to interpret each child's motivations, developmental tasks, and adjustment problems. We know that most teachers can become effective professionally in the highest and best sense of the word because we have seen so many hundreds of them achieve this development.

CHAPTER 2

Basic Assumptions

The Control of Human Behavior

Many people in the United States of America are badly frightened during these middle decades of the twentieth century. But it may well be that they are scared by the wrong facts. The most dangerous fact of our time is probably not that we know enough to blow our whole civilization to smithereens with hydrogen and uranium bombs, but that ruthless, empirically directed dictator groups have learned enough about human motivation and behavior to control the actions both of individuals and of masses of people. They deliberately produce fear, hatred, suspicion, and anxiety—the symptoms of mental ill health—as means of motivating and controlling children and youth. They withhold information and experience and substitute the reiteration of the big lie as a means of controlling the ideas of young people, thus warping and limiting their development. They plant informers in school classes and on school faculties. Through these informers they collect unfavorable bits of information about teachers in order to blackmail them into becoming communicators of propaganda and violating the friendship and mutual trust of professional colleagues, thus perverting human relationships and demeaning human dignity.

The only way a person can retain his sanity and self-respect under such stress is to rationalize his situation as that of participating in a great crusade for human good against terrible forces of evil. And this is exactly what happens to many people. I saw it happening in Czechoslovakia during a period in 1948 when I was in that country.[1] We should be very thoroughly frightened that, through the possession and use of knowledge about how to control human behavior, ruthless individuals and groups are able to seize and hold power within any social group or institution, within communities and nations, perhaps throughout the world. It is

[1] See Prescott, D. A. Two Months Behind the Iron Curtain. *Bull. Elemen. Principals Assn.*, 1949, **29**, 30–40.

very disturbing to have seen the beginning of the use of similar techniques in our own country.

Science and the Determination of Goals

In the United States we possess a great deal more valid scientific knowledge about human development, motivation, and behavior than any totalitarian country possesses. But the possession of knowledge does not guarantee its use in wholesome ways for the benefit of all. The purposes which scientific knowledge can serve do not inhere in the knowledge itself. They depend rather upon the philosophical, religious, and social assumptions about the meaning of life and about the nature of valid human self-realization that are held by the person, the group, or the nation that uses the knowledge. It is, therefore, obligatory for us to understand the assumptions that underlie our use of scientific information.

The child-study program about which this book is written is based upon a series of religious and philosophical assumptions, social values, and scientific axioms. All of us who, as consultants, guide the operation of this program with teachers or parents, believe that it is the right of every human being to initiate and develop his own assumptions about the meaning of life and the nature of human destiny and to derive his own social values therefrom; for this reason, we do not try to convince others that our own assumptions represent ultimate truth. But we also believe that in working with others it is only fair to reveal to them the basic assumptions by which we are living and the values we are seeking to enhance. From our point of view, the child-study program is an attempt to use scientific knowledge and the scientific method to enhance the values for which we stand. But we grant the right of any teacher or parent to reject any of these assumptions or values, and, therefore, we insist that participation in the program must be completely voluntary in every school and community.

The plan of this chapter is first to present succinct statements of the religious, philosophical, and ethical assumptions, the social values, and the scientific axioms upon which the program rests. Then we shall examine briefly the reasons why they may be considered valid and mention a few of their implications.

SOURCES OF VALUES

Religious, Philosophical, and Ethical Assumptions

The assumptions from which our child-study program derives its values are the following:

1. *Every human being is valuable,* regardless of his age, sex, race, creed, cultural background, social status, capacities, knowledge, or state of emotional adjustment. An individual's *value inheres in the fact that he is a living human being with potentialities* to be realized.

2. *Every human being has the right to strive for those conditions* of living, learning, and action, *for those relationships* with other human beings, *and for those experiences, which are necessary and appropriate to the achievement of his optimum development* as a person and *to his optimum usefulness within society,* providing always that these conditions, relationships, and experiences are at the same time consistent with the welfare and optimum development of other human beings. It is the proper function of all social institutions and of every individual to assist each person to achieve optimum development and usefulness.

3. *Whatever promotes wholesome development is moral; whatever blocks or prevents optimum development is evil.*

4. *Every human being has the right to be treated at all times in ways that show respect for his dignity and permit him to retain respect for himself as a person.* This is an essential condition to optimum development.

5. *The Golden Rule is the soundest ethical principle against which to evaluate the behavior of individuals, the programs of social institutions, and the policies of nations.* To love other human beings as one loves oneself, and to treat others as one would wish to be treated under similar circumstances ought to be fundamental goals constantly sought by members of the educational profession.

Social Assumptions

The social assumptions and values upon which the child-study program rests are derived from the philosophical and ethical assumptions stated above and from the traditions of our American society. They are:

1. It is axiomatic that *every child, inevitably and properly, internalizes the culture* of the family, the social groups, the community and the nation *into which he is born. Society thus gives each individual a large portion of his interpretation of reality.* The school's task is to facilitate, to correct, and to supplement the internalizations that the child is acquiring outside the school. At the same time *the school must accept, respect, and value every individual,* even when circumstances have caused him to internalize inappropriate ideas, attitudes, or action patterns. This is especially important because of the great cultural diversity that exists within the United States.

2. *Every individual has certain rights, which may not be abridged.* The Constitution and the common law seek to guarantee these rights. *Every individual must be made aware of these rights and must be taught to value and to defend them*—for himself and for others.

3. *The democratic process is the best procedure yet worked out for carrying on the decision making that is a part of all social living and* at the same time *safeguarding and guaranteeing to each individual the conditions necessary to self-realization.* The democratic process is defined as that process in which

each individual affected actually participates in making all the decisions that determine his conditions of life, of work, and of further development.

4. *Each individual must be* reared in such a manner that he is *capable and desirous of assuming the responsibilities that go with freedom to make* basic *choices* about the conduct of his own life and to participate in decisions about the conduct of government. Only responsible citizens can maintain and develop so complex a society as the current Western European–American one. Only free individuals can achieve optimum self-realization within this context of social responsibility.

5. *The scientific method is the best process yet devised for using the mind* to distinguish facts from fallacies, to discover relationships between known facts and to work out the implications of facts for action. Members of the educational profession should be trained consciously to use the scientific method when making judgments about what to expect from and how to deal with their pupils. Many young people will understand and adopt it, too, if they observe it daily in operation as the fundamental way their teachers approach their problems.

Scientific Assumptions

Integrating information from the dozen or more sciences that study human beings yields certain fundamental views about how children and youth develop and why they behave as they do. The group of axioms given below supplies a core of general concepts to guide the more explicit study of individuals. They are:

1. *Behavior is caused and is meaningful.* It is the resultant of the tensions set up by a series of forces operating within and upon the individual. The behavior that emerges usually makes sense when viewed through the eyes of the behaver.

2. *The causes which underlie behavior are always multiple.* Some of them are physical—within the body or acting upon the body. Some are relationships of love or hatred, of friendship or antagonism, with other individuals. Some are cultural, depending upon ideas, habits, and attitudes taken in from the family and the community or pressed upon the individual by the operation of various social institutions. Some grow out of participation in group activities with persons of the same maturity level. Still others grow out of the individual's own interpretations of his accumulating experiences, as he defines values, strives toward goals, and works out defenses against frustrations and limiting circumstances.

3. *Each individual is an indivisible unit.* The forces that shape him do not merely accumulate to produce a human being. Rather they interact. Consequently, one cannot take the individual apart, figuratively speaking, and deal with only one aspect of his dynamic make-up at a time. The whole will participate in and be influenced by all educative experiences.

4. *The human individual develops. No child or youth was born as he is or necessarily destined to become what he is. As the body grows and becomes more elaborate, new capacities* for experiencing, for learning, and for action

emerge. As experiences accumulate, more and more meanings and feelings aie differentiated. In other words, it is the interaction between the organism and its environment over a period of time that develops the individual personality. Hence *the developing individual must reintegrate, or reunify, himself from time to time at successively higher and higher levels of complexity both of structure and of meaning.* With successive reintegrations additional capacities emerge—capacities to remember, to perceive, to discriminate, to relate, to understand, to value, to plan and to act. This process of making successive reintegrations does not end with physical "maturity," but can continue to occur as experience adds new knowledge and understanding and as realized goals, related to fundamental values, open vistas of new goals and of long-term possibilities.

5. *Every human individual is a dynamic energy system, not just a machine acted upon from without.* The living oneness that is a human being develops self-awareness, concepts of and about himself, and a dynamic need to become, to realize his potentialities. This self-conscious personality becomes able to distinguish the direction of his own evolution, to envisage goals of his own, to discern and to create beauty, to discriminate between right and wrong and to choose the right, to find meaning and hope not only for his own life but also for that of mankind. This dynamic organization of energy that is *a human being is potentially a self-actualizing unity.* It emerges from the interaction of organism with world and society. But it always has the potentiality of going on from where it is, to participate in shaping its own further destiny, together with that of the society of which it is a part, and even that of mankind.

6. Dynamic *self-actualization is made possible* to an individual *by* the exist-ence of *an organizing core of meanings (values) at the center of the personality. These meanings govern the interaction between the individual and the succession of situations in which he finds himself.* They influence what he perceives each situation to be and to imply for him. They determine what he feels in each situation. They evoke criteria (desired goals and permitted means) against which the various behavior alternatives must be measured. Consequently, they regulate the individual's flow of behavior from situation to situation. Of course, this organizing core of meanings is built up gradually by experience and is modifiable at any time during life when the individual reintegrates himself. Usually it becomes quite strongly established during infancy, childhood, and youth. The development of this core of meanings should be a major concern of education. Its modification and reintegration are the chief tasks of therapy, when it has led to ineffective or inappropriate behavior.

7. *Each individual is different from every other.* The same basic forces and processes operate to shape all human beings and are available to all for self-realization. But these forces and processes vary both qualitatively and quantitatively from person to person. Consequently, an individual can be understood and intelligently assisted in his self-actualization only if one has very explicit information about him. The information needed concerns his circumstances and experiences in life and the meanings and accompanying feelings that these experiences have engendered in him. These meanings and feelings

are often discernible from systematic accumulations of objective descriptions
of his behavior.

The Gist of It

The five religio-philosophical and ethical assumptions presented above
affirm the value of all human life and the nurturing respect and love that
it should command from all of us, regardless of the background and circumstances in which this life is found. The five social assumptions and
values affirm that society is made for and by man, to assist his development; man is not made to enhance society at the expense of his development. But inasmuch as all members of society are interdependent, the
welfare of all must be protected and the participation of all must be
guaranteed, whether in the carrying out of responsibilities or in the
reaching of decisions. The seven scientific axioms show that, although
man is shaped by the world with which he interacts, he also becomes
dynamic and builds his own destiny and, to some extent, that of society
and the world.

Together these three sets of statements constitute a sort of biosocial
philosophy of human relations and education. In this philosophy man is
not only the apex of the evolutionary process, but a creature with special
value or significance in the universe. He is not a blindly operating machine but a creative being. Man appears to be, at one and the same time,
the partial fulfillment of a great creative dynamic in the universe and
a participant in the creative process.

THE VALIDITY OF THE BASIC ASSUMPTION

The scientific axioms presented above are reasonable inferences from
the facts now available in the sciences that study human life and human
behavior. The social values have been at least partially tested in Western
European and American societies. But what about the basic assumption
regarding the value of all human life? Whence did this idea spring? And
what reasonable ground is there for believing it?

Certainly the assumption is not universally accepted, for on a world-
wide basis life has never been held cheaper than in our twentieth century. Howard Mumford Jones writes, "If the entire population of the
United States were wiped out tomorrow, their number would be less
than the number of human beings who have died of violence or starvation
in war or as a result of it during the last half-century." [2] Yet the efforts
of governments and of individuals to prevent this shocking and terrible

[2] Jones, Howard Mumford, *Education and World Tragedy*, Cambridge, Mass.: Harvard University Press, 1946, p. 9.

destruction of life have been halfhearted and of dubious sincerity. Even in our own country we almost daily hear talk about the possible use of war as an instrument of national policy. Furthermore, totalitarian regimes certainly regard whole social classes, racial groups, and certain categories of individuals as expendable, or even as deserving extinction.

Nor is the value of life realized in its mere preservation; it is in the full realization of its potentialities that life's value is really to be found. Yet extensive observation of American teachers in the classroom and in discussion groups clearly reveals that many teachers, too, value children quite differentially. Some have much higher regard for children from certain social classes or ethnic groups than for children from others. Some are drawn to highly intelligent children or to persons with special gifts or driving ambitions. Others find it impossible to value the young of all races equally.

For these reasons it is necessary to explore briefly the origins of the idea that *every* human being is valuable and to discover why intelligent men have maintained this view. Our purpose in doing this is simply to open certain avenues of thought that can be followed by anyone with sufficient interest. Furthermore, we must accept the responsibility for validating the major assumption on which the child-study program is based.

People Agree for Different Reasons

Individual differences among readers create a difficulty at this point. The basic assumption that "all human beings are valuable" is examined here as a conviction that should underlie and to a considerable extent motivate professional work in the field of education. I know from experience that most school people accept this statement readily, but I am also aware that the reasons why different individuals are ready to accept it stem from three quite different religious or philosophical orientations. Some accept it because they believe in immortality—in the eternal life of each human soul after physical death. According to this view, life on earth is the necessary preparation for eternal living. Others accept it, though they do not believe in human immortality, because they believe that God exists and is working out a great plan or purpose in which man has a key role. A third group of people accept it, although they do not believe in human immortality or in the existence of a purposing deity, because they have great faith in man and in the capacities of human beings to love, to find truth, to discriminate wisely among alternatives, and to create beauty. These persons feel that man will build his own grand destiny.

Everyone will recognize, in turn, the orthodox Christian, the man who believes in God and purposeful meaning in the universe but doubts personal immortality, and the humanist. The three groups agree that every human being is valuable, but they arrive at this idea from quite different perspectives, or orientations toward the universe, and therefore accept it for quite different reasons. We have here a very vivid illustration of how an organizing core of meaning at the heart of the personality determines what each person perceives in a situation. Yet it is not surprising that people whose orientations toward the universe differ should agree on a value, because all are sincere searchers and finders of a portion of truth. One can perceive a portion of the truth according to each of these orientations. We shall now examine briefly some of the reasons people have for accepting the idea that human beings are valuable.

God's Relationship to Man

The concept that every human being is valuable has roots in the Jewish religion and has been extensively elaborated and developed by the Christian religion. The ancient Jews felt that the Great Architect of the universe and the Creator of Life stood in the same relationship to them as a stern but loving father toward his children or a tender shepherd toward his sheep. The psalmist in the Bible perhaps phrased it most cogently and beautifully:

The earth is the Lord's and the fullness thereof; the world, and they that dwell therein. For he has founded it upon the seas and established it upon the floods. (Ps. 24:1–2)

Know ye that the Lord he is God: it is he that hath made us, and not we ourselves; we are his people and the sheep of his pasture. Enter into his gates with thanksgiving, and into his courts with praise. . . . (Ps. 100:3–4)

The Lord is my shepherd; I shall not want. He maketh me to lie down in green pastures: he leadeth me beside still waters. He restoreth my soul. . . . Surely goodness and mercy shall follow me all the days of my life, and I shall dwell in the house of the Lord forever. (Ps. 23:1–3, 6)

Bless the Lord, O my soul: and all that is within me, bless his holy name. . . . Who satisfieth thy mouth with good things; so that thy youth is renewed like the eagle's. . . . Like as a father pitieth his children, so the Lord pitieth them that fear him. For he knoweth our frame. . . . (Ps. 103:1–5, 13–14)

Jesus simply extended this concept to make God the father of all mankind and not of the Jews only. And by all mankind He clearly meant all people within each nation as well as the people of all nations. For He explicitly called attention to the basic value of several kinds of human beings who were not highly regarded socially in His day: the meek, the unhappy, the humble, the infirm, the good Samaritan, the sincere publican, the peacemaker. Consequently, the Christian religion customarily has affirmed the value of every human soul, no matter how lowly, and

has devoted much effort and money to enhancing human development
by healing the sick and maintaining schools for underprivileged children
and youth. Of course, from time to time, Christian churches also have
acquiesced in social practices which obviously did not live up to this
belief. This occurs even today. For example, in our own country there
are many churches which do not admit Negroes into their fellowship
and communion.

Jesus, of course, not only affirmed the value of every human being
but of all living things as well:

Are not two sparrows sold for a farthing? And one of them shall not fall to
the ground without your Father. But the very hairs of your head are all numbered. Fear ye not, therefore, ye are of more value than many sparrows.
(Matt. 10:29–30)

Finally, there is added, in this tradition, yet another factor—man's relationship with God. Man is envisaged not only as the capstone of God's
creative organization of the universe, but also as the valued co-worker
with God in the further realization of His purposes in the universe:

For we are labourers together with God: ye are God's husbandry, ye are God's
building. (I Cor. 3:9)

Here, then, is a tradition that has given meaning to the lives of men
for thousands of years: God exists. He envisaged and brought order into
the universe. He created life. He evolved man as the apex of this creative
process and endowed him with great power to learn and to discriminate
between good and evil. Now man has become a co-worker with God in
carrying on the affairs of the world and even in the creative process itself.
In this plan, God's relationship to man is that of the loving, nurturing
father who finds pride and pleasure in his children's development and
self-realization. In such a scheme of things every person is valuable,
both because he is a child of God and because he is a potential creative
factor in the universe. Our society has inherited this tradition, which is
one of the main sources of our conviction of the value of human individuals. Note that this tradition concerns the relationship of God to man
here on this earth during each man's lifetime, and man's potential as a
creative force. It does not necessarily imply life after physical death.

The Doctrine of Immortality

The possibility of immortality for the individual personality supplies
a second very cogent reason for regarding every human being as valuable. Concerning this idea, which is very old, the early Jews were divided.
Many thought that eventually all their nation would be resurrected to
live again with their forefathers in the warmth and love of God's presence.

But the Sadducees did not believe in the resurrection, and the concept was still a controversial one at the time when Jesus lived. Jesus Himself spoke many times of life after death and predicted His own death and resurrection. The Gospel story concerning these events became the basis for our observance of Easter.

The Christian churches have built an elaborate dogma around the historical facts about Jesus. They have related the hope for immortality to the doctrines of salvation through declared belief, atonement for human sinfulness through Jesus' death, and the obligation of believers to sin no more. In this manner the hope for immortality and the belief in God's love for mankind have been used to motivate living in accord with the code of ethics enunciated by Jesus.

For the great company of sincere and orthodox Christian believers, then, one reason why every human being is valuable is perfectly obvious. Every person is possessed of an immortal soul or personality which will continue its existence after physical death. The quality of the life after physical death depends upon the kind of self that is developed during the organic existence. Thus the terrific importance of "belief," and of the development of "goodness" during the physical life as evidence of belief, is perfectly clear. Life on this earth is the individual's one chance to become an immortal soul that is worthy and, therefore, can be happy in the hereafter.

Humanism: The Upward Surge of Life

For humanists, the chief meaning and central motivation of life is the onward and upward push of human life toward a better world—the struggle to improve the human lot in every possible way. Humanists believe that every human being is valuable because they are challenged by human need, suffering, and frustration. Basing their convictions on the thinking of a series of philosophers, beginning perhaps with Aristotle and continuing through John Dewey, their trust is in the power of human reason to find solutions for the problems that beset mankind. They accept the idea that man is mortal and do not find it necessary to envisage a God as the creator of the universe and the shaper of the destinies of living things. For them the origins of the universe and of life remain mysteries which we do not have to explain in order to live the good life. John Dewey, for example, expresses this as follows: [3]

Man has constructed a strange dream world when they have supposed that without a fixed ideal of a remote good to inspire them, they have no inducement to get relief from present troubles, no desires for liberation from what oppresses, and for clearing up what confuses present action. Sufficient unto

[3] Dewey, John. *Human Nature and Conduct.* New York: Modern Library, 1930, p. 282.

the day is the evil thereof. Sufficient it is to stimulate us to remedial action, to endeavor in order to convert strife into harmony, monotony into a variegated scene and limitations into expansions. The converting is progress . . . progress means increase of present meaning, which involves multiplication of sensed distinctions as well as harmony and unification.

In other words, man does not need the vision of Heaven after death to motivate him; the problems that he and his fellow man face challenge him to strive for continuing human development. Dewey defines this challenge as follows: [4]

. . . good is always found in a present growth of significance in activity. . . . To make others happy except through liberating their powers and engaging them in activities that enlarge the meaning of life is to harm them. . . . Our moral measure for estimating any existing arrangement or any proposed reform is its effect upon impulse and habits. Does it liberate or suppress, ossify or render flexible, divide or unify interest? Is perception quickened or dulled? . . . Is thought creative or pushed to one side into pedantic specialisms? . . . To foster conditions that widen the horizon of others and give them command of their own powers, so that they can find their own happiness in their own fashion, is the way of social action. . . .

Morals is connected with actualities of existence, not with ideals, ends, and obligations independent of concrete actualities. The facts upon which it depends are those which arise out of active connections of human beings with one another, the consequences of their mutually intertwined activities. . . .

Erich Fromm perhaps expresses the current humanistic motivation and morality even more clearly: [5]

The need for a system of orientation and devotion is an intrinsic part of human existence . . . there is no other more powerful source of energy in man. Man is not free to choose between having or not having ideals, but he is free to choose between different kinds of ideals. . . . All men are idealists and are striving for something beyond the attainment of physical satisfaction. They differ in the kinds of ideals they believe in.

Fromm describes the ideals that he regards as appropriate for our times: [6]

Man must accept the responsibility for himself and the fact that only by using his own powers can he give meaning to his life. But meaning does not imply certainty . . . uncertainty is the very condition to impel man to unfold his powers. If he faces the truth without panic he will recognize that there is no meaning to life except the meaning man gives his life by the unfolding of his powers, by living productively . . . the one task that matters . . . [is] the full development of our powers within the limitations set by the law of our existence.

[4] *Ibid.*, p. 293.
[5] Fromm, Erich. *Man for Himself*. New York: Rinehart, 1947, p. 49.
[6] *Ibid.*, p. 45.

An Area of Agreement

Obviously humanists and theists are in agreement that every human being is valuable and that the full realization of the potentialities of the human personality is the major good in this world. It seems to make little difference whether one accepts the voice of religious authority, the fruits of feeling and contemplation in the individual religious man, or the disciplined reasoning processes of the humanist; in all these views of life, individual human beings are understood to be of fundamental value in the universe and their full development is seen as the chief aim of individual and social effort. These three views of the meaning of life, so commonly believed to be antithetical, may, in fact, be complementary to each other and, taken together, may lead to still deeper understanding of life and the universe.

Examination of the views of a number of eminent scientists reveal that individual scientists espouse one or another of these three points of view. The core of meaning common to all is therefore likely to have genuine validity and great importance. Many scientists agree that the focus of living should be upon the development of the human individual—upon facilitating the realization of the potentialities of every person. That this dynamic tendency to develop is present in all life processes seems, indeed, to suggest that the force in operation is as real as that which gives structure to atoms or draws the falling apple to the earth. The views of these scientists should be both suggestive and reassuring to most members of the educational profession, for these views make it clear that there is no reason for teachers to feel that scientific study and discipline must undermine their convictions and destroy their faith, no matter which of the three points of view presented earlier they may hold. The opposite may well prove to be true.

WHAT SOME SCIENTISTS BELIEVE

Beliefs of Max Planck

Max Planck, the great physicist who first announced the essential quantum theory, has the following to say in a paper titled "Religion and Natural Science": [7]

Religion and natural science have a point of contact in the issue concerning the existence and nature of a supreme power ruling the world, and here the answers given by them are, to a certain degree at least, comparable. . . . They are by no means contradictory but are in agreement, first of all, on the point that there exists a rational world order independent from man, and sec-

[7] Planck, Max, *Scientific Autobiography and Other Papers*. New York: Philosophical Library, 1949, p. 183ff.

ondly, on the view that the character of this world order can never be directly known but can only be indirectly recognized or suspected. Religion employs in this connection its own characteristic symbols, while natural science uses measurements founded on sense experiences. Thus, nothing stands in our way—and our instinctive intellectual striving for a unified world picture demands it—from identifying with each other the two . . . active and yet mysterious forces: The world order of natural science and the God of religion. . . .

Planck goes on to say that religion and natural science have different roles to play in human life. Natural science is to help men learn, religion to guide the use they make of their knowledge.[8]

We stand in the midst of life; and its manifold demands and needs often make it imperative that we reach decisions. . . . [Sometimes] long and tedious reflection cannot enable us to shape our decisions and attitudes properly; only that definite and clear instruction [guidance] can, which we gain from a direct inner link to God. This instruction alone is able to give us the inner firmness and lasting peace of mind which must be regarded as the highest boon in life. And if we ascribe to God . . . the attitudes of goodness and love, recourse to them produces an increased feeling of safety and happiness. . . . Against this conception not even the slightest objection can be raised from the point of view of natural science. . . . No matter where and how far we look, nowhere do we find a contradiction between religion and natural science.

These are strong, clear, and unequivocal statements from one of the greatest of modern physicists. Perhaps one of the reasons for their clarity and strength was that they were made in May, 1937, when Hitler had gained power within Germany and was outmoding all general human concepts in favor of cultural absolutes that served his immediate purposes. Those were days to test the stuff of German scientists as well as religionists. Perhaps that is why Planck closed his address with the following statement: [9]

Religion and natural science are fighting a joint battle in an incessant, never relaxing crusade against scepticism and against dogmatism, against disbelief and against superstition, and the rallying cry in this crusade has always been and always will be: On to God!

Planck obviously felt himself strengthened and reassured at this time by his experience of relating directly to the great forces of the universe—in other words, to God—as a source of inspiration and guidance. Certainly, the battle against skepticism, dogmatism, and superstition continues unabated. Perhaps the sense of a common task for religion and science may induce mutual tolerance and decrease dogmatism in individuals devoted to the enhancement of either science or religion.

[8] *Ibid.*, p. 185.
[9] *Ibid.*, p. 187.

Views of Du Noüy

Another eminent scientist, a biologist this time, also believes that God and a purposeful world order exist and that man can be aware of and can interact with God. Indeed, Lecomte Du Noüy believes that man is supremely valuable because man is himself a part of this great creative surge of life that is the spiritual aspect of the universe. Du Noüy has written two books about the nature of the dynamic cosmic force that is life and about the role of man in the universe. These books, which are delightful as well as rewarding reading, are titled *Human Destiny* and *Road to Reason*. Du Noüy sees the evolution of living things as the purposive expression of a great creative force that is God. He also sees man as sharing in the creating as well as in the realizing of cosmic purposes. For example, he writes: [10]

Man continues to play his part but wants to comprehend the play. He becomes capable of perfecting himself, and he is even the only one capable of doing this. But in order to perfect himself he must be free, since his contribution to evolution will depend upon the use he makes of his liberty.

Again, Du Noüy writes: [11]

We started rationally from the critical study of evolution, and were drawn to admit the criterion of liberty, the freedom of choice, implying conscience and the sense of human dignity. The idea of God emerged progressively as an absolute necessity.

A Mechanistic Universe

During the past fifty years there has been a sort of vogue among scientists to emancipate themselves from the authority and dogmatism of the churches and to become at least agnostic. Few of us who have studied and practiced some aspect of science during this period have failed to feel, at one time or another, a sort of requirement of skepticism, or of repudiation of religion, as necessary for acceptance into fraternal fellowship with scientific colleagues—as a sort of precondition to belonging among peers.

Actually this was simply the requirement of sincerity and of scholarship. If one understood physics, one "knew"—that is, was certain—that the universe was built out of basic "matter" and operated by the continuous transmutation of energy from one form into another without any destruction of that energy. Matter and energy behaved strictly in accordance with laws, and everything that happened was strictly "determined." Thus the universe was demonstrated to be entirely mechanistic,

[10] Du Noüy, Lecomte. *Human Destiny*. New York: Longmans, Green, 1947, p. 158.
[11] *Ibid.*, p. 107.

purposeless, and nonspiritual. Living things, including man, were composed of matter, and behavior was the result of the flow of energy through the organism. The human being, therefore, was a machine, responding to forces in its environment and adapting itself to the demands and conditions of the world around it. Since natural law, as discovered by the various sciences, proved this thesis, skepticism about things spiritual was more or less inevitable, if the scientist was a sincere and "adequate" scholar.

"Indeterminism" and Whitehead's Organic Theory

During the same fifty years, however, the basic science of physics has undergone a revolution. One of its present chief doctrines is that of "indeterminism," and many of its data are now seen as statistical, that is, based on probability and not on certainty. Extensive reading in the more recent discussions of science and philosophy by such men as Sir James Jeans, Sir Arthur Stanley Eddington, J. W. N. Sullivan, J. S. Huxley, Arthur H. Compton, Sir Charles S. Sherrington, John Dewey, and Alfred North Whitehead reveals that, although materialism and mechanism have not been ultimately disproved, two other views [12] of the universe are now equally tenable:

1. Underlying purpose or purposes are possible in the kind of physical universe that has now been demonstrated, and this view of the universe is now thought by some to be "more reasonable" than mechanism.

2. Nature is in essence organic rather than materialistic. The final real entities in nature are *not* substances which carry certain characteristics that determine the nature of the events in which these substances participate. Rather *the final real entity is an organizing activity*, fusing ingredients into a unity. Consequently this unity is the reality.

Such a unity could be a molecule of oxygen, a paramecium, or a man. Each is a fundamental unity or reality in the universe. An event is a unit in the experience of any organism, but the meaning of the event depends entirely upon the organism—molecule, animal, or man—that experiences it. J. W. N. Sullivan may have had some such idea in mind when he indicated that the next great step in developing a theory of the universe will probably be a contribution from biology.[13]

THE VIEWS OF EDMUND SINNOTT

In 1950 Edmund W. Sinnott published a very thought-provoking series of lectures titled *Cell and Psyche*, with the subtitle "The Biology of Pur-

[12] Whitehead, A. N. *Science and the Modern World.* New York: Macmillan, 1926.
[13] Sullivan, J. W. N. *The Limitations of Science.* New York: Viking, 1933.

pose." We will examine it at some length here partially because it contributes much meaning to our series of scientific axioms and partially because it so well illustrates Max Planck's dictum that scientists, beginning with evidence gained through their senses and aided by the measurements and processes of scientific research, can develop a concept of the wonderful order that rules the universe, may find meaningful direction and purpose within it, and perhaps will discover God as the initiating and creative force behind it. In such a system human beings, in fact all living things, are seen as having special significance and value.

Matter Is Running Down

The second law of thermodynamics is the logical place to begin thinking about the relationship of man and the universe, because humans, like other forms of life, can be accurately described as organized energy systems, albeit very complex ones. Inanimate objects also are energy systems—a bit of uranium, a piece of steel, a bridge, a house, the earth, the sun and the distant stars. Each is made up of energy, more or less organized within itself. Each derives its properties, that is, its characteristics, from the patterns of organization of the energy that constitutes it.

Now, according to the second law of thermodynamics, all inanimate objects have a common fate. All are gradually breaking down into simpler forms of energy organization, especially into heat, which is being spread more and more evenly throughout the universe. Uranium, being radioactive, breaks down ultimately into lead, giving off energy that, eventually in the process, turns into heat. Steel oxidizes and ultimately disintegrates, slowly giving off heat all the while. The same processes apply to bridges, houses, machines—to everything inanimate. The earth, the sun, the distant stars—all are slowly cooling. No energy is destroyed or lost in the process; it is all simply reduced to the common denominator of heat and dispersed through the universe. The result of this dispersion is that all things gradually lose the distinctive characteristics that were the effects of their earlier more complex patterns of energy organization. This is another way of saying that the material world is slowly running down and becoming less and less differentiated.

Life Is Building Up

The dramatic and significant fact that concerns us most, however, is the complete contrast between the actions of inanimate and animate energy systems. Living things are not running down. Life, in its evolution from simple and still-unknown beginnings up to man, has moved in just the opposite direction, and living things constantly are capturing energy from their environments and incorporating it into their own more and more complex forms of organization. "This great drama [of evolution] shows a continual increase in complexity, a mounting tension, a steadily rising level of organization." [14] "The fundamental thread that seems to run through the history of our world is a continuous rise in level of organization." [15] "The law of evolution is a kind of converse of the Second Law of Thermodynamics, equally irreversible but contrary in tendency." [16]

In other words, since the beginning of time, matter has been disintegrating and losing organization; but since the advent of life, living things have been building themselves up, increasing the complexity of their organization, and becoming more and more differentiated. It is this property of life which accounts for evolution and which has resulted in the development on this earth of all the varieties of plant and animal life that now inhabit the earth or have done so in times past.

The Human Individual Is Dynamic

The organizing force that characterizes life does not act in a vague general way throughout the world. It must operate in and through individuals, for the individual organism is the basic unit of reality in the universe, as Whitehead has suggested. And the story of the growth of the individual human being is one of the most fascinating and beautiful in all science.

The fertilized human ovum begins immediately to capture energy from its environment and to incorporate this energy within its own organized and dynamic energy structure; thus it multiplies itself into a host of identical cells grouped together. These small energy systems, related to each other, but also within and related to the larger energy systems of the mother's body and the world (especially gravity, perhaps), create an energy field within which each cell has a particular position. At appropriate times in relation to the growing whole, specific cells change their energy organization, or, in biological terms, differentiate themselves, to become nerve cells, muscle cells, and other kinds of special cells out of which grow the brain and spinal cord, the heart, the alimentary canal and other internal organs, the eyes and other sense organs, and so on. The position of each differentiating cell and the sequence in which the myriad differentiations occur present a spectacular picture of organization and timing, in relation to each other and in terms of what is necessary to produce a complete functioning human organism.

The goal of this growth, a functioning human being, is clearly envisaged, implied, or intended from the beginning. A sort of protoplasmic

[14] Sinnott, Edmund W. *Cell and Psyche.* Chapel Hill: University of North Carolina Press, 1950, p. 101.

[15] Needham, Joseph. *Time: The Refreshing River,* p. 185. Quoted in Sinnott, *op. cit.*

[16] Needham, *op. cit.,* p. 230. Quoted in Sinnott, *op. cit.,* p. 101.

purposing is occurring, and the fulfillment is exquisitely delicate, precise, and intricate. The persisting scientific riddle is how the initial organization of energy, the tiny fertilized ovum, can contain at the same time the blueprint of what it is to become and the dynamic, organizing power gradually to bring the complete organism into operational being within its particular energy field (the mother's body) in the larger universe of energy (the world). We know, of course, that enzymes are the catalysts that regulate the modifications of the energy structures in the individual differentiating cells. But what causes these enzymes to appear in cells in exactly the right positions at exactly the right times to ensure the progressive fulfillment of the blueprint of human growth remains a complete mystery. The organizing force eludes us. Nor is the operation of this force ended with birth; it continues as long as growth continues, perhaps, and even probably as long as life continues.

Sinnott has this to say about the organizing force that shapes growth and body maintenance and function: [17]

The basic question is the origin and nature of this organizing, goal-seeking quality of life. . . . This at bottom is a perfectly definite biological problem with nothing metaphysical about it. . . .

The plain fact is that in the present status of science, biological organization remains still unexplained. . . . I believe that we shall find that organization depends neither on the operation of only those physical laws which we now know, nor on some superphysical or vitalistic agent about which nothing can be learned, but that a more perfect knowledge of nature and man will tell us how the physical and the spiritual are linked in that ascending, questing, creative system which is life.

About the existence of this organizing force, or rather about the presence of these organizing processes, there can no doubt; hence our axiom that all human beings are dynamic and tend, in and of themselves, toward self-actualization. We are justified, then, in having strong faith in the continued effective operation of these organizing processes.

The Human Individual Develops

But there is yet more to be inferred from the manner in which the human personality is gradually brought into being over a period of time. *The human individual develops;* this axiom carries a number of meanings. Some of them are:

1. The pattern or blueprint of human growth is determined by heredity, but the growth process occurs through the interaction of the organism with its environment. The organism follows the blueprint meticulously and dauntlessly, even in the face of disease and undernourishment; even if the environ-

[17] Sinnott, *op. cit.*, pp. 104–106.

ment does not provide material to do a first-class building job, growth goes on. New body parts are added, and old ones grow and begin to function roughly at the time they are due, even if their structure is imperfect. This fact accounts for a considerable number of organic weaknesses and bodily imperfections among children who are undernourished or ill. The dynamic organizing force causes growth to continue regardless of difficulties; hence the importance of providing a satisfactory environment to cooperate with this great growth-dynamic throughout the growth cycle.

2. As differentiation and growth continue, new body parts develop, one after another. As they begin to function, their subsequent growth perfects them in response to the demands of the environment. This means that new potentialities for action and for learning frequently emerge—that new capacities constantly develop and seek to be exploited. The attempts of the individual to use these emerging potentialities constantly change his ways of interacting with the environing world. This is the basis of what we term "developmental tasks," such as learning to sit up, walk, talk, read, play group games, and attract and interact with persons of the opposite sex. The growing child or youth is actively driven, by the organizing dynamic regulating his growth, to undertake the use of his emerging capacities and potentialities.

3. With the emergence of new capacities, with growth in old capacities, with increase in knowledge and ability to conceptualize, with broadening of understandings, and with the development of a greater variety of behavioral alternatives, the task of unifying all the aspects of living, of maintaining self-consistency, and of developing a sense of personal adequacy becomes more difficult. Hence the individual must take stock from time to time in order to reintegrate his capacities at increasingly complex levels of organization. The organizing force that has guided the growth of the body usually ensures this series of reintegrations; indeed, it often makes reintegration virtually a continuous process, thus avoiding inner conflict and tension.

As the result of these reintegrations, the individual repeatedly develops new capacities. Thus, many of the so-called mental functions are not separate entities, independent of physical growth, but simply abilities that spring from body organization at successively more complex levels. These mental capacities, or functions, are as much implied in the dynamic structure of the fertilized ova as are the body parts, though mental growth, like physical growth, also depends upon the individual's interaction with his environment.

4. As a result of his new capacities and his accumulation of experience in employing them, the individual discovers new meanings and alters old ones. Thus his concept of himself and of his place in the world is enlarged and clarified, and he develops awareness of the ways in which he is likely to feel and behave in specific situations. Out of this process of dynamic interaction with the world and dynamic reintegration at successively more complex levels of organization, a *unique* self is ultimately formed. This self is simply the integration of meanings developed by interaction with the world: the concepts, the conduct codes, the values that guide the selection and development of behavioral patterns in specific situations. Not only in childhood and youth but

throughout life the process of development continues through reintegration at successively higher levels of organization.

Development, then, occurs as a succession of interrelated events: Growth causes new potentialities to emerge. These potentialities are used in interaction with the environment and, as a result, the individual gains skill, knowledge, and understanding. But unevenness in the development of these potentialities causes inconsistencies and confusion and makes it necessary to reintegrate the personality at a higher level of complexity. The reintegration itself causes new capacities and potentialities to appear, and the use of these in interaction with the environment makes subsequent reintegrations necessary. This process is continuous throughout life.

The Emerging Self

The dynamic self which emerges at the various levels of organization is not a separate entity or structure but rather a function of the organism as a whole. Our powers of reasoning, imagining and inventing, measuring behavior against criteria, discriminating between right and wrong, beauty and ugliness, wisdom and folly, are aspects of our functioning as complete organisms.

There is nothing mystical about the operation of these processes that produce a human personality, although we do not yet understand them fully. The story of how each human personality is created by the interaction of organized and organizing forces and of how man's creative capacities emerge in this process is truly a wonderful one. Even our sketch of these processes here is sufficient to show us how unacceptable is the idea that human beings are merely machines blindly responding to external stimulation and adapting to environmental pressures. Happily, this new idea of development is consonant with the common-sense view of life that the man in the street has always held regarding himself. We can safely respect our own dignity and value in the universe and that of all our fellow human beings!

Purpose and Freedom

Sinnott, who is also greatly impressed with the processes of human development and with the powers of integration of the organizing dynamic, makes the following significant inferences regarding the value of human beings: [18]

If we can show that mind and body, spirit and matter are held together in equal union as parts of that organized system which life is, then the idealist is

[18] *Ibid.*, pp. 109, 110.

encouraged to speak with much more confident voice. He can claim with assurance that mind is as real as body, for they are part of the same unity; that purpose and freedom are not illusions but are an essential part of the way in which events are brought to pass in protoplasmic systems; that the soul has a sound biological basis as the core of the integrated organism; that our sense of values is not arbitrary but results from the direction and preferences shown by such systems; and that the course and history of life, so different from those of lifeless matter, give hope that it may have an inner directive quality of its own.

If the goals set up in protoplasm, . . . the ends to which all living stuff aspires, have risen so high that in ourselves they now include the love of beauty and truth and goodness, may it not be that the organized system which man's spirit is, refined and elevated far above its simple origins, has grown the sensitive instrument through which he comes to recognize the presence of these same qualities in the universe outside him?

In other words, beauty, truth, and goodness are realities rather than mere mirages.[19]

If the responsive systems which we call our souls are found to be so stubbornly persistent in the flux of time and matter; *if our personalities are each unique and seemingly so valuable in nature,* does not this suggest that they may be of more significance, perhaps even of more permanence, than one would ever guess from a knowledge of the lifeless universe alone?

.   .   .   .

If each of us is thus an organized and an organizing center, a vortex pulling in matter and energy and knitting them into precise patterns; and if we are able, though in small degree, to create new patterns never known before, does not this suggest that we may actually be a part of the great creative power in nature and hold communion with it; and that, as James once said, we may come to recognize that this higher part of us is continuous with a more of the same quality operative in the universe outside and with which we can keep in working touch? Does not this, indeed, present as clear a picture as the scientist can draw of God, Himself, and our relations to Him?

Sinnott, an eminent biologist, is apparently moved by the same drama and sense of direction that Du Noüy felt when viewing the evolution of life forms: the development of increasingly complex patterns of organization and the perpetual emergence of new capacities for understanding and dealing with the world. He has affirmed his respect for life in general and his conviction that "our personalities are each unique and . . . valuable in nature." He has made it clear that available biological knowledge does not discredit belief in God and that it does positively affirm our right to expect further development and further creativeness from human life itself. On this major axiom concerning the value of human

[19] *Ibid.,* pp. 110, 111.

life, great physicists and eminent biologists are in agreement with our cultural tradition.

REVERENCE FOR LIFE

Albert Schweitzer

Having examined briefly some religious traditions regarding the significance of life, together with the views of eminent physicists, philosophers, and biologists, we may turn now to the views of one of the most evenly balanced and fully developed personalities of our times. A recent Nobel Prize winner, Albert Schweitzer has achieved eminence as a theological-research scholar, as a student of sociology and social ethics, as an artist, being one of the greatest organists and interpreters of Bach now alive, and as a physician and surgeon. In each of these diverse areas Schweitzer has achieved not only great profundity of scholarship, but matching skills in the practical application of knowledge to life situations. The story of his development and his accomplishments gives his views great weight.

Schweitzer believes in the existence of God, in purpose or meaning behind life's evolutionary process, and in the essential dignity and worth of every human being. He says: [20]

Man must bring himself into a spiritual relation to the world and become one with it. . . . Beginning to think about life and the world leads a man almost irresistibly to reverence for life. . . . [The] idea of love is the spiritual beam of light which reaches us from the infinite. . . . [In] God, the great first cause, the will-to-create and the will-to-live are one.

The organizing core of Schweitzer's personality is his tremendous "reverence for life." To him, life is God at work through protoplasm, and life is, therefore, essentially spiritual, or ultimate, in its meaning. That is, life has more value than any other reality. Consequently, Schweitzer set up a hospital in the heart of equatorial Africa to conserve and to further the realization of the life potential of the most underprivileged human beings he could find. Indeed, he feels respect, love, and reverence for life in whatever form it occurs and will not kill animals, insects, or plants unless it is necessary in order to conserve or develop human life. The world about him is so full, so vibrant with burgeoning life that Schweitzer "must make himself one with it" in order to express or actualize his own personality or self. He makes himself one with it by curing diseases that threaten life in some individuals, remedying chronic physical defects that have limited life in other individuals, teaching hygiene and

[20] Schweitzer, Albert. *Out of My Life and Thought.* New York: Henry Holt, 1949, pp. 225ff.

improved diet to foster more abundant life, and communicating to all around him this feeling of the sacredness of life and his reverence for life as a creative force. Schweitzer fully lives what he feels and believes.

A Biosocial Philosophy of Education

To me, teaching children or being a parent carries the same meaning, the same challenge, as the wonderful work Schweitzer is doing. Schweitzer has expressed his reverence for life day after day and year after year by helping humans in a primitive society to fight more effectively against eroding diseases and crippling injuries. As a representative of the more highly developed portion of humanity, he serves people whose environment includes many things that attack their bodies and thus limit the fulfillment of their potentials. Schweitzer's is the dual function of remedying, in some measure, the harm that physical, biological, and social environments have done to human beings and of exemplifying and demonstrating to them the warmth of love and the joy in helping that a privileged human being can feel and express toward less privileged fellow humans.

But teachers and parents can go beyond this. They, of course, prevent and cure illnesses, remedy accidental or hereditary defects, supply supporting love, and endlessly and graciously help children solve the troublesome problems of daily living. Then, with these things accomplished, their more difficult work begins. They must regulate or manipulate the physical and social world surrounding developing children and youth so that the new generation is positively and constructively helped to their fullest possible development—to more creative and self-fulfilling living. At this level, for persons who have genuine reverence for life, teaching and parenthood can become the most exacting, exciting, and spiritually developmental vocations that it is possible to imagine.

This is not, however, an invitation to teachers and parents to play the role of God. Teaching and parenthood are no proper vocations for those who enjoy a sense of power over others. They are only for those who love children with genuine humility, because children are life in the process of becoming. Teachers and parents must never think of or deal with children as clay to be molded into something true and beautiful according to the tastes of the parent or teacher. Nor is it appropriate to attempt to shape children into effective citizens according to the standards of the society. The role of the teacher who is imbued with reverence for life and with faith in the dynamic power of life to achieve fulfillment is that of nurturer and facilitator and not dictator and maker of decisions. For the kinds of decisions that teachers make in the classroom in situations such as those described in Chapter 1 depend fundamentally upon what the teacher feels his role to be in the life and development of the pupil.

At this point the basic assumptions that underlie our biosocial philosophy of education might well be restated in order to define more clearly the nature of the educative process and the implied functions of the teacher:

1. We affirm the fundamental value of all human life and believe that it should command nurturing respect and love from everyone, regardless of the background and circumstances in which this life is found.

2. We affirm that living things are dynamic energy systems with the tendency to elaborate themselves to the maximum complexity possible, considering their biological inheritance and the functional situations in which they exist. In other words, although the human individual is shaped extensively by heredity and by the world with which he interacts, he is also dynamic. He shapes his own destiny as a self and he participates actively in building that of his society and of the world. A teacher should have faith in this tendency of human beings to make the most of their potentialities.

3. We affirm that society is made by and for man and not man by and for society. This affirmation has these corollaries:

a. Inasmuch as all members of society, which is now world-wide, are interdependent, every individual must be trained to consider, to value, and to protect the welfare of all.

b. Inasmuch as society is changing at a tremendously rapid pace, as a result of increasing knowledge, invention, creativity, and human discontent, every individual must be trained to participate conscientiously and wisely in the social decision making by which these changes are brought about and regulated. This is the democratic process by which the welfare of all is safeguarded.

c. Inasmuch as democratically arrived-at decisions can be implemented only by effective and consistent action throughout society, every individual must be trained to feel and to act personally responsible for carrying out the intent of the decisions reached.

4. We affirm that it is the function of education to help each individual become at the same time a socially responsible and a self-actualizing person, thus achieving both his social and his biological destinies. There is no inherent antagonism or inconsistency between these two goals; rather they are complementary or are opposite sides of the same coin. Great improvement in working toward these dual goals in the educative process can now be made by helping teachers to see more clearly and deeply the effects and implications of their daily classroom decisions in interactions with individual children and by training them to make more valid decisions in the scientific sense.

Implications for the Educative Process

Given the validity of the affirmations just made, the opportunities and responsibilities that teachers and parents have in the education of children and youth are:

1. To maintain conditions appropriate for each individual's growth and development.

2. To establish and to maintain supporting, security-giving relationships with each individual.

3. To supply informative and developmental experiences as they are needed.

4. To accept and to give scope for functioning to the individual "selves" that emerge as the result of the interaction between individuals with their developmental dynamic and the world with its physical and social forces.

5. To provide social situations and group experiences through which the individual may learn to plan and carry out self-actualization through socially responsible actions and with consideration for the rights and welfare of other human beings.

CHAPTER 3

Mood and Timing

Education as an Empirical Art

While he was still president of Harvard University, James B. Conant
wrote a very thought-provoking book titled *Modern Science and Modern
Man.* In it he points out that such diverse activities as cooking and medicine, brewing and metallurgy, surveying and education all developed
first as empirical arts and are now rapidly being improved by the application of scientific knowledge and scientific methods. Among these arts,
Conant writes, surveying has now become extremely exact, with almost
no empiricism remaining in its practice, whereas cooking and even metallurgy still retain a high degree of rule-of-thumb operation. It is common
knowledge that empiricism in some aspects of medicine has been greatly
reduced, although other phases of its work are still highly empirical.

Education, however, remains very largely empirical, although here,
too, some progress has been made during the past forty years in applying
scientific information and procedures. Conant, of course, does not dis-
count the value to society of well-ordered empirical operations; in fact,
he recognizes that empirical developments in various practical arts have
been the bases of a great deal of our social progress. Thus Conant doubtless would agree that we can all be rightfully proud of the remarkable
progress our schools have made in bringing needed knowledge and skills
to all of the children of all of the people in the United States. No nation
has ever given so much education and such good training to such a large
proportion of its children and youth.

Conant goes on to point out, however, that the practical arts which rest
primarily upon empirical procedures periodically fail to produce the results intended. Persons pursuing these arts again and again find themselves "contending against unexplained perplexities"; that is, they do
their best, yet something goes wrong and they do not know why they
have failed. Consequently, they do not know how to change their practice
in order to prevent the recurrence of failure.

Certainly teachers are in exactly this situation. They conscientiously use approved methods and materials in teaching reading, for example, yet a certain number of their pupils become "nonreaders." They are genuinely concerned about children and careful in their methods of discipline, and they set a good example for their pupils. Yet, one out of every twelve children will suffer mental breakdowns later in life, according to recent reports from the U.S. Institute of Public Health. The number of alcoholics, delinquents, and criminals does not decrease in our population; a very large proportion of all marriages fail; and men and women continue to exploit and cheat, dominate and demean, insult and injure their fellows in many ways. As an empirical art, education clearly is unable to combat effectively many of the unwholesome influences that continue to play upon children and youth; hence, despite the generally dedicated efforts of teachers, the schools are still, in numerous instances, falling far short of developing healthy, socially responsible human beings. In other words, our teachers are still contending against countless "unexplained perplexities."

Scientific Theory and the Practical Arts

Conant uses the history of the last century and a half to show how scientific knowledge and the scientific method have eliminated more and more of these "unexplained perplexities" in the various practical arts. Specifically he points out that new theories in physics, chemistry, and biology have made possible the recent dramatic progress in medicine, agriculture, and invention. He writes: [1]

As these sciences became equipped with more and more satisfactory theories, the degree of empiricism in the arts related to these sciences diminished. As a consequence, in these practical endeavors it became more and more possible to attain accuracy of prediction. . . . New principles evolve which can be related to empirical observations; at that point it becomes possible to control with far greater accuracy than before what one is doing in the practical art and to predict the outcome of a large scale operation.

Child Study and "Unexplained Perplexities"

These statements by Conant describe very well what is just beginning to happen in education. The child-study program described in this book, for example, has been developed gradually during the past sixteen years. It illustrates, though in a limited way, the processes involved in attaining accuracy of prediction in education. The work done between 1939 and 1945 by the Division of Child Development and Teacher Personnel of the Commission on Teacher Education resulted in a new synthesis of

[1] Conant, James B. *Modern Science and Modern Man.* New York: Columbia University Press, 1952, p. 27.

knowledge, drawn from the sciences that study human beings, which constituted an inclusive theory of how children and youth learn and develop. It resulted also in the application of various elements of the scientific method in working out practical ways of communicating this knowledge to teachers in service, so that they in turn could achieve a better understanding of the children and youth with whom they were working.[2] This preliminary experimentation yielded such promising results in helping teachers to reduce the number of "unexplained perplexities" with which they were contending that the Institute for Child Study was established at the University of Maryland in 1947 to continue the work so well initiated under the Commission on Teacher Education. The remainder of this book will present in detail the processes that have so far been developed for guiding teachers in the study of their students and in their continuing assimilation of new scientific knowledge about human development and behavior as it becomes available.

Influence from Philosophy and Science

Before describing the ways teachers can be guided in their acquisition of needed knowledge and skills, it may be interesting to see how the mood and tempo of the educative process is affected when a teacher takes part in this type of group study. For, as indicated in the preceding chapter, philosophical assumptions and social values have been combined with scientific knowledge and methodology in the child-study program.

Science does not define the goals of education. It can only help professional workers resolve the "unexplained perplexities" that stand in the way of achieving goals already accepted. And in the American public at the present moment, there is probably as much confusion about the goals of education as about the means of achieving them. The purpose of this chapter is to show how a teacher's classroom decisions in working with a particular child are influenced by the philosophical assumptions and social values presented in Chapter 2, as well as by the scientific axioms and theories stated there and the scientific procedures to be described in later chapters.

THE CASE OF JANE

In Chapter 1 it was shown that the telling moments in the educative process come when teachers have to make decisions about what to say and do in particular situations involving individual children and groups of children. A number of situations were described to show the complex forces operating in them and the difficulty of making sound decisions

---

[2] Commission on Teacher Education, *Helping Teachers Understand Children.* Washington: American Council on Education, 1945.

with sureness. Just how difficult these decisions are will become more and more evident as we present the case of Jane in this chapter. It will be recalled that Jane is the twelve-year-old girl described in Chapter 1 as putting her arms around her teacher on the playground and declaring that she enjoyed playing only with children under six years of age. She wrote the story titled "Friendly Valentine," which really was the story of a lonely valentine. Jane's compositions were full of serious errors of language and spelling, and she openly defied Mrs. Summers, her teacher, by saying, "I'll get my book, but I won't read."

The case of Jane was selected to show the complexity of interacting forces that must be considered when making classroom decisions. It was selected also to show how hard it is for many children to "act right" at school and to succeed at their school tasks. It demonstrates the problems every teacher must meet, for most teachers have to deal with children of equal complexity every year. It shows that education cannot be a cut-and-dried affair of materials and methods alone, because it involves human beings each of whom has the right to the conditions, relationships, and experiences at school which will help him to take his next step in growing up to self-realization and social responsibility. Yet education is a mass enterprise, as it should be. It must go on in groups. Hence the teacher's task becomes that of making sensitive decisions from hour to hour that will modulate the mood and tempo of the group educative process according to the needs of individual children. In this chapter we shall show how Mrs. Summers accomplished this in working with Jane while she progressed in her child-study activities.

The Complex Problems Jane Presented

Recall for a moment the anecdote Mrs. Summers wrote on February 4 and imagine yourself in her situation:

> FEB. 4, 2:15 P.M. I asked the "Singing Wheels" group to get into their circle. Some of the children said, "Jane won't come into our reading group." I asked Jane to get her book. She said, "I'll get my book but I won't read." She joined the group but I didn't ask her to read because I was afraid she would refuse.

Every teacher will wonder whether Mrs. Summers was wise in letting Jane "get away" with refusing to read. Would this experience weaken her authority over Jane? Would it encourage Jane to feel that she had to do only what she felt like doing at any time? Was Mrs. Summers so afraid of creating a scene that she neglected her real job, that of teaching Jane to read? What could she have known about Jane that made her refrain from insisting that Jane read on that day? Did she perhaps see the situation through Jane's eyes to the extent that she knew that Jane had good reasons for acting as she did and really could not act differently at that moment? Could it be that the best way to help Jane learn to read was to permit her to skip trying to read on that particular day? Fortunately we shall be able to answer these questions, since Mrs. Summers was recording a great deal of information about Jane for use in a child-study group.

Various Facts about Jane

Mrs. Summers' record began with a description of Jane:

> Jane is a slender girl with blond hair, cut short and worn with bangs. She has large blue eyes and a very fair complexion sprinkled with freckles. She seems to have sensitive skin and cannot wear any coarse fabric without a rash appearing where the fabric touches.

The teacher added basic information which she secured from the cumulative record kept at school:

> The school records show that Jane's father was born in River City and her mother in Farmington. Her father works in the paper mill and her mother goes to a neighboring farm each morning to feed the livestock.
>
> Jane has a brother thirteen years old and a sister eighteen years old and in high school. Jane's birth date was October 24, 1939, making her almost twelve years old as I begin this record. She is the last in a family of three children.

From this point on the data gathered by the teacher are not presented in the sequence in which they came to her. They have been sorted and arranged to give the reader information which he needs in order to understand what her teacher actually faced as she made her daily decisions in working with Jane. Mrs. Summers was not always lucky enough to have all the information she needed in advance, as will be clear from the dates on the various entries.

Jane's Capacity for Learning

Upon entering the sixth grade, Jane took the short form of the New California Mental Maturity Test for elementary school children. Her score gave her an IQ of 60 on language factors, of 88 on nonlanguage factors, and of 72 on total mental factors. This would indicate only borderline mental capacity for school learning. On the basis of this test it would be easy to accept the idea that Jane is not very bright and to judge that this underlies most of her trouble and misbehavior. Fortunately, the school records showed many other testings, as tabulated below:

> Kindergarten, age 5 years, scored at the Grade 1 level on the Metropolitan Reading Readiness Test.
>
> Grade 1, age 6 years, scored at Grade-level 1.6 on the Metropolitan Achievement Test.

Grade 2, Kuhlman–Anderson Intelligence Test
    CA 7–6, MA 7–11, IQ 105
    Standard Achievement Test, Grade-level average 2.2

Grade 3, Stanford Achievement Test, Grade-level average 1.8

Grade 4, Otis Quick-scoring Mental Ability Test
    CA 9–5, MA 8–10, IQ 85
    Stanford Achievement Test, Grade-level average 3.2

Grade 5, Metropolitan Achievement Test, Grade-level average 2.7

Grade 5 (repeated the grade), Metropolitan Achievement Test, Grade-level average 2.2

Grade 6, New California Mental-maturity Test
    IQ total mental factors 72

These scores raised many questions in Mrs. Summers' mind. No person is ever able to do better on a test than his capacities allow, if the tests are valid and are properly administered. Jane's scores in the kindergarten and in the first and second grades show her making satisfactory school progress in terms of average mental capacity. But in the third grade her achievement score on the same test was much lower than it had been a year before, and in the fourth grade her intelligence quotient was twenty points lower than her score on a different test two years before. Of course, the two tests could vary somewhat in relative difficulty, but the slump in scholastic knowledge and skills along with the lower intelligence-test scores did suggest that something may have set Jane back in the third grade. The continued low accomplishment scores during the two years she spent in the fifth grade, when she seemingly learned nothing at all, and the low intelligence-test score at the beginning of the sixth grade indicated a continued arrest of mental development.

Jane's Home Situation

Further excerpts from the record follow. Mrs. Summers gathered these items over a period of several months and dated them as they were entered into her record about Jane.

Oct. 10, 8:50 A.M. Jane came to school this morning with deep scratches on her left arm. I asked her what had happened and she said, "I got into a fight with my sister and she did it." I asked her if her mother had put anything on it. She said, "My mother doesn't know. If she did, she'd side with Alice. She always does." One of the other children said, "She's always fighting with her sister."

Oct. 17 I met Jane's mother at the PTA meeting last night. She told me to let her know if I ever have trouble with Jane, because she "has her children right under her thumb." She also said that she realized that Jane hadn't been doing too well in school.

OCT. 23, 12:30 P.M.   As the children ran out to the playground Jane pushed one of the children hard and ran on. I said to the teacher walking with me, "I don't understand why Jane does things like that." The other teacher said, "If you ever saw Jane's home you would. Those children are totally undisciplined. They throw jelly into each other's hair and do anything they feel like doing. I was even there once when Alice threw a butcher knife at Jane. Luckily she missed." I asked her if the mother had any control over them and she answered, "Absolutely none. They call her every name they can think of."

OCT. 25, 12:30 P.M.   While we were out on the playground Jane started talking to me about her brother. (Her brother is in the seventh grade and seems to be a serious problem to his teacher. He is known throughout the community for his misbehavior.) She said that he could get anything he wanted at home because he was the only boy. She did have another brother, but he died from having whooping cough and now her mother is afraid something will happen to this boy.

NOV. 20, 2:00 P.M.   During recess some of the children were standing around me discussing younger brothers and sisters. Jane said, "I wish I had a younger brother or sister. I don't like being the youngest one."

DEC. 4, 12:30 P.M.   While I was on the playground this noon, one of the teachers asked me if I had heard the latest news about Jane's older sister. I said, "No." She proceeded to tell me that Alice is going out with a much older man. I asked if her parents knew about it. She said that Alice's mother had been told and that she said, "My Alice wouldn't do such a thing. She tells me everything." "What about the father?" I asked. She replied, "Jane's father is Mr. Milquetoast personified."

DEC. 14   I saw Mrs. A, a teacher, in the hall and asked if I might speak to her for a minute. She said that she wasn't very busy, so I told her I was becoming very concerned about Jane's actions. I told her about the various kissing episodes. [Jane had said to the other children in the room, "I don't need mistletoe to kiss Mrs. Summers, I just kiss her when I feel like it."] I asked her what I could do to restrain Jane without hurting her feelings. She suggested that I talk to Jane during a free period and tell her that as we get older we don't kiss our teachers. She added, "I think Jane is starved for affection. All the children are spoiled. As far as material things go, they get everything they want. But their mother just screams at them from morning to night and never gives them a kind word."

DEC. 29   I was in the midst of house cleaning when I heard a knock on the door. I found Jane and Florence on the porch. Jane's mother and sister were in the car. I asked them to come in. . . . Jane's mother again remarked that Jane could do better if she tried. She said that Jane just won't buckle down to do anything, that the first thing she did every morning was to go to the neighbor's to play with their children all day. I asked the girls if they had a nice Christmas and Jane said,

"I got everything I wanted." Some of the things she named were a bathrobe, sweater, locket, dress, coat, and things for her dollhouse.

JAN. 2, 10:15 A.M.   During lavatory period, Jane came up to me and said, "Alice's boy friend didn't show up during Christmas. She was supposed to marry him in July." I asked, "Were they engaged?" She said, "No one is supposed to know it, but I heard them talking when they thought I was asleep. I hear lots of things when they think I am sleeping."

JAN. 7, 1:15 P.M.   Jane had her head down on her desk. I asked her what was wrong. When she lifted her head, I saw that her face was covered with blotches and that she seemed to have a temperature. I decided to send her home with the janitor to go along. I gave her a note to her mother suggesting that they take Jane to their doctor.

5:30 P.M.   I telephoned Jane's home to see how she felt. Her mother hadn't thought it necessary to take her to a doctor but had given her a laxative and put her to bed. She thought that Jane might have poison sumac, since she had been playing in the woods Sunday with Florence. She went on to say, "I told her not to go playing in the woods, but she wouldn't listen to me. . . ."

JAN. 8, 9:00 A.M.   Jane didn't come to school today but sent a note asking for her assignments. I gave her brother her work.

JAN. 10, 8:45 A.M.   Jane came to school today. Both eyes were swollen nearly shut. She told me that her brother hadn't brought home her assignments and that Florence had told her he had them, so she made her mother bring him back to school, while the janitor was still here, to get them.

JAN. 12   A baby shower was given in the community and a number of school parents attended. One of the mothers remarked that Jane had certainly worked some kinks out of herself this year. I asked what she meant and she said that Jane used to be very rough. If someone said anything to her that she didn't like, she would call them a string of names and kick and bite them. In fact, she had bitten one of her former teachers quite badly.

Then someone said that she thought something must have happened to Jane while her mother was away for a year. I asked where the mother had been and they told me she had been in Capital City in a mental institution. She had had a serious operation and it had affected her mind. I asked who took care of the children and was told that the whole family lived with the maternal grandmother and that she took care of the children.

Another person remarked that you could still feel the tension in the home when you walked into it, because the father didn't speak to the grandmother. In fact, the grandmother cooked the food and she and the children would eat. After they finished the mother and father would eat.

One of the PTA officers said that she had gone to the home and asked the grandmother to help on a PTA project. The grandmother said that she would be glad to, but she wished they would ask her daughter, because it was time she accepted some responsibility for her children. Another person remarked that she felt sorry for the children when the grandmother died, because she was the only one who cared about the children.

JAN. 23, 8:15 P.M.   Jane was at the PTA meeting. I noticed that she had large black and blue marks on her arms. I asked her what had happened, and she said that she had another fight with her sister.

FEB. 21, 5.30 P.M.   Some of the children stayed after school to help set up chairs, etc., for the puppet show. . . . Jane said, "Florence and I are dying to see the twins' house because they brag so much about it." Florence said, "Well, to tell the truth, our house isn't very nice yet. We're still fixing up." Jane said, "Ours isn't either. We don't even have a bathroom or a kitchen sink."

MAR. 31   This evening my sister came to visit me. Sometime during the evening she asked me if I had heard about Alice, Jane's sister. I said, "No." She told me that Alice was pregnant and was accusing two men. Both of them are married. Could this be what has been disturbing Jane lately?

APR. 1, 12:20 P.M.   Jane came to school after being out because of illness. She told me that Alice had quit school. She added, "Wait until Daddy finds out. I pity her."

APR. 3, 12:25 P.M.   Jane came up to me and said, "Wait until you find something out. I'm going to feel awful." I said, "What do you mean, Jane?" She said, "You'll find out soon enough."

DURING EASTER VACATION—HOME VISIT.   Jane's home is an old farm house. It seems to be made of stone with stucco finish on the outside. The house is built against the hillside along the main road. A brook flows in front of the house, almost in the yard. There are several old buildings behind the house. They appear to have been farm buildings at one time, but are now in a dilapidated condition. The roof of the house seems to sag a bit, and there are some shingles missing.

The day I went to visit no one was at home except the grandmother. I introduced myself, and she said that she had been anxious to meet me and that Jane was at the neighbor's playing with their children. . . . The interior of the home was neat and clean. I noticed particularly that there weren't many windows so that the rooms looked a little gloomy. However, there were potted plants on the window sills. . . .

The grandmother asked me if I knew how much Jane adored me. I said that I realized that she seemed fond of me. Mrs. Z said that I was the first teacher who ever seemed interested in Jane and that she was most grateful because Jane had learned to read in my class. She went on to say that poor Jane had had a poor start in life. When she was about eight years old, her mother had suddenly gone insane. At first her son-in-law had refused medical care for her because he was ashamed of what the community might think. The period while the grandmother was trying to persuade the father to have his wife helped and until she actually went to an institution was a very hectic period for the children. The mother would think she heard someone coming for her and would barricade herself in the attic, screaming for hours on end. Finally the father realized that she needed some attention and took her to the institution in Capital City. She was there for a year and had electric shock and other treatments. The family went to visit her every Sunday. At times she refused to see them.

I asked where Jane's mother was now and she said that she had a new job doing house cleaning in the neighborhood. She didn't think Jane's mother should do any outside work, but she wanted to earn extra money. The grandmother thought she should stay home and accept the responsibility for her children.

Then she told me that this year was the first time Jane went to school without being forced. In fact, now Jane wouldn't stay home even when she was ill. I said that I was glad to hear that because I had tried to make school a happy place for Jane. I also added that I was fond of Jane. Since it was getting late and the grandmother had to prepare supper, I left.

The favorite comment of an English friend of mine comes to mind at this point: "Well, that's a bit much!" What Jane had been living through at home during all of her school life was indeed "a bit much." The accumulated evidence makes it clear that she had never enjoyed the security of love, had passed through many frightening hours while her insane mother was at home, and felt disgraced, ashamed, and looked-down-upon in the community because of her mother and now because of her sister; that home was a pandemonium of strife and aggression; and that she was, in truth, "starved for affection" as well as confused about how to meet life in her circumstances. Given these conditions, it is scarcely surprising that she had learned almost nothing in school after the second grade and that her responses on tests were such as to decrease her computed IQ from 105 to 72. Was it really rebellion and defiance that prompted Jane to say to Mrs. Summers, "I'll get my book, but I won't read"? Or was it defense from further hurt?

Jane's Situation at School

The question must be raised whether it was necessary and inevitable that all the things that happened to Jane at home should produce the effects they did on her schoolwork. Could not school have remained a bright spot in her life? Might she not have balanced off her fears and insecurity at home with feelings of adequacy, belonging, and accomplishment at school? We shall, in fact, see this begin to happen with Mrs. Summers' help, but the record contains only a limited amount of evidence as to what had happened during earlier years. Jane obviously began the school year in September, 1951, with a bad reputation.

Oct. 17, 8:55 A.M. All the children were asked to wait outside for a few minutes until the desks and chairs were moved into place. (They had been moved because of the PTA meeting the night before.) Jane came into the room crying. I asked her what was wrong, but she didn't answer. The principal came in and said, "Don't give her any sympathy. Jane has been out there acting like a wild woman. If she doesn't start behaving, she will have to go to another room."

I patted Jane on the shoulder after the principal left.

Oct. 30, 9 A.M. I formed a reading group in the fifth grade for poor readers. Jane asked to join the group.

Nov. 7, 12:30 P.M. Jane went for a drink and came back with a mouthful of water. I asked her to swallow. She did.

Nov. 29, 12:20 P.M. Some of the children were discussing the gifts they had made for their parents. This led to the discussion of the Christmas party at school. Suddenly Jane said, "You know those teachers in the other school didn't give us any Christmas presents and we had to sit and watch them open the things we gave them." I said nothing.

Nov. 29, 12:30 P.M. . . . Another teacher joined me so they [the girls] ran off to play. As they did, the other teacher said, "I don't understand why Mrs. X (another teacher, also principal) dislikes Jane so." I asked her why she thought Mrs. X disliked Jane. She replied, "Why, she told me so herself. When she found out that she was going to teach the sixth grade the year following the one she had Jane in the fifth, and that the fifth was going to be moved out to another school out of the township, she said she made sure she wouldn't have Jane again." I said, "Do you mean she deliberately failed Jane?" The other teacher said, "That's what she told me. There were others just as slow as Jane, but she just couldn't stand Jane."

Jan. 25, 12:30 P.M. Our pencil sharpener broke, so I sent Jane and Florence to another room to sharpen some pencils. The principal met them in the hall and told them she was tired of seeing them wandering in the hall and to stay in their room. Jane came back and started to cry. She said that Mrs. X hated her and she was afraid to have her for a teacher.

Feb. 4, 3:05 P.M. Florence sat next to me on the bus. She said, "Mrs. Summers, Jane won't read because the substitute teacher told her that she belonged back in beginners because she didn't know a lot of words during reading." I said that I hoped Jane would soon get over feeling the way she did. Florence said, "I'll call her tonight and talk to her."

Feb. 5, 8:50 A.M. Jane waited for me at the door. She said, "Mrs. Summers, I'll read today, but I'm afraid the kids will laugh at me." I told her none of the children had ever laughed at her and I didn't think they would start now.

Feb. 18, 9:30 A.M. I gave the sixth grade an arithmetic test this morning. When the papers were marked, Jane had failed the test. I put no mark on her paper, but she must have realized she failed, for she put her head down and cried when she saw the test.

The preceding anecdotes certainly show two things very clearly. The first is that Mrs. X, the teaching principal of the school, disliked Jane very much and lost no opportunity to blame her and hurt her feelings. This is most unusual. Out of the thousands of case records that our staff members have examined, we have found only a handful in which a teacher or a principal disliked a child to the point of rejecting or "picking on" him. This means that the emotional climate of the classroom had been particularly unfavorable for Jane during the preceding two years. Mrs. X was her teacher during the first of these years, and Jane was transferred to another school in another community during the second of these years as a result of Mrs. X's dislike. Remembering that Jane is organically so sensitive that rough cloth produces a rash on her skin, it is easy to understand that the daily experience of hostility from her teacher would create very strong emotional disturbances in Jane. One wonders whether Mrs. X was the teacher whom Jane finally bit!

These anecdotes also show that Jane is greatly disturbed by her scholastic failures. She feels her lack of skill in reading and arithmetic very keenly and is troubled about being different from the other children and inadequate to the school tasks. This was shown by the alacrity with which she volunteered to join the class of poor readers from the fifth grade; the many occasions, reported in the record but not included in these excerpts, when she asked to have this group meet for special work; her crying when she failed an arithmetic test; and her refusal to read aloud, even with Mrs. Summers, after the substitute had told her that she ought to be down with the beginners.

Incidentally, we are now able to see the wisdom of Mrs. Summers' decision not to try to make Jane read on February 4, when Jane said, "I'll get my book, but I won't read." Mrs. Summers had been out of school for almost a week because of illness, and this episode happened the first day that she was back with the class. She wisely reestablished her authority by making Jane get her book and join the group, but, with equal wisdom, she did not try to force Jane to read because she did not yet know the causes for the refusal. Florence gave her part of the reason on the bus going home when she reported the substitute teacher's sarcastic aggression against Jane. Then the supportive, reassuring handling by Mrs. Summers, with the help of Florence, brought Jane around by next morning and revealed more of the defensive nature of Jane's earlier refusal— "I'll read today, but I'm afraid the kids will laugh at me." It is now obvious that Mrs. Summers' decision not to force Jane on February 4 was the most "educative" decision she could have made. It facilitated

Jane's learning to read. Forcing Jane to read or punishing her as defiant could have set Jane back for weeks.

Jane and the Other Children

When any sizable number of human beings are brought together for any purpose over a considerable period of time, they inevitably become a society. That is to say, they relate to each other in terms of acceptance or rejection and in terms of finding things to do together "for the fun of it" or for the accomplishment of serious aims. They develop group codes of conduct, set up implicit rules as to how the activities of the group are to be carried on, decide what are good manners and what are bad manners, and set up ways of penalizing persons who violate these codes. Finally, the group becomes "structured," that is, they accord to each other varying degrees of prestige depending upon the roles they play, the degree to which they conform to the customs and codes of the group, and the kinds of personalities the individuals have. This tendency for groups to become a society is as true for children as for adults, beginning at least with the second or third grade.

One of the most meaningful and emotionally moving aspects of every child's school experience is his participation in this child society, his struggle to win belonging and then prestige in the group. Consequently, every school class has its high-prestige children; its "regular guys," or full members; its fringers, who get in on things from time to time; its isolates, who just don't matter at all; and its rejected children, who are annoying, aggressive, or obstructive to the group. This possibility for group membership is especially important to insecure children who do not know love in their own homes, for it gives them an avenue to immediate personal significance. At the same time, failure to achieve belonging and win roles in the group is doubly devastating to insecure children because it confirms their sense of lacking value to other human beings. It is easy to see that relationships with other children would be especially important to Jane, and we already have some clues as to what has happened to her from her "lonely valentine" story. Other excerpts from the teacher's child-study record follow:

> Oct. 23   As the children ran out to the playground Jane pushed one of the children hard and ran on. . . .
>
> Nov. 5   Jane was very quiet in school today. The children noticed it, too, and asked her if she felt well. She said that she did, although she didn't move out of her seat all during school hours. At the end of the day, she said, "I missed Florence today. I hope she comes tomorrow."
>
> Nov. 6, 8:50 a.m.   Jane met me at the door and asked me if Florence had come to school. When Florence came into the room Jane put her arm around her and said, "I missed you."

Nov. 7, 9:30 A.M.   Jane was rocking on the two back legs of her chair. I asked her to sit down because the floor was slippery and she might hurt herself. One of the children said, "There won't be much of a loss if she hurts herself." I said, "We don't want anyone in our room to get hurt."

Nov. 9, 1:15 P.M.   The children formed their social studies group. Jane was sitting next to the twins. Suddenly she started to cry. I asked her what was wrong. She said the twins were talking about Florence and she didn't want to work with them. I let her change groups.

Nov. 16, 12:40 P.M.   Jane and Ruth played on the playground together. They would snatch the boys' hats and run.

2:00 P.M.   Jane was chosen last for a relay game.

Nov. 27, 2:50 P.M.   Jane was absent today. At the end of the day one of the boys said to me, "I am glad Jane was absent today." I asked him why, and he said, "It's nice and quiet when she is not here."

Nov. 29, 9:15 A.M.   After our news discussion, one of the boys who had been absent the previous day asked if he might have a transportation booklet like those some of the other children had. I explained that John had only brought a few booklets and that there were no more. Jane said, "Robert can have my booklet. Florence and I can work together in her booklet." Robert smiled and said, "Thank you, Jane." I said, "That was a kind thing to do, Jane."

12:05 P.M.   After she had washed her hands, Jane returned to the room, opened her lunch box and put half an orange on Florence's desk. When Florence came in she didn't say anything, but opened her lunch and put a cupcake on Jane's desk.

Nov. 30, 2:50 P.M.   Florence and Jane were taking care of the library. One of the children went past Jane, and Jane pinched her. She saw that I was watching and grinned at me. I said, "Don't do things like that, Jane."

DEC. 7, 1:15 P.M.   The class decided to give a play for the Christmas program, and the children selected a play called "The Shoemaker's Gift." They chose children for the play parts, and Jane and a few others were not given parts since the play required only a few characters. We discussed ways of changing the play so that everyone might have a part. One of the children suggested a nativity scene, and I said, "Couldn't we use some angels in the nativity scene? I think Jane would make a good one." Then someone suggested that all the girls who didn't have parts be angels. . . .

DEC. 8, 10:15 A.M.   Jane was standing by my desk talking to Florence when one of the boys came up to her and said, "You certainly shouldn't be an angel in the play—you never act like one." There were some oak-tag strips on my desk and Jane picked them up and hit him across the face. The edges went into his eye. I was horrified and told Jane she could have injured him seriously. She said, "If he had done that to me, you wouldn't do anything to him." I couldn't convince her that she was being punished for what she had done and not because of the person she did it to.

JAN. 4, 10:15 A.M. Florence decided to move her seat to the back of the room. I told Jane she could move her seat back too, if she wanted to. She said she would rather sit by me.

2:30 P.M. Florence moved her seat back next to Jane.

JAN. 17, 1:15 P.M. I gave the children a *Weekly Reader* test called "The Wishing Star." . . . Jane came to me and I helped her finish. . . . Some of her wishes were:

I wish the twins weren't in our room.
I wish Florence could come over to my house more often.
I'd like to belong to a 4-H Club.
I don't like to play alone.

FEB. 6, 2:10 P.M. Ruth asked Jane to come to her house to play on Saturday. Jane said, "No, sir, I have been gypped out of playing with the kids all week and I'm going over Saturday." I asked Jane which kids she meant and she said, "Rolf, Wally, and Ann, of course." (Neighbor's children, all under six years of age.)

FEB. 7, 9:30 A.M. Florence was absent today, and so was one of the twins. Jane asked if the other twin could sit with her for the day. I said that she could. They worked together quietly for a long time. Jane suddenly said, "I get along better with the twins when Florence is absent." I said nothing.

FEB. 8, 8:50 A.M. Florence came to school today. She asked to move her seat next to Edith. I allowed her to do so. Jane also moved hers so that a group of four was formed, Edith, Doris, Florence, and Jane.

12:30 P.M. I was on the playground today. I allowed the children who had been ill with colds or who weren't wearing proper clothing to stay inside. These included Edith, Florence, and Jane. I hadn't been out there too long when Florence came out crying. She said that Jane had pulled her hair. . . . When I came in I noticed that Jane had pushed her seat away from Florence. I went over to her and put my hand on her shoulder. She shrugged it off and started yelling, "I don't care, she told lies about me." I said, "Jane, please come into the hall with me." She ran out of the room ahead of me into the cellarway and hid her face against the wall. I said to her, "Suppose you tell me your side of the story, Jane." No answer. "Are you annoyed because Florence played with Edith?" Jane started to cry and said, "I asked Florence to help me and she wouldn't do it. Then she said I was laughing in the hall and I wasn't. She wouldn't answer me when I talked to her, so I pulled her hair." I said, "Florence has to have other friends, too, and she won't like you any better if you do things like that. The best thing to do is wait quietly. She will come back to you. The two of you have been friends all year. It would be a shame to break up that friendship now." She stopped crying and asked me to send Florence out. I did, and as we came down the hall, Jane met us and said, "I'm sorry I pulled your hair, Florence." She took Florence's hand. Florence said, "That's all right, Jane. Let's go wash your face."

FEB. 11, 10:45 A.M.   During our puppet rehearsal Jane moved her chair next to Edith's and sat there quietly until Florence had finished her part. Then she moved next to Florence.

FEB. 12, 12:25 P.M.   I was on the playground with another teacher when Jane, Florence, and Ruth came running out to me. Ruth said, "The twins told Florence what Jane said about her when she was absent and they added a lot on." Florence said, "Jane told me what she really did say." I said to Jane, "Now you've learned the hard way that the things you say are sometimes multiplied when they are repeated." Florence said, "The twins are nasty."

MAR. 3, 12:10 P.M.   Jane showed me a piece of Florence's birthday cake. She had been to Florence's birthday party the day before and was the only girl from the room who was invited.

MAR. 12, 12:30 P.M.   Some of the children were playing hopscotch on the playground. They had formed two groups. Florence, Edith, and Doris were in one group, Laura and the twins in the other. Jane and Ruth went down the steps and ran through the hopscotch square that Florence's groups were using. The girls ignored them, so Jane ran through and scuffed the lines. Edith repaired them, still ignoring Ruth and Jane. Ruth and Jane finally stopped bothering them, linked arms, and walked around the playground talking and looking at the hopscotch groups occasionally.

MAR. 25, 12:30 P.M.   Edith had brought a jump rope to school and all the children enjoyed playing with it. Today, however, Jane snatched the rope and knotted it in big, thick knots. I sent Jane inside.

APR. 21, 10:15 A.M.   During lavatory period John picked up his lunch box and opened it and closed it. He said, "Jane, this is the way your mouth goes." Everyone laughed, including Jane.

The evidence seems to show that Jane was rejected by most of her classmates. She was the last to be chosen in the relay and originally was not given a part in the Christmas play. Her absence was welcomed openly, and a number of comments by children indicated their rejection of her. Much of her behavior obviously annoyed them. She was a disturber of the peace; when crossed, she responded with physical as well as verbal attacks, even against her best friend. At other times she could be generous. She felt her aloneness keenly, and in much of her behavior there was an undertone of resentment against children who belonged and of feeling that she was being done an injustice.

By and large, Jane's relationship with Florence offered moments of warmth in a cold climate of social disapproval by her peers. We do not have enough facts to know what made it possible for the two of them to get along quite well together. They must have lived reasonably close together, because Florence was the only child ever reported as visiting Jane's home to play with her there. The two of them may have had the same economic and social-class background, for they both reported that their homes were not very nice. But even though we do not know why it existed, we still can recognize the warmth of feeling for each other that existed between Jane and Florence throughout the year. Certainly this relationship was very precious to Jane. "Anyway," she felt, "Florence cares."

Any threat to this relationship with Florence naturally caused a strong emotional reaction in Jane for there was little else she could count on in her life situation. This made her overly possessive of Florence, and, of course, her possessiveness jeopardized the whole relationship. One can understand the jealousy that led Jane to pull Florence's hair during the noonhour after Florence moved to sit near Edith, to scuff out the marks when Edith and Florence were playing hopscotch together, and to knot up the jump rope Edith had brought to school for the children to enjoy. Edith was a terrific threat to Jane, whose natural reactions to this threat were socially the worst possible and threatened to drive Florence away from her. One wonders whether Mrs. Summers could have helped Jane develop readiness to be part of an intimate group that included Edith and Doris as well as Florence. Possibly Jane's experience of love and friendship was so limited that she could not as yet relate warmly to more than one age mate at a time. Certainly Jane faced the developmental task of giving up possessive friendships in favor of warm, group belonging. Was she aware of this? How could her teacher help her to accept and accomplish this task?

Jane and Her Teacher

We have seen Mrs. Summers interact with Jane in much of the material already presented. Other excerpts from the child-study record show Jane trying to establish and maintain a relationship that would give her much-needed basic security and reacting with panic or spite when she failed. Something about Mrs. Summers obviously gave Jane feelings of warmth and hope from the first moment of their acquaintance. The record begins with the first composition Jane turned in. It is reproduced here as it was written.

HOW WE GOT THE NICE TEACHER

It's monday Sept. 17, 1951. I walk in door and saw Mrs. Watson in the door for one said hell-o Jane and I said hell-o Mrs Watson and she told me the room I was to go in. and I saw Mrs summers and I said to Ruth and Ruth said I wish I had her you are lucky.

Material from the anecdotal record follows.

Oct. 12, 1 p.m. The children were lined up to go into school after their play period. Jane asked if she could hold my hand. I told her I had to walk behind the children.

Oct. 15, 9 A.M.   Jane met me at the door this morning and asked if she might have the job of hanging up my coat each day. I told her I thought it was very kind of her and allowed her to take the "job."

Oct. 16, 12:20 P.M.   Jane asked to move her seat in front of my desk. I suggested that all the children think about where they would like permanent seats and perhaps we could have a new seating arrangement at the end of the month.

Oct. 18, 12:45 P.M.   Jane came up to me on the playground, hugged me, and ran away.

Oct. 30, 9 A.M.   Jane asked to have her seat moved to the front of my desk. I told her to wait until November 1, so all the children could move their seats.

Oct. 31, 9 A.M.   Jane asked again if she could move her desk in front of mine. I repeated that she had to wait until November 1. Then she asked when we would have the next group reading.

6:45 P.M.   Jane came to my house to show me her Halloween costume. Unfortunately, I was not at home, but she went next door to show my sister her costume. . . .

Nov. 1, 9 A.M.   Jane was waiting at the door when I came to school this morning. She said, "You promised I could move near you today." We spent fifteen minutes rearranging the room. Jane ended up in front of my desk.

Nov. 7, 9:45 A.M.   Jane came up to my desk, got some Scotch tape and put it over her mouth. One of the children said, "Look at Jane." Jane said, "I can still talk."

12:00 Noon.   As the other children were washing for lunch, Jane came up to me and buttoned my jacket.

Nov. 14, 1:30 P.M.   In the middle of a planning period in social studies class Jane announced, "Mrs. Summers has a handsome husband. He always wears a white shirt." (Jane has seen my husband only once.)

Nov. 26, 1:15 P.M.   Our class has decided to make ceramics for their parents for Christmas. I asked Jane to tear up cloth for the children to work on. When the time came to pass out the cloth, Jane said, "I don't need any help," and sat down. I said nothing and went on showing the children how to make the pins. Jane sat looking at her desk and made no attempt to roll out her clay. I said, "I think Jane needs help." I helped roll out the clay and showed her how to cut the pattern. She smiled and said, "I like to do this."

Nov. 30, 12:00 Noon.   I went into the hall to see about some of my boys. When I returned Jane was at my desk. She had spread a napkin and was pouring soup from my thermos bottle. I thanked her and she said, "May I wash your bowl every day, Mrs. Summers?" I said, "All right, Jane, thank you."

8:00 P.M. We had open house tonight so all the parents could see the new addition to the school. As I walked in the door Jane met me. (My son was with me, since I had no baby sitter.) She said, "May I take care of little Mark?" When I said that she could, she took off his coat and took him to the first-grade room. I looked in on them about half an hour later, and they were sitting together playing with puzzles. When it was time to go home, Jane put on his coat and said, "I like to take care of him."

DEC. 3, 8:50 A.M. One of the twins came up to Jane and said, "Today is our turn to sit in front of Mrs. Summers." Jane answered, "I don't care, smarty, there are only fifteen days of school in December, so Florence and I sit here in January twice as long." I interrupted and said, "There will be six more months of school after December. You'll both have lots of time to sit here."

10 A.M. One of the seventh-grade boys came around selling mistletoe. I bought a sprig and put it on the desk. All the children were laughing and deciding where to hang the mistletoe. Jane picked it up and put it on my head, leaned down, and kissed my cheek. I said nothing, removed the mistletoe, and put it on my desk. None of the children remarked about the incident.

DEC. 7, 12:25 P.M. One of the teachers asked to see me in her room. When I returned some of the children told me that, while I was gone, Jane had been running around the room and that she had dropped an apple in Marjorie's milk. I asked where Jane was and someone said she was hiding under my desk. I asked her to come out, but she hid her face in the corner and refused to answer me. So I told the children to get ready to go out to play and then I said to Jane, "We're going out to play, Jane. When you're ready you may come out and join us."

We were out on the playground about five minutes when Jane came out. She and Ruth started walking around the playground for the rest of the period. When the bell rang, Jane said, "Mrs. Summers, I don't want the job of hanging up your coat any more." I said, "All right, Jane."

2:15 P.M. Jane asked me if she could have her job back of hanging up my coat. I told her she could.

DEC. 11, 10:15 A.M. Jane came to me during lavatory period and said, "Mrs. Summers, come and see me during Christmas vacation." I told her I would come if I could.

DEC. 14, 12:30 P.M. Today the children were discussing mistletoe again. Jane said, "I don't need mistletoe to kiss Mrs. Summers. I just kiss her when I feel like it." I said nothing.

DEC. 21, 1:30 P.M. As the children left for their vacation, Jane shouted, "Don't forget to come and see me during Christmas vacation."

JAN. 2, 8:45 A.M. As soon as I came in today, I noticed Jane had moved her desk in front of my desk.

JAN. 28, 3:15 P.M. I was sick in school, so I came home at noon. Jane telephoned and asked me how I felt. I told her I had a virus infection and would be absent the rest of the week. She said, "Well, don't worry about things at school. Florence and I will help take care of things."

FEB. 18, 10:15 A.M. I asked the children to be careful to keep our supply drawer neat. Jane said nothing, but came up to my desk and cleaned the drawer thoroughly.

FEB. 26, 10:15 A.M. Jane said to me during lavatory period that she wished she could sit in front of my desk again. I said to her, "Jane, you don't have to sit in front of my desk to make me like you. I like you no matter where you sit, even if you are in the back of the room." Jane said, "I know you do."

FEB. 27 Sometime ago the children chose chaperones for the trip to Metropolitan City. Jane and Florence chose Mrs. W. Today Jane decided she wanted to go with me. I told her she must go with the one she chose. I can't remember the exact things she said, but she really was very angry and said she was mad at me. Then I got upset and told her she had to go with the one she chose or stay at home. Later she apologized to me.

FEB. 28 We went to Metropolitan City today. After we got there and were all together, Jane remained very quiet all day and stayed close to me. She asked if she could sit with me on the way home. I said that she could. As soon as we left Metropolitan City she put her head on my shoulder and closed her eyes. I don't know whether she slept or not, but she didn't say a word until we got home.

FEB. 29, 8:50 A.M. Jane came to me this morning and said, "Yesterday was the best day I ever had." I asked her why, and she said, "Because I was near you all day."

MAR. 10, 10:15 A.M. During lavatory period this morning Jane told me all about Florence's visit to her yesterday. They had gone for a long walk and Jane said several times, "Boy, did we have fun!" She then said, "I wish I could call you Aunt Alice." I asked her why and she said, "Just because."

MAR. 24, 1:15 P.M. Some of the children were presenting their social studies report. Jane was not listening at all but was annoying Laura, who sat next to her. She giggled out loud. I asked her to pay attention. Next she pinched Laura. I asked her to take her chair to the back of the room. She took her chair and slammed it down in the back of the room. She yelled, "You always pick on me." Then she jabbed at a survey map lying on the work table, kicked at the closet and muttered to herself. I ignored her.

2:00 P.M. Laura came into the room crying. I asked her what was wrong, and she said that Jane had taken her necklace and was going to flush it down the toilet. I went into the lavatory and got the necklace from Jane. I said, "Why are you being so mean to Laura?" She said, "Because you punished me for something that was her fault." I told her that she was the one in the wrong, that Laura had tried to ignore her, and that she had persisted in annoying Laura. I asked her to go into the room and sit down. She did.

APR. 3, 12:25 P.M. Jane came up to me and said, "Wait until you find something out. I'm going to feel awful."

APR. 7 I planned to take my children to the county seat to take part in an educational demonstration. Some of the mothers volunteered to drive the group, and we tried to plan that each mother would take the children that lived near her. Jane decided upon the mother she wanted to go with. However, this mother was not going near Jane's home, only had a pickup truck, and didn't want any children sitting in the back. So I called John's mother, Mrs. Y, and asked her if she could take Jane. She said she would be glad to, so I came back to the room to give the happy (so I thought) news to Jane. She started crying and yelling, "I don't like Mrs. Y and I won't go with her. Why can't the twins go with her and let me go with Mrs. M?" I explained that the twins lived near Mrs. M, who already had arranged to take them, and that it was much easier for her to do so. Jane said, "Well, I'm going with Mrs. M. Mrs. Y is a horrible person." My patience snapped and I told Jane that Mrs. M could not go ten miles out of her way just to accommodate her and that if she didn't want to go with Mrs. Y, she could stay home. I also said that I was very much annoyed about the things she said about Mrs. Y and that she had to stay in at noon and talk to me.

During noon, while the other children were out playing, I asked Jane how she would feel if someone said such nasty things about her mother. She said that she wouldn't like it. So I said, "How do you think John felt when you said things like that about his mother? I don't think you have the right to make him unhappy just to get your own way." Jane said nothing.

1:15 P.M. I was putting up a bulletin-board display in the hall with a group of children helping me. Jane came out of the room and said, "Mrs. Summers, I'm very sorry about the things I said about Mrs. Y." I said I thought she should apologize to John. She did.

APR. 8. Jane went with Mrs. Y. Mrs. Y said that she was very well behaved the whole time she was in the car.

APR. 28, 9:15 A.M. Jane told me she heard I was leaving school next year. She asked me if it were true. I said that it was. She said, "If you leave, I'll cry for days." I said, "I'll be very unhappy if you do. I'll still be your friend even if I won't be close by. Besides, you still can come to visit me and write me letters." She answered, "If you go past my house each day, I'll wait by the road and wave at you." I told her I would stop in to see her occasionally. I added that I hoped that she would act next year just as if I were there. She promised that she would.

Mrs. Summers Gave Jane Security

Two objections commonly are made against certain aspects of our child-study work. The first is usually stated somewhat as follows: "Why should the teacher make home visits and find out what problems the child faces there? The chances are that his problems are caused by something at home. There is nothing a teacher can do about his parents, the way they treat him, or what goes on in his home. Why, then, should the teacher know about these things? It is much better merely to treat all children alike without knowing the unpleasant things that happen to each one."

The second objection is often presented as follows: "Suppose a teacher does find out that a child is not loved at home and is insecure and that this is basically what is the matter with him. His teacher can't make this up to him. She can't take the place of his parents and love him as her own child. If she tries this, the other children will notice it and will think that she is playing favorites. This will cause her a lot of trouble with the other children—more trouble than she will avoid with him. It will cause the child trouble, too, because pupils don't like teacher's pets. Anyway, the teacher's job is to teach children and not to love them; their parents are the proper ones to love them. But if they don't, you still can't expect a teacher to love every Tom, Dick, and Harry just because their parents have fallen down on their jobs."

The story of Jane and her relationship with Mrs. Summers certainly refutes both these objections, at least so far as Jane and Mrs. Summers are concerned. Fundamentally, to love a person is to value him, feel deep concern for his welfare, happiness, and development, and be ready to help him. It does not mean being sentimental about him, gushing over him, or babying him. Fundamentally, insecurity is the inability to value oneself. It means feeling that there must be something basically the matter with oneself, that one lacks worth. A child can never value and believe in himself until he has had the experience of being valued and believed in by another. Consequently, if parents are so maladjusted and preoccupied with themselves and their own problems that they do not make the child feel deeply valued simply because he is their child, the child will not be able to value himself. He will deeply doubt his own worth as a human being. This is one of the most enduring and persistently disturbing of maladjustments. Overcoming it requires great patience.

In one respect, Jane's case was typical of hundreds of others we have seen. No one in the family had sufficient insight, strength of character, understanding, and opportunity to pull the family together, harmonize the warring factions, neutralize the trauma, and induce the peaceful and harmonious living that begets psychological security. Although the grandmother was doing her best, her efforts were limited to maintaining the family routines and meeting the material needs of the family by cooking, washing, and sewing.

Are such children to be left unaided in their extremely unhealthy emotional situations? Of course, most of them actually never find help and simply become more deeply maladjusted. But we have seen dozens of cases in which such children were helped by their teachers—dozens of relationships like that which developed between Mrs. Summers and Jane. Analyzing the relationship between Jane and Mrs. Summers will identify some of the crucial factors in a security-giving teacher-pupil relationship. We know now that it is possible for a teacher to play this role without jeopardizing her relationships with the other children.

Mrs. Summers Valued Jane

The first factor in a security-giving relationship is a sincere valuing of the child by the teacher. This does not mean forming a sentimental attachment to the child or attempting to make up for his hard life situation by doing special things for and with him. It means having inner conviction that the child has good in him, has potentialities that can be realized, and is worth the thought and the effort involved in helping him. Someone must feel that a child is worth the bother he causes before he can ever really believe in himself.

How is this feeling on the teacher's part communicated to the child? Apparently, very seldom by words. More often it is done by understanding smiles, touches of the hand, taking the time at a busy or inconvenient moment to try to understand something, avoiding humiliating him, and especially not blaming him in one's own thoughts and feelings—a factor that will be discussed later. These factors are aspects of the mood of the teacher-pupil relationship, which is determined by how the teacher feels inside and not by any particular things she can learn to say or do to the child. Ultimately the child will know if he is genuinely valued. But he will be able to believe it only gradually.

Certainly one of the early cues Mrs. Summers gave Jane concerning her value in her teacher's eyes was on October 17 when she patted Jane on the shoulder after the principal had been severe with her. Others were her permitting Jane to do various personal services for her, such as hanging up her coat and washing her soup bowl, and accepting, albeit conservatively, little caresses—permitting Jane to hold her hand for a moment, to hug her on the playground, to kiss her cheek under the mistletoe, and to ride home from Metropolitan City with her head on her teacher's shoulder.

Of course, such direct evidences of affection must be limited in frequency and restricted as to time and place and must develop very slowly. Mrs. Summers was remarkable in the way she limited and timed her permissiveness. For example, on October 12 she refused when Jane wanted to hold her hand as the children lined up to go into the school. Throughout the month of October she refused Jane permission to move her seat up next to the teacher's desk. She permitted Jane to sit next to her for only a month at a time; then other children had their turns. She refused Jane permission to ride to Metropolitan City with her, and she met Jane's tantrum about Mrs. Y with firmness.

Managing Misbehavior

Another factor which in the long run goes far to prove to a child that he is valued is the way his misbehaviors are handled. There are three significant aspects of the handling of misbehavior. First, a person who really values a child never lets him "get away" with misbehavior. Persons who let children get away with misbehavior do so in order to save themselves bother or for some other personal reason. They do not do it for the child's sake. Children somehow know this. They exploit their privilege of misbehaving, but they do not derive security from it. They do not feel valued by the people who spoil them; quite the opposite, they feel that the person who won't take the trouble to correct them doesn't love them, although they are not able to put his feeling into words.

The second aspect of managing misbehavior is that a person who values a child is genuinely disappointed when the child misbehaves, but he does not reject the child emotionally, nor does he blame the child. He knows that the behavior was caused, and he may be able to sense some of the causes; consequently he does not reject the child as bad or unworthy. He is very sorry, however, that the combination of things evoked the misbehavior and disappointed that the child is not yet grown up enough and has not yet developed conscience, organized values, and perception enough to feel the undesirability of the behavior and avoid it. A person who values a child and understands that behavior is caused cannot reject or blame him, but is nevertheless compelled by his own valuing of the child to try to make the misbehavior an occasion for learning. Consequently, he deals positively with the situation.

In late March and early April, for example, Mrs. Summers knew that in addition to her other sources of insecurity and unhappiness, Jane felt threatened by Alice's pregnancy and the loss of family standing that the scandal would incur. Jane felt it doubly; not only would the other girls talk about her and look down on her, but Mrs. Summers, her new source of security, might also be alienated. "I'm going to feel awful, when you find out something," Jane had said to Mrs. Summers on April 3.

Nevertheless, all during this period, Mrs. Summers refused to let Jane get away with misbehavior. On March 24 she made Jane change her seat when she persisted in annoying Laura, and later she reprimanded Jane for taking Laura's necklace and threatening to destroy it. Mrs. Summers was firm and unequivocal in rejecting not only the behavior but Jane's rationalization of it. But she never suggested in any manner that Jane herself was unworthy or impossible to believe in.

Again, on April 7 Mrs. Summers did not let Jane get away with her tantrum about going to the county seat with John's mother. Eventually she even evoked from Jane an apology to John. Mrs. Summers also was angry about the way Jane acted and wisely let Jane feel her indignation. But it must be noted that Mrs. Summers was not expressing annoyance at being personally blocked in her plans for Jane; she told Jane that she "had no right to make John unhappy just to get [her] own way." Everyone must express this kind of indignation: anger at injustice, the violation of human rights, and the exploitation of others. But such anger does not involve the rejection of the misbehaver. Instead, it results in action to undo the harm he has done and to change him so that he will not wish to do the harm again. Mrs. Summers dealt with Jane so as to make her wish not to hurt John again in this way, and Jane responded by going to the county seat with John's mother and by behaving very well all during the trip.

The third aspect of managing misbehavior is in the timing of the disciplinary action and the demands made upon the individual who has misbehaved. A teacher must not be perpetually on the lookout for trouble. Judicious ignoring often gives a child the chance to think twice and not to persist in an undesirable pattern of behavior. This was admirably illustrated by Florence, Edith, and Doris, who ignored Jane when she ran through the hopscotch space several times and then scuffed out some of their lines—ignored her to the extent that her behavior was unprofitable as a way of annoying then and she finally went off with Ruth. A fight and many hard feelings were prevented by this unusually mature behavior of the three little girls. One wonders whether Mrs. Summers' quieting presence may have been an effective catalytic agent in this situation.

Mrs. Summers, also, tried ignoring Jane on March 24, when Jane was annoying Laura. This did not work, so she had to send Jane to the rear of the room. There Jane persisted for a time in expressing her unhappiness, but this time Mrs. Summers ignored her successfully, Jane subsided, and a crisis was avoided.

But the best of Mrs. Summers' procedures was her holding back from making immediate demands upon the child while she was excited or upset. The demands were never omitted, that is, Jane never "got away" with anything. On the other hand, the demands were made on her only when she was able to consider them, to see their reasonableness, and to respond to them. This was well illustrated on April 7, when Jane had her tantrum about going to the county seat with Mrs. Y. On the basic issue,

Mrs. Summers was firm: Jane would go with Mrs. Y or stay home. But Jane also had done wrong in talking publicly as she did about Mrs. Y. The consideration of this was put off till noon, when the pupil-teacher conference could be private. At noon Mrs. Summers raised the new issue and set Jane thinking about it. "How do you think John felt when you talked that way about his mother? You did not have the right to make him unhappy just to get your own way." Mrs. Summers made it clear that she rejected the behavior and stated the reason, but still she made no demand upon Jane. It was only an hour later, when Jane of her own volition came to Mrs. Summers in the hall, that she said, "I think you ought to apologize to John." By that time Jane was able to take the necessary action and was a better person for it. But demanding this in the morning might well have precipitated a crisis. Timing of demands upon children is an important aspect of helping them to learn to manage their behavior under stress.

Another excellent illustration of the same process came on December 7, when Jane misbehaved while Mrs. Summers was out of the room and then hid under the teacher's desk when she returned. In this situation Mrs. Summers let Jane find her own way back to rational behavior and a warm relationship by altering the situation instead of trying to make Jane change. She took the children out to play. Then she accepted Jane's expression of hostility—"I don't want the job of hanging up your coat any more"—without a countershow of hostility. And before the afternoon was over Jane sued for peace and asked for the privilege again.

Children feel that they are picked on when their teachers are too meticulous in spotting little items of misconduct. At the same time, moving too rapidly to correct misconduct does not give children the necessary time to think twice, to cool off, and to see their behavior in perspective. The actual making of demands upon the child is often better deferred until a later time. But on no account does this mean that the demands are not to be made. Children have to learn to measure up to the requirements of sound moral and social codes.

Teachers Can Give Security

We have seen that Jane began to gain a measure of emotional security through her relationship with Mrs. Summers and that the attitudes and actions of Mrs. Summers which made the security possible were in no way inconsistent with her professional role. Jane learned to read quite well during this school year, so much so that her grandmother was greatly surprised and very grateful to Mrs. Summers. Jane also changed much of her behavior toward other children and toward adults, as was observed by the neighbor who said that Jane had "certainly worked some kinks out of herself this year."

All this seems to have been accomplished because the teacher deeply and sincerely valued the child; accepted expressions of affection from her within reasonable limits and gave her genuine and patient help; refused to accept misbehavior, but did not reject the child psychologically along with the misbehavior; and helped the child to remedy her misbehavior by ignoring judiciously the behavior induced by emotion and timing appropriately the demands made on her. The teacher did all this without neglecting to respond to other pupils and without putting Jane in the unhealthy role of a pet.

Behavior Under Stress

Jane's case is rich in material about two types of behavior—one carried out impulsively under emotional stress and the other unconsciously designed to relieve or prevent emotional stress and lead to satisfactions. These two types are called emotional and adjustive behavior. Much of Jane's behavior in situations producing strong emotions has already been described: physical fighting with her sister, crying when reprimanded by the principal, hiding under the teacher's desk, striking the boy with the oak-tag strips, refusing to read, pulling Florence's hair, scuffing out the hopscotch markings, slamming her chair against the floor, threatening Laura, having a tantrum about Mrs. Y, and caressing the teacher on the playground.

Jane was very active under emotional stress and overt and direct in expressing her emotions. She tended to follow the behavior patterns of younger children, but according to the testimony of a neighbor, she changed these patterns greatly during the year she was with Mrs. Summers.

The Effects of Emotional Behavior. The idea that all emotions should be freely expressed as a means of avoiding the dangers to health and to orderly thinking that go with repression has been widely promulgated by some psychologists and mental hygienists. But I believe this to be an erroneous and dangerous principle. When Jane expressed freely the emotions which grew out of her insecurity and which burst out when she was frustrated, she simply got herself disliked by everybody, including members of her family, neighbors, teachers, and her peers at school. And this dislike deprived her of belonging, the roles that go with belonging, chances to build play skills, and friendships. In short, the uninhibited expression of certain emotions, especially of hostility, aggression, jealousy, and revenge, usually brings more rejection, frustration, and loss of love and status.

Managing Emotional Behavior. What, then, should the child or youth learn to do when he is angry, frustrated, jealous, vindictive, or full of hate? Obviously the first thing to do is to recognize that he has the emotion and to accept its naturalness, inevitability, and authenticity under the circumstances. The mistake so often made by teachers is to tell children that they should not feel angry, afraid, jealous, or vindictive. But all of us have these feelings under some circumstances; we are built that way. For this reason we must let children know that we accept their feelings as natural and do not blame them and that they can expect repeatedly to have such feelings and need feel no guilt about them.

But how to act when experiencing emotion is another question. Hundreds of case records show that when children freely act upon their emotional impulses, as Jane did, the result is always more trouble for themselves and others. For this reason I have been watching for records showing teachers and children dealing constructively with these feelings. We certainly need further research on this topic as soon as is feasible, but the tentative conclusion to be drawn from these records seems to be that the child should be restrained from carrying out the behavior implied by the emotion and given time to think twice about what it is best to do. In the long run this implies training the child according to a four-step procedure: (1) to accept his feelings of emotion as natural and justifiable under the circumstances, so that no guilt is implied; (2) to hold back from doing what he feels like doing because it will be better for him as well as for others not to act impulsively; (3) to think about what has caused the trouble and what can be done to solve this problem for him; (4) to act on the basis of the best plan he can conceive.

It should be pointed out, however, that this manner of dealing with emotion will not always avoid fights, for example. There are times when a boy knows that he has to fight for a number of reasons—to prove to himself and to others that he has the courage to risk pain and defeat, to show another boy and the group that he cannot be picked on or exploited with impunity, to defend a member of his group, or to participate with his group in defending a right. But under these circumstances a boy will know what he is doing and why he is doing it and will perhaps even be able to do it better because he has his wits about him. Holding back from the impulsive expression of emotion does not mean just "taking" whatever may happen to one; rather it means using better judgment about what to do. Obviously, developing the ability to manage emotions in this manner requires years of practice and a great deal of help from others. The first step is to accept the emotion itself as natural.

Scientific theory supports this way of managing emotion. The initial surge of feeling seems to narrow one's perception of reality; one experiences a sort of "blind" impulse to violence in order to break down frustrating barriers, to punish offending persons, or to escape immediately from the threatening danger or unpleasantness. These blind impulsive actions recur in case records. But once this initial action is restrained and the impulse inhibited, the individual's perception of his situation widens. He sees more of the factors involved and consequently is able to understand more of the consequences of his various possible actions. In other words, delaying action even for a short time gives evaluative processes a chance to operate. Codes of conduct, conscience, values, and reason come into play when the individual avoids impulsive, unexamined action and gives himself time to think.

Repression of Emotions

Repression of emotion is quite a different thing from inhibiting immediate impulsive action during emotion. It is indeed a dangerous thing, for it involves immediately putting out of consciousness all recognition of the fundamental nature and causes of the emotion. It means denying the existence of the emotion. This, of course, involves distortion of the individual's perception of reality.

Repression means that the individual does not permit himself to see his situation as it really is—to perceive that he is in real danger, genuinely blocked from realizing his purposes, or enmeshed in troubles that will do him harm. The emotion is rejected as an experience and the realities that give rise to it are denied. This is accomplished by putting the mind to work to manufacture an explanation of the situation, one's motives, or the relationship between oneself and the situation which will make the emotion unnecessary and inconceivable.

Some of the mental gyrations which make repression possible are rationalizations, projections, and introjections. All are mechanisms which permit one the comfortable but false feeling that he is right and that things are going to work out well. For this reason, repression and the consequent distortion of perception through which it is accomplished are very unhealthy and properly should be discouraged.

It is unfortunate that restraint of initial impulsive action during emotion has been confused with repression of emotion. The alternative to repression certainly is not to give all emotions immediate overt expression. In therapy, persons who are thoroughly habituated to repress their emotions must sometimes be brought back to the reality of their own natures and of life by being encouraged to let themselves feel emotion and to express it without guilt feelings. But this kind of therapy always includes a long period of reeducation in which the subject comes to understand the undesirability of the unbridled carrying out of impulses and learns to substitute socially reasonable conduct.

This confusion between restraint of action and repression of emotion can be eliminated if children are not blamed and made to feel guilty for having emotions. Indeed, maturity, social effectiveness, and the realization of sound values require that the individual learn to accept as natural and inevitable such feelings as anger, hostility, vindictiveness, and hatred both in himself and in other people. But it is equally important to learn to restrain the impulses that would express these feelings. Mental health in our culture requires that the individual adhere to patterns of action consistent with his social codes of conduct, including both self-realization and consideration for the rights and needs of others.

Mrs. Summers worked with Jane according to this developmental plan. She recognized the myriad causes of Jane's unpleasant emotions and so expected outbursts. She accepted the naturalness of the emotions, but she checked her impulsive action and gave her time to cool off and think a bit. Then she guided Jane to more sensible behavior. She could not, of course, revolutionize Jane's behavior in one short school year, considering the problems Jane faced. But she accomplished a great deal because the mood and tempo in which she worked with Jane were supportive and developmental.

The Easing of Persisting Tensions

Many children, like Jane, bring to school with them every day a terrific burden of tension and anxiety stemming from their home situations. Consequently, a moderate amount of failure, frustration, criticism, or jealousy will precipitate aggressive acts, tantrums, or withdrawal. One of the wholesome things a school can do for such children is to provide them with daily opportunities for relieving these tensions in creative activity. Music, painting and drawing, clay modeling, rhythms and folk dancing, games and sports, construction, and dramatic play all offer children fine opportunities to free themselves to give sustained attention to their school tasks.

It is interesting that Jane, entirely on her own, had discovered a tension-relieving activity. She had developed a program of therapeutic action which Mrs. Summers finally came to understand late in February. An inkling came when Jane did a *Weekly Reader* test called "News from Home." Jane wrote:

> I have a pet lamb. I take care of my pet. I would like to have a pet horse. The thing I like to do best at home is feed my lamb.

On the same test she also wrote:

> If I could have three wishes I would wish (1) I could have baby brothers and sisters, (2) I wish I had a lot of money, (3) Have lots of children when I grow up.

As Mrs. Summers read this material she remembered the many times Jane had talked about taking care of neighbors' children and her caring for Mrs. Summers' own little boy. She empathetically caught Jane's wistful feeling of longing for small brothers and sisters and for babies of her own to love and care for. Somewhere, somehow, Jane apparently had learned the joy of feeling love for others and of expressing it by caring for them. At first, Jane's desire to be with younger children had seemed unwholesome—a way of being important, getting control of a situation, and being powerful. But since a different interpretation was possible, Mrs. Summers pulled together all of her anecdotes about Jane's interaction with younger children and studied them. The anecdotes follow:

OCT. 29, 12:15 P.M.   Jane told me she liked to play with the neighbor's children.

NOV. 13, 9:30 A.M.   Jane told me she was going baby-sitting that night. She said, "I like to go and take care of Betty. She does crazy things like cutting off her hair in hunks."

NOV. 14, 1:30 P.M.   Jane told me she had been baby-sitting again with her grandmother. "I did all the work and she got the money."

NOV. 20, 2:00 P.M.   During recess time some of the children were standing around me discussing younger brothers and sisters. Jane said, "I wish I had a younger brother or sister. I don't like being the youngest one."

NOV. 29, 12:30 P.M.   When we got to the playground Jane put both arms around me and rubbed her chin against me. I said, "Jane, why don't you play with the other children?" Jane answered, "I only like to play with Rolf, Billy and Ann, or Wally and Francie." (All these children are her neighbors', and all are under six years.) Ruth said, "I guess she does like them. I went over to play with her one day and had to help cart three kids home."

NOV. 30, 8 P.M.   [Anecdote about caring for Mrs. Summers' son, Mark, during open house. At the end of the evening Jane put his coat on and said, "I like to take care of him."]

DEC. 10, 8 P.M.   Some of the children were making stuffed rabbits for Christmas gifts. Jane showed me some material she had bought. There was enough for five rabbits. She said she was making them for the neighbors' children.

JAN. 21, 1:10 P.M.   We decided to have our puppet show next month. Someone suggested that the smaller children sit in front so that they could see. I said that perhaps one member of the class could be with them and watch them in case they would be frightened and needed their mothers. Jane asked if she could have charge of them. The children said that they thought "Jane would be a good one."

FEB. 6, 2:10 P.M.   [Anecdote about Jane refusing to go to Ruth's house to play with her on Saturday. "I've been gypped out of playing with the kids all week and I am going over on Saturday." (Rolf, Wally, and Ann.)]

VALENTINE'S DAY, FEB. 14, 2:00 P.M.   Jane gave me a Valentine lollipop for my son.

2:50 P.M. My sister came to take me home from school and brought my son along. Jane asked if she could bring him in. I allowed her to get him. After he came in she asked if she could take him to the first-grade room. She did. After school was dismissed, she walked to the car with us.

FEB. 21, 8:15 P.M. During the puppet show Jane spent the whole time taking children to the bathroom, getting them drinks, etc. She had two by the hand in the hall at one time and she said to me, "This is fun." She was smiling every time I looked at her.

Of course, the causes that underlie behavior are always multiple; hence there were several reasons why Jane so much enjoyed the evening of February 21. She was being very successful at doing something at school, and after so much failure it must have produced a very pleasant glow in Jane to feel herself doing the right things so smoothly and well. Also, Jane was playing a role. The other children had felt that she would be "a good one" to take charge of the very young children and had given Jane this assignment. She was doing her part in a larger project. The feeling of belonging, of having a role, and of carrying it out successfully must have given Jane a feeling of self-realization.

But the record also supports the conclusion that much of the pleasure for Jane was intrinsic in what she was doing, that it sprang from doing things to make these little ones comfortable, safe, and happy. Even back in November, Ruth had observed her with small neighbor children and had concluded, "I guess she really does like them." On two occasions Jane had taken care of Mrs. Summers' little son, Mark, and each time she had taken him to the first-grade room for play appropriate to his maturity level. She had not merely fussed over him like a setting hen in the sixth-grade room where Mrs. Summers could see her taking care of him; rather, an empathetic concern for Mark's pleasure led her to take him to the first-grade room. On each of these occasions Jane had spoken as though it were a pleasant privilege to care for the young child. Every time Jane did any wishing, she wished for younger brothers and sisters, obviously because she would have the chance to care for them. She also wished to have lots of children of her own when she grew up. Peers often are very perceptive of one another's motivation, and the class had deemed Jane well fitted to take care of the little ones during the puppet show. Jane was smiling throughout the evening.

All this would seem to lead to the conclusion that Jane really did find pleasure in the activity itself. We see it also as a way Jane had learned to manage her tensions, to replace an unpleasant mood with an experience that gave genuine pleasure. She really did not need music and painting as an outlet when she was able to find little children to care for. It would be very interesting to find out just how Jane discovered this.

But, of course, such knowledge was not necessary to Mrs. Summers. It was enough for her to be able to recognize Jane's desire to care for little children a a wholesome adjustive process rather than a regressive tendency.

The Value of the Clinical Approach

From our discussion of Jane, the factors that prevented her learning and development, and the wisdom with which her teacher handled most situations, we can draw a number of conclusions. The first is that the effective teacher simply must have a certain measure of understanding of each child. In no other way will he be able to make the wise decisions that will foster the genuine development of each child, or modulate the emotional climate of the classroom so that it is appropriate to each child's adjustment needs. How well must he understand each child? Obviously, the degree of understanding required of a good teacher is not so great as that required of a therapist, but clearly the kind of understanding required is that which characterizes the clinical approach.

Clearly, too, the clinical approach requires considerable knowledge of the sciences that study human beings and considerable self-discipline in using the scientific method to make decisions about children. Here the relevance of Conant's comments, cited at the beginning of this chapter, becomes apparent. The science of human development and behavior is currently making enormous strides in its theoretical formulations, particularly with regard to the theory of selfhood, and good progress methodologically. Consequently the practical art of education can now reduce the number of "unexplained perplexities" involved in its practice. With adequate attention to the sciences that study human beings in the preservice education of teachers and with a careful follow-up training of teachers in service, we now can educate teachers to understand children. The teacher's understanding should be oriented toward wise classroom decisions, however, not toward successful therapy.

But the adequate education of teachers to relate themselves wholesomely to their pupils requires the study of philosophy and religion as well as science. For the clinical approach involves attitudes as well as information—sincere valuing of the child as well as sound reasoning about his developmental tasks and adjustment problems. In order to define these attitudes, it may be well to describe specifically the characteristics of the teacher whose approach is clinical.

The effective teacher will have the following characteristics in addition to adequate knowledge of subject matter and teaching methods:

1. *Active and sincere valuing of each child at all times.* Being sincerely valued as a person creates a haven of security for the child. It has a double

value: it helps the child to build and to maintain his own self-respect, and it removes barriers between the teacher and the child and promotes an easy two-way communication between them. Both are conditions vital to effective learning, as we have seen in the relationship between Jane and her teacher.

2. *Genuine expectation and acceptance of the fact that every child is unique.* The clinically oriented teacher does not regret or resent the uniqueness and individuality of each child even though it means that he must understand each child individually in order to teach him effectively in group situations. This idea has been axiomatic in his training. Valuing his own individuality, the effective teacher enjoys coming to know his pupils as individuals.

3. *Genuine expectation and acceptance of multiple or complex motivation behind behavior.* The clinically oriented teacher cannot accept a single, simple factor as the cause of a child's action or development. He knows that a great many factors, operating over considerable periods of time, have made the child what he is, and that there is no simple, single remedy for a child's difficulties, no "sure-fire" stimulator of his further development. The very complexity of the developing child gives dignity to the teacher's professional tasks. Complexity is welcomed because out of it spring potentialities for learning in the child.

4. *Acceptance of the necessity for trying many different approaches, in sequence or in combination, in order to evoke needed changes in behavior and the learnings necessary to further development.* The complexity of motivation, even in quite young children, is so great, and the variations in motivation from child to child in a given classroom are so vast, that it is completely unreasonable to expect any one method of instruction or discipline to work effectively with all children or even with a particular child at all times. The professional worker who realizes and accepts this principle does not feel annoyance toward a child or doubt about his own ability when his plans do not work out. Furthermore, he is always ready with alternatives, because he understands and accepts the complexity of human motivation.

5. *Genuine faith that, when enough causal factors favor it for a sufficiently long time, the necessary learnings and behavioral changes will occur.* The clinically oriented teacher not only knows that behavior is caused, but also has had the experience of seeing people learn, change their patterns of behavior, set up new developmental goals, and progress toward them. For these reasons he has faith that every child will respond to the educative process, provided he can influence enough of the causal factors that shape each child's life and learning. He knows, too, that human relationships in the classroom and the child's daily experiences in and about the school are powerful factors in development. In other words, he knows that his faith is well founded.

6. *Ability to discriminate between acceptable and unacceptable patterns of behavior and to help the child to discriminate without rejecting or blaming the child as a person while refusing to accept his actions.* This is a most important factor in the mood of education, because the child, through empathy, immediately feels the attitude the teacher holds toward him in any situation. The child will be able to sense whether the teacher sincerely values him even while he is refusing to accept a given pattern of behavior, expressing his refusal and per-

haps punishing the child. The child will feel, "This teacher likes me. He knows that this is wrong for me to do, so he won't let me do it. He doesn't like to punish me, but he does it anyway, to teach me not to do this again." With such handling a child tends not to repeat his misbehaviors, unless he has special adjustment problems of which this misbehavior is only a symptom.

In contrast, if the teacher rejects the child along with his unacceptable behavior and punishes in the mood of retribution for wrongdoing, then the child feels, "This teacher hates me. That is why he won't let me do the things I want to do. He doesn't want me to be happy, so he keeps picking on me about all these little things." With this kind of handling, the child will repeat his misbehavior whenever he feels that he can get away with it and so is checked in the development of self-discipline.

7. *Willingness to allow plenty of time for a child to learn, to change his patterns of behavior, his attitudes, or his goals.* The clinically oriented teacher knows that a child has to *grow* new knowledge, new behavior patterns, attitudes, or goals, and that growth takes time because it involves organic changes. He also knows that, while he may be creating optimum conditions for the child in the classroom and in his personal relations with the child, quite unwholesome conditions may persist at home, in the peer group, or in the child's own adjustment mechanisms. These persisting unwholesome factors may slow the child's progress or induce temporary regressions even after he has made a fresh start. Patience, which is in fact only the conscious recognition that time is required for learning, integration, and reintegration, is fundamental to the mood of effective education.

8. *Refusal to feel frustrated, inadequate, a failure, or otherwise threatened during the period before the child has begun to show improvement.* Few people realize that children's failure to learn and to realize their potentialities and their persistence in disturbing or undesirable behavior are very distressing to teachers. These tensions sometimes betray teachers into sarcasm or petty unkindnesses toward children, which, in turn, generate more trouble. But what hurts teachers most is the feeling of personal inadequacy and failure when their pupils do not learn and develop as they had hoped. A scientific knowledge of the forces that shape human learning, behavior, and development and a disciplined skill in figuring out the factors that are limiting particular children can prevent this tension. Teachers thus trained know what they are dealing with; they know what to expect in particular situations from particular children; they know what must happen before the desired changes can occur in the children. Teachers whose approach is clinical gain poise with experience. They are able to maintain the necessary relationships with children who are facing difficulties because they are not personally threatened with loss of self-confidence by the children's actions or failures.

9. *Scrupulous observance of a comprehensive and rigid code of professional ethics; ability to keep confidential all personal information about each child and his family in order to safeguard him from humiliation and loss of reputation or self-respect.* An appropriate code of ethics for members of the educational profession will be discussed later as a part of the description of a child-study program for in-service teachers. Here we need only to point out that

teachers need both extensive and intimate information about a child's background of experience and his home situation in order to understand him. Witness the insights into Jane that came with a knowledge of what had happened in her family life during the preceding four years. Such information is inevitably and properly a matter of great interest to the teacher, and the implications of such knowledge for the child's development are not immediately apparent. While the teacher is coming to understand these implications, nothing is more natural than to talk over the more interesting information with colleagues. This, of course, is precisely what must be avoided. Teachers must keep all information strictly confidential and communicate it only in formal case conferences with psychologists or psychiatrists or in committees of teachers organized for the specific purpose of assisting the child in question.

At first reading, this description of the clinical approach may seem a bit Utopian. Yet the case of Jane showed Mrs. Summers living up to these criteria. In fact, I have been emboldened to set down these criteria precisely because hundreds of teachers have actually learned to function in this manner as they progressed through the child-study program. Many do not, of course, even after three years of work. But so many do that we are sure it is feasible to base the mood and tempo of education upon an adequate understanding of the motivations and needs of the individual child.

On Understanding Children

PART TWO

On Understanding Children

CHAPTER 4

The Bases of Understanding

The case of Jane leads one to believe that harm rather than good had come to Jane through some of her earlier experiences at school. This could have happened again in the sixth grade if Mrs. Summers had not achieved a certain degree of understanding and acceptance of Jane as a person, for both were necessary before Mrs. Summers could make wise decisions when dealing with her in the classroom.

This understanding and acceptance of Jane, as we have seen, required a great deal of information about her capacities and skills, her home situation and accumulated experiences, and her feelings, attitudes, and needs. But it also required a great deal of scientific knowledge—a great many proven concepts that would explain Jane's behavior and clarify for her teacher the meanings and feelings that Jane's accumulated experiences had engendered in her. This chapter will describe briefly the scope of the information the teacher needs about the child and the range of scientific concepts he must grasp in order to achieve sufficient clinical understanding to make good classroom decisions about the child and about the group of which he is a part.

"Understanding" the Child

The understanding of the child that the teacher needs in order to make wise classroom decisions in interacting with him must have at least three components.

1. The teacher needs to be able to see situations through the eyes of the child, because children and youth often perceive situations quite differently from adults and because perception varies with the individual's unique background of experience. To understand why a child behaves as he does requires that the teacher perceive the situation fundamentally as the child does, *in addition* to seeing it in terms of the teacher's own experience, values, and intentions. This simultaneous double view is indeed difficult to achieve, but we have seen Mrs. Summers accomplish it successfully. Of course, it is absolutely impossible for a

teacher ever to see and feel a situation exactly as a child does; complete understanding is never to be expected.

2. To be able to "accept" a child despite some of his actions, the teacher
must know how the child learned to perceive situations as he does. How did
particular meanings and feelings grow in the child's mind in relation to particular objects, people, and situations? How did he develop the readiness to perceive things as he now does? This perception-readiness is, of course, a function
of the child's unique background of experience, which determined the "built-in"
meanings that are the bases of his present perceptions.

3. To make wise judgments in the classroom the teacher must have had experiences through which he *knows* that further growth, experience, and development on the child's part will change the meanings that objects, people,
and situations now have for him. Knowing how new relationships and experiences can change a child's perceptions enables the teacher to judge the kinds
of experiences and relationships that the particular child needs in order to
take his next developmental steps. And seeing this actually happen in children
over a period of time gives the teacher the necessary patience with the child
and faith in developmental processes to persist in his efforts long enough to produce the necessary changes. With some children this takes a long time.

Teachers must have scientific information if these three components
of "understanding" a child are to make sense to them. For example, many
teachers still think of learning and behavior simply as responses to outside stimulation. They assume that all children should respond in the
same way to a given pattern of stimulation. Hence they ask, "What can
I do to make my children learn to read?" "What can I do to make my
children pay attention?" "What can I do to stop certain kinds of misbehavior?" These teachers need information about the latest research
on perception, which shows that a child will see in a situation whatever
his earlier experiences have made him ready to see. This research also
shows that in so far as earlier experiences differ, children will see different things in and get different meanings from the same situation.
There is no single way the teacher can help all children learn to read,
spell, or figure. There is no single way to deal with children who lie,
steal, or daydream. In each case the kind of experience a child needs
to help him take his next step in learning or adjusting depends upon
what his accumulated experiences have been and thus varies from child
to child.

But mere knowledge of what a child has experienced in the past does
not automatically yield understanding of him. The teacher must have
scientific information about the processes by which accumulating experiences give rise to concepts, attitudes, feelings, emotions, ways of defending the self, and ways of maintaining the integrity of the self. Particular
attitudes do not necessarily grow out of particular experiences: much
depends upon the context of personal relationships, group role and status,

and concept of self, as well as upon the cultural background against which experience occurs.

Knowledge of the role played by time is equally vital. The factors that shape a child's present perceptions and behavior came into existence gradually by the customary processes of growth, learning, and developmental functioning. Hence changes can be effected only gradually through further growth, learning, and developmental functioning. Seldom indeed do children—or adults—learn simply by being told what is true. Nor do they change their behavior simply by being told what is "right" for them.

Factors That Influenced Jane's Perceptions and Behavior

Nor will merely reading the general truths presented above give the reader understanding of their meaning. These general ideas can best be clarified in relation to Jane's perceptions, behavior, and development as described in the case material presented in Chapter 3.

Concretely, there are at least sixteen distinguishable factors that contributed to Jane's perception of a variety of situations. As factors in her perception of life, they helped to prevent her learning to read and mastering other scholastic tasks and caused her performance on intelligence tests to decline until she appeared to be on the borderline of feeblemindedness, despite an average potential intelligence. These factors are enumerated below in much the same sequence in which they were revealed in the teacher's case record of Jane:

1. Jane's mother favored her older daughter and son. Jane experienced this discrimination almost every day; consequently she gradually came to expect that others would be preferred over her.

2. Jane's sister openly fought with her, that is, she took advantage of her greater size and her favored position in the family to make Jane do as she wished, and she punished her by physical force if Jane refused or attacked her in anger. Hence Jane gradually came to feel that she would not be dealt with fairly by others—that others would take advantage of her.

3. Jane's family was in a constant turmoil of bickering and blaming. There was no peace at home between the mother and the father, between the parents and the grandmother, between the parents and the children. Here blame set the mood, and the home was not a haven of love or security. Factors one, two, and three combined gradually to make Jane feel unloved and alone and led her to expect turmoil and quarreling as a regular part of life.

4. Jane was deeply worried for her mother and frightened for herself because of her mother's insanity. The screaming and other terrible episodes at home and the visits to her mother at the institution were causes of great and continuing disturbance to Jane. They made Jane feel that she and her family were actually different from other people in some undesirable way.

5. People in the community gossiped about the mother's insanity and were

inclined to consider the children as in danger of inheriting some of their mother's instability. Jane knew this, for it influenced the way neighbors, teachers, and other adults inquired about her mother's health, the attitudes they showed toward Jane in relation to other children, and what they encouraged or discouraged Jane from doing. Hence Jane felt that she was stigmatized and that other people saw her as different and unworthy, as having "something the matter with her."

6. The family as a whole had quite a low status in the community because of the occupations of the mother and the father, the kind of house they lived in, and the way family members acted both at home and in public. Jane knew the status of her family, and this influenced her way of interacting with other children. She and Florence admitted that their homes were "not so nice," but the twins "bragged" about how nice their home was. This helped make Jane see herself as different from others and somehow less valuable than others.

7. Some of the teachers at school disliked Jane, both because of her family background and because of the ways she acted when emotional. This gave these teachers the mental set of being quick to blame, of being hard on Jane, of not caring whether they humiliated her, or even of wanting to hurt her and put her in her place when she misbehaved. In other words, to avoid difficulties for themselves and for other children, they felt justified in hurting Jane both as a punishment and as a deterrent. They did not value her as a person. She felt alone at school because of this rejection and gradually developed the feeling that the world in general and the teachers at school in particular were "against" her.

8. Some of the teachers at school expected Jane to misbehave and revealed this expectation to her. This, of course, constituted a suggestion to Jane that she should misbehave; it is amazing how far children's actions correspond to what their teachers actually expect of them. These teachers, because of this expectation, found it easy to blame Jane without inquiring too much into situations and were on the lookout for opportunities to reprimand her. They thought of these reprimands as ounces of prevention. But Jane experienced all this as being "picked on," and she developed an inner readiness to perceive herself in many school situations as "picked on."

9. Many of Jane's classmates rejected her as a person and so would not accord her belonging in groups of which they were a part. Hence Jane felt she was an outsider, an unwanted person among her peers, an outcast.

10. Many of Jane's classmates humiliated her openly by expressing their rejection of her verbally and publicly in the classroom. This stirred her anger and at the same time hurt her self-esteem. She came to feel that the other children, like the teachers, regarded her as different, inferior, and unworthy, and she was angered by this.

11. Jane did not know, nor did she have a chance to learn at home, the skills she needed for group participation or the codes of conduct of children of her age group or of higher social classes. Consequently she often offended others, either accidentally or purposely, without realizing that this would only make things worse. So she frequently felt at a loss in facing situations at school

and knew only how to strike out impulsively and blindly against people who were hurting her, just as she did at home.

12. Jane had no roles which she played successfully in the classroom or in the class group. For this reason she had a constant sense of failure to measure up, of inadequacy, of inability to do what she saw others doing successfully.

13. By temperament Jane was excitable, and her emotions seemed to be extremely strong. Her labile, or rapidly fluctuating, temperament made it difficult for her to learn to manage herself in social situations—and she had had no sympathetic help either at home or at school. Her temperament made it easy for her to strike out impulsively and difficult for her to control her actions.

14. Basically, Jane seemed to have only average intelligence, or ability to learn. When the functioning of this adequate but limited intelligence was interfered with, as by emotion or by not being able to read, she became unable to understand either verbal or printed explanations unless they were gone over very carefully with her. In other words, during these periods Jane was in the situation of not being able to use the intelligence she actually had. She was pseudo-feebleminded.

15. Jane was physically an active child with lots of energy to spend. Consequently she often got herself into trouble by inappropriate or excessive action. For example, when emotionally disturbed she tended to attack other children physically—to strike others or to pull their hair—or to be verbally very aggressive. This, of course, intensified her rejection by her peers, increased the number of occasions she would be in trouble with adults, and deepened her rejection by both peers and adults. Because of her high energy output, reenforced by emotion, Jane always felt like being active, but her actions so often did not work out well. This must have made her mistrust herself and see herself as never able to do the right thing.

16. Because Jane experienced so many strong, unpleasant emotions in situations she herself had not caused, she developed a "chip-on-the-shoulder" attitude and felt that she was "picked on" by her teachers and that at school, as at home, she was discriminated against, especially when she was punished. This led to a generalized hostility toward teachers and peers and to the adjustment device of seeking out younger children to care for and from whom to gain acceptance.

Here, then, are sixteen different factors that tended to make Jane perceive herself and school situations in ways that interfered with her learning during the period between the second grade and the middle of the sixth grade. It should be noted that some of these factors were within Jane herself: the limited intelligence; the labile, easily disturbed temperament; the relatively high energy output; the discouraging feelings of insecurity, social nonbelonging, and personal inadequacy; and the "chip-on-the-shoulder" attitude about being "picked on." Of course, all these factors were caused before they, in turn, became part of the causes of Jane's difficulties with learning to read.

There were also outside causes for Jane's failure to learn. Her family, except possibly her grandmother, actually did not love her at home; they did discriminate in favor of her brother and sister; her sister did fight with her; the members of the household did constantly quarrel, bicker, and blame one another; teachers at school did reject Jane, expect the worst from her, look for chances to jump on her, and feel justified when they made her suffer; and the other children rejected her in their group, humiliated her publicly, and refused roles to her. So the forces that interfered with her learning were, many of them, things her teacher could do nothing about directly.

All these factors, whether they operated within Jane or from outside, shaped the way she thought and felt about herself and about people and situations at school. They organized her perceptions, formed the bases of the meanings that situations had for her and gradually shaped her concept of herself. Because the number of unfavorable factors was so great, Jane found herself unable to learn and her operational learning capacity actually decreased, though her potential intelligence, of course, remained average—as high as it ever had been.

Certain educators are reported to have said, "In order to teach a child to read you don't need to know anything about the child. You only need to know how to teach reading." If such a statement ever was made—and it seems improbable—Jane's case strongly refutes it. Jane would never have learned to read through the mere application of techniques, no matter how skillfully they were applied. What she needed to free her from the bondage of the way she saw herself was a supportive relationship with somebody who sincerely valued her. Building such a relationship is never a matter of technique and can never be learned as such. At the same time, it is doubtful that a child can feel love from a person who knows nothing whatever about him, for part of the proof of love is giving evidence of still valuing the child when he is misbehaving, or when adverse facts about his learning, his family background, his relationships with other children, or his unworthy motivations come out in the open.

Love, however, is not enough. Once the supporting, security-giving relationship has been built and the child's developmental motivation to learn to read has been released, then the teacher needs his best teaching techniques in order to facilitate the work of learning reading skills. This was illustrated by Mrs. Summers. To begin with, she decreased the blocking factors in relation to reading by facilitating the development and maintenance of friendship between Jane and other children, such as Florence, and by helping Jane secure roles in group activities which she had a chance successfully to fulfill, such as being an angel in the nativity scene at Christmas and taking care of the young children during the puppet show in February. In other words, every decrease in negative and blocking perceptions and every increase in positive ways of seeing herself, through success in personal relationships or in role playing, increased the probability of successful learning because they changed the way Jane saw herself in school situations. What the teacher had to do in Jane's case was to change the way the child perceived herself, the classroom situations and demands she experienced, and the relationship between herself and the opportunities for living and learning which the school offered. When these changes were accomplished, then the teacher could and did put her techniques for teaching reading into effective use. A child truly is an indivisible unit whose perception of his life situations are influenced by a whole constellation of forces.

Factors That Influence Perception and Behavior

We have tried to show through the case of Jane that the behavior of a child in the classroom is a function of the way he perceives himself, the situation, and the relationship between the two. A short way to say this is that behavior grows out of the meaning each situation has for the individual. But the way a child perceives a situation in relation to himself depends upon his developmental history, his organic dynamics, his relationships with certain persons, his innate capacities, and his views of his capacities as well as of his future—of his expectancies and goals.

All these factors are dynamic in any situation and should be viewed as "forces" that influence perception. A minimal list of these factors or forces is given below as a series of generalized scientific statements. They are the forces or factors that we have found, in our sixteen years of child-study experience, to be operative in the development and behavior of every child.

1. The child is a physical organism with certain innate and dynamic developmental patterns and certain developmental limits. These are established by biological heredity, and their unfolding depends upon innate cellular and hormonal dynamics that operate continuously.

2. The child is an organism at a particular growth level, with various physical structures and processes that are differentiated only to a degree. He is impelled from within to explore and to practice the behavioral possibilities implied by his current growth level or degree of differentiation.

3. The child is a physical being with particular momentary problems of maintaining physiological equilibrium. These momentary problems may give rise to hunger or thirst, the need to void the bladder or colon, to spend energy more actively or to rest quietly, depending on the metabolic situation, and a variety of other needs.

4. The child is a member of a particular family group in which he is psy-

chologically secure because he is loved by a number of people, is psychologically insecure because he is actively rejected, simply does not matter, or feels in rivalry for needed love.

5. The child is a member of a particular family which carries and which trains him to internalize, accept, and act in accordance with particular views of the roles of females and of males; a rural or urban pattern of living; the particular attitudes, ideas, and ways of acting that characterize the special region of the country in which they live; the language habits, the attitudes, and the customs of the ethnic groups to which his parents belong; and the attitudes, values, and ways of acting of the social class of which the family is a part.

6. The child is seeking to win and to play certain roles within his maturity-level peer group, to attain and to hold a certain status within this group, and to develop those skills of managing the body, adornment, and interacting with others that will enhance his role and status in his peer group.

7. The child perceives situations in terms of meanings engendered by his unique accumulation of experiences, molded by his hierarchy of values, colored by his feelings and emotions, and oriented toward the achievement of his specific developmental goals.

8. The child is presently equipped with certain potential capacities for remembering, abstracting, generalizing, symbolizing, reasoning, and imagining. These potentialities have been transformed into realized intelligence in so far as they have been given content by rich experience and called into action by the example and the expectancies of the adults who are guiding the child's development and of the peers with whom he associates. These potentialities have remained latent to the degree that his experience has been limited and to the degree that other persons in his environment have not called them into action by example and demand.

9. The child becomes an individual aware of himself as a physical entity; as having various relationships to other persons; as having certain knowledge, skills, abilities, and capacities; as believing in and adhering to certain codes of social, ethical, and aesthetic conduct; as being in a certain relationship to the universe, God, and the infinite and eternal; as deeply valuing certain aspects of life and of the world; and as having immediate and long-term goals to accomplish.

10. The child is a "self" with a particular background of emotional conditionings, feelings, and concerns, which color and influence the mood of all situations and experiences.

11. The child is a "self" that has worked out certain patterned ways, or adjustment mechanisms, for managing his interpretations of and feelings about situations and happenings so that he can maintain his self-respect and his feeling of adequacy for dealing with reality, at least up to a certain necessary minimal limit.

This, then, is a sort of minimum list of forces that operate constantly in every child's life. The interaction of these forces shapes the individual's perceptions and determines his motivations.

Scientific Knowledge Is Necessary

This list of forces defines the scope of the scientific knowledge the teacher must have in order to understand the children or youth he is teaching. Detailed description of the nature of these forces and the processes by which they operate to shape learning, behavior, and development cannot now be found between the covers of any single book and perhaps never will be. Rather, information about these forces must be obtained by selective readings from many books. An extensive bibliography has been included at the back of this volume in order to point to many valuable sources of scientific knowledge.

Extensive work with teachers indicates, however, that the necessary scientific knowledge can seldom be gained simply by reading scientific literature, no matter how extensively. Reading must be supplemented by the guided study of flesh-and-blood children and youth. For this reason, this initial description of the scope of the needed scientific information is somewhat elaborated in the analysis of the developmental tasks and adjustment problems of Timothy Thyme in Chapter 7. Also, scientific concepts are presented in a number of chapters throughout the book in connection with the discussion of specific children, where their meaning can be more clear-cut and explicit.

Information about the Individual Child

A re-reading of the eleven factors listed will show that, although all of them operate for all children, there are qualitative and quantitative differences from child to child with regard to each factor. For example, the second factor deals with the blueprint of growth through which all children pass. But in a specific first grade, even though all the children have chronological ages between five years and ten months and six years and ten months, there will be great differences in the level of physical maturity achieved by the different children. Some will be physically developed only to the degree usually achieved by four-year-olds; others will already be comparable to eight-year-olds in this respect. Most of the girls will be a good deal ahead of the boys in physical development because girls tend to grow up more rapidly than boys; but some of the girls will be less developed than the average boy. The teacher must, therefore, know the growth level of each individual child, because some children will be two years ahead of the average and others will be two years behind the average in physical differentiation and consequently in what they can learn to do with their bodies, especially their eyes and hands.

With regard to the fourth factor, some children in any classroom are emotionally secure because they are sincerely loved by a number of persons in their homes. But others are psychologically insecure because they are actively rejected by one or more persons in the home. Others will be neglected or ignored in the home; they do not really matter to the adults there, who may be greatly preoccupied with their own personal problems. Still others may rival older or younger brothers or sisters for the regard and affection of their parents. Still others may be overprotected or babied in the home and so robbed of many developmental experiences. The teacher cannot understand these different children until he has explicit information about the home situations of each of them, about the relationship of each with his mother, father, brothers, and sisters.

The same thing is true of each of the factors. In order to understand his pupils as individuals, therefore, the teacher must have explicit information about each of these factors as it applies to each child. Obviously this information should be put in the confidential cumulative record of each child as rapidly as the teacher obtains it, and changes with regard to any factor should be recorded as they occur. Chapter 6 concerns methods of gathering and recording these needed facts about individuals.

Learning the Clinical Approach

Obviously teachers can learn the scientific facts they need only gradually. Equally obvious is the fact that no teacher can gather each year all the facts he needs to understand each child as an individual. The gathering of the necessary facts has to be a continuous cooperative activity involving the school nurse and doctor, the visiting teacher and the school psychologist (if the school has these), and the teachers who, one after another, guide the child's learning.

However, even when teachers have the scientific facts they need and the necessary information about individual children, they have to be trained in scientific methods of interpreting these data. Clinical psychologists, psychiatrists, and psychiatric social workers require this training, and teachers are no different from other professional persons. Chapters 5, 7, 8, and 9 will demonstrate how teachers can learn, over a period of three years of in-service participation in child-study groups, to draw correct inferences about why children feel and act as they do and what they need to facilitate their learning, development, and adjustment.

CHAPTER 5

Interpreting Behavior

The crux of the educative process is what teachers say and do and how they feel when interacting with children in the classroom. How puzzling many of these situations are was demonstrated in Chapter 1 by anecdotes describing the behavior of Jane, Chester, Rodney, and John. How significant the teacher's mood and actions are was demonstrated in the case of Jane. The teacher's professional functioning is based upon his perceptions of the meanings of each situation for the child and his judgment as to what kind of response from him will best facilitate the child's learning and evoke desirable behavior. It is obvious, then, that the teacher's perceptions must be as valid as possible and his judgments as sound as possible if children's school experiences are to promote effective learning, conscious self-discipline, character improvement, and healthy adjustment.

The child-study program developed under the Commission on Teacher Education and perfected at the Institute for Child Study of the University of Maryland helps in-service teachers to sharpen their perceptions of children and to refine their judgments about how to help children learn and develop. The next five chapters will describe the processes that have proved effective for these purposes. A number of different kinds of activities and experiences are necessary. In this chapter we will begin to present these activities and experiences by describing some of the ways teachers learn to discipline themselves and one another in scientifically valid ways of arriving at clearer perceptions of the feelings, motivations, and needs that underlie the immediate behavior of individual children.

Common Errors of Judgment

It may be helpful at the outset simply to list the kinds of errors that the teachers who worked in our child-study groups often made in their perceptions of the causes of children's behavior and in their judgments as to what would be helpful to the children. In no sense can teachers be

99

blamed for these errors, since they are common throughout our population and can be overcome only by fairly rigorous and extensive training
in the scientific method and by broad grounding in the current scientific
explanation of human behavior and developmental processes. The most
common and widespread errors were:

1. Teachers identified one causative factor underlying a child's behavior
accurately, but they accepted this factor as the total causation of the behavior;
that is, they oversimplified their explanation of an action and consequently
could not make sound judgments about how to help the child.

2. Teachers reasoned by analogy from their own experience when, in truth,
the factors influencing the child's experience were quite different from those
influencing the teachers' experience. In other words, they lacked adequate information about the child and did not realize the need for it.

3. Teachers drew conclusions on the basis of mistaken ideas of what factors
actually influence behavior, that is, they lacked scientific knowledge of how
human behavior is activated and of what causative factors shape human development.

4. Teachers accepted a chance impression, a rumor, hearsay, or the statement of an unreliable or prejudiced person as fact—as a datum upon which to
base a judgment without further checking. That is, they did not discriminate
between facts and their own or their colleagues' mere opinions or prejudiced
interpretations.

5. Teachers drew a conclusion about some causative factor on the basis
of a single fact in a single illustrative instance, when in truth other facts existed
and were available which would have cast doubt upon this conclusion. In
other words, they came to a conclusion without considering alternative explanations.

6. Teachers generalized and characterized a child on the basis of a single
instance of his behavior, particularly if that episode had caused them unpleasant emotion. In other words, one strongly felt experience led them mistakenly to regard the child as characterized by that single unique situation.

7. Teachers accepted second-level inferences as true data, that is, knowing
that one thing was true they inferred something else to be true which, in fact,
could be true only if a second but unknown fact also were true.

8. Teachers accepted as always true of the child something which was true
only under certain circumstances, that is, something conditional. They failed
to perceive the conditions which caused the behavior and which limited the
application of their conclusion.

9. Teachers projected into the child's behavior motives which the child did
not have, but which the teacher himself had or which the teacher needed the
child to have in order to justify his feelings and judgments concerning the
child. Happily this error was much less common among teachers than most of
the other errors of reasoning and was, of course, always unconscious.

10. Teachers accepted as absolutely true something which was only possibly
true or, at best, probably true. This resulted in fixed attitudes and a closed

mind. In truth, it is hard for all of us to act decisively, as a teacher must, when we know that we are only probably right.

One recognizes instantly that these errors in reasoning are typical of most people in our society, even of well-educated people. When teachers make these errors they are only doing what most other people of their acquaintance habitually do, what we are all encouraged to do every day by advertising, political speeches and press releases, and organized groups seeking to promote particular ends. Much communication in our society is aimed at persuasion, at selling a point of view, justifying a position, defending an action, or propagandizing for something. The purpose of communication is seldom to bring out all the facts, reason soundly, and arrive at a consensus. Everything is slanted according to what the interested party wants us to think. Thus common social proc-esses daily teach us unsound ways of thinking, and teachers along with the rest of the population are the victims. Living in an age that is mate-rially greatly enriched by the fruits of scientific research, we are con-stantly pressured to avoid the scientific method in making financial, so-cial, political, and other judgments.

Of course, the procedure of child-study groups is not to enumerate these mistakes to teachers and urge them to refrain from repeating their errors. Rather it is to set up experiences through which teachers will dis-cover their own errors and help each other to discern and eliminate similar errors. These experiences consist of trying to figure out together in the group why a certain child did a specific thing in a particular situa-tion and, later, why the child repeatedly acted in a certain way in a sequence of situations. The "figuring out" is done by taking a specific series of steps that apply the scientific method to the analysis of the causation of behavior. We call this the "multiple-hypothesis technique." The experience of using this technique has many of the elements of un-raveling a mystery and is quite enjoyable to many teachers.

How the Study Groups Operate

Before illustrating the operation of the child-study groups with an actual case, some background information is necessary. Teachers in a given school system who wish to participate are enrolled in child-study groups of approximately a dozen persons. Each participant selects a child or youth whom he is teaching as the subject about whom he will gather information to be interpreted with the group. In other words, *the group undertakes to study intensively* and to understand during the year *as many children as there are participants in the group.* As the information about each child is being gathered from seven major sources, it is presented to the group for evaluation as to its objectivity, descriptiveness, scope, and significance; and the group, by discussion, helps the individual to discover additional opportunities for getting facts, to develop skill in valid ways of recording the data, and to determine what kinds of information still are needed to build a record that will yield significant conclusions.

Among the sources of information is the direct observation of the child in action in a multitude of situations in and around the school. Each participant writes, in descriptive anecdotal form, accounts of some five or six of these behavioral situations each week. In the course of three or four months each participant collects quite a body of objective descriptions of the child in action. Some of these descriptions deal with unique episodes that obviously were vivid experiences for the child being studied; others describe the child in action in routine situations. Others show the child interacting with his peers on the playground or in the classroom, and still others show him interacting with the teacher or some other adult or working or dawdling alone. These vignettes add up to a description of the child's experiences at school and his reactions to them.

The Multiple-hypothesis Technique

After the recording of data has gone on for three or four months the participants are somewhat disciplined in objectivity and are eager and ripe for interpretations. Then the multiple-hypothesis technique of interpreting behavioral episodes is introduced to them and practiced during four or five meetings of the group. They begin to observe recurring patterns of behavior in the various children and to seek explanations as to why these ways of acting recur. By means of the multiple-hypothesis technique the participants arrive at interpretations of behavior.

THE CASE OF CHESTER

The report that follows describes how one group of teachers worked out an interpretation of one boy's repeated avoidance of the tasks involved in learning to read. The group had been working together for about six months and already had learned how to make and test their hypotheses about the causation of specific behavioral episodes. No account will be given of how they learned to spot recurring patterns of behavior or of why they selected this particular pattern, exemplified by Chester's behavior, as their focus of attention in a particular group meeting.

Chapter 1 contained several anecdotes concerning an eleven-year-old boy named Chester, who was in the sixth grade. In one of these anecdotes Chester falsely reported to his teacher that Miss T, the principal, wanted him to‾do a chore for her. In a second he had begged his teacher to permit him to work in the sixth-grade workbook in arithmetic despite the fact that he had not yet completed the fifth-grade workbook. In a third anecdote Chester was described as having "played around all morning" instead of doing his work in reading. Consequently, when play-time came, his teacher told him that he could not go to the playground but must stay in the classroom and finish his work. Then, when the teacher went to the principal's office for a few minutes, he slipped out and started playing football with the other boys.

The final anecdote was a composition which Chester wrote and titled "My Family." In it Chester described and gave the ages of his mother and father, his brother Bill, who was nine years old, and his sister Sally, who was thirteen and in the seventh grade. Chester wrote, "He [Bill] isn't as old as I am but he's lots bigger. He is taller and weighs more. . . ." Chester's teacher was Miss C.

Selecting a Recurring Pattern of Behavior

The group studying Chester decided that the following items from the record constituted a recurring pattern worthy of analysis:

Oct. 10   While I was working with a group in reading, Chester's group was working at their tables. The work was a check-up on a story that the group had just finished reading with me. It was not long before I saw Chester with a game in a corner of the room. I went to him and asked, "Chester, have you finished your work so soon?" He answered, "No, ma'am, I was playing this game awhile." I said, "Go to your seat and finish your work." He looked at me with an expression that seemed to say either "I don't know what you mean" or "I don't want to." By this time my patience was a little ragged so I said, "Chester, go to your seat immediately and finish your work." He went to his seat slowly, looking back a time or two at the game corner and stopping a time or two.

When the period was up, of course, he had not finished his work, so when playtime came I said, "You have had part of your playtime. Now you can finish your work." He mumbled and whined, "What for?" I answered, "I believe you know why."

When the others started out the door to the playground, Chester started too. I said, "You may not go." He turned red and stuck out his lips in a pout. Then he started to cry. "Chester, if you will stop pouting and get down to work you will be finished in time to have some play." A few children who overheard the conversation said, "Miss C, that is the way he did all last year."

After all the children had left the room I stayed to see that Chester was settled to his work. After I was sure that he didn't need any more help I went to the playground. In about ten minutes he was there with his paper all finished. I commended him on his work. He smiled, thanked me, and went to play.

Oct. 27 . . . When Miss T came into the room he showed her
the books [new sixth-grade workbooks in arithmetic]. She told him
to work hard on reading so that he would be able to read and understand the problems. He promised to do so.

Chester is in the lowest group in reading. According to his cumulative record he has always had trouble with this subject. He says that he
does not like to read, and he proves his statement because he has
to have encouragement to get down to the work.

At times he has to be told that he must do the work.

Material from Chester's cumulative record, section on development of
abilities, knowledges, and skills:

2ND GRADE (latter part of year): Stopped looking at his book in the
reading circle and had trouble paying attention.

3RD GRADE: Attention span is short. Doesn't like to stay still long
enough to do the reading that he is capable of doing.

5TH GRADE: A poor reader. Does not read enough. Doesn't make
good on opportunities to read when asked to read in the group. Has
difficulty in "pinning himself down" to reading. Attention elsewhere
at reading time. Says, "I'll take it home and read it there."

Independent reading level—Second grade.
Instructional reading level—Third grade.

Nov. 6 Conference with mother. . . . Her first statement was, "How
is C doing in his work?" I told her that he showed improvement in
spelling and arithmetic. I added that he worked hard on both of
them. She said, "But his reading! He just can't read. I tell him that
he will never be able to do other work well until he learns to read.
You have to read before you can do anything else." Then I told
her that Chester did everything he could to get out of reading. He
invented every excuse imaginable. I asked, "What do you suppose we
could do to interest him in reading?" I had a feeling that maybe she
had pushed him and maybe this was one of the contributing factors
that had brought about a dislike for reading. She didn't have anything
to suggest so I proposed that we watch for a time to see if we could
find a solution. . . .

Nov. 19 [The episode described in Chapter 1 and again in this
chapter when Chester had been kept in at recess time to finish a reading assignment but went out anyway when the teacher went to the
principal's office.]

Nov. 24 Chester has not settled down to reading this year. He
always finds something to do when it is time for reading. I am still
trying to find a way to get him interested.

I was working with a group today while Chester was supposed to
be working at his table. His job was to answer questions about a
story on which he had worked with me. I was sure that the questions
were not too difficult. Soon I saw him go over to another table. He
perched on the corner and started talking to Charles. I said, "Go
back to your place and get busy." He went back and sat there a few

minutes. It wasn't long until I saw him at Sam's table. I decided to ignore it because I felt that I had taken enough time from the group for one child.

Not long before the end of the day, I found time to go to Chester. I asked for a piece of paper. I read the first question and wrote the answer on the paper. I did the second question likewise, put the paper down and walked off. When all the children were gone there was Chester, working away at his seat. I was curious but stayed away from him. Soon Sally (his older sister) came for him. (She continues to come for him every day.) He ignored her and worked on. I said, "Here is Sally." He remarked, "Wait a minute. I have just two more questions to answer." When he handed me the paper, I saw that he had answered all the questions.

Dec. 4 The group had just finished a work period and were cleaning the room. As each child finished cleaning his work place he was supposed to get a library book and come to the circle. He was to read until every child had finished cleaning. Chester got a book, came to the circle and sat holding it.

Soon I noticed him in another section of the room sweeping away. I saw John reach for the broom and say something. I moved nearer and heard John saying, "Give me the broom so I can finish sweeping my place." Chester swept on, so I went nearer to the boys. John said to me, "Chester got the broom while I went for the dustpan. He has finished his place. Now he is trying to do mine." I took the broom, handed it to John and guided Chester back to the circle. He sat down, ducked his head, and stuck out his lips.

I went to the shelf, chose a book which was easy and which I thought might interest him. I carried it to his chair which was beside mine. (He usually manages to sit by an adult.) I sat down, showed him the book, told him a little about it, and read the first paragraph to him. Then I asked him to read the next one to me. He took the book and read. I said, "That was good reading." He smiled as I left him and I continued to watch him out of the corner of my eye. He read on and by the time I returned to my chair he had read two pages.

At the end of the day he said, "I have read ten pages in that book. I'll take it home with me." And he went off with it.

Phrasing a Question

The child-study group saw in these anecdotes that over a period of three months during the current school year and apparently in earlier grades, Chester had used many devices to avoid working on learning to read. They felt that his teacher would have to recognize some of the causes of this behavior in order to work out a many-sided program for helping him to overcome his reluctance. The first step was to phrase the question. The group stated it as follows:

"Why does Chester so frequently and persistently avoid working at learning to read?"

Making Multiple Hypotheses

The second step was to make as many hypotheses as possible to explain Chester's behavior. The hypotheses were based both on their knowledge of Chester and on their knowledge of the common causes of avoidance behavior in other children. Thus the members of the group utilized
both their own teaching experience and what they had learned from
reading. The third step was to test each of these hypotheses against the
facts in Miss C's record about Chester, and the fourth was to consider
what additional facts about Chester or what additional scientific knowledge would be necessary to understand this behavior, in case the record
did not validate enough of the hypotheses. The final step was to figure
out ways of helping Chester to overcome his reluctance to work on
reading.

Since the group accepted the axiom that behavior always has many
causes, they sought to make as many different hypotheses as possible. As
each hypothesis was suggested, its wording was agreed upon and it was
written on the blackboard by the scribe for that day. At the end of about
forty minutes of discussion, the group found they had twenty-two hypotheses, as indicated by the accompanying list.

Reading the Record to the Group

After these hypotheses were listed on the blackboard, the teacher who
had recorded the anecdotes about Chester read the entire record to the
group, paragraph by paragraph. After each paragraph the group decided
which of the hypotheses were supported by the facts presented in that
paragraph and which ones tended to be refuted by the data. A plus
mark was placed by each hypothesis that was supported by the facts
and a minus mark by each hypothesis that was weakened. As the reading
of the record progressed, some hypotheses were supported by many facts
or were strongly supported by a few crucial facts. In the same way, some
hypotheses were refuted by many data, or doubt was cast on them by a
few crucial facts. Some hypotheses had both plus and minus data or no
data at all, so that additional facts obviously were needed. In other cases
it was found that the hypotheses as stated were not susceptible of proof
or refutation and should be either reworded or eliminated as scientifically
unsound.

In the pages that follow, Miss C's record on Chester will be presented
as she read it to the group. After each paragraph the numbers designating
the hypotheses that the group thought were supported will be listed, and
also the numbers designating the hypotheses on which doubt was cast.
The conclusions which Miss C reached and entered into her record after
this meeting will then be given.

THE CASE OF CHESTER

I chose Chester because he is a small restless boy who always seems to be seeking something. He has the reputation of being "slick as an eel" and can move from one spot to another in the time it takes to bat an eye. He never sticks to anything very long at a time.

OCT. 1   The first-grade teacher told me that Chester was always a poor eater while he was in her grade. But the second- and third-grade teachers said that he ate a good breakfast and always ate his lunch in their grades. Today at 9:30 while on a trip Chester started eating an apple. I asked, "Chester, are you eating so soon after breakfast?" He answered, "Huh, I ate breakfast at 7:30." Then he turned and smiled. "Guess what I ate?" "Oh, I suppose you ate an egg and a piece of toast." "No sir, I ate an egg, two pieces of toast, two strips of bacon, cream of wheat, and a glass of milk." All the time he was talking he had been walking beside the teacher with one foot on the curb and one foot off the curb.

I had been watching Chester at lunch for some time. He had been eating most of his lunch. I suggested, "Chester, let's keep a menu of what you eat for a week." He entered heartily into the plan with me. Some of the other children did too.

Later in the day I said, "Chester, you said that you eat breakfast at 7:30. I eat mine at 7:00." He remarked, "I don't get up until 7:00 so I eat at 7:30." "What time do you go to bed?" "Oh, I go between 9:00 and 9:30, for 9:30 is the latest Mother will let me stay up."

The study group judged that this anecdote indicated that Chester had good health habits with regard to eating and sleeping but that it did not have a direct bearing on any of the hypotheses about Chester's poor reading.

OCT. 4   When we started to lunch today, I was near the front of the group. I heard crying which sounded like a small child. I thought nothing of it, for we were passing a second-grade group and I thought it was one of them. After we reached the lunchroom, I missed Chester, so I inquired about him. Some of the children said he had gone back to the room. When I investigated I found Chester in the room with red eyes. I asked about the trouble and he answered, "Bill hit me." "Why did he hit you?" "I don't know." When I asked Bill why he hit Chester he answered, "He called me an ugly word." I looked at Chester who said, "I didn't call you an ugly word, and you hit me in the mouth." Then he hung his head and started off crying. Bill turned to me. "You can ask Gertrude and Joan. They heard him." The girls verified Bill's statement. "We were in the hall when Chester called Bill a son of a b——, and he meant the rest of it." I told Bill not to settle things alone next time but to let me help him, and I told Chester that it didn't pay to call people names. He jerked his shoulder and sat down in the hall with his face in his hand. I told him to go to the lunchroom and have lunch with the next group of children. When he looked up he was pouting and said, "I don't want any." "All right, then come on into the room with me." He came in and soon went to work at clay modeling.

The study group judged that this supported hypotheses 7, 8, and 22, concerning Chester's being rejected by the other children.

> OCT. 6   Yesterday after school, Chester went by a used-car lot that is located in the shopping center near the school. He got into a car, released the brake, and the car rolled into the porch of the office, tearing down the porch and breaking a window in the building. The owner of the lot previously had let Chester play in an old truck, but Chester had never tried getting into a passenger car before and no harm had been done.
>
> Chester's mother, not knowing my telephone number, called the principal that afternoon to tell her about it. She said, "I wanted to tell you about it so you would prevent the children from teasing Chester tomorrow at school." She also asked the principal to tell me about it and to ask me to keep Chester every afternoon until his sister in the seventh grade came by for him.
>
> This afternoon he slipped out, even though his mother had told him to wait for Sally, the sister, and I had told him at lunch to wait in the room for her. When Sally came by she said, "Mother will get Chester for this." She added, "I don't know what makes Chester do the things he does."

The group thought Chester's mother was very inconsistent in calling up the principal to ask that the children be prevented from teasing Chester about his accident and then having his sister bring him home from school every afternoon. They felt this showed that the mother lacked empathy with Chester and made him feel she expected him to do bad things and trusted his sister more than him. They concluded that this anecdote supported hypotheses 9, 10, and 15. A few members of the group felt that both these anecdotes showed that Chester lacked a good character, but most members disagreed.

> OCT. 7   Today I was prepared for Chester and was in the door as the children were leaving. As he came to the door I said, "Chester, wait a minute." After the other children were gone I reminded him of his mother's wish. He said, "I don't see why I have to wait. I don't want to." A frown accompanied his remarks. I answered, "It is your mother's request, and we will do as she asked." He said no more but went over to the record player and started a record. In a few minutes I saw him keeping time to the music. When Sally came he got his books, said good-by, and went out without another word.

The group thought that such close supervision by his thirteen-year-old sister must be very distasteful to eleven-year-old Chester and that he was taking it pretty well. They felt that this continuing situation supported hypotheses 9, 10, and 15 and tended to refute the idea that he couldn't discipline himself, hypothesis 21.

OCT. 10 [The anecdote about Chester's playing a game instead of reading and then crying when he wasn't permitted to go out to play at recess and the other children's reporting that this "was the way he did all last year."]

The group thought that crying about being kept in at recess was a mark of immaturity in an eleven-year-old and that Chester was perhaps overemotional. They felt that the tattling by the other children showed rejection of Chester. They voted plus marks for hypotheses 7, 8, 18, 19, and 22.

OCT. 11   CHESTER'S MENU FOR FIVE DAYS.

	Breakfast	School lunch	Evening meal
Mon.	grits one egg two pieces toast glass of milk	vegetable soup pimento-cheese sandwich piece of cake glass of milk	Irish potatoes slaw roll glass of milk
Tues.	one egg jelly two pieces toast glass of milk	potatoes with cheese green beans beets and onions stewed apples corn bread glass of milk	steak and gravy slaw two rolls glass of milk
Wed.	one egg two strips bacon two pieces toast glass of milk	spaghetti, meat balls slaw two slices bread blackberry pie glass of milk	ham, one slice Irish potatoes two rolls jello glass of milk
Thurs.	two pieces toast jelly glass of milk	tuna salad carrot sticks one roll apple pie glass of milk	two sandwiches apple glass of milk
Fri.	cream of wheat two pieces toast one egg jelly glass of milk	pork roast rice and gravy slaw two pieces bread jello and cream glass of milk	green beans sweet potato one egg biscuit glass of milk

The group thought that this diet had plenty of carbohydrates, fats—through the butter and margarine, which were not listed, and the gravy—minerals, and vitamins. They felt that the protein was perhaps rather scanty, but judged that the diet was not bad enough to support or refute any hypotheses.

OCT. 13   I have been noticing Chester stop in the principal's office door every few days to have a word or two with her as we went to and fro to lunch or the playground. Then every time she came into our room he would leave his place to go say a few words to her. At times he even went to the door or into the hall as she left. [Then followed the anecdote about Chester's telling Miss C that the principal wanted him to do a job for her and their going to the principal's office to find that this was not true.]

The group thought that Chester must be getting psychological support and a sense of security from his interactions with the principal, Miss T. His stopping at her office so often indicated to them that he must feel very insecure both at home and at school and that he was trying in this way to build up pleasant experiences to relieve his anxiety. They thought that the anecdote supported hypotheses 7, 8, 9, 17, and 22.

OCT. 15   Our class visited the homes in Chester's neighborhood today. That was part of the community study which the group had launched. When we were about a block from Chester's home, he said, "Let's go by this path. It's nearer." I asked, "Is it all right for us to use this path?" To which he answered, "I always use it." We still wondered about it but followed Chester down the path. He walked beside me most of the trip.

We had gone only a short distance when the path led us right through the backyard of a neighbor of Chester's. I had been seeing some indications of disregard for the property of others. Now I was seeing it again. I had observed Chester taking books from the desks of other children, looking at them, and putting them down again wherever it was convenient for him. I had seen him handle other people's work. One time he went so far as to spoil a piece of clay. He had borrowed pencils from me several times, and I never saw them again. One day he got a Manila folder from my locker and put his name on it. However, after I had talked with him about it he offered to pay for it, so I let him, since I thought it would be a good lesson for him.

When we got to Chester's home, his mother came out to talk with the group. She said, "I know a lot of these children." She began to spot first one and then another, calling the names as she did. Soon she saw two children whom she didn't know. She remarked, "I believe these are new children in the group." Then one of the children introduced them to her. About this time we heard a loud barking, so Chester went in to get his dog to show us. It was a large cocker spaniel. When we were ready to leave, Mrs. M invited the children to come back to play with Chester.

The child-study group noted that Chester walked with the teacher rather than with the other children on the trip and that the teacher reported numerous instances when he had shown disregard for her property and that of other children. They thought that this might be one reason why the children rejected Chester and held that it supported hypotheses

7, 8, and 22. They could not make much out of the contact with Mrs. M because the anecdote did not show her interacting with Chester. Nor could they tell whether Mrs. M was patronizing toward the children, or what the children's feelings toward her were.

> Oct. 17 [Anecdote about Chester's request to be permitted to work on the sixth-grade arithmetic workbook at school while he finished the fifth-grade one at home and his plan to sell doughnuts to pay for the new book.]

The group felt that Chester was humiliated by having to work in the fifth-grade workbook while most of his classmates were using a sixth-grade book, so he wanted to take the fifth-grade book home. They regarded this as concern for his own development and held that this anecdote supported hypotheses 7, 12, and 22. They felt that Chester's willingness to earn the money himself to pay for the workbook and his eager request to be permitted to try the more advanced work demonstrated that he sincerely wants to learn and threw doubt on hypotheses 1, 3, 5, 20, and 21.

> Oct. 20 Chester has been waiting for his sister for about two weeks. However, this morning he informed me that Sally was going to town after school and that he was going to go home with Billy, his younger brother. Soon after school Billy came by and Chester went out with him.

The study group felt that Chester must have been quite humiliated at having his older sister and now his younger brother escort him home, with responsibility delegated to them by the mother to keep him from getting into trouble. They thought it remarkable that Chester didn't make more fuss about it. Hence they concluded that this anecdote supported hypotheses 9, 10, and 22.

> Oct. 21 Today after school Chester said, "I am going home with Billy again. Sally has a meeting today." He went to Billy's room to go with him. Soon both boys came back into our room. Chester went to the record player and started some music. It wasn't long before he was doing rhythms to the music. He said, "I love to do rhythms."

The group thought that this anecdote gave further weight to hypotheses 9, 10, and 22 and that it also showed Chester using music and rhythms to neutralize and manage his unpleasant feelings.

> Oct. 25 Chester has stayed by my side much of today. As soon as he entered the room he came to ask for a free pencil that a company had left in the room for the children as an advertisement. He stayed by my chair while I collected lunch money. He sat by me while the group had a discussion in science. He asked to sit by me to operate the record player while we had singing. He stood at the back of my chair while I read a chapter from the storybook that we are reading together. After

school, while waiting for his sister, he followed me about as I mounted some new fingerpaints. This is quite typical of Chester's behavior.

The group interpreted this anecdote as indicating that Chester was greatly in need of acceptance and security and that what he was getting from the teacher was of real help to him. Obviously his relationships with the other children were not giving him the warm feeling of belonging that he needed, so he chose to be close to the teacher rather than to classmates. The group felt that this description of Chester's characteristic day-to-day behavior supported hypotheses 7, 8, 9, 10, and 22 and tended to weaken hypothesis 16.

Oct. 27   Chester came to me with the money for his workbooks. I had thought that he must have nearly enough to pay for them because I had been ordering the doughnuts for him. He was all smiles when I gave him the books. He said, "I will take my fifth-grade book home and let Mother start helping me. Can I start work in my new ones now?" I explained that he would have to read the directions first to be sure that he knew what to do and then he would have to try the sample to know how much he could do and how much help he needed from me.

When Miss T came into the room he proudly showed her the books. She told him to work hard on reading so that he would be able to read the problems. He promised to do so.

The group thought that this anecdote strengthened hypothesis 7 and weakened 21.

DATA FROM THE CUMULATIVE RECORD

Date of Birth, August 14, 1941
Physical Growth:

Grade	First		Second		Third		Fourth		Fifth		Sixth	
Month	Nov.	May	Nov.	May	Nov.	May	Nov.	May	Nov.	May	Nov.	May
Year	'47	'48	'48	'49	'49	'50	'50	'51	'51	'52	'52	'53
Age	6	6½	7	7½	8	8½	9	9½	10	10½	11	11½
Weight	39	41	43	45	45	47	48	54	55	58	60	62
Height	41½	42½	43½	44¾	45	45½	46	47½	48¼	49	50	50¾
Height Increment		1	1	1¼	¼	½	½	1½	¾	¾	1	¾

The increments of growth are all small, and Chester's growth was particularly slow between the ages of 7½ and 9. When plotted on the Wetzel grid he starts out in the "stocky" channel and moves into the "good" physique channel where he stays. In other words, Chester's growth is clinically good and his body is well proportioned. When his speed of growth is plotted on the grid, however, Chester is excelled by 70 per cent of the other children at the age of six, 84 per cent at eight, and 100 per cent at nine. From then on he is excelled by 95 per cent of all children of his age based on national norms. In other words Chester is naturally small and probably never will be as tall or as heavy as the average man, but in addition to this he is a very slow grower. His growth is perfectly normal and natural for him in the light of his heredity and is not unhealthy in any way. But the combination of being naturally small and at the same time a slow grower resulted in his being far and away the smallest child in his grade every year. Notes on his size in the cumulative record emphasize this.[1]

1st grade: So small he can wear his three-year-old brother's clothes. 2nd grade and all succeeding grades: Smallest child in the room.

The child-study group was much impressed with these growth data and discussed at some length their psychological and emotional effects upon Chester. They noted that Chester was excelled in growth level by 95 per cent of all boys of his age. He himself had mentioned his smallness in his composition, "My Family," in which he compared himself to his brother and pointed out that both he and his father had red hair and that his father had said that when he was a boy he was little like Chester but "when he did start to grow he really grew." They felt that these facts gave very strong support to hypotheses 11, 12, and 19, might partially account for Chester's frequent expressions of hostility to other children in his class, and might raise doubt in his mind about how his mother feels about him, thus giving additional support to hypotheses 7, and 8, 9, 10, and 22.

The cumulative record gave the following health facts: chicken pox at five years, no other childhood diseases. Missed no days whatever because of illness throughout his school life.

Medical examinations in May, 1948, toward the end of the first grade and in May, 1952, toward the end of the fifth grade showed the following:
No skin diseases or deformities.
Normal ears, throat, nose, mouth, heart, lungs, kidneys, and glands; eyes 20/30. Good nutrition and muscular coordination.
Bad teeth because of cavities.
Full-term, breast-fed, healthy baby.
First teeth came in late and soon decayed.

The study group judged this to be an excellent health record and found in it no support for any of the hypotheses about Chester's reading difficulties. They felt that it reaffirmed the idea that Chester's slow growth is perfecly normal in the light of his heredity. The vision test gave a strong minus to hypothesis 14.

[1] At the time when the case records presented in this book were being made, Dr. Nancy Bayley's graph sheets demonstrating the growth curves of height and weight for boys and girls maturing at average, accelerated, and retarded rates were not available. They can be obtained through the Institute of Child Welfare, University of California, Berkeley, California, and are highly recommended for public school use. (See references to Dr. Bayley's works in the bibliography.)

The cumulative record had the following entries with regard to Chester's characteristic rate of energy output:

1ST GRADE: Never still when in his seat, for his hands and feet move. Good in rhythms.

2ND GRADE: Seldom still.

3RD GRADE: Never still a minute, never seems to be tired. Enjoys active games.

4TH GRADE: No record.

5TH GRADE: Never still and can be in a different place every five minutes. Restless. Sits with feet in chair. Likes to play baseball and football.

The study group considered these facts along with Chester's health record and concluded that he is naturally a very active child who frequently needs to work off energy. They considered it likely that his naturally high rate of energy output had been augmented during the past several years by emotional tension. They felt that these facts gave a certain amount of support to hypothesis 13, but that they would not be crucial to his learning to read in his present classroom, where he had a good deal of freedom of movement.

The cumulative record contained the following data about the family and the interpersonal relationships within the family:

Family constellation during the 6th grade: Mr. C. M.—age 35; Mrs. N. M.—age 33; Sally—age 13; Chester—age 11; Billy—age 9. Pet dog named Tubby, pet cat named Blackie. Entries follow:

1ST GRADE: Chester talks about his family often. He slips off to Sally's room every chance he gets, and she comes to the first-grade room once every day.

2ND GRADE: If Chester is a few minutes late coming in from school, his mother calls his peers to find out where he is. If she can't find him, she begins to cry.

3RD GRADE: Chester's family seem very devoted. The parents usually include the children in their plans for evenings and holidays. Mr. M plays ball with the boys.

4TH GRADE: No record.

5TH GRADE: Chester says that his mother makes all his clothes and helps him with reading and arithmetic.

The study group decided the family must be close-knit, but were not able from these data to judge whether or not Chester felt secure in their love or whether he felt less valued than his sister and brother. He is the middle child of three. The group wondered whether Chester was not too much supervised by his mother and whether her constant checking up on him and her getting upset when she couldn't find him made him feel that she lacked confidence in him. Could it be that he was over-protected and was seeking independence? Could it be that his mother's oversolicitousness indicated her unconscious rejection of him? On the basis of these possibilities the group gave weak pluses to hypotheses 2, 9, 15, and 22.

The cumulative record gave the following data on Chester's relationships with adults:

1ST GRADE: Chester seems to love everyone and has been quite demonstrative with the teacher. He wants to help her with everything. He seems particularly devoted to Miss T, the principal, and goes to her office whenever possible. He always wants to show her his papers.

2ND GRADE: Chester is very fond of all adults. He is very affectionate with his teacher, putting his arms around her and saying, "Oh, I love you." He is especially fond of Miss T, the principal.

3RD GRADE: Chester is very affectionate. He still loves Miss T and often runs into the office to see her.

4TH GRADE: No record.

5TH GRADE: Chester likes attention from adults. He still loves Miss T. Chester's room this year is near the office of Miss A, the religion teacher for the school. When I miss Chester and look for him, I usually find him in Miss A's office. He will be busily engaged in talking with her. Chester brings me cookies and candy and gave me an apron for Christmas.

The study group considered whether these data indicated that Chester was an outgoing, naturally affectionate child or that he had a special need for love and attention. They were inclined to think that the persistence of his expressions of love and his seeking the company and attention of adults at school indicated insecurity at home and the need for constant reassurance as to his fundamental value as a human being. They also noted that most children are more preoccupied than he with winning roles and status with their peers throughout this period when Chester was cultivating adults so assiduously. Accordingly, the study group judged that these facts gave support to hypotheses 7, 8, 9, 10, 17, and 22.

The cumulative record contained results of friendship tests given at various grade levels, together with comments by his teachers about his peer-group interaction and status.

1ST GRADE: Chosen by five boys, rejected by two girls. Chose three boys, none of whom chose him. Rejected three boys, none of whom chose or rejected him.

Teacher's comments: Chester seems to be loved by nearly all of the children. He is frequently chosen to enter into their games and to accompany them on errands. He chooses to play with girls.

2ND GRADE: Chosen by six boys, rejected by no one. Chose three girls and rejected no one. One of the boys who chose him also had chosen him in the first grade, one who chose him had been chosen by him in the first grade, and one who chose him had been rejected by him in the first grade.

Teacher's comments: All of the group seem to like Chester. He received the second highest number of choices among the boys. He says, "Inez is my sweetheart," and he chose her on the test, but she did not choose him. This year *he has begun to play with boys.*

3RD GRADE: No friendship test.
Teacher's comment: Chester is loved by both boys and girls.

4TH GRADE: No friendship test or comments.

5TH GRADE: Chosen by one boy and three girls. Rejected by three boys. Chester chose two boys and one girl and rejected three boys. One boy and the girl also have chosen him. These are the first mutual choices recorded. One of the boys whom he had rejected also rejected him—the first mutual rejection recorded.

Teacher's comments: Inez and Gay chose Chester to be in charge of the Valentine box and the bookshelves. He is often seen talking to Madge and going to her for help. She rejected him in grade one, but they mutually chose each other on the test this year.

6TH GRADE: Chosen by two boys, rejected by one boy and one girl. Chester chose three boys and rejected nobody. There were no mutual choices with Chester.

Teacher's comments: One of the boys who chose Chester cries a lot. The three boys whom Chester chose are all good ball players but none of them chose him. The boy who rejected him is the most mature boy in the class. He said that he rejected Chester "because he acts like a baby."

Summary of friendship choices and rejections of Chester by other children:

Grade	Chosen	Mutual	Rejected	Mutual
1st	5	0	2	0
2nd	6	0	0	0
5th	4	2	3	1
6th	2	0	2	0

The child-study group felt that Chester had been well-liked in the first and second grades but noted that he seemed not to recognize who his friends were in these grades, for in the first grade he had chosen three boys, none of whom chose him, and he persisted in playing with girls. In the second grade, when he was chosen by six boys, he had chosen three girls as best friends. In contrast, in the fifth grade Chester had one mutual friendship choice with a boy and one with a girl and a mutual rejection with a boy. Here Chester seemed to have learned who his friends were and to be accepting them. By the sixth grade, however, Chester did not seem to matter much to the group. He aspired to friendship with three boys who were good ball players, but none of them accepted him. The one boy who chose him was babyish and cried a lot. The most mature boy in the class rejected him because "he acts like a baby." The group felt that Chester seemed always to have been more comfortable with girls. They judged that the peer group had never afforded him any real sense of belonging, so they concluded that these facts gave support to hypotheses 7, 8, 19, and 22.

The cumulative record gave the following material about the cultural background of Chester's family and about the ways in which the children were taught how to behave:

1ST GRADE: The M's home is above average for the neighborhood. It is clean and neat and the furniture is well cared for. They have a radio and a record-player combination and a collection of good records such as Strauss waltzes. They also have a recording machine, which Mr. M once used to make a record of our class saying poems. The home is heated with an oil heater and they own an electric refrigerator. They have no car but go riding in the truck Mr. M uses in his upholstery business. He owns the business.

Mrs. M makes all the children's clothes. She seems intelligent. She uses good English and apt words and tries to teach Chester to speak correctly. She encourages him to bring a clean handkerchief to school every day.

2ND GRADE: The M's have a new Pontiac and have had a telephone installed.

3RD GRADE: Mrs. M is a good housekeeper and cooks and sews beautifully. Chester's parents have taught him nice manners.

4TH GRADE: No record.

5TH GRADE: Chester's home is now on a new street in a new development. The interior has just been painted and a new television has been installed. Mr. M has sold his business and now works for an upholstering company. Both he and Mrs. M attended the local elementary and high school. Mrs. M sees to it that Chester studies every day. She tells him to come straight home after school, for she does not want him to stop at the homes of other children. She said that she was "after him all the time about eating a little, jumping up to do something else, and then coming back to eat a little more."

The study group noted that the family has prospered, moved to a new home in a new development, and acquired all the equipment that goes with modern middle-class living. The stress on cleanliness, good English, nice manners, and studious habits in the children, and the aspirations suggested by the kind of automobile they purchased also indicated middle-class attitudes. The group concluded that the family belongs to either the lower-middle or the middle-middle class and are constantly striving for improvement of their status. Under these circumstances, the group felt, Chester must be under constant pressure at home to do well in school and to behave with propriety by middle-class standards.

The group concluded that these facts concerning Chester's cultural background would support hypotheses 2, 4, 9, 10, 15, 17, and 22. They felt that Mrs. M's constant pressure on Chester to come straight home from school, to study hard, to stay at the table, and so on, might make Chester feel that his mother does not love him and doubts his basic worth. But they could not see enough direct evidence of this to put another plus by hypothesis 12 or to make an additional hypothesis covering his possible loss of self-confidence.

The cumulative record contained the following material about Chester's learning capacity:

1ST GRADE: The Metropolitan Readiness Test was given about six weeks after the opening of school. If a child scores under 60 he is regarded as not yet reading books. Chester scored exactly 60.

4TH GRADE: The California Test of Mental Maturity was given in January. Chester's chronological age was 113 months, his mental age 94 months, and his intelligence quotient 83. This would lead one to expect learning accomplishment a little below entrance into the third grade.

6TH GRADE: The California Test of Mental Maturity was given on November 11. Chester's chronological age was 135 months, his mental age, 105 months, his IQ 78. While the test was being given Chester squirmed and sighed often. At times he made no effort to attempt parts of the test until encouraged directly to do so.

A breakdown of Chester's scores follows:

Subtest	Possible score	Chester's score
1. Immediate recall	24	19
2. Delayed recall	20	4
Total memory	44	23
3. Sensing right and left	20	12
4. Manipulation of areas	15	9
Total spatial relationships	35	21
5. Opposites	15	9
6. Similarities	15	11
7. Analogies	15	11
8. Inference	15	7
Total logical reasoning	60	38

Subtest	Possible score	Chester's score
9. Number series	10	2
10. Numerical quantity	10	0
11. Numerical reasoning	15	4
Total	35	6
12. Verbal concepts	50	5
Total nonlanguage factors	114	50
Total language factors	110	43
Total scores	224	93

The study group noted the teacher's report of Chester's reluctance to try parts of the test without urging. They also noted that Chester had gotten more than half the items correct in the first three groups of subtests but only six out of thirty-five in the number concepts, one of his best subjects at school, and five out of fifty in the verbal concepts. They wondered whether he had not stopped trying about two-thirds of the way through the test. They recognized, of course, that they could make no accurate guess concerning Chester's mental age and intelligence quotient, but they could not accept an IQ of 78 as an accurate index of his brightness. They were at a loss to know how much of Chester's reading handicap was due to intellectual limitations and how far his low test score might be due to his reading and language handicap. They considered the possibility that both the test score and his accomplishment in reading might be lower than Chester's potential intelligence would imply, because emotional tension and a neurotic preoccupation with his small stature might interfere with his learning. On the other hand, they felt that the results of the two testings were consistent enough to indicate no better than a dull normal classification for Chester. They decided that the test results justified plus marks for hypotheses 6 and 19 and expressed the belief that an analysis of his actual school progress might help them appraise his learning capacities more accurately.

The cumulative record contained the following material about Chester's accomplishments in school:

1st GRADE: Likes to read; showed pride in his first reading book; reads very slowly; is learning to get words by himself. Can write numbers and count objects, add and subtract a few simple combinations. Enjoys hearing stories and poems; enters discussions. Forms letters and spaces words nicely. Is neat. Enjoys rhythms and listening time. Likes to work with crayons and paint. Is slow and deliberate in all of his work. Studies the following problems: How we care for our pets. Why we love Christmastime. Our part in the home.

2nd GRADE: Seems to enjoy reading and puts forth great effort. Has made progress; needs to work on speed and expression. Stopped looking at the book and had trouble paying attention during the last part of the year. Is making satisfactory progress in arithmetic. Knows most of

the addition combinations. Also has an understanding of many subtraction combinations. Needs to work on speed. Enters into discussions.
Has good ideas. Expresses himself well orally. Toward end of year could
write sentences and notes. Forms letters well and spaces words nicely.
Writes neatly. Shows ability in rhythms. Expresses himself well in
painting and modeling with clay. Is generally deliberate and thorough,
puts forth much effort in all his work and completes task. Chester
worked on the following topics: Spiders. Where we get our clothing.
How we get our mail.

3RD GRADE: Is making progress in reading. Speaks and reads very deliberately. Attention span is short. Comprehends what he reads.
Doesn't like to stay still long enough to do the reading of which he is
capable. His inability to read is a handicap when trying arithmetic
problems but toward the end of the year Chester did a better job of
thinking through problems. Has made a lot of progress in oral language
and some improvement in written language. Forms letters well, spaces
nicely and is neat with his writing. Shows ability in rhythms. Enjoys
listening to music. Likes to sing, but voice is not adequate for chorus
singing. Likes to work with paints and clay. Slow in all of his work.
Puts forth much effort. Happy as long as he can be moving from place
to place. Worked on the following topics: The food we eat. Our homes.

4TH GRADE: Reads slowly and is making better progress. Loves books.
Attention span is longer. Is learning to get new words independently.
Adds, subtracts, multiplies, and divides with average speed and accuracy. Needs to work on multiplication tables. Learns all spelling words
in the lesson and applies these words in his written work. Expresses
himself well in both oral and written language. Writes well. Participates
in all phases of the music program and in the art periods with interest.
Worked on the following topics: The library. The clothes we wear—
cotton, wool, leather, rubber, linen, silk.

Progressive Achievement Test was given in January. Chester got
the following grade-placement scores:

Subject	Grade placement
Reading vocabulary	2.4
Reading comprehension	3.6
Total reading	3.0
Arithmetic reasoning	3.5
Arithmetic fundamentals	3.8
Total arithmetic	3.6
Language	4.1
Total score	3.6

5TH GRADE: Chester is a poor reader and doesn't practice reading
enough to progress as he should. Has difficulty in pinning himself down
to reading. Attention is elsewhere at reading time. Says, "I'll take it
home and read it." Doesn't make good on opportunities to read with
a group. Independent reading level—second grade. Instructional reading level—third grade. Chooses hard books from the library truck. Likes
arithmetic. Can do long division and fractions for grade level but has

trouble with problems due to reading difficulties. Learns his spelling words and uses them in written work. Tells stories to the group but has trouble with sentence structure in written stories. Forms letters well but writing is not always neat. Participates in science activities. Locates simple materials. Works out easy experiments and enters discussions. Is interested in science experiences. Enjoys rhythms and listening time and participation in all phases of music program. Participates in art periods. Worked on following topics:

I. Early Explorers
   1. Which direction did peoples of long ago know about?
   2. How can we find directions on maps?
   3. How do we use the compass to tell directions?
   4. Where did people live before America was discovered?
   5. How does wind make ships sail?
   6. How long did it take to sail around the world?
II. Electricity
   1. How many things can we find that inventors gave us?
   2. How does electricity help us?
   3. How does electricity work?
   4. How does electricity travel?

6TH GRADE: Chester took the California Achievement Test on December 1 and made the following scores:

Reading subtest section	Possible score	Chester's score
1. Word form	25	20
2. Word recognition	20	17
3. Meaning of opposites	23	8
4. Meaning of similarities	22	6
Total vocabulary	90	51
5. Following directions	10	3
6. Reference skills	10	1
7. Interpretations	20	6
Total comprehension	40	10

Chester's placement for reading vocabulary is 3.6, for reading comprehension 3.7, and for total reading 3.6.

Language subtest section	Possible score	Chester's score
1. Capitalization	15	8
2. Punctuation	10	5
3. Words and sentences	20	5
Total language mechanics	45	18
4. Spelling	30	6

Chester's grade placement for mechanics of English and grammar is 3.9 and for spelling 3.9. Total language grade placement is 3.9.

Arithmetic subtest section	Possible score	Chester's score
1. Number of concepts	15	3
2. Signs and symbols	15	2
3. Problems	15	5
Total arithmetic reasoning	45	10
4. Addition	20	5
5. Subtraction	20	5
6. Multiplication	20	6
7. Division	20	8
	80	24

Chester's grade placement for arithmetic reasoning is 3.6 and for arithmetic fundamentals is 5.0. Total arithmetic placement is grade 4.3.

Chester's teacher figured that 2.5 was the grade-level accomplishment that would have been expected of Chester in the fourth grade if the mental age he earned on the California Test of Mental Maturity represented his full capacity for learning. His actual score on the Progressive Achievement Test gave him a grade placement of 3.6, or more than one full year beyond his indicated capacity. Then she figured the grade-level accomplishments that she had a right to expect on December 1 in the sixth grade if the mental age he earned on the California Test of Mental Maturity taken in November represented his full capacity for learning. She found that he should score at grade 3.3. His actual score on the California Achievement Test was 3.6 for reading, 3.9 for language, and 4.3 for arithmetic, or from three months to one year above his indicated capacity. Yet, on the basis of working with him from day to day, his teacher told the study group that she was surprised that his accomplishment scores were so low.

The child-study group weighed these test scores and the written evaluations in the cumulative record and came to the following conclusions:

1. Chester's real capacity for learning is probably indicated better by his school accomplishment than by his intelligence-test scores. In other words, his real intelligence quotient is probably between 85 and 90 rather than below 80.

2. Chester probably accomplished the maximum possible for him up to the fifth grade and may even be accomplishing all that is possible at present. Earlier reports that he put great effort into his learning were doubtless true.

3. Chester is a slow-growing, dull–normal boy. Even working his hardest he has fallen behind a little more each year. By the fourth, fifth, and sixth grades he is finding school expectancies so much ahead of his slowly developing capacities that he is greatly discouraged and tries to avoid failure by dodging assignments.

4. Chester's teachers have done the best that they could for him. In the light of his slow growth and limited ability he perhaps should have been held back in the third grade for an additional year, but this was not done.

In the light of these conclusions the study group decided that they had conclusive evidence that hypotheses 1 and 3 were not true and strong supporting evidence for hypotheses 4, 6, 15, and 19. They felt that the evidence also tended to refute hypothesis 21 and to support hypotheses 12 and 22. The group also expressed themselves as worried about the pressure Chester was under at home, fearing that this contributed still another factor to make him anxious in the classroom.

> DEC. 4 [Anecdote about Chester's sweeping another boy's work place when he was supposed to be reading, and actually reading ten pages after the teacher selected an easy book, got him started, and praised him.]

The study group, somewhat excited over their deepened insight into Chester, decided that they should make a twenty-third hypothesis. It is as follows:

23. Chester has not had enough patient, detailed help on easy reading in a climate of encouragement, praise for his success, and avoidance of criticism of his failures. To remotivate him, he needs success in the eyes of his parents, his classmates, his teacher, and himself.

As the group discussed this hypothesis they came to see that it had already been covered by the more negative hypotheses 2, 4, 7, 10, 12, 15, 17, 18, and 22; consequently they decided not to add it after all. Chester's teacher thought that the phrasing of the proposed hypothesis gave her good support in her efforts to help Chester and guidance for future conferences with Chester's mother.

> The cumulative record contained the following material about Chester's emotional behavior and self-adjustive processes:

> 1ST GRADE: Chester is quite affectionate. He loves to be near people. He pats and caresses those he seems to love. He pouts if reprimanded and cries at disappointments.

> 2ND GRADE: When Chester does poor work his face becomes very solemn looking. When he does good work he fairly beams.

> 3RD GRADE: No report.

> 4TH GRADE: No report.

> 5TH GRADE: When Chester is displeased over his work or when he is corrected, he pouts, makes faces, and says, "What was I doing, I was doing nothing." He likes his way, wants a lot of attention, and interrupts when the teacher is helping other children.

The study group wished that more had been included in the cumulative record about how Chester acted when experiencing emotion. They thought that his continuing demand for attention tokened anxiety from a number of causes but could not identify the causes from the material in the record. Consequently they judged that a plus mark should be placed only beside hypothesis 22. They regarded his pouting as evidence of immaturity and as justifying a plus for hypothesis 19. They thought that these descriptions showed that Chester was bothered every time he failed at some task and might justify a minus for hypothesis 5. Someone suggested that the interruptions of the teacher when she was helping other children might suggest a plus for hypothesis 16.

> DEC. 5   Miss T, the principal, was in the room today. I said, "Chester, show Miss T your book and tell her about it." He showed her how far he had read. It appeared to be around twenty-five pages. I am beginning to have hopes of interesting him in reading.

The study group thought that this promising accomplishment justified minuses for hypotheses 5, 20, and 21.

> DEC. 8   When it was time to leave today Chester came to me. His eyes were shining and he was wearing a smile. He said, "I have to hurry. I am trying out for basketball today. The coach told us to come right after school." Then his expression changed and he looked down at the floor. I waited; then I heard him saying rather slowly, "I sure hope I make it." I said, "I hope so too." At the beginning of the football season he had tried out for the team but he was too small. As he left the room I said, "Good luck."

The study group felt that this anecdote supported hypotheses 11, 12, 19, and 22.

> DEC. 9   The first thing this morning Chester informed me that he made the team. I think that I have never seen him more thrilled over anything. I told him that I was happy for him and he thanked me.

> DEC. 11   About 4:30 I left school. I met Chester coming down from the gym. "Where are you going?" I asked. I noticed that his sweat shirt was black and his face was streaked with dirt. "Oh, Sally is on the girl's team, and I am waiting for her so I can go home," he answered. "My, we have been practicing."

> DEC. 15   Soon after the opening of school Dick said, "Miss C, you should have seen the game Friday. Chester played part of the time." I said, "What, playing a game so soon?" "Oh, we played Harrison just to warm up a bit. They wanted to warm up, too. Chester substituted for a boy."
>   Chester heard Dick talking so he came over, too. As he came he smiled and rubbed his hands together in the expressive way that boys have when they have done something of which they are proud.

The study group thought that these anecdotes tended to refute hypothesis 21.

> DEC. 17   The following story was first written for thought. Then it was checked for arrangement of sentences and for capitalization and punctuation. Lastly it was rewritten in this form.

A DAY AT OUR HOUSE

Mother is the first one up at our house. The first thing that she does is to get the paper. Then she starts breakfast. Soon she calls to Daddy, "Get up." After he leaves for work she calls Sally and Billy and me. She says, "Wash your faces and hands and comb your hair." She won't let us come to the table before we look nice.

After breakfast we brush our teeth and get dressed for school. Mother helps us find our clothes and books. Soon we are on our way and mother is left alone to get the house in order and sew for us. She makes all our clothes.

When I get home after school my dog runs to meet me. I hear mother say, "Change your clothes." We change to play clothes. Then we go into the kitchen and eat a lunch.

We play until supper time. After supper we take a bath. We play games or watch the television until nine o'clock, when we go to bed. About ten or ten-thirty mother and dad come.

The study group decided that this material implied a minus for hypothesis 5 because the family reads a newspaper regularly and supports hypothesis 2 because Chester reports the mother as telling the children each thing they are to do.

JAN. 5   After school today Chester was talking with me about happenings during the holidays. I let him do most of the talking. The following are some of his remarks:

"We didn't get many toys this Christmas. We got mostly clothes. My brother and I got an electric train together. Mother told us Santa Claus brought the clothes and train." Then in a wise manner he added, "Of course I know that there isn't a Santa Claus, but we just say that."

"Santa Claus is the spirit of Christmas. It means the spirit of love and of giving. There were a lot of good programs on television about this. They said that Christmas ought to be the time for giving instead of receiving."

The study group thought that the parents were a little hard on Chester if they gave him no toys of his very own but gave him only necessary clothes and made him share the train with Billy. They thought that this might support hypothesis 9. They felt that Chester's comments on Christmas showed good moral sensitivity and tended to refute hypothesis 21.

JAN. 6   Following is a copy of the report I wrote today to send to Chester's parents. We give two written reports each year. This one covers a period of four months.

PROGRESS REPORT

X ATTENDANCE AREA   Y COUNTY SCHOOLS

NAME   Chester M   TEACHER   Miss C   GRADE   6
DAYS ABSENT   0   DAYS TARDY   0

READING.   Is reading independently on the third-grade level and instructionally on the fourth-grade level. Does not enjoy reading. Finds

many excuses to leave reading to do something else. Has trouble understanding what he reads. Is better able to find facts than to interpret
facts. Has trouble finding words in context when meaning is given.
Has trouble getting the main idea of a paragraph.

ENGLISH LANGUAGE.   Has a wide speaking vocabulary. Uses correct
English. Does not enjoy story writing. Understands sentence construction.

SPELLING.   Learns words in spelling lessons and uses them in written work. Enjoys spelling.

WRITING.   Spaces words well. Is practicing again on the formation
of letters. Is not neat in written work. Erases often.

ARITHMETIC.   Has worked again this year on addition, subtraction
and multiplication. Had some trouble with subtraction. Is now ready
for division. Has had experiences with problem solving. Enjoys arithmetic.

SOCIAL STUDIES (history, geography, and civics).   Has worked with
maps. Takes part in discussion. Showed interest in a study of his community. Shared materials. Is trying for a better relationship with classmates.

SCIENCE.   Experimented with the force of air. Has become interested in cloud formation. Likes dogs.

MUSIC AND ART.   Listens to music. Takes part in singing and
rhythms. Enjoys all phases of music. Works with clay, wood, paints,
and fingerpaints. Enjoys all media of art expression.

The study group thought that this report corroborated the earlier
discussion of Chester's capacities and school accomplishment. Obviously
he had not retained all the knowledges and skills that his cumulative
record indicated he had had. The group considered that in the light of
this report plus signs should be put beside hypotheses 4, 6, 15, 19, and 22.

JAN. 8   This is a copy of a story just as Chester wrote it:

MY DOG TUBBY

My dogs name is Tubby. When we are playing baseball we hit it
over the fence and he goes for it and brings it back. When we go
places he follows us. He follows us to the store. He follows us everywhere we go. He tries to follow us to school. One day he followed us
halfway and we carried him home. Mother made him go in the house
and she kept him there until we got to school, then she let him out
again. He plays with my cat. The cats name is Blackie. Tubby and
Blackie play ball with each other.

JAN. 12   Another story:

MY FAMILY

There are five of us. My brother, Bill, has blonde hair and blue eyes.
He is nine years old and in the fourth grade. He isn't as old as I am
but he is lots bigger. He is taller and weighs more. My sister's name
is Sally. She is thirteen years old and is in the seventh grade. She has
brown hair and blue eyes. Mother has brown hair and blue eyes. She

*is thirty-three years old and daddy is thirty-three too. He has red hair
and blue eyes. He said that he was little like me when he was a boy.
He said when he did start to grow he really grew. Mother says that I
may do like daddy did.*

When the child-study group had heard these two samples of Chester's
written language they agreed that he must be learning up to very near
the limits of his ability in language and wondered why he was not doing
as well in reading. The content of the two compositions was rather
stilted and stiff, but the realities described revealed both warmth and
anxiety. Tubby played ball with the children and followed them everywhere; when he tried to follow them to school, their mother managed
him. Chester used "we" in the story to refer to the family or the children.
Did this betoken a grand, warm unity in the family? Or did it indicate
that Chester was submerged—a fringer in his own family, who had to
say "we" because "I" had no role? Noting that he was supervised by the
other two children coming to and going home from school, that he was
a middle child, and that his younger brother was now taller and heavier,
the group decided that these anecdotes justified pluses for hypotheses
10 and 22.

But Chester did say "my cat." And the father did tell Chester that he,
too, was little as a boy but that "when he started to grow he really grew."
The mother also supported Chester's identification with his father by
saying that Chester might grow as his father had. The group thought that
this showed that the parents recognized the cause of Chester's anxiety and
were trying to relieve it. They felt that this justified strong minuses for
hypotheses 9 and 10.

On the other hand, the second story left no doubt about Chester's
anxiety concerning his size and growth. It also implied concern about
the fact that his brother had already excelled him growthwise. Whatever
the parents actually felt, the group judged that Chester thought himself
the ugly duckling of the family excelled by both his siblings in things
that the parents admired. His father's comments were only a solace for
an inferiority. So the group decided that this composition gave strong
support to hypotheses 10, 11, 12, 19, and 22.

JAN. 13–16 [The teacher was out sick.]

JAN. 19 After reports went out, Mrs. M wrote a note saying that she
would like to talk with me. I responded that I would call on her, and
I chose today because I knew there was a basketball game and that
Chester would be playing. I supposed that the other children would
see the game too. I wanted to go when all the children were away so
that we could talk uninterruptedly.

I had hardly taken my hand from the doorbell when the door was
opened by Billy. I asked, "Is your mother in?" and entered the living

room as he called, "Mother." Mrs. M came to the door folding an ironing board and said, "I didn't expect you today. I have just finished my ironing." She sat on the sofa and called to Billy, "You can turn off the TV and go out to play." He started out without a word. Then she called again, "Turn off the TV." Billy answered, "I did." (Why does she tell them the same thing over and over?)

Then, turning to me, she said, "Chester is playing this afternoon." "Yes, I knew he was," I replied. "That is why I chose this afternoon to call. I thought we could have more time to talk. Has Sally gone to the game?" "No, she has gone to Westville to my sister's. I told her that she could go to the game if she got back in time."

Hurriedly she asked, "How is Chester doing?" But before I could answer she went on, "I know he isn't doing well. He isn't at all like the other two children. They don't have any trouble. You would never know that he is any kin to them. I just don't know what is the matter with him."

She continued, "I have to tell him over and over to do things. Just the other morning I asked him about four times if he had brushed his teeth, and he would say, 'No, Ma'am, I was doing this and that but I am going to.' It is that way all the time. I know what you put up with at school but I don't know what to do about it. I have tried everything I know."

During the conversation she was tucking first one foot and then the other under herself. She was blinking her eyes and constantly moving in some way.

"How do you feel now about Chester's size?" I asked. She answered, "We were talking the other day. I told him I would rather have him slim like his daddy than big and fat like my brother. I asked him what he thought about it and he said, 'Oh, I suppose so.' I have tried to help him." "Well, he probably feels it more than he will say," I replied. "I think that because of his size he is always struggling for a place, wherever he is." Then his mother said, "I was so glad that he made the basketball team in spite of his size. You know he isn't a good sport, and I am so in hopes that playing on the team will help him to get along with other people. He has such a temper."

About this time Sally and someone else came in the back door. . . . Mrs. M introduced the lady as her sister. After the introduction the lady said, "May Sally go to the Smith Furnace Company with me?" Sally, who had followed her into the room, said, "I am going to the basketball game." "All right," replied the aunt, "but now I must be going." As they started out, Mrs. M asked Sally, "Is Billy going with you?" Sally answered that he was, and Mrs. M called, "Bring Chester home with you."

Mrs. M turned to me and said, "You know, Sally is only eighteen months older than Chester, but she goes ahead with things. Chester is not dependable like she is. He doesn't catch on to things like the other two. They have all of them had good teachers—I know it isn't that. I didn't have any trouble in school until I hit French and I finished X High School." I asked, "Did Mr. M finish X High School, too?" "No, he didn't finish high school; he went to Y High."

I got a chance to say, "Chester does like arithmetic." But she came back with, "Yes, he does, but he neglects other things to do it. And you know he can't do problems. He can't read them. Unless I just make him read aloud he doesn't know what he has read. When he is answering questions about his reading I never tell him the answers but I try to help him get them for himself. I make him read every afternoon but he reads so slowly that it takes about an hour for him to cover any ground at all."

I had been trying to get a chance to sound out Mrs. M about retaining Chester this year. Finally I got a chance. "How do you feel about Chester staying in the sixth grade for two years?" Immediately she said, "I don't see how he has made a grade every year anyway. I think maybe he should have been retained in the second grade. He certainly isn't ready for seventh. He has gotten the idea that he can go up whether he works or not." I commented, "Yes, I am thinking of his not being ready in many ways—in work habits, in skill subjects, in relationships with boys and girls, in interests, and so on." She agreed that she thought it a wise move to retain him this year.

As though the matter of Chester were now finished she started talking about the house. All the time we had been talking I had been getting a general idea of the house. In the living room was a dingy tan rug with dull, faded flowers. Under a window was a green sofa with dark, greasy spots on it. A cushion that had been yellow but was now black leaned against one end of the sofa. In front of the sofa stood a coffee table, the top of which was covered with inexpensive pieces of china and the bottom of which was full of Bibles and Sunday-school books all in a row. In front of the fireplace was a record cabinet full of records and books. Against one wall was a small bookcase containing a set of reference books. At either end of the sofa was an end table on which sat a lamp with big, bright, red roses on it. This completed the furnishings except for one upholstered chair, in which I sat. It, too, was a dull, dingy tan with flowers. The pictures were hung very high and the white curtains looked as if they had just been laundered.

Mrs. M said, "I am ashamed of the inside of the house, but we are still making payments and we have to improve by degrees. We have just about finished the outside. We have a new roof and new asbestos siding. We have had it insulated and weather stripped. Next, we plan to put on a cement porch, for the wooden one is wearing out." (I had noticed this as I entered.)

She continued, "I guess you notice how terrible the floors and woodwork look. My husband is scraping the old paint off the floors. He has just about finished the job. Then he will sand it and refinish it. The floors are just a sight. They were stained a dark color and we tried to paint them white. We have put everything we knew on them but the stain keeps coming through." (The doors, too, were a streaked pink and white.)

I remarked, "I notice you have a floor furnace. Is it oil?" "Yes," she answered, "we had that put in and it really heats. Of course we don't try to heat the three bedrooms. We just heat the three rooms on this side of the house. It is hard to pay fuel bills and other bills and keep three children going."

When she stopped to get her breath I said, "Mrs. M, I must be going. I have enjoyed my visit with you." "Do come again," she invited.

The child-study group felt that Mrs. M's comments showed that she was constantly expecting the worst from Chester, for she had said, "I know he isn't doing well. He isn't at all like the other two children. . . . You would never know that he is any kin to them. . . . I know what you put up with at school. . . . Sally is only eighteen months older than Chester but she goes ahead with things. Chester is not dependable like she is. He doesn't catch on to things like the other two." They considered that these and other comments gave strong support for hypotheses 9 and 10.

The group also felt that the way Mrs. M dealt with the other children during the teacher's visit and her accounts of what she said to Chester and of how she "helped" him with his homework indicated that she nagged him and gave strong support to hypotheses 2, 4, and 15. The presence of a good deal of reading matter in the home, they held, refuted hypothesis 5. The family's sustained effort to progress materially, the improvements on and in the house, and the general furnishings, the group members thought, indicated a lower-middle-class status with a strong drive to upward mobility. A strong desire for Chester to succeed in school certainly would accompany this and add further support to hypotheses 2, 4, and 15.

One of the group noted that none of the hypotheses really covered the point just made and suggested that a new one be added. The group discussed the matter and decided to add the following hypothesis to the list:

23. The strong drive toward upward social mobility that motivates Chester's parents is one of the causes of their constant and excessive pressure on him to do well in school.

The group felt that the home-visit report justified a strong plus for this hypothesis and recalled that the cumulative record contained the following facts, each of which justified a plus for hypothesis 23.

> 1ST GRADE: The M's home is above average for the neighborhood, etc.
> 2ND GRADE: The M's have bought a new Pontiac and have had a telephone installed.
> 5TH GRADE: Chester's home is now on a new street in a new development, etc.

Thus the group entered hypothesis 23 into the series with four pluses.

Summing up the whole visit, the group felt that the evidence was strong for maternal rejection of Chester, unfavorable comparison with siblings, maternal preference for siblings, constant pressure on Chester to learn, nagging about his reading, and too close supervision which undermined his confidence in himself. Even the parents' attempts to reassure him about his growth might well have miscarried, the group felt, because they occurred in this context of regarding him as a failure, as different from the others, and as a person from whom the worst was to be expected. They felt that the whole picture indicated a strong probability of the truth of hypotheses 11, 12, 19, and 22; they were uncertain from the evidence whether hypotheses 16 and 17 were strengthened by these data but decided not to put pluses beside them.

JAN. 22   Today I was talking with Miss T, the principal. She said, "Chester interests me very much. He can carry on a good conversation. He can discuss many topics, but he hasn't learned to read. I don't understand it. He is such a polite little fellow, and he wants to be helpful. I think his size has something to do with his disposition and his learning ability. He is so busy trying to find a place in the group that he can't work on reading skills." I said, "His mother isn't sure that she worries about it." Miss T remarked, "Oh, he wouldn't tell it for the world, not Chester!"

The study group took this as evidence that Chester had been putting his best foot forward with Miss T in the attempt to obtain greatly needed support and security from her. They took this conversation as support for hypotheses 4, 12, and 22.

JAN. 27   Today we were rushing to finish some painting before lunchtime because we were going on a trip right after lunch. I was at the sink helping to get jars and pans washed and packed away. The group had agreed that as each finished he would sit down and read for pleasure.

Chester came to me and said that Bob had torn his (Chester's) pants and that now he wouldn't be able to go. I asked, "Why did Bob do that?" Chester said, "I don't know." Then a child who was standing by the sink commented, "Chester was in Dick's chair and Dick was trying to get him out. Bob came over to help Dick." I told Chester to go to his seat. He went and started crying. On further investigation I learned that Bob had not torn them. Dick had been pulling Chester and the pants had caught on a nail. I told Chester that he could go because his coat would hide the torn place. Then I went out of the room for a minute. When I returned, Jack and George were at Chester's desk. A. H. (a girl) said, "They have fixed Chester's pants. They have pinned them. We told him to pull out his shirt too." I looked and saw that Chester's shirt had been pulled outside. I commented, "You look nice, for your shirt is the style that can be worn in or out." I thanked the children for helping Chester.

The study group held that this anecdote illustrated Chester's penchant for rubbing other children the wrong way. He had taken another boy's chair, resisted giving it up, and then falsely reported to the teacher that a boy had torn his pants when that boy had not been responsible. So they decided that the incident supported hypotheses 7, 8, and 22, but not very strongly because of the help the other children had given him in the crisis.

JAN. 29   Chester was spending too much time working in his arithmetic workbook. He was neglecting spelli*g and reading and using the
time for them on arithmetic. I had talked with him and tried to get
him to see that, to be well-rounded, he needed to have all the skills.
This same thing has happened over and over. So today I asked him to
let me keep his book for a day or so. I put it on my table. It wasn't
long until I saw that he had it again. I took it and this time I put it
in my locker. When he started home, I saw the workbook again under
another book. I asked, "Where did you get your workbook?" He turned
red, rolled his tongue, and stuck it out (in embarrassment and not at
me). I smiled, and then he grinned and ducked his head. I held out
my hand. He gave me the book, told me good-bye, and went out.

One member of the group suggested that this anecdote supported
hypothesis 1, that Chester was just stubborn and wouldn't work on reading unless forced to; but the group as a whole, after a discussion, came to
the conclusion that innate stubbornness was not really an explanation,
that he must have some motivation for this persistence. They looked over
the other hypotheses and did not find the necessary idea in any of them.
Hence they decided to add another hypothesis to account for this incident. It was:

24. Chester has failed so much in reading that he needs some successes
to bolster his self-esteem. Arithmetic is his best subject, so he is
working very hard to catch up with the class in this to compensate
for his failure in reading. He wants to prove to himself and to others
that he can succeed.

The group decided to enter this as hypothesis 24 and give it a strong plus.

FEB. 3   We visited the Coca-Cola plant today. The manager gave
each child a tablet, a pencil, and a ruler. Then he gave me one for each
pupil who had been unable to come. Chester had not heard him say
that they were for the absent children. He thought they were mine.
So he looked at them wistfully and then looked at me. Then he
counted them. I explained that they were for the children who couldn't
come. He turned red and grinned. That reminded me of the many
times Chester had shown the same behavior.
     Once the Coca-Cola plant had sent each child a booklet about
cotton. Chester got one. Then one day he saw some extra ones in my
locker. He looked long and hard at them, counted them, looked at
me, and fingered them some more. A few days later he asked me for
one. I gave it to him, and he thanked me.

FEB. 4   Chester handed me the following note as soon as he came
in this morning. It was in an envelope on which he had written, "To
Miss C."

Centertown
Feb. 3, 1953

Dear Miss C,

I enjoyed the trip to the Coca-Cola Botteling Co. today. I had a very nice time. Thank you for lettling me go with the class room. George, Bobby, Joe and I had a very nice time coming home together. I will try to do a good day's work tomorrow.

Senserly yours,
C.M.

The note is copied just as he had it on the paper.

FEB. 6   Each month a business concern sends us pencils as a form of advertisement. They came today and I gave each child one. Chester followed me around as I gave them out. As he followed me he looked at the stack of pencils and then counted the children who had not as yet received one. After school he asked me for one of the extra ones. Last month he went into my locker and got one of the extras without so much as asking for it.

One month, for one reason or another, I did not give out the pencils for several days. Each day Chester asked, "When are you going to give out the pencils?" He had several pencils at the time and therefore did not really need one.

The study group considered these anecdotes together and felt that Chester was showing an undesirable greediness that was somewhat inconsistent with his polite thank-you note. They debated whether this desire to get things for himself showed a character weakness or a life experience that was so lacking in success and rewards as to make him overanxious for possessions as a compensation. In the end they could not agree that this material clearly supported or weakened any of the hypotheses about why Chester avoided working at his reading. Most of them seemed to think that Chester wanted these little things so much because he had so few toys at home that were his very own and as a compensation for his many failures and rejections.

FEB. 11   After school Chester left to go next door to the community gym for basketball practice. About thirty minutes later he came back into the room and found me cleaning my locker. He looked interested and came over. I had started taking the things from the shelves and putting them on a table so that I could dust and rearrange. He began to help and as he took each thing from the shelf he examined it very closely. Evidently here was the chance to do what he was most anxious to do, namely, examine everything in that locker!

Suddenly he stopped to say, "I had better call Mother to tell her that I am helping you." I gave him permission to go to the office to use the phone. Soon he was back and resumed the work.

All the time we were working he was chatting away, commenting on everything he saw. He spied a walking cane and asked to use it at our pioneer fireplace. After receiving permission he hung it and turned to say, "How's that?"

When the job was finished he went to the record player and chose a record. It was a Christmas record that I had taken from the locker and placed on the record shelf. He said, "Oh, this is a Christmas record. That doesn't make any difference, I love to hear Christmas music any time. Isn't it pretty!"

Soon I had finished my other chores, so I said, "Let's go." He walked out to the car with me and then turned to go across the playground. I asked, "Are you going home alone?" He answered, "Sally has already gone. You see I went to the gym to practice." I asked, "Is your mother letting you come home alone?" His answer was, "She knows I am for she knows I have to stay to practice ball. I always go straight home now."

The child-study group interpreted this anecdote as revealing Chester's pleasure at the acceptance he received from his teacher as well as giving evidence of his curiosity about the contents of her locker. They conjectured whether this continuing acceptance by his teacher could supply him with enough security to free him to progress significantly with his reading, despite his mother's continuing too close supervision of his comings and goings.

FEB. 12   The library truck comes to our school every other week. Today was the day for it. When Chester came back from getting his two books, he came immediately to me to show one of them. It was *Something for a Laugh*. He started reading at once and stood by me for help. Now and then he would ask a word and now and then he would say, "Is this so and so?" Most of the time he was pronouncing the words correctly. I was very surprised at the words he was working out for himself.

The members of the group regarded this anecdote as showing that Chester wanted both to read and to be near his teacher to draw support and help from her. They thought that her acceptance and help might neutralize the fear of failure that apparently had deterred him earlier, so they decided that this anecdote implied pluses for hypotheses 4 and 22 and minuses for hypotheses 5 and 20.

FEB. 16   The children take turns being housekeeper for a day. The job is to sweep the corners that the janitor misses, dust everything, wash the sink, and keep things in general order during the day. It is a job that took the whole day.

Today was Chester's day. He started soon after he came in. He moved things and swept most carefully, going back to get the trash that he missed at first. He moved books, etc., from all the shelves and dusted them before placing them back in order. He washed the sink and the cleaning rags. He placed crayons, paints, brushes, etc., in order in the lockers and drawers. Now and then he stopped to scrutinize his work. There was a contented look on his face. Not once that day did I see the telltale frown.

During the day I saw him pick up papers that others had dropped. After we had done some work that required a lot of cutting of paper, he swept the whole room again to get up all the little pieces that had fallen from the tables. Toward the end of the day I whispered to him, "The room is the cleanest it has been for some time. Would you like to invite Miss T to see it?" He beamed and went to the office. She complimented him when she saw what a good job he had done, and he beamed again.

The child-study group saw this as a very happy day for Chester because being successful in cleaning the room gave him a sense of belonging, of having a significant role, and of being accepted and valued by his teacher and Miss T. They wondered whether he had used his tasks in order to avoid reading at any time during the day but were reassured on this score by the teacher. They took Chester's eagerness, industry, and good humor that day as evidence that the opposites of these characteristics, which he had previously shown, were due to his feeling rejected and to his failures. Consequently, they decided that his good behavior under the new conditions indicated pluses for hypotheses 4, 16, and 22 and minuses for hypotheses 5, 20, and 21.

FEB. 19 Chester stayed with me after school until I was ready to leave. We got into a conversation about his afternoons. I asked, "What do you usually do in the afternoons?" He replied, "I play with Tom Jones. He lives two doors from me and he comes over to my house." "Do you ever go over to his house?" "Yes, we take turns playing at each other's houses." "What do you like to play?" "Marbles or ball. We like marbles." "How old is Tom?" "He's twelve—just a year older than I am. He's in the seventh grade. He'll be out of school Tuesday, too. His teacher is going for observation with you." (Chester was referring to our going for a day of observation of work in another school.) "I'll bet you and Tom will have a good time that day." "We'll play all morning, but I guess Tom will go to the movies in the afternoon." "Will you go with him?" "No, Mother won't let me. She is afraid I'll get hurt." "Do you usually play all afternoon?" "Mother lets me play when I first come home, but then she makes me come in to do my homework."

The child-study group felt that this anecdote showed that Chester was deriving more and more security from being with his teacher, even though he was sacrificing playtime with Tom. They noted how freely he spoke, as though he did not need to be ashamed before her of oversupervision by his mother. The group felt that this anecdote supported hypotheses 4, 9, and 22.

FEB. 24 The class went on an all-day trip today to the campus of State College. We visited the mansion of Mr. D, who founded the college. Chester was particularly interested in the colonial kitchen of the mansion. He asked questions of the caretaker. He wanted to know all about the Dutch oven and the iron cooking utensils. We also visited the museum, the dairy, and an old stone church. Chester showed interest in a coach in the museum and asked me to read the placard on it.

On the way home a group of the boys conspired to see who could "get by" with sitting by various girls. They would slip in and sit by first one girl and then another. I would hear them saying, "I got by with that one," "She knocked me off the seat," "You try your luck," etc. Chester entered wholeheartedly into the game. He tried sitting by Nancy first. She rose immediately and started pounding him with both fists. One other boy had been allowed to sit by her. Two girls, Mary and Susan, let him sit by them without protest. Nancy said, "Look at Chester, he is sitting by Susan." Chester laughed and laughed.

Once Chester came and sat by me. I was in the seat that was over one of the wheels. Half of that floor space was built up to make room for the wheel. Chester stood up on this raised space and announced to the group, "Everybody look, I am the tallest one on the bus. I am even taller than Miss C."

FEB. 25   As soon as Chester came in this morning he came to me and said, "Thank you for taking us yesterday. I really enjoyed it." A little later Miss T came into the room to hear about the trip. Chester told her about the kitchen and the coach.

The study group noted that Chester was genuinely interested in what he saw and that he seemed to be somewhat more accepted by the group. They felt that the anecdote tended to refute the hypotheses based on lack of motivation to learn and decided on minuses for hypotheses 5 and 20. They felt that the episode when he claimed to be the tallest person in the bus implied support for the hypotheses based on concern about his growth and gave pluses to hypotheses 11, 12, 19, and 22.

FEB. 27   Chester was staying after school with me again. He was telling me about his plans for the school camp this summer. He added, "I am making the money to go." I asked, "What are you doing?" He answered, "I am selling doughnuts, coat hangers, and drink bottles. My aunt has promised to let me sell her flowers as soon as they start blooming. I run errands for the neighbors too."

Suddenly he looked at the clock. "I must be going," he said. "I have to deliver twelve dozen doughnuts today. I get them for twenty-eight cents a dozen and sell them for forty cents." Then I asked, "Do you know how much profit you will make on today's orders?" He immediately replied, "One dollar and forty-four cents." With that he calmly and slowly walked to his locker, got his books and sauntered out.

The group noted Chester's growing reliance on his teacher for warmth and interest in his day-to-day activities and his strong motivation to earn in order to enjoy the summer-camp experience. They also mentioned his functional use of his number skills. They felt that this anecdote tended to refute hypotheses 20 and 21. They were interested in whether Chester's good relationship with his teacher and his success in selling were resulting in greater effort with his reading.

> MAR. 1   After reading lesson today, Chester said, "That was a good story. I enjoyed reading it."

> MAR. 3   Chester came to a reading group that was not his own. He asked, "May I read in this group today?" I said, "Do you want to read in two groups today?" He answered, "Yes," so I let him stay. The book was too hard for him to read but he took part in the discussion. The group was reading from the book You're Growing Up. The particular story was called, "It Runs in the Family." It told of a boy who was shorter than his peers. Chester said, "That's me."

The study group noted that Chester wanted to read in two groups during the day and felt that this strengthened hypotheses 4 and 22 and tended to refute hypotheses 5, 20, and 21. They also judged that his sensitiveness to the content of the story and his comment, "That's me," tended to support hypotheses 11, 12, and 19.

> MAR. 4   I talked with Mrs. M at PTA today. Again she said that she didn't know what made Chester do as he does and that she didn't know what to do to help him. She commented that she is happy because he is reading better.

Members of the study group were impressed by the fact that Mrs. M still expressed rejection of and discouragement about Chester despite her awareness that he was reading better. They wondered whether Chester was ever praised by his mother. They agreed that this brief entry gave strong support to hypotheses 9, 10, 15, and 22.

> MAR. 5   Without permission Chester got Joe's arithmetic workbook from his table to see if his own examples were worked like Joe's. He also got Jim's Weekly Reader from his locker to copy Jim's work.

The study group felt that this behavior indicated the terrific pressure that Chester felt to succeed with his schoolwork and recognized that this very strong motivation might, in the long run, stunt Chester's moral growth. They felt that he should not be permitted to get away with actions like these; on the other hand they felt that he should not be rejected and punished for this behavior. The objective, as they saw it, was to teach Chester that copying does not succeed, but that he can succeed under his own power. They stressed Chester's need for positive praise for his little successes. The conclusion was that this anecdote tended to refute hypotheses 5 and 20, whereas it supported hypotheses 4, 12, and 23.

MAR. 12   My study of the record showed the need for more information on Chester's developmental history and on family relationships,
so I had another conference with Mrs. M at which I tried to get the
needed facts. Mrs. M gave the following facts as a result of my show
of interest, plus some promptings and questions.

Chester was breast-fed, and Mrs. M enjoyed nursing all her children.
She would sit for long periods just holding them while they nursed and
slept. The oldest and youngest would nurse and then fall asleep in her
arms where they slept for a while. Chester would nurse but would be
restless and not go to sleep until she put him in his bed. She did not
have the satisfaction of holding him. He was weaned by giving him
baby foods along with the breast until he finally stopped taking the
breast.

The group was very interested that Mrs. M remembered this difference
between Chester and the other children. She seemed disappointed in
Chester about this. They wondered whether there were circumstances
that led Mrs. M to reject Chester at this time and whether this unconscious rejection made her so tense that he couldn't go to sleep in her
arms after nursing, or whether something else might have made her tense
enough to prevent his going to sleep and this failure on his part deprived
her of a satisfaction that led to his rejection. At any rate, they judged
that this material gave strong support to hypotheses 9 and 19.

The other two children sat, crawled, stood, and walked earlier than
Chester, who sat at eight months, crawled and stood at ten months,
and walked at thirteen months. Toilet training required a long period.
"He would wet his pants rather than stop what he was doing," she
said. She scolded him for this.

The group noted that his mother made unfavorable comparisons of
Chester with his siblings and that she had scolded him in connection
with the difficult toilet training. They thought that Chester must have
felt his mother's rejection all during this infantile developmental period
as well as later. They decided that this gave strong support to hypotheses
9, 10, and 12.

When Chester was a baby and until he was a little over two years
of age the father was in the Navy. The family lived with Mrs. M's
parents. An aunt lived with them, too. Mrs. M's father "spoiled" Chester very badly, she said. The aunt helped to take care of him.

The group thought that Mrs. M might have been anxious about her
husband, since the war was at its height during this period. They also
thought that she might have disliked having to live with her parents
and having full responsibility for caring for the children. Also, she was
deprived of her husband's love and companionship all during this period,
and this was enough to make her tense, they felt. Perhaps this was why

Chester hadn't been able to go to sleep in her arms after nursing, or perhaps Chester became associated in her feelings with the anxiety and dissatisfactions of this period. They felt that these facts added further support for hypotheses 9 and 10.

> After the father's discharge the family moved into a home of their own, and then Billy was born. Apparently Chester was not jealous, the mother reported, because he would hug and kiss the baby. Mrs. M tried not to neglect Chester at this time.
>
> The boys have always been treated as much alike as possible. When clothes or toys were bought for one the same thing has been bought for the other. At one time Chester and Billy had boxing bouts and wrestling matches; but now since Billy is larger and rougher, Chester will not box or wrestle with him. But Chester still wants to be with Billy and will not go places without him.

The study group was impressed with the fact that Billy was born soon after the family moved into a home of their own. They noted that Chester's grandfather was no longer around to "spoil him" at the very time when his new brother came. The group felt that the fact that the same things were always bought for both boys or toys were bought for them together (the electric train) might mean to Chester that he had never enjoyed the status of elder son in the family. Chester's withdrawal from boxing and wrestling with Billy when the latter got larger and rougher made them wonder whether Billy had been admired at one time for getting rough and excelling his brother. All this, they felt, could have made Chester continue to feel rejected. It certainly would have made him sensitive about his small size and slow growth. In the minds of the members of the group the family was excused for these things because they did not understand at that time that Chester was a slow maturer. Still, they felt, the effects on Chester were to make him doubt himself. So they agreed that these facts gave further support for hypotheses 9, 10, 11, 12, 19, and 22.

> The father never spanks the children, but they usually obey when he speaks. He bought them balls, bats, gloves, goals, etc., so that they would stay home and play in their own yard. Many neighborhood children come to play with them. If they leave the equipment in the yard, he deprives them of it for a few days. When they are choosing sides for games Sally tells Chester, "You can do so and so, for you are as old as the rest of us." Chester answers, "Yes, but I'm not as large." The children have no regular jobs around home except to put away toys and make their beds. However, Chester will often ask his mother, "Is there anything I can do to help you?" Mrs. M says that Chester is helpful and polite.
>
> The family quarrel with Chester about being so slow. They say he is slow at everything he does. They rush him in the mornings so that

he will not make the other children late to school. He sits awhile at the table before he starts eating; then he eats very slowly, jumping up from the table now and then. They usually leave him at the table to finish. At night it is the same behavior. He has to be called and called to come to the table, and when he finally gets there he loiters over his eating. He generally loiters over eating, dressing, and obeying.

The child-study group tried to put themselves in Chester's place in his family situations. On the one hand there were the things to play with, the games and equipment. This seemed very good. On the other hand there was the insistence that Chester should at all times meet the standards of the other two children. Both of them were much larger than Chester and, in the light of Chester's score on the intelligence tests, perhaps they also were brighter and quicker to catch on. In contrast to Chester's apparent high energy output and swift movements at school, he was reported as almost unbearably slow at home. Everybody seemed to be after him all the time at home. Was his loitering a way of resisting their pressure? Or was he gaining notice—a role, so to speak—for being slow because he could not succeed at anything else? Or was he just living up to a reputation they had given him? Certainly, the group thought, Chester was living in a family where everybody else was recognized as doing "right," whereas he was always under fire for something. Had this not so discouraged Chester that he gave up trying? Had this not caused him to develop deep doubts as to his own basic capacities and worth? Was his slowness and loitering a defense against trying or an attention-getting and role-playing mechanism? The group thought that Chester's politeness in the home and his frequent offers to help indicated that he would have preferred to succeed in some positive, approved activities at home. So they considered that this material gave strong support to hypotheses 2, 4, 9, 10, 12, 15, 19, and 22. They thought that it tended to refute hypotheses 12, 16, 20, and 21.

> As punishment Mrs. M spanks, scolds, talks, and deprives of privileges. Talking seems to help Chester more than the other forms. She gets him alone and tells him why she must scold him more than the other children. She also says that she has scolded him too much.

The group was impressed with the fact that Mrs. M could do more with Chester when she took him off alone and talked to him. It made them wonder when and how, if ever, she caressed him or expressed love for him personally, individually, and directly. Chester's teacher had no information on this, but the record in general seemed to indicate that his mother felt she expressed her love by providing for, taking care of, teaching, and disciplining the children. For the other two this occurred in a context of general approval; for Chester it occurred in a context of failure to measure up, nagging, and constant unfavorable comparison with his siblings. In fact, for months the siblings had had the responsibility for "bringing" him home from school—this at the age of eleven and a half. The study group concluded that the way Chester was disciplined added further support to hypotheses 9, 10, 12, and 22.

> Chester slept well until he was in the second grade, when he started waking with a scream. This occurred over a period of months. Mrs. M does not know of anything that might have caused it. He now has the pattern of sleeping well again. Mrs. M said that she is so happy that Chester shows improvement in the control of his temper.
> During the entire conference the mother was moving in one way or another. Some of her movements were jumpy and jerky.

Someone in the child-study group remembered that Chester had "stopped looking at his reading book and had trouble paying attention" during the last months he was in the second grade. Someone else remembered that the mother had called up his classmates that year whenever Chester had not appeared at home immediately after school and that she had cried whenever she couldn't locate him promptly. Remembering these things, the group conjectured that Chester might have been under terrific pressure at home during that year to learn to read. They remembered that he had been reported by his teacher as "putting forth great effort" during the first half of the year. It was possible, they felt, that Chester had tried as hard as he could but that with his organic immaturity and intelligence limitations he simply had been unable to succeed and so had given up trying as the only adjustment he could make.

The group felt that his mother's crying and nagging and her jumpy, jerky movements showed that she was tense and perhaps neurotic and unable to empathize with Chester and give him the comfort and support he needed. Thus his nightmares, along with the other facts the group recalled, gave strong support again to hypotheses 2, 4, 9, 10, 12, 15, and 22. Someone remarked that it was a wonder that Chester hadn't acted worse than he had.

Evaluating the Hypotheses

This material completed the presentation of the case record up to the date of the group meeting, and its presentation had consumed the better part of two two-hour meeting periods. The group then turned to the tabulation study of pluses and minuses, eager to find out *what they had proved* about why Chester had so frequently and persistently avoided working at his reading tasks in the first half of the sixth grade. The tabulation of the hypotheses with their positive and negative scores follows:

	Plus score	Minus score
Hypotheses		
1. Chester is just stubborn and won't work unless he is forced to.	0	2
2. Chester's mother has kept after him about reading until he hates it.	7	0
3. Chester's earlier teachers have let him get away with not working on reading for so long that he thinks he can still get away with it now.	0	2
4. Chester has failed at reading for so long that he is thoroughly discouraged and avoids trying so that he will not feel like a failure again.	13	0
5. Chester has no real reason to want to read, since no one ever reads in his home.	0	10
6. Chester is not bright enough to read better at present.	3	0
7. Chester is not liked by the other children; he avoids trying to read because he doesn't want them to see him fail.	11	0
8. Since Chester is not liked by the other children, he avoids reading because he knows that the teacher will get after him and he can show that he has the courage to resist her. He thinks this will attract favorable attention from the other children.	9	0
9. Chester feels that his mother doesn't love him, and he is too preoccupied with his insecurity to keep his mind on learning to read.	21	1
10. Chester feels that his younger brother and older sister are preferred and get more attention and approval at home. Not reading is one of his ways of getting attention from his mother and father.	19	1
11. Chester is so worried about his smallness that he can't keep his mind on his reading lessons.	7	0
12. Chester feels that he is not like other children in growth and that there is something the matter with him that prevents him from learning to read.	15	0
13. Chester has so much energy to spend that he can't sit quietly long enough to master reading skills.	1	1
14. Chester may have something the matter with his vision which makes it very difficult for him to learn to read.	0	1
15. Everybody has expected Chester not to learn to read—mother, siblings, former teachers, classmates; consequently Chester also believes he can't learn to read. He is only living up to everybody's expectation of him.	11	0
16. Chester enjoys the attention he gets by not doing his reading. Since he has no other good ways of getting attention, he plays up his inability to read both at home and at school.	2	2
17. Chester knows that adults set great store by reading, and he wants to please adults so much that he gets panicky with fear whenever he starts to read, because it means so much to him.	3	0

Hypotheses	Plus score	Minus score
18. Chester's emotions are set off so easily that the least difficulty with a word in reading throws him into a panic. He prevents this by avoiding reading.	1	0
19. Chester is growing very slowly and really is quite immature for his grade. Everyone expects too much of him. . . .	14	0
20. Reading is not important to Chester because he can do all the things he really wants to do without reading—selling things, fooling with autos, playing games, etc. He therefore lacks motivation.	0	9
21. Chester lacks character. He does all sorts of bad things and will not discipline himself to learn to read because he hasn't been punished enough.	0	11
22. Chester has so many causes of unpleasant emotion—small size, criticism at home, rejection by other children, and repeated failure at school—that he has become nervous and emotionally unstable, and this prevents him from working effectively on learning to read.	32	0
23. The strong drive toward upward social mobility that motivates Chester's parents is one of the causes of their constant and excessive pressure on him to do well in school. . . .	4	0
24. Chester has failed so much in reading that he needs some successes to bolster his self-esteem. He wants to prove to himself and to others that he can succeed.	2	0

Seeking Valid Conclusions

The child-study group set about stating the conclusions that they felt sure of as a result of studying this case record of Chester. What impressed them immediately was the complexity of the motivation that led Chester so persistently to avoid reading tasks. They commented that there certainly was no single or simple causation for this behavior but that a number of factors produced it. They agreed that "the causes of behavior are always multiple."

Weighing the Evidence

When it came to specifying causes, the group saw at once that they could not treat the separate pieces of evidence as of equal weight and simply total up the pluses and minuses they had recorded. Some evidence obviously was conclusive: the table that showed Chester's growth in height and weight and the graphs of Chester's growth on the Wetzel Grid for Evaluating Physical Fitness were illustrations of this. They proved conclusively that Chester was a slow grower, physically immature for his age and yet physically sound and healthy, with a good body capable of effective action at his organic maturity level.

The tests of intelligence, the group felt, did not, alone, give equally sure conclusions. How far were they influenced adversely by Chester's inability to read? Still more important, how far were they influenced adversely by his adjustment mechanism of not trying things when he feared he might fail? His sixth-grade teacher had noted that he would not try some sections of the test until she encouraged him. And his subtest scores showed a much higher proportion of failure toward the latter part of each test than during the first half. Had Chester given up trying about halfway through? Only a carefully applied individual test by a professional psychologist could have answered this question satisfactorily. The group felt that "a child cannot have less ability than his accomplishment demonstrates," so they decided to consider his school accomplishment as well as his intelligence-test scores in figuring out what his "real" IQ probably was. In this way they concluded that Chester had an IQ of at least 85 despite the fact that he had never gotten this score on a test. Many members of the group felt that it might even be a bit higher than this, considering the emotional load he was carrying.

When it came to the question of whether or not Chester enjoyed the security of love at home, the group saw that they could not depend on a few facts but must evaluate many small happenings and expressions of feeling. They saw that they had to use the kind of evidence that is gathered gradually from direct observation, home visits, parent conferences, and conversations with the child himself. Thus they noted that when Mrs. M talked with Chester's teacher she invariably expressed her expectation of the worst from him, lost no chance to speak of his failures and misbehaviors, frequently compared him unfavorably with the other children, and always implied that he was a constant source of anxiety and unhappiness to her. As these expressions of attitudes accumulated, the certainty gradually developed that Mrs. M rejected Chester without realizing it. This conclusion was clinched by the information that she had felt frustrated when Chester could not, like the other children, go to sleep in her arms as a baby and that he had been "badly spoiled" by his grandfather.

Thus the group saw that understanding of matters of attitude and feeling results from a gradual accumulation of evidence rather than from a single direct statement of feeling. This is especially true when the attitude actually held is different from that considered acceptable in the cultural tradition. For example, nearly all parents claim to love all their children equally because they think that this is what is expected of them. Yet they are nearly always better pleased with one child than with another.

Restating Hypotheses

Another problem confronted the child-study group when they came to make a statement of their final conclusions about why Chester avoided working on his task of learning to read. It was the discovery that some of their hypotheses were "double-barreled" and others were ambiguous. For example, they discovered that they had proved, by the accumulation of friendship-test results and of anecdotes about his interaction with other children, that Chester frequently annoyed his classmates by his actions, that he had no persisting mutual friendships, and that some of the children actively rejected him as babyish. They recognized that this made it impossible for Chester to feel that he was an accepted, belonging member of the group. But, they asked themselves, on what basis had they inferred that this caused Chester to avoid his reading tasks?

In the discussion of this question it came out that some members of the group had read published reports about clinical studies of children who were having difficulties with their school learning tasks. These studies had demonstrated that children sometimes refuse to try things that seem difficult to them rather than fail repeatedly in the presence of their classmates. Other rejected or isolated children are known to have created disturbances in their classrooms in order to show courage before their classmates or to attract their attention. It was on the basis of these clinically demonstrated facts, the group decided, that they had written hypotheses 7 and 8. But now the question remained: Did it follow from the facts gathered that the same motivations activated Chester when he avoided his reading tasks?

The data about Chester, they felt, proved that he had been losing popularity with his classmates. This might have been a factor in his preferring at times interacting with other children to working on his reading. But did it prove that he was deterred by fear of failure before them? Or did it indicate that he was trying to show off or to appear brave before them? The group felt that these conclusions went too far, so they decided to rewrite their hypothesis on this point and to limit it to what they felt was reasonably well proved. The new statement follows:

7-8. Chester is socially immature in his behavior toward his classmates. This is due to many factors: slow physical growth, limited mental capacity, hostility toward other children stemming from being compared unfavorably with his siblings at home, limited experience in free-play situations because of being forced to go straight home from school, and continuous emotional tension. This social immaturity has resulted in Chester's being ignored by some children and rejected by others so that he knows that he is not a belonger in the group. This adds to Chester's emotional tensions in the classroom and is probably a factor in making it difficult for him to keep his mind on his reading tasks.

The group felt that they were on surer ground with this statement than with hypotheses 7 and 8. They recognized that many of the other hypotheses were double ones or were ambiguous, so they undertook to rewrite them all. They decided to list what they had learned to be true about Chester as an individual and to state as conclusions, or verified hypotheses, only valid explanations of factors that motivated Chester to avoid his reading tasks. The restated facts and conclusions about Chester's situation and motivations follow:

Facts

1. Chester is a slow grower, quite immature for his chronological age, yet with a good healthy body capable of effective action at his own organic maturity level.

2. Chester has limited capacity for learning. His intelligence quotient is probably around 85 but may be a little higher.

3. Chester has been emotionally rejected by his mother since infancy although she probably does not realize this.

4. Chester has repeatedly been compared unfavorably with his sister and brother at home and is certainly aware of this.

5. At home Chester has lived in an atmosphre of constant domination, nagging, and criticism from his mother and possibly from others.

6. More has been expected and demanded of Chester at home than he has been able to accomplish, particularly in the matter of scholastic learning.

7. Chester has tried very hard to win love from his mother and to accomplish what was expected of him at home.

8. Chester is socially immature in his behavior toward his classmates. This has resulted in his being ignored by some children and rejected by others, so he knows that he is not a belonger in the group.

9. Chester is still trying to win a place among his peers through participation in informal games and by trying out for football and basketball teams.

10. Although Chester is in the sixth grade his accomplishment in scholastic learning is at the advanced third-grade or early fourth-grade level.

11. More has been expected of Chester at school than he has been able to accomplish in the light of his slow growth, limited mental capacities and emotional preoccupations. He has been moved ahead to a new grade each year and has seen many classmates accomplish school tasks far beyond him.

12. From time to time Chester has tried very hard to accomplish what was expected of him at school.

13. Chester has experienced many things that always cause strong and persisting unpleasant emotions. Some of them were: unusually slow physical growth, being rejected by his mother, being compared unfavorably with his

siblings, being dominated and oversupervised by his mother and siblings, failing to win belonging in his peer group at school, and failing to learn well at school despite great effort. All these causes of unpleasant emotion have persisted and become more forceful as Chester grew older.

14. Chester's frequent moving about is probably more of an indication of emotional tension than of a naturally high energy output.

The group felt they had verified the following hypotheses concerning why Chester avoided working at his reading tasks:

1. Chester is emotionally preoccupied with his slow growth and finds it difficult to keep his mind on the task.

2. Chester is emotionally preoccupied with his lack of love and acceptance at home and finds it difficult to keep his mind on the task.

3. Chester is so oversupervised at home that he has gotten the habit of doing no task until he has been told many times to do it and until an adult forces him to get to work on it.

4. Chester is so emotionally preoccupied with his lack of belonging in the peer group that he finds it difficult to keep his mind on the task.

5. Chester is so eager to win attention and affection from adults at school that he works on this rather than on his learning tasks.

6. Chester is so eager to win attention and acceptance from his classmates that he works on this rather than on his learning tasks.

7. Chester has failed at reading so continuously for so long a time that he dislikes trying to read because he feels that he is sure to fail.

8. Chester feels that he is not like other children and so can't be expected to read like other children. He feels this inferiority because of his slow growth, rejection by his mother, unfavorable comparisons with his siblings, failure to win belonging with his classmates, and inability to learn as much as many of his classmates even when he has made a greater effort.

9. Chester finds the strong, unpleasant emotion to which he is subject unendurable. He has learned to protect himself from failure and from inferiority feelings by not undertaking tasks at which he feels the likelihood of failure.

10. Chester greatly needs and enjoys small successes. Hence he has worked on arithmetic and creative art activities rather than reading whenever he could get away with it.

Is Additional Information Needed?

The question came up whether Miss C needed additional information about Chester in order to understand him well enough to be of maximum help to him. This question usually is posed in connection with multiple hypotheses because of lack of data in some vital area. In this case the group felt quite sure of their conclusions and made no suggestions to Miss C about obtaining additional facts.

How Can Chester Be Helped?

After the meetings, Miss C found time to review the findings of the group and to think out and write down a number of constructive ideas about how to help Chester to continue to progress. Her list of things to do follows:

1. Continue to give Chester personal warmth, acceptance and support whenever it is appropriate.
2. Continue to give Chester concrete help in getting started on specific limited tasks, especially in reading.
3. Continue to give Chester responsibilities and roles in the day-to-day life of the classroom.
4. Give Chester more direct praise whenever he completes a task or does something reasonably well.
5. Have patience with Chester's slowness and deliberateness.
6. Utilize Chester's interest in music, art, and science as bases for activities to give him success and ways of working off emotional tensions.
7. Have a little talk with Chester about his growth, show him the graph of his growth on the Wetzel grid and reassure him that this shows that he is in the "good" body-development channel. Explain to him that it is natural for some boys to grow slowly and that slow growers develop just as good bodies as rapid growers or average growers.
8. Explain to the parents that Chester's slow growth is natural for him and help them to see the difficulties it has created for Chester both at home and at school.
9. Try to get Chester's mother to see Chester's life through his eyes, to see some of the good things he is doing, and to express praise and love directly to him.
10. Try to get Chester's mother to take the pressure off him and to give him more opportunities for self-direction.
11. Try to see Chester's father and to get him to see Chester's life through the boy's eyes and feelings.
12. Try to get Chester's father to arrange to do things or go places alone with Chester each week, perhaps in connection with Mr. M's work.
13. Hold Chester back in the sixth grade next year in order to give him time to catch up somewhat with his classmates in physical maturity, social maturity, and scholastic learning.

14. Encourage Chester to play baseball during the spring and basketball again next year.

15. Encourage Chester to go ahead with his plans for attending the school camp during the summer and try to get the parents to consent and to help Chester with this.

16. Brief Miss T, the principal, about the group's findings regarding Chester and get her to go over these plans for helping Chester in order to get her suggestions, criticism, and help.

17. Enter the findings of the study group and any plans for helping Chester into the cumulative record to help Chester's future teachers figure him out.

The Scientific Method

Doubtless the reader will have noticed already that the steps taken by the child-study group in seeking to understand Chester and by his teacher in planning ways to help him are the steps in what is commonly called "the scientific method." Briefly these steps and the sequence in which they are taken are:

1. Selecting a problem for investigation and defining it clearly.

2. Amassing an extensive body of objective and valid data concerning the problem.

3. Making as many tentative hypotheses as possible on the basis of current scientific theory and personal experience.

4. Checking the hypotheses against the data.

5. Testing the hypotheses in terms of the weight of supporting and refuting data.

6. Considering the adequacy of the data and gathering additional data if significant gaps are found.

7. Reevaluating the hypotheses in the light of additional facts.

8. Restating the hypotheses as validated conclusions.

9. Planning steps to take to solve the problem in the light of the validated conclusions.

This is the method by which scientific knowledge is applied to life situations by such professional workers as engineers, physicians, agriculturalists and research specialists. It is the process which has produced such rapid advances in industry, agriculture, and medicine in our society, and it is the method we must use if we are to make similar progress in education. Experimentation over a period of years has demonstrated that it is practical for average teachers to use the scientific method if they are carefully trained to do so. More than that, teachers enjoy functioning in an effective professional way through the use of the scientific method, once they have achieved reasonable proficiency. It relieves them of much anxiety, frustration, and sense of failure. It promotes easy and supporting relationships with children because it prevents teachers' feeling personally threatened by the success or failure of individual children. Because it permits teachers to know what they are doing and why, it enables them to be more flexible in their interaction with individual pupils, modulating their demands and teaching procedures to meet the needs and motivation of individuals instead of blindly applying the same method to all.

Obviously the teacher cannot gather as much material about each individual pupil in his classroom every year as Miss C did about Chester. Nor can he employ the multiple-hypothesis technique every time he has to make a judgment in the classroom. What has been described is a training procedure. The practical implications of this for the everyday operation of schools will be presented in a later chapter of this book, and the reader is asked to defer judgment as to the general practicability of utilizing this method until he has examined those implications.

CHAPTER 6

Obtaining Information

Specific bits of the behavior of Jane and Chester have been analyzed in detail in preceding chapters. Three factors necessarily were involved in reaching an understanding of why these bits of behavior occurred. The three factors were:

1. A considerable body of specific information about the individual child, including his health and physical make-up, family background, personal relationships, developmental history, accumulated experiences and their meanings for him, and ways of managing his emotions.
2. A considerable body of explanatory scientific knowledge that made it possible to understand the significance of the facts about the individual.
3. The conscious use of the scientific method of reasoning to arrive at explanations and to check the validity of these explanations against the facts.

This chapter will deal with the first of these factors, the obtaining of enough information about the individual child to permit interpretation of his behavior. It will describe seven sources of information that a teacher usually finds it feasible to use when studying a child and the procedure for tapping these resources. Perhaps the most expeditious way of presenting this material is first to list the seven sources of information, then to describe the way information from each of these sources can be obtained and recorded, and finally to suggest the probable significance of each kind of data.

The teacher usually finds it feasible to obtain the information he needs about a given child by the following means:

1. Observing the child in action in the classroom, on the playground, and elsewhere in and around the school and writing descriptive anecdotes about characteristic and routine bits of behavior, as well as about unusually significant or revealing episodes.
2. Studying the child's accumulating records at school and entering significant data from them into his own written record about the child.
3. Making visits to the child's home, conferring with the parents both at home

151

and at school, and recording descriptions of what he observed in the home and significant portions of the conversations with the parent or parents.

4. Observing the child's life space, recording descriptions of it and of things going on in it, and making notes of the child's references to his own life space in his classroom functioning.

5. Conferring with colleagues who have taught the child in the past or are currently teaching him or who have special opportunities for observing him in action, and recording the *facts* they can give rather than their evaluations of or opinions about the child.

6. Collecting and examining samples of the child's classroom work, including written work done in each subject of study or unit of work, drawings, paintings, and other products of manual or creative activity, and saving characteristic samples of these for inclusion in the study record.

7. Conversing with the child individually and informally after school, at recess, or during free time and recording significant bits of these conversations.

Obviously the needed information has to be gathered gradually as the teacher makes his initial intensive training study of a child. Where schools systematically have gathered records of this sort over the years, the teacher has immediate access to most of the data he needs; but such schools are, as yet, few and far between.

Our files at the University of Maryland now contain about fifteen thousand training records made by teachers as a part of their participation in the child-study program, and these records yield sufficient evidence that it is feasible for a teacher successfully to tap each of these sources of information. Of course, not all our records are complete in every area, but a goodly number are complete, and each of these sources has been adequately exploited by literally thousands of teachers in our program. So it can be done. However, one must remember that teachers are very busy people, and even during a training program they cannot be expected to tap all these sources immediately, or within less than the first three months of the school year.

OBSERVATION AND ANECDOTE WRITING

Learning to Observe

The cases of Jane and Chester have already demonstrated the way in which good anecdotal material which accurately describes a child's behavior in a number of different places and times focuses our thinking with regard to the child's motivations. Such material is concrete and real. One day when her group was forming a circle for reading, Jane said to her teacher, "I'll get my book, but I won't read." What seemed on the surface to be a surly defiance of the teacher, when examined in the light of many facts and many other bits of behavior, turned out to be a deeply hurt inner self crying out that it couldn't take any more at that moment —a plea to her teacher to spare her for today. Chester told the cock-and-bull story that the principal wanted him to do a chore for her. What seemed at first a barefaced protective lie turned out to be the result of extremely complex motivation. The boy was seeking much-needed supportive, security-giving contacts with the principal. The validity of this relationship and of his need accounted for his lack of guilt feelings when his fib was uncovered. But he also had deep doubts about himself because of slow growth, rejection by his mother, unfavorable status at home relative to his brother and sister, and failure to read adequately. Hence his behavior was also task avoidance, based upon this need to protect his self-concept from further damage by continuing failure with his reading.

To untangle such complex motivation and see clearly what the child is seeking or doing through his behavior, one must see the behavior clearly and record it descriptively. This is a most difficult task for teachers. Much in the tradition of our classroom practice and in the expectancies of the teacher's supervisors and colleagues implies that he must evaluate behavior immediately and react to it at once in such a way as to exercise control over it. Thus behavior is interpreted in relation to the teacher's goals rather than in relation to the child's motivation. The traditions and expectancies under which most schools operate give the teacher mental sets which influence his perceptions of what a child is doing in terms of how it affects the teacher's goals and plans for the group and for the individual and not in terms of the child's goals or developing concept of self. The first task of a teacher in child study, then, is to train himself to see what the child is doing—to overcome his mental sets to the extent of remembering and recording a description of the situation and of what was done and said in it.

Characteristics of a Good Anecdote

In order to help teachers learn to discipline their perceptions, we have developed a description of the characteristics of a good anecdote. Observing behavior with the idea of writing an anecdote about it changes the teacher's mental set, alters the way he views the behavior of a child, and thereby alters his perceptions. Discriminating the essential components of the anecdote he will write enables the teacher to be objective and to forget his feelings of being helped or hindered by the child.

The characteristics of a good anecdote are:

1. It gives the date, the place, and the situation in which the action occurred. We call this the setting.

2. It describes the actions of the child, the reactions of the other people involved, and the response of the child to these reactions.

3. It quotes what is said to the child and by the child during the action.

4. It supplies "mood cues"—postures, gestures, voice qualities, and facial expressions that give cues to how the child felt. It does not provide interpretations of his feelings, but only the cues by which a reader may judge what they were.

5. The description is extensive enough to cover the episode. The action or conversation is not left incomplete and unfinished but is followed through to the point where a little vignette of a behavioral moment in the life of the child is supplied.

The Time Involved

Studies at the Institute for Child Study reveal that the average amount of time devoted to writing an anecdote is about eight minutes. Of course, some situations and actions are so clear-cut that they can be written up in as little as five minutes; some are so complex or extensive as to require fifteen minutes for satisfactory description. Obviously this means that anecdotes must be written in the afternoon or evening after school is over. Some teachers make a few notes as reminders, but most do not.

Experience indicates that four or five good anecdotes a week build a very adequate picture of the child in action. Writing them requires from forty to fifty minutes each week and in twenty-five weeks results in a record of more than one hundred descriptions of action situations. This experience in objective observation and descriptive writing, supplemented by repeated group analysis of and help in evaluating the anecdotes, usually produces considerable skill in both these activities.

When and Where to Observe

We have found that it is desirable to get as wide a sampling of the behavior of the child as possible. Many anecdotes, of course, are written about classroom situations. But other very meaningful anecdotes may describe the child interacting with his peers on the playground or street or in the hallways or toilet. Lunch, assembly, gym classes, trips, and sports events are other excellent times for observation. The anecdotes should supply pictures of habitual and characteristic patterns of behavior as well as of unusual and dramatic situations full of meaning and feeling for the child. Initially many participants make records only of these dramatic events, and teachers sometimes say, "I can't find anything to write about. My child never does anything," meaning that he never creates disorder or acts dramatically.

A good way to find situations to describe is to time-sample the child's behavior. The teacher decides to write up whatever the child is doing at nine-twenty the next morning or at a quarter to two the next afternoon. Time-sampling swiftly reveals that the pupil is "doing something" at every moment in the day and that motivations and feelings operate in him continuously. Routine and nondramatic actions must be included to balance off the more vivid events and to prevent distortion of one's picture of the child.

What to Write About

The initial anecdotes should concern any situation or action on the part of the child that seems significant or interesting to the teacher. Most teachers have a reason for studying a particular child. It may be that the child seems not to be liked by his classmates, is having difficulty with some part of his schoolwork, is outstanding in all his schoolwork, is a leader among his fellows, or has a physical handicap or is atypical in some other way. We urge each teacher to select for study a child in whom he is interested; but we caution them not to choose a child who is seriously maladjusted, because such children present too many difficulties for the novice.

Whatever the reason for choosing the child, however, it is natural to begin writing anecdotes about situations exemplifying the characteristic that initially interested the teacher. This is certainly acceptable. But the teacher should seek consciously to notice other aspects of the pupil's behavior so as to build a balanced picture of him in action.

In general, the description should give a cross section of the pupil's life at school and show how he acts in a variety of situations. Some children behave so differently in different classes and with different teachers that one would hardly recognize them as the same individuals; a proper distribution of anecdotal material should demonstrate this. It is as important to see what bores a child as to see what excites his interests, and a good case record would reveal how he acts under both circumstances. It would show him in action when things are going well and when they are not going well; interacting with his teacher, the principal, other adults, his peers, and younger and older children; studying, loafing, creating, sulking, or pursuing an interest alone; interacting with his parents, siblings, and near-neighbor children; informal situations such as assemblies, celebrations, and parent visiting days, and in informal situations such as eating lunch or playing. In short, samplings from the whole range of his life experience in and around the school are needed.

Some Adequate Anecdotes

The anecdotes below, taken from the cases of Jane and Chester, illustrate the characteristics of a good anecdote and demonstrate variety in sampling. These case records can be reexamined for a more detailed study of descriptive write-ups based on observations of a wide range of situations. The first anecdote is taken from the case of Chester.

> Oct. 10 While I was working with a group in reading, Chester's group was working at their tables. The work was a check-up on a story

that the group had finished with me. [This is the setting or situation.] It was not long before I saw Chester with a game in a corner of the room. I went to him and asked him, "Chester, have you finished your work so soon?" He answered, "No, ma'am, I was just playing this game awhile." I said, "Go to your seat and finish your work." He looked at me with an expression that seemed to say either, "I don't know what you mean" or "I don't want to." By this time my patience was a little ragged, so I said, "Chester, go to your seat immediately and finish your work." He went to his seat slowly, looking back a time or two at the game corner and stopping a time or two. [Note that the description includes the action by Chester, the reaction of the teacher, direct quotation of what each said, the teacher's description of her own mood, Chester's reaction to her directions, and the mood in which he responded.]

When the period was up, of course, he had not finished his work; so when playtime came I said, "You have had part of your playtime. Now you can finish your work." He mumbled and whined, "What for?" I answered, "I believe you know why."

When the others started out the door to the playground, Chester started too. I said, "You may not go." He turned red and stuck out his lips in a pout. Then he started to cry. "Chester, if you will stop pouting and get down to work you will be finished in time to have some play." A few children who had overheard the conversation said, "Miss C, that is the way he did all last year." [Note the new setting, the actions, reactions, direct quotes, and mood cues.]

After all the children had left the room I stayed to see that Chester settled to his work. After I was sure that he didn't need any help I went to the playground. In about ten minutes he was there with his paper all finished. I commended him on his work. He smiled, thanked me and went to play. [Note that the episode is completed to reveal the outcome.]

The following anecdote is taken from the case of Jane:

FEB. 8, 8:50 A.M.   Florence came to school today. She asked to move her seat next to Edith. I allowed her to do so. Jane also moved hers so that a group of four was formed: Edith, Doris, Florence, and Jane.

12:30 P.M.   I was on the playground today. I allowed the children who had been ill with colds or who weren't wearing proper clothing to stay inside. These included Edith, Florence, and Jane. [Setting] I hadn't been out there too long when Florence came out crying. She said that Jane had pulled her hair. . . . When I came in I noticed that Jane had pushed her seat away from Florence. I went over to her and put my hand on her shoulder. She shrugged it off [mood cue] and started yelling [mood cue], "I don't care, she told lies about me." I said, "Jane, please come into the hall with me." She ran out of the room ahead of me into the cellarway and hid her face against the wall. I said to her, "Suppose you tell me your side of the story, Jane." No answer. "Are you annoyed because Florence played with Edith?" Jane started to cry and said, "I asked Florence to help me and she wouldn't do it. Then she said I was laughing in the hall, and I wasn't. She wouldn't answer me when I talked to her, so I pulled her hair." I said,

"Florence has to have other friends, too, and she won't like you any better if you do things like that. The best thing to do is to wait quietly. She will come back to you. The two of you have been friends all year. It would be a shame to break up that friendship now." She stopped crying and asked me to send Florence out. I did, and as we came down the hall Jane met us and said, "I'm sorry I pulled your hair, Florence." She took Florence's hand. Florence said, "That's all right, Jane. Let's go wash your face."

Each of our criteria of a good anecdote has been met in these examples. In the second, the meaning of the episode is made very clear by the excellent setting, including the account of what occurred at 8:50 A.M. Then the story is carried through to its happy ending, with enough direct quotes to show how the teacher played her role and Jane's reorientation of feeling resulting from it.

Identifying the Persons Involved

Another factor that often greatly increases the value of an anecdote is the clear identification of the persons involved. If Florence had not been identified in this anecdote it would have lost the greater part of its meaning. In relation to other anecdotes and to the understanding of Jane's interaction with her peers it was also important that Edith and Doris were identified. This gave much added meaning to a later anecdote, when Jane and Ruth ran through the hopscotch square and scuffed out the lines that Florence, Edith, and Doris were using in their game. Perhaps the identification of all the individuals involved should be a criterion for a good anecdote.

Cues from Other Children

Sometimes an anecdote can be very revelatory even though the child being studied is not himself the actor. This is illustrated in the case of Rodney.

> Nov. 10   It just dawned on me today when I saw Doris, one of our cheerleaders, to mention Rodney's cheer leading at the game. So I said, "Doris, I believe Rodney would make you a good yell leader." Doris replied, rather unconcerned, "Maybe he would; he's *too* lazy to play football." The *too* was emphasized; so I decided not to press the issue any further.

Again from the case of Jane:

> Nov. 27, 2:50 P.M.   Jane was absent today. At the end of the day, one of the boys said to me, "I'm glad Jane was absent today." I asked him why, and he said, "It's nice and quiet when she is not here."

> FEB. 4, 3:05 P.M.   Florence sat next to me on the bus. She said, "Mrs. Summers, Jane won't read because the substitute teacher told her that she belonged back in beginners because she didn't know a lot of words

during reading." I said that I hoped Jane would soon get over feeling the way she did. Florence said, "I'll call her tonight and talk to her."

The Value of Anecdotes

It was pointed out at the beginning of this section that anecdote writing trains child-study participants in accurate observation under difficult circumstances and habituates them in objective ways of looking at the behavior of their pupils. These values alone would justify considerable training in this activity.

But the anecdotes themselves yield much direct information about the child being studied which is scarcely obtainable in any other way. A single anecdote is seldom conclusive about anything, but the accumulation of anecdotes often yields insight. The following six types of information by no means exhaust the list of things that can be learned about a child through anecdotes, but they are certainly among the most important:

1. Anecdotes describe characteristic ways in which the child acts. It is easy for a teacher to be so impressed by the failures and undesirable actions of a pupil, because of the feelings they arouse, that he fails to notice many things that the child does well and the great preponderance of time when he is acting in an orderly and constructive manner. Time-sampling techniques, in particular, often reveal the child diligently at work and functioning in fully acceptable ways. Although these pictures of good behavior in no way "take the curse off" undesirable behavior, they do permit the teacher to analyze the circumstances under which good behavior and positive actions can be expected and to discern interests and other positive forces in the child's life which he can utilize in working with him.

2. One of the things that we most want in our study of a child is to see his school experience through his eyes, to sense what it is like to him to go through his daily school routine and to face the situations he finds there. In seeking empathy with the child, mood cues and the descriptions of the child's emotional behavior give us considerable insight. They make it possible for the teacher to discover his sore spots, the degree of his sensivity to hurt and frustration, his little joys, and, through these, the kinds of goals that have meaning for him. Evidences of affect, or feeling, also tell the teacher what his impact on the child is in various situations and, in the long run, show him how the child feels toward him.

3. The analysis of recurring patterns of behavior in an accumulation of anecdotes virtually always reveals some of the developmental tasks and adjustment problems on which the child or youth is working. A theoretical formulation of developmental tasks tells us at best, what all children face at different maturity levels in the course of growing up in our society. Recurring patterns of behavior, however, tell us which ones a particular individual is working on during a particular school year. They are likely to reveal which tasks he is having difficulty with and which ones he failed to accomplish at an earlier developmental level, with the result that they are now a source of adjustment problems. Recurring

patterns indicate what things a child is "up against," such as concern about his growth or about some physical limitation or oddity, parental rejection, sibling rivalry, quarreling between parents at home, rejection by or isolation from peers, a sense of inferiority due to racial, ethnic, or social-class origin, a sense of intellectual inadequacy, or any one of a dozen other adjustment problems.

4. Sociometric friendship tests and "guess-who" tests often give a valid picture of a child's status in his peer groups, but they do not tell us why he has this status. Anecdotes, on the other hand, show the child interacting with his fellows and permit us to see how he violates the peer-group code or where he is ignorant of it. They show us what game skills or social skills he lacks, and which of his adjustment mechanisms are inappropriate, alienate people, and make him ineffective or unwelcome in peer-group activites. They afford a basis for helpful conversations with him through which he may develop understanding of the effects of his behavior. They permit the teacher to judge how he may best be helped to win roles and belonging in the peer-group.

5. Anecdotes permit the teacher to see the pupil's adjustment mechanisms for what they are. Often a child's behavior is very irritating and seems unreasonable and senseless to an adult. But, subjected to situational analysis in the light of the child's experience background and current adjustment problems, these behaviors begin to make sense. Inappropriate as they may be, they can be seen as all that was possible to the child under the circumstances. By changing some of the factors involved—particularly by alterations in the teacher's attitudes as the result of deeper understanding—new meanings are added to situations for the child, with consequent modifications of his own behavior.

6. By re-reading anecdotes written about the child and noting the kinds of episodes selected for recording and the changes in the tone of the writing, the teacher often discovers his mood in dealing with the child and emotional reactions of which he had been previously unaware. One facet of the teacher's understanding of why the child acted as he did is the recognition that his own feelings have influenced the way the child behaved.

The foregoing statements indicate the value the teacher derives from keeping anecdotal records. But it must be emphasized that an anecdotal study alone cannot yield all of the information that is necessary to understand a child. Each of the seven sources of facts makes its own unique contribution and must be exploited if the teacher is to feel reasonably sure of the judgments he makes in the classroom.

STUDYING THE CUMULATIVE SCHOOL RECORDS

We look forward to the time when teachers of all grades after the first will find in the cumulative school records about each child all the information they need to achieve a good initial understanding of him. At present, school systems with adequate records are rare. Nevertheless, much valuable information is even now to be found in the available records, even though they are scattered and relatively inaccessible to the teacher. In the study of Chester presented in the previous chapter, a great deal of crucial information was found in his cumulative record. But subjective evaluations of his learning, relationships with his peers, motivation, and home relationships yielded almost nothing of value; only objective facts, test results, and descriptions of his home were usable. At present, cumulative records are cluttered up with subjective evaluations of children that are virtually worthless except as indices of how particular teachers felt about the child in question. What is needed is the conscientious and continuous storing up of facts and descriptions.

Here we can only list a number of things teachers should look for in the records; what they will find depends entirely on the practice in the particular school system. Data which are often included are:

1. Health and growth data, such as frequency of absence due to illness, acute-disease history, immunization data, physical anomalies and handicaps, limitations of eye and ear functioning, condition of teeth, measurements of height and weight (these should be made every six months), and sometimes a Wetzel grid. The last two are extremely valuable measures of growth and should be a part of the cumulative record of every child. These data usually are sufficient to indicate the general state of the child's health and the character of his growth; these, of course, form the vital organic basis of all mental activity and social functioning.

2. Family data. The full names of the parents often show the ethnic background or mixture of backgrounds into which the child was born. The names and ages of the siblings show the family constellation of which he is a part and the child's place in the birth order. The current address of the family and the sequence of addresses during the child's life give the teacher information as to his life space, the social class background of the family, and whether they are socially mobile. The occupation of the parent or parents and their educational backgrounds give additional information about the social-class patterns and cultural customs that the child is internalizing at home and in his neighborhood environment. Information about homes broken by divorce or death and the presence of a step-parent or of step-children helps in characterizing the persons whose feelings about each other determine the child's emotional security or insecurity.

3. Test results. Of course, the value of test scores depends upon the validity and reliability of the tests selected and upon the manner in which they are given. If good tests were selected and directions were carefully adhered to in administering them, they can be of considerable help in understanding a child. In general one can say that the mental age and intelligence quotient a child earns on a test represents the lowest possible estimate of his capacity, for many undetected factors could make him score below his innate capacity, but nothing could have made him score above his capacity if the test is valid and properly administered. In general, too, one knows that group tests do not have the reliability of individual tests. However, if the child has taken several group tests during his school life and no limiting emotional or experiential factors can

be discovered, it is probably safe to believe that the highest intelligence quotient he has earned is within ten points of his operational scholastic intelligence. His innate but undeveloped intelligence may, of course, be higher, but we have no way of measuring that.

The reliability of scholastic accomplishment tests, also, depends upon the way they are given as well as the way they are constructed. Many factors may prevent a child from demonstrating all he knows. Nevertheless, scholastic accomplishment tests are better than subjective marks for evaluating a child's accomplishment, particularly if they are analysed section by section to uncover his weaknesses. It is often desirable to use a child's mental age as the basis for estimating the grade expectancy of his accomplishment. This yields a rough measure of the knowledge one has a right to expect of a child if nothing is preventing his progress in learning and seems a much fairer basis for evaluating a child's actual accomplishment than comparing it with national grade norms, which are merely averages and do not take into consideration the mental capacity of the child in question. He may be at or above the grade norm and still materially below what we have the right to expect of him.

4. Ratings of traits. Many cumulative records contain ratings of children on the basis of specific traits; these are usually of little value. Research has shown that behavior is specific to each situation, depending on the meaning of the situation for the child and the intensity of the motivations that emerge from the meaning. No child is lazy or industrious, honest or dishonest, cooperative or uncooperative to an equal degree in all situations. His teacher needs to understand him in specific situations and may be seriously misled by trait ratings given by others under other conditions. In general, trait ratings do not seem worth the time and effort it takes to make and to record them.

5. Peer-group data. Sociometric-test data based upon friendship choices, work-group choices, or seating-mate choices sometimes are found in cumulative records and are helpful in showing how classmates regard the child being studied. But without anecdotal data that reveal why the child is chosen, rejected, or isolated they can only indicate a problem without giving clues about how to solve it. Facts about a child's participation in sports, clubs, and youth groups are very important because they reveal interests and sometimes the degree of skill developed. Children and youth give much weight to these activities in according belonging and prestige to their fellows. Records of offices to which a child is elected by his peers also are indications of the degree of prestige that he holds in their eyes.

HOME VISITS AND PARENT CONFERENCES

Home visits and conferences with parents at the school are perhaps the most important sources of significant information about the child. They have four major objectives:

1. To establish a friendly relationship with the parents and to develop a mutual feeling of partnership with them in the education and all-round development of the child.

2. To obtain a comprehensive and accurate developmental history of the child.

3. To obtain knowledge of the social status and cultural background of the family in order to understand the ways of living and the culturally based habits, interpretations of life, and attitudes that the child is internalizing at home.

4. To obtain knowledge of how the various members of the family feel about each other and interact with each other for the purpose of evaluating the climate of affection in which the child lives and the degree of emotional security or insecurity he feels.

Making the Initial Approach

In communities where home visits and parent conferences at school are not the custom, teachers are understandably shy about initiating such contacts. Traditionally, home visits and parental conferences portend some difficulty, some "trouble" to be ironed out. For this reason it is important to initiate such contacts before the child is having scholastic difficulties or is "in trouble." Of course, the initial contact should be before, or immediately after, the child first enters school. However, we have guided literally thousands of teachers in making successful home visits in communities where they have not previously been the custom, and in all cases except one the visits were welcomed by the parents. A simple direct approach seems to work best. The teacher sends a note home by the child with some such content as the following:

Dear Mrs. X:

I am Joe's teacher this year, and he is certainly an interesting child. I want to do as good a job with him as I can, so I feel the need to understand him well. I am sure that you know many things about him and have insights into his needs and feelings that I do not yet have and that would be of great help to me. I would like very much to come to see you and to have you tell me the things that you think it would be helpful for me to know about Joe. I have no complaints to make about him; I simply want to get to know him better. I could visit you any afternoon next week between 3:30 and 5:00.

Sincerely yours,

Such a note, or a telephone call using the same approach, almost always brings a quick and friendly response. The same procedure is effective at the secondary level, but here the teacher usually designates the subject he is teaching or explains that he is the homeroom teacher or extracurricular-club adviser of the child.

When the teacher enters the home he makes virtually the same statement and then listens expectantly. Usually the parent talks freely and easily and needs only a few questions to bring out the needed information. If the parents are hesitant, elementary teachers often ask to see pictures of the child when he was a baby and then get the story of when he began to sit up, walk, and talk, when he was weaned, and whether the birth was a difficult one. Questions about his early illnesses and their effects, about how he gets along with his older and younger siblings and what they do together follow easily. Mothers are usually glad to tell about a child's interests and the things the family has done together. If the family has lived in other communities, the teacher can ask for facts about the child's experiences there. The mother usually knows how he feels about himself and about his father. If a sensitive problem comes up and the mother hesitates, it is better not to ask a question but simply to wait or perhaps to repeat what she has said.

The teacher will learn much about the social status and cultural background of the family from what he observes of the furnishings of the home, the books and magazines in evidence, the arrangement of the furniture, the decoration of the home, and the nature and content of the yard. The family's favorite radio and television programs make interesting topics of conversation. The child's out-of-school activities also are worth exploring and often lead to information about hobbies, church affiliations, scouting, music and dancing lessons, movies, and favorite sports. Questions about the chores for which the child is responsible give ideas about how the family is organized and how well its members get along. The child's work outside the family—newspaper routes, babysitting, odd jobs—help to fill out the picture of the child's life. Pets, birthdays, and festivals such as Thanksgiving and Christmas often give clues to the climate of feeling in the home. Mothers are delighted to talk about babies in the home and in doing so often give clues to family relationships. The teacher should not, of course, ask direct questions about how members of the family feel toward each other.

With regard to schoolwork it is better for the teacher to avoid for the most part evaluations to the effect that the child is good at this or poor at that. It is better to describe what the child is working at and to indicate that time is required for the mastery of specific skills. Questions from the parent about the child's relationships with other children at school can be followed by questions about his friendships and playmates in the neighborhood and the character of his play activities.

The ideal home visit, then, is characterized by free-flowing, easy conversation based upon mutual interest in the child. It is far from a formal interview in which the visitor plies the parent with a list of predetermined questions regardless of the flow of feeling. The first visit, especially, should establish a relationship warm and friendly enough to cross social-class or ethnic lines because both persons have the welfare and development of the child at heart. If this is accomplished, later conferences at school or subsequent visits to the home can fill in gaps in the information, as was so well illustrated in the case of Chester.

Of course, the teacher does not make notes or write anything down during the visit. The record of the home visit should be written at home immediately after the visit, and the time required for the write-up has to be counted as a part of the visit. This means that, usually, only one home can be visited in an afternoon.

Some of the information sought during a home visit can, of course, be gotten during a parent conference at school. But it is never possible in such a conference to get the intimate picture of the child's out-of-school life that is gained by visiting the home. The home, after all, is the major point of focus and feeling in the child's life and must be experienced to be understood. Children in the elementary school usually are very pleased when their teachers visit their homes; it seems to create a new bond with them. Parents, too, get the feeling that "Joe's teacher is really interested in him" and take it as evidence that the school is trying to do the best possible for him. If difficulties, either scholastic or disciplinary, develop later, they are much easier to handle after this warm and friendly partnership in guiding the child's development has been established.

Examples of Home Visits

In making their first home visits, some participants will feel discouraged upon finding that they have not accomplished all four of the objectives listed. The purpose of this listing, however, was to establish these goals in the minds of participants, not to provide criteria for evaluating their initial experiences. One gets what one can from a home visit, and it is nearly always something very significant; but it is seldom, indeed, that all four objectives are fully accomplished during an initial visit. This will become clear from a reexamination of the visits already presented and from the study of others to be included.

In the case of Jane, it will be recalled that Mrs. Summers had already learned much about Jane's home life from the child herself, other teachers who had visited the home, and various mothers at the baby shower. Thus Mrs. Summers already knew that Jane's home life was hectic, to say the least, and that her mother had suffered some sort of emotional illness that required hospitalization for a time. But the information remained vague and the timing of events in relation to Jane's school experience was not accurate. It is interesting to see how Mrs. Summers' account of her home visit concretizes our understanding of what Jane had been up against since the second grade.

HOME VISIT

Jane's home is an old-fashioned farmhouse. It seems to be made of stone with stucco finish on the outside. The house is built against the hillside along the main road. A brook flows in front of the house. There are several old buildings behind the house. They appear to have been farm buildings at one time but are now in a dilapidated condition. The roof of the house seems to sag a bit and there are some shingles missing.

The day I went to visit, no one was at home except the grandmother. I introduced myself and she said that she had been anxious to meet me and that Jane was at a neighbors' playing with their children. . . . The interior of the house was neat and clean. I noticed particularly that there weren't many windows, so that the rooms looked a little gloomy. However, there were potted plants on the window sills. . . .

The grandmother asked me if I knew how much Jane adored me. I said that I realized she seemed fond of me. Mrs. Z said that I was the first teacher who ever seemed interested in Jane and that she was most grateful because Jane had learned to read in my class. She went on to say that poor Jane had had a poor start in life. When she was about eight years old, her mother had suddenly gone insane. At first her son-in-law had refused medical care for her because he was ashamed of what the community might think. The period while the grandmother was trying to persuade the father to have his wife helped and until she actually went to an institution was a very hectic one for the children. The mother would think she heard someone coming for her and would barricade herself in the attic screaming for hours on end. Finally the father realized that she needed some attention and took her to the institution in Capital City. She was there for a year and had electric shock and other treatments. The family went to visit her every Sunday. At times she refused to see them. . . .

It is hard to see how this concrete picture of a very traumatic period for Jane could have been gotten in any way except through this conversation with the grandmother in the actual setting where it occurred, and the fact that the slump in Jane's schoolwork was directly associated with it was established by the grandmother's statement that Jane was eight at the time. It also is worthwhile to notice the warmth of the grandmother's feeling toward Jane's teacher.

Of course, home visits do not always proceed as planned. Chester's teacher planned her visit for a time when she knew Chester would be playing basketball and the other children would probably be at the game. But the younger brother, Billy, greeted her at the door, and the older sister and an aunt arrived during the visit. Nevertheless, Miss C was able to observe much about the mother's attitudes toward Chester during this visit. Excerpts from the report of the visit follow:

. . . Mrs. M came to the door folding an ironing board and said, "I didn't expect you today. I have just finished my ironing." She sat on the sofa and called to Billy, "You can turn off the TV and go out to play." He started out without a word. Then she called again, "Turn off the TV." Billy answered, "I did." (Why does she tell them the same thing over and over?) . . .

Hurriedly she asked, "How is Chester doing?" But before I could answer she went on, "I know he isn't doing well. He isn't at all like the other two children. They don't have any trouble. You would never know that he is kin to them. I just don't know what is the matter with him."

She continued, "I have to tell him over and over to do things. Just the other morning I asked him about four times if he had brushed his teeth and he would say, 'No ma'am, I was doing this and that, but I am going to.' It is that way all the time. I know what you put up with at school, but I don't know what to do about it. I have tried everything I know." . . .

. . . Then his mother said, "I was so glad that he made the basketball team in spite of his size. You know he isn't a good sport, and I am so in hopes that playing on the team will help him to get along with other people. He has such a temper."

About this time Sally and someone else came in the back door. . . . Mrs. M asked Sally, "Is Billy going with you?" Sally answered that he was, and Mrs. M called, "Bring Chester home with you."

Mrs. M turned to me and said, "You know, Sally is only eighteen months older than Chester, but she goes ahead with things. Chester is not dependable like she is. He doesn't catch onto things like the other two. They have all of them had good teachers—I know it isn't that. . . ."

I got a chance to say, "Chester does like arithmetic." But she came back with, "Yes, he does, but he neglects other things to do it. And you know he can't do problems. He can't read them. Unless I just make him read aloud he doesn't know what he has read. . . . I make him read every afternoon, but he reads so slowly that it takes about an hour for him to cover any ground at all."

It is clear that Miss C accomplished three of her four objectives by this home visit. She established a friendly relationship with Mrs. M and made her feel that Chester's teacher was sincerely interested in him. She learned that Chester was rejected by his mother, constantly compared unfavorably with his siblings, and nagged about his schoolwork and many other things. Thus she got an excellent picture of the emotional climate in which Chester was living. She learned the nature of the culture that Chester was internalizing at home. But she failed to get any picture of Chester's developmental history. When the study group analyzed the home-visit report with Miss C, the need for the developmental history became clear, and it will be recalled that she was able to get significant information through another conversation with the mother. It is doubtful whether Miss C could have gotten this information during the first visit, even if she had stayed longer, since the mother had to realize her warmth toward Chester and her interest in him before she was willing to talk about these matters. Later in the year the mother was at last ready to communicate many intimate facts about the early years of Chester's life, and these were the clinching facts that made it possible for Miss C to understand him with considerable depth.

OBSERVING THE CHILD'S LIFE SPACE

When a child is born he knows nothing whatever about the world, people, society, himself in relation to the world, or how to live and act. All he will ever know or be able to do, he must learn. And what he learns will depend upon what he experiences, for experience is the fundamental basis of all learning. A child, then, can learn to know and to do only that to which he has access through experience.

As the basis for this experience, and consequently for his learning, every child has his life space—the area on the earth with which he comes in direct contact—and whatever this life space contains: people, physical happenings, the ways the people act, feel, and talk. The child's life space is his world, his universe. It contains the only society available to him, and it is, therefore, the culture of this society that he internalizes and that shapes his views of life and of how it must be lived. Equally, he gradually learns to understand and use in thinking and communication the language customarily employed by the inhabitants of his life space. Only as his life space is expanded by family trips from place to place, experiences provided for him at school, motion pictures and television, personal exploration of the larger community, and talking and reading can he acquire knowledge of things and events beyond his immediate life space. And he will interpret whatever he hears or reads about beyond his life space in terms of word meanings, concepts, and attitudes learned within it.

Many teachers seem unaware of this essential relationship between a child's life space and what the child himself knows, does, says, thinks, feels, and understands. They seem to expect all children of a given age to know more or less the same things, have the same interests, think and feel in the same ways, and associate the same meanings with words. This, of course, does not happen. Children's life spaces and the ways the people within their life spaces act, think, feel, and believe are dramatically varied, with the result that they vary widely in their concepts, attitudes, ways of acting, language patterns, and skills.

The reason for having teachers observe the life space of the children they are studying is to help them gain insight into and feeling for the world each child experiences. It is to help them sense the background from which the child tries to communicate and to understand what is communicated to him. It is to help teachers learn something of the experience content that underlies the concepts children reveal—to help them sense the relationship between concepts and the experiences of individuals. It is to help them understand the inevitable differences in concepts and attitudes among children and between children and themselves. Observation of a child's life space is laboratory experience in the study of semantics.

Clearly, a child's home is his most intimately and completely experienced life space. Home-visit reports should include full descriptions of what is in the home and what goes on there. However, the home does not constitute the entire life space of the child, although it is the most significant part of it. Initially in our child-study program, we found that many of our participants missed seeing that the home exists in the context of a neighborhood. Long before a child comes to school and throughout his school years, he explores, to the extent that he is permitted, the world outside his home. He builds a body of concepts about many aspects of life and society as a result of these exploratory experiences. Indeed, every child comes to school fairly loaded with knowledge—true, false, and partial—that is implied by his accumulated experiences within his life space.

We have wanted teachers to become curious about the content of each child's mind, for when they sense the eagerness with which the child has been actively investigating his world, it becomes fun to find out what he has learned through these explorations. The individual pupil always turns out to be much more grownup than one expects; he knows many things that one does not expect a child of his age to know. On the other hand, he lacks some of the knowledge that one has assumed all children of his age have.

To get to know something of the content of his mind, then, is to gain the power to build bridges from what he knows to what he does not know and so to make his learning easier. It is to gain the power to communicate with him, for example, by using illustrations out of his experience instead of out of one's own. It is to sense the kinds of direct experience, perhaps through excursions, that the child needs to fill in his knowledge. It is to become aware of what he has failed to notice within his life space, to learn how to guide his observations, and to sharpen his techniques of observation.

When a teacher gains this kind of insight into a child, he can "live with" the child in a genuinely developmental sense rather than in a restricted and artificial classroom relationship characterized by arbitrary tasks and pleasing children's games and songs. Living with the child in terms of his growing mind, his daily experience of the world, life, and society in and out of school, with sensitivity to the flow of his experience, can be valuable and rewarding to all teachers from the nursery school through the university.

Roger's Life Space

Roger Beach is eight and a half years old and is in the third grade. He is liked by his fellow students and was chosen by them to be king of the harvest carnival. He is an active boy, his favorite sport being basketball, but he dislikes all musical games. He is always eager to tell the latest community events and to recount exciting experiences on television. He talks freely and easily.

It may be interesting to the reader to test the degree to which he can penetrate into the content, texture, and feeling-tone of Roger's life by studying the following life-space material from the data his teacher gathered about him during the year she studied him. In other words, what is Roger's world like to Roger? How does he interact with it? We will begin with an autobiography Roger wrote as a language assignment.

AUTOBIOGRAPHY

My name is Roger Beach. I am 8½ years old. I was born in this town. I was born on March the 8th. I am a boy. I am not a girl. There are six in my family. I have three brothers and no sisters. I go to Allen school. I have gone to two schools, they are Hughes in Florida and Allen. I go to Allen Baptist Church. I live at the bottom of Green Wood Mountain. I am an American. I have brown eyes. I have brown hair and I am light skinned.

I feed the mules and hogs and carry in coal and draw water. I like school very much. I like language and arithmetic best of all. I am 4 feet tall and 2 inches. I weigh 63 pounds. My eyes are 20/15.

Nov. 3, 1952 I approached Roger with the following question at the clean-up period. "Could you go with me up to Green Wood?" (Green Wood is an old cemetery and church on top of a hill beyond Roger's house.) Roger nodded his head and said, "Uh-huh, I can go." I replied, "Well, I haven't been up to that old place for about twelve years."

When school closed, Roger and I left the room together. We walked out the back door to my car. When I started the motor, Roger said, "Gee, your starter is in a funny place; it's connected with the switch, isn't it?" My answer was, "Yes." As we drove down the school drive to the public road, I stopped the car for the school bus to pass. Roger waved at some school chums on the bus.

Both of us noticed the new sawmill across the field from the school. I said, "Those sawmillers sure worked today. Just look at the lumber they sawed." (Today was the first day it was in operation.) Roger said, "I mean they worked hard. Part of the time today, I couldn't half hear what you said, it made so much fuss."

We drove on down the road. When we passed Rev. Murphy's son Joe, I said, "Joe is moving to a new place to live." Roger said, "Yes, I heard he was moving. Joe's daddy told Ed, my brother, that he would give his eyeteeth if he could stay at Allen." (Joe is a fourth-grade boy; Joe's father is the Methodist minister and is moving to another community this week.)

I knew there were two ways we could go to Roger's and to Green Wood. Roger directed me to turn to the right so we would miss an old covered bridge.

As we passed several houses, six to be exact, we discussed who lived in each house. The seventh house was Roger's. He said very proudly, "I live here, Mrs. Watts." I said, "Oh, you do. Oh, I like your new green house; it looks so pretty." "It ain't no new house. We fixed up a old one," was Roger's comment on their home. "Say, Roger, do you think I should stop for us to tell your mother that you are going with me to Green Wood?" His response, "No, Mamma and Daddy are away over in the big field picking cotton; they don't care for me to go, for I go up there lots. Mamma and Daddy are going to get done picking cotton today."

We turned up the hill a few yards from his house. There were woods on both sides. I made a comment on how pretty the autumn leaves were. Roger said he thought the leaves were pretty, too.

We reached Green Wood. I made several comments on the remodeling of the old church. We stopped the car, walked out in the cemetery, and read the markers on some of the tombs. We walked back to the car, and then I asked Roger if we could see inside the church. He said, "Me and Daddy, my uncle, and David came up here not long ago. You can see inside; it's not locked."

We left Green Wood and drove down the hill to Roger's house. He got out of the car, and I said, "Roger, could you get me some water? I am so thirsty after eating that piece of candy and getting no water at school." "Yes, I'll get some water," said Roger. We got to the front porch. Roger opened the door and led the way to the kitchen and back porch.

We walked through the living room. It was in order, neat and tidy. The kitchen was clean. I noticed two cookstoves. The water bucket was on a table on the cement back porch. "The bucket is empty, but I can draw some water for you to get a drink," said Roger. He picked up the bucket and dipper and started walking to the well, some ten feet from the porch. Roger started to let the bucket down into the well when I said, "Roger, let me draw the water." He gave me the ropes.

The family dogs made their way to the well for a greeting. We talked about the number of dogs, the kind, etc. Roger offered to give me one of the puppies, but I assured him that I had one dog at home and that one dog is all that I can care for.

I poured the water into the water bucket. Roger was holding the dipper while I drew the water. He handed me the dipper for me to drink first. I said, "Thanks, the water is so good, and I was so thirsty."

We walked into the living room, and I remarked that I would like to see the mother, daddy, and little brothers. Roger said, "If you see them, we will have to walk to the back field, 'cause they don't quit work 'til sundown." "Oh, no, Roger, I can't stay that long. I'll go for this time and come back again sometime to see your mother, daddy,

and little brothers." I thanked Roger for going with me up to Green
Wood and for the nice drink of water.

He stood on the front porch while I walked to the car. I started the
automobile, said good-by, and drove away. Frankly, Roger was a perfect
host.

Appearance of the Home

The farm consists of several acres of farming land, and there is also
some woodland. The house is a remodeled old house which gives the
appearance of a new home. The outside is green asbestos siding. The
porches are cement. The house is underpinned with cement blocks.

The front yard is bare. There is no grass except tall Bermuda grass
in the back yard that needs to be mowed down. The boys' wagons, tri-
cycles, and other playthings were under one of the big trees in the
front yard. The well is about ten feet from the back porch. Its curb
is made of brick. Clapboards are laid across the top of the brick. The
top hasn't been fixed yet. The back yard is comparatively small. The
pasture fence comes to the edge of the yard. Inside the pasture are the
truck garage, barn, and pigpens. The outdoor toilet is at the edge of
the yard and fence, under some trees.

The house has six rooms: two bedrooms, a living room, a kitchen,
a dining room, and a place for a bath.

Apparently Mrs. Beach is a good housekeeper. She has the shades,
curtains, rugs, and furniture arranged neatly. The rugs were clean and
the floor waxed. There was no bed in the living room. The living-room
furniture had some type of cover over it, probably old bedspreads. The
covers were clean. In one corner was a tall cabinet radio. A heater
(Warm Morning) was in the living room. In the kitchen Mrs. B has
two stoves—one wood and one gas. There were built-in wooden cabinets along one wall. A dinette set was in the kitchen.

There are six members of the family. Roger is the second child. No
outside relatives live with the Beaches. All four of the children are
boys. Since my visit a friend has told me that the stork will soon pay
another visit there.

Roger has responsible chores at home. He has two mules to help
feed. At the moment there are no pigs on the farm because the last
one was recently butchered for meat. There is one milk cow, and there
are about a hundred chickens which demand some care from Roger.
His pets are: ten chickens, two cats, and five dogs.

Roger's appearance in school is good. His skin and clothes are neat
and clean. His hair gets cut often. His wearing apparel consists of dungarees and shirts all the time. He dislikes overalls. They are clean and
ironed nicely.

STORY ABOUT MY PETS (language assignment)

*I have three little puppies. They are Cocker Spaniels. Mrs. Jones
gave them to us. I have the mamma dog, too. The mamma dog carried
one of the little puppies off and lost it. The mamma dog came back
home without the little puppy.*

Interview with One of Roger's Former Teachers

Nov. 8, 1952 Saturday noon. Mrs. Jones and I had luncheon together at Walgreen's. After we gave our order I remarked, "Tonight
is our big night; it is our annual Harvest Carnival." Mrs. Jones asked,
"Do you have a king and queen this year?" I replied, "Yes, my king
is Roger Beach, and the queen is Alice Barton. They are cute children."

Mrs. Jones was Roger's first-grade teacher and has lived in this
community many years. So I furthered my investigation by asking what
Roger's mother's maiden name was. Mrs. Jones replied, "She was Sarah
Proctor, Luke Proctor's daughter, at Loon Hill. Sarah's brother Norman painted the Lord's Supper picture at Loon Hill. He was quite an
artist. Have you seen the picture?" I answered, "No, I'm sorry I
haven't, but I would like to see it."

I told Mrs. Jones that Roger and I had visited Green Wood one
afternoon previously. I said, "Apparently Mrs. Beach is a good housekeeper." Mrs. Jones said, "Oh, yes, she comes from a good home. She
was taught good housekeeping at home." I said, "Did you ever teach
either Mr. or Mrs. Beach?" She said, "No, I never taught them, but
I know that neither of them went very far in school because of lack
of interest by their parents. Fred and Sarah had so many chores to do
at home, therefore neither had a chance. Both Mr. and Mrs. Beach
were smart in school," continued Mrs. Jones. "They could have gone
far up the educational ladder had they had the opportunity. Both were
smart."

Mrs. Jones said she thought Mr. Beach got to or maybe finished the
sixth grade, but she didn't know how far Sarah went because she lived
in an adjoining community.

"When did the Beaches move to Florida?" was my final question.
"Oh, they lived down there about three years. They were living in
Florida when Roger started school. He was in the first grade when
he entered Allen school the first of April, 1951, and was in my room."

Health Habits—Second Grade

Brushes his teeth. Does not visit the dentist. Sleeps eight hours
every night. Does not sleep with windows open. Eats three meals every
day. Drinks little milk. Drinks coffee and tea. In his diet every day he
eats eggs, meat, fruit, vegetables, and bread.

Interview with Roger's Sunday-school Teacher

After school, Miss W, a member of our faculty, Roger's Sunday-
school teacher, and the leader of our child-study group, was discussing
child study with me. She said, "Watts, you should visit our Sunday-
school class sometimes. Roger comes practically every Sunday, and you
would think he is a perfect angel. He knows all the answers."

Anecdotes

Oct. 16, 1952 Thursday afternoon at 3 o'clock Roger and Tom
were discussing breakfast menus. I heard Roger say, "I like milk, meat,
jelly, and full cream flour biscuits for breakfast." I entered into the
discussion by asking, "Roger, do you use full cream flour, too?" He

replied rapidly, "Yes, do you use that kind of flour?" I said, "Oh, yes, I like it very much."

I had my things ready to leave. Roger said, "Say, Mrs. Watts, have you seen the big full cream biscuit in the show window at the hardware in town?" I said, "No, I haven't seen it, but I heard an announcement on the radio about a contest—to guess how much flour it took to make one biscuit." Roger seemed so enthused with the contest and the grand prize. He took several seconds to explain the rules. Here are the rules he gave, counting them on his fingers:

1. You get one guess when you buy a 25-pound bag of flour.
2. You get two guesses when you buy a 50-pound bag of full cream flour.

If you guess the amount of flour, you will win a big Crosley TV set; the second prize is a good radio. After he put emphasis on the rules Roger said, "One woman I heard of guessed 12 pounds but I believe it took a 25-pound sack myself." He stretched his arms outward and tried to measure the size of the biscuit.

Nov. 5, 1952, 8 A.M. Immediately following the morning bell, all the children were getting adjusted, hanging up their coats, etc. Roger skipped and came to my desk, clapped his hands, and said, "Hot dog, Mrs. Watts, I am so happy." "Why are you so happy, Roger?" I asked. "Ike is our President. He is the one I hoped would be."

Nov. 21, 1952 Roger and seven boys—all late-bus riders—had been using profane language out on the playground. Most of the boys were fourth graders. On Friday all the boys were called out of their classrooms for a conference. Roger cried because it appeared that he received much of the blame from the older boys.

Dec. 2, 1952 Tuesday morning Roger came back to school from the Thanksgiving vacation. He had a sore on his face. I said, "Roger, how come that sore on your face?" Roger replied, "I climbed up in a bush and slid down, and a limb scratched my face." I asked him if he would like for me to put some methylate on the scratch. Roger said, "Yes, I don't care for you to paint it." While I was painting the scratch I told him to tell his mother he was a clown. He said, "Thank you," and walked away.

Here is a description of some of Roger's likes and dislikes that he handed in as part of a language assignment:

1. Foods he likes: candy, cake, and ice cream
   Foods he dislikes: turkey and dressing
2. Books he likes: reading good library books
   Books he does not like: Snow White and the Seven Dwarfs
3. Classes he likes: arithmetic and language
   Classes he dislikes: "There isn't one."
4. Work at home he likes to do: "Feeding the animals on the farm."
   Work at home he dislikes: "Toting in stovewood."
5. Sports he likes best: baseball and basketball
   Sports he dislikes: softball

6. Favorite colors: red, blue, and green
7. Cars he likes best: Chevrolet and Hudson Hornet (his cousin has a Hudson Hornet)
8. Pets he likes best: puppies and chickens
9. Favorite TV programs: "The Web."
   Programs he doesn't like: "Squalling women."
10. Things he sees around home: a nice home, farm animals, pets, brothers, trees, woods, pasture, a truck, toys.
11. What Roger saw on the way to school this morning: houses, mules, cows, woods, a store, Methodist Church, sawmill, two little creeks.

DEC. 5, 1952   Roger sat across the table from me in the lunchroom. He asked if I saw "Dragnet" last night. I replied, "No." Then I said, "Roger, you mean you went out in the rain to go down to your uncle's to see 'Dragnet' last night?" He answered, "Yes, I went down there by myself. I went early enough to see 'Lone Ranger' at 6:00, then I stayed until 9:30." He told the group that he wrapped up good but, after all, he got wet. His final remark, "I mean I was soaking wet when I got home."

DEC. 11, 1952   Thursday at 2:45, during the clean-up period, Roger walked up to me and asked, "Did you hear about a man shaking hands with Mrs. H (one of the high school teachers) and taking her diamond?" I said, "Yes, I heard about it." Roger said his brother Ed came home telling about the thief. Ed is a junior in high school. Roger finished his news by telling that Mr. Y, the principal, had called the sheriff. His final remark, "Boy, the sheriff and his deputies got busy and found the thief."

DEC. 12, 1952   In the lunchroom I sat at a table with Roger and four other children. Roger said, "My daddy has gone to town today to look for us a TV set." He smiled and added, "I hope he finds us a Philco, 'cause that's the best kind, I think." He asked what kind I own. I answered. He asked what size screen mine was. I answered, "A seventeen-inch screen." Roger said, "That's the size we want."

DEC. 15, 1952   Monday at 9:45 I was standing by the radiator warming as the children were returning from the toilets. Several of the children circled around me and general conversation was in progress. When Roger got a chance he asked, "Mrs. Watts, guess what I bought for my mother for Christmas?" I answered, "I have no idea." He finally said, "Well, Saturday I went to town and I bought Mother a manger, stable, angels, shepherds, and all. You know—the Christmas story. It costed me fifty-nine cents. I bought it at the ten-cent store." I told him I thought it was such a sweet gift for Mother. Roger made this final statement, "Mamma set it on the radio in the living room." All the other children seemed anxious to know what the gift was. They stood in the circle and listened.

DEC. 16, 1952   After school, about 3:15, the principal visited our room. There were six late-bus riders in the room, including Roger. . . . Roger said, "Mr. B, did you know Pamela Carter's brother was a guard for General Eisenhower the other day at Guam?" Mr. B answered, "No, I didn't know it, Roger." Roger was half-sitting on one knee and leg; he rubbed his hand through his hair and said, "Well, he was."

DEC. 20, 1952   Recess at 9:45. Roger walked up to me and asked, "Have you seen one of the new Bibles that costs six dollars?" I said, "No, but I knew a new version was being printed." He continued his story, "Well, in one place it says Jesus was born by another woman instead of Mary." "Where have you seen the new Bible?" I asked. Roger said, "A preacher came to our house the other day selling them."

JAN. 1, 1953   During the Christmas holidays, Roger's uncle, aunt and three cousins came home from Florida. They are living at Roger's house until their house is in livable condition. At 8 o'clock the children were getting ready to settle down following the bell. Roger called me and said, "Guess what I did last night." To make a wild guess I said, "I guess you saw '52 go out and '53 come in." Roger nodded his head, rubbed his hand through his hair and said, "Uh-huh, me and Ed went to the show and didn't get home till 1:30 this morning." I laughed in a joky mood and told Roger, "Better be careful today or you will have to get toothpicks to help keep your eyes open." Roger joked back, "Hope not, I'm not sleepy now."

1:15   During activity period Roger called, and I answered, "Yes, Roger, what do you want?" "Who is your preacher?" he said. Then without any response from me he said, "Well, your preacher can't preach at all. When he gets to preaching his teeth falls down; he just can't preach." (He was guest speaker at Roger's church.) I looked at Roger and told him he shouldn't make remarks like that, that it sounded as though he was making fun. He blushed and said, "Well, I wasn't making fun. I was just telling how he did."

JAN. 2, 1953   In the dining room today I overheard a group of children tell what they would like to be someday. Roger's ambition was to be a wrestler. "When I get through high school, I want to go to a good training school. I want a good trainer to train me," he said.

JAN. 5, 1953   Monday about 8:15 Roger called me by name and asked the following question, "Did you hear about Jean Floyd getting killed?" I answered, "No, tell us about it." Roger said, "Well, Jean was a nineteen-year-old girl, and she was going to work. She walked across the road, and a car hit her. A woman was driving the car. She was going about twenty miles an hour. She put on her brakes, but she hit Jean anyway. That woman that run over Jean is about crazy. You know, she hollers and screams all the time. She says she can see that beautiful girl. I mean she was pretty."
One of the students asked Roger if he was kin to her. This is his reply, "Jean was kin to me, a cousin, I think. Daddy and some more kinfolks went down to there after it happened. That woman didn't mean to hit Jean. She blowed the horn, put on the brakes, and skidded into Jean." Roger stood on the floor as he described the tragic accident. He seemed to have been emotionally upset, I thought, from the

tone of voice he used. It sounded solemn and sincere. The expression on his face was sorrowful.

During the period, Roger's expression changed somewhat. Later he said, "Oh, yes, did you know a thirty-seven-year-old singer died?" He scratched his head and said, "I can't think of his name." A third-grade girl said, "It was Hank Williams." Roger said, "That's right. He was riding in his new Cadillac when he had a heart attack."

Jan. 13, 1953   Tuesday morning as I was turning into the school drive I noticed a boy leap from one of my classroom windows. A fellow teacher who was with me remarked that it looked like Roger. I slowed my car to a standstill and then saw Stan jump. About 8:15 I asked the two boys why they jumped. Roger replied, "Oh, we was just playing and decided to jump out the window." I asked for another explanation. "We just did." Roger and Stan seemed to act as if they thought the jump was cute. Both grinned, swung their shoulders sidewise, gave a silly grin, and replied again, "Oh, we just did." I told the boys of the danger of falling and asked them to report to their parents what they had done.

Jan. 14, 1953   Morning. A few minutes of 8:00 we were adjusting the lights, heat, shades, etc. I asked Stan and Roger if they told their parents what happened yesterday. Roger said, "Yes, and I mean they told me that it had better not happen again. The bad part of it all was, Uncle S and them and us all went down to Uncle D's to watch TV and Mamma and Daddy told them about it too. I didn't like it so I left and went down to Jack and Ellen's to get them to come and see TV."

Jan. 19, 1953, 10:55.   At preparation-time for lunch, Roger said, "I went to church last night (Sunday) but I didn't even hear a word the preacher said." I asked, "Why not?" "Oh, me and Pete sat in the back of the church with our mamma's Bibles, and we read; oh, I forgot how many chapters we did read during the preacher's sermon." The conversation closed there as we went to lunch.

Jan. 20, 1953   As I entered the room some minutes before eight, I heard Roger and Sam having an argument over whether the baby in "I Love Lucy" is real or whether it is a play baby. Roger said in a strong and loud voice, "Lucy's baby is real, isn't it? It's a boy, isn't it?" My answer was, "Yes." Roger turned to Sam and said, "I knew it was so." Sam had not seen Lucy's program the night before. His argument was that it was a play baby. Roger had seen the program. I suggested that Roger borrow my Newsweek magazine from the first-grade teacher because it contained some information on Lucy's home, family, husband, and their success in radio, TV, and the theater.

Roger left the room to borrow the magazine. When he came back he was holding the magazine in his hands and looking at Lucy's picture on the cover. He said, "This is that red-headed Lucy all right." Roger sat down in his chair and read the article. Some thirty minutes later he returned the magazine to me with this comment, "That magazine is good."

JAN. 21, 1953   Early Wednesday morning before books, I was noti-
fied that Roger with three fourth-grade boys had been smoking the
night before at a school entertainment. The report came from the
fourth-grade teacher. The problem was met by having the boys report
to their parents what they had done.

JAN. 26, 1953   When I entered the room, Roger was near the door.
We said, "Good morning." I complimented Roger on his new fresh
haircut. He said, "Thank you. Daddy cuts my hair. He has some electric clippers."

JAN. 29, 1953   At 2 P.M. I was checking spelling papers and a group
of third-graders were standing around watching. Roger spoke up, "Boy,
Saturday night I'm going to laugh until my belly hurts." I asked, "Why
are you going to laugh so much?" He told the group that he was coming to the ball game Saturday night and that all the money will go
to the March of Dimes. I corrected Roger on using the word "belly."
He grinned and never said a word. He didn't seem to show resentful-
ness.

JAN. 31, 1953   Roger turned in the following story on his language
assignment:

BED-TIME FUN

I write on my blackboard.
I go to Uncle D's to see TV.
*The programs I like best is boxing, Gene Autry, Roy Rogers, Amos
and Andy.*
I eat supper before bedtime.
I go to bed at 9:30 o'clock.
I read books before bedtime.

JAN. 31, 1953   Saturday. Tonight at the March of Dimes at the
Allen gym I observed Roger during the first game. He stood for thirty
minutes on the sidelines. He put his weight first on one foot and then
on the other. During the third game I saw him again. He was sitting
on the edge of the stage yelling, "Rah, rah, come on, men." The married men were playing the wives.

FEB. 2, 1953   Monday morning on the way to school, Miss S, a
fellow teacher, asked, "Watts, did you see Roger Saturday night at the
ball game?" I answered, "Yes." She said, "Once he helped some older
boys keep score. He told the big boys how to put the scores down."

FEB. 9, 1953   About 4 P.M. another teacher and I were driving by
and stopped in at Roger's home. The reason we were driving by was
to overtake the bus because a fourth-grade girl got left and couldn't
find her way home. When we got near Roger's home we saw him at
the basketball goal and blew the horn at him. The mother and two
of the brothers were at the front door on the porch. Ed was in the
1938 truck in the driveway. The father was not at home. When we
got to the door Mrs. Beach very kindly invited us in. She apologized
that the living room was not very tidy because she had been sewing.
Threads and small pieces of material were on the floor. We told her
that was all right. . . .

After about twenty minutes we decided to go. Mrs. Beach asked us to stay longer. As we went out the front door I noticed a milk can sitting on the front porch. I asked Roger if the family was selling milk. Mrs. Beach and Roger both answered, "Yes." The mother said, "We haven't been selling milk very long. We have three fresh cows." Roger said, "We have three new calves.". . .

We said our good-bys and left.

FEB. 16, 1953   At 9:45 the children were eating mid-morning lunch when Roger walked up to me and said, "Mrs. Watts, Walt like to have got killed this week end." "How come?" I asked. He replied, "He was running in the yard, then he ran up on the front steps. His foot slipped and he hit his head on the corner of the cement steps." "Oh, I'm sorry to hear that. Did you take him to the doctor?" I asked. "No, we didn't. Mamma doctored him at home."

MAR. 4, 1953, 3:05 P.M.   After school, Roger's table of boys had room chores today. When Roger and Sam were sweeping the cloak-room Roger suggested that the two of them move the baby bed (sick cot). Sam laughed and told him that wasn't a baby bed, it was a sick bed. Roger said, "Well, I say baby bed so much at home, I want to say it here at school." I said, "Roger, you don't have a baby bed at home, do you?" He nodded his head and said, "Hmmm." "Well, who sleeps in it then? Does Jerry or Walt?" His final answer was, "Oh, nobody." Then he looked at Sam and grinned.

MAR. 23, 1953   Monday morning. Roger told about Jim's getting pushed down the steps at church Sunday. Jim then, in turn, told about Roger and Stan's fight Sunday at church. I said, "Boys, don't tell me that you had a fight at church." Both the boys said, "Yes." Then I asked, "Why?" Roger did the talking. He said, "Well, when Stan pushed Jim down the step, I told him that was dangerous. Stan called me a baby, and I wasn't going to take that, so I hit him." Roger continued, "We had a pretty good fight. I mean I was mad. I knocked Stan against a truck. I made him cry." My question was, "What did your parents say?" His answer was, "I don't reckon they knew it."

APR. 6, 1953, 8:15 A.M.   Current-events period. Roger said, "My news is about Alan Beach. He almost got killed Sunday. A bunch of us boys was playing in the barn. I threw a pitchfork at a wasp's nest. The wasps was flying everywhere. Old Alan ran, fell down the feed hole out of the loft, and landed on the old mule's back. The rest of us boys opened up the stable door and let Alan out. The old mule kicked him twice. He laid out on the grass a long time." Roger laughed while he was telling his news. There were tears streaming down his face. Several of the other children laughed, too, at his news.

APR. 9, 1953   Thursday. Roger was absent from school because he and Ed, the older brother, helped fix a pasture fence at home.

APR. 10, 1953   Roger brought some assorted cards to school that I had ordered from him. When I arrived the two boxes were lying on my desk. When he came in at 8:03 he said, Mrs. Watts, I laid your cards on the table." "Yes, I found them; thanks a lot," I replied. "May I carry Miss B's stationery to her?" he said. "Yes, you may go."

About 10:15 in social studies class a general discussion was in progress concerning the release of prisoners in Korea. Roger's contribution was that he saw some news on TV showing the names, places, etc. His final comment was, "More prisoners will be released tonight. I want to hear it on our radio if I don't get down to Uncle D's."

APR. 27, 1953 Monday morning the class was discussing current events. One child said, "Lots of the programs on the radio and television will be on one hour earlier." I said, "Yes, why?" The child who told the news didn't seem to know why. Roger raised his hand and I recognized him. He said, "Well, that's called daylight-saving time. We don't go on daylight-saving time."

The discusion continued. Roger's contribution was on the release of prisoners in Korea. He gave the news that two or three men from our state were included in the release. Roger then asked if the Americans had Reds for prisoners. Some member of the class said, "Yes, that's why swapping is going on."

APR. 28, 1953 Roger stayed out of school to drag land for his daddy.

MAY 4, 1953 Monday morning, current-events period. Roger's contribution was telling about going to two funerals on the previous day. He said the elderly lady did not look natural, but the man did. He commented on the large crowd at the funerals.

MAY 6, 1953 When Roger entered the room after the 8 o'clock bell, he was wearing a white T shirt, dungarees, and was barefooted. He had a badge about the size of a quarter fastened to his shirt. He sat down in his chair and immediately called out, "Mrs. Watts, see my badge I got in the mail yesterday from the Kellogg Company. You know I drew a picture and sent it to the Kellogg people. They sent me this here badge. I don't know if I will win anything else or not. They didn't send or say anything about it." Then he sat down and began on his arithmetic work.

Roger's Interaction with People, Things, and Events

An individual's concepts of himself and of the relationship of this individual self with people, things, and events are the product of his interactions with what is in and with what goes on in his life space. It may be worth enumerating some of Roger's concepts of himself and his world and listing some of his experiences to see how these factors depend on each other. The autobiography, for example, emphasizes certain concepts of self that have great meaning for Roger. "I am a boy. I am not a girl." "I am an American." "I feed the mules and hogs and carry in coal and draw water. I like school very much. I like language and arithmetic best of all. I am 4 feet tall and 2 inches. I weigh 63 pounds. My eyes are 20/15." Here Roger is saying that he is a male and that this implies he is something very different from a girl; that he looks at events through American eyes and feels belonging to a nation and concern for it; that he is a worker responsible for specific tasks; and that school is a valued experience and it is a pleasure for him to use language and to learn numbers. He also thinks of himself in terms of tallness, weight, and the limitations his eyes set for him.

Does other life-space material corroborate these concepts of self and ways of relating to the world? Such material as we have included shows Roger losing no opportunity to act as a male should in terms of the peer-group code. For example, on November 21, Roger is one of eight boys called up for using "profane language" on the playground. Among his listed likes are two sports, two automobiles, two kinds of pets, and a horror and mystery program on television. Among his dislikes are the story "Snow White and the Seven Dwarfs" and "squalling women" (possibly singers) on television. He mentions "Dragnet" and the "Lone Ranger" as enjoyable programs. He is interested in what is dangerous in his community: the thief who stole a diamond, Jean Floyd's tragic death, the death in his car of the singer. He even enjoys taking part in dangerous activities: jumping out of windows, scratching his face while sliding down a bush, smoking at an evening entertainment, Walt's accident on the steps, his fight with Stan at the church, settling the fight without letting his parents know anything about it, and the escapade in the barn when he threw a pitchfork at a wasp's nest (perhaps hornets) and Alan was kicked by the mule. This is all very much in line with the male peer culture. So is his interest in sports. He prefers hard-ball baseball to softball, likes basketball best, likes boxing very much on television and hopes to become a professional wrestler. He attends local ball games and even helps older boys keep score. As a male American he is interested in the war in Korea, the release of American prisoners, and the man who was one of the President's honor guards on Guam. He is aware of the larger America and so knows about daylight-saving time, although it is not practiced in his region of the country.

Two areas in which Roger's mind is open to experience show the imprint of his regional culture. One is religion and the other language. In religion Roger is a Baptist, but he nevertheless knows the Methodist custom of rotating pastors, is interested in the old church and graveyard, and knows that the church is not locked. He always knows his Sunday-school lesson and behaves properly in class. (He knows male culture limits.) He knows the Christmas story well and buys a Christmas-story present for his mother. He is aware of a new translation of the Bible and of its controversial content. Mrs. Watts' preacher comes in for criticism for his oral delivery. Roger and Pete read extensively from the Bible during a long sermon, and he goes to two funerals in one day and comments on how the corpses looked.

Roger speaks the dialect of his area: "Uh-huh," "it made so much fuss" (noise), "it ain't no new house," "he would give his eyeteeth," "they don't care for me to go" (meaning they don't care if I go), "going to get done," "don't quit work 'til sundown," "toting in stovewood," "squalling women," "it costed me fifty-nine cents," "Mamma set it on the radio," "Well, your preacher can't preach," "Jean was kin to me," "she blowed the horn," "that woman . . . is about crazy. You know, she hollers and screams," "we was just playing," "I mean they told me that it had better not happen again," ("I mean" always emphasizes what follows) "the bad part of it," "me and Pete," "laugh until my belly hurts," "like to have got killed this week end," "I don't reckon they knew it," "old Alan ran," "old mule's back," "get to go to Uncle D's."

It would be a mistake to think of many of these expressions as incorrect or as representing inadequate command of the language. Roger's speech is extremely effective as communication in his life space. Of course, he needs to learn the other, more formal and academically approved language, too, in order to communicate more widely and with more precision to a larger number of people and as a social-class status symbol in case he is upward mobile. For his age and area, however, Roger communicates extremely well, and it would be a pity to school all of the picturesqueness out of his speech.

Roger conceives of himself not only as a worker but as a member of a family team whose combined efforts earn their daily bread. "I feed the mules and hogs and carry in coal and draw water." He knows the work plans and work habits of the family: "Mamma and Daddy are away over in the big field picking cotton. . . . [They] are going to get done picking cotton today." "They don't quit work 'til sundown." At the moment there are no pigs on the farm because the last one was recently slaughtered for meat. There are two milk cows and there are about ten chickens which demand some care from Roger. He likes "feeding the animals on the farm," but he dislikes "toting in stovewood." Roger reports noticing farm animals, the pasture, the truck, mules, cows, a store and the sawmill on his way to school. He notices the cost of things, such as his present and the new Bible, and he earns money selling stationery. He stays out of school to help fix the pasture fence and "to drag land" (harrowing).

It is hard to realize that Roger is only eight-and-a-half years old. He seems like a boy of twelve or even fourteen in terms of the work he does, his independence, maleness, and knowledge of what is going on in his community and in the world. We are reminded of his real age when he begins crying when blamed by the older boys for using profanity, when he reports that he made Stan cry in their fight, and when he comes in wearing a badge from the Kellogg Company. Roger's record shows a personality, a self composed, as always, of both good and regrettable traits, in the process of becoming.

The child's life space, then, is a significant area for investigation. A teacher studying a child must examine it for himself and see what is in it, what is going on there, and who the significant people are. But since the teacher's perception of a child's life space is influenced by his own background of experience, it is difficult for him to see it through the child's eyes. For this reason he should have the help of other observers—Roger's Sunday-school teacher, first-grade teacher, and mother, for example. How much we would have liked to see Roger in his life space through his father's eyes, his brother's, or his uncle's eyes! But most of all it is important to see a child's life space through his own eyes, as we did in the autobiography, the listing of likes and dislikes, the story of "Bed-time Fun," his reports during the news periods, and conversations with him before school in the morning, after school in the afternoon, and on the trip to Green Wood. One learns much about a life space by direct observation, but one alters one's perceptions through the child's descriptions and reactions to it in language assignments, class discussion, and personal conversation. Traversing the child's life space with him is, of course, immensely rewarding, especially if one lets the child direct the conversation, accepts all expressed feelings and interpretations, and reflects these feelings back to the child in an accepting mood.

CONFERRING WITH COLLEAGUES

Colleagues who taught the child in the past or who are currently teaching him in a departmentalized school are important sources of information, though not primary ones like the home, the cumulative record, and direct observation. They are especially good for describing how the child acted at earlier stages in his development, recalling significant events in the child's life and how they affected him, giving supplementary information about the family, and describing the child's current behavior under the influence of different interests or interpersonal relationships.

It is necessary to remember, however, that teachers are in the position of constantly making evaluations and judgments about their pupils, and when asked about a child, they naturally respond with an evaluation. A teacher who is studying a child objectively will record such an evaluation, not as a fact about the child, but as revelatory of a portion of the climate of opinion and feeling under which the child lives and learns, with the particular teacher. After noting such evaluations, the child-study participant must try to get his colleague to describe rather than to evaluate. A series of questions such as, "Give me an illustration of that sort of behavior" or "Try to remember one specific instance so that I can write it up as an anecdote" will usually accomplish this. Having evoked anecdotal descriptions of concrete situations, the participant can then follow up with questions such as, "How often do you remember this as occurring?" or "Would you say that the child did this every day, every week, once a month, or less frequently?" or "Can you tell me about where you first noticed this, how often it has happened, and when you last noticed it?"

When a colleague reports some fact about the child's family, it is always desirable to ask, "How did you come to learn this?" When the colleague mentions an informant, the same question applies, "Do you know how he learned this?" In this way gossip and hearsay can be distinguished from information based on experience or communication directly from a parent, nurse, or social worker.

Sometimes a colleague will report a child as insolent, upset, fearful, repentant, or resentful. The participant must check these interpretations by asking, "What did the child do that led you to feel that this was his reaction?" or "How did he look or act in showing that reaction?" The teacher does not question the validity of his colleague's report, but does ask for more concrete descriptions of the child's posture, voice quality, facial expression, and other behavior.

Often a child-study participant, by talking with the principal and two or three of the child's former teachers, can discover the reputation that the child has carried from year to year, from classroom to classroom. This is valuable information because it reveals the climate of opinion in which he has had to do his learning and which has significantly influenced his behavior. It is important to evaluate the extent to which the reputation was justified by getting specific facts and determining whether anybody knew what had motivated the child's behavior. It is equally important to discover any changes in reputation, for it is not unusual to find that a child has been "marked" for years by a single episode. Stealing, especially money, and overt sexual play or conversation can so mark a child. Unacceptable behavior by a sibling or a parent sometimes produces a halo effect, and contrast with a sibling may also influence the climate of opinion concerning a child.

Cooperation in Gathering Data

In many departmentalized schools—junior and senior high schools for the most part—groups of three teachers select three children who are in the classes of all three. Then each one observes and writes anecdotes about all three children, and they exchange material periodically. Teacher A will receive all anecdotes and other data about child A from teachers B and C; teacher B will receive all anecdotes and other material about child B from teachers A and C; and teacher C will get all material about child C. Such cooperative studies of children afford interesting experiences for the teachers. They soon discover that children act differently when working with different teachers and dealing with different subject matter. They also discover that different teachers tend to notice and record, and hence to emphasize, different characteristics or ways of behaving in the same child. The fact that different teachers perceive the same child so differently is very convincing evidence that a single individual never perceives the total reality, the whole truth, about any person or event. The result is that each broadens the base of his observations so as to include more aspects of the child's behavior, or a larger sampling of his actions. Invariably the teacher's attitudes toward the child are changed as he gradually spots some of his own preoccupations, biases, and pet likes and dislikes.

Of course, the major purpose of having three people cooperate in building the records about three pupils is to get richer records. When a teacher is with a young person for only one period a day for one or two semesters, he has little real opportunity to get to know that student. But when three teachers band together to study three students, each young person is under observation at least three periods a day and may also be observed in such diverse situations as extracurricular clubs, homeroom activities, athletic practice, and foreign-language study, and in such diverse places as the cafeteria, hallways, playground, assembly, gym, shop, and science laboratory. Through this wider sampling, teachers are able to see how differently a young person behaves when working at a subject in which he is doing well and is vitally interested and when working on something he dislikes or finds difficult. Sometimes he scarcely is recognizable as the same individual.

The effect of this experience on the teacher of the subject in which the student is not interested is usually to stimulate the teacher to help the student build a bridge from his own life experiences or needs to the subject-matter area that has held little meaning for him. And when the teacher succeeds in doing this with one individual, he is likely to try the same process in interesting other students, for he has learned that student interest cannot be taken for granted. At the same time, teachers learn that, in reality, individual students do have different limits of learning capacity and different aptitudes; it is deadly for student and teacher alike arbitrarily to require a student to take a course that is beyond his capacity and to deny him access to courses for which he has real aptitude, no matter what the general curriculum requirements are.

Another cooperative enterprise in studying secondary school students also has led to very stimulating and valuable discussions. Teachers in a particular school sometimes agree to follow several individuals throughout a whole school day to find out what the day is like to them, how it adds up as a day in the developing individual's life, and how well balanced it is. Each teacher who teaches the student on that day agrees to write one or two anecdotes describing his work in that particular field, some to observe his interactions with peers on the playground or in the gymnasium, cafeteria, and hallways during recess periods, and still others to report on extracurricular activities in clubs or athletics. Then, in a group meeting, all the records are read in the correct time sequence in an effort to see the day in school through the student's eyes. The findings are often quite surprising and have implications not only for ways of helping the student concerned, but also for curriculum planning, school organization, guidance work, physical arrangements, and so on.

Such studies are particularly illuminating when the school days of very able students are contrasted with those of borderline or failing students. They may reveal, for example, that it is developmentally unsound to heap failure upon failure for a particular student and that his course of study should be altered to give him the opportunity to achieve a fair balance between success and subject matter that is extremely difficult for him. Equally illuminating is the contrasting study of the day of a student who is extremely popular with his peers and that of a student who is unpopular or rejected, though perhaps academically successful.

Of course, it goes without saying that some training in objective observation and the writing of descriptive anecdotes must precede such studies, for a series of evaluative judgments from the different observers can lead only to endless arguments. It also goes without saying that such case conferences have to include more than just the anecdotes; cumulative-record data and descriptions of earlier parent conferences supply invaluable material to the working group.

Illustrative Material

The case histories already given supply numerous examples of significant information obtained by child-study participants from their colleagues and illustrate the informal way in which such information usually is obtained. In the case of Jane, for example, on October 23 her teacher was walking on the playground with another teacher when Jane "pushed one of the other children hard." Then her teacher said, "I don't understand why Jane does things like that," and the colleague replied. "If you ever saw Jane's home you would." The colleague then went on to describe how Alice threw a butcher knife at Jane one day when she was visiting them and how the children put jelly into each other's hair and called the mother all kinds of names. In December another teacher reported that Jane's sister Alice was going out with a man much older than she, and later in the year this had very significant reverberations in Jane's mood when Jane said to her teacher, "Wait till you find something out; I'm going to feel awful." Mrs. A, another fellow teacher, counseled Jane's teacher about the kissing episode and helped her to see that Jane was "starved for affection," adding that the mother "just screams at them from morning to night and never gives them a kind word." Still another teacher reported to Mrs. Summers that the principal hated Jane and had failed her in the fifth grade to ensure her transfer to another school. These communications from other teachers alerted Mrs. Summers to the child's deep insecurity long before she was able to get the information she needed about Jane's home situation. It also helped her to understand the principal's interaction with Jane and to soften the effects of these impacts.

Again, in the life-space material about Roger, we find colleagues making significant contributions, even to Mrs. Watts' partial case record. Mrs. Jones revealed much about the background of the parents that would account for their attitudes toward Roger and for their expectancies of him at home. His Sunday-school teacher described his knowledge and exemplary behavior in Sunday school: "You would think he is a perfect angel." Miss S had noticed Roger showing older boys how to keep score at the basketball game, something his own teacher had missed.

Such information comes easily and informally from fellow teachers. But it must be recorded in order to be recalled when it is needed for interpreting the child's motivation and needs and for finding ways of helping the individual. It is, of course, also proper to sit down for half an hour with a former teacher in order to canvass somewhat more systematically what happened to a child during an earlier year. Although these more formal interviews yield less, on the whole, than informal contacts, considering the time spent, both types of contact are needed.

COLLECTING AND EXAMINING
SAMPLES OF THE CHILD'S WORK

Teachers are, of course, professionally concerned with each child's development in basic language and number skills. Participants in child-study groups are therefore interested in watching the growth of each child being studied in spelling and punctuation skills, knowledge of number combinations, and skill in arithmetic processes. Participants should periodically enter into their records characteristic samples of the classroom work of the children they are studying. Results of objective tests should also be entered in the interest of periodic evaluation of pupil progress.

But we are not content to have our participants stop their analyses of children's learning when these evaluations show satisfactory individual progress in relation to the children's respective capacities. Sound growth toward understanding the quantitative aspects of life, for example, involves growth in mathematical concepts as well as skill in manipulating numbers. Consequently we encourage participants to listen to and record children's interpretations of what they are doing in arithmetic, algebra, or geometry, and to analyze the concepts that underlie these explanations in order to discover absence of or vagueness in necessary concepts. Discussion in the study groups will help teachers to plan individual and group experiences which will result in the development of clearer and more accurate concepts.

In the language field, too, we are interested in developing understanding of the semantic aspect of language rather than stopping with word recognition and spelling. For only when the meanings of words are accurately discriminated can children grow in the power to think, to reason clearly, and to reach valid conclusions. For example, in one of the communities in which we organized child-study groups, participants noticed that children consistently were scoring higher in reading comprehension than in vocabulary. Analysis revealed two very significant factors: the parents of the children were quite limited in the vocabularies they used in the homes and in the reading matter they made available; and the children's experience was limited largely to their own neighborhoods, which were essentially lower class. The net effect on the children was that they lacked many words for the things and processes and for the qualities and characteristics of things that existed and went on even in their limited environment.

But the schools were using excellent teaching methods. The children constantly were seeking, through reading, the answers to questions which they themselves had posed in the classroom. The consequence was that they got many word meanings from contexts even though they did not know the dictionary meanings of many of the words that occurred in their reading materials. Once the participating teachers understood this, they began a series of excursions into the neighborhood and more widely over the state in busses. They encouraged the children to observe and describe everything they saw and to find the words they needed for accurate naming and description of things, processes, characteristics, and qualities. Significant vocabulary growth resulted. We like to believe that there was also a considerable increase in the accuracy of the pupils' thinking, though we must recognize the drag of the language habits of the home and the neighborhood. At any rate we do feel that the teacher's tasks include a sensitive awareness of the concepts that underlie mathematical and language development so that they are not content with mere recognition, manipulation, and reproduction of symbols.

Language Work as Autobiographic and Projective Material

In the cases already presented, language assignments provided many significant insights into the child's state of mind. Jane's poignant story, "The Friendly Valentine," turned out to be the story of how lonely Jane really felt. Chester's "A Day at Our House" revealed his mother's dominating role in the life of the children. His story "My Family" revealed his preoccupation with his small size and slow growth and his hope that he would grow rapidly, like his dad, once the growth spurt began. Roger's "Autobiography" not only gave many important facts about his life space and experience background but also affirmed his preoccupation with maleness: "I am a boy. I am not a girl." His "Story About My Pets" identifies the kind of dogs he has and recounts the loss of a puppy. His list of likes and dislikes shows how he reacts to some of his home tasks and his keen interest in the experiences available to him, such as reading books, looking at television, evaluating automobiles, participating in sports, and reacting to farm animals, trees, woods, creeks, churches, and the work of the world—the sawmill, truck, and store. "Bed-time Fun" indicates more of his interests and further establishes his maleness.

In the secondary school, young people frequently permit their inner concerns and deeper feelings to express themselves in writing before they are ready to talk about them freely with adults. Writing is a way of discussing things with themselves, seeking meanings, clarifying values, considering their own relationships with the world, and pondering the meaning of life and its implications for their own future. The following essays and poems are from the case record of Margaret Anne Aldrich, a sixteen-year-old eleventh grader who did not like school despite the fact that she made A's on all subjects. Seemingly poised, she showed tenseness in her voice and avoided social activities.

DANCES

There have been many dances held during the time I have been in high school. Weeks of preparation with practicing entertainment numbers, preparing decorations, refreshments, etc. There is always a hurry and hustle with people flying here and there doing this and that. To a bystander, they may seem rather silly in all their haste and hurry, and excitement, but that excitement, that hurry, that work they do, all can be slated up to experience, good experience. This experience in working and cooperating with others, of hurdling difficulties, of making whatever materials you have do, of learning that the show must go on, come what may, when the big night comes, nothing can match the satisfaction those kids feel at having done their job well. They have a lot of fun, which is their just reward for their hard work. I believe in dances, because the dance and the preparation for it fosters a companionship between youth that is necessary. It provides a good outlet for the energy and initiative of youth. It is one prevention against juvenile delinquency. A student may be an excellent scholar, but if he does not take part in such extra activities he will miss something that is rightfully his, something that all the learning in the world can't make up for. You can't hide behind a book all your life. You have to meet people on sound grounds and the student must learn that this will be different than meeting someone in his well-known education world, where he has already made his mark. He must make his way in the social world and he may as well learn, while he is young, by taking part in the dances and other social activities of his school. Otherwise, he will be a misfit in society, which will only lead to his own unhappiness. You can't be happy if you feel you don't belong and the only way to belong is to take your own part in the world.

A few weeks after she had received this essay, Miss Corey recorded the following anecdote:

> DEC. 3   When I asked M. A. why she didn't like to go to dances or plays or lectures, she said, "Well, I know it's hard to believe, Miss Corey, but I'm scared. I've never met anyone on a social level. I don't know what to do or say."

From this anecdote we can understand that in her essay Margaret Anne was arguing with herself about the importance of rounding out her development by more participation in social events.

A WHITE PAPER

A young girl sat in a school desk with its usual marred top. Her slim figure bent over the desk was clothed in a clean, white blouse and a neat, tailored blue skirt. One tawny-hued curl fell unrestricted over her one eye, which like its blue-grey counterpart was staring into space, while her hand clutching a yellow pencil rested motionless on the sheets of white paper marred only by a few black figures. Strange thoughts were passing through the mind, that rested behind that uncomprehending gaze. Thoughts of a day in Spring, when a young girl had signed up for her schedule for the coming year. The thoughts materialized into the familiar schoolroom scene with the students listening quietly as the principal explained in a powerful, almost frightening voice that the students must take a certain number of subjects the next year. Different phases of worry, confusion and indecision passed over the faces of the youngsters, as one by one, they were called upon to give their choice of subjects. The scene faded as a girl's voice murmured the word "Chemistry" through trembling, red lips. Almost indefinable in form, each had a central figure, a girl of about 15 running away from black horrible symbols and formulas, that reached out to grab hold of the tawny hair or flailing arms and always the same voice seemed to come from those grotesque figures, a harsh, demanding voice that grew louder and louder as the terrible numbers and symbols seemed to multiply and appear everywhere, closing in tighter and tighter like a steel band around the figure of the girl, who finding no escape, had stopped running and stood cowering like a frightened beast, while the band grew even tighter about her, the harsh voice was becoming echoed, a loud clanging one. Then, more noises, the rustling of paper, the tramp of feet, but above all these noises, the same familiar harsh one rang out and the blue-grey eyes focused on the form of the short eagle-eyed man and the thoughts fled in terror from the mind as the sharp voice reechoed with, "Celia, hand me your paper! If it isn't any better than previous ones, I promise you'll fail this course." A trembling hand extended the paper, white except for the few black figures and letters and a few, tiny round wet spots that reminds one of the misty dew that veils a blue-grey sea.

In this essay Margaret Anne reveals the emotion that can accompany seemingly routine situations at school for sensitive young people. Obviously her straight A record did not mean that school was an easy and triumphant experience for Margaret Anne. One wonders how many of her teachers sensed the inner turmoil she was experiencing and whether appropriate reassurance might have let her like school more. The same inner trepidation is revealed in the following poem.

ASSEMBLY SPEECH

The people were silent,
The room was still.
I pulled myself to my feet
Much against my will.

Stumbled to the front
And up the stairs,
While zealously saying
My silent prayers.

Nobody moved,
And everyone stared,
I knew I was dying,
But nobody cared.

I clasped my hands firmly,
My fingers like ice,
And I crumpled my notes
In a death-like vise.

I took one deep breath
And straightway began
To explain all about
The School Social Plan.

And there before me
The audience sat,
As I delved into this
And I talked about that.

But as I was talking,
I had one great fear,
That all I said passed
Out the opposite ear.

I ran out of words,
As the seconds flew past,
And I knew the torture
Was ended at last!

I ran down the steps
And fell into a chair,
And took my first free
Breath of fresh air.

The weeks passed by,
I forgot my ordeal;
The assembly bells
Again started to peal.

The assembly was fine,
I was without care,
Then Mr. Biehl really
Gave me a scare.

I squirmed in my chair
And wished I'd fall dead.
After two weeks he's asked me
To repeat what I'd said.

So with faltering voice
And smile, weak and wane,
I went through that torture
All over again.

Now at the word Social Program,
I get out of reach,
And all because
Of an assembly speech.

Adolescents are vitally interested in emotional experience, and they frequently imagine what they have not themselves experienced. This is one of their ways of exploring life. In these imaginative projections, however, they reveal something of the nature of their emotional experience through the situations which have significance for them.

A DREAM

Blessed is he who possesses a dream;
More blessed than a king enthroned in wealth,
For wealth may be swept away in life's grim, black tide,
But a dream is a sturdy island in the midst of life's turbulent ocean.
More blessed than a maiden of virgin beauty,
For the lashing rains and shrieking winds of life wash away the beauty
    and leave only a scarred, eroded visage;

But a dream drives its roots deep in fertile soil and draws life and lasting beauty from the black earth.

More blessed than a powerful despot,

For power can be destroyed by the greater power, the searing flame, the sun that lights the way from the dark dungeon of slavery to freedom and light.

But a dream remains a quiet spectator of the inferno that rages at its very feet.

For a dream is of the earth and of the Heavens;

Of the sweat that coats and cools the furrowed brow.

Of the toil that bends the weary back and is a child of the wrinkled calloused hand.

Of the tears that fill the eyes, which beseech help from the awe-inspiring starlit skies.

Of the inner strength that lifts the exhausted body and despair laden soul.

Of the hope that springs anew into a heart where hope was but a smoldering ember.

Of the happiness born of a kind word, sweet smile or helping hand.

Of the love that warms an empty, aching heart.

Of the pride that lifts again the head bowed in despair.

Of the fears that lurk within the mind and soul which shrink in agony from this unseen, merciless torturer;

Of the black, furrowed earth, a grey-blue sky, apple blossoms, a baby pink dawn, which heal the heart stabbed by fate's piercing blade and open the eyes, blinded by tears, that they may see again life's beauty.

Of robin's song and the gentle patter of spring rain which cures the deafness that contrived to shut out earth's hard cruel sounds and in so doing, prohibited the entrance of soft, sweet notes, of such material, durable and strong material are dreams made.

Without a dream a man is like a ship in a gale without a star to steer her or the comforting gleam of the light-house to proclaim the end of the long voyage.

Like a weary traveler who walks a road that stretches through verdant valley, dusky dale, over massive mountains and high hills, ever onward into the horizon, a lonesome road without an end.

A traveler who must keep walking because his own shadow is close at his heels, breathing down his neck, ever prodding him onward.

His feet may slip and he may fall in agonizing exhaustion, but he will rise again to go on.

He passes others along the road who turn off on little byways along which sign posts say: pay, college, occupation, business, home and others, the most predominate being success and happiness, but his constant companion of gypsy blood reaches out and prevents him from stopping, so he continues to run and stumble along, always running away from himself, running where? No one knows.

He who has no dream to give him hope as he makes his weary way; no dream to call his name that he may proudly answer present;

No dream to say well done, no dream to introduce him to that one who treads upon his heels; that they may dwell together in peace and friendship.

Take a man's money, but give him a dream and it will lead him up
from the dregs of poverty; take a man's health, but give him a
dream, and it will heal his mind and body; take a man's power,
but give him a dream and it will inspire him to cooperate and
yield to the will of others; take a man's dream and he is lost forever,
an unknown number amid the hurrying multitudes, of those without
a home at the long day's end, without a haven, without a dream.

Young people feel the impulse to escape at times, especially if their
efforts to achieve maturity are great and the obstacles difficult to overcome. But at the end of the next essay, Margaret Anne embraces the
struggle again.

ESCAPE

I often try to imagine what it would be like if people could escape
from the tasks and duties, the hurry and bustle of our modern world.
To a place where they might do as they wished. Where they might
find a quiet companionship with the study pages of a friendly book or
stretch out in the sweet, green grass and build castles out of the gold
of the sun rays that strike the city, white clouds drifting in the ozone
blue above the gentle swaying tops of the majestic pines, or, see their
own reflection mirrored in the laughing brook and find again the
quick, easy laughter that they had lost in the whirl and hardness of
modern life. Or, find again in people they really love the gentleness
that has become a foreigner in our impersonal world; a land where
every man might find his dream whatever it might be and then again,
I suppose without the stimulus of competition and quick tempo of
this world and the striving to reach a goal that is always over the next
hill, life would be pretty boring and we would long for a good, thrilling crime movie or a noisy ride on a street car.

FEAR

Fear is one of the most potent enemies of mortals. It creeps on
stealthy, felinelike tread into the fartherest recesses of the human
mind and there begins to unfurl its unscrutable curtain, so that the
mind gropes in a realm destitute of light, vainly, frantically seeking
sunlight and laughter. Finding none, it cringes in shuddering horror
as this hideous monster, with taunting laugh, creates from a throbbing
pulse, strange footsteps; forms from a lonely wind, a heart-rending sob;
and out of a normal existence, molds a living, torturous hell.

Young persons sometimes feel very old and quite experienced. They
have felt so vividly and tried so earnestly to face life that they begin to
feel that they know what it is about. If they seem cocky and unduly independent at times, one must understand that it results from the attempt
to discover a basis for self-confidence—for trusting themselves and their
perceptions. Fear, uncertainty, and the desire to escape reality will return, and again the young person will need reassurance. The ways of
Nature seem basic, so young people often feel that they are close to
truth when they observe Nature and sense the guiding hand of God
behind it.

THE CALENDAR

Man with all his wisdom of the world,
May only count the days in numerals bare,
Devoid of the elements that fashion from a year,
A creation, strange, magnificent and fair.

A number black upon a parchment white
Can never justice do unto a January sky,
Where etched in granite Spires and verdant pines,
Forever watches life's turbulent river flow by.

For there in a steel grey winter dawn,
Ancient yesterday folds its hands carved with toil
And humorously watches his merry grandchildren,
So fresh from the sterile soil.

When the winter sky begins to gain new light
And lantern flames devour less yellow fuel,
The farmer about his daily, vilesome chores,
Needs no aid to identify February's clear cut cool.

March's own lusty heralds
In gusty shrieking torrents bide,
Like dashing cavaliers, who daunt
The trembling hepatica upon the bleak hillside.

April is the springtime of the year
When apple blossom scented rain becomes a part
Of the freshness of the face revealing
The sweet springtime in the heart.

May is wild forget-me-nots
That send their message across the brown
And starry nights when the hand of God
Seems to turn back the hands of time.

June is one full-blown scarlet rose
Missed by lips no less red
And clutched to the bloody breast
Of a Soldier lying dead.

July is the time when moss gentians
Lift their exquisite petals of blue
And their petite _____ the sea _____
Exhibit their splendid hue.

August is the river of wheat
That flows through the western plains
And the heavy paler smell of ripened fields
Mixed with the scent of other grains.

September is a cool morning mist
That cloaks the far off mountain range

Where, but a mere hour before
The great Bear stalked the skies.

October bids stern frost walk its valleys
With strides ravishing and bold
Chasing away the laughing children
In Hallowe'en dress of crimsen gold.

November announces its arrival
By blue haze, reminescent of the summer of yore
And receiving no immediate welcome
Impatiently rattles the door.

December again lights the lanterns
To show the way in crisp snow all about,
And the stars come out as the lights blink off
And guide the old year out.

So man may count the days and months
Each by a specific name be known
But the sensitive pulse of nature
Is regulated by God alone.

Learning to get along with all sorts of people in all sorts of situations
is another of the developmental tasks with which young people wrestle.
As they develop concepts of fairness, justice, mercy, and love, they discover that many traditional practices in our society violate these ethical
ideals. Consequently they feel that one of their significant roles will be
participation in the creation of a better world.

HOW WE CAN HELP OVERCOME INTOLERANCE

Before presenting the ways in which we can help to overcome intolerance, I wish to explain that I do not restrict intolerance to certain
races or religions, but I am speaking of the intolerance that is present
in our routine everyday life. If we are to eventually overcome the intolerance between nations and races, we must start as all great things
are begun, from a humble foundation. We must work in the classroom,
the home, the street, everywhere we come into contact with others.
We must try to analyze the words and actions of our parents, our
brothers and sisters, our friends, our teachers. That we may understand what circumstances or emotions motivate them in their speech
and deeds. We must realize that people are a product of and affected
by their environment. We must recognize father's anger as a result of
a big deal that he failed to put through for the office and sister's
melancholy moods as indicators of her quarrels with her best beau;
and teacher's bad temper as the result of an especially noisy class.
When we are able to connect people's attitudes and behavior with
the causes for them, we are more easily able to understand them and
understanding is the key that will unlock the barred door of intolerance. When we are able to cooperate, work, live and play with the

members of our family, our friends, and the people we meet every day, then we will be well on the way to combating intolerance for those of a different color, language or creed.

The case record about Margaret Anne demonstrates the circumstances at home and at school and the experience background that underlay her essays and poems. Most of her specific motivations cannot be discerned, and no depth analysis of the specific origins of her emotions and inner conflicts can be given without the material contained in the case record. But one can sense that Margaret Anne is writing about herself, and the presence of the broader adolescent developmental tasks is clear.

The purpose of including this material is to suggest the wealth of projective material that participants in our child-study program will find in the daily classroom work of their students. How far a specific study group can go in interpreting such material depends, of course, on the extent of their knowledge of the literature of psychiatry, psychoanalysis, and genetic psychology. But even teachers who lack such a background at the beginning of their study can sense the realness and the vividness of the emotional struggles of young people seeking the inner organization that will permit them to live good and fruitful lives.

Drawings and Paintings

Most children love to draw and paint. If the necessary materials are available to them and they are free to draw or paint what they wish whenever they have spare time or become restless, they will go to the easel frequently and produce much interesting work. The subject matter, form, organization, and colors used are all worth noting because this creative work nearly always relates to preoccupations and interests significant in their emotional lives. One of the major reasons for drawing or painting is to relieve tension, to achieve a catharsis of blocked feelings, to express what cannot yet be said in words or through actions. Sometimes the content of the drawing or painting is a direct statement of the child's feelings; most often it is symbolic, centering around some idea related to the preoccupation. Another reason why children draw and paint is to clarify an idea or a feeling, to find out by expressing it what one actually does feel or think. Apparently the movement, the colors, and the form of the expression help to organize the individual's ideas or expressive pattern in relation to the emotion-producing situation, relationship, or self-concept.

There do not appear to be clear-cut standards teachers can use in interpreting the significance of content, colors, or organization, because the significance of each symbol varies from child to child. But after the child has expressed himself through the drawing or painting, he is often able to verbalize more freely. The teacher can ask him to show his picture to the class and tell them the story of it or go to the easel with him and encourage him to explain what it is about. It goes without saying that whatever the child says is to be accepted without criticism. If what he says does not have a significant meaning for the teacher, it is a good technique simply to repeat the last thing the child said as a means of encouraging him to speak further.

Of course, it frequently happens that the child does not succeed in expressing his feelings, or in accomplishing the clarification he unconsciously is seeking, through a single drawing or painting. I once received from an able nursery school teacher a series of sixteen drawings done by a four-year-old child over a period of six or eight weeks after a new baby had been born into the family. Up until this time the four-year-old had been the adored only child in the family, and he gave many evidences of finding the new brother hard to take and of being considerably disturbed emotionally by his coming. The first picture was a crude painting of a house with a tree nearby. Each successive picture elaborated this initial picture, until the final painting of the series showed a mother and father walking down the walk from the door pushing a baby carriage before them but with a boy walking between them holding a hand of each parent. The series was a beautiful story of a child coming to terms with the presence of his little brother through the continuing experience of receiving love from and having time alone with understanding parents, encouraged by a vitally interested and empathetic nursery school teacher.

Teachers should not try to read a great deal into a single piece of creative work; rather they should give children the opportunity regularly and often to work out their feelings through painting, drawing, clay-modeling, dramatic play, dancing, and the like. Then by observing how the child uses space over a considerable period of time, the teacher frequently can sense constriction of emotions, feelings of personal inadequacy, and excessive restraint of feeling. Sometimes the colors the child uses suggest the violence of pent-up emotions or the gloomy and dark mood in which the child's life is lived. Often from the content of the pictures the teacher can gradually sense the matter which the child is trying to understand, the inner conflict that he cannot resolve, or the vague fear that is tormenting him.

On the other hand, it is all too easy for an adult to project into the child's creative expression an emotional content and quality which simply are not there; much creative expression is done simply for the joy of doing it. I have on my desk a ceramic figure of a baby hippo done by a very talented four-year-old. On a trip to the zoo, the youngster was entranced by the baby hippo; when he came home, he molded a very beautiful one in clay, simply for the joy of reliving his experience. His mother put it in the kiln and helped him apply the glaze. It is important for teachers to learn to appreciate and share these pleasurable creative experiences of children, to tune themselves to happiness as well as to see possible indications of conflict, fear, hatred or aggression.

In summary, then, we have found that the drawings, paintings, and other creative expressions of children are very valuable sources of information about their inner lives and feelings. This inner richness is expressed by both the content and the method—form, color, balance, organization, and use of space. Teachers can use creative expressions to best advantage by encouraging children to talk freely about them in an atmosphere of complete acceptance. Interpretations can be sought in terms of whether or not the child, as he created, was:

1. Reliving the pleasure of an earlier experience for the simple joy of it.

2. Trying to clarify the meaning of a situation, relationship, or experience both intellectually and emotionally, that is, to get at its meaning for himself.

3. Relieving his tensions (catharsis) by expressing, directly or symbolically, an inner fear, aggression, hostility, anxiety, self-doubt, or some other emotion.

4. Simply playing with ideas and feelings, or with color, form, and organization in the expression of ideas and feelings, because it is pleasurable to rearrange them in new combinations and relationships and to express them in new ways. Creation is self-enhancing because it tests one's power to express ideas and feelings.

Because the child can create only out of his own experience and feelings, all free creative productions are excellent projective material. But a considerable background knowledge of the child's life is necessary to understand what he is saying. There is always the danger of projecting into a child's work something that one has discovered to be true for another child or for oneself.

INFORMAL CONVERSATIONS WITH THE CHILD

In our present consulting practice, we guide child-study groups in tapping the six sources of information that already have been described. But many teachers are using a seventh source of information, namely, informal conversations with the child before school, after school, during recess periods, and at odd times when the child seeks out the teacher. They are writing up these experiences as anecdotes. However, the information gained often is so significant that the staff is considering whether such conversations should be highlighted as a seventh source of information. In any event, it seems wise to point out here certain cautions to be observed in these little interviews and the special conditions under which they can be fruitful.

When teachers work with child-study groups, their attitudes toward the children they study undergo a rapid change. Initially most of them tend to blame children who fail to do their work properly, disturb the class, or violate school rules. But as they become convinced that behavior is caused by the interaction of forces operating within the child and impinging upon him from outside, they become interested in trying to find out what these forces are and how they can be modified. As they progress in this search, and without being aware of it themselves, their attitudes toward children change. First they stop blaming individual children. This leads them to overlook some of the lesser misdemeanors, defer judgment, and try to get the child's story of what happened. They avoid direct conflicts with the child, take more trouble to involve him in interesting activities, give him roles by getting him to help out in various ways, and, all the while, listen more carefully to what he has to say and observe more closely the way he feels. Children nearly always respond to this change in attitude by improved behavior.

Then the child begins to take the initiative in approaching the teacher. He brings things up to her desk to show her, sits near her at luncheon in the cafeteria, and, finally, appears at school early or stays late in the afternoon to help her do little chores. The most fruitful conversations occur at this time.

We are most anxious not to interfere with this natural and desirable evolution in the relationship between the teacher and the child. We are fearful lest highlighting these informal conversations as an important source of information should lead the teacher prematurely to try to initiate them. Usually it is the child who should initiate the contact; the teacher should simply make the most of it when it comes. We are also afraid lest the teacher, in his eagerness to understand the child better, may quiz him, ask him questions which he is not yet ready to answer, and so drive him away from such contacts just when they could be most helpful. Again, the teacher must avoid using these moments to admonish the child or to try to exert a "good influence" upon him before he is ready for it and while he is still testing the quality of the new relationship between them.

It has to be remembered that the child has unconscious reasons for seeking these contacts. Usually he is seeking reassurance. He wants to be with someone who really values him as he is. He wants to feel accepted and to experience real interest in him and in what he does, thinks, and feels. When the teacher listens to and accepts what he has to say, when he can feel some warmth in the relationship, then he feels deep inside that he is valued, that he has a friend. The maturing of this relationship should be the first and primary purpose of these informal conversations; the information and insights gained are the valuable by-products of this most important personal relationship.

Perhaps a few examples from the case of Chester will illustrate these informal conversations.

DEC. 8   When it was time to leave today, Chester came to me. His eyes were shining and he was wearing a smile. He said, "I have to hurry. I am trying out for basketball today. The coach told us to come right after school." Then his expression changed and he looked down at the floor. I waited; then I heard him saying rather slowly, "I sure hope I make it." I said, "I hope so, too." At the beginning of the football season he had tried out for the team but he was too small. As he left the room I said, "Good luck."

DEC. 9   The first thing this morning Chester informed me that he made the team. I think that I have never seen him more thrilled over anything. I told him that I was happy for him. He thanked me. . . .

JAN. 5   After school today Chester was talking with me about happenings during the holidays. I let him do most of the talking. Following are some of his remarks: "We didn't get many toys this Christmas. We got mostly clothes. My brother and I got an electric train together. Mother told us Santa Claus brought the clothes and train." Then in a wise manner he added, "Of course I know that there isn't a Santa Claus, but we just say that. Santa Claus is the spirit of Christmas. It means the spirit of love and of giving. There were a lot of good programs on television about this. They said that Christmas ought to be the time for giving instead of receiving." . . .

FEB. 19   Chester stayed with me after school until I was ready to leave. We got into a conversation about his afternoons.

TEACHER: What do you usually do in the afternoons?
CHESTER: I play with Tom Jones. He lives two doors from me. He comes to my house.
TEACHER: Do you ever go to his house?
CHESTER: Yes, we take turns playing at each other's house. Sometimes I go down to his house. Sometimes he comes to mine.
TEACHER: What do you like to play?
CHESTER: Marbles or ball. We like marbles.
TEACHER: How old is Tom?
CHESTER: He's twelve—just a year older than I am. He's in the seventh grade. He'll be out of school Tuesday, too. His teacher is going for observation with you. . . .
TEACHER: I'll bet you and Tom will have a good time that day.
CHESTER: We'll play all morning, but I guess Tom will go to the movies in the afternoon.
TEACHER: Will you go with him?
CHESTER: No, Mother won't let me. She is afraid I'll get hurt.
TEACHER: Do you usually play all afternoon?
CHESTER: Mother lets me play when I first come home from school. Then she makes me come in to do my homework. . . .

FEB. 27   Chester was staying after school with me. He was telling me about his plans for camp this summer. He added, "I am making the money to go." I asked, "What are you doing to make the money?"

He answered, "I am selling doughnuts, coat hangers and drink bottles. My aunt has promised to let me sell her flowers as soon as they start blooming. I run errands for neighbors, too."

Suddenly he looked at the clock. "I must be going," he said. "I have to deliver twelve dozen doughnuts today." I asked, "Where do you get them?" He answered, "From the Krispy Kreme Doughnut Co. I get them for twenty-eight cents and sell them for forty cents a dozen." Then I asked, "Do you know how much profit you will make on today's order?" He immediately answered, "One dollar and forty-four cents." With that he calmly and slowly walked to his locker, got his books, and sauntered out.

Although Miss C began her study of Chester on October 1, it was December 8 when Chester began to come to her to divulge things that mattered deeply to him, and it was after Christmas before he began to stay around after school in order to be with her. On January 5 Miss C states explicitly that she let Chester do most of the talking and learned that the children got few toys and that his electric train had to be shared with his brother. Chester's effort at formulating a philosophy of Christmas giving then came out very easily because Miss C had accepted everything that went before. Perhaps Miss C asked Chester too many questions when Chester was staying to talk with her on February 19, for she got only the bare outline of his relationship with Tom Jones and not too much about Chester's feelings, except the wistful admission that Tom probably would be leaving him to go to the movies on Tuesday afternoon. Again on February 27 we find Chester telling Miss C about plans close to his heart—how he would go to the summer camp. Then he showed some pride in the fact that he was earning the money to go and revealed much initiative in the various ways he described for earning this money. Perhaps there was even a little justified swagger when he looked at the clock and said to his appreciative friend, "I must be going. I have to deliver twelve dozen doughnuts today." Certainly it was pleasant to him to recount the success of his business venture to a person who valued him and would make no unfavorable comparison with his brother in response.

The other case records presented earlier also include good examples of informal conversations, such as those of John Anderson presented in Chapter 1. His conversations with his teacher about his worries, the hoped-for birthday party, and what followed revealed his effort to make her think of him as valued at home. Then his developing security with her made it possible for him to get the psychological relief of confessing frankly to her that his birthday had not been nice, that he had had no party, nor even a cake prepared especially for him. It is difficult to communicate to teachers the emotional healing that comes to children when they have someone with whom they can converse in this open and frank way about their feelings, anxieties, aspirations, and plans. Such conversations frequently provide the emotional catharsis and ensuing reassurance about their own value and worth which frees children for learning in the classroom.

GENERAL CONSIDERATIONS

It has been pointed out several times that the development and behavior of a child or youth can be understood only by persons who have three resources, namely, valid scientific knowledge, a considerable body of facts about the individual to be understood, and self-discipline in carrying out the specific steps in the scientific method of arriving at judgments. We have found that there are seven sources of information which a teacher can tap in order to understand the child to the depth required for good judgments when dealing with him in the classroom. Learning to tap these sources of information effectively constitutes and involves training in the scientific method.

It is our practice in our child-study groups to have participants read to the group the material they have gathered about the children. If a teacher reads a succession of anecdotes, each one in turn is evaluated by the group as to the extent to which it meets each criterion of a good anecdote. In this way each participant gradually is disciplined by the group to be objective, to be specific, and to include descriptions of the clues that influence his judgment and feeling about the meaning of the situation for the child. In like manner, cumulative records are combed for facts rather than recorded opinions about the child. Reports of home visits are analyzed to discover things which the visitor observed but failed to record, and recorded evaluations are questioned until the supporting facts are brought out or the opinion deleted. Conferences with other teachers are scanned by the group in the same manner. Thus the group process is utilized constantly to train participants to value and record facts, to be specific and descriptive in what they write, and to defer interpretations until they are systematically canvassed in the group by agreed-upon scientific methods of manipulating data to get validated conclusions.

CHAPTER 7

Organizing Information

It goes without saying that no teacher ever will have a perfect understanding of each of his pupils. Not even therapists achieve this with their patients; and we are far from desiring to develop teacher-therapists. What we are aiming at is simply to help teachers get a professionally functional understanding of their pupils, an understanding deep enough to permit a preponderance of wise decisions in the classroom. Of course, every teacher will continue to make mistakes, but the number of mistakes can be greatly reduced. Concretely, what the school is striving for is to promote the effective learning by each child of the specific knowledge and skills he needs and to help each one take the developmental steps necessary to the realization of his potentials as a self and as a socially useful person.

In order to help in this process, the teacher must identify the positive forces in the child and in his life situation which can be counted upon to facilitate the needed learnings, adjustment, and development. Equally, the teacher must understand the negative forces which are blocking or hindering the child, for these forces must be eliminated, neutralized, or compensated for in order to make the necessary learning possible and to relieve maladjustments already operating.

The Importance of Organizing Information

Understanding cannot be achieved in a hit-or-miss fashion. The teacher needs some sort of guide for analyzing each child which will call attention to the major dynamics that are operating to shape his behavior and adjustment. The use of such a guide will enable the teacher to discover how each of these forces is operating in the particular child's life, whether or not he has enough information about the individual to assess each dynamic, and specifically what further information he needs. Given the necessary information in each area and the necessary scientific background, the teacher will be able to describe the forces that are operating within each child's body and self-organization, the relationships with other persons that are affecting his security, belonging, and social functioning, and the expectations and demands that are impinging upon him in his home, school, peer-group, and community.

When the teacher has such a definition of operating forces, he can then proceed to study their interaction to shape the child's behavior in various situations. The ensuing understanding of, or insight into, the child as a dynamic unit or self will then make it possible for the teacher to identify ways of utilizing constructively his motivations, avoiding pressures that antagonize him or paralyze his learning, and eliminating or neutralizing the forces that evoke undesirable behavior or block learning. These understandings and insights and these identified ways of helping the child will constitute the bases for the teacher's perceptions of the child in the classroom. The meaning or significance of the child's words or actions in the classroom will then be "understood" correctly by the teacher, and his quick reactions to what he perceives will have a high probability of being helpful to the child.

A FRAMEWORK FOR ANALYZING A HUMAN BEING

In the case of Jane we identified sixteen factors or forces that interacted to inhibit her learning and to evoke the undesirable ways of behaving which her teacher described in the anecdotal material. Then we listed eleven factors operating in all children and youth to shape their motivations and behavior. This list of forces was arrived at empirically through years of experience in studying the learning and behavior of school children by means of the case records their teachers prepared about them. The problem now is to define a framework of concepts that will be most serviceable in guiding teachers in their practical analysis of children and youth.

If one examines the sixteen factors which operated to shape Jane's behavior, or the eleven which operate in all children and youth, it will be clear that all of these can be subsumed under three general headings which identify the points of origin of these forces. The three general headings could be: physical organism, society, and self. In experiments with an organizing framework which employed these three major headings, we found that the necessary subheadings under these chief categories are so many and so diverse that teachers become confused by the complexity of the interrelated parts and are unable to bear them all in mind when thinking about a particular child. We have also tried out organizing frameworks with ten major headings and with six major headings. Our experience indicates that the six-area framework is the most workable of the three, although there still remain areas in it where teachers often become confused. Teachers find it possible to remember easily the six major topics, together with most of the subheadings that must be subsumed under each. Accordingly we are presenting in this chapter the six-area framework that we have been using for some time, but we by no means feel that it is final or the only useful framework that could be developed. We recognize that the choice of area topics is entirely arbitrary and for convenience. We have been influenced by the desirability of highlighting certain dynamics in children's development which often have been missed by teachers in their efforts to understand the pupils with whom they work.

The framework followed in the third year of our child-study program varies slightly in details from that used in the second year because in the third year we can count on certain insights which may still have to be learned during the second year of work with us. Consequently the framework given below more closely resembles that used in the third year than that used in the second year. Also the details of our framework have not heretofore been committed to writing, so the details also will vary from those presented by one or another of our consultants.

A FRAMEWORK FOR ANALYSIS

1. *Physical Factors and Processes*
   a. Growth rate and physical-maturity level.
   b. Characteristic rates of energy output, of fatiguing, of recovery from fatigue, and characteristic rhythms of activity and rest.
   c. State of health, health history, and health habits.
   d. Physical limitations and handicaps, how they are managed by the individual, and how the individual thinks and feels about them.
   e. How the individual uses his body, including game skills.
   f. Attractiveness of face, physique, and grooming in terms of their impact on adults, peers, and self.
2. *Love Relationships and Related Processes*
   a. Relationships of the individual with each parent and sibling and how these relationships are expressed.
   b. Relationship between the parents, between each parent and each sibling, and between the various siblings, and how these relationships are expressed.
   c. Relationship between each of the above individuals and any other adults living in the home and how these relationships are expressed.
   d. Relationships of the individual with pets and how these relationships are expressed.
   e. How difficulties in relationships within the family are managed by the individual and by others in the family.
   f. Relationship of the individual to any person outside the family who sincerely values him personally and who becomes a source of security to him, such as teacher, neighbor, relative, scoutmaster, priest or pastor, psychiatrist, nurse, etc.

3. *Cultural Background and Socialization Processes*
   a. Subcultures carried by the family and the characteristics of these cultures: masculine–feminine, rural–urban, regional, ethnic, social-class, caste.
   b. Processes by which the child is internalizing these cultural factors.
   c. The functioning of the individual in the school as a social institution.
   d. The functioning of the individual in other community institutions and social processes: church, play and recreation; earning, saving, and spending money; scouts; 4-H clubs; museums, etc.
   e. Progress in the individual's internalization of the wider American culture through school-mediated, family-guided, and community-available experiences.
   f. The individual's concepts of and feelings about the American society, his sense of how its present institutions and processes have evolved gradually through the roles played by individuals and groups in the past, and his sense of his own responsibility for playing roles that will maintain and develop it further.
   g. Inconsistencies which may exist between the cultures the individual is internalizing at home, or in his neighborhood, and the expectancies that are pressed upon him at school, in his church, in business or industry, or by the government.
   h. Special pressures felt by the child if his family is geographically or social-class mobile or if he elects to become mobile himself.
   i. Special pressures felt by the child if his family belongs to an ethnic group in a minority in his community or to a caste-discriminated racial group.

4. *Peer-group Status and Processes*
   a. Characteristic activities of the individual's peer group, roles available in these activities, knowledge and skills required for these roles, customs and codes of behavior of the peer group, and personality characteristics esteemed by the peer group.
   b. Roles sought and won by the individual in his peer group, and the status accorded him through this role playing.
   c. Failures of the individual to win desired roles in the peer group and the causes of these failures in terms of lack of knowledge or skills, failure to follow peer-group customs or codes, lack of the necessary personal characteristics or the possession of unacceptable personality characteristics, or inappropriate behavior.
   d. How the individual manages himself when he fails to win peer-group roles or when he fails to play accorded roles successfully.
   e. The effects of physical, affectional, and cultural factors upon the individual's peer-group status and role playing.

5. *Self-developmental Factors and Processes*
   a. The individual's *conception of himself and feelings about himself*, as influenced by physical processes and factors, love relationships and related processes, cultural background, socialization processes and social experiences, peer-group status and processes.

    b. How the individual's many-sided *conception of himself influences his perception* of situations, or the meaning that each successive experience has for him.

    c. The individual's unique accumulation of experiences and the *meanings,* including both knowledge and skills, which he has *distilled out of* these *experiences,* meanings which *constitute his conceptions of the universe, of society, and of events.*

    d. How the individual's many-sided *conception of the universe, of society, and of events influences his perception* of persons and situations and his perception of their meanings for him.

    e. The *conceptions* and feelings the individual has *of the relationships* that exist *between himself* (as he conceives himself) *and the universe, society, other individuals and events* (as he conceives them). These conceptions of relationship between self and universe, self and society, and self and others are the bases of the individual's attitudes, codes of conduct, philosophy of life, and values.

    f. The individual's potential and operating capacities and aptitudes for learning and doing, as evaluated objectively through tests and subjectively by persons who have interacted functionally with him through time.

    g. The mental processes which the individual habitually uses to work out the meanings for himself, for others, and for society of various experiences and situations, including symbolizing, abstracting and generalizing, reasoning, and imagining.

    h. The long-term purposes and the immediate goals which the individual reveals through his behavior; and the patterns of action which he permits himself to use as he works toward these goals and purposes.

    i. The conceptions which the individual's parents, siblings, teachers and peers have of him as a person and the expectancies as to his behavior and competencies which result from these conceptions.

6. *Self-adjustive Factors and Processes*

    a. The quality of the individual's feelings about his own physical adequacy. Whether he feels: abundantly adequate, physically sufficient to meet situations, physically limited as to what he can undertake, physically handicapped in what he must undertake, physically inferior to others, or physically ill.

    b. The quality of the individual's feelings about his love relationships: is completely secure in his sense of being loved, intermittently feels loved and unloved, is uncertain and confused about whether he is loved, feels unloved and therefore essentially alone, feels actively rejected by those whom he wants to love him.

    c. The quality of the individual's feelings about being socially significant: constantly feels socially important, intermittently feels socially important, feels himself to be without social importance, feels in conflict with the expectancies and demands of social processes, feels actively excluded from social roles, feels antisocial.

d. The quality of the individual's feelings about his status among his peers and about the roles accorded him in peer-group activities: feels that he is a high-prestige person privileged to play leadership roles, feels that he belongs and effectively plays roles in the group, feels anxious about his belonging because he only intermittently wins roles, feels isolated and without significance to the peer-group, feels in conflict with peers about his roles and status, feels actively rejected by peers who refuse him roles.

e. The quality of the individual's feelings about his adequacy as a total person, as a self: feels he can face successfully whatever comes, feels reasonably adequate to meet life, feels that he may fail to achieve some goals but will succeed in others, feels that success or failure depends upon luck, feels he is more likely to fail than to succeed in any task, feels he is sure to fail at everything.

f. The individual's way of acting when he is experiencing any of the feelings listed above, or particular combinations of them.

g. The adjustment patterns used by the individual when some of the unpleasant feelings listed above are experienced repeatedly or at a high level of intensity: rationalization, withdrawal, projection, compensation, fantasy, creative activity, sublimation or others.

h. Whether the individual is facing continuing adjustment problems that are limiting or damaging his conception of self, distorting his conceptions of the universe and of society, warping his felt relationship with persons, group, or society.

i. Whether the situations giving rise to continuing adjustment problems are being altered for the better or worse by known factors, and whether the effects of these continuing problems are being neutralized by known factors.

j. Whether the individual's continuing adjustment problems are of such severity that therapeutic assistance is necessary.

Synthesis and Planning

When participants are able to describe the child adequately in each of the six areas of the framework, they are ready to look again at the child as a whole, as a functioning person, and to make some professional judgments about him. These judgments are implied by the following questions:

1. On what developmental tasks is the individual working?

2. What adjustment problems is the individual facing?

3. What assets are available to facilitate the accomplishment of his developmental tasks and the solving of his adjustment problems?

4. What liabilities are making it difficult for him to accomplish his developmental tasks and to solve his adjustment problems?

5. What constructive action is possible at school to assist the individual in his development and adjustment?

6. If the constructive action possible at school is clearly inadequate,

what therapeutic resources are available and what steps must be taken to ensure the use of these resources?

Organizing Knowledge

In practice we do not call the framework presented above "A Framework for Analyzing a Human Being." We call it simply "An Organizing Framework." Everything that has been included in the framework is there because research or clinical study has shown that it is a vital factor or process underlying the flow of behavior or shaping the development of the individual. Teachers already know many of the scientific facts and concepts concerning the causation of behavior and development, but rarely is their knowledge organized into an integrated explanatory system which they can use for analyzing and understanding an individual child. Usually this knowledge is piecemeal and unorganized. This is one reason why teachers so frequently oversimplify their interpretations of why a child acts as he does and accept a valid partial explanation as the entire cause of behavior. Consequently, a major use of the framework presented above is to help school people organize their knowledge according to a system of concepts which can be used as a basis for the valid analysis of a child's motivations and needs.

Locating Areas of Ignorance

A second important use of the framework is to help the individual teacher discover what needed scientific knowledge he lacks. Reading the framework usually reveals to the teacher that he is ignorant of a number of the factors or processes mentioned or does not understand their significance for school learning and human development. Such discoveries define for the individual the scientific knowledge he must seek. In other words, the framework makes it possible for the individual to diagnose his areas of ignorance and to undertake a systematic program of reading and study to fill the gaps in his knowledge.

Organizing Information about the Child

A third use of the framework is to help the participants in the child-study program organize the facts they are gathering about a child in such a way as to facilitate the analysis of him. This can be done either individually or as a group activity. The teacher reads what he has recorded about a child from each source used and asks himself concerning each item: What does this tell me about the child, and why might it be important? Does it tell me something about him in physical terms, such as growth, energy, health habits, handicaps, skills, or attractiveness? Or does it tell me something about the climate of feeling in which he lives and how it affects his sense of security and his concept of himself? Does it tell me something about the culture he is internalizing at home or at school, or about how he is meeting cultural expectancies and demands at home and in the community? Does this material show the child playing roles in the peer group, reacting to failure to win the role he wanted, or trying to attract favorable attention from his peers and so build himself up with them? Does this item reveal something of how the individual thinks and feels about himself? Does it indicate a capacity greater than I had expected or show a failure to use a capacity which I know to exist? Does it reveal a goal he is pursuing, a code of conduct he is following, or a value that is beginning to be clarified in his self-organization? Does it betoken a persisting adjustment problem that is bothering him, or demonstrate an adjustment pattern on which he has become dependent?

When the participant sees that the item tells him something about one of the six areas in the framework, he inserts the number of the area on the margin of the page beside the item to remind him to use this item when he is pulling together his information about the child in this area. More often than not an item will be relevant to several areas, and when this is true the teacher writes the numbers of all the areas about which the item gives information. This procedure makes it unnecessary for the participant ever to reorganize his child-study record by rewriting data under appropriate headings. It also makes it unnecessary for him to read irrelevant data when trying to analyze a specific group of forces operating in a child's life. In other words the numbering of the items permits the quick scanning of the total record whenever the teacher wants to interpret some aspect of a child's life situation or the totality of forces (motivations) that are interacting to shape his behavior and development.

Interpreting an Area within the Framework

In practice, our study groups utilize this framework to take a specific series of steps leading to an understanding of the forces that are acting within and upon the individual. At any time after a significant quantity of data has been recorded and classified with the aid of the designating numbers, a teacher or the group can begin to form hypotheses about the dynamics operating in any or all of the six areas.

The first step is to formulate a series of specific questions to be answered by the facts in a given area. These questions, of course, are based upon our synthesis of knowledge derived from the sciences that study human beings. The available data in an area are then canvassed to see what answers they support for each of these questions, and the answers in turn describe the forces that are acting upon or within the child in this area. The procedure for classifying the data and for formulating answers on the basis of available data will be illustrated shortly in the case of Timothy Thyme, as will the later steps of analysis and planning.

Spotting Gaps in Information

When each question in an area has been answered as well as possible on the basis of the available data, it will become clear that additional data are needed to validate tentative answers and to provide new answers. The specific data needed and the possible sources are then defined for the guidance of the teacher who is gathering the data. Usually this process is carried on area by area throughout the framework.

Discovering Developmental Tasks and Adjustment Problems

When a reasonable number of tentative answers in each area has been found, the process of synthesis is begun. The individual who has been artificially segmented for purposes of analysis is put together again and viewed as a functioning unit. This process takes the form of listing the developmental tasks and adjustment problems upon which the child or youth is working. Then the various assets and liabilities in the child's life situation are listed, and the group arrives at a fair picture both of the individual's motivations and needs and of the forces that have made him what he is and are shaping the flow of behavior which confronts his teacher. With this knowledge, the teacher can begin to see a child's school experiences through his eyes and can perhaps even share his feelings in specific situations.

Planning How to Help the Child

The next step consists of considering what changes in conditions and relationships and what new experiences would be most helpful to the pupil in taking his next developmental steps and in working out a healthy adjustment to his life situation. This, of course, is the practical pay-off of the analysis. We have already seen in the cases of Jane and Chester that it is entirely possible and practical for a teacher with insight to help children who face formidably difficult life situations. Teachers are always able to figure out a practical way of helping a child once they understand him. Ordinarily, when consultants first begin to work in a school system, they are faced with a stream of teachers who ask, "What can I do about a child who . . . ?" Naturally we are unable to respond because the undesirable behavior is only a symptom. It is, then, really thrilling, after two or three years of work with these teachers, to hear one say, "You are going to hear the case record of my Joe today in our meeting. You will see what he is up against and that he has improved somewhat. But I am anxious to find more ways of helping him, because I know that he is capable of doing still better. After you have heard the record, please make a lot of suggestions about things I could do to help him."

Continuing Guided Observation

The continuing task in the work of child-study participants is perpetually to record descriptions of the child in action and needed facts about his life situation throughout the year. This continual guided observation has a number of important purposes. It supplies facts which ultimately may refute certain tentative hypotheses and confirm others, thus yielding deeper insight into the dynamics that shape the child's behavior and development. It provides the most practical way of testing the validity of all the hypotheses that have been made about him. And, most important, it provides the means of evaluating the effectiveness of the steps that are being taken to facilitate his learning, his development, and his adjustment. Finally it records changes which are occurring in the dynamic constellation of forces playing within and upon him and demonstrates that the individual is growing, changing, and fulfilling his potentialities to the degree made possible by the factors in his private world. For there is no final solution to any child's problem, just as there is no complete or ultimate self-realization for the individual. Instead. there are processes operating over a period of time, and the teacher is privileged to become, for a period, the source of significant dynamic elements in each child's constellation of developmental and limiting forces.

Using the Dewey-decimal System

The processes of case analysis by which a teacher can arrive at insights into a child's developmental tasks and adjustment problems and see the forces that shape his behavior are illustrated in the case of Timothy Thyme. The group classified the material gathered by Timothy's teacher under the six areas of the framework already described, using a Dewey-decimal system of classification in which the first number indicates the area to which the material is relevant. The numbers after the decimal point simply tell which item this is in the series of items classified under this area. The serial number permits easy reference back to a specific bit of material and also ensures against leaving out any items when making hypotheses.

THE CASE OF TIMOTHY THYME

I shall study Timothy Neil Thyme, a member of my seventh-grade English and history classes at X Junior High School. I chose him simply because he appeals to me—he has a sparkling personality that seems to reach out.

VITAL STATISTICS: Born June 11, 1939. Age 12 years 3 months.

PHYSICAL DESCRIPTION: Tim is in the shorter half of the class. He has dark-blondish straight hair and round blue eyes. His cheeks are
1.01 ruddy except when he is tired or ill. Tim has a high forehead and a
3.01 short, straight but not patrician nose. His mouth is not large, except
4.01 when grinning, and two dimples appear when he smiles. Tim's build is
6.01 stocky. His fingernails are stubby and chewed. He does not wear blue jeans as so many do, but wears corduroy pants, usually blue or blue-gray.

The study group classified this introductory paragraph under area 1 because it told so much about Tim's appearance and gave his birth date and age. They classified it under area 3 because his clothing betokened family taste (cultural or social class) a shade above his fellows, and under area 4 since he appeared different from his peers because of this clothing. The group felt that they would want to remember the chewed fingernails when they evaluated his adjustment problems because nail biting usually indicates emotional tension (area 6).

SEPT. 14 I have a great number of similar first names in my section
5.01 including two Timothys. Hence it becomes necessary to use nick-names. So Timothy Thyme volunteered to be called Tim in prefer-ence to Timmy. He said that he had been called Timmy all through elementary school and wanted it stopped.

The group classified this paragraph under area 5 because they thought it suggested Tim's concept of self and indicated that he was aware of himself in somewhat new terms. They felt that he was trying to use his entrance into junior high school as the occasion for establishing him-self at a higher maturity level both in his own mind and in the minds of others.

SEPT. 27 History Exam. Tim is writing busily; his lips move silently
1.02 as he writes. Occasionally he gazes into space; occasionally he bites a
5.02 nail, not in a nervous manner but as if a snag bothered him and he
6.02 wanted to get rid of it.

The group classified this anecdote under area 1 because it showed lip movement and nail biting, physical manifestations of tension. They classi-fied it under 6 for the same reason, and under 5 because it showed Tim holding himself to a task.

SEPT. 28 Standard procedure in the auditorium is to file out in a single line. Tim gave the boy in front of him, Bob, a healthy shove,
3.02 and a small tussle ensued. I motioned them out of line and back to
4.02 their seats and made them wait until the auditorium was clear. It wasn't necessary to lecture or punish them. Having to wait was suffi-

cient, for it was lunchtime and their entrance into the cafeteria was delayed.

The study group saw this episode as peer-group interaction that ran counter to good order in the school, so they classified it under 4 (peer group) and under 3 (adapting to a social institution).

OCT. 1   I passed by Tim's table at lunch. He was chatting with Sue,
4.03   who is in a beginning music class with him.
          Half an hour later Tim came into English class flushed and literally
1.03   dripping. Water was running down his face and dripping off his ears.
5.03   When I asked him what he had done, he grinned and said that he
          had stuck his head under a faucet to cool himself off. He also was
4.04   humming to himself. Then he got up and whispered to Bob and both
          of them giggled.

The group felt that this anecdote dealt mostly with peer-group matters—interaction with Sue and Bob and perhaps showing off a bit for his peers by coming in dripping. They also classified it under 1 because it showed him flushed from activity and finding a way to cool himself. Area 5 was mentioned because Tim obviously generalized that evaporating water cools the surface from which it evaporates. He was showing knowledge.

OCT. 2   Nominations for homework chairman were made. Tim was
4.05   nominated among others. He received three out of a possible thirty-
          four votes. Did not see who voted for him except that Sue was one.

It was recognized by the group that peer-group popularity often influences the way children react to each other in situations that are not strictly peer-group activities. They thought that this anecdote might help evaluate Tim's peer-group status.

3.03   OCT. 3   Tim stopped by the room on the way to gym, stuck his head
4.06   in the door and whispered "Hello" to me. I replied in kind. At
6.03   luncheon I observed that he was eating alone. After luncheon, before
          English, the rest of the children were moving around, talking, and
          some were reading over their assignment. They are not required to get
          quiet until the bell rings. Tim was gazing into space, his lips moving.

The study group classified Tim's friendly "Hello" to the teacher under area 3 as showing how he related to his teacher, an aspect of socialization. They noted that he was aloof from peers both at luncheon and afterward and so classified this in area 4. They wondered whether his absent-minded gazing into space indicated an emotional preoccupation, and so added area 6.

OCT. 8   Tim was asked by Bob to read something that the latter had
4.07   written. Tim made a quick comment but didn't exhibit much interest.
          Comment by math teacher at lunch: "That Tim Thyme of yours

is a sketch. The other day when we were having the standardized math tests in the auditorium, he raised his hand. But when Mr. Lanham

3.04 went to him to answer the question Tim patted Mr. L on the back and said, "Oh, that's O.K., I've got it now." Then in math class later he said, about a certain problem, "My father says it can't be proved."

2.01 He was really amazed when we did prove it and said, "Boy, wait 'till I tell him."

Tim watched eagerly as I filled the big desk inkwell. I deliberately

3.05 dribbled a little on the side to see what he would do. He became very

5.04 excited, leaped up from his seat and quietly asked the class, "Any-

6.04 body got a blotter?" I handed him a Kleenex and he carefully wiped it off.

The study group classified the first paragraph under peer-group inter-action. They felt that the second paragraph showed how he related him-self to a teacher and so classified it under socialization. Tim's mention of his father showed his relationship to the latter permeating his school-work; hence was classified as area 2. The last paragraph showed Tim helping Miss Riley and was classed as socialization. His initiative in be-ing useful was thought to indicate an attitude and was placed in 5. His excitement was classified as area 6.

5.05 OCT. 9 Tim quietly came in and sat during the time before the

4.08 9 o'clock bell, reading *Microbe Hunters* by Paul deKruif.

3.06 Oh, the powers of mental telepathy. I had fully made up my mind to invite myself to Tim's lunch table today when he stuck his head in the door and asked me to sit with them. (I had informed the class on the first day that I didn't want to intrude on them and would come to their tables only on invitation.) I still can't quite believe this coin-cidence.

Tim's reading of *Microbe Hunters* was classified under 5, the self-de-velopment area, as indicating an interest, and under 4 because he was behaving differently from most of his classmates at this time. His invita-tion to Miss Riley was classified under socialization.

AT LUNCH. When I arrived most of the children were at the table, but Tim was not. About five minutes later he came running up but took no notice of my presence. He put his lunch by a chair at the

4.09 opposite end of the table and quietly said to Mary, "Save me a seat."

3.07 When he returned with his milk he saw there was no stool at the place where he had put his lunch. He also saw me. He asked if there

1.04 were a chair next to me. I nodded, so he sat down and took out a tuna sandwich. He also felt the bag. "Bet there's a banana." Then, looking, "Yep. That means one every day for three weeks."

The study group noted that Tim tried to sit by Mary but she did not save a place for him. This they classified as area 4. His interaction with the teacher they classified as socialization, and the content of his lunch as area 1, bearing on his eating habits.

"Where were you?" I asked. "Music," he replied. "What have you
5.06   learned?" "Two notes." I laughed, and he grinned. "I'll play those
6.05   notes until I know them well!" "Do you play alone?" "No, Sue,
4.10   Ed, Bob, and Jim are all playing flute. Al is learning trombone. We
all play together."

The study group felt that this conversation indicated Tim's interest in
music, which they classified in the self-development area. His manner
of replying to Miss Riley they took to be humor and therefore classified
as area 6, and the naming of the peers with a common interest they put
under area 4.

1.05   Bob came up and asked Tim if he was going skating, and when Tim
4.11   said yes, they made arrangements to meet. Tim then said to me, "I
3.08   have a hard time with these clubs 'cause I have a paper route." "That's
nice," I said. "What do you do with the money?" "Put it in the
bank," he replied. When I looked surprised, he said, with twinkling
eyes and a grin, "I'm going to college, you know." "Oh," I said,
3.09   "where?" "I'm not sure, but I'll probably do as my father did—
5.07   Brown, M.I.T., and then Harvard." "Good land, why three colleges?"
2.02   "Brown for general education, M.I.T. for electrical engineering, Harvard for physics. I may not do the last; may get some pre-med and be
half doctor and half scientist, like a microbe hunter."

The study group considered that the skating showed a physical skill
—area 1; the arrangement to go with Bob was peer-group interaction—
area 4; the paper route showed effective functioning in society, area 3;
the family tradition of going to college indicated cultural background,
also area 3; the tendency to follow the father could be cultural or
affectional, so area 2 was included; and the planning for the future was
an aspect of self-development, area 5.

4.12   Al leaned over and said, "Tim's father is Father Thyme." "Yeah
5.08   and I'm T.N.T.," said Tim, and the first one of us who has a kid is
6.06   going to have Thyme on his hands."
Tim said that his father is working with a Mr. S—"He's the man
3.10   who invented the ignition coil and the only man who's richer than
5.09   he is is Ford." Then, snapping his fingers, Tim said, "Got to remember
to plant that corn!" He went on to say that he was going to experiment
with it at home this winter. Then he excused himself and threw away
his trash, explaining that he had used the same bag for his lunch for
five days and that he thought that was enough. With that he went
outside.

The joking by Al about the family name was considered peer-group
interaction, area 4; and the further play on words by Tim was seen as
humor, area 6. The work of the father and Tim's knowledge about Mr.
S was regarded as socialization, area 3, and Tim's interest in science was
classified as area 5. Tim's thriftiness in using the same bag five times
was taken as a self-developmental characteristic, area 5; his politeness

in excusing himself and disposing of his trash properly was seen as more socialization, area 3.

4.13   When I remarked about something, "You'll do that over my dead body," Bob leaned over and asked Tim, "How many points?" "About fifteen, I'd say," replied Tim. "What goes on?" I asked. "You get 10 points for knocking down a lady, 15 for a lady with glasses, and 20 for a lady on crutches with a seeing-eye dog," said Tim. "What in the world . . . ?" They both giggled and Tim said this was something that hot-rod drivers had thought up. "My brother drives one."

The study group regarded this as peer-group lore, area 4, and as peer-group humor.

5.10   Oct. 11   Just corrected standardized spelling tests. Tim has fifth grade minus, which means that he didn't quite make the fifth-grade score. The highest score made was 6 points above ninth-grade ability, the lowest was at fourth-grade level. So Tim was second from the bottom of the group. 12 of the group scored at the ninth-grade level, 9 at the eighth-grade level, 3 at the seventh-grade level, and 3 at the fifth-grade level. Tim's IQ is 120 on Otis Alpha and Gamma tests.

The group classified this material in area 5, as showing Tim's capacity for learning (IQ) and his very low relative accomplishment in spelling.

2.03   I forgot to record earlier that I met Tim's mother at P.T.A. As there were forty parents there I didn't get much chance to talk with her. She did say, however, that she was surprised that he wanted to be called Tim.
Most of the mothers are around thirty-five to forty, or else look to be that age, so I was surprised that Mrs. Thyme looks more grandmotherly.

The group classified the mother's attendance at P.T.A. and her comment on the use of the name Tim as area 2.

4.14   Oct. 15   Before a.m. class. Tim is sitting at his desk reading The
5.11   Twenty-one Balloons, by duBois. The other members of the section are visiting and catching up on week-end news.

1.06   Later.   Tim came rushing up to me as I entered the room. He had been outside, cheeks ruddy, panting, excited. "Have a very dear little present for you," said he, opening his hands, which were cupped.
3.11   There was a black and orange, fuzzy caterpillar. I oohed and ahed
5.12   and admired it, accepted it upon my finger. But I drew the line at
6.07   letting it eat the plant on my desk and said it had best return to its home outside. When I put it out the window, Tim was pseudo-upset about this being done.
2.04   After class Tim told me that he has two brothers and a sister, Mike, Susan, and Jeff, each of them four years apart. "You see when one gets out of college another goes in. My father planned it that way."
6.08   "What is today? Monday? Papers [in a groaning voice]! I'm so darn sick . . ." and he broke off.

Tim's tendency to prefer reading to mixing with the other children was classified under areas 4 and 5. His bringing the caterpillar to the teacher was taken as indicating his relationship to her, area 3, and his interest in living things, area 5. His comments about his siblings and father developed the group's picture of the family constellation—area 2. The fact of delivering papers was also area 3, whereas the groans over delivering papers showed the emotional cost of continuing his money-earning project—area 6. His excitement over the caterpillar was area 6.

4.15   Oct. 16 We were playing "Twenty Questions" before class. Tim guessed one subject (my glasses), and was the one to give the next topic. His topic, guessed in eleven guesses, was the banana in his lunch.

           Vocabulary review. Tim missed "consternation" and "ecstasy."
5.13   He pronounced both but didn't know their meanings.

           After school. The local roller-skating rink is reserved for our school on Tuesdays, so some of our section went skating. When I arrived,
1.07   Tim was whizzing around the rink like a small tornado, weaving in and out, paying no attention to the music. He was not, however, rough-necking. As he swept by, he urged me to get on the rink. I had not
4.16   been skating for over ten years, so I was enjoying comparative safety
3.12   on the sidelines. When I did venture on, Tim would skate up to within six inches of me in back, dodge around in front and then zoom on.

The group saw Tim's success at "Twenty Questions" and his skating skill as peer-group assets, hence the 4.15 and 4.16 classifications. The vocabulary-review report helped define his knowledge limitations, area 5. His skating skill showed how well he can manage his body, area 1; and his interaction with Miss Riley gave further evidence of his feelings for and good relationship with her, area 3.

           Various bits of information were gleaned. Tim said that his sister
2.05   is now at Stanford and one brother is at U. of Wisconsin. The other
3.13   brother is attending Grant High School. The one at Wisconsin is
5.14   going to go to Princeton to study theology. "He doesn't seem very religious to me. I can't imagine him a minister. He doesn't belong in the family. I don't like church—it makes me sleepy."

The character of the expectancies that family members hold for each other begins to appear. It would seem in part to be a function of their cultural level. Hence the group classified this material under areas 2 and 3. Tim's own attitude toward church and having a minister in the family was classified in area 5.

           During one of the periods of relaxation, I smoked a cigarette. Tim
3.14   came flying by and registered pseudo-horror. On the next trip around he yelled, with a grin, "Fiend."
           Bob and Tim came up. Bob said that Al was mad because he had

4.17   skated with Al's girl. "Is he mad at Tim, too? Tim skated with her."
"No, everyone knows who Tim's girl friend is—Sue." Sue is in another
class section across the hall. She lives down the street from Tim.
1.08   There was none of the usual adolescent boy–girl reaction—no giggling or sighing. It was more like the younger children who come
home from the first grade and say, "So and so is my girl friend."
About five minutes before we had to leave the rink, the wheels on
1.09   the front of one of Tim's skates came loose, making it impossible for
him to skate on it. He promptly sat down, removed the defective skate,
and went on skating on one skate, the other foot covered only by a
stocking. He went faster on one skate than most were going on two.

Tim's kidding of his teacher about smoking was taken as further evidence of the character of his relationship to her. The comments about
his skating with Al's girl friend and about Sue as his girl friend showed
more about the peer-group structure. The distinctly childlike pattern
of this marked Tim as still in his childhood rather than approaching
pubescence; hence it was classified as area 1. His great skill in skating
on one foot was further evidence of his ability to manage his body and
so was given another 1.

3.15   Oct. 18   Tim came up from lunch carrying a pocketbook. He grinned
4.18   at another teacher and me and said, "Us girlies gotta have our pocket-
6.09   books." He returned it to Nancy to whom it belonged.
Tim then made a remark about having no time to study. "Too
much radio and television, eh?" I said. "We don't have a radio or
3.16   television," he replied. I expressed surprise. "Well, we live in a neighborhood of ten lawyers, that ought to tell you," he countered. I said
that I didn't understand, and he explained that in comparison with
lawyers, scientists are poor.
Tim's science teacher reports that Tim came into the room singing
1.10   doo-de-doo-de-doo in a very childish voice. He then sang a child's
song in a high squeaky voice. When he left the room he did the
same.

The group saw the pocketbook episode as peer-group activity (area
4), socialization (area 3), and humor (area 6). They saw the conversation about the radio and the lawyer neighbors as internalized from comments at home, area 3. They felt that Tim's singing was spontaneous and
not show-off; his voice quality they took to be evidence of his level of
physical development, area 1.

3.17   Oct. 19   Tim held out his hands. "Look, I'm growing nails." "Good,
6.10   any special reason?" "Nope, just decided I needed them."

The group thought this exchange indicated Tim's growing security
to say what was on his mind to his teacher. They raised the question
whether this freedom to mention matters of intimate concern indicated
a growing affection—a close personal relationship that should be classified in area 2. They finally decided that this conversation was not dif-

ferent from what he might have said to most of his teachers; hence they classified it as area 3 rather than 2. They also thought that the anecdote showed Tim to be concerned with managing the ways he expressed his tension and so classified it in area 6.

OCT. 22   Tim brought a note this morning which said:

Dear Miss Riley,

Please excuse Tim at 11:45 A.M. after he finishes his lunch. We are going to see a surgeon about his thumb, which needs attention.

1.11   Very sincerely yours,

2.06   Anne R. Thyme

I have noticed this thumb, which has a discolored nail. I thought he had smashed it. I inquired about it and he said he "knocked a piece off it three years ago." "How?" I asked. "Oh, I was holding a boat away from the dock as we were coming in and . . ." here made a slicing motion which gave me a graphic picture.

The group thought this anecdote concerned a physical difficulty—area 1. They wondered why it had been permitted to run on for three years and so wanted to consider it when evaluating family relationships —area 2.

OCT. 23   Tim was absent this morning. He came in about eleven and gave me the following note:

Dear Miss Riley:

Please excuse Timothy as I am sick in bed and he had to stay home to help me.

2.07   Sincerely,

                                                                     Anne R. Thyme

I told Tim I was sorry and asked what was wrong. "Oh, it's something
5.15   like pa–pt–pa. . . ." "Ptomaine?" said I. "Yeah—comes from eating something." "By the way," I asked, "what did the surgeon say?" "Oh,
1.12   he chopped off part of the nail. He may take the rest off and just leave me a skin thumb." The discolored part was gone.

A home relationship, Tim's difficulty with words, and a physical factor were touched in this anecdote, the group judged.

OCT. 26   "Miss R, what happens if you forget your report again?"
3.18   "Fifteen minutes after school." Tim thereupon, with a pleased expression, placed his report card on my desk.

Report card:	English C+	Workshop S
	Art S	Math B
5.16	Gen. Science B+	Music S
	History B+	Gym S

LATER. I asked the class to write down their three greatest wishes. "Do you have to write three?" said Tim. "I only have one wish."

5.17 "O.K., just write down the one thing you want." Tim wrote: "Peace
6.11 on earth, good will toward men."

OCT. 29 I asked the section to write about their families. Below is what Tim wrote. All spelling, lack of punctuation, and insertions are exactly as were on his paper. The crossed-out word is supposed to be physicist.

> My family is made up of six people, Michael Thyme Jr. my oldest brother he is married He will graduate from the U of Wis. in Feb.
2.08 > with a Master's degree and hopt to go to Princeton and get his D.D. (He is 26 I think) Susan is the second 21 years old She is at Stanford
3.19 > Univ. Jeff is 16 has a hot rod (1937 Ford) is in Grant High takeing 5 Majeurs—He like cars and plans on the machanical side. Mother is
5.18 > 52 (I think) is the best cook as you can see (my stomach) Dad is 53 or 54 he is a ~~pishistis~~ scientis and a member of the Nateonal Ac. of Science He enjoy everything except war and some other things.

OCT. 31 Class was deciding on amounts to be given to the Red Cross. Tim said, "I think anyone who can't give twenty-five cents must
3.20 be awful poor and shouldn't be living in this area. They ought to be down in the slums or something." I spoke to Tim, explaining that
4.19 maybe some people didn't have a quarter. He said, "Then they ought to get a job. I work." "Maybe they don't have time to work because
5.19 they have to take care of younger brothers or sisters," I continued. "Then they should be paid for that," Tim replies. "Perhaps their parents can't afford to pay them." "Then they shouldn't live in this neighborhood."

The study group discussed Tim's tendency and capacity to go to the heart of things. Someone called attention again to the way Tim had summed up everything he wanted in life in terms of "Peace on earth, good will toward men." Evidently Tim is beginning to work on the task of establishing in his own mind the values to be sought in living. A certain altruism seems to be a central theme in his valuing, and obviously the Red Cross is an expression of it. He sets rather high the amount which he feels each one should give and is perhaps a little self-righteous when he says others should work to earn it if they don't have it. "I work."

Nov. 2 At the end of a conference with the principal, I asked if she remembered any of the Thyme children. "Oh, yes, I know them all."
3.21 "All? Tim is only in the 7A," I replied. "Oh, yes, he stopped in my office the other day and introduced himself." (This is most unusual
5.20 for any child in this school, as we have over 1,200 children. It is especially unusual for a 7A.)

4.20 Nov. 7 Other children busily straightening room, talking, picking up
1.13 trash. Some sitting quietly. Tim slid down in his chair, head resting on back, stretched, and yawned.

Nov. 8   The *Lincoln News*, the school newspaper, was on sale this
morning. The student representative sells it for 5 cents. The opening
3.22   period usually ends at 9:07. About twenty-eight out of the thirty-four
4.21   present bought a copy. Tim did not. All who bought a copy were
5.21   reading it, with others looking over their shoulders.

Tim and Bob had their books all ready to leave at 9:07 and waited
6.12   impatiently all the time until the bell rang. It was delayed in order
to give time to sell the papers. When it did ring, they rushed from
the room.

Members of the study group wondered whether this incident betokened lack of interest in peer-group activities, lack of school loyalty
and spirit, concern for more mature things than are usually printed in
school papers, or just plain stinginess on Tim's part.

The remainder of the record is reproduced with the classifications
which the group made recorded in the margin. The reasons which led
the group to classify the data as they did are not given. Readers may
wish to decide for themselves how they would classify the material.
Many of Tim's cumulative record and report cards were included in the
record. Many of the reports are not classified because we regarded them
as subjective opinions rather than facts. Wherever a fact has inadvert-
ently been included in such statements of opinion, it has been classified.
Of course, the reports do show the climate of feeling about him under
which Timothy was working with his various teachers.

Nov. 12   The assignment was to write an original composition on
Halloween or related subjects, such as ghosts, haunted houses, etc.
This is Tim's:

MASKS FOR HALLOWE'EN

*Halloween was probably first celebrated by the Romans on the first
day of November in honor of Pomona, the goddess of fruit trees.*

In England the Druids, probably from Italy, had the same celebra-
5.22   *tion but for the sun god. Then at Thanksgiving the same celebration
was held again.*

*In later times it was believed that the spirits of the dead arose and
came back. When food was left outside on the steps for the spirits it
was picked up by the beggers. This explains why the people believed
the spirits returned. At these celebrations masks were worn.*

*The first masks were used by the Egyptians to make the dead look
like they were alive. The mask was placed upon the mummy to aid
it in returning to life.*

*The Greeks used the mask in their plays because the arena stage
was so large people couldn't see the expression on the actors faces,
unless they were exaggerated. And so the idea of mask spread to other
parts of the world.*

*At Halloween we like to wear a mask because it changes our char-
acter and appearance.*

*This Halloween children in their Halloween costumes and here
in Park City (Eastern Metropolis) and other places will collect winter
clothes for the people in Korea.*

COMMENT AS ENGLISH TEACHER: Remarkable improvement in spelling. This probably indicates either copying or parental aid as he has not yet reached the stage where he can spell "exaggerated."

5.23

Nov. 15   The results of the Standardized English Test (reading) show Tim as 8A reading ability. In Vocabulary he ranked 7.5 (grade level) and in Comprehension 10th (grade level). The range of the class: lowest in ability, 8A, highest, 10B+; in Vocabulary, lowest, 7.5, highest, 10.7; in Comprehension, lowest, 6.2, highest 12.

5.24

The children who were interested in learning their scores were invited to remain at 3:00 today to learn them. About 12 stayed. Tim did not.

ELEMENTARY RECORD

Nov. 12   The cumulative record shows that Tim was living at the address where he now resides and attended the same elementary school from kindergarten through 6th grade.

3.23

Teachers' comments:	Talent & trait	Ones needing improvement
Kng. A	Sp. Tal. & Desirable char. traits well dev., very friendly, self-con- fident, industrious	Talkative
1A	" (these ditto marks	"
3A	" put in by teacher of 1A)	" but not annoying
4AB	Alert; industrious	Talkative
5B	" interest in poetry	
6B	Industrious, alert	

Attendance

	Days Present	Days Absent
Kng. A	66	10
" B	82	6
1A	84	6
1B	81½	12½
2A	81	3
2B	79½	11½
3A	80	4
3B	92	3
4A	80½	5½
4B	88½	2½
5A	not given	
5B	" "	3
6A	" "	1
6B	" "	1

1.14

Standardized Achievement

In 4A—Reading, 4B; Vocab., 4A
In 5A—Reading-Comp., 6½A; Vocab., 7½B; Arithmetic Fund., 7A; Prob., 11½A.
In 3A: IQ 116

In 4B: IQ 116
In 6A: "   120² (small 2 indicates 2 tests)
5.25   No names of standardized tests given. Spelling in 4B, 2½B.

REPORT CARDS

3.24   KNG. Nov. 1944   Timmy has adjusted nicely to the kindergarten
4.22   group. He seems to play and work happily with the other children.

APR. 13   Timmy is a very alert and responsive little fellow. He par-
5.26   ticipates in all the activities and has a cooperative attitude. His working habits are good.

FIRST GRADE—Nov. 15   Timmy is a well-rounded little boy. He
reads well, does his work neatly and accurately. He has a great deal
5.27   of poise—and a wealth of ideas.
Encourage Timmy to work without talking while other children
are in their reading groups.
Parent's comment: Timmy says he will try hard not to talk so much,
but "it is really difficult."

APR. 5   Timmy has not shown the growth in reading I would like to
see. He is attentive but does not seem to grasp the new words we
learn from day to day. If he could read a story every evening at
home from a book on his level, I am sure that improvement would
follow quickly.
No parent comment.

SECOND GRADE—DEC. 2, 1946   Timothy is a fine student—conscientious, cooperative. Full of enthusiasm and an insatiable curiosity. One weakness—unsatisfactory manuscript. However, he's been
striving toward improvement with great fervor.
Parent's comment: I am surprised Timmy has a check in "known
2.09   number facts." Dr. Thyme considers he has a very keen sense about
3.25   number facts. He shows other children how to do their number
work and can do some third-grade work. Maybe you have him confused with some other boy in the room. He also reads a great deal
at home.

APR. 14   Timmy continues to show great enthusiasm, alertness,
originality, and qualities of leadership. However, I'm sorry to report
5.28   a "slump" in spelling. His grades on weekly tests are quite low. May
I suggest one or two nights a week of study in that area?
Parent's comment: We are going to do our spelling so that we
will get A on the Friday test.

JAN. 30   Timmy is showing steady progress. I am pleased with the
effort he is making to improve his reading. He attempts new words
and is steady in his work habits. Timmy has been very helpful to
me. He is always willing and cheerful. He uses good judgment.

THIRD GRADE—APR. 8, 1948   Timmy's work shows steady progress.
6.13   He seems to enjoy his work and takes pride in doing it well. His
reading is improving. Timmy is very honest. He readily admits his
part in any difficulty and is always willing to share in his part of the
blame.

Timmy does help me a great deal, and I appreciate it.

Parent's comment: Timmy is very happy in your room. He seems to be so interested in everything and will hate to leave in June.

JUNE 23, 1948   Timmy has satisfactorily completed the 3B.

5.29   Timmy has been a fine student. He has been a great help to me, a very willing assistant.

Timmy's work has shown steady improvement. His spelling record has gone backward. He becomes impatient. A little more effort and it would improve.

FOURTH GRADE—Nov., 1948   Timmy is adjusting nicely to the work of his grade both in spelling and arithmetic. He needs, however, to improve in reading so that he may have more fluency in this subject.

Parent's comment: Timmy is reading at home so he should improve in reading.

JUNE 16, 1949 . . . completed work of 4B and has shown definite growth in all areas of activity. I am sure T will carry into 5A the

5.30   fine attitude of cooperation he has displayed with me. I wish him success in his new work.

FIFTH GRADE—APR. 4, 1950   We are all glad that Timothy is back

5.31   and have enjoyed hearing about the trip as well as seeing his well-made scrapbook. The class (as well as Timothy) has profited by his experiences. His classwork continues to be satisfactory in every way.

JUNE, 1950   I have enjoyed having Timothy in my class this year and wish him continued success in the sixth grade.

His scores in the recent standardized tests were excellent.

SIXTH GRADE—Nov., 1950   Timothy is interested. He wants to do well. His marks are very satisfactory. Timothy must try to control his lips. His talking is at times very disturbing and a great waste of class time.

Timothy's work continues to be satisfactory. He is trying to control his lips and there is decided improvement along this line.

JUNE 14, 1951   I have enjoyed the youngest of the Thyme's very much this year—he is really a live wire. Timothy should do very fine work at junior high. I know he will enjoy the new school, and my very best wishes for his success go with him.

Nov. 13, 1951   In English class, Tim's section was discussing nouns

5.32   —common and proper. The book gave a list of common nouns and the child was to give a proper noun—from general to specific.

2.10   Tim volunteered for "man" and gave "Dr. Thyme."

Nov. 16   Everyone is reading a story. Some are slouched in their chairs. Some have their books flat on their desks. Some are wiggling

6.14   while reading. Some are copying assignment from board. Tim is sitting up straight. Occasionally he nibbles a finger, brushes his hair off forehead, shades eyes with hand. Now he is writing. His lips move as he writes. He seems to be sounding out words, as I can hear a faint whisper and he sits four desks from my desk.

1.15   HEALTH RECORD. Had measles, tonsils out, eyes, teeth okay in elementary school.

1.16

Kng.	1st	2nd	3rd	4th	5th	6th	7th
Wt.	44	50	60	65	64½	75	missing	79
Ht.	43½	45½	49	51	52½	55	57	58½

Nov. 16

ME

5.33   I believe that life on earth is given to a person so that he might improve the world. Every one must die and we have no control over death. If a person is going to die he will if it is the will of God. I think a person should be doing something all the time. It is posiable for me to do this on week day but my mind stopps and I play during the week end. There is nothing that I don't like to learn about because I think a person shough know every thing that he can learn in the short time he is on earth.

6.15   The only thing I am afraid of is God.

I believe that war is to kill off the week and dumb and leave a better world.

4.23   I am week phyically I like sports but I cannot play them well.

I am one nervest reck.

Timothy

"Tim, I wanted to see you because of some things I wondered about. In reading over your analysis of yourself, I wondered about two things. One was about your statement about fearing God. What did you mean about it?"

5.34   "Well, I guess because God's the truth, and aren't you more afraid of the truth than the false?"

"Then you don't fear God as a power that causes death?"

"No, just because he's truth."

"What do you mean by that—what does it mean to you?"

Silence. He looked off, with a slight frown.

"Is it clear or vague?"

"Sorta vague."

"What about being a nervous wreck? Do you really feel you are?"

6.16   "Yes, I bite my nails."

"What makes you nervous?"

"I just feel that I oughtta keep doin' somethin'. When we're in history class and you're talking, I just gotta do somethin', so I bite my nails."

"You mean something physical?"

"Yeah, I guess so. But it's just doing something. That's why I don't want my father to get a television, 'cause then I know I'll be cooked! Guess I only have a week of freedom."

"Are you getting one next week?"

"Yeah, I guess so. I know I'll never get anything done."

"I wish I could do something to help this nervousness."

"Well, I just have to do something. F'instance, on Wednesday night, I had Scout meeting, I had English make-up, I had history and math homework, and it was wonderful. I had something to do."

I almost fainted! This is most unusual. We discussed a few more things, and he left.

Nov. 21 "Will you please eat lunch at table 28 today?"

3.26   "O.K., thank you."

"But I don't have a banana today."

6.17   "Well, in that case, I'm afraid I must refuse."

Delighted laugh.

The three things that have given me the most happiness in my life:

5.35   *1. My trips to the west coast.*

6.18   *2. The feeling of accomplishing some things while I have been*

2.11   *living.*

    3. That my father has been safe.

Nov. 26 I informed the class that their desks must be cleaned out—

3.27 that the fifth-hour class would empty all trash found in the desks on

5.36 the floor. Each one began to clean his or her desk. Tim went up and down his row and cleaned out each empty desk in his row. He was the only one who did this.

Tim is writing. The whole class is taking an exam. His lips are

6.19 moving, as if carefully sounding out words. It is not a slight movement, but more like someone learning to speak or as in singing when lip movements should be exaggerated.

We have made a chart showing tallest and shortest in the room.

1.17 The tallest boy—68½ inches; shortest—56½ inches. (Tim is fourth

4.24 from the shortest, 58½ inches.)

Weight goes from 134 to 64. Tim is second from bottom in weight.

Nov. 28 We were discussing poetry and the fact that people seldom

5.37 learn poems by heart any more. So they decided they would like to. Tim said he knew one and would like to recite it next Wed.

DEC. 3 The class was playing "Truth or Consequences." Contestants

4.25 were volunteers. Tim was third to volunteer, with shrinking and chewing his nails (faked). But, it was decided that it was a girl's turn, and Tim never did get called on.

DEC. 4 Volunteers for Santa Claus were called for—Tim volun-

4.26 teered. Since there were four who volunteered, it was decided to draw for the privilege.

Class was discussing price for Christmas tree. Tim raised his hand —"I don't see the sense of a Christmas tree. What do you accomplish by it?"

4.27 Bob, who was chairman of the social committee, said, "If you can't

5.38 afford to chip in twenty-five cents for a tree, you ought to be in the slums."

6.20 "I can chip it in, but I don't see what we accomplish by it."

It was put to a vote and five voted against it.

When voting for ice cream, Tim voted for five-cent cups. The choice was five-cent, ten-cent, and fifteen-cent cups.

5.39   Topic for panel discussion suggested by Tim: "Christianity versus Communism. Which will rule the world?"

          I was invited by a table, not Tim's, to eat lunch. I came out of
3.28   the teachers' cafeteria, carrying my tray and passed Tim's table. He looked up, smiled, and indicated a stool. I shook my head and pointed to the other table. He nodded and said, "Tomorrow?" and I said, "Yes."

          One of the members of a class who heard my case study helps in
3.29   the nursery school in the Episcopal church attended by the Thymes.
2.12   She spoke to the minister, who said, "She [Mrs. Thyme] is a very domineering person. She has great drive and pushes everything out of the way of her goal. Dr. Thyme is a complete scientist and rarely attends church."

4.28   DEC. 5   They drew for Santa Claus today, and Tim lost. So he becomes a mailman and delivers the cards.

          JAN. 8   Tim volunteered for maintenance man. He received eight
4.29   votes and was therefore eliminated from the first round of votes.

          JAN. 11   Tim was watching the rain turn to snow. He shouted, "It's
3.30   sticking," and was joined by Mike. Their conversation was general.
4.30   The row captains were reminded to mark rows. Tim looked around and said to Mike, "Edna [his row captain] never does anything 'cept sit on her ass."

          I reminded them of three things they must remember, one of which was to remind parents to attend P.T.A. to discuss a possible swimming pool for the area.
5.40   "If you want a pool, you'd better get your parents here," said I.
          "I don't," said Tim.
          "Don't want a pool?"
          "Nope."
          "Why not?"
3.31   "It just costs too much money. Put out a lot of money for that and some dumb president will come along and send more money to Europe or something, and taxes go up."

          JAN. 14, P.T.A.   Dr. and Mrs. Thyme came in to find out how Tim was doing. When I explained that his work was fine—average and
2.13   steady—Dr. Thyme was perfectly satisfied, but Mrs. T expressed a
3.32   desire that it would be higher.

          Dr. T asked about spelling, because, "as I remember mine, Tim's is very good."

          I replied that it must be congenital as Tim's is very poor, but improving.

          I remarked that he was very philosophical, and we discussed the
5.41   fact that he seems to have absorbed much of the family's thinking. "Tim seems to be the most serious one."

          Mrs. T said he was the youngest and therefore babied—"perhaps he's closer than the rest."

          Has regular jobs—cleaning floors, setting table, which he does
5.42   regularly and happily. He loves to cook and makes biscuits for dinner.

          Experiment with the corn is set up and when I expressed a desire to see it, Dr. T said I could if it's successful. If not, not another word will be said about it.

Dr. T was abrupt and definite in views: "There shouldn't be homework." "Tim's spelling was a result of too much experimentation in the schools"; "There shouldn't be a swimming pool—could better use the money to pay teachers a higher salary."

2.14

Mrs. T wasn't at previous P.T.A.'s because of illness.

(Sure hope I make it into that home.)

Forgot that I spoke to them about television set. They bought one mainly (according to them) to keep Tim home. It seems he was always visiting in neighbors' houses and watching.

Dr. Thyme mentioned that Tim was the only one who seemed interested in science and willing to do any scientific research.

JAN. 15   The class decided that they were not behaving as well as they should in math. They discussed ways and means of control and finally decided to institute a system of fines, to be administered by the sergeant at arms. They voted on the sum and five cents was suggested.

4.31
5.43

Tim arose and said, "I think it ought to be ten cents. Everyone has five cents and ten cents would mean more."

His motion was defeated.

Names were put up on the board as to those who were to be fined, and Tim's was there. He was fined ten cents, which meant he had been caught twice.

JAN. 17   Conversational items at random:

Not many at home interested in science. Learn so much there they don't need to study more.

4.32
1.18

First corn he planted died. "Don't know why; I kept them covered with water."

"Maybe you used too much," I suggested.

"Well, I did water them sorta vigorously. Mom can testify to that. She had to change my bed when I sprinkled too hard one day."

JAN. 21   Children were playing "Dr. IQ." Tim was chosen and asked a technical question about baseball. He just shook his head and said, "I don't know a thing about baseball."

5.44
3.33

FEB. 4

THE THREE PEOPLE I LIKE BEST

5.45
2.15

1. God because he is my creator.
2. My dad because he has taught me more about what I want to know than anyone.

2.16

3. My mother because she has taught me to like more things.

FEB. 12   I brought a planetarium, a setup with sun, earth, and moon which all revolve simultaneously. Tim said, "That's good, but you should see the one at the Planetarium in New York."

3.34
5.46

I suggested that some of the people houseclean their notebooks. "Why don't they buy these separators?" said Ed. "They only cost ten cents."

5.47

"I can't afford it," said Tim.

FEB. 12   "My mother's really a wheel at church. She's always up there.
She practically runs everything—secretary of this, treasurer of that.
2.17   She's never home. Sometimes she disagrees with the minister. She
3.35   thinks he doesn't run things right, and she really tells him off."
6.21   He also told me the second batch of corn for the experiment died.
5.48   A third batch is on its way.

FEB. 14   Tim gave one boy a valentine signed, "Guess by the writt-
4.33   ing." Ronnie came over to Tim and said, "I didn't have to guess the
5.49   writing. Look." He pointed to the spelling.
6.22   Tim asked me how to spell "writing" and I told him.
3.36   He laughed uproariously and said, "I guess I'm the only one in the
5.50   room that spells it that way. He didn't have to guess."
        (Opinion: He didn't seem embarrassed.) The whole group laughed
heartily.
        Tim gave me a very lovely valentine. I said I was highly compli-
mented that he felt he could afford it. He said, "I opened the second
vault!"

FEB. 19   All the children do their homework on a clean sheet of
paper. Each assignment is on a fresh sheet. Tim utilizes the space
5.51   below and will use a paper over and over until it is full. In my five
years of teaching, this is only the second time I have ever seen this,
and in junior high I've dealt with about two hundred children a
semester.

FEB. 20   Lincoln News (school newspaper) went on sale today. Two
people did not buy one. Tim was one of these people. He sat while the
purchasing was going on, with a look of patient disgust on his face—
mouth turned down, slightly pursed.
        I offered him mine to read. He shook his head.
6.23   "Are you sure you don't want to read it?" I asked.
5.52   "I don't, particularly. I know what's in it."
        But he took it and read it carefully.

FEB. 21   The boys reported to the gym for one half hour of free
play (i.e., not regular gym period). There were about sixty-five to
seventy-five boys. They were divided into teams and put on either
side of the gym.
1.19   In the center of the gym at regularly spaced intervals were six soft
6.24   volley balls. When the whistle blew, both sides rushed en masse,
4.34   grabbed the balls, and played dodge. Little skill was involved at first.
The boys just threw the balls into the crowd and hit at random. Who-
ever was hit was honor bound to leave the play space.
        At first Tim was reticent. He hung back and dodged any balls com-
ing his way. He caught a ball however, and then appeared to be more
aggressive. He ran toward the other team, throwing, and dodging. He
was finally eliminated for going over the foul line, i.e., going into
enemy territory.
        When on the sidelines, he jumped up and down in a very excited
manner. Every time someone was hit, he cheered loudly. He continually jumped up and down. Other boys merely stood and watched.
        Somehow church came into the conversation.
5.53   "My father doesn't even go to church on Christmas. Mom goes

2.18   to 9:30 and 11:30 services."

For lunch he had a boloney sandwich, banana, cup cakes, and lemon-meringue pie. I have noticed that he frequently gets dishes of mashed potatoes and gravy, always a banana in his lunch, and lemon-

1.20   meringue pie whenever it is available.

He also eats Grape Nut Flakes every morning for breakfast.

FEB. 25   Tim has a part in the class play, he was chosen by the class.

4.35   The class wrote it. He is a rookie with a "big brother."

They were having a rehearsal today. When I entered the auditorium, it was dark, but in the gloom, I could see a figure flitting along the rows.

"Who's that?" I called.

"Me," replied Tim.

1.21   "What are you doing?" asked I.

"Putting up the seats of the chairs."

FEB. 28   I was absent the day before. As Tim came up to get the

3.37   Bible to give out, he said quietly, "I'm glad you're back."

5.54   I thanked him. Only about six others out of a class of thirty-eight inquired about my health.

MAR. 4   Glee-club teacher was asking for sopranos for Boy's Glee

2.19   Club. Tim interrupted with, "Do we have time to think it over?" "Certainly," said Mr. B, "In fact it would be best as, . . ." Tim interrupted again with, "When do I let you know if I want to join?"

"Tomorrow."

"O.K., I have to ask my mother and father."

The school has a roller-skating club. People wishing to go sign up. Recently people have been signing up and then not coming. This means the rink is reserved for too few people. Now people will have to pay and be given a ticket. This was explained in homeroom. The class president said, "And then if they don't show up . . ." "There

5.55   goes their quarter down the drain," finished Tim.

During a discussion of the Korean War, Tim remarked, "This country is going down because all the smart people are being killed

5.56   off."

(It may be remembered that earlier he said wars were to kill off the weak and the dumb.)

I was in doctor's office and leafing through a magazine put out by the community in which Tim lives. This community is considered one

3.38   of the socially elite in this city. I came across this:

RETURN FROM CUBA

Dr. and Mrs. Michael Thyme have just returned from Cuba after an important meeting. Dr. Thyme addressed the organization and re-

2.20   ceived the Distinguished Service Award and plaque. . . . The award

3.39   recognizes the scientific research and leadership of Dr. Thyme.

Tim has been entering the room for the past two days whistling, but not the usual kind of whistle. This is more birdlike, more of a canary imitation. He has done it six times in two days. No tune, just birdlike.

"I want to stop and get some eighth-grade reading from you so I can read some this summer."

I explained that he was reading above eighth grade when he was
5.57   reading *The Mysterious Island* by Jules Verne.

"My trouble is that I understand what I read very well, but I can't
6.25   read fast."

MAR. 5   "Are you joining the glee club?"
4.36   Tim: "Nope, can't get up. I'm too lazy." Glee club meets at 8:15
5.58   Mon., Wed., and Fri.

Boys and girls are visiting, talking; Tim is cafeteria supervisor. He
4.37   was elected to this position. It entails posting the names of the three children who check their individual table each day. Tim is talking with Ronnie, the boy to whom he sent a valentine, Ronnie accompanies him to the back of the room to see who's on duty. There is a chart there.

He stops on his way up front, visits with a group of boys, continues
3.40   to his seat. "Come to lunch, Miss Riley?" I refused as I had a previous invitation.

MAR. 9   Bell rang. Tim: "Got to get busy." He still gives out the Bible every morning. He looked, couldn't find it. Turned, went down to seat of person whose turn it was to read. "Got the Bible?"

"No."

"Who stole the Bible?"
4.38   "Here it is," said Agnes, pulling it out from books. He had just overlooked it.

MAR. 10   Tim was absent this morning. I saw him in the hall at 12:00.

"Well! Where were you?" said I.

"Had a real sore throat. I could hardly talk. But I gargled all morning and it's better."

Tim's table got a cafeteria ticket, which means fifteen minutes after
1.22   school. The children usually sit with bored expressions, waiting for teacher's back to be turned so they can whisper. Tim put his head down on his desk. He didn't look well, not having the ruddy color usually found in his cheeks. So, as he was not here at lunchtime anyway, I excused him.

He was absent the next day.

Composition

THE DECLINE OF AMERICA AND THE ROMAN EMPIRE

Our Country was founded by hard working people. They had to
3.41   work for what they got. Because of them, only the Roman Empire
5.59   became great. People had to work and suffer and nothing was free or
6.26   easy. The Romans' and Americans' dollar at one time was worth a dollar and it's value had not be decreased. Our country just like the Roman Empire couldn't be strong for ever. Corruption entered in many ways and applies to both countries.

Dishonesty and corruption started in 1932 when F. D. Roosevelt was elected president of the United States. He came in on a beer platform and put the greedy people in power. The greedy lawyers wanted money. So they would get a client, which might not have even thought of going to court but was encouraged by the lawyer. One lawyer would fight the other until they drained their client of his money then they would come to an agreement, this applys to the majority of the lawyers. In this way patents were no good. If a company stole your patent you would have to go to court and hire a lawyer. Your money would be legally stolen by the lawyer and if you did win your suit you would just make a little money because the lawyer fees are so high.

In Rome the dishonest and greedy wanted to get in office. The dishonest had money. With their money they bought grain and gave it to the people as a bribe for votes, thus the dishonest got in office.

Poor government was the main reason for the fall of Rome. Poor government is something we really have in America. Our country has people in important jobs that are communists. With people running the country that plan to destroy it, how can it remain stable?

The majority of the politicians and lawyers here have luxury because they lie and cheat to get money. Luxury is another reason for the fall of America. Those with luxury don't give a darn whether the country goes to pieces. They have their money and food and they don't care about the future. They are not thinking what kind of a country their grandchildren will have to live in.

The buying of votes was done in Rome and is done in America. The $100 a plate dinner is the same idea. Greedy men in our country will do any thing to save their jobs even though it is not for the best interest of our country. This time it's not the lawyers but the government workers, except those whose job can not be filled by anyone else. With the lawyers and the politicians keeping the bad in office the little people are pulled in too.

Surely we have depopulation which Rome had. We have a war now in Korea which many people feel could be stopped. Today people smoke, drink and use strong medicines. Nature doesn't have a chance to build up its defences and the body when attack by a disease has no power and the person gets very sick or dies.

Our country has many other things Rome had like: High taxes and conquering the world and leaving the home unprotected and enemies within.

Grades for 7A semester:

English B	History B	Music C
Art B	Wood Shop B	Gym B
5.60 Science B	Math B	

Tim went to N.Y. a short while ago. He saw "Paint Your Wagon"
3.42 and "The King and I." Of the latter he said he knew the author. He
5.61 also saw "The Greatest Show on Earth" and visited the Planetarium. Also, there was good news. The experiment has begun.

MAR. 26 Tim volunteered for a place on the forum. He received
4.39 six votes; the highest for any one person was ten and that boy is the president.

A subject for the forum was suggested and Tim said, "Oh, pumper-
6.27   nickel!"
        "Hey, that's good. That's better than 'peach fuzz.'"
3.43   ("Peach fuzz" came out as a substitute for "damn" and "hell"
        when we had a talk on swearing.)

        "Nancy and Eve never stay when they're table checkers. They leave
6.28   all this slop, and I have to clean it up." Complaining and querulous
        tone.
        "It's not your responsibility."
        "I know it's not, but we'll get a ticket if I don't."
        "I'll speak to Nancy."
        I did so, and she reported that Tim clears away the trash before
4.40   they have a chance and bosses them around.

        The class went out to have its picture taken. Coming in, when
        I reached the top of the stairs, there was Tim, holding the door and
4.41   swatting each boy as he went through. Each grinned as he did it. He
        was grinning all the time.
        He left as I approached the top of the steps. I heard his "delighted"
        laugh as I entered the hall, and he then apologized for closing the door
3.44   in my face, which I didn't think he'd done.

        Mar. 24   Tim's row was in charge of entertainment. They chipped in
        their own money at Tim's instigation and bought balloons and bubble
        gum. The various volunteers had to do stunts with the balloons, all of
        which ended with the balloon bursting. Tim was in seventh heaven;
4.42   he yelled, he shrieked, he giggled, he roared, he ordered people around,
        he gave instructions at the top of his lungs, he bustled around in be-
6.29   tween stunts preparing. Altogether, I would say he was very excited.
        The children accepted his orders and none of the committee at-
        tempted to assume leadership except when Tim gave it to them.

        Apr. 2   "Who's the little blond boy in your room who brought a
        note to me?" asked a teacher of me in the lunchroom.
        "I don't know. Why?"
        "He brought a note and I didn't know who wrote it, so I asked him.
        'Oh, some teacher that's substituting in math. I'm not even sure if
3.45   she can send me around like this. I don't think it's legal.' He said it
5.62   in a perfectly serious tone," continued the teacher.
        I inquired and found out it was Tim.

        Apr. 22   Opened conversation with: "How's the corn coming?"
        "We're using ordinary garden plants now that spring has come.
        Pop spent all Sunday working out a formula. Anyway, you couldn't
2.21   come over as there's only two of us. Mom's gone to Wisconsin. You
3.46   see, I'm Uncle Tim now (with a wide grin), so Jeff and I are alone."
        "You know, I have a feeling you're going to come in here the last
        day of school and say, 'The experiment's fine, but it's too late to
        come over now.'"
        "Nope, I won't be here. I'll probably leave five days early. Susan's
        getting married."

Told Tim I wanted to see him to talk over that composition of his. Asked him to stop by at 8:45.

"O.K., I'm usually here at 8:00."

5.63   I was surprised as he said he couldn't join glee club because he couldn't get up early enough. "Where are you at 8.00?"

He pointed to the floor, meaning downstairs. "I work in the metal shop and help Mr. S." He left the room and then leaned in and said, "For an A."

I asked for a volunteer to help with library basket. Tim was first. When he finished, he brought the key to my desk.

3.47   "Dankeschön," said I.

"Wie gehts mit ihnen?" said he.

When he got to his seat, he asked what it meant.

I have observed Tim frequently during the recitation of the "Lord's Prayer" in opening exercises.

His voice is the only one clearly heard. The other thirty-seven mumble or speak very softly.

3.48   Only one other person besides Tim folds his hands. The other thirty-six merely bow their heads.

5.64   When the words "For thine is the Kingdom" are reached, there is a general tensing so that as soon as the "Amen" has rung out, they

6.30   may quickly leap to their feet, the idea being to see who can be first. I have never seen Tim do this. His head remains bowed and hands folded until the end!

APR. 29   Tim was nominated for moderator in an assembly-forum. He

4.43   received seven votes. The class was voting on the time to meet for a picnic; 10:30 was nominated. Tim asked that it be later because,

5.65   "I have a lot of work to do in the morning, and I don't get up so early."

SECURITY

Let me start by saying that there are two ways to face life A. Religious, B. Political. I try to keep on the side the Religious I think that I should accomplish some thing every day but I fall to the po-

5.66   *litical side and cuss the government.*

6.31   *1. A. A person feels secure unless some thing makes him feel unsecure so I don't think a person can make you secure unless you are unsecure at the time. Parents can make me unsecure by when things that are amusing come up about me I get imbarist which make me insecure.*

B. Teachers make me unsecure by doubting things I say that are resenable.

C. By not playing with me or asking me to play. (Not that I can't find something to do.)

2. Yes because they listen to what I say

Yes because I can chose my friends and they listen to what I say.

MAY 2   Read them a story as basis for paragraph on Conflict. It was about an honor-roll boy in a situation where, in order to get a hundred,

5.67   he had to cheat. Tim said, "I'd rather have a clean C than a dirty A."

This sounds a little "sticky," but it has its purpose:

We had an evening affair at school at which all music organizations performed. Tim was in the band, which was excellent.

3.49   I was greeting all my performers outside the auditorium when Mrs. Thyme came up to me.

2.22   "Oh, Miss Riley, I can't tell you how much Tim is going to miss you next year. He just loves you."

I told her the feeling was mutual.

"I do want to have you over for dinner very soon."

I'm afraid my face lit up, and I told her it would be delightful.

(My point in including this is that to me it indicates that when you study a child and maintain interest in him or her, this interest and concern are communicated and it gives the child a sense of security and affection.

Sure hope the invitation comes before this record goes in.)

MAY 5   Composition:

MOUNTAINS

Mountains are beautiful. In the mountains the bear, deer, rabbit, mt. goats and many other animals live. Untouched by humans the mountains are a place of beauty and interest. Have you ever thought
5.68   about how the mountains were started? Why they are where they are where they are in relation to water, volcanoes, plains and other mountains? I am going to try to tell you just that. The diagrams will help.

At one time the earth was smooth with no mountains. At different places under the earth two points would try to push together. Then the earth's crust would crack at an angle like this [drawing] the arrows showing the pressure. Also shown in the diagram. The land on one side was pushed up according to the position the crust cracked at. The opposite side was pushed as shown. The side which was forced up became a mountain.

Because the mountain was high than the valley, in time rain and weather wore down the sides of the mountains and made gullies. The dirt from the mountain fills up the valley, caused by the over riding crust. With the dirt came shells and the bones of water animals. This valley was usually 10 miles deep not including the height of the mountain. This deep valley was called, after it was filled with dirt, a geosyncline. When this geosyncline is filled up, its weight causes such pressure that a second break is caused. Almost instantly a new mountain is formed where the geosyncline had been. As soon as a geosyncline is filled it might take only 1,000,000 years to make the rest of the mountain, this is what is ment by instantly. The geosyncline pushes up because this second break releases all the pressure which had kept the geosyncline down so it poped up to its equilibrium.

This second break caused another geosyncline not a nother mountain too. This second geosyncline make an ocean deep and in time will fill up and cause a nother break.

Now the sid that originally over rode turned the crust up and bent it like a board You'll notice the bottom of a board starting to break.

Well this happened to the earth. And where these cracks started up up came volcanoes.

The best example of mountain like that above is in western Mexico. (Following was a diagram of the above explanation.)

MAY 6   Tim came rushing up. "You're gonna have to do something about Ann." Face was red, frowning, voice very loud.

6.32   "Calm down. Take a deep breath. Now, tell me."

He started lower and slower, but built up and built up.

"Well! I went by our table, and there was junk all over it, so I said to Ann, she's the checker—Clean this up! I'll be back in five minutes to check up. So I left and came back and, Miss Riley (here he was almost spluttering), it was *still* a mess and Ann was *gone.* So, I cleaned it up."

"Why?" I asked.

"Well—'cos—well, we'll get a ticket and have to stay after. They know I'll clean it up, so they just leave it."

"O.K.," I said, "let's look at two things. You really have a personal interest in the clean tables, haven't you? The main reason for concern is that you wish to leave at 3:00. Right?"

4.44   "Yeah."

"It's evident that they have no fear of remaining at 3:00 because of your diligence."

"What's that?"

3.50   "Hard work."

"Boy, it sure is. I'm just a sucker."

5.69   "There's only one solution that I can see, Tim. You know, I've talked to the girls and it doesn't seem to do much good. You take away any proof by covering for them. I suggest you leave the table and let the whole table take the consequences. Or, if getting out at 3:00 is more important, bear the consequences."

"O.K., guess I'll keep it up."

"Now, for the second point. Tim, what was wrong with the way in which you approached Ann?"

"Nothin'. I told her and I meant it."

"Was there *nothing* wrong?"

"Nope. What do you think is wrong?"

"Suppose I say to you, 'You do this, you do that.' Would you like it?"

"Oh, yeah, I see what you mean. I'll try to remember, but—they'd better clean up!"

MAY 7   Hallelujah! Tim has invited me to dinner Saturday night, so I have hopes of including it in the records.

3.51   The class was discussing, "Learning by experience *vs.* learning by instruction."

Tim said, "Ya gotta have both. My mother told me to watch out

5.70   for salesmen who fill you full of bull. I didn't pay any attention, and did I get gypped. I bought two knives, and they weren't any good."

6.33   "Why?" asked the kids.

"Well, they were great big, hunky things and how could you use them?"

"How was the man using 'em?"

"Aw, he was cutting up oranges, and radishes and stuff."

"Why can't you?"

"Well, who wants to use a carving knife for an ole radish. At least that's what my mother said, and my father said they could make forty of 'em for the price I paid."

"How much?" chorused the class.

Delighted laugh, "That's my secret!"

4.45   "Aw, come on 'n' tell us."

"Well—a dollar and twenty-five cents."

Gasp from the class. During the telling of this, the class was going into gales of laughter because of the manner in which Tim related the story. They were laughing more with than at him.

He also was enjoying himself.

MAY 8

WHO I WOULD LIKE TO BE

2.23   *I would like to be as much like my father as I could. Because he has good ideas always. He is understanding. He knows a great amount*

5.71   *of Science and Math which I would like to know.*

MAY 9   Tim seems to consider me his private property ever since

2.24   the invitation and has been most affectionate. He sticks his head in the door and says hello in "squeaky" voice.

3.52   He said good-by as he left at 3:00, and again stuck his head in after going to his locker. Each time he grins his widest.

MAY 10, HOME VISIT. I arrived at 6:00. The house is a fairly large one in the more fashionable district. It is two blocks from an elementary school. Each morning, Tim walks half a block up and two over

3.53   to catch his bus. He passes this elementary school, which he attended, and a few stores whose exterior decoration resembles that of early colonial days. The rest of the area is purely residential, with private detached homes of high worth.

The house is comfortably furnished in no particular style. The

2.25   sofa was antique and uncomfortable. This fact was commented upon several times by Dr. Thyme. There was a new chair, which Dr. Thyme also made reference to as impractical as it was of gold color. A small table-model TV set was in one corner—about 17-inch screen.

We were joined by two neighbors and shortly thereafter went in to dinner: tomato juice, crackers with shrimp spread, celery, cucumbers,

1.23   and carrots for a beginning. Dr. left the juice. Tim had two glasses. Tim then helped his mother clear.

The main course consisted of roast beef, potatoes, string beans, gravy, and homemade rolls. A fruit salad was already by our plates. Dr. had a lettuce and tomato salad. For dessert we had ice cream and cake, the latter being for Dr.'s birthday in two days. He would then be away.

When we had finished the main course, Dr. arose and cleared the

5.72   table, Tim assisting for the main plates.

Following is information such as I can remember it:

Mrs. T's father was one of six. He was reared on a farm. He suffered an injury and was confined to the house and as a result learned to cook. He was a far better cook than his wife who used to make samples for him to O.K. Mrs. T is an only child. Her father was a doctor.

Jeff came in while we were eating He'd been working for a florist delivering Mother's Day flowers. He got $2.50 an hour.

They have a rather rigid schedule for graduation. Jeff graduates from high school. Susan graduates from Stanford and gets married the next day. Mrs. T wants to spend the preceding week end at Mount Holyoke for a reunion. Jeff is to be best man on Tuesday and graduates on Wednesday. Somehow they must get to their summer place in Minnesota, but Jeff insists on going to the local beach area for one week

2.26   with the high school gang.

Mike and his wife are using the family house for the summer and both working for the recreation department. He will then go on into theology, his family paying tuition and his wife teaching.

Jeff has a scar on his neck—rather it may be a scar or it may be a birthmark. If a scar, it resembles a large burn.

Mrs. T brought up a forum which is to take place at her church. After some good-natured kidding on Dr. T's part, it came out that one of the members of the panel is a former beau of Mrs. T's, whom she hasn't seen in thirty years.

Dr. remarked several times that Tim is a very serious thinker and the only one who seems interested in science.

He definitely hates Roosevelt and blames all the corruption in the present regime on him. Called attention to the fact that a lake in Michigan now called "Roosevelt" was formerly called "Crooked."

The trouble with the world today is that the so-called leaders refuse to adhere to the "fundamentals" but what these are were never stated.

3.54   However, he feels that they are embodied in the constitution. After a discussion of this, I brought up the fact that the constitution was

5.73   not what the people wanted and therefore could not technically be called a people's document arrived at through democratic principles. He said the people didn't know what they wanted, and it was therefore perfectly permissible for a group of intelligent men to foist on them what they believed sound. I felt this a good point for debate, but being a guest desisted.

We looked at slides of the many places he and the family had been, i.e., Yellowstone, Grand Canyon, Mexico, Arizona, Michigan, California, etc.

Tim showed me the workshop, which seemed to have every conceivable tool—a lathe, drill press, enlarger, and others I can't remem-

3.55   ber. I was shown various things which his father invented, plus several degrees, plus a membership in the American Academy of Scientists.

The basement has a Bendix and the kitchen an electric dishwasher.

I didn't see Tim's room, as "all the junk down here was moved upstairs."

Dr. thinks the U.S. is definitely following the path of all other past

5.74   great countries and sees no hope for recovery as no other country has survived inner corruption.

He would like to vote for MacArthur or perhaps Taft. Both are honest and stand for democratic principles.

1.24   During the discussions, Tim moved around restlessly and was told several times to sit down.

Mother T is afraid of mice and once fell down the loft stairs trying
6.34   to escape from them. At this time she was carrying the eldest child, and had just recovered from a serious abdominal operation.

All their summers are spent on a large and deserted lake in Minnesota.

5.75   Grace was said at dinner by Dr. Thyme. It was not one of that
3.56   "pat" kind that one hears rattled off. It was composed on the spot and pertained to that particular dinner and guests.

Brother goes "steady" with girl in high school.

This concludes the record of Tim and the demonstration of how the Dewey-decimal system can be used in conjunction with an organizing framework to classify all of the data available about a pupil. Chapter 8 will demonstrate how the child-study group interpreted this record in relation to the organizing framework.

CHAPTER 8

Seeing Development

Once the material about Timothy Thyme was classified, the child-study group began at once to analyze the factors affecting Tim's behavior and development. They did this area by area, first phrasing a series of questions about Tim to be answered in each area and then consulting the numbered items in the record to find out whether they had the information necessary to answer each question and what the answers might be. Each area will be presented in turn.

PHYSICAL FACTORS AND PROCESSES

The group phrased the following questions to guide them in analyzing how physical factors and processes were influencing Tim's behavior and development.

1. What is Tim's present growth rate and maturity level?
2. What is his characteristic rate of energy output, fatiguing, and recovery from fatigue? What is his characteristic rhythm of activity and rest?
3. What is his present state of health? Does Tim's health history indicate that he is a generally healthy child or that he is prone to frequent infections? Has he recovered readily from all illnesses? What good or bad health habits does he have?
4. Does he have any specific physical handicaps? Does he have any general physical limitations? If so, how does he feel about these handicaps or limiting factors?
5. How well does he manage his body? What physical-game skills does he have? What physical-game skill common among his peers does he lack? If he lacks any of the customary physical skills, why has he failed to develop them?
6. How attractive are his face, physique, and grooming? To teachers? To his peers? How does he feel about his own physical attractiveness?

In order to make hypotheses about question 1 the group turned to item 1.16, the record of Tim's height and weight at various grade levels. They noticed at once that Tim had grown 4½ inches in height between

241

the first and second grades, only 1 inch between kindergarten and the first grade, 2 inches between the second and third grades, and 1½ inches between the third and fourth grades. The next three years showed 2½ inches, 3 inches, and ½ inch respectively of growth in height. In other words, even taking into consideration the possibility of errors in measurement from one cause or another, Tim seems to have grown in height in little spurts rather than evenly. His growth in weight was much more regular, averaging about 5 pounds a year except between the third and fourth grades, when no increase is reported, and between the fourth and fifth, when a 10-pound increase is recorded. The possibility of an error in the fourth-grade measurement was noted, as well as the fact that Tim had increased but 4 pounds in weight between the fifth and seventh grades. It was noted from item 1.16 that Tim was the fourth from the shortest boy in his room and second from the bottom in weight. The group wondered whether Tim simply had inherited the tendency to be short and slim or whether his growth was being interfered with by some unrecognized factor.

In order to understand Tim's growth better the group decided to plot his height and weight on the Wetzel grid. When they did this, they found that his body build from kindergarten through the third grade would be classified as stocky and that from that point on he had grown progressively more slender, until in the seventh grade his body build would be evaluated clinically as only fair. When they plotted his growth on the age schedules of development, they found that only 10 or 12 per cent of boys were more developed than he up to the third grade, but that his relative rate of growth had declined after that time so that about 70 per cent of boys were more mature than he in the seventh grade. So great a shift as this in growth rate over a period of four years gave them concern about Tim's health, particularly about the factors that regulate growth, and led them to think that he should see his physician for a check-up on his physical condition. Remembering evidences of tensions in Tim they felt that this question should be brought to his parents' attention. The reader will notice that Tim's case is quite different from that of Chester, who was a slow grower throughout his life, because the change in the pace of Tim's growth indicated the need for clinical attention.

With regard to Tim's present maturity level, the group felt that the picture of his increments of growth plus items 1.08, 1.10, and 1.17 indicated quite well that he has not yet entered his pubescent growth spurt. In other words, Tim is still in his late childhood.

When the group considered Tim's characteristic rate of energy output, they found items 1.07, 1.09, 1.13, and 1.24 significant. But none of these items gave any clear picture of Tim as an energy system. So the group concluded that they lacked the information needed to rate Tim as high, average, or low in available energy. Nor were they able to judge his characteristic rhythm of activity and rest or his rate of recovery from fatigue.

The third question had to do with Tim's health. Item 1.14 showed that his school attendance has been quite regular. Item 1.15 reports only measles, among the possible childhood diseases, and the removal of his tonsils. It was apparent, therefore, that Tim had not been a sickly child. Item 1.22 shows him with a sore throat, pale, and resting with his head on the table. Aside from this brief illness there is no evidence of ill health; yet the unusual pattern of Tim's growth still gives some cause for anxiety.

The fourth question concerns physical handicaps and limitations. Item 1.15 reports that his eyes and teeth are all right, and no mention is made in the health record of any handicap or physical anomaly. Items 1.11 and 1.12 show a bad thumbnail which received attention from a surgeon after several years of difficulty, but implies no limiting factor. Only Tim's small stature, slow growth, and uncertain energy supply seem to be limiting factors.

Items 1.05, 1.07, 1.09, 1.18, and 1.19 deal with the way Tim manages his body. Here we find him skating with great skill but knowing nothing about baseball and appearing ill at ease in the dodge-ball game. The implication seems to be that he can use his body quite skillfully in individual sports in which he is experienced but that he is inept at group games. Perhaps this is partially due to the fact that Tim spends all his summers with the family at an isolated lake in Minnesota and so has not had much opportunity to learn group-game skills. At any rate, we find him saying that he knows nothing whatever about baseball, and the record contains nothing which shows him successfully participating in group games.

The description of Tim's physical appearance in item 1.01 shows a boy somewhat better dressed than most boys in the class and generally of good appearance. His "sparkling personality" mentioned in the introductory paragraph of the record seems to stem from what he is as a person rather than from outstanding handsomeness of face or figure, though he does show two dimples when he smiles.

The child-study group evaluated this record toward the end of the year and found themselves only partially satisfied with the insights it yielded concerning Tim as a physical being. They felt that, much earlier in the year, the following additional information should have been sought:

1. The mother should have been consulted as to the history of Tim's physical development. This would have shown whether he really was a slow

grower from babyhood or whether, as the physical measurements seem to show, something unfavorable happened in his growth process during elementary school. It also would have given a more adequate picture of Tim's customary flow of energy and of his physical recuperative powers from fatigue.

2. Tim should have been observed frequently on the playground to find out more about how he managed his body and about his game skills in particular. Conversations with him about his physical activities also would have enriched the record greatly in this area.

3. The pattern of Tim's physical growth, as revealed by the Wetzel grid, together with the unfavorable indications there, should have been brought to his parents' attention as soon as his seventh-grade physical measurements were made. The parents should have been urged to consult their physician. Had this been done in time, his teacher might have learned the outcome of the physician's investigation. Most important of all, Wetzel has found that changes in growth pattern such as that Tim showed often indicate and forewarn of later illness. Something may be wrong with Tim's general body economy. If so, it is important to recognize it and to undertake remedial measures promptly.

LOVE RELATIONSHIPS AND RELATED PROCESSES

The study group phrased the following questions to guide them in analyzing the ways in which love relationships and related processes are influencing Tim's behavior, development, and adjustment.

1. What is the nature of the relationship between Tim and his mother, especially in view of his being the youngest child in the family?
2. What is the nature of the relationship between Tim and his father?
3. What is the nature of the relationship between Tim and each of his siblings?
4. What is the nature of the relationship between Tim's mother and father?
5. What is the nature of the relationship between Tim's parents and each of his siblings?
6. What is the nature of the relationship between each of Tim's siblings?
7. What is the general emotional climate within the family?
8. To what degree is Tim emotionally secure?
9. Does Tim's relationship with Miss Riley add to his security?

Hypotheses about question one depend upon items 2.03, 2.06, 2.07, 2.08, 2.09, 2.12, 2.13, 2.16, 2.17, 2.19. This material concerns Mrs. Thyme's surprise that Tim wants to be called Tim rather than Timmy; Tim's thumb, which went without surgical attention for three years; Tim's staying at home to help his mother when she is ill; Mrs. Thyme's desire that Tim do better schoolwork, although Dr. Thyme is perfectly satisfied with the boy's accomplishments; Tim's mother's saying that he is babied and is perhaps "closer than the rest"; the parents' buying a television set to keep Tim home more; Tim's describing his mother as "really a wheel at church. . . . She practically runs everything. . . . She's never home." Finally, Tim must ask permission to join the Boys' Glee Club. The group found it rather hard to evaluate the relationship between Mrs. Thyme and Tim on the basis of this material. She seemed to want to keep him close to her, called him the baby of the family, and spoke of being closer to him than to the others. But Tim's comments about his mother were that she is a good cook, is active at the church, and is never at home. So the group decided that they could not really tell what part Tim's mother plays in his life apart from pressing him to do better at school and general supervision of his activities. They wondered why his thumb had gone uncared for during three years and presumed that it was not seriously painful. They remarked that Tim did not speak of his mother in the loving terms that most children do.

If the group was uncertain about Tim's relationship with his mother, they were never in doubt about that with his father. Item 2.01 showed Tim "amazed" that his father could be wrong. Item 2.02 showed him planning his life according to the pattern set by his father. Item 2.04 showed Tim boasting about the way his father planned the spacing of the children, as though his mother were not equally concerned. In item 2.08 we see Tim identifying his father as a scientist, proudly pointing to his membership in the National Academy of Science, and writing of his father's likes and dislikes. Item 2.10 shows Timothy identifying Dr. Thyme with the word "man." In 2.11 Tim says that one of the three things that have given him the most happiness in life is "that my father has been safe." In 2.13 Dr. Thyme is "perfectly satisfied" with Tim's work, whereas his mother wants him to do better. He describes Tim's poor spelling as very good compared with his own at the same age. Dr. Thyme also says that Miss Riley may see Tim's experiment with the corn "if it is successful. If not, not another word will be said about it." Here, in item 2.14, Dr. Thyme again protects Tim from possible humiliation over failure. In item 2.17 Tim is encouraged to try a third experiment with the corn after two failures. Item 2.20 gives an additional reason why Tim is so proud of his father. Tim really goes "all-out" for his father in his choice of people he likes best (2.15) and in his essay (2.23) "Who I Would Like To Be," he writes, "I would like to be as much like my father as I could. Because he has good ideas always. He is understanding." Item 2.26 shows Dr. Thyme characterizing Tim as "A very serious thinker and the only one who seems interested in science." Thus an identification seems to exist between them.

From these data the group inferred that Tim is very close to his father, almost idolizes him, and desires more than anything else to be like him. They found his father accepting Tim's shortcomings in spelling, protecting him against feelings of failure, and expressing confidence that Tim would develop soundly. The two of them shared many mutual interests. The group felt that Tim was drawing real security from his relationship with his father.

The relationship between Tim and his siblings was assessed on the basis of Tim's frequent comments about them to Miss Riley, found in items 2.04, 2.05, 2.08, 2.19, and 2.24. The group was unable to find any trace of rivalry or antagonism between Tim and any of his siblings or among the siblings. Tim seemed proud of what each was doing, knew about their plans and aspirations, and was proud of becoming an uncle.

The group found itself unable to assess clearly the quality of the relationship between Dr. and Mrs. Thyme. Each clearly was an individual with a strong personality and vigorous views. They differed greatly in views about religion, how well Timothy should do in school, and home furnishings, but seemed in accord in the encouragement of their children's plans for careers and marriage. Apparently the family functioned as a team with each one helping to carry out mutually agreed-upon plans. Dr. Thyme's teasing of his wife about meeting an old beau was good-natured, he said grace before meals, and the two of them agreed on buying a television for Tim. So the group inferred that the climate of the home was warm, loving, and characterized by mutual support among all members of the family. They felt it was a climate in which Tim could feel secure.

Under such adequate security-giving conditions at home, the group felt that Tim did not really need love from Miss Riley. On the other hand, when a child is fully loved at home it is easy for him to learn to love others and life is always enriched by such relationships. The group noticed that Tim's warmth toward Miss Riley seemed to increase as the year progressed, with regard to his sharing his intimate feelings with her. Mrs. Thyme reported that he would miss her sadly during the ensuing year; "He just loves you," she said. And, in truth, Tim did come to express his affection directly (2.24).

CULTURAL BACKGROUND AND SOCIALIZATION PROCESSES

The child-study group found the record very rich in the area of cultural background and socialization, since it contained fifty-six items. They phrased the following questions to answer in interpreting it.

1. What subcultures within the larger American culture does Tim's family carry?
2. By what processes is Tim internalizing these cultures?
3. What roles is he playing in social institutions outside the home?
4. What does he know of the larger American culture?
5. What does he feel about the current American society, about how it got

that way, and about his present and future responsibilities in maintaining and developing it?

6. Do inconsistencies exist between the various cultural factors he is internalizing at home and elsewhere, or between these internalized factors and the expectancies and demands he is facing at home and at school?

7. Is he subjected to any special pressures due to geographic mobility, ethnic identification, or caste?

In answer to question one, the group found it necessary to make tentative inferences from the available data rather than to affirm positive proof. For example, they inferred from the family name and from the given names of the children and wife that the family was Anglo-Saxon, probably English, in origin. Consequently the group felt that the family probably carries the Early American–English culture pattern. From the section of the city in which the family home is located, Dr. Thyme's occupation and success, various family attitudes (Timothy's argument that anybody who couldn't give a quarter to the Red Cross "should not be living in this neighborhood"), the plans for graduate study for each son, and the choice of a profession by each son, the group inferred that the social-class status of the family was lower-upper-class with roots in New England and the Middle West. The family likewise carries a mixture of rural and urban cultures but is basically urban in its current setting. (Mrs. Thyme's grandfather was a farmer.)

Without too much evidence, the group also inferred that the family is upward mobile in social-class terms, because the mother's grandfather was a farmer with six children, her father was a physician with only one child (upper-middle), and her own present family is lower-upper class. The group regarded the mother's attitude of wanting Timothy to get better marks in school regardless of other factors as a distinctly upper-middle-class characteristic that might indicate some anxiety on her part about the children's maintaining their present status. The group recognized that the family's social status might even be upper-upper class if Dr. Thyme's family is an old one with great influence and prestige in the community where he grew up; but they felt that, if this were true, it undoubtedly would have been mentioned somewhere in the teacher's contact with the family. Lacking this knowledge, the group inferred that the family is upward mobile from the middle class. Timothy, then, is faced with the continuing developmental task of internalizing an Early American–English, New England–Middle Western, urban, and upper-middle- or lower-upper-class culture and of living up to the expectancies and demands of this cultural background in his daily actions and in his school accomplishment.

The processes by which Tim is internalizing this culture are chiefly those set going at home and reenforced at school. They include much interaction with his father, "good" books as a constant factor in family life, encouragement to maintain a paper route and save his money, the assignment of regular tasks to do at home, the family expectancy that he choose a profession and prepare for it by graduate work beyond the bachelor's degree, extensive travel with the family, going to the theater, visits to museums and the Planetarium, participation in family discussion of politics and of national and world events, the expectancy that he will "accomplish something" in life, encouragement to try to understand the present in the light of the past ("The Decline of America and the Roman Empire") and to understand the causes of everything around him ("Mountains"), and encouragement to think out his religious position for himself. Add to this the family discussion of Dr. Thyme's many professional successes, of the recognition he received for his work, and of the professional plans of Tim's older brothers and their steady progress toward the realization of them, and one finds an environment that is constantly stimulating Tim to learn, to adopt a pattern of life similar to that of his father and older brothers, and to measure up everywhere to the standards set by them.

When the group had finished analyzing these processes by which Tim is internalizing the culture carried by his family, they realized that they also had the answer to question seven. Tim is under special pressure, that is, he is under more pressure than most boys in school experience. To live up to and to maintain by his own development the status achieved by his father is a formidable task. And to begin to see his tasks as clearly as Tim has by the age of twelve-and-a-half years is a big task even for a boy with an IQ of 120.

Question three asked what roles Tim is playing in social institutions outside the home. The group quickly spotted his paper route as one such role, together with the use of the bank as the repository of his savings. Attending the theater, visiting the Planetarium, using the skating rink, going to church, and using travel facilities and hotels on trips to California, Mexico, New York, the Grand Canyon, Yellowstone National Park, and elsewhere were noted as additional instances of his functioning in the wider culture.

School, of course, is the chief institution outside the home in which Tim is functioning. Here the group found him introducing himself to the principal when he entered junior high; playing in the band; doing poorly in his spelling, very well in general science, history and math, and unusually well in reading comprehension; avoiding the school newspaper; volunteering for Santa Claus and for maintenance man but not being chosen; stating strong opinions on a variety of topics; being a cafeteria supervisor; having a part in the class play; choosing not to be

in the glee club; doing errands for teachers; volunteering for the forum
and suggesting topics for discussion; directing the work of an entertainment committee at a party; and participating freely in discussions
and making frequent personal contacts with his teacher. The group
evaluated this as quite full functioning in intellectual terms. They noted
that his behavior often attracted favorable comment from the adults
in contact with him and less frequently evoked approval from his peers.
Summing up their information in this area, the group felt that Tim has
unusually wide contacts with the larger American culture, is utilizing
these contacts to learn a great deal about it, and is functioning well from
the adult point of view.

In answer to question four the study group listed the following events
and aspects of American life of which Timothy showed knowledge: science, medicine; colleges; religion; radio and television; boating; National
Academy of Science; Red Cross; Greek, Roman, and English history in
relation to current American life; the Korean War; the value of money
and the costs of public facilities; governmental aid to European countries; political corruption; the role and incomes of lawyers; patents;
devaluation of the dollar; F.D.R.; buying of votes; taxes, empire building, "enemies within"; the ways of salesmen; the world-wide conflict
between democracy and communism.

The group agreed that, although not all of Timothy's knowledge and
ideas are valid, he is nevertheless alert to an extraordinarily wide variety
of aspects of life in the American culture for a child of his age.

Question five is concerned with what Timothy feels about the current
American society, how it became as it is, and what responsibility he
has for maintaining and changing it. The group was impressed with the
similarity between the attitudes Tim expressed in his various papers and
comments at school and the attitudes expressed by his father to the
teacher at school in the Thyme's home. Timothy wrote that he wants
to be as much like his father as he can because his father "has good
ideas always." Obviously, then, Tim sees the society of which he is a
part largely through his father's eyes and regards his father as right
about these matters. In other words Tim is adopting his social attitudes
ready-made. But the group was quite impressed with the degree to
which he not only has made these attitudes his own but supports them
with reasoning. Tim clearly abhors political corruption, dishonesty,
greed, luxury, selfish disregard for the public welfare and the country's
future, and vices that weaken the body. He sees in these evils the chief
threat to our nation's welfare. And Tim applies these values as a citizen
of the school: "I'd rather have a clean C than a dirty A."

Although there is no report in the record that Tim is determined to
do something about the political and social evils he sees, the group

judged that he feels personally involved, because one of the three things that has given him greatest happiness is "the feeling of accomplishing some things while I have been living" (this at the age of twelve!), and because in his essay on security he says, "there are two ways to face life: A. Religious, B. Political. I try to keep on the side [of] the Religious. I think that I should accomplish something every day *but* I fall to the political side and cuss the government." In other words Tim is driven by a strong sense of personal duty and cannot be satisfied simply to do what is right as an individual but feels personally involved with government, so much so that sometimes he must "cuss" it because of his felt dissatisfactions with its functioning. Surely, here we see not only the development of character but the gradual affective involvement of the child in the dynamics that underlie the functioning of his society.

Question six gave the group some difficulty. It asked whether inconsistencies exist between the various cultural factors Tim is internalizing at home and elsewhere and between these internalized factors and the expectancies and demands he is facing at home and at school. The group noted first that Tim feels a conflict between the religious and the political ways of facing life and judged from the record that his mother represents the religious view and his father the political. So Tim is bringing this conflict to school with him. It was felt that the school and the home both supported Tim in the things he abhors, such as corruption, dishonesty, greed, selfish disregard for the public welfare, and the like. On the other hand, the group noted that Tim states all his attitudes with great force and bluntness and that Dr. Thyme also is extremely positive in all of his attitudes. They wondered whether Tim ever looked to see whether there were possibly two sides to any question (the swimming pool, aid to Europe) and whether he might be becoming a very intolerant person. They could not quite accept his wholesale condemnation of social and political trends in the United States and thought that he ought to see recent events as a mixture of good and bad things. They doubted whether the country is going to the dogs so completely as Tim feels it is. But they realized that more temperate attitudes would have to be suggested to Tim very carefully lest they precipitate either a direct conflict with the home or doubt on Tim's part about his idealized father. So they decided to stress with Tim the importance of facts, to encourage him to look for facts which tended to refute as well as to support his conclusions.

Summing up this area, the group felt that Tim is quite advanced for his age in his internalization of the culture of which he is a part, that he is under heavy pressure to live up to the standards and expectancies to which his family holds, that his present tendency is to identify with his father and to accept the latter's ideas and attitudes ready-made as sure truth, that he is in danger of being intolerant of the diverging ideas and attitudes he may find among his peers and too strong in the statement of his own opinions. They felt that his abhorence of evil was sound and that he had a strongly developed sense of his own social duty. But they could not find suggestions of any clear-cut directions in which he might take constructive social action. They hoped that the school will be able to encourage him to undertake thoughtful factual analyses of social problems and a greater readiness to look for two sides to social questions, without decreasing his strong dislike for what is morally and socially evil.

PEER-GROUP STATUS AND PROCESSES

The child-study group worked out the following questions relating to Tim's peer-group status and processes:

1. What are the chief group activities engaged in by Tim's peers, what roles do these activities afford, what knowledge and skills are required to play these roles, what customs and codes of behavior do the members of his peer group follow, and what personality characteristics are esteemed by his peers?

2. What roles does Tim seek in these activities, which ones does he win, and what status is accorded him by his peers?

3. Does Tim fail to win any roles he seeks? If so, why?

4. How does Tim manage himself when he fails to win desired roles or when he fails to play a role successfully?

5. What are the effects of physical, affectional, and cultural factors upon Tim's peer-group status and role playing?

6. Is Tim's status with his peers satisfactory to him? Does he know why he has the status which his peers have given him?

The child-study group had some difficulty in answering the first question because not all of the participants understood the degree to which children at each maturity level have a society of their own which operates according to its own codes and customs rather than according to adult-approved standards. They found it hard to distinguish between the adult-directed activities of groups of children at school and the peer group—mediated activities that mean so much to the developing child or youth. Many of them recognized that, in a sense, going to school and taking part in its activities is itself a peer-group matter because their peers expect all children to act in accord with their own codes and customs in and around the school rather than in accord with the expectancies and demands of the adults who are running the school. They saw that school-operated activities, like the band and various athletic teams, are important peer-group activities despite the fact that they are set up and administered by the school authorities. Some of them saw that a classroom in which children are permitted to deliberate together and to make their own decisions about such matters as rules of behavior, extracurricular activities, and organizing for effective daily living together becomes a place where the peer-group society can operate openly and effectively under adult observation and guidance. The autocratic classroom where all decisions are made by the teacher, they felt, tends to drive the child society underground into less desirable activities and to lend prestige to the more aggressive and rebellious children who dare to show their fearlessness of adults through their behavior in the classroom.

The group knew that late-childhood and prepubescent male peer groups, such as that to which Tim belongs, regard sports and group games as the core of their significant activity. They knew that good skill in these active games is almost required for full peer-group belonging. They also knew that joking and general horseplay are characteristic of boys at this maturity level. Personality attributes that are esteemed include daring, ability to withstand pain without crying, a measure of unkemptness of clothing and hair, and the avoidance of playing with girls.[1]

But the group remained troubled about their ability to distinguish between school-mediated activities and peer group–mediated activities. A consultant who was visiting them had to admit that these are not easy distinctions to make, that there are certainly significant overlappings, since the peer group expects that children will act in the classroom in accord with their own codes, unless coerced by adults. So the group decided to list all peer-group items from the record on the blackboard and to see whether putting all this material together in this fashion would help clarify their interpretations about Tim. The items were listed as follows:

4.01   Tim doesn't wear blue jeans as the others do. Wears corduroy pants.

4.02   Tim gave Bob a healthy shove coming out of auditorium. They tussle.

4.03   Tim was chatting with Sue at table during lunch.

4.04   Tim came in with head dripping water; whispered to Bob; they giggled.

4.05   Tim nominated for homework chairman. Got three out of possible thirty-four votes. Sue voted for him.

4.06   Most children moving around, talking, before English class. Tim gazed into space. Ate his lunch alone.

4.07   Asked by Bob to read something latter had written. Made quick comment. Showed no interest.

4.08   Tim sat alone, reading *Microbe Hunters*, before 9 o'clock bell.

[1] See Tyron, C. Adolescent Evaluations of Adolescents. *Monographs of the Society for Research in Child Development*, 1939, **4**.

4.09   Asked Mary to save him a seat at lunch table. She didn't.

4.10   Told about learning to play flute. Sue, Ed, and Bob studying same instrument. Al is learning trombone. All play instruments together.

4.11   Arranges to go skating with Bob. Says paper route interferes with his club activities.

4.12   Al jokes with Tim: "His father is Father Thyme." Tim jokes back: "I'm T.N.T."

4.13   Bob and Tim joke over hot-rod point system: "Twenty points for knocking down a lady on crutches with a seeing-eye dog."

4.14   Tim sitting alone reading *Twenty-one Balloons*. Others visiting together.

4.15   Playing "Twenty Questions." Tim guesses right and gives next topic.

4.16   Tim skates well—like a small tornado, not roughnecking.

4.17   Al is angry at Bob for skating with his girl. Not angry at Tim for doing same thing. "Everybody knows Sue is Tim's girl friend."

4.18   Returned pocketbook to Nancy; joked about it.

4.19   Tim said, "Anyone who can't give twenty-five cents to Red Cross shouldn't be living in this area. They ought to be down in the slums."

4.20   Tim slouched alone in chair while others chatted and straightened up the room.

4.21   Tim refused to buy the school newspaper. Twenty-eight out of thirty-four did. All read it except Tim and Bob.

4.22   Tim reported as playing happily with other children when he was in kindergarten.

4.23   Had Scout meeting Wednesday night. Wants to be kept busy; finds homework wonderful because it gives him something to do over week ends.

4.24   Tim is fourth from shortest and next to lightest in weight in class. Still a little boy.

4.25   Tim volunteered but not selected when playing "Truth or Consequences."

4.26   Volunteered for Santa Claus; didn't get it.

4.27   Tim objected to getting Christmas tree for party and to getting ice cream that cost more than five cents. Voted down.

4.28   Tim is "mailman" to deliver cards at party.

4.29   Tim volunteered for maintenance man. Got only eight votes and so was eliminated.

4.30   Tim criticized Edna, his row captain, to Mike. "Edna never does anything 'cept sit on her ass."

4.31   Tim advocates fine of ten cents for misbehaving in class instead of five cents as approved by others. Voted down.

4.32   Playing "Dr. IQ," Tim unable to answer question about baseball; said, "I don't know a thing about baseball."

4.33   Tim gave Ronnie a valentine. Ronnie guessed sender from misspelling. Whole group laughed; Tim not embarrassed.

4.34   Tim first held back, then joined dodge-ball game in gym. Didn't play well. Eliminated for crossing foul line.

4.35   Tim chosen by class for part in play—rookie with a big brother.

4.36   Tim decides not to join the glee club.

4.37   Tim elected cafeteria supervisor; talks to Ronnie; visits with a group of boys.

4.38   Tim says somebody stole the Bible. Agnes finds it for him.

4.39   Tim got six votes for a place on forum. Highest for anybody was ten.

4.40   Tim clears up tables for Nancy and Eve. Complains about it to teacher. Teacher speaks to Nancy who says Tim does it before they have a chance and that he "bosses them around."

4.41   Tim holds door open, swats each boy as he enters. All grin.

4.42   Tim's row in charge of entertainment. He took command, and they bought balloons and bubble gum. Tim very excited, noisy, bossy. His assumed role accepted by all the group.

4.43   Tim nominated moderator in assembly forum. Received seven votes.

4.44   Tim complains to teacher about Ann not cleaning up in cafeteria. Teacher helped him to see he had been too bossy.

4.45   Class group enjoyed Tim's story on himself about being gypped by salesman.

The group went over these forty-five items carefully to see what peer-group roles Tim had sought and won or failed to win. They found that the following roles had been refused to him by the group: homework chairman, seat beside Mary at lunch, "it" in "Truth or Consequences," Santa Claus, maintenance man, and moderator of forum—a total of six roles. They found that he had won the following roles: played flute in band, played "Twenty Questions" successfully, went to skating club and skated well, attended Scout meeting, played mailman at Christmas party, acted a role in the class play, was cafeteria supervisor, won a place on the forum, directed entertainment when his row was in charge—a total of nine roles. The group also noted that Tim tended to win more roles during the second half of the year than during the first part. In other words, Tim's status seemed to improve as the year progressed.

The exact status given Tim by the group was not easy to assess, because, as with all children, his status varied somewhat with the activity. Only once did he have a real leadership role—on March 24, when he got balloons and bubble gum for the class and took charge of the party. Four of his nine roles—playing in the band, playing "Twenty Questions," going to skating club, and attending the Scout meeting—required no assent from his peers; they were activities organized by adults, and Tim needed only the desire and capacity in order to participate. Being mailman at the Christmas party, having a part in the class play, being a cafeteria supervisor and having a place on the forum were voted to him by the group. The group noted that mental capacity and devotion to duty were important requisites for three out of four of these roles and felt that the class recognized and admired, to a certain extent, Tim's ability and conscientiousness. Putting together this whole picture of roles won and refused, the group decided that Tim's status was that of a "fringer." Only once had he led; and half his roles could not have been denied him by the group because they were adult-mediated and did not require much group cooperation with Tim. The roles they voted him were roles he was qualified to play, and this implied a recognition by the group of Tim's assets.

The group then turned to the question of why Tim had the status only of "fringer" rather than of "full belonger" or "leader." They first listed the actions reported in the record which were in accord with the peer-group code and customs. They found these to be: shoved Bob in auditorium, came in with head dripping water, joked with Al over family name, joked with Bob over "hot-rod point system," guessed right in "Twenty Questions," skates well, uses male vocabulary in criticizing Edna, got a laugh from the group about his misspelling, played part in class play successfully, visited with group of boys in cafeteria, held door open and swatted each boy in turn, got balloons and bubble gum for party, plays well in band, and got a laugh about being gypped by a salesman. There were fourteen such favorable items among the forty entries.

Next the group listed the characteristics or actions which violated peer-group codes and customs or failed to promote peer-group aims. These items were: dressed better than the rest (corduroy pants), sat alone and gazed into space while other children visited, took no interest when approached by Bob, sat alone reading while others visited, again read while others are having fun together, wants homework to keep him busy week ends and evenings, ate his lunch alone, is physically small, objected to buying Christmas tree which group wanted, objected to spending more than five cents for ice cream, advocated twice as big a fine for misbehavior as group wanted, showed he has no knowledge of baseball, is unskilled at dodge-ball, opposed swimming pool, complained to teacher about Nancy and Eve, is bossy to helpers in cafeteria, complained about Ann to teacher, and remained bossy in cafeteria. This is a total of eighteen items, many of which are strong violations of peer-group standards at this maturity level, for example, dressing better than the others; remaining aloof while the others have fun together; not playing with the others after school and on week ends; objecting to things that the others love, such as the Christmas tree and big servings of ice cream; tattling to the teacher about the failure of others to do the work he was supposed to supervise; and being overly bossy. Worst of all is his lack of knowledge about baseball, as well as his lack of skill in playing it and dodge-ball. It appears that Tim can swim, manage a boat, and skate, but he knows no group games and is therefore out of all sports during the afternoons and week ends. It is probable that he will always remain only a "fringer" with his peers until he begins to participate in team play. The group wondered what Dr. Thyme's history had been in such activities and what his present attitudes are. They suspected that Dr. Thyme's attitudes might have been an important factor in Tim's failure to mention football during the autumn and in his failure to have any knowledge of baseball or any skill in playing it.

The data available did not show anything about how Tim acted when his peers failed to elect him to roles for which he had volunteered. The record did show, however, that he became very bossy when he had the role of cafeteria supervisor and was directing the party. He became very excited when he did participate, as when he played dodge-ball and directed the entertainment. For this reason the group inferred that Tim really does desire peer-group roles and that getting them is important to him. They inferred, furthermore, in answer to question six, that Tim is not satisfied with his fringer status but wishes to be a full belonger, as most children do. They doubted whether he understood why he did not have a higher status, felt that his teacher had helped him by pointing out that he was too bossy in the cafeteria, and believed that she could help him further by analyzing with him the code and customs of his peers and by encouraging him to learn to play baseball.

In answer to question five, the group felt that Tim's small stature was something of a handicap to him but that this would not interfere with his playing baseball successfully if he were interested in it. They felt that Tim's identification with his father might be holding him back in the peer group because his father always expressed himself so positively and possibly because his father did not value sports, although they had no proof. They felt that the tendency of his family to dress Tim better than the others was not a help to him with his peers and that his social-class consciousness, expressed on several occasions, was not appropriate in the prepubescent peer group although it would be acceptable in the late-adolescent peer group.

Summing up the area, the group thought that Tim's intelligence, readiness to joke, and willingness to keep trying for roles were assets, and that his strong individualism, his tendency to bookishness rather than sociability at odd moments around school, his physical smallness, and his lack of interest in group sports were distinct liabilities. They felt that Tim made real progress during the year toward being accepted by his peers and thought that he should have private guidance from his teachers on how to get along better. They hoped that a male teacher could be interested in teaching him to play baseball and that he could perhaps be involved in touch football during the next autumn. They felt that winning belonging was becoming an adjustment problem for Tim and that his fringer status might account, in part, for his symptoms of tension.

SELF-DEVELOPMENTAL FACTORS AND PROCESSES ✗

The child-study group developed the following questions about factors and processes involved in Tim's development as a self:

1. How does Tim think of and feel about himself as a person in the light of what we have learned about him in the four preceding areas of analysis?
2. How does Tim think of and feel about people, events, society, the world, and the universe in the light of his unique background of relationships and experiences?
3. How do Tim's conceptions of himself, society, and the universe influence his perceptions of persons, situations, and events?
4. How does Tim see himself in relation to other persons, events, society, and the universe, to be evaluated in terms of his attitudes, codes of conduct, philosophy of life, and values and goals?
5. What do we know about Tim's potential and operating capacities for learning and for doing?
6. What mental processes does Tim habitually use in working out the meanings of situations and events for himself?
7. How effective are Tim's actions in working toward his goals and purposes?
8. What conceptions of Tim are expressed by his parents, brothers, teachers, and peers? What expectancies and demands upon him grow out of these conceptions others have of him?
9. Are there inconsistencies between the conceptions Tim has of himself and the demands made upon him by the various people who are significant to him?

The child-study group devoted three meetings—a total of six hours—to analyzing Tim's development as a self and felt that they were well rewarded by their increased insights into the forces that shape the development of all children. Because there were seventy-four items in this area, the group decided to pull together and list on the blackboard all the items under each of the following subtopics: (1) Tim's capacities, (2) Tim's experiences, (3) knowledge and skills, (4) interests, (5) attitudes and values (including ethical code of conduct), (6) conception of the universe, (7) philosophy of life, and (8) conception of himself and his place in life and the universe. The classification of the data led to much discussion, of course, and resulted in many insights into Tim's self-organization and into the dynamics that spring from this self-organization. It also led to considerable clarification of the participants' ideas about the processes by which the self-concept is differentiated, becomes

structured, and then becomes dynamic in its own right in shaping behavior.

Angyal has pointed out that genuine understanding of a person does
not amount to shrewd analysis to spot his weaknesses; rather it is perception of the organizing forces that are his essential or central values,
for these deep central meanings ascribed by the individual to self and
the universe are the real organizing forces within the personality. The
study group sought to discover these inner organizing forces in Tim in-
ductively, by analyzing each set of factors in the logical sequence suggested by the numbering of the topics above. I am afraid to try to repro-
duce on paper the essence of this six hours of laborious yet stimulating
experience. Rather, I must be content with presenting summaries of
what they concluded.

Many of the seventy-four items in this area were listed over and over
again under the various headings and so were considered in different
conceptual settings. Rather than attempt to discuss the entire list of items,
we will consider what the group felt Tim is as a self, especially how he
conceives of himself; second, how his values and his ensuing self-concepts
influence his perceptions and behavior; and then how he got to be the
self he is.

Tim's Conception of Life and the Universe

In the essays titled "Me" and "Security" and in several conversations
with Miss Riley, Tim stated the essence of his conception of life and the
universe. The following items are in his words:

5.33   "I believe that life on earth is given to a person so that he might
improve the world."

5.17   "I have only one wish, peace on earth, good will toward men."

5.33   "The only thing I am afraid of is God."

5.34   "I guess [I fear God] because God's the truth, and aren't you more
afraid of the truth than the false?"

5.45   "[I like] God because he is my creator."

5.66   "There are two ways to face life: A. Religious, B. Political. I try to
keep on the Religious side [for] I think that I should accomplish something
every day but I fall to the political side and cuss the government."

5.33   "There is nothing that I don't like to learn about because I think a
person should know everything that he can learn in the short time he is on
earth."

5.33   "Everyone must die and we have no control over death. If a person
is going to die, he will if it is the will of God."

We shall soon have the opportunity to decide whether these concepts
really are the organizing core of Tim's self. If they are, they will constantly influence his daily perceptions, attitudes and acts; for this reason
we should be very clear about them. He has said he believes life is given

to a person so that he may improve the world. He defines improving the world, his one wish, as bringing about peace on earth and good will among men. He feels that being alive carries the obligation to be doing something all the time; he regards this as the religious way of facing life, which he contrasts with the political. (Apparently Tim thinks of "doing something all the time" as working to bring about a better world, in contrast with political activity, which is doing something to promote one's own selfish interests. This seems clear from the attitudes he expressed after making this statement.) Tim feels that learning everything one can is part of this obligation imposed by life, apparently because it prepares one to become useful in improving the world. Consequently, his current obligation is to be constantly learning something. God, as Tim conceives Him, is truth. Perhaps we can infer from this that to learn portions of the truth is to become like God, to become good. Here we come to Tim's somewhat enigmatic statement that he "fears God because he is truth and that truth is more to be feared than the false." Perhaps this is a backhanded way of saying that he fears not to know the truth when he needs it. If this is what Tim means, it could be a partial basis for his strong feeling of obligation to be doing something at every moment, to be learning constantly. Tim recognizes and accepts the fact that death must come to all and feels that the time when one dies depends upon the will of God; but he stoutly affirms that this is not the basis of his fear of God. God as truth is what he reverences and fears. We shall have to check the validity of this conceptualization of the inner organizing core of Tim's make-up by seeing whether Tim's behavior confirms it. A preliminary confirmation lies in the fact that it is not based upon a single essay or interview. The relevant items were dated October 26, November 16, and April 29.

Tim's Conception of Himself

Of course, Tim has a many-sided conception of himself, and we are fortunate that his teacher recorded the words in which he presented many of these facets.

5.01　Tim sees himself as being at a new maturity level upon entering junior high school and so wants to be called Tim instead of Timmy, as he has been called in the past. This surprised his mother (item 2.03).

5.07　Tim sees himself as a person who will go to college and graduate school and finally get a doctorate. Perhaps he has decided this because he feels he must live up to the family pattern set by his father and brothers; perhaps he sees it as the necessary way of preparing himself for maximum usefulness; or perhaps both motives are operating.

5.08　His initials make him think of himself as a bundle of energy. "I'm T.N.T."

5.20   Tim sees himself as a person of social consequence who should know and be known by the highest-status person at school, so he goes to the principal's office and introduces himself early in the year.

5.49   Tim sees himself as a very poor speller but apparently isn't bothered by it because his father, who has achieved outstanding usefulness in the world, has said that he was a still worse speller at Tim's age (item 2.13).

5.33   "I am weak physically. I like sports, but I cannot play them well." When the study group analyzed Tim's fringer status in the peer group they wondered why he participated so little in sports. His conception of himself supplies a partial answer, for no one doubted that he could learn to play games like baseball to an acceptable degree.

5.35   Tim sees himself as having accomplished much that is laudable, for he says that one of the three things that have given him most pleasure is "the feeling of accomplishing some things while I have been living."

5.33   Yet Tim also feels that he is falling short of his obligation, imposed by his being alive, to be doing something constructive at every moment. "I think a person should be doing something all the time. It is possible for me to do this on week days but my mind stops and I play during the week end."

5.34   "I feel that I oughtta keep doing something. . . . That's why I don't want my father to get a television, 'cause then I know I'll be cooked. Guess I only have a week of freedom. . . . I just have to do something. For instance, on Wednesday night I had Scout meeting, I had English make-up, I had history and math homework, and it was wonderful. I had something to do."

5.42   This drive to be doing something constantly was not merely a desire to escape boredom. If it had been, Tim would have welcomed a television set, for his mother reported that they bought one mainly to keep Tim at home, since he had been going to neighbors' houses to watch theirs. So Tim's concern about "doing something all the time" seems rather to grow out of a compulsion constantly to be learning, to be getting to know truth, to be developing his power for good.

5.33   Tim obviously is very self-demanding and sincerely feels that he is not living up to his obligations to the degree he should. He is even concerned about the effects of the inner conflict between duty and pleasure, for he says, "I am one nervous wreck."

5.34   Miss Riley, in a conference with Tim, probes to find out how genuine is his feeling of being a nervous wreck. She asks, "Do you really feel you are?" Tim replies, "Yes, I bite my nails." She questions, "What makes you so nervous?" and Tim responds without hesitation, "I just feel that I ought to keep doing something." He elaborates this. "When we are in history class and you're talking, I just gotta do something, so I bite my nails." Obviously the group process in class is too slow to satisfy Tim's need to be learning at every moment.

5.71   Next to conceiving of himself as obliged constantly to be doing something useful, the most significant way Tim sees himself is as resembling his father. In his brief essay on "Who I Would Like to Be" he says: "I would like to be as much like my father as I could. Because he has good ideas always. He is understanding. He knows a great amount of Science and Math which I would like to know." Here, again, Tim is consistent. He wants to have good ideas. He wants to understand. He sees knowledge of science and mathematics as the way of getting these good ideas, this understanding. His father to him represents a sort of epitome of capacity for usefulness through knowledge to which he himself aspires. So Tim wants to be as much like him as possible. The group wondered whether Tim had not internalized his core values, to know and to be useful in the world, directly from his father by emotionally identifying himself with the latter.

The group summarized Tim's conceptions of himself as follows:

1. Sees himself as growing out of childhood.
2. Sees himself as going through college and graduate school.
3. Sees himself as a person of social significance and high status.
4. Sees himself as physically weak.
5. Sees himself as accomplishing something significant in his development toward great social usefulness.
6. Sees himself as like his father.
7. Sees himself as falling short of meeting his obligation to be doing something valuable at all times.
8. Sees himself as a nervous wreck because of these shortcomings.

The study group felt that Tim's perceptions of himself strongly confirmed their judgment as to the core of meanings that seem to be organizing him as a self or personality. They wondered whether the attitudes and actions he displays daily would give added support to their interpretation of his inner values.

Tim's Perceptions, Attitudes, and Actions

In this section we shall test the degree to which Tim's perceptions, attitudes, and actions are consistent with his feeling that a person is given life in order to help develop a better world, should be doing something useful at every moment, and should seek knowledge as a basis for learning how to be of help. We shall test his consistency in relation to money, taking responsibility, and perception of social events, because the data are relatively rich in these matters.

The following items dealt with money:

3.08   Has a paper route; banks the money to use when he goes to college.

3.10   Father works with a man who made an important invention and is now very rich.

3.16   The family has no radio or television. They live in an area inhabited by people who are better off than they. Scientists don't make as much as lawyers.

5.20   "Anybody who can't give twenty-five cents to the Red Cross must be awful poor. . . . They should get a job. I work."

5.21   Wouldn't buy a school newspaper, though most of the children did.

5.38   Objected to assessing each one as much as twenty-five cents for a Christmas tree.

5.38   Voted for five-cent cup of ice cream instead of ten-cent or fifteen-cent cups.

5.40   Objects to community swimming pool. Says it would cost too much money.

5.43   Wants fines for misbehavior set at ten cents instead of five cents in order to make fine a greater deterrent. Later is fined twice.

5.47   Says he can't afford to buy separators for notebook; they cost ten cents.

5.50   Gave teacher an expensive valentine. Says he opened a second vault.

5.51   Economizes by using the same paper over and over until it is completely covered.

5.52   Was one of two people who refused to buy school newspaper, but he read the teacher's copy.

5.55   Says, "There goes their quarter down the drain," when commenting on persons who don't skate after signing up for it.

5.59   Describes how he thinks greedy lawyers bleed their clients of money.

5.59   Describes how politicians cheat to get money.

5.59   Is against $100-a-plate political dinners. Says government workers must attend to hold their jobs. Also speaks of politicians' buying votes.

4.42   Chipped in money to help buy bubble gum and balloons for class entertainment which he managed.

5.70   Tells about buying two knives that weren't good at a cost of $1.25. Points out he hadn't heeded his mother's advice.

These items show Tim working each day to earn money with his paper route and saving it to help himself through college. At first glance he appears stingy about spending it, for he refuses to buy the school newspaper, objects to paying twenty-five cents toward a Christmas tree, and votes for the cheapest and smallest cup of ice cream for the party. He says he can't afford to buy separators for his notebook, although they cost only ten cents. On the other hand he pressures others to give twenty-five cents to the Red Cross and seemingly has done so himself, wants fines for misbehavior doubled, gave the teacher an expensive valentine, chipped in to help buy bubble gum and balloons for the class, and bought two special paring knives for use at home. Thus he is willing to spend when the end seems socially valuable (Red Cross, fines, and paring knives), when it will give pleasure to someone he loves (teacher), or when it will result in direct enjoyment to himself (skating and party fun). He strongly condemns shyster practices among lawyers, political corruption, and luxury as signs of national decadence. Although one wonders whether there is social rivalry between his family and neighborhood lawyers, one must recognize that Tim is consistent everywhere in standing for an ethical code that would lead to social betterment. He seems more discriminating in his ways of spending money than most twelve-year-olds.

The following items deal with carrying responsibility:

6.08   "What is today? Monday? Papers [in a groaning voice]! I'm so darn sick . . . [breaks off]."
5.04   Leaped up to help teacher wipe off spilled ink.
6.09   Complains over having no time to study.
2.07   Stays home to help mother when she is ill.
5.19   Feels people should work to earn money for Red Cross. "I work."
4.20   Rests in his chair while others straighten up room.
5.36   Cleaned out all empty desks in his row as well as his own. He was the only one who did this.
4.29   Tim volunteered for maintenance man in the room.
4.30   Tim complains that Edna does not fulfill her responsibility.
5.41   Tim has regular jobs at home—cleaning floors and setting table. Makes biscuits for dinner. Does all chores happily. Loves to cook.
5.44   Overwatered his corn experiment. It died.
5.48   Second batch of corn died. Tim started third batch.
1.21   Tim put up seats in auditorium on own initiative.
4.37   Tim carries responsibility as cafeteria supervisor.
4.38   Tim carries responsibility for giving out the Bible every morning for opening exercises.
5.59   Tim complains that persons with luxury don't care about whether the country goes to pieces.
6.27   Tim complains that his table checkers, Nancy and Eve, do not do their tasks.
5.63   Tim wouldn't join glee club because it met at 8 o'clock three days a week, but he comes at that time almost every morning to help Mr. S in the metal shop—"for an A."
3.47   Tim first to volunteer help with library basket.
6.32   Tim complains Ann doesn't do her work properly as a table checker, so Tim does it himself.
5.72   Tim helped clear the table at home.

Tim really does seem to find self-fulfillment in carrying out responsibilities which other children might not care to do, but he does it at some cost to himself emotionally. Still, he does come through in most instances and often goes beyond the call of duty as usually interpreted, as when he cleaned out all the empty desks in his row and put up the seats in the auditorium. He has little tolerance for people who do not have the same sense of social obligation, for he complains about children who do not give enough to the Red Cross, about persons with luxury who don't care about what is happening to the country, and about Edna, Nancy, Eve, and Ann, who do not carry out the responsibilities they have accepted. Thus, Tim is consistent in holding both himself and others to a high level of social responsibility. It is remarkable that we see him faltering in this only twice during the year (when he said of his paper route, "I'm so darn sick . . ." and when he rested in his seat while the others picked up the room). Tim would hardly be human without these little slips. Indeed, as we see this terrific sense of social responsibility operating in Tim, the question has to be raised whether it is not too absolute for his own good, whether it is making him unduly intolerant of his peers and of other persons in the community.

The following items deal with Tim's perception of social events and with the meanings he attaches to them.

3.10   Tim recognizes the roles of invention and of research in social progress.

5.22   Tim writes that Halloween is a time for children to collect winter clothes for people in Korea.

5.33   Tim says war is to kill off the weak and dumb and so leave a better world.

5.39   Tim suggests as a topic for panel discussion: "Christianity versus Communism: Which Will Rule the World?"

5.40   Tim sees aid to Europe resulting in higher taxes. Disapproves.

5.56   Tim says in a discussion of the Korean War, "This country is going down because all of the smart people are being killed off."

3.41   Tim writes: "Our country was founded by hard working people. People had to work and to suffer and nothing was easy."

3.41   Tim writes: "Our country couldn't be strong forever [because] corruption entered in many ways."

3.41   Tim writes that dishonesty started in the United States in 1932, when greedy people were put in power.

3.41   Tim writes that sometimes patents are no good because if a company steals your patent, the services of a lawyer in a court suit would be so high that you wouldn't make money even if you won the suit.

3.41   Tim writes that "our country has Communists in important jobs. With people running the country who plan to destroy it, how can it remain stable?"

3.41   Tim writes that "the majority of lawyers and politicians here have luxury because they lie and cheat to get money."

3.41   Tim writes that "government workers who are incompetent pay politicians and parties to hold their jobs."

5.68   Tim writes: "Untouched by humans, mountains are a place of beauty and interest."

The meanings that arise as a part of Tim's perceptions of social events appear fully consistent with his conviction that "life is given to a person so that he might improve the world." Tim is solidly opposed to everything that he sees as bad for our country and solidly in favor of things that appear constructive to him. But an important problem for us to consider is whether Tim's perceptions of social events are simply reflections of what his father thinks or whether they are significantly shaped by his central life values.

The report of the home visit indicates that Tim's basic thesis in his essay "The Decline of America and the Roman Empire" is shared with his father. One can imagine family discussions in which instances have been cited of every evil that Tim abhors. But the probability is that these examples of corruption and dishonesty have come out piecemeal over a period of time in connection with discussions of the news of the day. It is doubtful whether Dr. Thyme has ever put together all the factors mentioned by Tim as contributing to the decline of America. Separately he has probably mentioned all of them. But why did they all fit together for Tim and come out as his supporting evidence for the decline of America?

What, according to Tim, are the factors militating against a better America? He maintains that America is declining because people no longer have to suffer and work so hard as formerly, the dollar has less value than it used to have, dishonesty and corruption were introduced into government by F.D.R., greedy people came into power, lawyers' fees are high, there are Communists in government posts, people with luxuries don't care about the future of the country, lawyers and politicians are able to get luxuries through lying and cheating, incompetent government workers pay in one way or another to hold their jobs, people smoke, drink, and use strong medicines, and high taxes enable us to conquer the world while we leave the home unprotected from enemies within.

It seems probable that Tim has heard of valid instances of each of these things. And each instance horrified him because it seemed to him to threaten what he valued—a world constantly growing better. Learning of one evil after another must have made him feel the world is growing worse rather than better. Before Tim assembled these instances in his essay, they became related to each other in his mind because they threatened what he valued.

Since Tim is only twelve years old, he tends to generalize too broadly and to think too much in terms of absolutes. Things are black or white to him, and people fall too easily into groups to be characterized as wholes. With appropriate guidance at home and at school, he will gain sufficient knowledge and insight to outgrow this habit. Otherwise, he might become a fanatic. At present, however, he has a good, solid core of values about which to organize his ever-growing body of knowledge.

Of course, Tim still has some attitudes that are inconsistent with each other. For example, at one time he sees war as making for a better world by killing off the weak and "dumb" and at another time he sees war as damaging our country by killing off the able. He sees it as good to collect clothes for needy Koreans, but sees government help for the rehabilitation of Europe as bad. One suspects that he is somewhat prejudiced in favor of one of our political parties. But this is the way attitudes evolve; they are often adopted ready-made and then gradually modified as new facts are revealed by experience and assimilated into the individual's concept-feeling system.

A number of these ideas about Tim's self-developmental processes were not formulated by the child-study group, for the record was rich enough in this area to permit extended analysis. These ideas do, however, provide answers to questions one through four which the group raised.

Tim's Capacities and Skills

The study group felt that they would be better able to see ways of helping Tim with his development if they appraised his capacities and skills for learning. With regard to general intelligence, they found that on group intelligence tests he had scored intelligence quotients of 116 in the third grade, 116 in the fourth grade, and 120 on each of two tests in the sixth grade. The consistency of these scores, together with his rich home background, led them to judge that this probably represents his real capacity. These scores place him well above average in intelligence, but not among the unusually gifted. Thus Tim has good but not brilliant capacity for learning.

In skills Tim achieved the following levels of ability at various grades:

> Spelling ability at grade 2½B in the fourth grade, at 3B in the sixth grade, and a little below fifth-grade level in the seventh grade. Reading comprehension at grade 4B in the fourth grade, at 6½A in the fifth grade, and at the tenth-grade level in the seventh grade. Reading vocabulary at grade 4A in the fourth grade, at 7½B in the fifth grade, and at 7½A in the seventh grade. Arithmetic fundamentals at the 7A level in the fifth grade. Arithmetic problem-solving at the 11½A grade level in the fifth grade.

The group noted a number of inconsistencies in these skill levels. Spelling, of course, stood out as his only deficiency, for here he was more than two years below his grade level. They noted Tim's identification with his father and wondered how long it would be before Tim would recognize that it was not useful to play up this likeness to his father and would seriously accept the task of learning to spell correctly. Given his obvious learning capacity, they felt that it would be useful for someone whose opinion he valued to counsel with him about this. The group noted his brilliance at problem-solving in arithmetic and decided that his motivation already was adequate in mathematics.

In reading, Tim's rapid growth in capacity to comprehend what he read was not accompanied by a similar development in reading vocabulary. The group thought that this should be brought to his attention and that he should be encouraged to use the dictionary more extensively. They also remarked that Tim himself had spoken of his major problem in reading when he said (item 5.56), "My trouble is that I understand what I read very well, but I can't read fast." They noticed that the record contained several allusions to lip movements accompanying his writing or reading (items 5.02, 6.11, 6.16) and that there were many evidences of tension connected with these activities. It was clear, they thought, that Tim could profit greatly from working with a remedial reading teacher who would help him build up his speed.

Tim's Mental Processes

One process that Tim uses to work out the meanings of situations and events seems to be to consider what his father thinks about it. "He has good ideas always," Tim wrote. Consequently, if Tim's poor spelling did not trouble his father it would not trouble Tim either. The group also found that Tim's attitude toward a community swimming pool was identical with that of his father; so were most of Tim's political and social ideas. Thus his father's ways of thinking seem to have become a major influence on the way Tim's mind works.

A second major process is to measure situations against the hard core of his own inner values. His sense of the obligation to keep busy doing useful things, to become useful in building a better world, to learn constantly, to be frugal, to support worthy causes, and to live up to his responsibilities seems to supply him with many cues to meaning. So we see him cleaning out all the empty desks in his row although responsible only for his own desk. He was only the second child among the thousands in Miss Riley's teaching experience who used paper over and over until it was completely covered. He stood out against his peers for larger contributions to the Red Cross and larger fines, but for a smaller Christmas tree and smaller dishes of ice cream. He valued books as sources of experience and knowledge, and sought the eighth-grade reading list for summer reading. He blamed his table checkers for their laxness in tidying up the cafeteria. He was always reverent during the Lord's Prayer. Although Tim adopted his father's views about matters in which the latter's experience was richer than his, his life at school was marked by doing his own thinking and standing for what he valued, no matter what his peers' attitudes might be. Perhaps we can say that this habit of finding the meanings of situations in relation to his value system made him see a deeper significance to situations and events than his peers were seeing.

How Effective Were Tim's Actions?

The study group found it very difficult to decide how effective Tim's actions were. For teachers, the most obvious way to measure the effectiveness of a pupil's actions is by his marks in various school subjects. The group felt that with an IQ of 120 and a stimulating home background, Tim should make strong B's in most of his subjects. Actually Tim's marks during the first half of the seventh grade were B in all subjects except music, in which he received a C. Consequently Tim was judged to be effective in his school learning.

But measuring Tim's effectiveness in managing his body presents a spotty picture. He skates very well, but cannot play any group games and was awkward at dodge-ball. He is always under tension when he writes and always very jumpy when excited, as he was during the class party and when he was eliminated from the dodge-ball game.

If the effectiveness of his actions is measured in terms of their impact on his peers, the outcome is again uneven, in fact, somewhat unfavorable. Tim volunteered or was nominated for a number of roles in class activities which were refused to him. The group voted him only those roles where he clearly would do well, according to their evaluations. He was far too bossy on his job as cafeteria supervisor. On the other hand he was able to joke very successfully with some of his fellows, and his status seemed to improve somewhat as the year wore on.

Tim also measured his own effectiveness, and despite his good marks, wide knowledge, and his father's satisfaction with him, in his own eyes he was far from measuring up to what he thought he should be. He saw himself as physically weak. He saw himself as failing in his duty to do something useful at every moment. He recognized that he was handicapped by his slow reading. Curiously enough, however, he was not bothered by his real spelling deficiency and only once mentioned his fringe status with his peers (item 6.31).

How Others See Tim

Tim's teacher was attracted to him as "a sparkling personality that seemed to reach out." A quick glance at Tim's cumulative record will show that most of Tim's earlier teachers responded in a similar manner. We did not classify most of this material because it was subjective and evaluative rather than factual, but reading through it does show the climate of opinion about him throughout his school experience. Sample comments include:

> KINDERGARTEN: "A very alert and responsive little fellow."
> 1ST GRADE: "A well-rounded little boy."
> 2ND GRADE: "Timothy is a fine student—conscientious, cooperative. Full of enthusiasm and an insatiable curiosity."

3RD GRADE: "Very sincere about his work . . . refreshing enthusiasm . . . very honest, does help me a great deal."

4TH GRADE: "Has contributed much by his reference work carried on in his free time . . . fine attitude of cooperation.

5TH GRADE: "Is interested, working hard. He is really a live wire."

MATH TEACHER: "That Tim Thyme of yours is a sketch."

213.   Dr. Thyme was perfectly satisfied with Tim's work. Mrs. Thyme expressed a desire that it should be better. Miss Riley remarked that Tim was very philosophical. Dr. Thyme said, "Tim seems to be the most serious one." Mrs. Thyme said he was babied, "perhaps he's closer than the rest" [to us adults]. Dr. Thyme mentioned that Tim was the only one who seemed interested in science and was willing to do any scientific research.

2.24   During the home visit Dr. Thyme remarked several times that Tim is a very serious thinker and the only one who seems interested in science.

Three significant points came out of this material as the group discussed it. The first was that Dr. Thyme is fully satisfied with Tim and sees Tim following in his own footsteps to a career in science. But Tim's mother is not satisfied with him and wants him to win higher marks. A second point is that Tim's conception of himself as falling short of what he should be doing is not shared by his father or by any of his teachers. Only his mother agrees with him in this. Can this be a part of her upward-mobile social ambition to see Tim stand out in competition with others? How far is his mother's evaluation of him the basis for Tim's discontent with himself? How far is Tim's self-devaluation the result of his own values? The third point is that all the adults now in close contact with Tim agree that he is very serious-minded, philosophical, and thoughtful.

If one takes into consideration Tim's capacities, it is clear that he is making fine progress in accomplishing his intellectual developmental tasks. In other words, Dr. Thyme and his teachers are realistic in their evaluation of his abilities, and Mrs. Thyme and Timothy himself are not.

It is also clear from the facts in the record that the adults around him, interested in his mental processes, are unaware of his need for developing greater physical adequacy and of a possible disturbance of his physical-growth processes. His parents equally are unaware of his need to function adequately in his peer group so that his sense of belonging can be enhanced. In other words, Tim has wonderful potentialities but is being stimulated by his environment and by his inner value-system to a somewhat lopsided development. Sports activity would enrich and balance his experience because through it he could gain a sense of physical competence and ability to get along with his peers. One foresees considerable difficulty for him when he has to serve his time in the Army, both physically and in his relationships with his fellows.

SELF-ADJUSTIVE FACTORS AND PROCESSES

The study group decided to try to answer the following questions about Tim's self-adjustive processes:

1. Is there evidence that Tim is frequently or continuously under tension?
2. What is the quality of Tim's feeling about his physical adequacy, love relationships, social significance, peer-group belonging, and adequacy as a total person?
3. What adjustment patterns does Tim characteristically use to reduce tension? Are any of these patterns unwholesome?
4. Does Tim have any continuing adjustment problems? What assets and liabilities does he have in relation to these problems?
5. Does Tim need clinical help?

In order to find out whether Tim is frequently under tension and to see what the situations are under which he shows tension, the group listed all the recorded indications of tension and strong feelings. The tabulation follows:

6.01   His fingernails are stubby and chewed.

6.02   His lips move as he writes; he occasionally bites a nail.

6.03   Eats alone; after lunch sits gazing into space, his lips moving.

6.04   Gets very excited when teacher dribbles ink.

6.07   Very excited over caterpillar he shows teacher.

6.08   Groans, "Papers! I get so darn sick . . ." and broke off.

6.12   Waited impatiently while school papers were sold and read.

6.14   Nibbles a finger, brushes hair off forehead, shades eyes, lips move as he writes.

6.15   Writes in the essay titled "Me": "I think a person should be doing something all the time. It is possible for me to do this on weekdays, but my mind stops and I play during the week end." "The only thing I am afraid of is God." "I am weak physically. I like sports, but I cannot play them well." "I am one nervous wreck."

6.16   Says he fears God because He is truth, that one fears truth more than the false, that he does feel he is a nervous wreck, that he bites his nails, that he feels he ought to keep doing something, that he just has to be doing something, and that it's wonderful when he is extremely busy.

6.19   Lips keep moving while he is writing, an exaggerated movement as though he were just learning to talk.

6.23   Has look of patient disgust as others buy the school paper.

6.24   Tim at first reticent in dodge-ball game, then very excited; jumps up and down on sidelines after he was eliminated from game.

6.25   Says, "My trouble is that I understand what I read very well, but I can't read fast."

6.26   Writes forcefully about the decline of America because of corruption, dishonesty, greedy lawyers, poor government, luxury, buying of votes, buying of jobs, smoking, drinking, using strong medicines, high taxes, conquering the world and leaving the home unprotected from enemies within.

6.28 Complains in a querulous tone about Nancy and Eve not staying to clean up in cafeteria.

6.30 Tim is very reverent during the "Lord's Prayer."

6.31 Tim writes in his essay on "Security" that a person feels secure unless something makes him feel insecure. "Parents can make me unsecure by when things that are amusing come up about me I get embarrassed which makes me unsecure." "Teachers make me unsecure by doubting things I say that are reasonable." "[Children] make me unsecure by not playing with me or asking me to play. (Not that I can't find something to do.)"

6.32 Tim rushes up, face red, frowning, very loud voice, to complain about Ann's not cleaning up cafeteria table.

6.34 Tim often moved about restlessly during teacher's home visit and was told several times to sit down.

The study group felt that there is abundant evidence of almost continuous tension in Tim. Tension is apparent when he writes and it appears as undue excitement when the teacher dribbles ink or examines the caterpillar he brought her and when he is on the sidelines watching the dodge-ball game. Trivial matters bother him: for example, the delays while the school paper is sold and read. He has to repress his statement of how he feels about his paper route. He also expresses much deeper concerns, about keeping busy doing things, fearing the truth, being physically weak and poor at sports, and being a nervous wreck. He also is worried about reading slowly. He feels very deeply about the "Decline of America." Tim's essay on security shows that he is vulnerable to being laughed at at home, doubted by a teacher, and excluded from play by his peers. He grows quite angry with Nancy, Eve, and Ann when they fail to do their duties in the cafeteria, and he is very restless at home during the teacher's visit. Putting it all together, the group judged that Tim is under greater tension than is desirable.

On the other hand the group found many evidences that Tim releases tension by joking:

6.05 Jokes that he has learned to play two notes on his band instrument.

6.06 Jokes about his father's name and his own initials, T.N.T.

6.09 Jokes "us girlies gotta have our pocketbooks."

6.17 Jokes about not having a banana for lunch. Laughs.

6.22 Laughs uproariously about his misspelling on the valentine.

6.27 Jokingly says, "Ah, pumpernickel!"

6.33 Gets a big laugh over the story about being gypped by the salesman.

The group also noted that Tim expressed some very deep positive bases for happiness. The three things that he reported as giving him greatest happiness were:

1. My trips to the West Coast.
2. The feeling of accomplishing some things while I have been living.
3. That my father has been safe.

Tim also was very excited and happy the day he took over the direction of the class party. "He yelled. He shrieked. He giggled. He roared. He ordered people around and gave instructions at the top of his lungs." So the group evaluated Tim as living rather vividly, as finding a considerable amount of real happiness, but as still carrying a larger load of tension than is necessary or desirable.

Qualitative Evaluation of Tim's Feelings

The group found that they already had answered the second question, dealing with the quality of Tim's feelings. He feels that he is physically weak and unable to engage successfully in sports. He feels secure in belonging to his family and identifies strongly with his father. Perhaps he sometimes feels threatened by his mother's pressure for a higher level of accomplishment. He feels that he is a socially significant person and is very much at home with adults. He seems to sense his status as a fringer with his peers and is hurt by their excluding him from play groups. But he keeps volunteering for roles, wins some, and plays them successfully. His exaggerated delight at successfully directing the class party shows how much he longs for a more sure belonging in the peer group. He is happy and proud of the things he is able to accomplish as a person but is tormented by the feeling that he should keep busy at useful things. This recurring pattern of feeling is strong enough to have a compulsive element in it, but the group could find no adequate explanation for it, except perhaps his father's outstanding accomplishments and his own longing to be as much like his father as possible.

Tim's Adjustment Patterns

When the study group looked for the defense mechanisms that are so common in children, such as making excuses, blaming others for their own failures, shyness, daydreaming, aggressions against others, joking, and the like, they were amazed. They could not find evidence that Tim habitually used any of these adjustment patterns except joking. When he was aloof from the group it was to follow an interest of his own, such as reading. Though he was at first reticent about participating in the dodge-ball game, he quickly overcame it and soon was strongly involved. The rebuffs he sometimes received when he volunteered for roles led to no storming or aggressions. When he reported in anger the failures of his table checkers in the cafeteria it did not seem to be to get even but rather to invoke authority so as to get the job done. In other words Tim's positive desire to pursue his goals make it possible for him to sublimate most of his frustrations. The group noted that when he reported that other children made him feel insecure by not inviting him to play with them he added, "Not that I can't find something to do." Indeed this seems to be Tim's major adjustment pattern. The world is so full of interesting things to do that he is not vulnerable to rebuffs and frustrations of the sort that bother other children greatly. If Tim is overly serious, it is not to compensate for peer-group rejection, but because of his genuine and continuing interest in a central life theme, getting to know the world in order to make it a better place.

Continuing Adjustment Problems

The study group felt that Tim has four continuing adjustment problems:

1. He needs to get the feeling of mastery over his body, to feel that he can manage it in a wider variety of situations, as in sports. This is very important for him to learn before he has to enter military service. Otherwise, he will experience great difficulty in measuring up successfully to the demands of military training.

2. He needs greater skill in getting along with his peers. This also will become crucial when he enters military service and when he goes away to college. Sports seem to offer a good avenue to this adjustment, too.

3. He needs to learn consciously to seek to know the several sides that exist on all controversial issues. Tim's habit is to look only for the "right" answer, and he equates the right answer too certainly with his father's views. He will not become able to understand others well enough to negotiate with them successfully in the future if he does not try to see situations from their perspectives as well as from his own.

4. He needs to become less compulsive about "doing something" at every moment. Participating in recreational activity to a reasonable degree ought not to cost him twinges of conscience.

Tim's liabilities, which will retard the solving of these adjustment problems, were seen by the group to be:

1. His small stature and the possibility of some growth difficulty.

2. Tim's belief that he is weak physically and his apparent acceptance of this as a permanent characteristic.

3. Tim's limited experience in playing successfully with peers—he is "behind" in his peer-group experience and knowledge.

4. Tim's great success in winning the approval of adults at home and at school, which makes it seem unnecessary for him to please his peers or to achieve competence in sports.

5. Tim's strong desire to know as much as possible. Perhaps he already is beginning to see that a lifetime is too short for learning all one wants to know. This is beginning to make him bookish.

6. Tim's compulsive feeling of obligation always to be doing something useful.

The assets that will help Tim solve these adjustment problems were listed by the group as:

1. A really attractive, spontaneous personality.

2. Good capacity for learning and thinking with resulting good ideas for the peer group as well as for society.

3. An unusually rich background of experience.

4. Security in his relationship with his father.

5. Success in a number of peer-group activities.

6. A real liking for sports and pleasure in using his body well, as illustrated by skating.

7. A real wish to be a full belonger in the peer group, illustrated by his volunteering for many roles.

8. Confidence in his own capacity to learn and to think.

9. A comprehensive orientation of self in the universe, involving the acceptance of God as his creator, the feeling that God is truth and that he can know truth, the feeling that he is significant as a living being and has the obligation to function in such a way as to make the world a better place.

10. The habit of relating all his experiences, learning, and activities with this central self-orientation.

Does Tim Need Clinical Help?

When the group reckoned up Tim's liabilities and assets in relation to his continuing adjustment problems, they concluded that he could profit from wise guidance but was not in need of clinical help. They felt that any teacher who had a real understanding of him and a genuine affection for him could take advantage of the many opportunities afforded by school situations to guide him into the attitudes and activities that he needs. They saw in him an unusually well-knit personality and did not sense any need for reorganization or therapy. However, they did see a need for better balance, which could be accomplished by guiding his activities and helping him, privately, to analyze his attitudes and actions. They felt, too, that a conference with his father might help, particularly if it included an analysis of Tim's physical-growth pattern, using the Wetzel grid, and a discussion of what he will face when he enters military service, based on the supposition that he will be preparing for an officer's role and that more participation in sports would be good preparation for this role.

The Teacher's Task

As shown in Chapter 1, teachers have a formidable number of decisions to make each hour as they deal with children in their classes. Miss Riley felt much surer of being helpful to Timothy as she progressed in her study of him throughout the year. Especially, she looked forward to teaching him again the following year. She felt that her study of Tim had validated for her the postulates set forth in Chapter 2. She could begin to see why he acted as he did, and why situations had for him the meanings which they did. Certainly his developing self was an active agent in his own evolution: his conceptions of himself, his world, and his relationships with his world determined the meanings situations had for him and became the active bases for his motivations.

Miss Riley began to have confidence in her capacity to understand Tim and to guide him. She wished greatly for equivalent material about many of her students and actually found more available than she had anticipated. This she put to good use. Miss Riley also discovered that she lacked certain basic scientific knowledge and began to round out her knowledge by reading and by further graduate study. The organizing framework became a basis for self-evaluation. Against it she measured both her information about individual young people and the scope of her scientific knowledge. Thus it became a tool which she has continued to use.

CHAPTER 9

Analyzing Group Dynamics

When children go to school they are placed together in groups or "classes" of thirty or more to do their learning. These class groups become miniature societies with the customary characteristics of societies, namely, goals, activities, customs, codes of conduct, roles, status, and individual strivings. Consequently each child does his curricular learning, that is, learns to read and figure and studies science and social studies, in the context of a miniature child society. This child society becomes very important to him, for it offers him the possibility of belonging and perhaps even a prestige status. Unlike the home, however, the children's peer-group society does not offer belonging to the individual just because he exists. In the peer group, belonging must be won. It must be won by playing roles effectively and by conforming in behavior to the customs and code of the child society. For any given child in school, then, classroom experiences have two kinds of meaning: one relating to the skill, information, and attitude learnings expected and demanded by the child's parents and teachers, the other relating to the child's status and roles in the peer group.

Inevitably, each school class has its own unique structure as a group. This structure depends upon how the individual children feel about each other, relate to each other, and accord roles and status to each other. For example, a class that is well integrated into a unified group around one or two leaders who mutually respect and value each other is quite different in its way of functioning from a class broken into three or four relatively independent cliques which are rivals for status and power in the group as a whole. Also, the characteristics of the leaders influence the way the group operates and the kinds of experiences that individual children have within it. The peer-group structure and dynamics are also very powerful factors in determining the kinds of experiences the teacher has with the group as he tries to facilitate their learning and their functioning as a class within the total school organization. Some groups are unusually "difficult" to work with, others are much easier to work with than the average class.

Factors Determining Structure and Dynamics

⟨The teacher has a double need to understand his class as a miniature child society. Its character as a society can make his work pleasant and easy, or it can create difficult problems for him. Also, the character of the peer-group structure and dynamics sets important conditions within which each pupil must live and learn during the year. For certain individuals, the task of winning belonging in this peer group or achieving certain desired roles and status may be the most compelling interest of the school year, the major developmental task upon which to work. Hence it becomes very important for a teacher to know explicitly what factors determine the structure of each class and what are the dynamics of interpersonal relationship which operate in the group. Some of the factors that must be considered are:

1. Quite apart from the adult-determined curriculum of the school, peer groups have their own activities in which they engage whenever opportunity offers. These activities may be copied from the preceding group of children or spontaneously generated. They usually are related to the developmental tasks on which the children are working, hence they vary considerably from one maturity level to another. Most of these activities are called "play" by adults, but they are very important to the children and youth, involving a great deal of new learning and evoking vivid interest and tremendous efforts to succeed.

2. To participate successfully in these activities a child must possess the necessary specific knowledge and skill in, for example, rope skipping, jacks, marbles, baseball, football, prisoner's base, dodge-ball, social dancing, dating, basketball, etc. A child can win belonging in the peer group only by using his knowledge and skill successfully in a series of these peer-group activities.

3. Each peer-group activity is carried out in accordance with a set of customs and a code of conduct apparently handed down from each generation of children to the next. To win belonging, a child must obey the code of the group and act in accord with the customs of the group. At many developmental levels the code of conduct and the customs of the peer group are at variance with the code and customs of adults. So a child following the code of the peer group may get into difficulties with his teacher and yet win approval from his fellows. Fighting among boys and secret whisperings among girls are illustrations.

4. Each peer-group activity provides a number of roles for participants, and each role successfully played carries its particular degree of prestige. This is well-illustrated by baseball, where pitcher and heavy-hitter are high-prestige roles and outfielder and poor-hitter are lesser-prestige roles because they require less skill. An individual's status within the group depends upon the

number of different roles he plays successfully in the whole gamut of peer-group activities and upon the prestige value of these different roles.

5. Children who are outstandingly successful in playing many peer-group roles become the high-prestige persons in the group—the leaders—and exercise a powerful influence over the attitudes and actions of their peers both in and out of the classroom. Children who conform to peer-group customs and codes and play a number of roles effectively become full belongers in the group and feel themselves "one of the gang." Those who have but limited knowledge and skill at playing peer-group roles and, consequently, often fail at these roles become "fringers." They will be accepted as participants when only a few children are available for an activity, or they will be given only those roles in which they can succeed and in which they will not diminish the success of the group. A few unfortunate children who lack the knowledge and skill to play peer-group roles successfully, who are timid or lacking in courage, have physical disabilities, lack judgment, or are "dumb," will be refused peer-group roles and will become isolates or nonbelongers. Although they are constantly a part of the class group, these isolates simply do not matter to their peers; it is almost as though they were not present. On the other hand, children with objectionable personality traits such as selfishness, the habit of tattling or appealing to adults, the tendency to quarrelsomeness, an unjustified air of superiority, overbossiness, or the inability "to take it" and children who are "teacher's pets" will be actively rejected by the group even though they may be intelligent and possess the requisite skills for role playing.

6. It is one thing to know how to get along well with parents, teachers, and other adults and to please them by obedience, good learning, and conformity to adult mores. It is quite another thing to know how to get along with one's peers. Hence peer-group activities at each successive maturity level are important sources of learning for every child and youth. Through these activities each individual is disciplined by group processes to subordinate personal desires to the success of the group, to accept group customs and codes, needs and roles, to achieve personal success and status through successful group activities, to respect the rights of others, and to promote the purposes of the group as a whole. To a considerable extent it is through peer-group activities that leadership capacities are developed, the concept of teamwork is established, and a sense of personal adequacy based on sure belonging is engendered.

7. The preferred activities of peer groups, like their customs and codes of conduct, change with the maturity level. For boys, skill in games is an important factor at virtually all maturity levels; so is a sense of humor. But in middle childhood a boy does not have to "take" a joke on himself to the degree that he must in early adolescence. In middle childhood he may become angry and still hold prestige roles, but in early adolescence he will be regarded as a poor sport and will tend to lose status if he becomes angry at a joke at his expense; he must laugh at himself along with the others. Interest in the opposite sex is more or less taboo in middle childhood, but in early adolescence learning to get along with the opposite sex is an important developmental task and success in attracting members of the opposite sex brings prestige.

Classrooms, therefore, are places where children and youth systematically learn important knowledges and skills that prepare them to earn a living, to be socially responsible, and to enjoy the better things in life. But they also are the settings in which a very vivid life develops among peers who are gradually learning how to get along with their fellows, to be effective group members, and to subordinate selfish desires to the accomplishment of group goals. The teacher must be equally aware of both aspects of classroom living, for it frequently happens that peer-group processes interfere with the more widely recognized curricular learnings. Furthermore, what a particular child learns during a certain year about getting along with his peers may be more important for his success in later life than his standard curricular learning. This may be particularly true of some of the more privileged and gifted children whose parents are pushing them overly hard for academic superiority at the cost of balanced physical and social development.

This chapter will present the case record of a seventh-grade girl from the time she was twelve years and eight months old until she was thirteen years and three months old. Anne Hart was "one of the larger girls in her group, not as tall as one or two, but of heavier build and well-developed." She was about to begin to menstruate, so she was in the transition period between late childhood and early adolescence—a time when young people usually alternate between acting like children and acting like adolescents. It is also the time when individuals move out of late-childhood peer groups and into early-adolescent peer groups, two types of groups which differ greatly from each other in activities, codes, and customs. Along with a few of the other girls in her class, Anne faced the developmental tasks of early adolescence. Because these tasks are so pressing for the individual and because they were not shared by all the girls in the group, an awareness of them is important to an understanding of Anne's behavior and how her classmates felt about and reacted to her.

The Developmental Tasks of Early Adolescent Girls

Some of the developmental tasks faced by the early-adolescent girl in our society are:

1. Learning the significance of the physical changes occurring as a result of growth, especially of the maturing of her reproductive capacity, and learning how to maintain health at the new maturity level.

2. Learning ways of grooming, dressing, and behaving that are appropriate to her sex and effective in attracting favorable attention from boys, other girls, and adults.

3. Learning how to get along well with boys in the light of her new body dynamics and maturity level.

4. Learning how to get along well with girls in the light of her new hetero-sexual roles and maturity level.

5. Winning and effectively playing adolescent peer-group roles in the school and community.

6. Winning from parents the right to make more decisions and to be respon-sible for a wider range of her own behavior.

7. Maintaining security-giving love relationships with her parents despite her striving for greater freedom to make decisions for herself.

8. Continuing her successful accomplishment of school tasks and winning adult approval in and about the school.

9. Learning about and participating in social institutions and processes, and learning her duties and responsibilities as a citizen.

10. Exploring possible adult roles such as homemaking, caring for children, taking part in community affairs, and choosing a vocation.

11. Exploring questions about the meaning of life and about the values to be sought in life.

12. Continuing the development of a code of ethics as a measuring stick for evaluating her own attitudes and her actual behavior.

13. Setting up goals for immediate accomplishment as a step toward long-term purposes.

It must be stressed that Miss Thornton, Anne's teacher, was studying her *during the early days of Anne's adolescence,* a period when every individual fluctuates repeatedly between the feelings, attitudes, and be-havior of childhood and those of adolescence. In other words, the devel-opmental tasks of early adolescence were sometimes strongly present in Anne's awareness, and at other times she laid them aside to be a child again for a while.

The Social Structure of the Class

On October 21 Miss Thornton told the children that they would con-tinue to do a great deal of their study in small committees which would report the results of their investigations to the class as a whole. She said that often children like best to work with their closest friends, but that this could not always be done because it is important for everyone to learn to work with everyone else and for no one to be left out. It would help her, she told the group, if each one would write on a piece of paper the three people whom he or she would choose for best friends and the three people whom he or she would choose last as friends. The girls' choices are graphically presented in Figure 1. Wide, solid two-way arrows indicate mutual choices between children as best friends; one-way slender arrows indicate one-way choices of best friends, and broken ar-rows signify last choices, which are really rejections. Such a graphic presentation of choices is called a sociogram—a diagram of the social structure of the class.

The Girls' Sociogram

An analysis of the girls' sociogram reveals the following facts:

1. There are three major subgroups among the girls, identifiable by mutual choices. The largest is made up of four girls: B.W.–A.H.–M.M.–S.T. Two additional girls, S.M. and J.R., chose only members of this group as their friends and obviously identify themselves with this group. So, operationally, the group is made up of six girls, though two of them are "fringers."

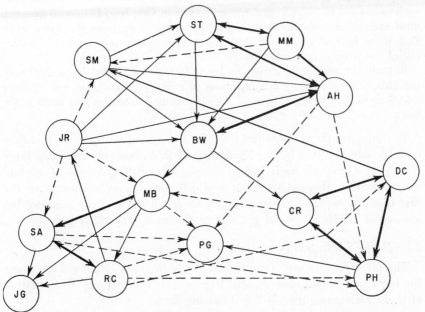

Fig. 1 Girls' sociogram—friendship choices and rejections

2. A second subgroup of four girls is made up of M.B., S.A., R.C., and J.G. J.G. was absent the day the choices were made, but she certainly belongs to this group because she was chosen by every member of it. None of these girls chose any full member of the first group, though one of them, R.C., chose J.R., who identifies herself with the first group, rejects two members of the second group, and was chosen only by R.C.

3. The third subgroup is a triumvirate made up of P.H., C.R., and D.C. None of them chose a member of the first group or the second group, but D.C. did choose S.M., who identifies herself with the first group.

4. The two most chosen girls are B.W. and A.H., the girl whom we are studying. Each was chosen by the five other persons who make up this first group. But there is a contrast between the choices made by these two girls themselves. A.H. is clannish and chooses only within her own group, but B.W. chooses A.H. in her own group, M.B. in the second group, and C.R. in the

third group. B.W. is the only child in the class who chooses a best friend from each of the three groups.

5. P.G. is the most rejected girl in the class, for four of her classmates rejected her, including three members of the second group. She was, however, chosen by P.H.

6. C.R. chose a boy, J.P., the most popular boy in the class. No other girl chose a boy.

7. There was a total of twenty-three rejections of boys by girls, although this is not shown on the sociogram. This would seem to show that the boys are quite important to the girls in this grade; but the peer-culture mores are such as not yet to favor formal recognition of it. One boy, J.H., who also was most unpopular with the boys, drew seven rejections from the girls, while D.B. drew four rejections and A.T. drew three. So three boys drew fourteen out of the twenty-three rejections.

8. Only two girls were chosen by boys—A.H. and P.H. But in contrast with the girls, there were only five rejections of girls by boys against twenty-three rejections of boys by girls. Most of the girls seemed to matter very little to the boys.

In summary, the girls do not constitute a unified group except as they may be held together by the leadership of B.W. Instead, there are three closely knit cliques, each bound together by strong bonds of mutual choices within themselves. S.M. and J.R. are fringe adherents to the first group, whereas P.G. is a fringer to group three if she has any belonging at all. However, no girl was unchosen by any other girl.

The Boys' Sociograms

The boys' choices are presented in two sociograms. Figure 2 diagrams the boys' best-friend choices, and Figure 3 their rejections. Examination of these sociograms reveals the following facts:

1. There is only one major grouping of the boys. The high-prestige persons in this group are J.P., who was chosen as a best friend by nine other boys, and H.F., who was chosen by eight others. The two of them mutually chose each other, so this one group determines the operations of the whole boys' peer group; there are no cliques to fight amongst themselves. The nearest approach to a subgroup is found in the mutual choices between G.T. and L.N. and G.T. and L.Mc, but G.T. ties these other boys to the central group by his choice of H.F. D.S. was quite a popular boy, being chosen by four other boys, but two of his three choices go to the two leaders of the group, J.P. and H.F., so he is no rallying point for an opposition clique. E.C. and F.C. seem close friends because they mutually chose each other, but they are not a split-off pair because both chose J.P., the most popular boy in the group. J.H. and A.T. were absent when the friendship choices were made.

2. When we turn to the rejection sociogram of the boys, Figure 3, it is easy to see which ones are unable to win peer-group belonging. J.H. was rejected by seven of his fellows, and R.F. and T.C. were each rejected by five

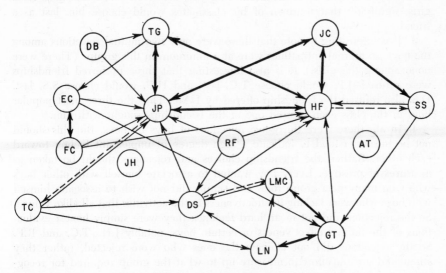

Fig. 2   Boys' sociogram—friendship choices

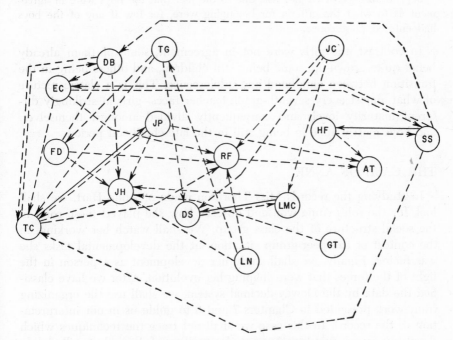

Fig. 3   Boys' sociogram—friendship rejections

of the boys. It will be remembered that J.H. also won seven rejections from girls, signifying that fourteen of his classmates would choose him last as a friend.

3. It is interesting to note that there were only two mutual rejections among the boys, so mutual antipathies were at a minimum in this group. (There were none among the girls.) It is also interesting that three preferred friendships were refused—J.P. would choose T.C. last, and H.F. would choose S.S. last. D.S. also refused the friendship offered by L.Mc. Thus the three most popular boys in the class each refused one of the friendships sought with him.

4. In all, there were thirty-five rejections of boys by boys. But this should not be misunderstood to indicate a high degree of unpleasant feeling toward each other. Rather, the friendship choices and rejections should be taken as measures of prestige. Every boy wanted to associate himself with other boys who won many peer-group roles and simply did not wish to associate himself with boys who were lacking in effectiveness in the activities that all alike valued. So the rejections did not mean hard feelings; they were simply honest evaluations of the limited effectiveness of certain boys, notably J.H., T.C. and R.F. So the rejections did not alienate the ones who were rejected, rather they stimulated greater effort to measure up to what the group required for recognition and belonging.

5. The absence of cliques was due to the fact that the boys were in agreement as to what the criteria for belonging were, for few if any of the boys had entered pubescence.

In contrast, the girls were not in agreement, some of them already being quite grown-up, some being still children, and others being in the transition between childhood and adolescence. This is a classic picture of what almost every seventh-grade teacher faces—girls at strikingly different maturity levels and consequently divided amongst themselves, and boys mostly alike in being still in the late-childhood period.

THE CASE OF ANNE

In studying the records Miss Thornton made of Anne Hart, we shall look for the roles Anne won and observe how she played these roles in the social structure of the class group. We shall watch her working, in the context of the peer-group situation, at the developmental tasks she was facing. Finally, we shall study her development as a person in the light of the forces that were shaping her evolution. After we have classified the data by the Dewey-decimal system, we shall use the organizing framework presented in Chapters 7 and 8 to guide us in our interpretation of the record. In this case we shall not trace the techniques which the study group used to gain an understanding of Anne, but will simply present the material as gathered by the teacher, together with the interpretations she made with the aid of the group. We have selected this case not only to demonstrate the interplay of the individual and the group, but also to show the great value of an adequate cumulative record, since such a record permitted Miss Thornton, with the aid of the study group, to get the insights she needed very early in the year.

> I chose Anne Hart because she appears to be a stable, poised child who enjoys her schoolwork, associations, and life in general. She laughs readily and often, has a good sense of humor, is efficient, cooperative, and intelligent.
>
> I feel that she and I will have fun together and that she will contribute a great deal to the group and to me this year.
>
> B. L. Thornton, Grade 7
> Oct. 15, 1953

1.01 4.01	Oct. 18 *Descriptive Sketch.* Anne is one of the larger girls in her group—not as tall as one or two but of heavier build and well developed.
1.02 2.01 1.03	Her skin is clear and her hair a glossy light brown. Her large expressive hazel eyes often seem full of mischief or sparkle with amusement. Her face lights up whenever she catches my eye and her ready smile reveals white, well-cared-for teeth.
1.04	Her hair is parted on the left side and the ends are slightly curled. A dark tortoise-shell barrette holds the hair back on the right side.
1.05 4.02 3.01	On this particular day she is wearing a yellow wool skirt, a white cotton blouse trimmed with dainty lace and pin tucks. The Peter Pan collar is pulled outside of her navy blue sweater. Her socks are heavy, white, ribbed ones, rolled at the top and with these she wears gray suede loafers with a dime under the tongue strap of each. Her clothes are always neat, in good taste and rather more expensive than those of a majority in our community.
4.03 6.01 4.04	Anne was separated this year from some of her friends with whom she has come up through school. This came about because the seventh grade is housed in a new building and includes children from two different schools. Since there are three sections of the seventh grade it was decided not to keep each group intact from the earlier schools but to mix the children from the two schools about equally in each room. Anne has felt this keenly and often talks of the children in the other rooms. She has a kodak and brings many snapshots to school to show me, remarking, "This is so-and-so. She is in Mrs. A's room this year. We have always been together."
4.05	At play period, if any of these children are on the playground, she runs to them and shows much pleasure at the reunion. Indeed during the first few weeks of school she limited her playground activities to the aforementioned group or to a small group from our own class. Lately she has become interested in teacher-led games and has played baseball with a large group of boys and girls despite the fact that her two closest friends in our class have not been playing.
1.06 5.01	She repeatedly says, "Miss T, I can't hit a ball," but nevertheless she seems to have good muscle coordination and always is quickly chosen.
5.02	In class, Anne is in the top group in her studies, assumes many responsibilities and is a leader. She was chosen doorkeeper and has never yet been tardy or absent. She made all telephone arrangements

4.06   for our doughnut sale last week, headed the committee for checking
5.03   with the salesman and the children. They sold 193 dozen at one time
and 63 dozen at another time.

    Anne takes music and subscribes with a few other children in the
5.04   class to "Keyboard Jr.," an educational magazine for music appreciation.

4.07   Her mother was elected one of the three grade mothers by the
3.02   children.

3.03   Oct. 20   Anne is always at her post as doorkeeper when I arrive.
She smilingly opens the door and makes some pleasant remark about
the weather or tells a bit of news about one of her peers. Once or
2.02   twice she has pinned a rose on me, and once she had a second rose
and pin for Mrs. Z.

    She and Sallie, the school maid, often laugh and chat together.
Recently Sallie said she needed a brown hat, so Anne brought her
3.04   one. Anne told me, "It has a real wide brim and Sallie said, 'That's
5.05   just what I need.' " Anne added, "Sallie says she only goes to church
every other Sunday."

    Anne went on to say that she and her family attend the First
3.05   Assembly of God out at Highlands. "Joel Perry goes there, too. He
lives just back of me." (Joel is the most popular boy in the class ac-
4.08   cording to the sociogram.)

    Anne also talks often of Jenny, one of the cooks. She was amused
3.06   that Jenny and Sallie both ordered doughnuts from her and laughed
5.06   at Sallie's haste in coming for hers. In class she often quotes Sallie
6.02   on our science exhibits—"Sallie says if that spider bites us we'll be
dead before we can get to the hospital." Or, "Sallie says that a snake
5.07   will kill you right now if it bites you. Miss Thornton shouldn't allow
you to keep such things in the room." Anne often takes Sallie on a
tour of our room to show her our "critters."

    Oct. 24   Today on the playground, as Anne was waiting her turn to
bat, she said, "Miss Thornton, Daddy used to ride a man to work
3.07   every day. The car was parked on our driveway and Joe [brother]
2.03   and I were playing in it when we found a bottle of liquor. Mother
5.08   has always told us it was wrong to drink it and all, so Joe and I broke
it on the driveway. Daddy whipped us for it because he had to buy
6.03   the man another bottle. He doesn't ride that man any more, though."

    Oct. 25   Anne has the solo part in a choral reading for P.T.A. She
5.09   and a committee chose the songs and she came to me to say, "Could
3.08   Sara change and play 'Faith of Our Fathers'? She already knows that,
4.09   and it will be easier."

    When we practiced with the piano, Anne played her song, a rather
5.10   difficult patriotic one, very smoothly and skillfully. The other two
had difficulty with theirs.

    For several days children have been saying, "Miss T, Anne and
4.10   Danny Sutton are sweethearts." Anne giggles, sways from side to
6.04   side with head lowered and fingers over her lips. Yesterday and today
I noticed that Mary M. is with Danny and Anne on the playground.
4.11   Both Anne and Danny have dropped out of the ball game and stand

6.05   talking and laughing together. Today he pitched a small football to
the two girls in turn. Then they would stop for long talks.

    Several times during class I saw Mary leave her table to talk with
4.12   D. Anne appeared puzzled but always grinned when she caught my
2.04   eye. Betty W. said to me, "Mary doesn't like D., but he can't decide
6.06   whether he likes Anne or Mary best."

    Oct. 27   Anne met me as usual at the door. I had purchased a
5.11   parakeet for another teacher in the building. She said, "Oh, let me
see!" Followed me down the hall and talked for a moment or so
before returning to her post.

    During the morning I noticed her standing by Clara Richmond,
6.07   who had her head on the table. When she saw me looking, she
4.13   quickly changed the frown to a smile and went over to the files.
(Clara has recently moved to the table with Anne and the others at
her own request; see sociogram.)

    Anne chose Janice G. to help her serve in the lunchroom next
4.14   week instead of either Mary or Sara. I was surprised, as this was the
first deviation from the usual relationship.

    Again today, Anne passed up the ball game for companionship of
4.15   Mary and Danny. This time Sara joined them.

5.12   Oct. 29   We went to the lot today to see a small circus unload and
set up the tent. Three elephants were the center of attention. Anne
6.08   came over to me giggling and looking up from under her lashes to
2.05   say, "Betty says those three elephants are Mary, Sara, and me."
4.16   "She did! Which is which?" I asked.

    "I'm the one on this end, the big one is Sara [who is plump], and
the little one is Mary."

    "Why is the middle one Sara?" I asked.

    "Because she is so self-satisfied."

    Sara looked up with bright eyes and a half smile. In a moment,
Anne sat down on the grass beside her.

3.09   Nov. 1   Met me at the door this morning with a merry laugh and
a comment on the chilly weather. She was wearing a lightweight pink
1.07   pleated wool skirt, navy blue sweater, angora collar and cap, white
socks, and gray loafers.

    At play period she asked, "Do you know how you wash this cap
5.13   and collar?"

    "No, how?"

    "Just wash them by hand, roll them in a bath towel, and put them
in the refrigerator."

    "Miss Thornton, you know when Mary and I first saw each other
4.17   we were four. I threw a stick at her, and she threw a brick at me."

    "Well, you were just trying to get acquainted, weren't you?"

    She laughed and continued, "Yes'm. Then another time she climbed
the fence and I told her to get off because it was mine. She said it
wasn't—it was her grandmother's. Mother had to come out and tell
us it was both of ours."

2.06   As we were coming back to the classroom she moved close to me,
giggled with her hand over her mouth as she said, "Danny said a
1.08   girl kissed him twice Halloween night at the carnival."

6.09   "Did you care?"
4.18   "No'm. He's Mary's sweetheart now."
         Mary who was walking with us, cut her eyes around and said, "I'll
4.19   bring you some notes she wrote him."
         "No, you don't."
         The two appeared on the usual friendly basis. At lunch Anne,
4.20   Mary, and Betty sat alone at a table. Sara was absent that day. Anne
         tells me she first met Sara in the third grade. Sara, the daughter of
         one of the leading preachers in town, is widely traveled for a child
         in our community. She has visited most of the states, Mexico, and
5.14   Canada. Anne has been to New Orleans and Florida.

         Nov. 4 Anne is wearing a scarlet sweater, angora collar and cap,
1.09   navy skirt, and scarlet coat with heavy velvet tabs at the collar.
1.10   She came to me to whisper, "Miss T, Frank blew me a kiss just
4.21   now. He must be getting interested in girls." She giggled, hand over
2.07   mouth, chin tucked down, body swaying from side to side in what
         I would label coy amusement.
             At lunch she told me her mother had found several "love notes"
         of hers and had destroyed them. "She tore them all up in little
3.10   bits."
         "Where were they?"
         "In my pocket."
4.22   Later, when a child reported that eight love notes had been passed
         during the day, I asked, "How about your other written work? If your
         notes slow you down with the papers you need to write or check,
         how about making copies of your notes so you'll have some written
         work?"
             Anne cut her eyes around and said, "Oh-o-o-, Miss Thornton!" Then
6.10   she joined in the laughter.
             She appeared greatly amused over the chapters in *Stuart Little*, by
         E. B. White, which I read to the group. In these particular pages
6.11   Stuart is preparing for his date with Miss Ames. He writes her a letter,
1.11   gets a canoe, changes his shirt every hour, combs his hair, fidgets, etc.
         At last he appears indifferent when she arrives. Then he finds the canoe
         damaged too badly to use and is disconsolate, but Miss Ames suggests
         going to the country club to dance.
4.23   Anne said, "Girls can always think up something."

EXTRACTS FROM THE CUMULATIVE RECORD

NAME—Anne Elizabeth Hart
1.12   DATE OF BIRTH—Jan. 19, 1941

Physical Growth

Grade	I		II		III		IV		V		VI		VII
Month Year	Nov. '47	May '48	Nov. '48	May '49	Nov. '49	May '50	Nov. '50	May '51	Nov. '51	May '52	Nov. '52	**May** '53	Nov. '53
Age	6½	7	7½	8	8½	9	9½	10	10½	11	11½	12	12½
Weight	48½	54	54	61	64	70	79	80	83	87	99½	107	115
Height	48	49	50¼	51¾	52¾	54	55	57	58	59	60⅛	61⅜	62⅞

1.13 (row marker for Age line)

Health Record

1.14
Small pox vaccine, 1947, 1953
Typhoid vaccine, 3 shots in 1947, 3 shots in 1949
Boosters in 1950, 1951, 1952, 1953

Anne tells me she has had most of the childhood diseases except scarlet fever.

1.15
Medical examination in first grade shows following are O.K.: both eyes, both ears, nose, mouth, throat, glands, heart, lungs, and kidneys. No skin diseases, nutrition O.K., muscular coordination O.K., no deformities. Teeth decayed, dental care recommended. Four teeth were filled in 1953.

Physical Growth: Descriptive Data

Form suggests data should cover: preschool developmental history, health and physical handicaps as reported by parents, nutrition as reported by parents, energy output based on teacher's observation, growth compared with peers, body build, motor and game skills, posture, and grooming.

1.16
GRADE 1   Anne was a normal baby. Mrs. Hart told me she began feeding her a formula at an early age. She has no physical handicaps. Anne eats well, nearly everything put before her. Her energy output is great. She likes active and rough games. She often plays boys' games

1.17
1.18
with them. Compared with her peers she seems in the same growth stage. She is a tall, well-built girl with light hair and eyes. Her hair is well kept and her face and hands clean. She is graceful and seems to like

1.19
rhythms. Her motor coordination is very good indeed. (Miss A.B.C., '47)

GRADE 2   Anne does not eat all her food this year. She will say,
1.20
"I don't like that." I have insisted on her trying some of everything.
6.12
Mother says she has a time making her eat eggs at home. Anne is
1.21
very energetic and is always one of the leaders in a game. She likes
4.24
to pick at Jim and Joe. She is tall and well-proportioned. Well-dressed
1.22
and always clean. She sits and stands erect. (Mrs. D.E.F., '48)

GRADE 3   Anne has good skin but little color. Eyes are bright and
1.23
skin glossy. She eats well in lunchroom. She is very active and plays like a little girl. Today at play period she and some of the other girls
1.24
found some large pieces of cardboard. They put them on a bank and
4.25
slid down; "Had more fun." Anne is one of the largest girls in class.
1.25
She is tall and slender. She is very erect. She is quite skillful in
1.26
games and very graceful in movement. Her mother makes her many
1.27
lovely clothes. She is always clean. (Miss G.H.I., '49)

GRADE 4   The above continues to be true except that she seems to
1.28
be slightly stooped in the shoulders. (J.K.L., '50)

1.29
GRADE 5   Anne turns up her nose at some of the foods served at
6.13
lunch but tries to eat them anyway. Her skin is a little pale but hair
1.30
and eyes seem to reflect health. She plays active games and is always
4.26
one of the leaders. She is the tallest girl in her group but is well-

1.31   proportioned and quite graceful. Comes to school attractively dressed
1.32   and well-groomed. Good posture. (Mr. M.N.O., '51)

1.33   GRADE 6   The above is still true. (J.K.L., '52)

        GRADE 7   Eats "everything except spinach and broccoli and I'm try-
1.34   ing to learn to like these." Plays active games under teacher leader-
1.35   ship. Bad posture referred to in fourth grade is not noticeable to me,
        but both the mother and Anne are exceedingly conscious of it. She
1.36   is one of the most mature, physically. Is meticulously well-groomed.
1.37   Face is beginning to break out. Misses no time from school. Had a
        few colds. (B.L.T., '53)

Affection

        GRADE 1   Family constellation: Father, Claude, age 40 years
2.08   Mother: Carol Melton Hart, age 40 years
                    Brother: Joe Hart, age 9 years
                    Anne Hart, age 6 years
2.09   Grandparents on mother's side live with them. (A.B.C.,
                    '47)

2.10   GRADE 2   Grandparents have moved away.
2.11   Pets—one dog and four cats. (D.E.F., '48)

Affection: Descriptive Data

        Form suggests data should cover relationships among family mem-
        bers, relationships between the child and other adults, relationship
2.12   between the child and teachers and relationship with pets.

        GRADE 1   The family get along very well. Both Mr. and Mrs. Hart
        work and the grandparents take care of the children. Mrs. Hart says
        she wants both children to take music lessons and this is why both
2.13   parents work. For a while both children brought their lunches to
        school. Joe would throw his away and do without food until he got
3.11   home. Anne would put hers in her lap under the table and eat from
6.14   there. Both children seem to push themselves forward. Every time we
        had company in the room, Anne would do something to call atten-
        tion to herself. Once there were four adults in our room during library
6.15   period. Anne was not ready to read, but she rushed forward to read.
5.15   She didn't know many words but she knew the story, so she sub-
        stituted words and made up part of the story.
2.14   Anne has many pets and knows how to care for them. (A.B.C., '47)

        GRADE 2   The fourth-grade teacher remarked that when Anne enters
3.12   her room she "feels like spreading down a carpet." Adults find Anne
5.16   entertaining. She tells a good story. Anne is the child who can be
        asked to check on something and will do her best to do the job as
5.17   well as the teacher could. She is a treasure. (D.E.F., '48)

        GRADE 3   Anne loves her parents but she knows they won't allow
3.13   any foolishness. Often she has said, "My daddy will whip me if . . ."
        or "My mother will punish me if . . ." There is no doubt in her
6.16   mind that she must behave or else. She is very affectionate. Has a

tendency to get angry if other children can do things better than she can. (G.H.I., '49)

GRADE 4 All the above is still true. Anne has initiative seldom
5.18   seen in a child of her age. (J.K.L., '50)

No entries for grade 5 or 6.

Peer Culture

Form suggests sociograms or results of friendship tests, membership and offices in clubs, church, and school.

GRADE 2 Anne was chosen by ten children as best friend. She was
4.27   rejected by no one. She chose as her best friends Susan, Mary, and Ned. She stated that she liked to play with everybody. (D.E.F., '48)

GRADE 3 Chosen by two boys and four girls, including Mary. Re-
4.28   jected by three girls and one boy. Chose Sara, Mary, and Carrie. Rejected May, Caroline, and "boys in general." (G.H.I., '49)

GRADE 4 Chosen by Sara, Carrie, two other girls, and three boys.
4.29   Rejected by Virginia. (J.K.L., '50)

4.30   GRADE 5 Chosen by Sara, Esther, Lena, Mary, and Carrie. Rejected by Susan. (M.N.O., '51)

4.31   GRADE 6 Chosen by Milly and Jane. Rejected by: Lurline, Esther, Mary, Sara, and Carrie. Chose: Lurline, Jane, and Harry. Rejected: Esther, Carrie, and Mary. (J.K.L., '52)

Form suggests additional descriptive data such as:
1. Roles and status within groups
2. Knowledge of peer-culture codes
3. Variance from codes and customs of group
4. Boy-girl interaction and relationships

GRADE 1 Anne seems to want to be a leader and generally in some
4.32   way or another she will be "it." Plays well with both boys and girls. They never seem to resent the fact that they generally play what Anne wants to play. (A.B.C., '47)

GRADE 2 No one in the group resents Anne's being the leader. She
4.33   makes a very good one. There's never a dull moment, and they play and work well together. She plays with girls more during recess and likes to sit at the table with girls. When we form a group she likes to sit by Ned, and this seems to please him. (D.E.F., '48)

5.19   GRADE 3 Anne is by far the best leader in the class. She can do al-
            most anything. She is not conceited because of her unusual abilities.
4.34   She is too busy helping others. They appreciate her. Anne and Ned were sweethearts for a long time. They worked well together, were never silly—just sincere in their admiration for one another. Then Jack began claiming Anne as his girl, and Mary liked Ned. Suddenly
6.17   Mary and Anne were having a few words over Ned. Then Anne and Ned were sweethearts again. (G.H.I., '49)

4.35   GRADE 4   Anne is still a leader. For example, she selected a story
5.20   to dramatize, chose the people for roles, and directed the play. It was
          good. She was sweet to all in the room. (J.K.L., '50)

4.36   GRADE 5   On any and all occasions, Anne has some kind of a story
5.21   to tell to the group. (M.N.O., '51)

          GRADE 6   Anne's ability seems to be recognized by the children, for
          she is always one of the first to be chosen when there is a job to be
4.37   done where leadership is involved. But since February she has been
          rejected by the girls at the table and on the playground. She now
6.18   plays with Lucia and Kathy. (J.K.L., '52)

Socialization Data

Community	Street and Number	Telephone No.	Date
1. Bethel	16 Shady Lane	none	'46–'47

2. Family continues to live at same address

3.14   Schools attended elsewhere: none
          Date pupil first entered school: 9/15/47

Name of School	Year	Grade
Bethel	'47–'48	1
"	'48–'49	2
"	'49–'50	3
"	'50–'51	4
"	'51–'52	5
"	'52–'53	6
"	'53–'54	7

5.22

          Form suggests record should contain data giving information about
the following: conveniences in the home, standard of living of the
home, ways and content of child training in the home, family attitudes
and values, interests and activities of members of the family outside
the home, social status of family in the community, social mobility
of the family, social mobility of the child, and cultural variations
within the family.

3.15   GRADE 1   Anne's family lives in a five-room house with three bed-
          rooms. Anne sleeps in the room with her grandparents. Joe has his
          own room. They have an electric stove, washing machine, two radios,
          and a piano. Mother works in the weaving room at the A Mill. Grand-
          mother keeps house for the family. They attend the Assembly of God
          Church. Parents are pushing the children forward, giving them private
3.16   music lessons and very good clothes. Mr. H told me he wanted his
          children to have everything he didn't have. (A.B.C., '47–48)

          GRADE 2   Family still attends Assembly of God Church. They drove
3.17   over to Capital City several week ends to hear an evangelist at a heal-
          ing meeting. Anne says they went five times.
3.18   Mrs. H has been to P.T.A. meetings most of this year. Anne comes
          with her. Anne says she made her mother come so we would win the
          dollar prize for best attendance for our room. Parents are strict with
3.19   Anne. She was a few minutes late going home one afternoon. Father

6.19   came to school to get her and said her mother was going to whip her. Anne was spanked. Father was mad—didn't talk a bit pleasant. (D.E.F., '48–49)

        GRADE 3   Family resides at same place this year. Mother no longer
3.20   works. Father has had regular work and children are continuing with their piano lessons. Mr. and Mrs. Melton, Mrs. Hart's parents, have
2.15   moved out of the home and the family are by themselves. The children are carefully trained. They know they must behave, and if they are
3.21   disciplined at school they will receive no sympathy at home. The parents are very anxious for the children to learn all they can. Mother attended P.T.A. a few times but stopped rather than bring the children out at night when they should be abed. The mother will not allow the children to play with a certain little boy in the neighbor-
3.22   hood because "he uses bad language and fights," but she will let
4.38   them play with this boy's sister because "she is nice." (G.H.I., '49–'50)

        GRADE 4   The children are carefully supervised, and a whipping is given if the parents feel one of them needs it. Still there is a good
3.23   spirit of camaraderie among them all. Anne is quite relaxed when she
2.16   is with either one or both of her parents. (J.K.L., '50–'51)

3.24   GRADE 5   Anne's mother is very anxious that Anne be well-prepared in her work. She has visited school several times to talk about Anne's work. (M.N.O., '51–'52)

3.25   GRADE 6   Mrs. Hart continues to show interest in Anne's work. She always says, "If there is anything I can do, I'll be glad to do it"—and she does. (J.K.L., '52–'53)

        GRADE 7   Father told me he did not have as much education as he
3.26   wanted the children to have. Said he felt the need for more education. Anne said, "Mother and Daddy went to about the tenth grade. Joe, fifteen years old, is in his second year at College Prep—a private
3.27   school. The family talked of sending Anne there, too, but she begged to stay at Bethel.

        Occupations of family: Father—mechanic at the mill. Sells some-
3.28   thing on the side this year. Mother—worked for a while as a weaver at the mill. Has been a housewife since 1950. Mother was a regular
3.29   P.T.A. member in '48–'49 and a grade mother this year ('53–'54). The family continues to attend the Assembly of God Church in another community. They often go to musical programs at the college.
3.30   (B.L.T., '53–'54)

Self-developmental Data

Mental Maturity Scores

Date	Name of Test	CA	MA	IQ	GE
11/9/50	California Test of Mental Maturity	117	132	113	5.7
5/3/53	Davis–Eels Games			105	

(5.23 appears in left margin at the 11/9/50 row)

NOTE: GE means grade expectancy and is called grade placement in the California Mental Maturity Test Manual.

Achievement Scores

Date	Name of Test	Reading				Arithmetic		
		Vocab.	Comp.	T.		Reas.	Fund.	T.
5.24	2/20/52 Progressive Ach.	4.2	4.4	4.3		4.7	4.3	4.5

Language   Grade
5.2   4.7

LIST OF UNITS STUDIED BY GRADES

5.25   GRADE 1   Trips, airplanes, pets, Christmas, milk, vegetables, farm
animals, library. Anne made a trip to New Orleans, where her father
was working in a shipyard. She has read for information and was very
5.26   helpful to group in information found. She has shown an active interest in all units this year.

5.27   GRADE 2   Summer vacations, transportation, boats, weather changes,
Christmas toys, community helpers, homes, what is happening, animals, people, and flowers in the spring, and library. Took a trip to the
city library. Anne has done outstanding work in reading. Has shown
5.28   some talent in music and art.

GRADE 3   What we have learned from the Indians of North America.
5.29   How mail is brought to us. What workers help us build our homes.
Made trips to the circus grounds, around the community to see mail
5.30   boxes and to the station to see a mail car, around the community to
see homes and grounds, to the Air Force base, and to the city park.

GRADE 4   Why do leaves change in autumn? How is glass made?
5.31   Why is Alaska important to us? Anne is good in everything. She reads
well, adds much to discussion, has good ideas in construction, writes
5.32   well, and paints well. Plays songs for children to learn and then plays
them while they sing.

5.33   GRADE 5   How people got scattered to America. Anne continues with
5.34   piano lessons. Learns new songs that the class wants to sing and
5.35   plays for them. Continues to write and relate interesting stories.

GRADE 6   Are trees important to us? Why did the early settlers
5.36   push farther west? How has transportation improved since 1620? Has
5.37   done much research, headed committees, and led discussions.

Self-adjustive Processes

Record suggests data that show what makes the child emotional,
both pleasant and unpleasant, how he acts under emotions, and how
he manages his emotions.

GRADE 1   No entry.

6.20   GRADE 2   Anne has shown no emotional strain.

6.21   GRADE 3   No unpleasant emotions shown.

6.22   GRADE 4   Anne pouted one day. The following morning she asked
the teacher if she wanted to know why. When the teacher replied

4.39   "Yes," Anne said, "Sara made fun of me because I said, 'Mother, she. . . .' "

6.23   GRADE 5 Anne continues to have tendency to pout when Sara is
4.40   able to do something better than she does.

        GRADE 6 Anne has become more quiet—not as much sparkle and
6,24   enthusiasm since Sara, Carrie, Lurline, and Mary have rejected her
4.41   in the room and around the playground.

        This concludes the cumulative record.

HOME VISIT AND LIFE SPACE

        OCT. 18 Anne called her mother about noon at my request to see
        if it suited her for me to visit that afternoon. After school, she waited
        as I finished up a few odd jobs so she could walk home with me.
5.38   We left by the rear school door and cut across the yard, up an embank-
        ment to a tar and gravel road. We then took a small dusty path
        through weeds and grass across a vacant lot. There was a wire coop,
        with a number of black and white bantams in it, near the path. I
1.38   commented on them and Anne took a skipping step as she said, "Joe
2.17   used to have some." She said that her mother was so glad to know
3.31   I was coming "because last year when Mrs. L came she was ironing."
2.18   She said, "Now, Miss Thornton, you'll get to see our cockers!" She
        chattered of Joe's years at College Prep—"Mother wanted me to go
6.25   there, too, but I'm so glad she didn't send me. I'm glad I'm in your
4.42   room, and I'm glad I'm with Mary."
        Suddenly she broke off to say, "Miss Thornton, look at that hill
5.39   with those lovely trees. I've been wanting you to see that; I told
6.26   Mother I wanted to show it to you. Look at that one little tree off
        to itself." The hill was lovely and the trees had begun to turn. They
        were beautifully shaped, too, for they were uncrowded. "It's just per-
        fect," I replied.
        "This is my street," she said, as we turned into a very pleasant and
        attractive side street. The houses were neat and many had fences
3.32   around them. Most of them are heated by oil, as the tanks are visible
        on stands in the rear. Three houses in the neighborhood have tele-
        vision antennas, but the Harts' does not. A few late roses were in
        bloom in the yards.
        Anne's front yard is quite small—only a step or two to the red-
        painted cement steps and the front door. But the side yard is spacious,
        with no fence between the Harts' and their neighbor's on the left.
3.33   Here there is a large shade tree, and there is another directly behind
        the house. Back of the house is the garage, the clothesline, and a large
        house for the cockers.
        To the right of the Harts' is the home and shop of a public-roads
        maintenance man. His mother lives with him and is Mary's grand-
        mother. In a vacant lot across the street from Mary's grandmother
        are some of the road machines Mary's uncle maintains. Next door to
3.34   this vacant lot is Mary's father's shop, and farther along is Mary's
        house.
        Neighbors directly across the street from the Harts' have lovely,
3.35   deep-red roses. Anne pointed them out to me, saying, "That's where

I got those roses I gave you." Anne says that another neighbor poi-
6.27 soned one of the cocker spaniels. She told me about the birth of some
5.40 of the cocker puppies. I heard a number of the dogs barking in the
rear.

Anne opened the door and ushered me into the living room. Mrs.
Hart immediately appeared, smiling, and invited me to sit down.
3.36 She appeared older than I expected. Her hair was partly white, and
she rolled it high with combs. Her eyes were warm and bright behind
shell-rimmed glasses. She wore an aqua gabardine dress with a green
1.39 patent-leather belt. In build she was short and stocky.

Anne disappeared for a moment and then came back to say she
4.43 was going to run over to Mary's and that they would be back to see
me before I left.

The room in which we sat was ceiled and painted apple green. A
large radio cabinet stood just inside the front door. The furniture
was overstuffed, with worn gray plush upholstery. A table in the
opposite end of the room held a large framed photograph of Anne.
3.37 Over the mantel was a long rectangular picture which drew my eye.
It was very unusual and appeared to be painted on plush, or velvet,
or maybe black felt. A whatnot in the corner held numerous china
and glass articles. There was a parakeet in his cage on a small straight
chair. Two pictures, one a small copy of "The Angelus," hung on one
wall and a small plaque with a Bible verse over the radio. On top of
the radio were two Bibles. A rather worn rug in neutral tones covered
the floor.

We talked about the cockers they are raising. She said they were
a good deal of trouble right after they were born but she has one she
wouldn't sell for $50.00. Finally the conversation came around to
Anne. Mrs. H laughed as she said, "I've been meaning to send you
2.19 a note to get after her about the way she stoops." "Why, I hadn't
noticed it," I replied. "You haven't! Well, Mrs. L and I talked
1.40 about it last year and I even bought her a brace—but it's been so
3.38 hot and it shows so through her thin dresses that I haven't made her
wear it. So I just keep after her. She'll hold up for a few minutes and
then she'll droop her shoulders again. I even thought of writing the
principal a note about it. You know, they're sort of afraid of the
principal."

"Since you've told me about it, why don't you let me see if I can
help her first. I'd like to tell her about a speech teacher I once had
who did more to help me with posture than anyone," I replied. Mrs.
3.39 Hart said, "I'm so glad you are helping her to improve her writing,
2.20 those r's and those s's. I tell her, too, that she knows better grammar
than she uses."

Mrs. Hart went on to say that she wants both children to go to
college. "But you can't tell about them! My sister's son went to
3.40 Alabama a year and then to Auburn and then he quit and joined the
Navy. But Mr. Hart's sister's son is in his junior year in Oglethorpe
and while he finds it hard I think he'll finish. He's engaged to Dr.
3.41 W's daughter of Savannah." (She named a prominent physician.)

Just then Anne and Mary joined us and soon Joe came in, and
we all talked awhile. Joe released the parakeet from his cage, and
2.21 it flew to Mrs. Hart's shoulder. There he recited nursery rhymes and

greetings and whistled the wolf call. Joe said he had taught him that, and everybody laughed.

As we walked out to the gate together Mrs. Hart mentioned that they owned their home, having bought it seven years ago. "But," she 3.42 said, "I'd like to move. I don't drive, and this is so far from the bus line. So Mr. Hart has to drive me back and forth. I want a larger house, but nothing too modern. I want a house that is a home!" (Anne had 3.43 confided in me on the way over that her mother often talked of moving. She said, "She wants to move, but I don't!")

Mrs. Hart then said, "I don't believe Anne practices enough on 2.22 her music. I tell her that lessons are too expensive unless she does. I want her to have music if she makes the most of her opportunity."

Anne and Mary walked down the street with me pointing out places and things of interest as we went along.

Oct. 18   Talk with Anne's sixth-grade teacher.

I approached Mrs. L on the playground. I said, "I'm quite interested in Anne this year and would like for you to give me some of your memories and knowledge about her that may not be recorded."
5.41   She replied, "Well, I think Anne is a very dependable child. Last
4.44   year, though, she seemed lost in her group. There was some friction
6.28   between those three close friends—Anne, Sara, and Mary."

"What seemed to be the difficulty?"

"Well, I never did get to the bottom of it, but I thought maybe
5.42   it was due to letting Anne assume responsibilities and the others getting jealous. I talked with her mother and she said, 'Well, maybe she is doing more than is good for her.' So for a while I just said 'no' without giving any reason."

"Tell me about the family," I said.
2.23   "There is something unusual about the family, I don't know just what it is. The grandfather came to school one year the last day before the Christmas holidays and brought Anne and her brother five dollars each. He came in the room and sat down. Said he wouldn't be visiting the Harts' that Christmas but wanted the grandchildren to have some money. Anne seemed embarrassed almost to the point of tears, so I
6.29   felt the whole episode was too personal for me to push matters.

"Joe and Anne are quite different. He isn't nearly as dependable as she. For a while he attended College Prep, but now he is at high school. Once I was substituting here. Joe was in the grade, and when we came in from the playground he didn't come with the others but stayed on the bars. When he did come in, I told him to stay after school, but he went home. Then his father brought him back. Said, 'I don't mind his staying, but I'd like to know what for.'

"I don't know what it is, but there's something odd in the family. I've been in the home a number of times. Mrs. Hart is nice but seems—you know—just a little different. Her sister married a lame
3.44   man in Auburn. She said the family opposed the marriage, but it's
2.24   worked out real well. Anne visits them quite often."

SCHOOL REPORT

An evaluation of Anne's work was sent home in January and May of each year. These evaluations proved to be very much alike, so only the one sent in May, 1951, at the end of the fourth grade, is included in this record.

Final report—Grade 4—May, 1951

1.41   Days absent 2, Tardy—0

5.43   Reads rapidly with smoothness and comprehension, sometimes careless. Can relate clearly what she reads. Has wide vocabulary. Gets many new words independently.

5.44   *English.* Is learning sentence structure, to paragraph, and use of capitalization and punctuation in written work. Written stories are good, but she is sometimes careless and does not use learned rules. Oral work is very good.

5.45   *Spelling.* Rarely misspells a word in weekly assignments; is careful in all written work. Uses dictionary daily.

5.46   *Writing.* Is forming her letters more neatly. She is capable of better writing.

5.47   *Arithmetic.* If she takes time she has little trouble with this subject. She can add, subtract, multiply, and divide by two numbers. Solves most problems with ease.

5.48   *Social Studies.* Uses maps and globes well. Brings worthwhile news to class. Takes an active part in discussions and does well in research. Has done well on Alaska and on Early Explorers.

5.49   *Science.* Showed intense interest in problems of "leaves" and of "Glass." Made good reports on them. Has learned about the water cycle and about air, sun, steam, and clouds. Enters into discussions.

5.50   *Music and Art.* Does well in both. Has made many of the charts in the room. Among the most interested and able members of the class.

A First Analysis of Anne

Early in November Miss Thornton decided to analyze the information she had gathered about Anne in order to see more clearly the developmental tasks and adjustment problems on which Anne was working. She felt that this would verify or refute the "hunches" she had about Anne and provide her with deeper insights to guide her efforts to facilitate Anne's further development and adjustment. She also recognized that she would probably find some areas in which she did not yet have adequate information and planned to use these gaps as guides for gathering further data.

Miss Thornton first tabulated all the information she had under each of the six areas and then tried to answer the significant questions posed in the study group under each area. (See the questions in Chapter 8 preceding the interpretation of each area in the case of Timothy Thyme. The reader can check the validity of any interpretation by scanning the appropriate numbered items in the preceding material about Anne.) Miss Thornton's conclusions follow:

Physical Factors and Processes

1. Anne seems to have inherited her mother's stocky build and will soon slow down in her rate of growth. She is an early maturer and will menstruate before the average girl does. She has always been one of the tallest girls in her class but will be of only average height as the other girls catch up to her. She is now facing the developmental task of adjusting to her new body functions in terms of the way she feels about herself, the way she relates to boys, the way she relates to other girls, and the way she manages her health problems.

2. Anne seems to have a relatively high rate of energy output, for she has always been one of the more active girls in her class in games and the like. She has good endurance and does not seem to fatigue easily.

3. Anne seems to be an essentially healthy child. She has seldom missed any time from school because of illness, except for a few colds. Her health habits seem to be good in terms of eating, sleeping, cleanliness, and immunizations. There may be a question as to the care of her teeth; it is possible she does not see the dentist regularly.

4. Anne has no apparent physical handicaps or physical limitations. Her mother's concern over her posture does not seem justified to me.

5. Anne has always managed her body with skill and grace when compared with other children. She has played all the children's games well; but it is true that she was an early maturer and that this made it easier for her to gain these skills at a given age.

6. Anne is a very attractive child, provided with better-than-average clothes by her mother, skillful in her grooming, showing excellent taste in what she wears, and caring for her clothes. She usually dresses better than the other girls.

Love Relationships and Related Processes

1. Other teachers have reported that Mrs. Hart loves Anne and that the child is relaxed and happy with either or both of her parents. I did not notice any tension between Anne and her mother when I visited the home, but I did notice that every comment her mother made about Anne was a criticism to the effect that Anne was not doing as well as she could. Is it possible that Mrs. Hart is so anxious for Anne to excel that she fails to give her the warmth she needs, particularly during the stressful period of early adolescence? I remember that Mrs. H tore up the "love notes" she found in Anne's pocket. This makes me wonder whether Anne confides everything to her mother the way she babbles to me about Frank blowing her a kiss or Danny telling about being kissed by two girls on Halloween.

2. Anne does not seem to fear her father despite the fact that he has whipped both her and Joe on occasion. Both the mother and the father are quite strict with Anne. Anne seems to accept the discipline as proper; still I am a little troubled by the lack of positive expressions of affection between

Anne and her mother. The latter seems preoccupied with "getting ahead," with "doing the right thing." Does Anne feel that she must earn her parents' love by outstanding accomplishments?

3. Anne and her brother seem to get along with no more than the usual number of squabbles. I see no evidence that she regards him as preferred in the family, though Mrs. L says Joe isn't as dependable as Anne. I need more information in this whole area.

4. The record reveals very little about the relationship between Mr. and Mrs. Hart. They seem consistent with each other in training the children. I do not see evidence of preference for either child.

5. Something seems to have happened between the Harts and Mrs. Hart's parents. It was odd that the grandfather brought money to the children at school as a Christmas gift. I suspect that the Harts wanted them to move out of the home, but I know nothing of any unpleasant emotional climate in the home.

6. To sum up, Anne does not seem to me to be emotionally insecure, yet I cannot be sure that she has adequate companionship with her mother. The latter seems overly concerned to have Anne excel. Does this bother Anne? Anne seems rather to share her mother's ambition to be on the top of the heap! This is an area in which I need more information. I'll have to listen carefully to the things Anne says.

Cultural Background and Socialization Processes

1. Anne's family is of Anglo-Saxon and German-American stock. Their background is rural, but they now live "in town." They carry the culture of the Deep South and are of the lower-middle class. But they share the American dream and want their children "to have what they did not have," in other words to be upward mobile, with a good education as the chief means of gaining a better status.

2. Rather strict training, with physical punishment to insure obedience, is the basis for rearing the children. The mother keeps after Anne all the time about her schoolwork, and both parents supervise Anne's activities carefully. They always know where she is and what she is doing. The religious training also is rather rigid and "Fundamentalist."

3. Anne participates fully in the life of the school and goes to church and to evangelistic services regularly; the family goes to many musicals at the college, but Anne is forbidden by religious taboos to attend many movies and to dance.

4. Anne has done well in social studies, but I haven't heard her comment on the wider American culture. This is something I must listen for.

5. The rather rigid religious attitudes in the home will create some problems for Anne as an adolescent if she shares her thoughts and experiences extensively with her mother. Still she dresses and grooms herself with more style than most of the other girls and doesn't yet show signs of conflict between parental standards and adolescent peer-group standards.

6. Anne is under special pressure to excel in schoolwork, in music, and in all sorts of extracurricular school activities as a means to upward mobility.

Mrs. Hart mentioned a number of Anne's cousins who are in college and one who is marrying the daughter of a prominent physician. Her parents expect her to go to college and certainly will want her to "marry well." I expect that this pressure on her will increase as she goes through high school.

Peer-group Status and Processes

1. Anne has always been skillful in participating in peer-group activities and has been called a "leader" in peer-group activities by all her teachers. Yet periodically she has had trouble with members of her in-group. Mrs. L thought that this was because she showed too much initiative in seizing leadership roles. Her mother agreed.

2. The difficulties Anne had with her peers last year were within her own clique or in-group. There seemed to be some rivalry for status, for in the fifth grade Anne was reported as pouting when Sara was able to do something better than she. Then the sixth-grade teacher reported that the others got "jealous" when Anne assumed too many responsibilities. But these girls and Anne mutually chose each other as best friends again in the seventh grade. So the friction may be due to rivalry and may not represent any real rejection of Anne.

3. Anne's early maturing may be altering her relationships within the peer group, particularly within her own clique, where the other girls are not maturing physically with equal rapidity. As a result of this early physical maturity, Anne faces new developmental tasks which many of the other girls do not yet share. How will this influence their relationships during this year with me? Will she gradually drop out of some of the late childhood peer-group activities?

4. Anne's mother is pushing her to excel and to be upward mobile. Do Anne's efforts to live up to this family expectation lead her to be too aggressive in seizing responsibilities and leadership roles at school? Or has Anne had so many leadership roles in the past that she takes her leadership status for granted and has become too directive with her peers?

5. Will the real peer-group leadership go to Betty this year? I notice on the sociogram that she was chosen by every member of Anne's clique and had a mutual choice with Anne. But Betty also chose a key person from both of the other cliques and was the only person in Anne's clique to choose outside that particular in-group. If Betty becomes the real leader of all the girls in the class, what effect will this have on Anne and on the latter's feelings toward Betty?

6. Anne's new maturity level should make interactions with boys a more important aspect of her peer-group life this year. In the third grade Anne rejected "boys in general," and this was natural for her maturity level at that time. But in the same grade her teacher reported that Anne and Mary were "having a few words over Ned"; then Anne won out and Ned became "her sweetheart again." This year Anne and Danny Sutton have been identified as sweethearts by the other children, and she has often dropped out of the ball game to talk with him on the playground. Sometimes Mary and Sara have joined them. One day Anne said, "He's Mary's sweetheart now." Will a new kind of rivalry develop here? "Love notes" now loom large in her conversation.

So there is evidence already that she is working on the developmental task of learning how to attract and interact successfully with boys.

7. It will be interesting to follow the interaction between Anne and Sara, because Sara is the daughter of one of the most successful ministers in the community, pastor of a large church. Sara's family is upper-middle class, the status to which Anne's family aspires and which some of her relatives have attained. Will this desire for social mobility influence the relationship? I note that in the fourth grade Anne was reported as pouting one day and then telling the teacher it was because "Sara made fun of me because I said, 'My mother, she . . .' "

8. Anne's peer-group friendships obviously mean a great deal to her. When her last year's group was split up in the new school this year, she eagerly sought her old friends on the playground during the early weeks of the year. When her mother wanted her to go to College Prep, Anne resisted, and she also resists the idea of moving to another house as her mother wishes. She told me, "I'm glad I'm with Mary."

Self-developmental Factors and Processes

1. As I go over the material, I discover that I do not have the information necessary to understand how Anne thinks and feels about herself as a person, how she thinks and feels about people, events, society, the world, and the universe, or how she conceives of herself in relation to society and the universe. Beyond seeing that she thinks of herself as a person who can lead in classroom activities and in programs attended by parents, I have little information about what life means to Anne. Is this all that it means to her as yet? Or are there other meanings to be discovered?

2. With regard to values, I can see that Anne constantly seeks to be prominent in classroom activites, that she values friendship with Mary, and that she wants to earn good marks in school. Doubtless she has other values. It will be a challenge to see whether I can discover them.

3. According to test results and on the basis of reports by other teachers, Anne has a bit better than average learning ability. According to reports in her cumulative record, she must be using her capacity quite fully, because she usually is reported as excelling most of her classmates. Has she really done better work than they, or have her many leadership roles created a sort of halo of excellence about her? Specifically, she is reported as reading exceptionally well and as remembering what she reads. Spelling and use of the dictionary were reported as excellent. She has been successful with every unit of work in social studies and has been interested in science. She is very skillful in oral presentations and in discussions. Her number work has been satisfactory, and she has excelled in reasoning out arithmetic problems. So her skill learning has been very effective in the light of her capacity. Yet she did not measure up to her grade expectancy on the objective test. Perhaps her early maturing has caused her to appear advanced.

4. As to her mental processes, Anne has been reported as doing much research and reporting her findings accurately, as solving problems with ease, as writing and relating interesting stories, and as showing talent in music and

art. It will be interesting to see how much of a creative spark she has in her writing and art work.

5. Anne is reported as being very effective in carrying out activities toward the achievement of her goals. Certainly she did an excellent job selling doughnuts. In the past she has organized dramatic presentations, headed research committees, led in presenting programs for parents, etc. All of this she has done effectively. There do not seem to be emotional factors, or concepts of herself, that hold her back from doing what she sets out to do.

6. Obviously Anne's parents and teachers alike have high expectations for her and constantly have pressed her to do well. How far has her good work been a response to these expectancies, and how far has it been the accomplishment of goals she set for herself? Everyone seems consistently to expect Anne to do well.

Self-adjustive Factors and Processes

1. There is no evidence that Anne is under frequent or continuing tensions. Emotion-producing problems that have been reported so far seem to be mostly concerned with relationships with her peers. I shall have to find out whether this really is a persisting problem with which Anne needs help. I feel that there must have been other factors in her life situation that gave rise to temporary emotional disturbances from time to time, but, if so, they have not been reported. Perhaps I can learn to see somewhat more deeply into Anne's feeling life.

2. Despite the fact that Anne said, "I never can hit the ball," she has been very effective in games, manages her body with grace, and is very well dressed. So she must feel physically adequate. About the quality of her love relationships at home I know little, but all Anne's former teachers have felt that the home was characterized by love and that Anne is therefore emotionally secure. Anne has never mentioned her own significance in society, but she certainly has been kind to Sallie and Jenny and on good terms with her teachers and the principal. She cannot ever have had a doubt about her belonging in the peer group, but she may be emotionally involved in a struggle to maintain a high-prestige status. She has done so well in her schoolwork and activities that she should feel adequate as a person to face life, but I shall have to evaluate the impact of her mother's continuous pressure on her to do better.

3. When under emotion Anne has been reported several times as pouting. Her way of reducing tension when in conflict with her peers seems to be to withdraw. Last year she chose new playmates when she was in difficulties with Mary and Sara. This year she did not participate in games until they were led by the teacher; then she participated well. Perhaps this indicates that she turns from peers to adults when under stress and seeks satisfaction from pleasing adults as a substitute for peer-group approval.

4. I therefore see no continuing adjustment problems for Anne just now except in the peer-group area. Her assets in meeting this problem are a fine capacity to do things well, her strongly established belonging in the group, and her background of experience in successful leading. As to liabilities, I do not see that she is egotistical but she may be overly directive or overeager

to seize leadership roles. I shall have to watch for these factors. She certainly does not need any special or clinical help with her adjustment problems at present.

Having made this preliminary analysis of the factors and processes affecting Anne's learning, development, and adjustment, Miss Thornton continued to build her case record and to interact with Anne in the classroom in the light of the insights she had gained and in the endeavor to fill in the gaps in her understanding.

The Case of Anne, Continued

Nov. 8   Today Anne is wearing a russet corduroy skirt, maroon windbreaker, gray slipover sweater, mustard-seed necklace and bracelet to match. She is carrying a tooled leather bag, with a scarf, lipstick, which she uses very sparingly, and other articles. At play period I suggested that she and a group of girls not playing games practice walking around with plyboards (9 by 18 inch) on their heads. I explained that this might help with our walking and posture. Anne was very enthusiastic and ran to get the boards from the room, saying, "You'll walk with us, won't you?" Eight or ten girls practiced the entire time.

As Anne walked along beside me, she asked, "Did Mother say anything to you about my shoulders?"

"Yes, she did," I said, "but I told her I hadn't noticed."

"Oh, she and Mrs. L fussed at me all the time last year. Mrs. L would make me walk, then she'd let Geraldine walk to show me how, and I'd be so embarrassed. She compared us all the time."

At lunchtime she sat across from Danny, Sara, and Mary. They giggled a lot, and she looked across the table at them without her usual smile. Completing her meal, she rested chin on hand and eyes staring out of the window and appeared deep in thought. When we came to the circle and I read them a chapter from The Yearling, she sat across from the same three and looked troubled. As she left to go home, I asked, "Is everything all right?" She half smiled and said, "Yes'm," but I felt she was not too sure.

Nov. 9   Our group gave the devotional at P.T.A. Anne announced a group of three songs—two were spirituals which Sallie, the maid, sang with the group. Anne wore a burgundy velvet dress. She had a solo part in the choral reading of the 24th Psalm.

After the children's part in the program, the principal thought they should either go home or stay in the classroom. A picture on emotions was being shown and discussion was to follow. Anne said, "I wanted to see that picture." I explained that it was not an entertaining picture. She showed her disappointment by hanging her head. Her usual smile was missing. But she stayed in the classroom and "did a lot of work."

PARENT CONFERENCE   Anne met with her mother and me. Did a fine job of explaining the day-by-day work and the materials in her folders on science, vocabulary, arithmetic, etc. Talked with us for thirty minutes, then left for her music lesson. We sat at her table with all her materials before us.

The marginal numbers in the left column: 1.42, 1.43, 4.45, 2.25, 1.44, 6.30, 4.46, 6.31, 5.51, 5.52, 5.53, 5.54

Nov. 11   At the door Anne said, "I have a surprise for you this
2.26   morning." I found a brown paper sack with a jar of peach preserves
inside. She reminded me at day's end. "Now, don't forget your pre-
4.47   serves." At lunch Anne sat beside Danny. Mary was absent, and Sara
sat at another table. At my table one of the children said, "Miss T,
Frank has been blowing kisses at Anne all morning."

WRITINGS

(Science)   THE CORN SNAKE

4.48   Sara and I looked in the National Geographic Magazine and we
5.55   saw a snake that looked like our snake. The name of the snake was
North Carolina Corn snake. The North Carolina Corn snake is a
favorite among naturalists because of its handsome colors. To keep
our snake alive we need to look in magazines and books to find out
what kind of snake it is and what it eats and where it lives.

(Science)   RICHARD'S GRASSHOPPER

Today Richard brought a large grasshopper to class. This grass-
5.56   hopper is green with a yellow stripe down his back. He has compound
eyes. His power is in his jaws and his hind legs.
Richard said he had him in a jar so he could jump around and he
jumped straight up and knocked the lid off. His hind legs are green
with yellow spots on them. His front legs are green and very short. He
has a very odd mouth.

(Science)   THE FLYING SQUIRREL

This morning Jack brought a flying squirrel. It is brown with gray
spots on it. It has very unusual legs. Its front and hind legs are connected by winglike folds of skin. It can make long gliding leaps through
the air.
5.57   He eats nuts and apples. He holds it in his front paws and sits on
his hind legs and pushes it in.
The flying squirrel lives in a hollow tree in the winter and in the
summer he usually is thirty feet from the ground in the crotch of a
tree.

(Science)   MY SPIDER

This morning Emmy called me to the door and showed me a garden
spider. It had spun a web on the front porch of the school. Mrs. L
5.58   came and looked at the spider and I got a jar and caught it. It is a
beautiful spider. It is yellow and black. We named it Charlotte. We
hope it will make an egg sack. I went out on the front porch and
found some of Charlotte's web. It is sticky.

(A Story)   JAZZ SESSION

5.59   This story takes place in the large city of Chicago, Illinois. My
2.27   name is Susan and I am going to tell you about my 15 year old
6.32   brother. He's a regular pest.
This morning when I left the house for school I never intended
2.28   to meet my brother down the street. Just as I turned the corner who

did I meet? Nobody but my brother! He yelled and said, "Mike, Joe, Bill and I are going to play our instruments for a jazz session on T.V. Will you play the piano for us?"

All through school I thought about the wonderful jazz session.

When 3:30 came I walked home with Elizabeth Marryweather. She is my best girlfriend. We live in a big white three-story house and Elizabeth lives across the street from me and she has said her family is going to build on to their big two-story house. Her brother Mike is going to practice with my brother Tommy and Joe and Bill this evening. She thinks it is perfectly ridiculous that Mike and Tommy are going to try to play the trumpet and the trombone for a jazz session because of the small amount of time they have been taking lessons. I think so, too, but I suppose if they make a mess of it, it won't be me.

We had been practicing two hours when I heard dad come in. I heard him say, "I'll be glad to get on my slippers and go into the den and read the paper and then take a nap until the fights come on T.V." But as it happened we were practicing the song "Make Love To Me" and in the den.

When dad came to the door of the den, mother began to help dad take off his coat as she said, "Now you can go upstairs in the sitting room and rest and look at T.V. up there. Let the children practice." I could hear dad grumbling as he went upstairs.

About 8:00 mother called dad and we stopped practicing so we could eat dinner. We had rolls and rice and gravy with fish, and for dessert we had strawberry short-cake. After dinner I helped mother with the dishes and then we all went back into the den to practice while mother and dad watched Life of Riley on T.V. After dinner the boys and mother and dad and I watched the fights. The Marryweather family came over and the grown-ups played Canasta while we went into the den and played some records. About 10:00 we went out in the kitchen and ate what was left of the strawberry shortcake.

(Story)   DON'T SAY NO

Monday morning Sallie was standing by me at the door and got to telling about her son, how he got married the first time. Sallie began telling the story: "Well, when he was dating this girl he never would stay out later than 10:30. One day I came in and I noticed a piece of white paper laying on the table and, boy, when he sees me a-coming he got to rolling it up and stuck it in his coat. I didn't one time think about him getting a marriage license."

"About a week later he told me not to expect him until late. And 10:30 passed and I went to bed. He didn't come in until the next morning. When he came in I said, 'Boy it's about time you're getting home.' He said, 'Well mother, don't fuss at me now. I'm a married man.' I said, 'Son, why in the world didn't you tell me you was going to get married?' He said, 'I's scared you'd say no!'"

(Essay)   MY HOME

The first place I step when I go in is the living room. The walls are a light shade of green and the top of the room is white. Over the mantle is a long but pretty picture. It favors an oil painting.

Margin values (left column):

3.45
4.49

5.60

2.29

3.46

3.47

6.33
5.61

3.48

5.62

This room is not a rectangular shape; it is broken because of another room. In one corner we have a line of shelves that contain figurines. This room as a whole contains a sofa, two chairs, a large radio, and a small table. At the front of the room is a large heater.

3.49

As you turn to the left you go into my room. The walls are dark rose and the ceiling is white. Over the mantle hangs another painting almost like the one in the living room. This room is a rectangular shape. The curtains are organdy. This room contains a bed, dresser, and a cedar chest.

The next room is my mother's and daddy's bedroom. It is a light shade of blue. This room is also a rectangular shape. The floor is covered with a wool carpet. It is designed with all kinds of flowers. This room also contains a bed, dresser and a chest.

The next room is my brother's room. His room is the same shade of green as the living room. This room contains a piano, bed, table and a bookshelf with many brightly colored books.

The next room is the kitchen. It is yellow. The room is a long narrow room. The floor is covered with tan tile. Our kitchen contains a heater, a stove, refrigerator, sink, cabinets, table and chairs, and the birdcage. We have yellow curtains.

The last room is the bath. It is dark rose and has rose curtains to match. The bath contains a tub, lavatory and commode.

(Essay)   *HOW I FEEL ABOUT MYSELF*

This morning Miss Thornton asked us to write about ourself. She said to put what we like and what we dislike.

6.34

I don't like the color of my hair. I wish it was black and wavy. I think I would like for my eyes to be dark brown. I'd like my complexion to be a shade darker. I wish I were smaller.

6.35

I like my personality very well and I have many, many friends and if I have any enemies I don't know it.

5.63

I like to go to school very much, I like spelling, geography and history best of all, I like English very well but, I want to learn more about it. I especially like to read good books. I also enjoy Miss Thornton reading to us. I think she can read better than anyone I have ever heard.

5.64

I do not enjoy arithmetic very much but I think I need to improve on it. I also need to improve on my writing. I think I do fairly well in school, but I could do better.

2.30

I love my principal and my teacher very dearly. I have enjoyed this year more than any other year I have been in school.

1.45
4.50

I like all my school friends and I like most of the boys. I like some boys better than others.

I like dogs and parakeets more than any other kind of pets. I love dogs more than anything.

3.50

I think Queen Elizabeth is the pretiest woman in the world. I collect things on all of the royal family of England. I have been doing this for four years. When the Coronation was taking place I heard it seven times and saw it three. Carl Compton went on a trip and when he came back he brought me a cup and saucer with her picture on it.

I wrote the Queen a letter and I waited about five months, then I

gave up hope of ever getting a letter. About a year later, when I came
in from school, mother said I had a letter from England. When I
saw it, I thought I would faint. I loaned the letter to a person and
6.36   I thought for a while I wasn't going to get it back. When I did it was
battered and torn. I treasure it very much.

Miss Thornton brought some coronation books for me to see and
I thought she was very kind to think of what we like.

I like small children very much. I would like to have a baby sister
5.65   although I don't think I will ever have one. I like to hear them talk
1.46   and sometimes they say things I would never even dream of saying.
6.37   I love them very much. I want two children when I am grown and
married.

3.51   I like my home and I am thankful for it. I would like for our house
6.38   to be larger. I wish it was two stories with a side terrace to it.

I think I have a wonderful family. My father works on the second
shift so he isn't with us but one evening of the week. Every night
2.31   we have devotional together. Mother reads the Bible and we pray.
5.66   I think my mother and father are especially good to us. On Sundays
we attend church together and we do on Sunday night too.

Sometimes I get daddy to tell me of when he was a small boy. The
2.32   stories he tells me are very interesting. I like to compare the way the
children lived then and the way we live now. Mother doesn't tell me
about the things she used to do as much as daddy. I love my whole
family.

3.52   I get a weekly allowance and then daddy will give me money for
other things I need, like when I go to the football game or other
5.67   things. I would like for daddy to raise my allowance but I might not
save as much as I do now.

I like my clothes very much. I would like to have more jewelry and
3.53   more dresses. I would like to have a yellow evening dress and a white
5.68   one.

I take piano lessons and I am in the fifth grade in music. I like
5.69   to play popular songs but I don't like to practice every day. Mother
6.39   says "it takes practice to make perfect."

I like secret clubs and secret codes. I do not belong to any as of
now but I have sent some blanks in to join some. Last year Sara,
4.51   Mary, Betty, Carrie, Lurline and I had a secret club. We all enjoyed
it very much. I think I would like to belong to the Scouts more
than to any other clubs or organizations.

5.70   I want to be a school teacher when I grow up because I like people.
I would want to teach the seventh grade because you can play with
your children and I believe it would be fun.

(Essay)   FUN WITH DADDY

4.52   Yesterday I asked Josephine W. home with me from church. After
dinner we wanted to go get us a Dairy Queen. Daddy said, "No."
2.33   Finally we got him cornered and begged him to take us. He finally
said, "O.K."

While Josie and I were getting our coats, daddy slipped in his
6.40   room and locked the door. When we came back we couldn't get in.
He said he was going to bed. Then we heard the key turn in the lock

and we hid behind the door. We were watching him but he didn't know it.

When he went out the front door to get in the car we were right behind him. He then took us over and got us an ice cream. We came home and washed the dishes.

(Story) CAPTAIN ON THE BOWLING TEAM

My name is Elizabeth Howard. I am 17 years old. I am a senior at Mulberry high.

5.71

All the girls in the senior class this year want to be captain of the girls' bowling team. We were to be practicing and then we would have the finals.

3.54
6.41

My dad gave me a new Pontiac for my graduation present and I already have it. I went by and picked up Dottie to go down to the bowling alley. Today was the finals. Dottie wanted awful hard to win and so did I.

We arrived and went right to practicing. At first I lost all hope of winning and then I began to make more scores and then Dottie would make more than me. About 6:00 P.M. the senior class had gathered, all except the teacher and the principal.

Finally at 8:00 the principal called and said that he had been called out of town to a school banquet. We decided not to have a team, just to meet every Thursday and bowl for fun.

(Essay) MY COLORED FRIEND

My colored friend is Jennie, the cook. Last year when I came to know Jennie, Sara and I were serving in the lunchroom. We served all year and, while we were serving, Jennie would talk to us.

3.55
5.72

I think a colored friend is the best friend you can have.

When Sara and I would come down to the lunchroom late, Jennie would have all the plates served so all I would have to do was put the plates and milk down. Clara would already have the forks and napkins down.

2.34

This year I let the cooks and Jennie in every morning. I will miss all my colored friends next year when I go to another school. Maybe I will see them even then. I think I have the nicest colored friends anyone could have.

3.56

Nov. 23 Today Anne said, "You know last night when I was looking at those London Illustrated News that you loaned me, I remembered that I saw some of them in the public library. Mother said to tell you she enjoyed them.

4.53

At lunch Jerry made a dive to sit beside Anne. Danny with a wry smile sat down beside me. When I said, "That's new, isn't it?" he grinned and said, "Yes'm." Frank, on my right, said, "Most every one of the boys likes Anne."

1.47

Nov. 24 Complained of sore throat today but played dodge-ball with group at play period. Was wearing a straight black skirt, garnet sweater and short, soft yellow coat. Asked me to hold coat when she found game too active.

5.73
3.57

Took record player and records up to share with other seventh grade. Managed player for the group.

5.74   Said she cooked hot dogs for family last Saturday, washed dishes
        and cleaned the house.
5.75   Each day she sits close beside me as I read *The Yearling*. Laughs
2.35   often at humor, is ready with explanations of some remarks or mean-
6.42   ings of words when I stop for clarification.

Nov. 29   I took our new symphonic record player to school for first
time. (The children raised most of the money for its purchase.) Anne
seemed greatly pleased. She placed her chair quite close and leaned
over to see as I explained each direction for its use. She held records
5.76   on her lap and listened attentively with a smile of apparent appreciation as I played several organ selections to demonstrate use of bass and
treble and volume controls. She said in an aside to me, "That's what
I want to play, the organ."
        Today I noticed that Tommy beat Richard to a seat by her in the
4.54   circle as he said, "Better luck next time, old boy." T also sat beside
her at lunch. She looked at me and smiled as he made a quick slide
4.55   into a seat beside her. She played dodge-ball with the group at play
1.48   period. Once she was pitcher on one side.
        Group is planning trip to see Disney's "The Vanishing Prairie." She
4.56   wrote purposes on blackboard as children gave them. When I said
that unless almost every person planned to go, we'd have to take the
trip after school hours, she said, "I'd like to go with you after school."
        I said, "If anyone feels that he or she doesn't want to go because
you don't attend picture shows, I'll understand." Anne said, "I don't
go, but I'd like to see this picture." I asked them to discuss the matter with their parents and then we'd work out our plans accordingly.

MY DINNER

(Story)
        *Saturday Mother asked me if I wanted to go to town with her.
I told her, "No." She asked me if I would cook dinner if she wasn't
home. I told her I would. She left and I started cleaning house.*
5.77   *I started dinner at eleven. I was going to have some hot dogs. I
made my chili and put a potato on to cook to go in my chili and
fixed my wieners and put my rolls on to warm. While everything
was cooking, I peeled my onions and cut them up.*
        *I finally thought I was finished. I looked at the clock and it was
twelve. I started fixing my hot dogs. And then I thought about my
potato that I was supposed to mix with my chili. I took all of my
chili off the hot dogs and mixed it with potato. I finally got my hot
dogs fixed.*
        After dinner I washed dishes and finished cleaning house. Mother
5.78   *came back about one. She said she had a very good time and thanked*
6.43   *me for fixing dinner but I didn't think I did so well.*
Dec. 1   Yesterday we went as a group to see Disney's "The Vanishing Prairie." When we came out the children asked if we couldn't
walk back to school. The day was crisp and cool—ideal for a walk.
Then, too, I thought this would be another opportunity for carrying
out some of the purposes the children had listed—good manners in
public, skill in observation, learning to appreciate each other, having
fun, applying knowledge of traffic rules.

We set out walking in groups, which interested me. Anne was on my left and close beside her was Lester N, a new admirer. On the

4.57   outside beyond Lester was George T (see sociogram). Betty was on my right. There was much bantering, laughter, and chattering back and forth between the groups.

Lester bought Anne a drink and crackers when we stopped at a

4.58   drugstore. She giggled and cut her eyes at me as she sat beside me. Lester, of course, sat at our table.

Just as we arrived at school Anne's father drove up, stopped his

2.36   car, and chatted with us. He laughed about our long walk. He is of medium height, rather heavy and with a ruddy complexion. Said he was on his way to work. Anne told me later that he had been to a friend's to help him kill a hog and was given some "good meat."

I have been telling the children bits of *The Roosevelt Family* of *Sagamore Hill*—particularly about Teddy's close relationships with his children and about his standards regarding sportsmanship and

5.79   responsibility. Anne asked today, "Would you be willing to lend me that book?" I said that I would when my sister had finished reading it. "I can hardly wait," said Anne. "Why don't you borrow *Circus Doctor* while you are waiting?" I said.

DEC. 2   Today Anne brought *Circus Doctor* back, saying, "I could hardly get any of this read last night. Joe borrowed it and wouldn't

5.80   give it back."

"I meant for you to keep it until you finish," I said.

"Oh, thank you. I like it," she replied.

Anne made a charming picture on the yard today as she again

1.49   played a very active game of dodge-ball. She wore a full black wool skirt with scarlet woven threads, twin scarlet sweaters, black suede loafers, white socks, and the grain-of-mustard-seed necklace.

6.44   When I read the chapter in *The Yearling* relating Fodder-Wings'

5.81   death, her eyes filled with tears. She handed in a very fine written account of our trip and of the picture, saying, "I sat up till twelve-thirty I got so interested writing this."

I had given her some sheet music to try at home. She brought it

5.82   back saying, "I can play these." I asked her to sing the words of one, which she did. I then said, "We will get you to help us learn these, and I'll give you these copies for your music folder." One was a prayer and one a rather difficult hymn.

DEC. 3   Asked me today if I had a copy of *The Little Princesses*.

5.83   "I did have," I replied, "but I loaned it to a cousin who never returned it. I'll see if she still has it." "Thank you, I want to read it."

"Miss Thornton, how would you write to Crawfie?"

"She lives on one of the king's estates," I replied. "He gave her a cottage for life, after she married."

"I believe it's Kensington," said Anne.

"I don't remember, but I believe she would receive any letter addressed to her maiden name."

When we went to the library truck a sudden thought struck me and I said, "Anne, get *Mary, Mother and Queen*. Tell the librarian you can easily read it and that I would like for you to have it." She

5.84   returned with the book, and I noticed her poring over it for some

time. Later I said, "If you like, I can help you with the royal line."
"I think I understand it already," she replied. A few moments later
she brought me the book to show me Mary's full name, and we
laughed together over the length of it.

As she was reading, Nancy said, "Miss Thornton, Jack said, 'Anne
4.59   is reading about herself.' What did he mean?"
        "I think he means that she is a queen." I looked at Jack and he
6.45   only smiled. Anne giggled, tucked her head down and said, "He has
a good imagination."

1.50   DEC. 6   I thought Anne looked a little pale today and I noticed a
small breaking out on her face.

She said they bought a television over the week end.

When I asked the meaning of the word "devout" and several other
5.85   difficult words she defined them easily.

DEC. 7   Today I read from *The Roosevelt Family of Sagamore Hill*
to the group, about the fun the father and children had together in
hiking, camping, boating, etc. Afterward I handed the book to Anne.
5.86   When she had completed her work, she sat in a sunny corner of the
room in our rocking chair and read it. I had told her that much of
the book was political and she might not care for all of it. So I
watched with interest as she read. There was no skipping. Later she
came to me smiling and said, "This is the best book! I like it better
than the one on Mary the Queen."

DEC. 10   Today I saw that a game of softball was going on, also a
game of football. Several children were playing on the bars. The day
was crisp and sunny. I approached the group on the bars and said,
2.37   "I'm walking around the whole yard. Who wants to come along?"
4.60   "I do," cried Anne, and we set out on a brisk walk together, talking
as we went.

"Miss Thornton, do you know Daddy likes to cook? Last year he
decided to bake a fruitcake, so he bought the fruit and nuts and cut
2.38   up a dishpan full. Then he baked a huge cake and when he cut it the
slices were so big! He served it to all our friends when they came to
5.87   the house. I believe I'll make a fruitcake myself this year."
        "It's lots of fun," I said. "I cut all the fruit for mine last night."
        "Ooooh, Miss Thornton, I think I'll go home with you."

We walked five times around the large yard, pausing now and
again to talk to various children or to watch groups at play. Thus
we had time for much interesting conversation.

Anne said, "Joe was burned real bad with hot water when we lived
2.39   in North Carolina—third-degree burns. And he still has bad scars
on his hip and leg. . . . You know, Miss Thornton, Mother used to
make Joe practice his music in the third grade, and he would just
cry and cry."
3.58   "Does Mother play?"
        "No'm, that's why she is so anxious for us to be able to play. I'd
go in and shut the door and play for Joe. Mother would think Joe
was getting along fine. She would be in the kitchen, and he would hit
a wrong note every now and then."
        "You're doing fine with your music, aren't you?"

5.88   "Yes'm—I'll soon be in another book. I only take once a week now, and I don't like to practice. I like to play popular songs, and Joe plays the trumpet. Mother says, 'That's just too much.'"

2.40   "I was looking at TV last night, and Mother made me stop. It was a murder play and she said she didn't want me to spend too
5.89   much time with TV. But you know, while I was reading about Teddy Roosevelt I didn't even think about TV."

"Do your grandparents live in town now?"

2.41   "Yes'm. We see them every week, and Mother made Grandpa a cake for his birthday. It was real good—better than Grandmother's. It was fresh cocoanut. But chocolate is my favorite."

1.51   I noticed today that her heavy red winter coat is four inches shorter than her dress and the sleeves well above her wrist. She kept tugging at her sleeves as though trying to stretch them.

3.59   Anne said that she is not a church member but is a regular attendant with her family.

Dec. 13   Night of P.T.A.

A raw rainy night. Anne was the only girl among the group of nine
3.60   children who had volunteered to come and present a reading lesson for parents. Her mother sat with the other parents just behind the
2.42   group, and I noticed that she smiled constantly in a most pleased
5.90   manner. Anne took the lead in the beginning, although shyly, as
6.46   shown by low voice and rather brief replies to questions put to start the group to reasoning and put them more at ease under unnatural conditions.

The lesson chosen was one that I felt would more particularly interest boys, being on the Antarctic. But they appeared much more self-conscious, and so Anne recalled other information we had studied, on the training of airmen to survive in the Arctic. For a few minutes she and I worked hard to get the interest of the eight boys—two or three of whom did not usually read in the same group. Finally interest was stimulated and every child became active in participation. Parents commented on how much they had learned from the children and several expressed amazement when the children evaluated the lesson and showed the relationship of the subject matter to the various things they were studying. Mrs. Hart said, "I'm so glad I came. I wish I could come and stay. I've learned so much tonight."

2.43   Anne handed me a package after P.T.A. She said, "You said we were not to give you presents, but Mother said I could slip this to you tonight."

Dec. 17   Today several children brought small gifts. Sara and Mary appeared to be in some sort of a conspiracy. Sara had given me a
4.61   package. Finally Anne came to me and said, "Miss T, open your presents." "No," I said, "I'm sorry, but I'm sure you understand why I can't." She smiled and said, "Yes'm." Walking to her seat, she
6.47   exchanged glances with Sara, then hung her head unhappily. I noticed that Sara and Mary paired off all during the day.

I commented to the principal that I was concerned over what appeared to be unhappiness on the part of the child and an apparent
4.62   teaming up against her of her two closest friends. I recalled what
6.48   Mrs. L had told me—also the material in the cumulative record.

Miss C said, "She had a time last year. Mrs. L said there was so much jealousy."

5.91   When we went to the bookmobile, Anne came to me saying, "Miss T, help me get some good books." So I selected one or two for her, and then I saw a brand new book on the adult shelf—*Spies for the Blue and Gray*. I pulled it out eagerly and Anne said, "I bet that's good." "So do I," I replied. "Let me read it first and if I think it would interest you I'll check it out for you."

4.63   She offered to keep one of our plants over the holidays, and when she left Danny was carrying it for her.

WHAT CHRISTMAS MEANS TO ME

Christmas is a time when we are supposed to worship the true and living God, because over 2000 years ago He sent His Son into the world to pay for our sins.

To a lot of people Christmas means holidays from work and school, big dinners and parties and lots of gifts.

5.92   *But to me Christmas means a time when we stop our daily living for a few days to reverence the birth of the Christ-child. I believe everyone would have a happier and merrier Christmas if, when we give gifts, we wouldn't give to receive but to give to make someone happy.*

6.49   *When Christmas comes I enjoy it very much but one thing I don't like about the holidays is that we have to be out of school. I like school very much and when I am out of school I miss Miss Thornton and all my schoolmates. Another thing I like about Christmas is when you give someone something and it makes them happy.*

I like to pop firecrackers and set off cherry bombs and rockets. I like to see the colors in Roman candles and sparklers. I always have fun with fireworks when Christmas comes.

4.64   *Last year some children up the street came down to our house and my brother and I went with them to set off some fireworks. We wanted to hear a real big noise so they told me to throw a cherry bomb in a concrete drain pipe. The drain pipe was about three feet in diameter.*

I was going to be the one to get hurt if anyone did. All the rest backed off and held their ears. I got two cherry bombs and set them

6.50   *off one right after the other, then I ran back to where the others were. Then all of a sudden a noise sounded like a big explosion. We*

5.93   *all laughed and ran to see if it had done any damage. It hadn't.*

I am looking forward to this Christmas and I hope it will be a happy one for everyone, everywhere.

1.52   JAN. 3   Anne opened the door for me with her usual smile. "I'm glad to be back at school," was her greeting. She wore a new navy and yellow plaid skirt, navy sweater and a long knotted strand of gold

4.65   beads, which she later told me belonged to Clara. "She asked me to wear them." I was interested, as I had never noticed any evidence of close relationship between these two.

2.44   She sat close to me in the large circle, handed me my pencil, my roll book, and my glasses, in anticipation of my needs. Had little to

4.66   say. At play period she ran to me and began to talk.

Had I had a good Christmas? Then she told about purchasing my gift. "You know Mother and I didn't know what to get for you for
3.61   Christmas, so Mother told the clerk 'She's an old maid and keeps house.'" (The gift was a set of emerald-green bath towels.)

Anne said, "Daddy has a new job now. He is working on the first
2.45   shift at Calloway. He says he likes the second much better. He has
3.62   always worked at night. You know Joe is going out at night now, so Daddy said, 'All right, young man, now I can keep an eye on you!'" She giggled and said, "O-oo, that made Joe so mad."

"Did you make your fruitcake?" I asked.
5.94   "Oh, yes, and it was so good."

I noticed that her face is quite broken out today. While she talked
1.53   with me she occasionally ran bases for a child who had a bad foot.
4.67   Sara, Mary, and Clara Richmond were in a huddle on the far side of the yard.

During arithmetic today I suggested that the group use Christmas spending in making up a problem of their own. Anne told me that she cashed one of her government bonds and she had twenty-eight
3.63   dollars to spend. "But," she said, "I bought some stock in the Old
5.95   Line Insurance Company with part of my money. Daddy and Mother bought some too, but Joe said he wasn't going to take a chance."

Anne told me today they had sent the TV back. "Oh," I said, "aren't you getting it back?" "I don't know. The man said the cur-
3.64   rent was too strong." Dora C, who was listening, said, "you ought
4.68   to get an RC. They're good." "Well, ours was a GE," replied Anne.

Anne looked at Dora, giggled, and said, "Miss T, when we were
4.69   in the third grade I told Dora I'd teach her music for five cents a lesson." Dora laughed and said, "I was taking from Mrs. E." Then Anne giggled and said, "She paid me for one lesson, then her mother called my mother and asked if I was really going to teach her music. Mother said, 'No, they're just playing together, and Anne will give Dora back her nickel.'"

CONFERENCE WITH ANNE'S FIRST-GRADE TEACHER Ever since I began this record I have been trying to talk to the first-grade teacher. I approached her yesterday and she asked for time to think. So today I went to her room and said I would like to ask a few questions about Anne.

"What do you remember about her relationship with other children?"
4.70   "Snooty."

"When you visited the home, what was your feeling?"
"Very peculiar people."

"Why did you feel so?"
3.65   "They felt they were better than anyone else."

"How about the parents—were they actively interested in the child and in the school?"
2.46   "Oh, yes, she was a grade mother, and the father always came to P.T.A. But later they quit.—Think they are better than anybody else. They sent Joe to College Prep, you know."

2.47   JAN. 4 At play period Anne was beside me as usual. She was wearing
4.71   new brown suede sling-heel slippers—a Christmas present. Said her
1.54   daddy is going to start on his new job Thursday. "He's going on a
          cut, though. He's tired of all that riding. Then, too, he's not getting
2.48   along with his boss, who is a real nervous man and everybody hates
          him. Twice people have tried to kill him.
              "Daddy says that he may get the TV back now so that he can
          enjoy it in the evenings. Everybody's pleased over his being at home
3.66   except Joe," and she giggled. "Mother said she'd just as soon I didn't
          have it to look at as I read more now."
              She giggled again and asked, "Miss T, did you know that I've
6.51   always been real shy? Mother said I used to be real bad."
              "Do you remember your first school days?" I asked.
6.52   "Yes'm. I was scared, and I hated my teacher. Now I love her.
          Mother told me that I would. I always loved you though!"
              Anne told me today that Mr. Hart will take a carload of the chil-
          dren to the Audubon lecture and movie Thursday night. She also re-
4.72   ported that Mary spent last night with her. However, she named no
          children to go in their car—just said, "We have room for three."
          Mary spoke up and said, "I'm taking Sara."
              Mr. Hart was the second child in his family. One sister was just
3.67   older and there were three younger sisters. One of them lives in a
          restricted well-to-do section of the city. Anne said, "Miss T, her
          house is a dream." A second one lives in a small nearby town. She
          is married to a man who was a professor in a small Junior College.
          He now teaches in the neighboring town. A third sister works at
          Montgomery Ward. "She had a bad wreck about a year ago."

          JAN. 5 Signed papers today with her full name—Anne Elizabeth.
5.96   Came to me to say, "Miss T, you checked my spelling, but I had
          erased on this word. I thought you would see it."
              I asked the children to exchange seats today with those who sit in
          the rear of the room where the lighting is not good and the tables
          are far away. I explained I thought it only fair to accept some of the
5.97   discomforts. Anne moved with apparent cheerfulness to a seat not
          nearly so desirable. She smiled and went immediately to work, whereas
          Dora showed her displeasure by sitting for some time with idle hands
          and a pouting expression.

          JAN. 7 Today I purposely delayed my appearance on the playground
          to observe the behavior of Anne, Sara, Mary, and Clara R. The day
4.73   was warm with a very high wind. When I came out Anne and Betty
          were in the far corner of the playground, sitting huddled on a log.
          Sara, Mary, and Clara had climbed the bars and were sitting on top.
              I called them over to me and said, "Would you three talk with me
          for a few minutes. I'm puzzled about why you three and Anne, who
          are such good friends, seem so unhappy much of the time. It has
          bothered me all year and I feel that we need to talk together."
              A glance was exchanged; then Sara said, "I'd like to be friends,
          but Anne is so bossy."
              "Tell me about it."
              "Well, I don't know. She just wants to have her way all the time."

"Are you sure it's all on her side or is it perhaps a fifty-fifty situation?"

Sara shrugged and said, "Mother worried about it last year and went to Mrs. L."

"Do you think maybe it's a situation best not discussed anywhere else, but something all of you could come together and talk over in an earnest effort to work out a better relationship?"

All three agreed so I asked, "Would you like to come together in the office where we can be alone to talk?" "Yes'm," all three said.

We went in and sat down in a circle. Anne did not seem surprised. I think she had guessed from seeing me talking with the three in the yard. They said that the trouble between them began in the third grade and became serious in the fifth—perhaps reached a peak there, but there was still trouble in the sixth. Mary said, "We fought the first time we ever saw each other when we were four."

"Anne told me about it once, but I thought it was just a way of getting acquainted, the way small children often do. Didn't you spend night before last with Anne?"

Mary tossed her head, flushed, and turned one of several Christmas rings around on her finger. "Yes'm."

"And you remember the day I went to visit her home, you were there; and the day I went to your home she was there. And another time you were sitting on the curb so lonesome because neither Anne or Sara was at home. You seem to want to be with her outside of school but here things seem different. Is that right?"

Mary tossed her head again and glanced at Anne. Then she said, "If she is willing to forgive me, I'm sorry."

"But it isn't as easy as that," I said. "Something must be the matter and we ought to try together to make it right."

Anne spoke up saying, "Miss Thornton, if they would tell me just what is wrong I'd really appreciate it."

4.74   Finally it came out that the three of them considered her a "teacher's pet."

"Well," Sara said, "getting to do lots of things. I like to do things too."

"What are some of these things that she gets to do that trouble you?"

"Ah, nothing, I don't want any of her jobs."

"Well, what should we change? What would you like to have different?"

"Shall we think it over carefully, not discuss it with anybody else, and then talk about it again tomorrow?"

Sara fought tears as she said, "I've tried to get it straightened out."

"I guess we're jealous," said Mary.

"I know what's the matter with me," said Clara. "When I quit playing games and went to sit with Sara and Mary I got into trouble. I'm going back to games. And I don't think you pet Anne any more than the rest of us."

"Can you think why she spends so much time with me at play period and sits with me at lunch?"

"Yes'm, it's because we are together and don't want her."

"Has this made you unhappy, Anne?"

6.53   "Yes'm, and the only reason my mother knew about it last year and talked to Mrs. L about it was because I went home crying so often."

"My mother was worried too," said Sara.

"My mother told me to be nice to her," said Mary.

"Do you think the boys have anything to do with the situation?" I asked. Clara grinned. Betty nodded. Sara was noncommittal and Mary again flushed and tossed back her hair.

"Well, I liked Danny before she did!" Mary said.

"Did he know that?" "No'm."

6.54   Anne sat in a big red leather chair with her head back. She spoke only once. She appeared pale and concerned. The conference is hard to record because so much came out. I had asked them to be frank regarding any incidents this year in which my relationship might seem unfair, because I didn't want to make things more difficult either for Anne or for them.

Finally I said, "Well, if you feel like it, write out your feelings and conclusions about this. This will give you time to think. Then, if you want to, you can give me what you have written, to help me know what to do. But you don't have to write anything or give it to me unless you really want to. Meantime, I'll try to help any way I can, and you must tell me if anything seems unfair to you."

2.49   EVENING OF THE SAME DAY   Tonight ten children and two fathers
5.98   met me at the high school to see the Audubon film. Anne came with
4.75   her father alone. Mary, instead of bringing Sara, came in Sara's car with the latter's parents. They dropped the girls, and Sara's father (who is pastor of the largest church in the community) asked when the lecture would be over so he could come back to get the girls.

I went in with the seven boys and two fathers and chose an aisle seat. This placed all the boys at my end of the row. Anne and her father sat at the other end of the row, and there were several vacant
4.76   seats in between. When Sara and Mary entered, Anne swapped seats with her father and sat next to Mary. They talked together quite animatedly.

After the lecture I sought Mary and Sara in the hallway and asked them if they didn't want me to wait with them at the lower gate until Sara's dad came for them. Sara said, "No, my parents will be there." Then Anne and her father came along and insisted that I ride with them. Mr. Hart said he thoroughly enjoyed the evening.
3.68   "When I was in New Orleans I spent all my spare time in Audubon park." Then he laughed as he said, "You know my wife said tonight, 'Why is it that Anne can get you to go anywhere and I can't?' I do enjoy things like this film, but, you know, she won't go! I wish she would."

"Anne, you'll have to make a date with him for the next one in April."
2.50   "Oh, I have another date before then—for P.T.A. Monday night," laughed Anne.

4.77   JAN. 8   A child in my group was sick so I stayed in to minister to him during play period, but I could see the group through the windows. Anne, Mary, Sara, Betty, and others played dodge-ball. Clara joined the softball group. The games appeared to be going with zest.

Anne, Mary, Betty, and Clara gave me written accounts of their difficulties which are recorded later. Sara also handed me one. She said she wrote hers after the Audubon lecture, as did Anne and Mary.

As I was going home I passed Sara's home. Along the circular driveway in front, a line of six or seven girls was roller skating in 4.78 single file, led by Sara. A hasty look showed Anne in the line, also Mary. They saw me and waved.

Checking some arithmetic problems on Christmas spending, I no-4.79 ticed that Sara gave Mary a gift but didn't mention Anne. She also gave gifts to Esther and Bill—friends in the group last year.

Mary's Account of the Difficulties:

In the first grade Anne and Carrie were in my room. We all got along just fine. We always played together and stuck close by.

In the second grade we were all together except Carrie and she had rheumatic fever. We always played together then too.

In the third grade we all sat together and did just fine. Later in the year Sara A. moved here. We all made friends with her and our teacher put her at the end of our table. About the end of the year we all got roused up but we got over it.

In the fourth grade we were not together.

In the fifth grade Mr. O was our teacher. We started playing paper-4.80 dolls. He let us build paper-doll houses. Anne and Sara shared a room and I shared a room with Esther. That roused things up because everyone wanted a separate room. Anne and Sara got into a fuss and didn't speak for a while. We had no more fusses that year.

In the sixth grade, everyone had to write who they liked best and who they disliked. It somehow got around to everyone and that is what started our trouble mainly. We wouldn't get along the rest of the year.

In the seventh grade we are all separated. Anne, Sara and I are together in Miss Thornton's room. We get along now just fine, except a few small instances, such as I would speak to Anne and wouldn't get a reply. Maybe she didn't hear me and I guess she has spoken to me and I didn't hear her and that might have caused a mix-up.

My conclusion is that we all join in and play together and forget the past and try to do better in the future years to come.

Sara's Account of the Difficulties:

The first fuss I had with Anne was in the fifth grade. It all started like this. Our teacher, Mr. O, let us play paper dolls. When we played together we didn't get along.

One day we decided to make a doll-house. We made it out of paste-board boxes. It was a hotel. Anne and I let our paper dolls live 4.81 on the top floor. After a while we got tired of playing and Anne and I got into a fuss because she wanted to take the house and I did also. We had a few words and didn't bother to play with each other for a few days. After a while we got over it and did better for a while.

In the sixth grade we each seemed not to be able to get along to-gether. I tried and tried to be nice to her. She was just as nice to me as she could be. We had our little differences but they didn't mean anything. Sometimes in the afternoon we played together. Mrs. L talked to us about it too.

I am not jealous of Anne or anybody else. Around the last part of the year we seemed to get along better.

This year I am glad Lena, Esther and Carrie and the rest of us are separated. We are getting along better than we did last year. Anne and I have not said anything to each other about anything.

I have talked to my mother about it a few times and she has told me to be nice to Anne and not fuss. I have tried to do that this year. I want to be friends with Anne and everybody else.

While thinking it over I see that I am part of the blame and that we should get together and be friends. I have said Anne likes to boss but I guess it's partly me instead of all Anne.

CLARA'S ACCOUNT OF THE DIFFICULTIES:

I think my trouble with Anne started in the third grade.

Well, after I left this school and went to Washington School, I didn't think much about it. Now that I'm back here I still don't get along with her. I have tried but it doesn't work. I don't like Anne 4.82 like I like other girls. I've tried to like her but I can't, so now I'm just going to stay away from her completely and play with other girls. I have more fun with the others, playing ball and getting exercise. You told us to tell what we thought about it and I have.

BETTY'S PAPER Betty is new in the group this year, also younger, having skipped a grade.

OUR PROBLEM

The first day of school I noticed Anne, Sara and Mary kinda stuck together. About a week later Anne acted friendly and acted like she wanted to be my friend so I started playing with her. Our friendship lasted quite a while.

The time before the last time we all changed tables, Clara came 4.83 to our table and Anne acted kinda like she didn't like me as well and started running around with Clara. She then didn't have much to do with me but I feel that was her business. Later we all got to be friends again but Anne continued not to be too friendly.

When we went Christmas caroling I didn't have anyone to walk 3.69 with for a partner and neither did Anne so I asked her to walk with me. Clara was supposed to have walked with Anne but she walked with Mary and their little gang. Anne and I had a good time together that night.

Tuesday I left school because I was sick and after I left some sort of fuss got started between Anne, Mary, Sara and Clara. Anne told me that while she was on the play ground that she sat with Miss Thornton and talked to her. She said that Sara and the other two just got mad at her for some unknown reason.

Wednesday when I came back to school Mary and the others were mad at Anne. I ran around with Anne but was as friendly as I could be to the other three. When we went out to recess, Anne and I went to the log. Mary, Sara and Clara went out under the tree. Anne and

I talked a while and thought maybe the others would come out there to the log but they didn't. Then we went to the bars and then Mary and the rest went to the log.

Anne is my best friend and I like her very much. I used to say she was the pet because everyone else did but now I don't because I realize why Miss Thornton lets her do what she does. I believe that
4.84   the thing that started it all was that I quit playing with the other girls so that I could be with Anne. The other reason is jealousy.

ANNE'S ACCOUNT OF THE DIFFICULTIES:

When I was in the fifth grade, Mary, Sara, Esther, Carrie and I sat at a table together. Mr. O was our teacher and he would let us bring paper dolls and other things to school to play with. We really played more than we worked.

Along about the sixth month we were in school, Mary, Sara, Esther, and Carrie picked a best friend and that was the one she played with. Mary, Sara and Esther ran around together and Carrie and I ran around together. Then Carrie started running around with Mary, Sara and Esther. I would be sitting at the table and while I was doing my
4.85   work they would be writing notes about me. When I would speak
6.55   they wouldn't speak to me.

In the sixth grade we all sat at the same table again. Ruth sat at the table with us. She and I started running around together and doing everything together. Then Ruth started running around with
5.99   Esther. I didn't like it and I said something about Ruth, which was wrong. Then I went to Ruth and apologized. About a month later none of them would speak to me.

Sara and I served in the lunch room every day and while we were gone to serve Mary, Esther, Carrie and Ruth would write notes and then pass them to each other when they came to lunch. They would have secrets and would whisper to one another and say, "don't tell
6.56   Anne."

[Note inserted by Miss T: All year I have worked to help Mary break a habit of whispering behind her hand. I have told her that if the conversations are so very private they should not be carried on in the group. She continues to whisper with hand over mouth and eyes on me. When I remind her that this is very impolite, she flushes, tosses her head, and in a few moments is whispering behind her hand again.]

I would ask them why they were mad at me and nobody would know. They would call me Mrs. L's pet and said she likes me better than them.
3.70   One day the principal came in the room and asked Mrs. L to let her have a girl for a while and Mrs. L told me to go. The principal wanted me to go show some lower grades from Washington School where the auditorium was. They were coming to see a puppet show.
4.86   When I came back to the room everybody at my table was calling me the principal's pet. I didn't know what to do. I would tell them I couldn't help it because Mrs. L asked me to help Miss C. When we would go out to play they didn't want me around, so I would play with the other girls.

Lots of time Mrs. C would want someone to keep her children on

the playground so Mrs. L would ask Sara and me to do it. Mary,
4.87   *Esther, Carrie and Ruth wouldn't like it because I helped keep them.*
Mrs. L would get us together and ask us what was wrong and I
wouldn't know.

This year we were separated and we all thought we could get along
better. Then one day while we were having arithmetic I came to a
problem I didn't understand. I went and asked Miss Thornton to
explain it to me. She did and when I came back to the table every-
one was saying that I was teacher's pet, or that Miss T took up more
4.88   *time with me and that she let me do more things than anyone else.*
I said I wasn't the teacher's pet—that if they went and asked for
help Miss T would help them—that was her job. Everybody insisted
I was a teacher's pet and I suggested that we stay after school and
get it cleared up. Nobody wanted to do that. Clara apologized and
6.57   *I said that was all right. But the next day they were unfriendly again.*
It worried me. Clara started playing with us at play period and they
(Mary and Sara) didn't have anything to do with me.

One day after school I went to see Mary and she didn't seem to
have much to say to me. And so I didn't know what to say. Then
after school about a week later Mary and I played together and had
a real good time. But the next day in school she wouldn't speak to me.

JAN. 10   A rainy day. A group was planning to help with the P.T.A.
program tonight. When I asked if all had transportation, Anne said,
"I may not have, as Daddy may have to work late."

"Perhaps I can pick you up," I said. Then on second thought I
asked Sara, "How are you coming?" "Daddy will bring me." "Who
will be with you?" "Mary." "Then wouldn't you be able to bring
4.89   Anne? I'd be glad to but I have all the music books, records, chart,
and record player to bring." "Yes'm, I guess so." I thought Anne
looked none too happy.

1.55   EVENING   Anne came with the others. She wore her pale-pink pleated
flannel skirt, white blouse edged with tiny lace, and navy sweater.
5.100   Anne handed the records to me as I needed them—unasked, but
2.51   a tremendous help! She sat between Sara and me and participated in
all the music activities.

JAN. 11   The sun came out today and Anne played "Pop the Whip"
1.56   for a while with Sara and Mary. Then they got the bean bags and
4.90   a small group together to play dodge-ball. Later they practiced with
batons.

Mary told me Anne spent Friday night with her. Anne said, "Mary
4.91   ate supper with me. Then I spent the night with her."

Mrs. L noticed the girls together and commented at play period.

JAN. 14   After school today a group of boys stayed awhile to work
and play with some musical instruments. They finally moved over to
a table and I saw them conferring with their heads together. Finally
4.92   Joel called, "Come here, Miss T, I want to show you something."
Moving across the room I noted that they had a story folder and were
going over its table of contents.

"Look, Miss T, Anne said she had written fifty-five stories up to now. Look! This is one she wrote last year! And she's counting some things as stories when they aren't. Here's the 'Pledge of Allegiance to the Flag.' "

4.93 "Do you know what?" Richard asked. "Last year she wrote a story about Sara and it got back to her. Sara really got mad! Anne said Sara thought she was better than anybody else because she was the preacher's daughter and she had more clothes than anyone else."

Recognizing that the boys knew of the feuding, I asked what they felt might really be the cause. "Well," one of them said, "every one of us has *liked* Anne at one time or another."

"Yes, sir. We sho' have!" with much slapping of shoulders and shaking of hands.

"Anne likes Danny, though."

"You mean she still likes him best?"

"Yes'm. But he likes Ruth in Mrs. G's grade."

4.94 Tommy said, "You know, it looks like when one boy starts liking a girl, they all do," and he laughed heartily.

As the group broke up, I told Joel I thought he had done something not very fair or sporting in checking Anne's stories and questioning them when she was not present. He agreed.

5.101 I went to the office and when Mrs. L came in I asked her if she remembered the story Anne wrote and then "repeated" this year. She said, "I believe I do." I then asked if she remembered the one about Sara and she said, "I don't know—it seems to me that I remember something—I just don't recall right now."

1.57 JAN. 17 Anne at the door as usual. She ducked out of sight as she opened the door, and I saw that she had cut bangs. She giggled. I said, "I like your bangs. Who cut them?" "Mother."

4.95 At play period almost the entire group played softball; every girl participated. At lunch Anne, Sara, Mary, and Betty sat together. The principal reported seeing Anne, Sara, Mary, Carrie, and Esther all skating together after school Friday afternoon.

JOBS I VALUE

I think there are quite a few jobs I value highly.

I think the jobs I value highest are keeping Miss Thornton's desk and going on errands for Miss Thornton and for Miss C [the prin-
5.102 *cipal]. The reasons I like and value these highest is that I know I am helping someone else and I enjoy it. Another reason I like to keep Miss T's desk for her is that I can do that when my work is caught up and I don't have time to worry about what someone else is doing.*

I like to go on errands because it helps me to prove myself willing and be able to accept responsibility.

5.103 *I enjoy my job as doorkeeper very much. I value it secondly although I think it is very important.*

Another job I enjoy doing is serving in the lunchroom. I think you get experiences serving in the lunchroom that you couldn't get anywhere else.

I enjoy doing all the jobs I am asked to do but I value some higher than I do others.

1.58   JAN. 20   Today the children whispered that it was Anne's thirteenth
2.52   birthday so we all sang for her. She giggled and cut her eyes around.
4.96   She said she had received another piece of luggage for her birth-
6.58   day.

       JAN. 21   Entire group played together—racing, relays, and runs
4.97   around the playground. Ground was cold and wet so we did not
       stay more than fifteen minutes.

From this point on only selected materials from Miss Thornton's record
about Anne will be presented. She found these items especially significant in making her final interpretation of Anne's development and adjustment problems.

5.104   JAN. 26   Today Anne told me she went to the city library last night
        and took out five books. They are: An Old-fashioned Girl by Louisa
        M. Alcott, Elizabeth and Philip in Canada, King George VI, Cross-
        roads for Penelope by Howard, and Meg's Fortune by Malvern.
        Sitting beside me today she asked in a low voice, "Miss T, have
        you ever watched people go into the Grand Hotel to a dance? All
3.71   those beautiful evening dresses—the young girls and older women
6.59   all wrapped up! And the men with dress clothes!"

        FEB. 1   Came to me with Mary to say, "Miss T, tomorrow is my
2.53   mother's birthday. Mary and I want to make her a cake, but if we tell
4.98   her she won't let us. Would you assign us a cooking lesson so we
        could say you said to do it? We can take all the materials down to
        Mary's and make it."
        "Surely," I said. "Tell her I want you to make something using
        fractions."
        A few days ago while reading on Brazil, I found that only one
5.105   child in the room had ever tasted tapioca. So I urged them to buy a
        package and make the family dessert—combining arithmetic with
        learning a new food. Mary and Anne followed through and Anne said
        she thought it was delicious.

1.59   FEB. 8   Yesterday I noticed that Anne and Mary both had had their
4.99   hair curled. Today I asked, "A permanent?" Anne giggled and re-
3.72   plied, "Yes, Mary and I both got one. The lady up the street gave
        them to us."
        During a discussion about TV in class today, the story was told
        about a young boy who tolerates no conversation among his elders
3.73   during a TV program. He says crossly, "Will you hush!" Anne said in
2.54   an aside to Sara but loud enough to be heard, "My mother would
        slap me out of the chair if I said that!"
        The girls made the cake for Anne's mother and reported that it
4.100   turned out well. Anne asked if she and a group, including Mary and
        Sara, might plan a Valentine party for the class.

        FEB. 14, VALENTINE'S DAY   No heat in the room, so we finally went
        into the auditorium and huddled around the heater there. Anne and
        her committee slipped out and went back to the room to arrange for

5.106   the party. When we had returned after lunch, the chairs were arranged in a large circle and on every chair was a pretty napkin and a plate. Anne had made heart-shaped cookies, attractively iced. The others furnished punch and heart-shaped candies. The group had decorated

3.74   the rocking chair with a large red heart. They had pulled it to the front of the room and escorted me to it. Then, with much ceremony, they crowned me "Queen of Hearts" with a lovely white and red crown. After refreshments they asked me to give out the valentines.

I would guess that Anne received five to one over anybody else. Many times the same boy would give her three or four. She received

4.101   several pink envelopes sealed with red hearts. I said, "Those certainly look interesting." She giggled and later told me they were from Danny and that each envelope contained several valentines.

She then asked if Sallie, the maid, might be invited in. She served Sallie herself and was one of several remembering her with a valentine.

5.107   She also carried a plate to Will, the janitor. She thanked me for my
3.75   valentine although I did not sign my name—just used a question mark.

FEB. 16

BOOKS I HAVE READ THIS YEAR

Step-sister Sally, Wings Around South America, Nellie's Silver Mine, Operas Every Child Should Know, Sandra's Cellar, Keys To The City, It Happened in England, Teeny Gay, Mother and Queen,

5.108   *Circus Doctor, Tales of Wonder, Whispering Girl, by Means, The King's Spurs, The Hurricane, An Only Child, Crossroads for Penelope, King George VI, Meg's Fortune, The Royal Tour of Canada, Mary Mapes Dodge, Enchanting Jenny Lind, Bright Side Up, Great Tradition, Single Stones, Debbie of the Green Gate, Sensible Kate, Debeta Ann, Little Women, The Little Princesses, and Margaret, The Story of A Modern Princess.*

FEB. 18   Today at lunch three boys moved their plates from the table where they usually sit back to a half-filled table where Anne was

4.102   sitting. "Look, Miss T," said another boy near me, "Look at the boys at Anne's table." Several turned to look and one explained—"Ooo— popular." Sara was with her. Mary was absent today. Sara and Anne seem much closer in their relationship recently. Sara had on a new plaid skirt and red pedal-pushers today for the playground activities.

FEB. 24   Today Anne wore a new black cotton skirt with gold and

1.60   aqua design, white blouse, and black sweater. While making a chart
5.109   she turned over a full bottle of India ink. A great deal splashed on her brand new skirt. I gave her a clean cloth to wipe it off and advised

6.60   putting a pad of paper towels under her skirt to keep it from her petticoat. I went on with a reading group but then I noticed that she was having quite a time—the ink was all over her hands and on the fresh blouse. She said, "It went through on a new petticoat my aunt sent me."

"You'd better go home, I think, and let your mother take care of it

while it's fresh," I said. "Will she understand it was an accident?"
"Yes'm."

Anne was back in about twenty minutes, a trifle breathless.

"Could she get the ink out?" I asked.

"Yes'm, she got it out," Anne giggled. "Mother was ironing, and
she said, 'Lord 'a mercy, how can I keep you decent looking?'

"I told Daddy I wasted a whole new bottle of ink, and he said, 'Well,
if Miss Thornton never spilt any ink, I'll buy her two bottles.'" She

2.55   laughed as she said, "You see, you can get yourself two bottles."

"No, I'm afraid I can't," I replied.

"Daddy told Mother, 'Little boys tear up their pants and little girls
have to spill things.'"

"Did he bring you back to school in the car?" "Yes'm."

FEB. 25 Worked with a group writing a play. When they asked me

5.110   to listen to what they had completed, several turned to Anne and asked

4.103   her to report. Afterwards she made suggestions for costumes which
others suggested. She was one of a group of six children who were
writing invitations to administrators and grade mothers to attend
activities winding up our study of coffee, our national drink. She received a large package of books from the Pan American Union today
in reply to a letter she had written. She distributed these to the group.

Anne made a very attractive place mat from a coffee bag we received
at National Coffee Company when we went there Tuesday. The bag
was a good quality tow, almost like heavy monk's cloth, and came from

5.111   Santos, Brazil. She stenciled a map of Brazil on it with crayon and
pressed it after raveling the edges.

Anne helped me a few minutes after school and as we worked I
said, "Do you still feel you'd like to be a teacher?" "Yes'm." Then

5.112   after a pause, "Mother doesn't want me to be a nurse, she says she

2.56   wants me to be a teacher." Another pause; then she straightened up

6.61   and, looking full at me, said, "But I think I want to be a teacher
anyway."

MARCH 8 I took a pair of gold ear bobs to Anne today at her request.
She wants them for the play in which she has a part. It culminates our

3.76   study of coffee. She said, "Mother doesn't wear them." Neither does
Mrs. Hart drink coffee, and she is hesitating over coming to the coffee
time preceding our program. I told her she need not drink coffee,
but as our grade mother I would so much like to have her here to
meet the guests. She still has not said she will come.

Anne said today, "Mother wants Joe to be a doctor but she doesn't
want me to be a nurse. Last night Joe was working on his English, and

3.77   Mother said, 'Joe, you shouldn't have any trouble with that; I skipped

2.57   a grade when I was in school.' And Joe said, 'Yes, but I don't have
your brain.'"

Anne and one other child were not permitted by parents to go to
a magician's show in the auditorium today. She stayed in the room

3.78   and worked.

3.79   MARCH 9 Anne's mother did not come for the program.

3.80   MARCH 17 Anne came to me early and said, "Mother told me to
bring all my books home over the week end. . . ."

5.113　MARCH 21　Today Anne walked in and put a pile of books down so
2.58　noisily that my attention was attracted. I noticed that she had taken
6.62　every textbook home over the week end. . . .

MARCH 22　Mrs. Hart came for a conference. . . . I asked her to sit
where Anne had left all her materials. As we began to examine them
I sensed an utter lack of interest in all the folders. Finally, she drew
2.59　back in her chair and said, "I'm awfully disappointed in Anne's work.
3.81　She doesn't know a thing!"

"What are you basing your statement on, Mrs. Hart?" I asked,
remembering the books over the week end.

"I checked up on her. She doesn't know a thing in the language
book."

"Are you sure? Do you mean rules and definitions or what?"

"Well, yes—she can't tell you anything. Do you expect to finish this
arithmetic book this year?"

"No, I don't, and I don't think—"

"Well, what will happen when she goes to high school? What will
happen if she hasn't gone through the geography book? Frankly I am
very much disappointed."

"Mrs. Hart, how have you felt about Anne's learning in previous
years?"

"Well, with some I was pleased and with some I wasn't."

"I'm sorry you feel disappointed and particularly sorry that you have
waited so long to tell me. I have urged you and the other parents to
visit and to know the children's work."

3.82　"Yes, I know—but if I came would I see a schedule?" and her eyes
went to the daily work plans of the children on the board.

"Do you mean thirty minutes of this and thirty minutes of that?
No, that isn't the way children learn best, Mrs. Hart."

We talked for an hour and a half. She kept reiterating her dis-
2.60　appointment and I kept trying to tell her that I was proud of Anne's
work. But I felt that I was getting nowhere, so I urged her to talk
to our principal and to our supervisor.

I said, "Mrs. Hart, you know this can be so difficult for Anne. She
is trying to gain both your approval and mine in her work."

"Oh, I'm not trying to teach her."

"No," I said, "but you are examining her, checking up on her."

"Oh, yes, and do you give examinations and tests?"

"Not the old-fashioned ones such as you and I used to have," I
said, "but we do check up on the work in many, many ways, and every
day."

She drew back and exclaimed, "You don't! So how is she to learn
3.83　all of these things?" Then she said, "I guess you just don't under-
2.61　stand. You've never had any children. I want the best for mine." She
continued, "You know I took Joe out and sent him to College Prep
and I started to send Anne."

As she left she agreed to talk with somebody else and made an appointment to talk with the principal at eleven the next morning.

5.114　MARCH 23　Today Anne missed several spelling words. . . .
6.63

5.115   MARCH 25   Anne missed words on the final test. Does not usually
6.64   do so. . . .

APRIL 1

MY LAST TWO WEEKS OF T.V.

          Saturdays: 7:45   John Cameron Swayze
3.84   8:00   Red Buttons
5.116   8:30   Life of Riley
                     9:00   Big Story
                     9:30   Amos and Andy
                     10–11:15   Wrestling
          Thursday: 8:30   Justice
                     9:00   Dragnet
                     9:30   Ford Theatre
                     10:00   Lux Theatre
          Sunday: 5:00   Oral Roberts—Evangelist Healer
                  5:30   Ramar of the Jungle
          I usually go to bed about 10:00 or 10:30.

3.85   APRIL 5   Today Anne said, "Miss Thornton, Governor Folsom is a
        cousin of mine."
        "He is? On your mother's side?"
        "Yes'm. He is my grandmother's cousin."

        APRIL 6   Anne remarked, "Miss Thornton, I had a cousin who went
3.86   to Annapolis, but he dropped out his second year." Several of the boys
        grinned at each other. One had been reading a story of a plebe at
        Annapolis and was reporting on the book at the time.
        Today in oral language Anne recounted to the group the story of
        a fight she once had with Mary (when they were four years old). She
4.104   was sitting just to my right and Mary to my left. Then Sara told
        the story of the fight she had had with Anne over the paper-doll house.
        These came out as oral stories following the reading of the story a
        child had written, suggested by a Norman Rockwell painting. There
        was much giggling among the girls involved and a few interjections.
        I felt that this time the telling lacked the stings that went with the
6.65   conference. The unpleasant emotions seemed to have been drained
        out of the memories.
        Anne said today that, "Joe gets into my room sometimes and gets
        my things. He got my diary once, out of the cedar chest, and Daddy
2.62   really got after him. I didn't give him a Christmas present or a birth-
        day present. We always get mad with each other right before Christ-
        mas and birthdays."
5.117   Anne is getting ready for her music recital.
        She asked this afternoon if she might take her language book home.

MAY 5   ESSAY

WHEN MY PARENTS DON'T UNDERSTAND

        Many times children our age think our parents don't understand.
        In their way I think parents do what they think is best for us and we
        don't know how to accept it as the best.

I remember when I was about three years old I liked to help mother in the garden and mother wouldn't want me to. I would get angry and think she wasn't treating me right. Mother just didn't want me to hoe up her plants but I thought it just wasn't right because I couldn't work the same place in the garden as she did.

5.118
6.66

When we moved to Forestville daddy bought some rabbits to kill and can for the winter. Joe and I took a sudden liking to two of the rabbits. The day daddy was killing the rabbits, I took these two rabbits around on the front porch and hid them because I thought it wasn't right for daddy to kill them.

2.63
5.119
6.67

When daddy got ready to kill them I thought he didn't understand that I wanted to keep these rabbits. Finally he consented to let us keep the two and I felt better.

Joe used to carry daddy's lunch to the mill and I wanted so much to go with him. Mother forbade me to go and I would sit and cry because I wasn't allowed to go with Joe to carry daddy's lunch. I always thought mother didn't understand.

2.64
3.87
6.68

After we came to Bethel things were different. I was always wanting to go over to Mary's house. Mother would say, "Some other time" and when I would keep begging she would get impatient and say if I didn't hush she would spank me.

6.69
2.65

I remember one time Mary wanted me to go to the store with her and her mother. I thought she meant the store right below us and I went and told mother. When we left I found out she was going to the Jackson Mills store and then going visiting. We didn't get back until early afternoon and when I did come back mother spanked me. She didn't understand that I didn't know that we were going to be gone that long.

4.105
3.88
2.66
6.70

Not long after that I had to go to the dentist. Mother made an appointment with Dr. W. When we got there he had a patient in the chair. We had to wait about fifteen minutes. All the time I was getting more and more scared. When he finally did take me I was almost scared to death. I hollered and cried and finally mother and daddy became impatient with me and said I was going to get a spanking when I got home. They didn't understand why I was crying. Dr. W really wasn't hurting, it was that I was so scared I could hardly stand it.

6.71
2.67
5.120

When I was in the fifth grade I stopped on the way home to ask Mary's mother if she could go play with me. When I got home I got a whipping for stopping on the way home from school.

2.68
6.72

Again while I was in the fifth grade I was going home with Sara and on to town. I thought Sara and I were going to ride to town with her father and I told mother that. It turned out that we were going on the trolley by ourselves. When mother found out we went by ourselves she thought I told her something that wasn't true. She didn't understand at first, but finally I made her realize that I didn't know we were going by ourselves.

4.106
5.121
2.69
6.73

MAY 25   ESSAY

MY CONSCIENCE

A conscience is a wonderful thing to have at times and at other times it can be quite a pest.

I have heard it said, and I am sure you have too, "I don't think he
or she even has a conscience." I think people are quite wrong in saying
5.122   this because in my estimation everyone has a conscience. At all times
people hear their conscience but, don't heed it.
I think you can get into trouble by not listening to your conscience.
When I was real small I would start out of my yard without permission
and my conscience would tell me this was wrong but I would go on.
The result was that I was punished for disobeying.
I also think people can act on impulses and then think about what
they've done and find they were wrong.
My conscience helps me to tell right from wrong and then it's up to
me to decide which I will do.

Anne's language folder contains 93 compositions written during her
year in the seventh grade, a total of 237 pages. Of particular interest are
the twenty-page "My Life Story" and the six-page "We Declare War"
story of Anne's fight with Sara over the paper dolls. Of course, Miss
Thornton had intimate knowledge of all this material as she made her
interpretations of the record, and perhaps two factors in the autobiography must be mentioned here. One was the account of the time when,
as a toddler, Anne had licked the icing off her father's birthday cake.
Anne wrote:

That night at dinner mother found it out and spanked me. Daddy
2.70   only said, "Anne, be ashamed, licking all the icing off of Daddy's
6.74   cake." But that hurt more than mother's spanking because I loved
him.

Again, at the end of the autobiography, Anne diagrams her family
tree through five generations on both sides of the family. Then, in discussing her family background, she wrote:

Five generations ago my father's great-great grandfather sailed from
3.89   Germany to America and settled here in the South. Mr. ———— Hart
5.123   founded M———— County in this state. The plantation in M County
was handed down to my great-grandfather. He enlarged it. My great-
grandfather was killed in the Civil War and the plantation was burned.

The fact of this plantation-owning, old-family background stands out
in many of Anne's writings and in a number of unreproduced teacher
conferences with the mother as a central awareness in the mother's feelings and as a constant spur to family accomplishment and a cause of
family aloofness in the community.

This completes the material about Anne and her interaction with her
classmates. It remains now to see what we are able to understand about
the structure and dynamics of the class as a group, Anne's motivations,
and how these factors influenced the interaction between Anne and her
classmates.

THE STRUCTURE AND DYNAMICS OF THE CLASS

Perhaps the first question that comes to mind is whether the sociogram represents the dynamic social structure of the class in any valid and significant fashion. Do we see evidence of the structure portrayed by the sociogram in the actual natural groupings of the children in their day-to-day actions? Since the positive friendship choices were almost entirely among girls and among boys, and since the case record is about a girl, we shall deal with the structuring of girls' interactions first.

Interaction among Girls

The first material showed Anne regretting that some of the girls who had belonged to her in-group during the previous year were no longer in the class (4.03, 4.04). She sought them out frequently on the playground during the first weeks of school, or spent her time with her in-group of the current year (4.05). Then, as the year advanced, we have numerous instances of the in-group to which Anne belonged being together: 4.16, 4.19, 4.20, 4.46, 4.51, 4.57, 4.61, 4.65, 4.67, 4.73, 4.76, 4.77, 4.78, 4.80, 4.90, 4.95, 4.98, 4.100, 4.102, 4.104. Thus the record contains twenty instances in which this particular little clique functioned together on the playground, in the cafeteria, or in the classroom. Of course, there were numerous other incidents in which these same girls also played, visited, or went around together out of school. The inference is clear that a friendship group of this sort is a very real social phenomenon and that being accepted and valued in such a group is a very vital part of life for all children. We are greatly in need of more descriptive research material such as that supplied to us by Miss Thornton's record to demonstrate the scope of the interaction among children with others of their particular in-group and also with children not in their in-group. The record does show Anne interacting with children who were not a part of her clique, but such interactions were much less frequent in the record. One suspects that most children, experientially, do not go to school with all the children in their classrooms but are largely aware of and find special significance in the actions of members of their own in-group. The other children in the classroom matter very little to them.

Interaction among Boys

Because Miss Thornton's record was about a girl there is a minimum of description of groupings among the boys. Nevertheless it is worthwhile to examine the record to see how the boys did group themselves in the situations described. We shall want to see whether the boys' friendship pattern influenced such groupings or whether they interacted with Anne and her group entirely as individuals. On November 23 Jerry, Frank, and Danny, all boys who chose Joel as a best friend, sat at the table with Anne and Miss Thornton (4.53). On November 29 Tommy, a member of the boys' in-group, beat Richard, a rejected boy, to a seat beside Anne (4.54). On December 1 Lester N. and George T., mutual friendship choices, were together with Anne and the teacher on the way home from seeing "The Vanishing Prairie" (4.57). On January 14 Joel, the most-chosen boy in the group, was the spokesman for the boys' group (4.92) in going through Anne's story folder and pointing out that she was padding it with the "Pledge of Allegiance to the Flag" and a story she had written the year before. Identified in this complaining group were Richard and Tommy, both of whom had chosen Joel as a best friend. So while material about the boys is necessarily meager, what we have shows that they, too, tend to act with the other boys whom they admire and choose as friends.

The more anecdotal material I read, the more I am impressed with how much peer-group friends mean to children in school. Sometimes life seems hardly worth living to them when they cannot win a place in the group to which they wish to belong. And they seem willing to risk much displeasure from teachers and parents in the effort to attract favorable attention from admired peers. Hence the evidence from our accumulated anecdotal material supports the idea that the peer-group life of children in school is vigorous, vital, and full of meaning for them.

Anne's Place in the Group

Anne's place in the group can be evaluated by means of the sociogram and the roles she was described as playing. The sociogram shows Anne securely established within the dominant clique of girls. She had three mutual friendship choices within this group and was chosen also by two other girls who desired to belong to this group. Her leadership roles, however, related more to classroom activities than to playground activities. The other children seemed to accept and value her capacity for planning, directing, and carrying out group projects. Illustrations are numerous: she engineered the doughnut sale (4.06); she planned the songs and choral readings for P.T.A. (4.09); she chose Janice G. to help her with a lunchroom task (4.14). In the cumulative record her first-grade teacher felt that she wanted to be a leader and usually achieved it, since the other children did not resent playing what Anne suggested (4.32). Her second-grade teacher gave the same report and remarked that Anne "made a very good leader" (4.33). Her third-grade teacher described her as "by far the best leader in the class"; "she can do almost anything," and that "they [the other children] appreciate her" (4.34). In grade four the teacher described Anne as "still a leader" and told how she planned and directed a class play (4.35). In grade six the teacher reported: "Anne's ability seems to be recognized by the children, for she is always the first to be chosen when there is a job to be done where leadership is involved (4.37). Yet this was the year in which Anne had so much trouble with members of her own clique. On November 24 she managed the record player for the other seventh grade (5.73). She wrote the purposes of the trip to see "The Vanishing Prairie" on the blackboard for the group (4.56). She played new songs for the group to learn (5.82), and on the night of December 13 she helped the teacher involve a group of boys in a discussion of the Antarctic at a P.T.A. meeting. In her essay on "Jobs I Value" (5.102), Anne reported helping the teacher and the principal as her most valued tasks and rated her post as doorkeeper second and serving in the cafeteria third. She did not mention her leadership of peers as a valued task. Nevertheless, she took the leadership in organizing a Valentine's Day party and followed through to make it a success (4.100, 5.106). On February 25 she had a leadership role again in writing a play with a committee and making suggestions about costumes (4.103). She also had a part in the play.

Certainly this is an impressive record of leadership in classroom activities, and the other children seem to have given these roles freely to Anne and not merely to have acquiesced to the teacher's nominations. Nevertheless, real peer-group belonging is most often won in other ways—by effective participation in active games and sports appropriate to the maturity level of the group and by adherence to the customs and code of behavior of the group. The record shows that Anne was skillful and effective when she chose to take part in the games of the children. Illustrations are: baseball (4.05); dodge-ball (4.55); setting off fireworks (4.64); dodge-ball (4.77); roller skating (4.78); dodge-ball (4.90); skating (4.95); and relay races (4.97).

On the other hand, Anne was developmentally in the transition to early adolescence. Adolescent-girl peer-group activities involve less-active play, preoccupation with clothes and grooming, much interaction with boys, and concern with dances and parties. An examination of the record shows Anne moving into these interests somewhat ahead of most of her classmates. The record is replete with descriptions of her unusually well-selected clothes and of her careful grooming. Closer study shows numerous occasions when she did *not* participate in the active play of the other children—sometimes to be with the teacher, sometimes to be with Danny, and sometimes simply to talk with other girls: 4.11, 4.15, 4.60, 4.66, 4.67, 4.71, 4.73. So there are about as many recorded instances of her failing to take part in active games as of participation.

Relationship with Boys

But Anne's new interests and the transitional phase of her peer-group identification are most strikingly illustrated by her evolving relationship with boys. This is demonstrated by her interactions with them and by their reaction to her: other children identified Anne and Danny as sweethearts (4.10); she and Danny dropped out of play to be together on playground (4.11); Anne's reaction to interaction between Mary and Danny (4.12); with Danny, Mary, and Sara on playground (4.15); talks to teacher about Danny being kissed at carnival (4.18); tells teacher Frank blew a kiss at her (4.21); reacts to passing of "love notes" (4.22); says, "girls can always think up something" (4.23); sat with Danny at lunch (4.46); again with Danny at lunch (4.47); reports liking boys (4.50); Jerry sat by her at lunch (4.53); Tommy sat by Anne at lunch (4.54); Lester squired her back from "The Vanishing Prairie" and bought her a soda (4.57, 4.58); Jack said, "Anne is reading about herself" (a queen) (4.59); Danny carried plant home for her (4.63); Mary claimed she liked Danny before Anne did (4.74); a boy commented, "Every one of us has liked Anne at one time or another" (4.93); Anne got many valentines from boys (4.101); many boys at Anne's table (4.102). These incidents far outnumber the ones that show Anne playing at children's games and certainly establish her interest in and attractiveness to boys. It is clear that she is moving into adolescent behavior in advance of most of her girl classmates. Unfortunately we do not know Mary's physical-maturity level, so we cannot judge how genuine is her rivalry with Anne over boys.

Other Adolescent Interests

Interest in other adolescent peer-group concerns is evidenced in Anne's writings, in her comments to the teacher, and in her activities at home. For example, on November 1 she describes to the teacher the proper way to launder her angora cap and collar (5.13); on October 18 she calls the teacher's attention to the great beauty of some trees they pass on the way to her home (5.39); her paper on "The Jazz Session" and other comments reflecting her interest in popular music are strongly adolescent (5.50); her plans for motherhood and interest in young children are characteristic of the transition period into adolescence (5.65); the story "Captain on the Bowling Team" places her at age seventeen, possessed of a new Pontiac, and a senior in high school (5.71).

The account of preparing a dinner for the family describes another growing-up role that Anne is exploring (5.77). Her altruistic views about Christmas giving, mixed with accounts of setting off fireworks, is a perfect example of the alternating orientation toward grown-up values and toward childhood interests (5.92, 4.64). Making the fruitcake was another exploration of the home-making role (5.94); so was the purchase of insurance stock (5.95). Anne's comment about watching people go into the Grand Hotel to a dance and their beautiful evening dresses suggests a role to which she may be looking forward in fantasy (3.71). Her serious consideration of a choice of occupation was mentioned several times (3.77). Anne's self-analysis in 'When My Parents Don't Understand" shows her at work on the adolescent developmental task of a new relationship with her parents (5.118); the essay on "My Conscience" carries on this adolescent self-analysis (5.122). Her preoccupation with social status and family background and her obvious desire for social mobility also mark the emergence of adolescent attitudes (5.123). At the same time the reader will recall numerous evidences of remaining childish interests, such as her interest in clubs with secret codes.

Clearly Anne's inner concerns were moving rapidly away from those of the late-childhood peer group. The factors described above made it impossible for Anne to function consistently and wholeheartedly in the late-childhood peer group, and this was sensed by her classmates, although they were not yet able to put it into words. They were aware of increasing separateness or distance between themselves and Anne, and it made them increasingly critical of her. Doubtless this began even back in the sixth grade.

Crime and Punishment

We know from Tryon's research [1] and from our own accumulation of case material that late-childhood peer groups have a certain code of conduct to which all group belongers are expected to adhere. We also know that this code is enforced among group belongers by various kinds of punishment administered by the group. The most severe punishment, of course, is expulsion from the group and rejection of association. The late-childhood–girls' peer-group code includes such items as: participating in active play, taking turns in choosing what is to be played, maintaining a certain social distance from nonbelonging children, maintaining a certain distance from adults in authority, such as teachers, not tattling to teachers, not seeking special privileges from persons in authority, and joining other group members in punishing nonconforming members.

The girls in their conference with Miss Thornton and in their write-ups of the causes of the difficulties with Anne described the latter's violations of the code, and Anne herself elaborated this in describing times when she was punished. In the conference with Miss Thornton, Sara

[1] Tryon, Caroline M. Adolescent Evaluations of Adolescents. *Monographs of the Society for Research in Child Development,* 1939, **4.**

said, "Anne is so bossy . . . she just wants her way all the time" (4.73). All three said that they considered Anne a "teacher's pet." Asked to define what made her a teacher's pet, Sara said, "getting to do lots of things" (that the rest of us don't get to do); "I like to do things too" (4.74). Clara said, "I know what's the matter with me. When I *quit playing games* and went to sit with Sara and Mary I got into trouble. *I'm going back to games.* And I don't think you pet Anne any more than the rest of us" (4.74). When Miss Thornton asked, "Do you think boys have anything to do with the situation?" Clara grinned, Betty nodded, Sara was noncommittal, and Mary flushed and tossed her head, saying, "Well, I liked Danny before she did" (4.74).

In the write-ups of the causes of the difficulties, Mary alleged that the first trouble came at the end of the third grade after Sara joined the group, that in the fifth grade Sara and Anne had quarreled over space for their paper dolls, that in the sixth grade information about friendship choices on a sociometric test had gotten around and caused trouble, and that Anne had not responded when spoken to in the seventh grade. Her solution was for all of them *"to join in and play together* and to forget the past." She obviously felt that Anne's failure to participate regularly in their games was a trouble-causing factor (4.80).

In her write-up, Sara told of her quarrel with Anne over space for the paper dolls, said that the difficulties in the sixth grade "didn't mean anything," and cited as her solution, "If we could *get up a good game of dodge-ball* or something else . . . and forget the past." She admits to wanting to be boss herself as well as finding this trait in Anne. Here again the basic demand is for Anne to participate in their active games (4.81).

Clara's account is very straightforward. "I don't like Anne like I like the other girls. . . . I'm just going to stay away from her completely and play with the other girls. *I have more fun with the others, playing ball and getting exercise.*" Here again is the affirmation that active play is the proper activity of the peer group (4.82).

Betty's write-up affirms that Anne was not constant in her friendship, that she neglected Betty in favor of Clara when the latter moved to their table (4.83). She admits that she called Anne a "teacher's pet" because the others did, but affirms, "I believe that the thing that started it all was that *I quit* playing with the other girls to be with Anne. The other reason is jealousy" (4.84).

Anne's account of the difficulties centers around problems of pairing off—rivalry for partners for "running around together." "Carrie and I ran around together. Then Carrie started running around with Mary, Sara, and Esther" (4.85). This was in the fifth grade. Then in the sixth, "Ruth sat at the table with us. She and I started running around together and doing everything together. Then Ruth started running around with Esther" (4.85). "The principal wanted me to show some lower grades from the Washington School where the auditorium was. They were coming to see a puppet show. When I came back to the room everybody at my table was calling me the principal's pet" (4.86). "Miss C would want someone to keep her children on the playground so Mrs. L would ask Sara and me to do it. Mary, Esther, Carrie, and Ruth wouldn't like it" (4.87). "One day while we were having arithmetic I came to a problem I didn't understand. I went and asked Miss Thornton to explain it to me. She did and when I came back to the table everyone was saying that I was teacher's pet" (4.88). Anne felt that rivalry for intimate friendships and being given an unusual number of special assignments by adults were at the root of her difficulties.

So the indictments against Anne were that she did not play games regularly as a good group member should, she attracted other girls out of their games, she was bossy and wanted her own way, she was too close to her teachers and accepted too many special roles from them and from the principal, she was after Danny on whom Mary had a priority, and she didn't always respond when spoken to. And on all of these counts Anne was certainly guilty in terms of the late-childhood-peer-group code.

It is not surprising, then, that members of her in-group punished her. Their manner of punishment is well described by the girls themselves and by Anne. In the conference Miss Thornton asked, "Can you think why she spends so much time with me at play period and sits with me at lunch?" "Yes'm, it's because we are together and don't want her" (exclusion, 4.74). Mary's account says that Sara and Anne "didn't speak for a while" (4.80). Sara's account says that she and Anne "didn't bother to play with each other for a few days" (4.81). In these cases refusing conversation and refusing participation are the punishments, but the evidence is that Anne punished Sara as much as Sara punished Anne. Betty reported that when the group went Christmas caroling Mary, Sara, and Clara got together and excluded Anne, who then walked with Betty (4.83). Mary, Sara, and Clara again separated themselves from Anne and Betty on the playground, keeping up the pressure on Anne. They all called Anne teacher's pet (4.83). Anne's own account of things that hurt her include the following: "They would be writing notes about me. When I would speak they wouldn't speak to me" (4.85). "Mary, Esther, Carrie, and Ruth would write notes and then pass them to each other when they came to lunch. They would have secrets and would whisper to one another and say, 'don't tell Anne'" (4.85). This exclusion from "secrets" is a most tormenting punishment among girls in late childhood. "They would call me Mrs. L's pet . . . everybody at the table was calling me the prin-

cipal's pet" (4.86). This epithet implies disloyalty to the group and consequent unworthiness of in-group membership. "When we would go out
to play they didn't want me around, so I would play with the other
girls" (4.86). It is to be noted here that just playing is not rewarding in
itself; it is important to play with the members of one's own group.
These, then, are the peer-group punishments. They can be the source
of much unhappiness.

Anne's Motivations

Anne, of course, was more or less aware of her peer-group code. Why,
then, did she not conform to it fully and so cement her high-prestige
status with the group? The reason is that a human being is an indivisible
unit, and Anne had numerous motivations in addition to maintaining
status in the peer group. Some of these other motivations led to behavior that was inconsistent with the peer-group code; but these motivations were strong in Anne because she was moving into early adolescence
and needed to slough off some forms of childish behavior in order to
work at her new developmental tasks. So Anne persisted in responding
to them.

Two factors were of primary importance in the development of these
motivations. One was her early maturing, which made her an adolescent
while most of her classmates remained in late childhood. The other was
the strong family-instilled desire for upward social mobility in the community, toward which academic success, playing important roles in the
school as a social institution, and pleasing the upper-middle-class teachers and principal contributed. The demands and expectancies of the
parents and teachers, then, were very forceful factors in shaping Anne's
motivations. And she had been rigorously taught to obey these demands.

Anne's Developmental Tasks

Early in the present chapter we listed thirteen developmental tasks
that are usually faced by adolescents. Perhaps the best way to gain satisfying insights into Anne's motivation and behavior in the seventh grade
is to examine the evidence in the record about her status and progress
on each of these tasks.

1. Learning the significance of the physical changes occurring as a result
of growth and learning to maintain health at the new maturity level.

The record shows that Anne was a healthy girl except for a few respira-
tory infections, that the physician found no physical handicaps, that she
was average or better in her usual rate of energy output and of physical
endurance, and that she developed acne during the stressful seventh-
grade year. It tells us nothing about Anne's knowledge of the repro-

ductive process, but it does show that she loved little children, planned to be married, and hoped to have two children of her own. The record reveals little about how physical maturing affected Anne's concept of self.

2. Learning ways of grooming, dressing, and behaving that are appropriate to her sex and effective in attracting favorable attention from boys, other girls, and adults.

The record shows that Anne had a very lively interest in clothes and grooming. In this she was greatly aided by her mother. Her clothing was feminine, modest, and attractive, and she combined fabrics and colors to good advantage. She used lipstick sparingly, cut her hair in bangs, and got a permanent wave. In comparison with her peers, Anne seemed well advanced in this developmental task.

3. Learning how to get along well with boys in the light of her new body dynamics and new maturity level.

The twenty or more recorded incidents of Anne's interaction with boys show that she was already fully successful in attracting boys and in getting along well with them. "Every one of us has liked her at one time or another," said one boy. There was a whole succession of boys who sat beside her at lunch, and there was much good-natured rivalry among them in getting this place. It is not surprising, then, that her interest in playing children's games with the other girls began to fade during the year, and she preferred pairing off with Danny. The new, higher level of gonadal hormones in Anne's bloodstream supplied the necessary motivational dynamic.

4. Learning how to get along well with girls in the light of her new heterosexual roles and new maturity level.

Unfortunately the record does not tell us how many of Anne's classmates also were about to pass the menarche and consequently to enter early adolescence. In particular it is important to know the maturity status of Sara, Mary, Betty, and Clara, the members of Anne's in-group. One cannot judge the physical-growth level of these girls simply from their behavior. It does seem safe, however, to believe that most of these girls were not growing up as rapidly as Anne and therefore did not share her new motivations or understand their meaning for her. Hence Anne did not get along too well with her girl classmates. In another year, many of them would understand her better and might again want to follow her leadership as they explored their new roles in the light of their new maturity levels. But the seventh grade was a difficult one for Anne because most of her peers did not face the same developmental tasks.

5. Winning and effectively playing adolescent peer-group roles in school and community.

In the seventh grade the peer group was a late childhood one rather than an early-adolescent one, as indicated by the activity choices of the girls. So Anne had few opportunities to learn how to win roles and function effectively in a post-pubescent, heterosexual peer group. Her work on this developmental task must await her entrance into high school the following year.

6. Winning from parents the right to make decisions and to be responsible for a wider range of her own behavior.

Anne's family was closely knit, with the mother seeming to play a dominant role and attempting to manage the direction and details of the children's development. The mother's drive for upward mobility through the children, her lack of faith in youth ("You can't tell about them!" 3.40), her interference in Anne's schoolwork toward the end of the year, and her attempts to make vocational choices for both Joe and Anne indicate that Anne will have difficulty in achieving this development task. The whole family pattern of training has been rather rigid. Freedom has been given within the areas approved by the mother, as when Anne got dinner for the family, made a fruitcake, etc. But freedom to explore friendship and life values was another story. Anne already had experienced the problem. At one time she apparently had considered becoming a nurse, but this was tabooed by her mother, who insisted that Anne should become a teacher. Later, when Anne began to identify psychologically with Miss Thornton, she herself wanted to become a teacher and dropped the significant remark, "Mother says *she* wants me to be a teacher. But I think *I* want to be a teacher *anyway*" (5.112).

7. Maintaining security-giving love relationships with her parents despite her striving for freedom to make decisions for herself.

Anne has always had a warm and security-affording relationship with her father. They "have fun together," he told her many stories about his childhood, he has ever been ready to defend her against the school or even against the mother, as in the case of the spilled ink. He was able to understand her love for the rabbits and permitted her to keep them. It was he who shared her appreciation of the beauty of a lake near their earlier home in North Carolina and who provided many of the most meaningful experiences of her life, including the visit to a ship about to be launched, trips to Florida and New Orleans, fun at an amusement park, a trip to the beach, a boatride at Silver Springs, and other experiences, in many of which the mother refused to share. So it is to be expected that Anne will be able to hold this security-giving relationship with her father during all the vicissitudes of growing up and winning independence. In time he may appreciate her need for it and help her win it.

With regard to the mother, one feels that her strong drive for mobility made successful achievement by Anne the price of approval and affection. During the first home visit, all the mother's comments about Anne were critical of her accomplishments. Toward the end of the year, Mrs. Hart was very bitter and hostile toward the school and toward Miss Thornton, because, she maintained, Anne "hadn't learned anything." She apparently gave Anne a hard time about her scholastic accomplishment during the last part of the year and rejected the teacher's estimate that she should be "proud" of Anne's work. Anne obviously will have trouble holding her mother's affection when she makes a strong bid for the right to make her own decisions.

8. Continuing her successful accomplishment of school tasks and winning adult approval in and about school.

The record shows that Anne met this developmental task successfully in the seventh grade. Most of her writings during the early part of the year were stilted and trite, but as the year progressed Miss Thornton seemed to free Anne to write what she really thought and felt. Anne was ever a leader on research committees with her fellow pupils and was an effective participant in concept-forming discussions. But if her mother is successful in transferring Anne to College Prep, with its formal recitations and examinations, its fact-cramming textbook study, and its neglect of analytic thought processes, Anne may have difficulties. It may be that her mother is right, that this is what she needs to prepare her for success in formal college courses; but one cannot help feeling that her growth as a person—her developmental education—would be arrested by such dreary experiences, for she has been trained to accept rather than to struggle against the demands of persons in authority.

9. Learning about and participating in social institutions and processes and learning her rights and responsibilities as a citizen.

The record contains very little about Anne's accomplishment of this developmental task. It shows Anne participating in church activities, using the public library and the bookmobile, shopping at downtown stores, going to Audubon lectures, and attending musicals at the College, as well as participating in a public music recital and in P.T.A. meetings. She went with the class to a coffee company and to see "The Vanishing Prairie." She was intensely interested in the royal family of Great Britain, but made scant mention of current political, social, or economic affairs in her own nation. Perhaps it is too early to expect this of Anne, for this developmental task has greater importance in middle and late adolescence. Her expressed attitudes toward her Negro friends, Sallie and Jenny, showed appreciation and warmth.

10. Exploring possible adult roles such as homemaking, caring for children, taking part in community affairs, choosing a vocation.

Within the possibilities open to her, Anne had quite an active year in terms of exploring possible adult roles. She attended church regularly, practiced cooking, cleaning, and other homemaking roles, considered the possibility of having children of her own, and thought about the vocations of nursing and teaching. She probably had little or no opportunity to know about women at work in civic, political, business, and charitable activities. But her burgeoning interest in her future as a mother and as a teacher were apparent and can be expected to grow soundly with advancing maturity.

11. Exploring questions about the meaning of life and about the values to be sought in life.

Here, again, we have seen Anne only in the transition period between childhood and youth, as evidenced by her essay on "What Christmas Means to Me." In this essay she begins to glimpse spiritual values expressed through human relationships rather than the enthronement of material values. But more often her writings reveal the context of social-status values in which she lived. In her stories she lived in a big three-story house, was given a Pontiac for a graduation present, vied with a classmate for the captaincy of the bowling team, practiced with her brother and his friends to appear on television, and got a tremendous thrill from a letter from someone in the British royal entourage. She once wished that their own house had two stories and a terrace on the side.

Thus, to Anne, the glamour of a higher social status was currently strong. She was, however, busy exploring human relationships and seeking to understand them, as evidenced by her writing "When My Parents Don't Understand." Her identification with Miss Thornton was in part an exploration of a teacher's role and in part an exploration of a richer life and wider appreciations, as evidenced by her asking Miss Thornton to choose books for her and her sincere and deep interest and enjoyment of the books chosen. She obviously relied more on Miss Thornton than on her mother in exploring the implications of her new maturity level, for she babbled to her about Danny's being kissed at the carnival and about "love notes" which her mother had destroyed. Thus her identification with Miss Thornton may well have been a way of exploring the possibilities of friendship with a mature person, intellectual companionship, and ways of gaining access to the experience and appreciation of beauty and spiritual values. For so young a person, this identification suggests the search for sound values. It is doubtful that she sought Miss Thornton's company chiefly because she was excluded by her peers; she may even have sought these contacts at the expense of peer-group relationships because she valued them more.

12. Continuing the development of a code of ethics as a measuring stick for evaluating her own attitudes and her actual behavior.

Anne's choice of "My Conscience" as a topic about which to write an essay indicates that she was aware of the continuing developmental task of building a code of ethics against which to measure her own attitudes and behavior. But the content of this and other essays shows that actually she was only on the threshold of building a real conscience, a code of ethics based on convictions of value. Rather, Anne's conscience had so far been built into her by parental teachings and punishments. "I think you can get into trouble by not listening to your conscience. When I was small I would start out of my yard without permission and my conscience would tell me this was wrong, but I would go on. The result was that I was punished for disobeying" (5.122). The record shows that Anne had been taught primarily to obey her parents, her teachers, and the rules of life laid down at church and by law. Disobedience, she had been taught, brings punishment. Your conscience is a built-in, unerring guide. You must decide to heed it, or you will be punished. She also had been taught always to be truthful (5.121). On numerous occasions, as revealed by "When My Parents Don't Understand," Anne had broken the letter of the law in response to adequate and legitimate motivation, but she had always been spanked—because her parents "didn't understand."

There is always danger that a conscience based on external rules and regulations enforced by punishment will get in the way of the development of an inner, self-derived code of ethics based upon the thoughtful analysis of experience according to a set of values. In such instances, whatever the individual can get away with becomes permissible. Anne showed traces of this when her strong desire to please Miss Thornton with many writings led her to pad her language folder with a story written during the previous year and the "Pledge of Allegiance." Perhaps it was not sporting of the boys to point this out to Miss Thornton, but it could have been a useful lesson to Anne to know that other people could not condone this. After all, she was really fooling herself and not promoting her development by this padding. Of course, nothing could have been more natural for a thirteen-year-old than to behave this way. But it demonstrates what Anne had not accomplished on the task of developing an adequate code of ethics and indicates a legitimate area of attention and concern for her future teachers.

13. Setting up goals for immediate accomplishment as steps toward long-term purposes.

Anne's behavior, conversation, and writings seem to imply four long-term purposes: becoming a teacher, becoming an effective homemaker and mother, improving her social status in the community, and understanding more about life and the world by experience gained through books. We cannot tell whether exceptionally good subject-matter and skill learning at school seemed to her to be an important step toward the first of these goals. But we do know that she both read and wrote an extraordinary amount during her year in the seventh grade. Considering the fact that her intelligence level as revealed by tests was good but not exceptional, we must rate her scholastic accomplishment as adequate. She certainly did practice the development of homemaking skills regularly at home. Her continuous efforts to please her teacher and principal may, in part, have been goals related to her desire for higher community status. Finally, she read prodigiously quite a range of both fiction and non-fiction, especially biographical material.

Educational Implications

This chapter has demonstrated the importance of a number of aspects of the educative process in relation to the development of individuals.

1. It demonstrated that, with adequate cumulative records and with adequate in-service training, a teacher can achieve a depth of understanding of individual pupils which far surpasses that found in most classrooms. By the last of November Miss Thornton had come to understand Anne's motivations, needs, developmental tasks, and adjustment problems at a depth which permitted her to make very wise decisions in the classroom and elsewhere about how to help Anne take her next steps in learning and in becoming what she had the potentialities to become as a person. She then had six full months in which to interact with Anne on the basis of these insights. In a later chapter it will be my task to show that this can be accomplished by most teachers still earlier in the year, not concerning one child but concerning most of the children in a classroom. Miss Thornton actually had such insights into a number of the children in her class and accomplished even a great deal more in helping certain other pupils than she did with Anne.

2. It demonstrated that a child society existed in Miss Thornton's classroom, as in all other school classrooms beyond the first or second grades. This child society had its own set of activities which afforded roles and status to the children admitted to belonging. These roles required knowledge, skill, and personal characteristics for successful fulfillment. The society had its own customs

and code of conduct, enforced by punishments. Winning these roles was an important goal of every child, and failure to be accepted was accompanied by anxiety and other unpleasant emotions. Rivalries within groups existed. Altogether, the children seemed constantly aware of and motivated by these peer-group forces no matter what the classroom activity in which they were involved. It is apparent, then, that school learning always occurs within a context of peer-group dynamics and so the latter is a matter of important concern to every teacher.

3. It demonstrated that by using sociometric techniques and keeping anecdotal records a teacher can come to know the structure and dynamics of this child society within the first three months of any school year. From that time on he can make classroom decisions on the basis of insights that include these peer-group factors. It must be clear that this can be accomplished in most classrooms only if administrators understand that this is a necessary part of the professional work of a teacher and provide the teacher with time and assistance for accomplishing it.

4. It demonstrated that physical-maturity level was a vital factor in determining the developmental tasks on which Anne was working and, consequently, some of her dominant motivations. This factor is equally vital in the dynamics of every child and youth. No single item of information about a child or youth is more important for a teacher to know if he hopes to do a really professional job of guiding the learning, development, and adjustment of his pupils as individuals. Very few school systems regularly gather the information about individuals which is necessary to know each child's maturity level at any given time. Yet this information is relatively easy and inexpensive to secure.

5. It demonstrated that using an organizing framework helped Miss Thornton to understand factors in Anne's motivation and needs which she might otherwise have missed. The use of the six-area framework presented in Chapter 7 as the basis for her initial analysis of Anne in November gave Miss Thornton a well-balanced view of Anne's motivation and needs. It also revealed areas in which she lacked adequate information to make judgments and so guided her in her further information gathering. The use of a developmental-tasks framework in the last interpretation of Anne's dynamics gave perspective on the meaning of Anne's behavior in the seventh grade and on what she will face during the coming three or four years. Every person has his own preoccupations and blind spots about development and behavior, so it is very important to have several organizing frameworks to use at different times to guide one in the interpreting of information about children whom we hope to understand. The use of such frameworks helps the teacher to avoid the effects of personal bias and the pitfalls of oversimplified interpretations.

6. It demonstrated how understanding Anne made it possible for Miss Thornton to guide her learning as an individual although she was one pupil in a class of more than thirty children. The record shows how this was done in language work through guided reading and through both free and guided writing of essays and stories. Material not included in this report showed the same method being applied in arithmetic, science, and social studies, for Anne

kept folders of her work in each of these areas, and in music as well. Actually the only effective way to "provide for individual differences" is to know each child well enough to be able to judge what experiences he needs in each subject-matter, developmental-task, and adjustment-problem area.

7. It demonstrated that, at school, Anne was constantly working on some of her own developmental tasks and adjustment problems as well as on formal curriculum content. It is always so in school, whether administrators and teachers will it to be so or not. The curriculum of a school for an individual child is everything that he experiences in and around the school—physical conditions, interpersonal relationships, peer-group structure and dynamics, cultural expectancies and demands in operation in the school, textbooks, assignments, drill and practice periods, committe work, participation in discussions and in evaluative sessions. He learns whatever meanings and skills arise out of the cumulative effects of these experiences as he perceives them in the light of his own unique experience background, concept of self, and orientation toward society and the world.

This chapter showed that Mrs. Hart, like many parents and teachers, unfortunately did not understand the educative process. She did not know that what a given child learns during a particular year in school depends upon the developmental tasks and adjustment problems he is facing as well as upon the experiences provided by the school, the tasks set by the school, and the expectancies according to which the learning and development of the child are evaluated.

Actually, school people do not have the choice between teaching subject matter and guiding the learning and development of children. For it is natural law that children are preoccupied with and constantly work at their own developmental tasks and adjustment problems. Of course, all children need certain basic skills and subject-matter knowledge. At appropriate times in relation to their maturity and in appropriate situations in relation to their experience background, these learning tasks become vital parts of their accepted "developmental tasks" and children become keenly interested in them. But this does not happen in the same grade or at the same chronological age for every child with regard to any specific skill or subject matter. This is the fundamental reason why teachers have to understand their pupils as individual developing persons in order to make sound judgments about how to help them in the classroom.

PART THREE

On Human Development

CHAPTER 10

The Individual Is Shaped

The preceding chapters have demonstrated how teachers, by a three-year in-service program of studying children, can gain adequate knowledge of and insights into the developmental levels, current motivations, adjustment problems and developmental tasks of their pupils. We feel quite sure that this program accomplishes its aims. Subjectively, our assurance grows out of having guided more than forty thousand teachers in fifteen states through this program since 1940. With our own eyes we have seen these teachers gradually change in the ways they related to children, sought to facilitate necessary learning by the children, interpreted and evaluated the behavior of their pupils, and "managed" the class as a group or "disciplined" individuals when needful. We know from direct observation and from extended conversations with them and their supervisors that a considerable proportion of these participants in our child-study program became better teachers. Fortunately we also have objective evidence that supports the same conclusion; a summary of this evidence has been published separately.[1] Consequently we now feel that, taken together, the case material presented in the earlier chapters of this book and the objective data presented in the monograph summarizing the findings of the research studies have demonstrated and proved that teachers can learn to understand their pupils as developing individuals when given appropriate and adequate training.

Nevertheless, two questions are asked over and over again by educational administrators when they hear us talk about the program or see the motion picture which portrays it in operation.[2] The first of these questions is: "Granted that teachers who participate in the child-study program do learn to understand several children a year quite deeply, is

[1] Brandt, R. M., and Perkins, H. V. Research Evaluating a Child-study Program. *Monographs of the Society for Research in Child Development*, 1956, **21**, 62.

[2] "Helping Teachers to Understand Children," prepared for overseas use, USIA, Part I, 21 minutes ($38.29); Part II, 25 minutes ($43.63). Both may be obtained from United World Films, Inc., 1445 Park Avenue, New York 29, New York.

it actually feasible for them during any one year to get to understand to this degree nearly all the children in their classrooms?" This is a very proper and necessary question. Happily it can be answered in the affirmative. Chapter 12 will be devoted to describing the practical steps by which teachers can understand nearly all the children in their classes.

One question, however, is always asked and must be answered at the outset: "Is it really necessary that teachers and principals understand children as individuals?" Is it not possible for the scientists who understand human development and behavior to provide educators with a series of general principles, applicable to most children, which can guide teachers and principals in making their hundreds of daily decisions? Cannot the scientists also work out and present to educators a clear-cut statement of the implications of their scientific findings for such educational problems as how to group children for most effective learning, when to introduce various subjects into the curriculum, how to motivate children to learn when they are disinterested, what kinds of discipline are most effective at various maturity levels, how to guide young people into the occupations that are most appropriate for them, and how to deal with children and youth in such a way as to prevent delinquency and mental illness?

Unhappily these questions must be answered in the negative, for one scientific truth has persistently negated every plan and device educators have developed for finding a single method of schooling that will adequately serve all children. It is the fact that every child is unique and differs from every other child in many ways that affect his learning. Confronted with a roomful of children, most teachers find it difficult to accept this fact. Confronted by a building full of children, principals find it even harder. But once teachers and principals expose themselves for a time to the direct study of individual children and youth, they become convinced by their own experience that every child is unique and are even glad of it because it confirms their own uniqueness. Once convinced, they are always able to work out general curricular plans for specific groups and general rules of conduct for all children in a school and yet carry out these plans and administer these rules in ways that take account of individual differences. To do this, it is necessary only that school people have available both the necessary scientific knowledge about human development and the necessary information about individual children, that they be adequately trained to interpret this material in relation to individual children and youth, and that time be assigned for the teachers to use in "figuring out" individual pupils.

Actually every teacher and principal with a few years of school experience has often recognized the uniqueness of individual children and youth and often has shown insight in helping individuals who faced

special problems. But often they have waited to do this until the child
in question was in serious difficulties through scholastic failure or grossly
unacceptable behavior—for school people usually are very patient with
children. Sometimes, to be sure, the problems have worked themselves
out, but in too many cases the child's concept of himself, or of the
school, already has been badly damaged. We urge that every child be
regarded as unique from the moment he enters school and that the
necessary steps be taken at once to get to know him in terms of the
several factors that are shaping his development, motivation, and adjustment. When this is done, most scholastic failure can be prevented,
and so can most undesirable behavior. Nor is the task of gathering and
interpreting the necessary information about individual children and
youth as monumental as most of us have feared, providing we plan for
it systematically and follow up on its interpretation regularly.

Perhaps these statements can be made more convincing and the scope
of the task revealed by a description of the ways in which children differ
significantly. Chapter 8, which deals with the interpretation of Timothy
Thyme's record, contained a series of questions that should be answered
about every child, indicating the factors that vary most widely from
child to child. These questions will be repeated here, and a few of the
scientific facts which establish their importance will then be given to
show that they really are significant questions. The questions will be
grouped under the six major topics that our synthesis of explanatory
scientific information indicates are necessary.

PHYSICAL FACTORS AND PROCESSES

Growth and Maturity Level

1. What is the child's present growth rate and maturity level?

We know from a mounting body of research evidence that all children
pass through approximately the same pattern of body development in
terms of the sequence in which the different organs and tissues develop
and begin to function. This pattern is established by a heredity that is
common to all members of our species. We also know that children
follow family patterns of inheritance with regard to many details of
growth, such as body build and size and shape of various body parts.

But one of the most significant inherited characteristics is generally
ignored by parents and school people alike. It is inherited differences
in the rate at which individuals move through the blueprint of growth—
differences in rate of maturing. For example, the amount of body differentiation and development between birth and pubescence is roughly
the same for all normal, healthy children. Yet girls on the average be-

come pubescent at thirteen-and-a-half years and boys at fifteen years and five months. Thus, on the average, it requires two years less for girls to accomplish this amount of growth than for boys. Nor is this something which has happened suddenly, for girls mature more rapidly than boys throughout childhood. X rays of the wrist and hand area show that girls on the average at the age of seven already have about the same skeletal maturity that boys achieve at eight. So girls are usually almost a year ahead of boys in maturity when they enter school and gain still another year in development by the age of thirteen and a half.

But the variation within the sex is much greater than the average difference between the sexes in rate of maturing. Shuttleworth, using data from the Harvard Growth Study, has shown this graphically.[3] Stolz and Stolz, on the basis of data from the California Adolescent Study, give an even more detailed analysis of rhythm and patterns of growth during adolescence.[4] They show that one boy may be entering adolescence at the age of ten, whereas another equally normal boy may continue in childhood until he is fifteen and a half. So, among boys, there is a five-and-a-half year variation in the amount of time required to grow from birth to the entrance to the pubescent growth phase. There is also a variation among boys of from two to four years in the duration of the puberal phase of growth. Some boys are quite grown up by the age of fourteen, whereas others are not really mature until after they are eighteen. The same degree of variation exists among girls, except that each phase is reached earlier. This means that teachers in every grade from the fifth throughout high school are confronted with classes in which their pupils of the same chronological age *vary as much as six years in physical maturity level.*

Other research data, cited by Stolz and Stolz, and studies done by Zachry,[5] Blos,[6] H. E. Jones,[7] and Tryon,[8] to cite only a few, show that the development of the body is significantly related to other aspects of development, such as muscular strength, social relationships, concept and acceptance of self, and emotional adjustment problems of various kinds. The Forty-third Yearbook of the National Society for the Study

[3] Shuttleworth, Frank L. The Physical and Mental Growth of Girls and Boys Age Six to Nineteen in Relation to Age at Maximum Growth. *Monographs of the Society for Research in Child Development*, 1939, 4, 3:1.

[4] Stolz, Herbert R., and Stolz, Lois M. *Somatic Development of Adolescent Boys.* New York: Macmillan, 1951.

[5] Zachry, Caroline. *Emotion and Conduct in Adolescence.* New York: Appleton-Century, 1940.

[6] Blos, Peter. *The Adolescent Personality.* New York: Appleton-Century, 1940.

[7] Jones, H. E. *Motor Performance and Growth.* Berkeley: Univ. of California Press, 1949; also, *Development in Adolescence,* New York: Appleton-Century, 1943.

[8] Tryon, Caroline. Evaluations of Adolescent Personality by Adolescents. *Monographs of the Society for Research in Child Development,* 1939, 4, 4:88.

of Education summarizes much of this material.[9] Actually, physical growth establishes a sort of base line against which each individual's developmental tasks and adjustment problems must be evaluated. Chronological age is of very little value in measuring these tasks and problems, so great is individual variation in the rate of maturing. So the first datum every teacher needs about each child is a valid measurement of his maturity level and current rate of growth. Stolz and Stolz have shown how this can be estimated during adolescence from graphs of increments of growth in standing height. Wetzel has developed a grid graph that many of the school systems working with us have found most useful throughout the individual's school life.[10] And experimentation is now going on in a number of New Jersey schools, with the help of Dr. Wilton Krogman of the University of Pennsylvania Medical School, using X rays of the wrists and hands of grade school children. We know, then, that it is possible to measure the maturity level of each child with relatively little expense of time or money; but very few school systems currently are obtaining and using this most necessary datum about each child.

Energy Output

2. What is the child's characteristic rate of energy output, fatiguing, and recovery from fatigue?

The human being can be accurately described as a very complex energy system. At each moment of life, energy is being transmuted in every cell of the body, and all mental, feeling, and behavioral phenomena rest upon these basic energy-transmutation processes. Girard's book *Unresting Cells* gives a very interesting account of these basic energy processes.[11] Interestingly enough, the basic rate of energy transmutation per unit of body weight is highest in infancy and gradually declines during childhood, adolescence, and adulthood. Consequently, children in school constantly are having energy released in their bodies at a much higher rate than are the adults who are guiding their behavior. Yet it remains traditional in so many schools for the pupils to remain relatively inactive and for the adults to be constantly in action. It is no wonder that teaching is such a fatiguing occupation, when one considers the vast quantities of energy released every hour in a roomful of children.

Of course, the release of free energy for motivated action is quite a

[9] Forty-third Yearbook: *Adolescence*. Chicago: National Society for the Study of Education, 1944.

[10] Wetzel, N. C. *The Wetzel Grid for Evaluating Physical Fitness*. Cleveland: National Educational Service, 1948. See also references to Nancy Bayley in the bibliography.

[11] Girard, Ralph. *Unresting Cells*. New York: Harper, 1949.

different matter from basal metabolism, which is the measure of the amount of energy required simply to maintain cell processes when the individual is at rest. Yet even basal metabolism varies enormously from person to person; [12] in fact, physicians count as normal any basic metabolic rate from 20 per cent below the average for the individual's sex and age to 20 per cent above the average. In other words, a variation of 40 per cent in basal metabolic rate is regarded as healthy and normal among human beings. This is an enormous variation and indicates that the autonomic and hormonal factors which regulate energy output operate at very different rates in different healthy persons. Once it is called to his attention, every teacher recognizes a fundamental variation in energy output as characteristic among children. He can spot the four or five children in his classroom each year who are constantly in motion or who are tensely spending energy by holding still, and the equal number of pupils who are sluggish in movement and can remain relatively inactive for long periods of time. He can also observe which children fatigue rapidly and which have boundless endurance.

The subjective rating of energy output and fatigability does have one pitfall, however. Some children are keyed up by persisting strong emotions rather than high in energy output, whereas others are experiencing continuing depressive emotions which make them lethargic and nonresponsive. So emotional factors in the child's life must be considered in evaluating his energy output.

Health

3. What is the child's present state of health? What is his health history? What desirable and undesirable health habits does he have?

The child's health affects his classroom mood, learning, concept of and feelings about himself, and relationship with parents and with other children. Consequently it is a matter of concern to his teacher. Happily the school physician or nurse usually can give the teacher the information he needs, and school medical records should be readily available to the teacher. Conversations with the child's mother also will help. Pertinent information about each child's health should be placed in his cumulative personnel record for the use of successive teachers.

Handicaps and Limitations

4. Does the child have any specific physical handicaps? Does he have any general physical limitations? If so, how does he feel about these handicaps or limiting factors?

[12] See Shock, Nathan, in the forty-third Yearbook of the National Society for the Study of Education.

Answers to the first two of these questions should be available in the child's health records, but the weakness in most schools is in follow-up. Handicaps in hearing, sight, speech, and dentition sometimes remain uncorrected for years, to the detriment of the child's school progress and with damage to his feelings about himself and to his relationships with others. Our records, however, are replete with instances of the good results of teachers' discussing the child's need for corrective measures with parents over the telephone or in conferences at P.T.A. meetings. Sometimes children are so adroit in their adjustments and parents so accustomed to their ways that remediable defects do not seem serious to the parents and a word or two from the teacher on several occasions really is needed to secure the necessary action.

Skill in Using the Body

5. How well does the child use his body? What physical-game skills does he have or lack? If he lacks customary skills, why has he failed to develop them?

The playground and the gymnasium are places where teachers can readily observe and evaluate each child's large-muscle skills. The classroom offers innumerable opportunities for the development of finer coordination and general grace of movement. The ability to manage the body well in a wide variety of activities and the possession of specific game skills are major assets for each child in winning peer-group roles and greatly affect relationships with other children. They also greatly affect the individual's feelings about and concept of himself and therefore play an important part in his emotional adjustment. Anecdotal material based on direct observation and regularly entered into the cumulative record can give an excellent picture of the child's development in this area from year to year.

In evaluating this material, two factors must be taken into consideration. The first is the child's developmental level. Slow growers will be correspondingly slow in learning to use their bodies well, so the teacher will need to help each child find physical activities at which he can have a measure of success. This is particularly important for children who are very intelligent and who may tend to overcompensate for lack of physical skills by scholastic accomplishments. It is very hazardous to a child's later adjustment to push him ahead into grades where he cannot participate successfully in the physical activities of his classmates, because success in these physical activities helps a child to feel adequate, whereas failure makes him feel inferior to and different from other children.

The second factor to be considered is whether the child has had the opportunity to learn to manage his body as well as other children of his own maturity level and, if not, to consider what can be done around school to help him catch up. The life space of some children who always have lived in small apartments or in crowded areas in large cities simply has not been adequate to permit them to learn to manage their bodies skillfully in a wide variety of situations. Other children have been restricted in what they could do by physical handicaps that were subsequently corrected. Still others have been overprotected by parents for fear that they would be hurt or play with "undesirable" playmates, or for other reasons. To such children, school sometimes offers the first real opportunity to gain a mastery over their bodies. If this does not seem important, it may be well to remember that each boy, at any rate, must look forward to military service, where skill in managing his body will be most important for safety and success.

Physical Attractiveness

6. How attractive is the child's face, physique, and grooming to his teacher and to his peers? How does he feel about his physical appearance?

The physical appearance and grooming of a child or youth have a considerable influence on the way his teacher and his peers feel about him and on the attitudes they express toward him. In our society these factors are taken to reveal something about an individual's quality as a person and about the quality of his family background. So teachers, consciously or unconsciously, respond favorably or unfavorably to children on the basis of facial features, body form and proportions, hair appearance and grooming, clothing, and general neatness and cleanliness. And classmates do, too. The appearance of some children, on the other hand, fails to have an impact on teachers and peers and tends to isolate them.

Inevitably, the child senses the way the teacher and other children feel about his appearance. This influences both the way he feels about himself and the way he interacts with the teacher and with his peers. This is true throughout childhood, but it becomes especially significant during adolescence. L. J. Elias studied about six thousand high school seniors in the state of Washington and found that 17 per cent of them worried about appearance, as many others about being overweight or underweight, and another 13 per cent about having a poor complexion.[13] Stolz and Stolz, in the study already cited, reported that about one-third of the adolescent boys studied were worried about some aspect of their physical growth. These matters can be quite tormenting, especially to adolescents; because of them, some become shy and withdrawing, whereas others overcompensate by fighting, roughness, nonconformity,

[13] Elias, L. J. *High School Youth Look at Their Problems.* Agricultural Experiment Station, State College of Washington, 1947.

or overemphasis of scholastic success. Teachers who understand how they feel can be most helpful.

LOVE RELATIONSHIPS

Emotional Insecurity

Psychiatrists frequently use the term "emotionally insecure" in relation to maladjusted persons. It seems to mean that the individual in question lacks faith in himself as a person, doubts the validity of his own inner selfhood, and so feels continuous anxiety. This feeling must be contrasted with feelings of "personal inadequacy," which refer to doubt of one's ability to learn and to do things. Many "insecure" persons attempt to compensate for this doubt of their own inner worth by conspicuous accomplishment. They seem endlessly driven to gain one kind of recognition after another, but their anxiety is not diminished by their accomplishments, no matter how great, because they have a deep inner feeling of being valueless or unworthy. As psychiatrists have sought to discover the basic cause of "emotional insecurity," they generally have found that it occurs in children and youth who have not been loved or whose experiences have convinced them that they are not loved, no matter what the reality may be.

The Nature of Love

Some seven years ago I was quite bothered by the fact that the term "love" occurred so infrequently in psychological writings dealing with human motivation. Scientists seemed to have a deep distrust of the term. This led me to read extensively in psychiatric literature in the attempt to discover whether love is a genuine human reality or only a romantic construct within our culture, for cultures do exist in which love is not practiced. My search was very rewarding and led not only to the conclusion that love is a genuine human reality but also to the conviction that it plays a most important role in human development.[14] Very cogent affirmations of the nature of human love appear in the writings of Harry Stack Sullivan[15] and Erich Fromm.[16]

Perhaps it will be worth the space here to include a brief summary of my conclusions regarding the nature of love so that teachers may know what to look for in relationships between parents and between

[14] Prescott, Daniel A. The Role of Love in Human Development. *Journal of Home Economics,* 1952, 44:3, 173–176.

[15] Sullivan, Harry Stack. *Conceptions of Modern Psychiatry.* Washington: W. A. White Psychiatric Foundation, 1947.

[16] Fromm, Erich. *Man for Himself.* New York: Rinehart, 1947.

parents and children. Valid love seems to include the following components:

1. *Love involves* more or less *empathy* with the loved one. A person who loves actually enters into the feelings of and shares intimately the experiences of the loved one and the effects of these experiences upon the loved one.

2. One who loves is deeply *concerned for the welfare,* happiness, and development *of the beloved.* This concern is so deep as to become one of the major organizing values in the personality or self-structure of the loving person. Harry Stack Sullivan wrote, "When the satisfaction or the security of another person becomes as significant to one as is one's own security, then the state of love exists." [17]

3. One who loves finds *pleasure in making his resources available* to the loved one, to be used by the other to enhance his welfare, happiness, and development. Strength, time, money, thought, indeed all resources are proffered happily to the loved one for his use. A loving person is not merely concerned about the beloved's welfare and development, he does something about it.

4. Of course the loving person seeks a maximum of participation in the activities that contribute to the welfare, happiness, and development of the beloved. But he also *accepts fully the uniqueness and individuality of the beloved and,* to the degree implied by the beloved's maturity level, *accords* to the latter *full freedom to experience, to act, and to become what he desires* to become. A loving person has a nonpossessive respect for the selfhood of the loved one.

The Role of Love in Development

Out of these conceptions of the nature of love spring a series of hypotheses about the role of love in human development which may help teachers to understand the effects of known home relationships upon the development and behavior of individual pupils.

1. Love is customarily and most readily achieved within a family circle, but it can include many other individuals or even whole categories of people.

2. Love is not rooted primarily in sexual dynamics or hormonal drives. It is rooted in the individual's value dynamics. But it often includes large erotic components when it occurs between parents and children, between children, or between adults.

3. The good effects of love are not limited to the beloved, but promote the happiness and further development of the loving one as well. In other words to *love is not altruistic but self-realizing.*

4. Being loved can afford any human being a much-needed and basic psychological security. To feel that one is deeply valued regardless of how one looks or acts is to have a haven of safety in case of failure, indiscretion, guilt feelings, or social rejection. If one is truly loved there is always somebody to turn to; the place of residence becomes a "home" when love is there. Inner conflicts can be shared without fear of exposing oneself to ridicule or to blame.

[17] Sullivan, Harry Stack, *op. cit.,* p. 20.

5. Being loved makes it possible to accept (love) oneself, provides the necessary experience basis for learning what love really is, and so opens the door to learning how to love others. We suspect that a person who has never been loved cannot fully respect and love himself, but must always restlessly be reassuring himself as to his own fundamental worth. Nor can an unloved person really love other people.

6. Being loved and loving in return facilitate the psychological identification of the loved child with the parents, relatives, teachers, or peers who love him. He internalizes the culture more readily and develops culturally favored attitudes and values more easily through these identifications. When one enjoys the security of mutual love with an older person it is much easier to learn what that person wants or expects one to learn. In contrast the unloved child often is so full of hostility that he tends to reject what he is told and to refuse to meet the expectancies laid upon him as a way of expressing this hostility. The great readiness of loving persons to provide meaningful experiences for beloved children and to aid them at every step in the learning process gives a great advantage to loved children in accomplishing their developmental tasks of internalizing the culture and adopting socially acceptable codes of conduct, values, and goals.

7. Being loved and loving others facilitates winning belonging in groups. It promotes the development of personality characteristics that make the individual easy to get along with and attractive in group situations. A child or youth who is secure through love has little reason to "lord it" over others, to be aggressive and hostile, or to be shy and withdrawing. Such children do not need constantly to climb in status by calling attention to the failure and inadequacies of others.

8. Being loved and loving others facilitate adjustment to situations that involve strong, unpleasant emotions. For example, when a loved child fails at something, the failure does not cut so deep as to make him doubt his basic worth. Knowing that he is loved, he can be easily reassured and encouraged to try again. In contrast the unloved child who fails is in double jeopardy. To his insecurity is added the feeling of inadequacy, and he becomes more and more reluctant to try again with each failure. Consider the impact on children of the expectancies and demands of the school. Punishments, penalties, and the demands of authority are bearable for loved children because for them they do not imply either rejection or fundamental lack of worth. But to the unloved child these things may seem to be indications of rejection or low valuation. Consequently resentment, rebellion against authority, or hostility against peers who seem more favored may ensue. The loved child is thus better prepared to meet the vicissitudes of life that stir strong, unpleasant emotions than is the unloved child.

9. Love can be a great aid to the individual in his developmental tasks of orienting himself toward the remainder of mankind, of seeing his place in the limitless universe, and of orienting himself toward God. The "fatherhood of God" necessarily must mean one thing to a well-loved child and something quite different to a rejected or neglected child whose father is cold, harsh, or punishing. "The brotherhood of man" cannot but mean one thing to a child

from a warm, well-knit, mutually supporting family and something else to a child from a family characterized by constant jealousy, bickerings, or exploitation.

Needed Information about the Individual

It is hoped that these ideas about the nature of love and its role in human development will help teachers to read between the lines of what is said during home visits, conferences with parents at school, and informal conversations with the child himself in such a way that valid answers can be found to the following questions that must be answered in this area:

1. What is the nature of the personal relationships between the child and his mother, his father, and each other member of the family?
2. What is the nature of the personal relationships between the child's mother and father and between each of the other members of the family?
3. What is the general emotional climate within the family?
4. To what degree is the child emotionally secure or insecure?
5. Does the child's relationship with me, his teacher, add to his security?

✗ Factors Inducing Insecurity

In our accumulation of case records to date we have found numerous instances of children suffering the anxiety that goes with emotional insecurity due to the following types of home conditions and relationships:

1. Parent rejected the child.
2. Parent preferred a brother or sister over the child.
3. Parent was so preoccupied with his or her own adjustment problems that the child was neglected.
4. Parents were inconsistent with each other or with themselves in the ways they treated the child, with the result that he became confused and anxious.
5. Parents used withdrawal of affection as a means of punishment to control the behavior of the child.
6. Parents so overstressed the importance of school learning and success for a child of limited capacity that the child felt he was not loved when he could not excel at school.
7. The home was broken by desertion, divorce, or death, and the child had depended for security upon the absent parent.
8. The child was identified in one parent's mind with the other parent or a relative who was immoral or a failure or who showed some especially undesirable characteristic or behavior pattern.
9. Parent overprotected the child and kept him from having needed experiences or relationships with other children or adults.
10. Parents were unusually severe in their punishments in their efforts to insure "right" behavior.

Doubtless this list could be extended greatly. It is intended only to suggest some of the situations that can make a child feel unloved and insecure, whatever the real relationship may be.

Religion and Security

A word also must be said about the relationship of emotional security to religious experience. Sooner or later in their development, all children in our culture are faced with ultimate mysteries, such as: How was the world created? What is life? What is the meaning of my life? What happens to a person when he dies? Why are some actions right and others wrong? What is beauty? How can one know what is true? Is the universe orderly? Were the world and life accidents, or do they have some purposeful meaning and some direction in which they change? Is there a God? If so, what is He like? Ultimately each person must choose for himself what he will believe to be sound answers to each of these questions. Nevertheless, it cannot be doubted that the kind of answers a child learns from his parents and from his church do affect not only his basic orientation in the universe but also his emotional security.

There are moments in every life when one has only faith to rely upon. At any rate, I am personally convinced from direct and intimate experience of the ways some individuals with faith faced both living and dying that they had an unassailable emotional security through their religious convictions of the existence of God and of a personal relationship to Him. I am equally impressed by direct and intimate experience of the ways some other individuals with no faith suffered unbelievably in both living and dying that they were without a resource which could have been of great help to them. Lacking quantified research data, I accept this intimate knowledge of what other persons have experienced as indicative of an area of great scientific importance to understanding emotional security in human beings. Of course, dogma and faith are not the same thing; and the inculcation of dogma does not necessarily give rise to faith in God, man, or oneself.

If their ears are attuned to it, teachers usually have the opportunity to hear children express their concepts of the universe and of God and to discover whether their pupils are coming to regard the universe as operating in orderly fashion under natural laws which man gradually is learning and as a place where each person has a significant destiny. They also can learn what kind of God each child conceives of and what kind of relationship each has to God. In this way teachers can come to know whether the individual's religious experience is creating for him a secure relationship to a loving Father-God, whether he is developing anxiety and guilt feelings in connection with his little sins, or whether he feels alone and without significance in a vast universe, except as he may find security with his family and friends.

CULTURAL BACKGROUND AND SOCIALIZATION

Internalizing the Culture

1. What subcultures within the larger American cultures does the child's family carry?

At birth children have no knowledge of the world and no instinctive patterns of behavior for living effectively in it, as have the young of so many of the lower forms of animal life. But the child is not born into an unknown and unexplained world which lacks tested patterns of behavior. Rather he is born into a society which for generations has developed its own explanations of phenomena, interpretations of the meaning of life, and distinctive ways of carrying on life processes. These ways are always in some degree influenced by and appropriate to the geography, resources, and climate of the region of the earth controlled by the particular society and depend equally upon the history of the society. They constitute the culture of each society and must be learned (internalized) by each successive generation of children and youth. This learning is guided by the child's family, by schools and churches, and by many other agencies, such as voluntary groups (Scouts, 4-H clubs) and mass media of communication (television, newspapers, motion pictures, etc.).

The Culture Is Changing

As new knowledge is added and new ways of carrying on life processes such as tilling the soil and manufacturing valued commodities, are developed by succeeding generations, they are incorporated into the culture. So children of each new generation do not repeat all the learning processes of their parents but learn to live according to the behavior patterns of the latest developmental stage of the society. They learn to see things in the latest perspective, and this may occasion some strain between youth and their elders. Children born in the United States during the last half of the twentieth century will take for granted flying, television, the use of atomic energy as a source of power, a high school education, military service, and "social security." None of their great-grandparents and few of their grandparents could do this.

Furthermore, a world-wide culture is developing in the arts and sciences, accompanied by international tensions and stress as different societies gain the new knowledge. Each society adopts different social and economic arrangements and different political processes for regulating their lives as these artistic and scientific changes occur. Consequently our children are internalizing both the new way of life developed in our own society and the tensions generated because other societies, interdependent with ours in many ways, view life differently in the light of their respective historical backgrounds and geographical settings. In fact, there are regional tensions of this sort within our own country. In the meantime, change continues everywhere at a rate which tests human learning power and adaptability to the utmost. And there is always the danger that, under the stress of assimilating new ways of living, some of the old wisdom about life and its meaning may be lost, may remain uncommunicated to the new generation.

Cultural Diversity in Our Society

A further complication in this continuing developmental task of internalizing the culture, as faced by different children, is that not all children throughout our country are internalizing an identical culture. Ours is a country of great cultural diversity, of many and varied acceptable life patterns; the child must assimilate the culture carried by his family, his social subgroup, and his region of the country. In fact, although there are common elements that permeate all groups within our society and characterize us as "Americans," the acceptance of cultural diversity has been historically one of the foundation stones of our society. It was written into the fundamental law of the land in the Bill of Rights, which guarantees such basic freedoms as freedom of religion, the press, assembly, and speech. Let us list, then, some of the cultural diversities which children bring to school with them and which produce significant differences in attitudes, ways of talking and acting, and interests and goals among the pupils in every school in the country. There are six of these major kinds of cultural differences with a number of subheads under each.

Masculine and Feminine Cultures. Our society fosters a masculine culture and a feminine culture. In other words, men are expected to dress, talk, feel, and think differently from women and to play somewhat different roles in society from women. A very important factor in socialization is that the child internalizes the sex-appropriate masculine or feminine patterns. Boys are greatly handicapped when they happen to take on too many feminine ways of feeling and acting and are rejected as "sissies" alike by both boys and girls. Girls suffer somewhat less from internalizing masculine patterns and seeking to play social roles usually allotted to males, but they nevertheless face innumerable difficulties and limitations unless they are characteristically "feminine" in appearance, speech, attitudes, and actions. One of the first ideas built into each child's concept of self by the people around him is that he or she is a boy or girl, and from that moment the sex-appropriateness of language, attitudes, and actions is stressed. And, although there are many jokes about the "war between the sexes," most people are glad that this distinction exists culturally as well as biologically. They enjoy being men or women, and they enjoy each other.

Rural and Urban Cultures. People who live in cities are marked by different attitudes, interests, language habits, and ways of acting from those who live in the country. We still have a rural culture and an urban culture, though the differences between the two are less marked now than they were a generation or two ago. These differences are, however, still great enough to give politicians cause for concern when they make television appearances or radio speeches on national hookups. For the things they say carry different meanings in the country and in the city, and their manner of speaking and the words they use may appeal to or repel either the city or the country audience because of cultural differences. Thus country and city children are not the same in attitudes, language habits, patterns of courtesy, background of experience, or interests.

Regional Cultures. Different regions of our country have different historical backgrounds, resources, climates, kinds of housing, traditions, and language patterns. In other words, our society is marked by a number of regional cultures. People in New England, the Deep South, the Middle Atlantic states, the Middle West, the mountain states, the Pacific Northwest, California, Texas, and the Southwest are all characterized by differences in language, attitudes, and habit. Each region is rightly proud of its own distinctive history, traditions, attitudes, and way of life. And each child must be understood in terms of the regional culture he has internalized. In recent years the geographic mobility of our population has been such that a child with any given regional background may appear in a classroom almost anywhere in the country. He will need the same sympathetic understanding of his background, language, and folk habits as the other children in the region into which he has moved. Furthermore, because there has recently been much intermarriage between individuals from different regions of the country, many children carry curious mixtures of attitudes and ways of doing things. Teachers are now beginning to see regional cultural differences as enriching children's lives and personalities rather than as stamping them with "peculiarities." Regional cultural differences usually make sense when they are understood, and living together in the classroom helps to break down traditional sectional prejudices.

Ethnic Cultures. Our country is particularly rich in variety of ethnic backgrounds within its population, for nearly all of us have roots somewhere across the seas. English, Scotch, Irish, French, Italian, German, Scandinavian, Czech, Slovak, Polish, Balkan, Greek, Armenian, Russian, Spanish, Jewish, Japanese, Chinese, Philippine, Puerto Rican, and Mexican and other Latin American cultures are represented in concentrations in various cities and regions of the country—and this list is far from complete. Religion, family patterns of living and rearing children, language habits, attitudes, recreational patterns, and traditional values all vary from one group to another. I once studied the language habits in the homes of the pupils in one school in Perth Amboy, New Jersey, and found twenty-seven different languages spoken by the parents in the homes. Customs, fete days, ways of celebrating festive occasions, and concepts of what constitutes "success" in living vary greatly among these ethnic groups. Altogether the result is the great enrichment of the culture of the United States. Consider, for example, the variety of foods obtainable in any major city or the variety of music available and appreciated across the country.

Each child must be understood in terms of his particular background, the way his family seeks to realize the "great American dream," and the vicissitudes and successes it has met. Researches utilizing social-distance scales have shown that prejudices are widespread among the different ethnic groups within our society and, of course, teachers initially carry these prejudices. But as teachers have more contact with and understand better the ethnic backgrounds of their pupils, these prejudices fall away and they learn to see common human values, social worth, and cultural enrichments in these diversities. Each individual pupil comes to be valued as a person possessing a certain developmental potential.

Social-class Cultures. Our society, like most others, is divided into cultural strata on the basis of socioeconomic levels and in terms of group participation. Most social scientists call these strata "social classes" and distinguish five social classes in the United States, each carrying its own distinctive culture. Following the European tradition, and for want of more satisfactory descriptive terms, these classes are usually called upper, upper-middle, lower-middle, upper-lower, and lower-lower. But it is not the names that are significant. It is the fact that families classifiable under these different headings differ with regard to the neighborhoods they inhabit within a community; language habits; methods of training their children—rewards and punishments, for example; values; expectancies for their children as to behavior, school accomplishment, and vocation; churches; social and civic groups; recreations; means of relieving tension; routine living habits; and, as a consequence of all these things, the experiences and life space provided for their children. Each child, of course, must learn to feel, talk, and act in terms of the social-class culture his family carries, since this is the chief culture to which he has access. Consequently children come to school with widely varying experience backgrounds, attitudes, language habits, ways of relating to other persons, ethical codes, life goals, and self-concepts, for all these are shaped by their social-class backgrounds.

One of the characteristics of the middle-class culture is that people who carry it believe that it is the "right" way of life and that its ideals, standards and customs are really the only proper ones. Middle-class persons also believe that from 60 to 80 per cent of our population belongs to this class and that virtually all people could be like themselves if they had ambition and "right attitudes." Yet the fact is that over 50 per cent of the people belong to the lower class, as defined by social scientists, and that upward mobility in terms of social participation, marriage, and vocation is not possible for the vast majority of lower-class persons. Of course, this does not mean that the living standards of lower-class persons cannot be raised; in fact, such a rise has occurred widely during the past twenty years as wages have risen. But this improvement in living habits does not automatically make lower-class persons middle-class, for social class is primarily a matter of social participation, friendship circles, vocations, and neighborhoods.

Another characteristic of middle-class persons is that they mistakenly believe that all lower-class persons are marked by certain undesirable characteristics such as liking to be dirty, vulgar, unambitious, and immoral. Almost all teachers are middle-class people, who automatically have internalized all these ideas about the unerring correctness of the middle-class way of life and the worthless and undesirable characteristics of lower-class people. It is therefore difficult for them to understand the attitudes, language habits, and behavior patterns of lower-class children and to accept these pupils as socially valuable persons. Happily most teachers do accept this task and overcome their middle-class views to the extent that they value each child for himself, but they still often find it difficult really to understand lower-class children's behavior and attitudes.

Social-class Mobility. Society in the United States contrasts sharply with European societies in that the path of upward mobility is much more open to children of the upper-lower and of the middle classes. For lower-lower class children it is still very difficult. The "American dream" for many families is to gradually improve their status through giving the children a better education than the parents had, helping the children to get better jobs than the parents held, and gradually raising their standard of living. And this dream is being realized by millions of Americans to the extent of moving from one social class to the next higher. Schooling plays a large part in this mobility, along with intelligence adequate to the necessary learnings.

But upward mobility is always difficult because of the unlearning that has to be accomplished, because of the disruptions of personal relationships involved, and because of the anxieties and emotional strain entailed. For upward mobility requires more than mere industriousness and desire to "get ahead"; it involves tearing up one's roots, changing ways of doing things to which one has been accustomed from birth on, and breaking personal relationships that are dear and security-giving. Nor is it just to say that anyone who wishes can be upward mobile or to feel respect only for those children who show ambition, for many children lack the requisite intelligence, and many others have never lived in environments that permitted them the necessary vision or the experiences that would make such a vision realizable. Still others are not willing, or even able, to pay the necessary price of anxiety. Therefore, one of the tasks a teacher faces is that of helping those for whom upward mobility is feasible and appropriate to envisage it as a goal. And an equally important task is that of sensing the social value and individual worth of pupils for whom upward social mobility is neither feasible nor appropriate. These children must be accepted as valuable human beings with potentialities for a good life still to be realized. And the school has an important role to play in helping them to become effective in their vocations, civic responsibilities, health habits, appreciation of the beautiful, ethical distinctions, and personal and social relationships.

In the light of all these considerations, it must be evident that the social-class subculture a child carries and the problem he faces of whether or not to strive for upward social mobility are basic facts about each pupil. Differences between children in these characteristics have great significance both for understanding and accepting them as persons and for influencing what justly can be expected or required of them in the way of learning and behavior at any particular grade level.

Caste Discrimination. Unhappily, our culture has set up caste discriminations among our population on the basis of pigmentation of the skin. The concepts on which caste is based are that anyone whose skin is white is innately superior to and entitled to privileges denied to persons whose skin is pigmented black, yellow, brown, or red. Scientific research reveals that *there is no factual basis* whatever for believing that persons with white skins are innately superior in intelligence, physique, creativity, emotional stability, or capacity for ethical discrimination to persons with pigmented skins. This means that such differences as exist between the races in our society *are due to the effects of caste discriminations* applied through time. They are not a justification for caste. Given identical experiences and living conditions with members of the white race, colored peoples will produce the same proportion of gifted individuals, idiots, artists, criminals, inventors, paupers, statesmen, insane, athletes, and day laborers as the white population. Yet caste-based discrimination continues to operate in our society, although, happily for our sense of justice, these discriminations gradually are becoming less severe.

It is nearly impossible for white persons to know what it feels like to grow up a Negro, Indian, or Oriental in our society, for they have never known the humiliations, fears, and frustrations suffered daily by persons experiencing the effects of caste in operation. One of the most obvious effects of caste is segregation. Persons carrying the caste stigma are limited as to where they can live, where they can go, what cultural and recreational experiences they can have, and what they can look forward to as self-realization. Often they are given inferior educational opportunities, although this is not always true either in the South or in the North. Doors are closed to them in many occupations throughout the country, their opportunities for playing civic roles are limited, and often they may not even worship God in the company of white people, although according to the tenets of all the major faiths, colored as well as white people will live together in bliss throughout eternity. People all over the world are aware of our caste system and, because of it, doubt the sincerity of our professed desires to help them achieve a richer life and a more significant role in international affairs. Caste at home is a severe handicap to our government's influence abroad in the struggle against totalitarian Communism.

It will, of course, take years to achieve full integration of the children of all races into our public schools, but the process has been well begun and school people have most significant roles to play in its accomplishment. In the deepest sense, integration requires that teachers see each child simply as a human being in the process of realizing his potentialities for development. Yet pigmentation of the skin, social class, ethnic background, and other cultural factors cannot be forgotten or ignored by the teacher, because they affect what the child says and does, how he feels about himself and others, how he relates to others, and how he thinks and feels about himself and our society. These factors have shaped his experiences, built his concepts, and molded his attitudes.

In summary, to understand the attitudes and actions of a particular pupil, a teacher needs to know whether appropriate masculine or feminine attitudes and actions characterize the child's behavior, whether the family background is rural or urban, in what region or regions of the country the parents grew up as well as where they are now living, the ethnic background of each parent, the social-class background of each parent, the current social status of the family, and whether the family is attempting upward mobility, experiencing downward mobility, or suffering from a low-caste status.

How Culture Is Internalized

2. By what processes is the child internalizing the subcultural elements carried by the family?

A wide variety of processes operate in internalizing the culture. Central in the experience of any child, of course, are the patterns of feeling, thinking, and doing things that characterize his family life. Naturally these will vary with each of the subcultural factors described in the previous section; but instead of describing each of these variations here, we will present a list of the processes which customarily shape the learning of the child. The teacher should seek to learn how each of these processes function in each child's family life in order to assess its influence on the child's ideas about society and his ways of functioning in it. Both home visits and conferences with parents at school are necessary to obtain and record this information. But such information usually is valid for a considerable period of time, unless the family is experiencing a rapid change of fortune.

Factors that influence the child's internalization of the culture include the following:

a. Living amid and using the physical means of carrying on family life, including furnishings, food, clothing, playthings, books, music, etc.

b. The example of parents, presented through daily-living habits, talk, interpersonal relationships, and parents' direct precept teaching.

c. The expectancies of parents regarding the behavior of the child as supported by praise and rewards and enforced by reprimands and punishments.

d. The example set for the child by the behavior of older brothers and sisters, other adults living in the family, and relatives who have prestige in or close relationships with the family.

e. The religious life of the family, including church and Sunday-school attendance, Bible reading, prayers, grace before meals, and religious and ethical principles emphasized in conversation and carried out in action.

f. Materials available and family habits of reading newspapers, magazines, books, comics, children's literature, storytelling, etc.

g. The availability of and family habits concerning radio and television, including favorite programs, time devoted to these media, and amount of attention given to special public events such as political campaigns, congressional hearings, and the like.

h. Family habits regarding attending motion pictures, including frequency and content of the programs.

i. The example set for the child by his peers in neighborhood, playground, and school play groups and in preadolescent and adolescent gangs; the ideas presented in conversations and "bull sessions" in these groups, at slumber parties, etc.

j. Participation in organized groups for children and youth, such as Scouting, 4-H clubs, service club—sponsored athletic teams, community centers, church-organized youth groups, YMCA, YMHA, and the like.

k. Attendance with family members, alone, or with peers at sports events, circuses, rodeos, folk dances, theaters, concerts, opera, zoos, art galleries, museums, and the like.

l. Attending a public or private school, participating in curricular and extra-curricular activities, and experiencing the manner in which these institutions are organized and operated, including participation in planning and evaluating, visits to community institutions, student government, disciplinary measures, school spirit, etc.

m. Psychological identification with a succession of loved or high-prestige persons, such as parents, priests, pastors or rabbis, teachers, Scout leaders, actresses, athletes, political leaders past or present, military heroes, gangsters or criminals, scientists, artists, etc.

n. Sharing in traumatic or deeply moving experiences, such as natural catastrophies, wars, economic depressions, victory celebrations, and festivals.

Naturally a teacher cannot know in detail how each of these processes is affecting each pupil, but keeping adequate records over a period of time certainly can make clear the major influences that are shaping the child's internalization of the culture of which he is a part.

Roles in Social Institutions

3. What roles is the child playing in social institutions outside the home?

In seeking information about the processes by which the child is internalizing his culture, the individual's roles in such institutions as church, youth groups, YMCA, and sports programs should be ascertained. But there are other experiences through which invaluable learning also comes to children and youth. Some of these are suggested by the following questions:

a. What work experiences outside the home is the child having, such as paper carrier, errand boy, delivery boy, baby-sitter, berry-picker, lawn-mower, leaf-raker, or part-time employee in commerce, industry, or service occupation for adolescents?

b. Does he have a bank or postal-savings account?

c. Does he buy his own clothes, toys, or sports equipment or go to the stores to make purchases for the family?

d. What travel experiences has he had with his family? Alone? On visits to relatives or friends? With groups of young people? In summer camps?

e. Has he had experiences with welfare or social-service agencies? The juvenile court? Clinics? Hospitals? Police?

f. Has he had opportunities to observe closely at firsthand such adult operations as building construction, road construction, boat operation, animal care, plant culture, well drilling, machine repairing, preparing exhibits for fairs, preparing church dinners, etc.?

Conceptions of the value of money, the processes of commerce, industry, and agriculture, codes of conduct, and visions of possible roles for the self grow out of experiences such as these. So do ideas about the relationship of the individual to society, of neighborhood to state, and state to nation. Direct experiences of society in operation give much more meaningful learnings than ideas from books and classroom discussions. When a teacher knows some of the experiences the child has had, he can more easily build a bridge of meaning from these experiences to textbook and classroom knowledge and so make the latter functional for the pupil.

Concepts of Self in Society

4. What does the child know and feel about the current American society, how it got that way, and his own present and future responsibilities for maintaining and developing it?

Lower-class children, whether rural or urban and regardless of region, are amazingly limited and provincial in social knowledge and outlook, despite the earnest efforts of their social-studies teachers. Their world is largely that of their own experienced life space. The knowledge and concerns of Timothy Thyme certainly contrast sharply with those of Jane and Chester. The cases of Anne and Roger were between these extremes and demonstrate how a sensitive teacher who listens insightfully to what children say can help individuals broaden their social perspectives. This happened also with Margaret Anne. Teachers are not mere purveyors of information; they are openers of doors, awakeners to reality. If they listen to and record what pupils with limited life space and experience say, they will discover their experience limitations, envisage the next steps necessary to broaden their awarenesses, and watch them follow up and explore new aspects, to them, of the wider national scene. Schools are on the threshold of the wider use of motion pictures and television to provide these broadening experiences. However, just any visual aid will not do, nor just any book for supplementary reading. Proper selections have to be made for each group, and sometimes for individuals, to touch experiences already gained and interests already kindled and to broaden the perspective of the pupil by connecting a number of his experiences and interests. Education is a developmental process rather than a matter of completing one task after another. Such teaching can grow only out of listening to, recording, and interpreting over a period of time the comments, questions, and concerns of individual pupils and of groups.

Culturally Induced Emotional Conflicts

5. Do inconsistencies exist between the various cultural factors the child is internalizing at home and elsewhere, or between these internalized concepts or attitudes and the expectancies and demands he is facing at home and at school?

In so complex a society as ours, few children, and very few adolescents, can escape internalizing ideas and attitudes that are inconsistent with each other. This leads to inner conflicts and to uncertainty as to where to fix one's loyalties. Teachers hear many expressions of anxiety over questions of loyalty to ideals, and concern about what is right or true or what it is practical and realistic to do or believe. Many times, too, teachers are appealed to as authorities or rejected as authorities when they undertake to set pupils right. Here teaching becomes an art, for the teacher must recognize that the conflict and the problem are the child's and not his own. What is the right answer for the teacher is not always the right answer for the pupil, who has a different background and a different total life situation, involving his emotional security and his sense of belonging and adequacy. So the teacher's task is that of guiding the individual pupil to work out the answers that are appropriate to him. This may require weeks, months, or even years of learning and thinking for the pupil and is not possible through the magic of a right answer given by the teacher. For there are ways of thinking, of using the mind, to resolve uncertainties and inner conflict; a teacher who can guide the child to learn to use these processes of truth-seeking for himself may contribute much more to the mental health and intellectual development of the pupil than one who gives glib answers and uses clever techniques for temporarily convincing pupils to accept the teacher's answer.

Awareness of these inner conflicts regarding truth and loyalties in children and youth also is important to teachers as a guide to how to react when a pupil rejects some assigned school task or behaves in a difficult manner in the classroom when discussion touches a sore spot. These rebellions can be seen as protective or defensive devices, and too much need not be made of them on the spot. Rather, a later personal conference can be used to clarify the meaning of the behavior difficulty with the child and its significance for the teacher in the management of the class as a whole.

Above all, the instant assertion of authority is dangerous, for the mishandling of situations involving deep inner conflicts regarding truth and loyalties on the part of pupils can prejudice an individual for a long time against the very subject-matter area where he can most profit from wider knowledge, or against a teacher who has the rich background of experience which, when properly shared, would greatly enlighten the pupil. Nor does a lower-class pupil mean to insult the teacher when he questions some stated truth or attitude. He simply sees life differently, from a contrasting background of experience. But these inner conflicts are not limited to lower-class individuals; they may occur in children from any social class, regional, ethnic, or caste background.

Cultural-adjustment Problems

6. Is the child subjected to any special pressures or tensions due to geographic or social mobility, ethnic identification, or caste?

The information gathered by the teacher in relation to earlier questions in this section will supply the answer to this question. Yet it is important for the teacher to ask himself this question in relation to each pupil. Hostilities between children, resistance to school tasks, rebellious or show-off behavior, truancy, daydreaming, "tall stories," shyness, or other defensive behavior often result from tensions generated by uncertainties about how to talk, act, or believe when one has moved to a new section of the country, when one's family is rising in the social scale, when activities at school are incompatible with ethnic customs, when one experiences ethnic prejudices, or when caste-based discriminations humiliate or frighten the pupil. Understanding acceptance and positive valuing by the teacher and opportunities for successful functioning in classroom activities are all neutralizers of the effects of these tensions. So are successful play and sports on the playground or in intramural or interscholastic contests. But before the child can be helped, the causes of his tension must be understood.

The discussion in this section devoted to socialization processes has demonstrated that children vary enormously in the cultural backgrounds they bring to school and that a knowledge of these factors in relation to individual pupils is invaluable to their teachers. The gradual accumulation of this information in each child's cumulative record therefore becomes a significant professional obligation and its interpretation by each teacher in turn an avenue to deeper understanding of the child and so to more effective developmental teaching.

PEER-GROUP STATUS AND PROCESSES

The Child Society at School

Research carried out during the past twenty years has shown that a child society exists within the larger adult-operated society. Participation in this child society provides a very significant basis for learning how to get along with peers during childhood and youth. The chief known features of the operation of this child society were described in Chapter 9 and need not be repeated here. But the questions that a teacher must be able to answer about the individual child in order to be able to evaluate the significance of his efforts to win roles and secure belonging in peer groups will be listed. These questions are:

1. What are the chief group activities engaged in by the child's peers? What roles do these activities afford? What knowledge and skills are required to play these roles? What customs and codes of behavior do his peer group adhere to and follow? What personality characteristics are esteemed by his peers?

2. What roles does the child seek among these activities? Which ones does he win? What status is accorded him by his peers?

3. Does the child fail to win any of the roles he seeks? If so, why?

4. How does the child act when he fails to win desired roles or when he fails to play a role successfully?

5. What are the effects of physical, affectional, and cultural factors upon the child's peer-group status and role playing?

6. Is the child's status with his peers satisfactory to him? Does he realize why he has the status his peers have given him?

Individuals Vary in Roles and Status

A re-reading of the case materials already presented will show that answers to these questions vary from child to child and that individuals differ enormously in this area. It will reemphasize the importance of these factors to the child's mood in the classroom. It will demonstrate that peer-group factors are constantly present among the motives that underlie each child's behavior in the classroom, on the playground, and in all school situations. For peer-group status and roles are of immediate concern to the child, in contrast to the more remote interest that much of the traditional subject matter has for him. Peer-group belonging is a constant source of pleasure to successful children, an enormous factor in helping them to enjoy going to school and in making them willing to put forth effort to succeed there. Conversely, being rejected by the peer group or being isolated from the peer group generates strong unpleasant emotions, makes the child reluctant to attend school, and stimulates the development and use of defense mechanisms such as fighting, withdrawal, daydreaming, misbehavior in the classroom, vandalism in relation to school property, truancy, tattling, and a host of other undesirable behaviors. Lack of successs in peer-group activities also may lower an individual's general level of aspiration; for it profoundly affects his feelings about and concepts of himself and his ideas of how other people think and feel about him. The teacher needs explicit information in this area in order to understand the motivation and behavior of each individual child.

In the area of peer-group status and processes individuals vary so greatly that ways of dealing with episodes must be different for different children. Certainly this was beautifully illustrated in the cases of Jane, Chester, Timothy Thyme, and Anne Hart. Children who have been overprotected at home have to be reassured and given the chance to develop the necessary physical game-skills and appropriate social ways of acting at school. Children with special disabilities need to have potential peer-group assets perceived by their teachers and to be given opportunities to display these characteristics and competencies in classroom or special group activities where they will win recognition and respect from their fellows. Children whose defensive behavior only widens the gap between them and their peers need the opportunity for repeated informal supportive conferences with the teacher through which they are helped to see both the reasons for and the undesirable social effects of their actions, in contrast to the more customary arbitrary punishment of the child for his behavior, which only serves to deepen his hostility to the school in general.

Two kinds of children are perhaps in greatest need of special study and help by the teacher and are least often given the help they need. One is the isolated child who "never gives any trouble." The other is the rejected child who compensates for not being liked by scholastic accomplishment and a constant striving to please adults.

The Isolated Child

The socially isolated quiet child tends to be unnoticed most of the time by both teachers and peers and often already is seriously maladjusted. Insecure because of lack of love at home, or feeling inferior or inadequate because of physical, social, or mental limitations, such children often are deeply unhappy and may be headed for later mental breakdown or even for unexpected delinquency unless they are helped. The avenue to such help is first of all to know enough about them to understand the basis of their quietness and isolation. Then a personal relationship with them which reassures them and gives them a sense of being valued and valuable is needed. Finally, unused aptitudes and capacities can nearly always be discovered and the child encouraged to use them. This stimulates him to believe in himself, increases greatly the number of pleasant moments in his life, decreases his depressive emotions, and encourages him slowly but steadily to increase his level of both social and intellectual aspiration and effort. It is amazing how much some of these utterly drab children can be "brought out" and developed over a period of three or four years when teachers understand and help them. There can be little doubt, too, that this is good mental hygiene—a way to decrease mental illness during adolescence and adulthood. Best of all it enriches the lives of human beings who otherwise might never realize their potentials for becoming. But remedial effort seldom shows spectacular immediate results, so helping these children becomes a matter of team play by a succession of teachers.

The Rejected Child

The very bright child who gives up efforts to win friendship among his fellows and roles in peer-group activities and compensates by scholastic accomplishments and toadying to adults also is often on the road to unhappiness and even to emotional illness. One is naturally pleased by the earnest efforts and good academic learning of these individuals and may even be inclined to double-promote them to "save them time" and avoid boring them with classroom associates below their level of intellectual functioning. But it is important to remember that later professional, industrial, or commercial success depends significantly upon the ability to get along well with peers and the possession of skill and know-how for developing and maintaining friendly interpersonal relationships with equals and subordinates as well as persons of higher status. These skills, and the personality characteristics that win acceptance and friendship, do not "come naturally," nor are they automatically accorded to "big brains." They have to be learned gradually and developed out of rough-and-ready interaction with peers at successive developmental stages. It is difficult to cultivate them successfully as an adult, after the need for them has become painfully apparent.

Endless stress constantly is being created in industry, commerce, education, and government by adults who are intellectually fully competent and prepared for their work, but who have never learned how to get along well with associates and to play roles as part of a team rather than as shining soloists, or who have an insatiable lust for power over others because they have never known the pleasure of being "one of the gang." So teachers in elementary and secondary schools have a special obligation to understand and help the isolated or rejected gifted child or youth learn to accept and play minor roles in peer-group activities and gradually to improve their status as they gain social skills, more self-discipline with regard to the ways they interact with peers, and warmer, more accepting personality characteristics.

The curriculum appropriate to a given child is never limited to scholastic studies. Full and balanced development of an individual's potentialities for social usefulness and for personal happiness depends upon successful learning of how to function well with peers. So much that is termed extracurricular in modern school practice actually offers the developmental experiences most needed by certain pupils.

SUMMARY

Research has shown that every child is unique. Four of the factors that contribute to the uniqueness of each individual are physical processes that affect the body and its operation, love relationships and the emotional climate in which the child lives, the various cultural elements that the child internalizes from the family, neighborhood, and social groups of which he is a part, and the peer-group processes to which the child is exposed as he seeks to win belonging among the children with whom he goes to school.

Physical factors that contribute to his uniqueness are: his inherited pattern of physical growth and the rate at which he matures physically, his characteristic rate of energy output and his normal rhythm of activity and rest, his health history, health habits, and state of health at any given time, his physical handicaps and physical limitations, the skills which he develops in managing his body, including game skills, his physical attractiveness to others, and his grooming. Each of these factors influences his concept of himself and the way he feels about himself. Each affects the way other people feel about him. His rate of maturing determines the age at which he will face certain developmental tasks and affects his readiness for certain learnings at school and in his peer group.

Love relationships and affectional processes that contribute to his uniqueness are: relationship to his mother, father, siblings, pets, and other adults; the emotional climate in which he lives as determined by relationships between his parents, relationships between his parents and each sibling, relationships among his siblings, and between his parents and other adults who are significant to him. Given the full feeling of being loved, a child feels "emotionally secure" and can face the vicissitudes of life with courage and equanimity. Given doubt as to whether he is loved, he becomes emotionally insecure and his behavior is characterized by a continuing and pervasive anxiety about his own worth. This leads to various attempts at adjustment, such as withdrawing, daydreaming, negativistic behavior, aggression and hostility toward other children or toward adults, or overcompensation by excessive compliance or by striving for scholastic excellence. So a child's security or insecurity profoundly influences his concept of himself, his feelings about himself, and his capacity to accept and love others. The behavior that he shows as a result of his "security" or his anxiety about himself influences the way other people think and feel about him and the kind of relationships others are willing to have with him.

The various elements of our complex culture that the child internalizes from his family, neighborhood, and community shape his concepts of the world and of society, his language skills, and his daily-living habits and influence his attitudes toward everything he experiences, his codes of conduct, his values, and his goal definition. They give him his initial orientation in the universe. They influence his conceptions of himself and of others and his feelings about himself and his relationships to others. They form his concepts of right and wrong and shape his appreciation of what is beautiful. They establish his initial loyalties and teach him what he should strive toward. When the cultural elements that he internalizes are inconsistent, they generate mental and emotional conflicts. When cultural demands and expectancies are incompatible with his capacities or maturity level, they result in a sense of failure and inadequacy and engender doubts about himself. Caste and ethnic discriminations give rise to severe adjustment problems and have profound effects on the child's concept of and feelings about himself and others.

(4) Whenever children are thrown together for a considerable period of time, as at school, a child society develops. To win roles and belonging in this child society is an inevitable need and motivation for every child, and the activities involved in doing this are the essential processes by which children learn to get along with other persons as peers. But all children do not possess the knowledge, skills, and personal characteristics necessary to win full and satisfying belonging. Some children become high-prestige persons and leaders in their peer groups; others become full belongers; others can be only "fringers," admitted to some roles but excluded from others to which they aspire. Some are isolated and have little or no significance to their fellows, whereas others are actively rejected because of ineffective or objectionable behavior or characteristics. The roles and status a child wins in the group influence greatly the concept he has of himself and the way he feels about himself. His roles and status are recognized by his fellows and shape their concepts of him and their feelings about him. Isolation or rejection by the peer group give rise to serious adjustment problems in all children experiencing them, with consequent strong emotions and attempts at adjustive or compensatory behavior to relieve the tensions.

These four kinds of factors do not operate independently, but are all parts of a dynamic constellation of forces which interact to give rise to a steady flow of motivations and feelings and gradually shape the developing self. But the self also becomes dynamic and has a part in shaping its own destiny, as we shall see in the next chapter.

CHAPTER 11

The Individual Shapes Himself

Self-developmental Processes

For quite a long while the term "self" was almost unused in psychological literature, but during the past fifteen years it has come into vogue again, because it has not been possible to explain either perception or behavior without envisaging some continuing and organizing core in the human personality. However, it is still very difficult to describe this organizing core adequately without seeming to turn it into some kind of entity—organic, innate, vitalistic, or mystic—that contradicts known scientific principles. I suspect that this is because we are still unaccustomed to think in terms of processes persisting over a period of time and changing with use and because we think too much in terms of entities which act. I see *the self* as best described *in terms of* the mental *processes* that characterize the person *and* in terms of the *meanings* for the individual that result from these on-going processes.

Both experimental and clinical studies have given us clues to the nature of "self-processes" and so have helped eliminate mystical interpretations. For example, they have shown that *people carry ideas about themselves* that are powerful factors in shaping their levels of aspiration, ways of defending themselves from loss of self-respect, and, indeed, choice of behavior patterns in many situations. This has led to the widespread use of the term "self-concept"; and phenomenological psychology, recognizing the uniqueness of every human being, has enthroned the "self-concept" as the factor which primarily influences everything a person perceives and all his choices of action patterns.

But this term does not seem to be fully descriptive of how self-processes operate. For clinical studies have shown that *feelings about self are quite as important as concepts of self*. Recent research into perceptive processes and the outcomes of the use of projective tests have shown that each individual is unique in what he perceives ambiguous situations to mean, and that his background of experience, including emotional conditionings or referents, is a factor influencing these perceptions.

Furthermore, concepts of self are always relational; that is, they are not just ideas about what one is, but about oneself in relation to other persons, and so imply concepts of others and feelings about others as well. Self-concepts relate the self to physical things and energy processes in the material world and so *imply both knowledge of and feelings of relationship to* these material and energy factors. They also relate the self to other persons and to groups of persons.

But it seems to me that selfhood includes even more than was implied above. It does, indeed, include concepts of oneself, feelings about oneself, and concepts of relationships between self and world and self and others. It includes *awareness of the knowledge one has* gained about the world *and of the skills one has* developed for dealing with things, people, and situations. And *it also includes* the *attitudes* one has formed, the *codes* of behavior to which one adheres, the *values* one has enthroned as worth striving for, the *goals* one defines as steps toward the realization of values, *and* the *operations* one has worked out *for maintaining integrity and self-respect* in the face of emotion-provoking experiences. Actually, *these are all meanings* that have come to the individual as a result of experiencing, doing, feeling, and thinking. *Consequently I would define the self as the meanings that are possible—indeed, inevitable—to the individual.*

Of course, these meanings are the result of the experiences through which the person has passed, and so the self changes as new experiences accumulate and are assimilated. They are dependent upon the individual's capacities for learning, symbolizing, abstracting and generalizing, sensing relationships, and reasoning. They are influenced by the ways in which the individual habitually carries on his mental processes, which are learned and can be conditioned. These meanings also are influenced by the emotions evoked by experiences and accompanying thought about experiences. They are further influenced by the habitual ways in which the individual defends his integrity and self-respect in his own thinking—by his "defense mechanisms." It seems to me that individuals are startlingly different, even unique, in the meanings a given situation or experience can have for them; the character of these meanings constitutes the essence of selfhood.

According to this conception of selfhood, the self-developmental processes are those through which the individual comes to know his world, his society, his universe, himself, and other people, in their myriad interrelationships. They also are the processes by which he reaches decisions as to how to act in the places and situations in which he finds himself. And both kinds of processes involve feeling as well as knowing, and doing as a part of experiencing. Furthermore, there can be no static self-entity because meanings change as experience broadens. Nevertheless, there is a dynamic quality to these self-processes because meanings shape behavior. Knowledge, customs, attitudes, codes of conduct, values, and goals all are meanings that have grown out of experience; yet they all help shape the patterns of action that characterize the individual and which, in turn, provide the further experiences that change meanings. They may even cause the individual to initiate action to change a situation, invent a new machine, create a work of art, or seek power or prestige. And the results of these actions may give rise to new meanings leading to new ways of acting or to creativity. Thus the self evolves while life endures, yet it always has continuity.

The Emergence of Self-awareness

In trying to get insight into how the self-processes emerge and give rise to these various kinds of meanings, which in turn become dynamic factors underlying behavior, it has been helpful to me to re-read certain books by George Herbert Mead,[1] which, in turn, have led me to formulate a statement of how self-awareness develops in the infant.

For some time after birth, the infant appears not to have any consciousness of self as such. Functioning as an organism, it interacts again and again with things, people, and physical processes in its immediate field. This interaction continually activates psychological processes within the organism, including sensation, feelings, perception, and generalized emotion. Gradually these psychological processes ripen to the point where memory ensues. With the functioning of these processes, at least four aspects of the interaction between the infant and its environing world can operate to produce the dawning of awareness of self as differentiated from the rest of the world.

1. From birth, events in the immediate environment constantly produce effects within the organism, at first as diffused sensations. As these sensations are differentiated and organized in relation to each other, the first perceptions occur. Objects, persons, and events in the external world are gradually distinguished from one another. In the same way, the infant gradually becomes aware of the dimensions and properties of his body and eventually perceives his body as an object distinct from other objects, such as clothing, mother, or bottle.

2. Internal tensions, recurring rhythmically within the organism, lead to such actions as waking, moving, crying, bladder and bowel evacuation, nursing and resting. Each of these actions is accompanied by sensations and effects on the internal tensions; and these sensations and qualitative effects determine the affect (feelings or emotions) the infant experiences along with the act. Affect involves awareness of physiological tensions and flows on continuously, changing qualitatively from moment to moment according to whether the tensions are being increased, relaxed, or altered in character. Thus awareness

---

[1] Mead, George Herbert. *Mind, Self, and Society.* Chicago: Univ. of Chicago Press, 1934. Also, *The Philosophy of the Act.* Chicago: University of Chicago Press, 1938.

of pleasantness or unpleasantness is a basic attribute of the infant's body and a basic factor in his experience of his body. Indeed it is one of the primary elements in experience and enables the infant to distinguish his body from other objects. The body can be felt, and it also feels; other objects can only be felt. And affect—pleasantness or unpleasantness—is a continuous, primary experience.

3. As time passes, certain objects and persons, perceived as external to and separate from the body, become associated with changes in internal tension and in feelings and emotions. This is the beginning of learning and memory. The result is a clearer and clearer awareness of a distinction between "me"—the body and its feelings—and other objects. (Of course, the infant does not yet use the symbol "me"; he only gradually becomes aware of what is later symbolized by this word and concept.) But he also inevitably develops feelings of relationship between the "me" and the objects that influence his feelings. So he tends to accept or approach objects that yield pleasant affect (he grasps for his bottle and reaches out toward his mother), and to reject or avoid objects or persons that have produced unpleasant feelings and emotions. This tendency to react to people and things on the basis of pleasant or unpleasant effects on internal tensions eventually builds memories that include differential awareness of a "me," an "it," or an "other" which presently will emerge as generalized concepts. Thus the self is differentiated as a "me" whose feelings are subject to changes caused by contact with external objects and processes or by the actions of persons. In other words, the infant's awareness of "me" brings with it relational feelings toward whatever makes up his experiential world, depending upon the effects produced in "me" by that world in operation.

4. But the actions of the infant, which spring from his own internal tensions, also produce many effects in the world around him. Crying babies are picked up, fondled, nursed, "changed," etc. Persons around them do things when infants cry, so the infant gradually learns to signal to them the way he feels. He can also produce effects upon inanimate objects—balls, dolls, or other toys make noises when grasped and often disappear from view when thrown. On the other hand, if the baby does not act or signal, neither persons nor objects may change their position with relation to him over a considerable period of time. A mother or nurse may sew, read, or move about the room paying no attention to the infant until it begins to cry; then she may immediately approach. A ball will make no noise until squeezed; a block will remain in place until thrown. Repeated experience of these effects makes the child aware that he can produce effects in his world. The sense of an active "I," who can initiate events and do things, emerges.

To summarize, an infant becomes aware of "self" as an entity when:

1. It has defined the dimensions of its own body and differentiated it from other perceived objects.

2. It has recognized pleasantness and unpleasantness as attributes of this body and knows that these feelings are differentially influenced by perceived objects and persons.

3. It has developed patterns of acceptance and rejection, seeking and avoidance in relation to these objects.

4. It has recognized that it is able to originate events, produce effects in other persons, and utilize objects.

The factors that build self-awareness include the body as an aspect of self; unpleasantness and pleasantness as aspects of all self-experiences; the sense of "me" as as object acted upon by the world; and the sense of "I" as an active agent able to produce effects in the world. The self-concepts of children and youth in school continue to carry these same meanings, and it is worth the teacher's effort to try to understand how children differ in their self-concepts with regard to each of these meaningful factors.

Basic Orientation of Self toward the World

The term "emotional security" is very vague in its meaning for most teachers, yet psychiatrists and clinical psychologists know that emotional security or insecurity refers to the individual's most basic orientation toward the world. Teachers sometimes wonder why it is so difficult and requires so long a time to help a particular child become "secure"; and when it has been accomplished, they often feel they have not really contributed significantly, that the child has done it himself. In the hope of clarifying what emotional security really is and of making clear to teachers that they really can and do help insecure children reorient themselves to their world, we will attempt to describe how children become secure or insecure.

"Security" is an aspect of the child's concept of himself. Whether or not a child is loved by the persons who care for him and guide his behavioral development influences greatly the ease or difficulty with which he attains security; indeed, it may be the determining factor. To understand this, one must recall the characteristics of love: empathy (sensing how the loved one feels), concern for the comfort, well-being, and development of the beloved, willingness to use all of one's resources to contribute to his comfort, well-being, and development, and willingness to let the loved one be himself. How do these factors influence the way a parent deals with an infant or young child? To answer this question we must trace the ways in which love influences the infant's experiences while he is developing his basic concepts of self and the world in relation to self, as described above.

1. The experiences of a newborn infant do not immediately yield perceptions, only sensations not yet organized in relation to each other. Yet the infant has a rich sensory life, arising both from internal physiological tensions and from stimulation from the outside world. And these sensations all carry affect, that is, they are pleasant or unpleasant in varying degrees of intensity.

2. As experience accumulates, these sensations gradually fall into related patterns, and perceptions of self and of various aspects of the environment result. These perceptions carry affect consistent with the accumulated pleasantness or unpleasantness of the sensations that underlie them. So the baby may evidence pleasure when he is taken up and given the breast, because this has always given rise to pleasant sensations. Or he may evidence distress as he is taken up and undressed for his bath, if this usually has meant unpleasant sensations for him.

3. As affectively toned perceptions accumulate, the world gradually takes conceptual form for the baby as he senses its relationship to him, to his comfort and well-being. Qualitatively, his world is determined by the feelings of pleasantness and unpleasantness he experiences. This is his basic orientation to the world.

4. But the affect carried by an infant's sensations is determined primarily by the way he is handled. If his position is changed suddenly and if he is handled tensely and jerkily, he may frequently feel loss of equilibrium, a sort of dizziness. If his clothing catches on his nose or ears as he is dressed or undressed, he may feel pain or a momentary sense of smothering. If soap gets into his eyes or if his ears and nostrils are cleaned roughly, the affect will be unpleasant. If the bath water is too hot or too cold, he will experience unpleasant shock, and if the washcloth is too abrasive or too roughly applied, it will hurt. If he is not properly "burped," he will experience gas pains, and if his formula is inappropriate he will have colic.

In contrast, if he is always lifted gently, if the body with which he has contact is relaxed, soft, and warm, if the breast yields refreshing nourishment, if he is lovingly and supportingly cuddled and rocked while he nurses, then his accumulating sensations will be predominantly pleasant and the world will seem to him a loving, nurturing, permissive, safe, and satisfying place. On the other hand, if he has experienced more unpleasant than pleasant sensations, he will perceive the world as a place where threats abound and pain and discomfort are the price of the satisfaction of needs. Who can deny that some babies experience this kind of world, whereas others know a world of mostly pleasant feelings?

5. The mother who loves her child, unless she is emotionally disturbed, usually handles it differently from the mother to whom the child is only an unwelcome chore. The reason for this lies in the nature of love itself. The mother who loves her baby has empathy with it. She shares its sensations and feelings, so she knows how each bit of handling makes the infant feel. She values the baby's comfort and happiness, so she finds pleasure in sensitively adapting each handling process so that the baby will get a maximum of pleasant sensation and a minimum of unpleasant feelings. She feeds him when he is hungry rather than on a rigid schedule. She cuddles and sings to him. She attends to him frequently so that he does not long remain wet or soiled and thus protects his skin from chafing and irritation. Indeed, there are a thousand little ways in which an empathetic, loving mother can add pleasant feelings to an infant's day. And these thousand opportunities are missed by a preoccupied or rejecting mother.

It follows that there is a high probability that the baby of a loving mother will accumulate a preponderance of sensations that carry pleasant affect and that the baby of an unloving mother may accumulate a preponderance of sensations that carry unpleasant affect. Hence the initial perceptions of the world for both children will be affectively loaded in opposite directions. For one child the world will be pleasant, supporting, nurturing, and comfortable; for the other it will be a hurting, threatening, unpleasant world of discomfort.

6. Perception of self as distinct from and as affected by the world comes gradually, and with it come feelings about self as well as about the world. The child of the loving, sensitively nurturing mother not only feels that the world is comfortable and values him highly; he also feels that he is acceptable and worthwhile and that he is what he should be. In contrast, the child of the unloving, nonempathetic mother not only feels that the world is unpleasant and hurtful, but also that it does not value him or is actively hostile to him. In consequence he feels that he is worthless or that he is not right for his world, or he reflects hostility back toward the world.

7. The emotional aspects of the child's perception of self and the world strongly influence the way he acts in relation to his world. If he perceives the world as loving and valuing him and consequently as supporting, comfortable, and nurturing, then he will trust the world and be unafraid in it. He will expect to have his needs satisfied and to find pleasure in the process. In short, he will be psychologically secure.

In contrast, if a great amount of unpleasant affect has accompanied the infant's experiences, he may seek to avoid interactions with the world except those necessary to survival. His tendency may be to withdraw, to evoke as little notice from the world as possible. Or, if he has felt hostility from the world, his tendency may be aggressively to make insistent demands upon the world, to react violently to discomfort, to put up a howl at the slightest provocation. Both withdrawal tendencies and aggressive attention-seeking may be evidences of emotional insecurity, for they indicate that the world is not right for the individual. Certainly kindergarten and first-grade teachers can instantly remember children whose behavior at the outset indicated feelings of security or of anxiety and insecurity.

8. For most children, the home conditions and experiences that produce security or insecurity continue throughout childhood and adolescence. Empathetic, loving parents do not press the child for learnings until his physical growth has made these learnings possible for him. Toilet training, dressing himself, proper use of tableware, respect for property, learning to read, and the accomplishment of other developmental tasks are demanded and expected only when the child has shown readiness for them. Consequently these tasks do not become areas of ceaseless struggle and conflict between the parent and the child, and the child's security is never threatened by them.

In contrast, unloving parents or parents who respond readily to custom and social pressure frequently press the child to learn these things before his physical maturity and mental development make them possible. In such cases the child senses continually that he is not pleasing the parent when he makes mistakes or fails to learn; hence his insecurity is continually deepened.

9. Patterns of discipline used in the home affect the security of the child. The child is more likely to be secure in the home in which "the punishment fits the crime" and the child always knows why he is disciplined. He knows that his parents do not like to punish him but that they must for his sake, and so he does not feel unloved even when spanked. Insecurity often results when the child is punished in anger, arbitrarily, and as a way of relieving tension in the parent. The child frequently takes this arbitrary punishment as evidence that the parent does not love him. Some parents even tell their child directly that they are ashamed of him and do not understand how a child of theirs could act that way, or that they cannot love a child who acts in this manner. Parents of a secure child do not withdraw love as a means of controlling behavior; they use other, more direct means, including spanking.

10. Parents who love and have empathy with a child recognize and accept the unique individuality of each child. Consequently they do not favor one child over another, do not compare children unfavorably with each other, or urge one child to be like another. Rather they enjoy the differences that exist among their children, praise each one for his own learnings and proper behavior, and encourage each to learn at the time and at the pace that is natural to him.

To sum up, emotional security is a fundamental relationship to the world. It is developed largely because of the way a child is treated. It grows out of the feelings toward him of the persons most intimately related to him. If they love him they will treat him tenderly and show sensitive consideration for the way experiences make him feel. Insecurity is an equally fundamental relationship to the world and likewise is developed because of the way the individual is dealt with. It results from the parents' not wanting the child, being somehow disappointed in him, treating him harshly or unfeelingly, pressing him for learning and actions he is not yet able to accomplish, or demanding characteristics in him that are not natural to him. The inevitable result is a continuing and pervading anxiety in the child.

Helping Insecure Children

When a child has lived through a period of six or more years under conditions which make him feel that he is not loved, valued, and respected, it becomes very difficult for him to believe that a teacher really accepts and values him. It will take a long time for him to find security through classroom relationships. Nevertheless, a teacher can do much to help an insecure child come to believe in himself and to learn that the world values him. Valuing him as a human being and seeing good in him and potentialities to be realized, she will seek ways in which he can win little successes deserving praise, which she will then bestow. Like Mrs. Summers in the case of Jane, she will not let him "get away" with hostile and unworthy behavior, but he will nevertheless know that her concern is for his happiness and development. Children have an empathetic capacity of their own which enables them to sense when they are really valued. Basically, this is what matters most. For when a child senses that he is valued by a teacher, he will seek opportunities to be near her and to do things for her, and eventually he will change his ways of acting in order to get her approval, unless the pressures at home are simply too great for him to overcome. Actually, one need never feel hopeless about an insecure child.

PROCESSES INVOLVED IN DEVELOPING AS A SELF

Born with no knowledge of the world and with almost no action patterns ready for use, the human being is still wonderfully equipped for living and for becoming, through his learning capacities. He is endowed with capacities for perceiving the world, deriving meanings from these experiences, symbolizing these meanings, and formulating and testing possible patterns of action based on these meanings. As the result of organic maturation, the accumulation of experiences, and the functional evolution of behavior that occurs partially in response to the demands made upon the individual, additional psychological processes emerge. Symbolizing, abstracting, evaluating, reasoning, emotional identification, and introjection are examples of these processes, which permit more complex interpretations of the significance of the self and its roles in relation to objects, events, and persons. But it must be remembered that the orientation toward the world built up during the child's first few years of life continues to influence his approach to and interpretation of experiences. In this section we will describe some of the more important aspects of the individual's interaction with the things, people, processes, and ideas that make up his environment.

Interacting with the Physical World

The child continually makes contact with, manipulates, and explores the properties of all physical objects and processes to which he can gain access. At first he seems to remember these properties only in terms of their effects on the organism (me). But a little later he remembers them also in terms of their uses (I); and still later he observes the attributes of the objects and processes themselves. Gradually he distinguishes interactions among external objects and processes, and eventually concepts of cause and effect and of orderliness in the universe. Thus the self "internalizes" the physical world through interaction with it, or experience; that is, it comprehends the fundamental properties of physical objects and processes not only in relation to the self but also in their ordered relationships toward each other. Thus the self attains control over physical objects and processes and learns to manage them to its own ends, to the degree that the physical world becomes understood. It is a wonderful experience to observe these meanings being developed and put to use by children and youth in the school, on the playground, and at home.

Learning What the Body Can Do

The child continually uses his own body in interacting with objects, persons, and processes in his environment. Gradually he gains a measure of control over his body and learns its potentialities and limitations. Gaining control over bowel and bladder evacuations are major accomplishments during infancy; so are learning to walk, eat with conventional utensils, dress oneself, climb, dodge, play ball, and use various tools. Learning to talk, like learning to read, write, draw, or play a musical instrument requires great skill development. Such learnings place a wide variety of skills at the disposition of the child, and they lead to the formation of concepts about the self—"I can do this" and "I cannot do that." Experiences with others also lead children to compare themselves with each other and to rate themselves as stronger or weaker, more skilled or less skilled, fully equipped or handicapped, attractive or ugly in comparison with others. Thus concepts of self and readiness to attempt things are profoundly influenced by the quality of the child's body and the kinds of skills he develops in using it.

Learning to Symbolize and to Communicate

Early in his interaction with other persons, the infant learns to give signs of his needs and tensions and to react to signs from them. Later he learns to communicate conventionally through language, gestures, facial expressions, and the like. Through this interaction with others, the child learns the conventional symbols for objects, processes, and persons. As rapidly as concepts are formed, they are named; as rapidly as abstractions are made, they are symbolized. Names are given to sensations, actions, the properties of things, explanatory principles, relationships, events, ways of doing things, time, and so on.

The process of assimilating experience (gaining meanings) is speeded up tremendously when the child communicates with other persons who answer his questions, help him to name things accurately, and show him how to use language in thinking. Soon language and other kinds of symbolization become means by which the experiences of others can be shared and the experiences of self greatly extended. In middle childhood, when the child learns to read, this possibility is still further broadened because reading permits one to share the experiences of persons who are not physically present, even of persons who have been dead for centuries.

Language also becomes a tool the child can use in recalling his cumulated experiences, manipulating concepts, and projecting possible patterns of behavior in thought. Most of the more complex psychological processes that are differentiated during development depend upon the use of symbols of one sort or another. Thus, growing skill in accurate symbolization and the manipulation of symbols results in greater development of self by increasing the number and complexity of the meanings that constitute it. At the same time it places at the disposal of the individual effective means for evaluating situations and events, defining goals, and developing plans of action.

Symbols Must Be Conventional. It must be remembered, however, that each developing individual does not work out his own symbols. Skill in symbolization is so essential to social living that society long since has conventionalized a wide variety of symbol systems. These it undertakes to communicate to children and youth by the teaching of languages, mathematics, music, and other arts, so that each child has the opportunity to acquire at least the requisite minima of these skills. But in helping a child to acquire these skills certain limitations on what he can learn at any particular time have to be kept in mind.

1. A certain level of physical and mental maturity must be reached before a child can acquire some of these skills, such as reading.

2. The child's motivation to acquire a given skill will depend on his home background and experiences. It will be influenced by the functional use others make of these skills in his experienced world.

3. A child can glean from the symbols used by others (teachers, books, paintings, orchestras) only the meanings associated with those symbols in his experiences. So children with meager backgrounds will need new experiences before they can develop large vocabularies and fine distinctions of meaning and understand the significance and value of mathematical symbols, for example. Equally, children with meager language backgrounds will need much patient guidance to build word knowledge and to recognize subtle differences in meaning.

4. Children vary enormously in the richness of their experience and in the language habits which they bring to school; consequently all children cannot be expected to show the same degree of symbolization skills at any grade level.

"Internalizing" the Culture

Interaction with other persons, including the use of language and other symbol systems, results in the child's "internalizing" the culture into which he was born. Each child's interpretation of physical objects and processes, management of his body, and use of language are circumscribed and ordered by this culture as it is transmitted to him by the expectancies, demands, habits, and explanations of other persons.

But the culture involves and transmits much more than this. Interaction with others soon causes the child to develop concepts of property, money,

work, wages, cost, home, school, church, hospital, factory, Congress, newspapers. It also transmits concepts of roles played by human beings, such
as father, mother, brother, boy, girl, grocer, laundryman, policeman,
farmer, nurse, priest, teacher, banker, judge, senator, artist, manufacturer,
repairman, boss, owner, official, soldier, gangster, cowboy, leader, captain,
referee, etc. In other words, interaction with others and the experience of
events acquaints the child with social institutions, social processes, and
social roles and reveals to him the behavior required of him by these institutions and processes. It also shows him the wide variety of roles that
he as a person may play.

Thus the individual comes to see the world and its processes, people
and their roles, and himself and his significance largely in the terms which
his cultural background ordains. At the same time, the child gradually
learns to act in accordance with the demands of society and to use social
institutions and processes in achieving his ends. Thus the self not only
"internalizes" the accumulated knowledge, habits, and values of the culture; it also comes to have at its disposal a complex series of social institutions and processes that can be exploited to its own ends, within culturally approved limits. We have seen these processes actually working
in the cases of Chester, Timothy, Roger, and Anne.

Playing Social Roles and Winning Belonging

When the child interacts with others and takes part in social activities,
he experiences social relationships and plays social roles. These experiences profoundly affect the child's conception of himself and feelings
about himself. In the home the child may be dominated and punished;
he may be encouraged to learn, guided into experience, and assisted in
interpreting what he has experienced; or he may be permitted to dominate and exploit others. In interacting with children outside the home,
he may find himself sought, avoided, or merely ignored. He may find
himself organizing and directing group play, or following the suggestions
and directions of other children. He may find himself teased and bullied.
Thus the child constantly sees himself evaluated by others, winning roles
in social groups based on these evaluations, and functioning in the kinds
of relationships with others that are implied by these evaluations.

In contrast to love, which comes to an individual just because he exists,
social roles come to him on the basis of what he can do and how he behaves. If he wins roles that carry prestige and plays them successfully,
these experiences enhance his confidence in himself and his eagerness to
undertake more difficult roles. If his social experiences and relationships
demean or isolate him, they produce strong emotions that impel him to
work for more satisfying roles and relationships, to withdraw from unpleasant relationships, or to punish the other children involved. Obvi-

ously, participating in group activities and experiencing consequent evaluations by others are powerful factors in shaping the child's conception of his own worth and importance to others, the roles he can hope to play, and how these roles can be won. This, too, has been illustrated vividly in the case records.

Developing Codes of Conduct

As children interact with other persons, they continually experience the evaluation of their behavior by others in terms of certain principles or codes of conduct. "A good boy doesn't do that; he does this." "A nice girl wouldn't act like that; she would always . . ." There are many such codes in our society—codes of courtesy and hospitality, right and wrong, "good taste" and "socially correct" behavior, the beautiful and the ugly. There are also codes for boys and for girls, for different age groups, social classes, and caste-status groups. There are varying codes for members of different churches and professions, business entrepreneurs and members of trade unions, government officials, persons living in certain regions of the country, and persons in specific social situations.

As the child experiences the reactions of others to his behavior, he learns the codes of his family, sex, peer group, social class, caste, and region of the country. He learns them by being told what they are, being praised, blamed, or punished according to them, observing others acting in conformity with them, hearing the praise or blame and observing the reward or punishment others receive for their behavior, and participating in this praising, blaming, or punishment. Thus the codes become internalized and circumscribe the child's conception of the behavior appropriate to him. When he violates these codes, feelings of guilt, shame, vulnerability, and unworthiness result. In contrast, behavior in accord with these codes strengthens the individual's self-assurance and his feeling of the essential rightness and unassailability of the self.

Identifying with Other Persons

As the child interacts with others, his relationship with or admiration for a particular person may become especially intense. The bond of love with mother or father may enthrone one of them in the child's mind as an almost divine object of emulation. Or the child may be drawn strongly toward some other adult or toward some peer who is especially attractive or enjoys great prestige and power in the child's world. Small tokens of love or interest from such a person, or the possession of an experience, interest, or aptitude shared with a person of high prestige may be sufficient to give the child a special feeling of relationships to that person. The child then is said to "identify" himself with that person, for he continually seeks to make himself identical with the person he admires by introjecting into himself the attitudes, codes of conduct, postures, habits, and ways of behaving of the other person. He does this without any effort to validate these attitudes, habits, codes, or ways of behaving on the basis of his own experience. Thus he takes unto himself whatever the other person seems to feel and believe and copies his actions. Sometimes a child identifies in this way with a group of persons rather than with an individual. In any case, the processes of identification and of introjection have a marked influence on the self that is being differentiated and developed, and the influence touches not only behavior patterns but also the goals, purposes, and aspirations that characterize the self.

As we have seen in the outline above, the seven processes by which the developing child acquires the meanings that differentiate and develop him as a self are:

1. Interacting with the physical world
2. Learning what the body can do
3. Learning to symbolize meanings and to communicate with others
4. "Internalizing" the culture
5. Playing social roles and winning belonging
6. Developing codes of conduct
7. Identifying with other individuals or with groups

Since each child's experiences in going through these developmental processes are different from those of every other child, great differences in concepts of self and of the world are found among children. Different behavior patterns result, and different roles are sought. Individuals become organized by these unique constellations of meaning.

The Self Becomes Dynamic and Purposive

The "self" is a specific organization of meanings that have grown out of accumulated experience and the operation of psychological processes for dealing with the implications of experience. Human beings tend to differentiate meanings to the utmost possible to the organism and its intellectual capacities. This tendency brings into action additional psychological processes directed toward the further development and expression of the self. These self-mediated, self-oriented processes continue to set new goals for experience, learning, role playing, and inventing or creating and direct the behavior of the individual toward their realization. The individual no longer merely responds to stimulation in predictable ways. He becomes dynamic; he initiates events to accomplish goals which he himself has set. Totalitarian governments do not like this human tendency; they seek to orient people against it and repress it when it occurs. But I do not believe that purposiveness and creativeness can be eliminated from the human personality, because the tendency toward greater differentiation seems to be a law of nature. It occurs in the growth and development of the body, and it seems equally characteristic of mental functions and the development of the meanings that underlie selfhood.

The dynamic, self-mediated psychological processes that make it possible for each individual to have a part in determining his own destiny are:

1. Purposing, or the setting of immediate goals for behavior to accomplish.
2. Evaluating, or the taking of attitudes toward situations, persons, and processes in terms of their relationship to the goals of the self.
3. Reasoning, or deducing the meaning of previous experience for the solution of a problem met in achieving a goal, and developing a plan for accomplishing the purpose despite the problems encountered.
4. Imagining, or combining remembered elements of experiences into new constellations, in the search for more adequate concepts or in the effort to create more satisfying experiences.
5. Valuing, or abstracting highly generalized conceptions of what would be optimum for the self and for others for whom the self is concerned.
6. Aspiring, or envisaging a long-term pattern of personal development and accomplishment, or envisaging ways of altering environing conditions, relationships, and processes in the direction of one's values.

Anyone who analyzes the life and accomplishments of persons like Gandhi, Pasteur, Beethoven, Franklin, Jefferson, Lincoln, the Wright brothers, Schweitzer, and a thousand others who have contributed vitally to human betterment must see these processes at work and realize that the human personality is dynamic and can initiate significant events. Nor are these capacities given only to persons of genius. Those of us with more limited gifts can still use these processes to develop beyond our limited circumstances, uncover new knowledge, apply old knowledge in new and more fruitful ways, keep human progress in motion, and give children and youth a better chance to realize their potentialities for becoming.

Evaluating Differences Due to Self-developmental Processes

It is hoped that the preceding discussion of self-developmental processes has demonstrated convincingly that each person has a unique conception of the world in which he lives and a highly significant conception of himself and his possible roles in this world. Child-study participants seek to discover the nature of these private views of the world and the self which mark every child as different from every other child. The questions they seek to answer are:

1. How does the child think of and feel about himself (a) as a developing physical being, (b) in terms of the emotional climate in which he lives, (c) in

terms of the cultural elements he has internalized, and (d) in terms of his efforts at role playing in his peer group?

2. How does the child think of and feel about people, events, society, the world, and the universe in the light of his unique background of relationships and accumulated experiences?

3. How do his conceptions of himself, society, and the world influence his perceptions of persons, situations, and events?

4. How does he see himself in relation to other persons, society, events, and the universe? That is, what are his current attitudes, codes of conduct, philosophy of life, values, and goals?

5. What do we know about the child's potential and operating capacities for learning and for doing?

6. What mental processes does he habitually use in working out the meanings of situations and events for himself and in defining his goals and the steps to be taken in working toward them?

7. How effective are his actions in working toward his goals and aspirations? How could he be helped to become more effective in realizing his plans?

8. What conceptions of the child are expressed by his parents, siblings, teachers, and peers? What expectancies and demands upon him grow out of these conceptions others have of him?

9. Are there inconsistencies between the conceptions the child has of himself and of his place in the world and the conceptions of him and demands made upon him by the various people who are significant to him?

If the necessary information about the child is available—and we have demonstrated that it can be gathered—then a teacher with appropriate training can answer these questions. His decisions about how to deal with the child in the classroom will be more insightful when he has found these answers, and he can guide the child's learnings in each subject-matter area in such a way as to help him take his next steps in becoming, in moving toward realization of his potentials for selfhood and social usefulness. Under such conditions teaching is a thrilling and satisfying profession.

SELF-ADJUSTIVE PROCESSES

Emotions

Unpleasant emotion is experienced when the individual's processes of becoming, or of realizing himself through action, are blocked or threatened. Pleasant emotions are experienced when barriers are broken down or threats removed and when the individual is able to act freely toward goal accomplishment.

Emotions are valuable because by means of them the rate of energy release within the body is made appropriate to the demands of the individual's situation. Thus emotions occur at different levels of intensity in different situations and are classifiable as mild, strong, and disorganizing (hysteria) according to the degree of change in the energy-releasing processes of the body. Strong emotions also are classifiable as active, when great quantities of energy are relased rapidly, and as depressive, when the rate of energy release is markedly slowed. The real usefulness of emotions to the human being is perhaps best understood in terms of energy; and certainly the behavior of a person experiencing emotions is much more understandable when one knows how his body is operating.

Physical Processes during Routine Living—Feelings. A person's action in any situation must be carried out by the body and involves the use of energy. The body is a very intricate energy system; each cell must take into itself, transmute, and give out a certain amount of energy continuously during its span of life. The task of maintaining a dynamic energy equilibrium in all the parts of the body is cared for by a wonderfully coordinated set of physiological processes. These include: respiration, intake of food and fluid, digestion, transportation of the necessary nourishment by the cardiovascular system, distribution of these materials throughout the body with the aid of the lymphatic system, osmosis wherever membranes intervene, the clearing away and elimination of waste and of the by-products of the metabolic process, the storage or release of certain useful materials, the production and dissemination throughout the body of a tremendous number of catalytic agents and enzymes essential to the operation of various biochemical processes, and the over-all coordination and regulation of these processes.

Ordinarily, all these processes go on at characteristic basic rates which maintain life in each cell, provide for the repair of damaged tissue, permit growth until full maturity is reached, and release additional energy into sensory, neural, and motor tissue for routine activities. But the course of routine living does not always involve the same rate of energy expenditure in any particular muscle system. Rather, periods of considerable activity alternate with periods of rest or of relatively little activity. So there is provision in the body for a rhythm of activity and rest. During activity, fatigue gradually increases as the biochemical state of the muscle systems and blood changes with the accumulation of waste products. During rest, the homeostasis, or dynamic biochemical equilibrium, of the whole body is restored. So both activity and rest are essential aspects of this rhythm in the energy dynamics of the body. The affect that accompanies the ordinary processes of body functioning and the usual rhythm of routine activity and rest is called "feeling." Feelings, of course, vary a good deal according to whether one is fresh or tired, interested or bored.

Physical Processes during Mild Emotion. Some situations call for unusual rhythms of energy transmutation and release. All emotion-producing situations require special modifications and adaptations of the energy-transmuting processes, and the adaptations required vary with the intensity and nature of the emotions.

Mild emotion, whether it is pleasant or unpleasant, produces modest increases in the rate at which all processes involved in the ingestion, digestion, distribution, assimilation, and metabolism of energy-releasing materials are carried on. Specifically this means that the rate of the following organic processes will be somewhat stepped up: respiration, secretion of saliva and of gastric digestive fluids, peristalsis in the stomach and all along the intestines, rate of heartbeat, and level of blood pressure throughout the body. The sense organs also function more discriminatively, so that perceptions are sharpened. The over-all effect of these functional changes in body processes is to increase alertness and to focus the person's attention upon the meaning-producing factors in the situation. It also increases moderately the amount of energy being transmuted in the brain and central nervous system, the muscles generally, and the visceral organs. In other words, the effect of mild emotion, both pleasant and unpleasant, is generally tonic to all normal body processes. So the person feels "pepped up" and invigorated.

If more people realized the tonic effect of mild emotions, we might well use them more in the educative process both at home and at school. For children and youth naturally seek mild emotion. It makes life more vivid and does no harm. This is probably why research has not revealed detrimental effects from moderately exciting motion pictures, radio programs, and television shows. It is a possible reason why moderate punishments can be of help in developing self-discipline in children. Also, mild emotional disagreements between children may focus their attention upon and help to fix in their minds the conclusions that end the argument when they seek adult mediation or group decision. Certainly peer-group processes frequently evoke mild emotions, and this may be one reason why these group processes are so effective in their influence on the codes of conduct and the behavior of children and youth. Perhaps the participation of the pupils themselves, together with parents and teachers, in establishing the goals of their schoolwork can give these goals more emotional significance and result in more rapid and effective learning. A measure of excitement, then, seems to be good for both body and mind. And adults need this as well as children.

Physical Processes during Strong Emotions. Strong emotions are of two kinds, active and depressive. Examples of strong active emotions are fear, anger, jealousy, joy, vengefulness, elation, acute anxiety, frustration, hatred, and worship. Those that we term grief, remorse, failure, self-pity, relief from anxiety, awe, inadequacy, inferiority, and despair are examples of strong depressive emotions. All strong emotions, whether active or depressive, present a sharp contrast to mild emotions in the kinds of adaptations in organic processes that accompany them.

Strong Active Emotions. The general effect of the changes in organic processes that occur during strong active emotions is to mobilize the body for immediate intense mental and physical activity. On the one hand, this requires the immediate cessation of all momentarily unnecessary expenditure of energy. On the other hand, it involves the immediate stepping-up of all functions upon which rapid and sustained energy release depends, effective distribution and utilization of energy-supplying materials, and a number of concomitant safety-insuring adjustments in organic processes.

Specifically, strong active emotions *conserve energy* by a general cessation of activity all along the alimentary canal. The flow of saliva and of other digestive fluids almost stops, and peristalsis in the stomach and all along the intestines ceases. Spastic contractions may occur in the intestines. Then comes the maximum stepping-up of functions favorable to rapid and sustained energy release. These include increased rates of heartbeat, blood pressure, oxygen supply and carbon-dioxide elimination through respiration, and adrenalin production, and immediate release into the bloodstream of red-blood cells stored in the spleen and sugar stored in the liver. We do not have data on thyroid functioning but could logically expect a considerable increase in the rate of thyroxin production. The best logistic distribution and use of energy-supplying materials is obtained by the contraction of all blood vessels, especially capillaries, along the alimentary canal, thus reducing the supply of blood there to a mere trickle. At the same time, there is a widening of capillaries in the brain and large muscle systems so that a full blood supply in these areas is assured. Safety-insuring mechanisms include the rapid increase in the clot-inducing factor in the blood and the increase in hormones, particularly adrenalin, which supplement the work of the autonomic nervous system in speeding up heart action, increasing blood pressure, and stimulating metabolic functions. The sweat glands are opened to cool the body during the anticipated action.

This whole dynamic mobilization of body resources to provide maximum energy for action is coordinated by adaptive changes in the autonomic nervous system, regulated from the hypothalamic section of the brain. These adaptive changes are made with terrific speed, and the body is immediately ready for whatever action may be implied by the situation. The emotions producing such an adjustment seem almost to require some form of action to utilize the energy so dramatically released. This may complicate things under modern social conditions, in a classroom, for example. These details of what goes on in the body during strong active emotions may help teachers realize what the child is up against during such experiences and enable them to help him find socially acceptable ways of using the energy that is generated.

Strong Depressive Emotions. The general effect of the changes in organic processes that occur during strong depressive emotion is to reduce action to a minimum by reducing the rate of all body processes involved in energy transmutation and release. Specifically, the rate of heartbeat and the level of blood pressure are greatly lowered. Respiration becomes slow, superficial, and often irregular. Carbon-dioxide production is lowered by more than 30 per cent. The appetite is light, the temperature often falls below normal, the hands and feet may become cold and bluish, and available muscular strength is found to be at a minimum in dynamometer tests. In contrast to active emotions, depressive emotions reduce the capacity and need of the body to spend energy.

This reduction of energy output makes sense in terms of the meanings for the individual of the situations that produce depressive emotions. There usually is nothing much that can or should be done about situations evoking grief, remorse, relief from great anxiety, awe, despair, and the like. More likely, the individual must assimilate some very significant happening and reassess his life situation quite thoroughly before launching into a new program of activity. Consequently action is postponed and the life processes are maintained at a minimum level until new circumstances or changes of thought give rise to new plans of action. Of course, mental processes are slowed down by these changes in energy dynamics, too; hence depressive emotion is not favorable to creative thought. Reduction of energy does, however, prevent the individual from throwing himself into undesirable or fruitless action and allows time for the stabilizing of factors operating in the world around him. This interval also permits other persons to intervene, perhaps to give counsel or other help to the depressed person.

Physical Processes during Disorganizing Emotions. Disorganization of either physical or mental processes, or of both, occurs in certain genetically susceptible persons when cataclysmic happenings come suddenly or pile up over a period of time. Perhaps everyone has his breaking point, but certainly some individuals are much more likely to go to pieces under great stress than others. No regular pattern of changes in physical functioning is seen when this disorganizing level of emotion has been reached, for disorganization implies loss of adaptation, that is, pathology. Uncontrollable trembling, weeping, laughing, fighting, loss of control over the sphincter muscles of the bladder or colon, paralysis, hallucinations, and loss of ability to comprehend reality or to sense the results of behavior may appear. The individual can no longer function effectively or take care of himself. Other people must take over; perhaps the person must be hospitalized. Disorganizing emotions seldom occur at school, and dealing with them is not the responsibility of a teacher. They must be treated by physicians or psychiatrists.

Traditionally, emotions have been regarded as undesirable, even dangerous. But our analysis has shown that they are a part of the adaptive capacity of the organism and actually adjust the body functioning to the wide gamut of demands which may be made upon it. Mild emotions are tonic to physical and mental processes alike. Strong active emotions equip the individual for extraordinary and sustained action in crises. Strong depressive emotions remove the possibility of action when action would be fruitless. Only disorganizing emotions represent a breakdown of mental and physical processes, and these seldom occur at school.

The Causes of Feelings and Emotions

In earlier days it used to be thought that emotions were separate patterns of behavior set off from the usual occurrences of life and initiated by specific stimuli from outside the organism. Now we recognize that feelings or emotions (affect) are a natural part of all behavior and experience. The kind of feeling or emotion experienced depends upon what the situation means to the individual and how his behavior works out in relation to the goals that are aroused in the situation. Earlier in this chapter, five kinds of processes were described as interacting to produce the meanings which situations have for individuals and as the evolving bases for attitudes, codes of conduct, goals, and aspirations. These processes, then, give rise to the feelings and emotions the individual experiences. We will now study the interaction of these processes somewhat more specifically in order to help school people understand the factors that are constantly entering into and shaping the way children feel in the classroom and around the school.

Physical Factors. Everything one does involves body functioning, so the condition of the body and the state of its physiological processes have a part in determining how one feels. A child's mood and feelings will always depend, in part, upon factors such as the following: whether he is hungry or full; whether his body nourishment is adequate, inadequate, or inappropriate; whether he is tired or fresh; whether he has free energy to spend and is not permitted to do so, or whether the situation demands more energy than he has; whether he has a headache, a cold, indigestion, or some acute or chronic infection somewhere in his body; whether his sense organs are functioning effectively, or whether he strains to see or hear; whether his body is growing at the same rate as the other children and whether it has reached the same maturity level or is conspicuously different in size or shape or has obvious defects; whether his skills in using his body surpass, equal or fall short of those of the children with whom he is compared or compares himself; whether his hair, facial features, general appearance, and grooming are attractive to others, repellent to others, nondescript, or conspicuously different. These are a few of the physical factors that influence how a child feels about himself, his susceptibility to emotional disturbance, and his tendency to carry anxiety.

Free and effective physical functioning of a healthy, appropriately developed body gives rise to joy and pleasant emotions. Any threat to safety or to appropriate growth, appearance, and functioning brings unpleasant feelings and emotions. Every child has six continuing physical needs:

1. Physical health and safety
2. Appropriate timing and symmetry of growth
3. Proper rhythm of physical activity and rest
4. Opportunities to function physically in ways appropriate to the structure, dynamics, and maturity level of the body
5. Opportunities to develop skill in managing his body in its full functioning
6. A physical appearance that is socially attractive

A child's feelings or emotions in the classroom will be influenced in part by the degree to which each of these needs is met, unrealized, or blocked. Every child faces the continuing developmental tasks of satisfying these needs, and if he is handicapped or blocked in the fulfillment of any of them, he faces a continuing adjustment problem that will be accompanied by anxiety and recurring unpleasant emotions.

Love Factors. The role of love in the achievement of emotional security already has been discussed at length and need only be recalled here. Every teacher knows that the child "brings his family to school with him." That is, the emotional climate in which he lives at home constantly influences his mood, susceptibility to emotional disturbance, and feelings in the classroom. Hence the teacher can understand the feelings and emotions of the child only if he knows about such threats to a child's security as quarreling at home between mother and father, separation or divorce of the parents, death of a parent, birth of another child into the family, inconsistencies in demands on the child by the parents, illness of a parent, overprotection by a parent, interference by a grandparent or other adult, or living in a foster home. Every child has a need for emotional security based on the assurance that he is loved and valued by those who are responsible for him. If this need is met, his feelings of security can carry him through many difficulties and failures. Lacking it, he has a persisting adjustment problem that gives rise to continuing anxiety and self-doubt or to hostility and aggressive demands for notice.

Cultural Background and Socialization Factors. The great diversity of subcultures in our society has been described. Each child's view of the world, attitudes, and ways of acting are profoundly influenced by the particular subcultures he has internalized, for these cultures are his doors to what mankind has learned about living through thousands of years. Yet each pupil in our elementary and secondary schools—already acting, thinking, and feeling in terms of his own limited cultural background— must grapple with the developmental task of learning more about our society and how to function in it. The problem of maintaining consistency and unity within himself as he grows in experience and knowledge is a terrific one, beset by many emotion-producing situations. Some of the problem situations that produce stress for many children and youth as they grow up in and into our society are the following:

1. The child or youth may internalize sex-inappropriate ways of thinking, feeling, and acting, resulting in disapproval by peers and adults, difficulties in winning peer-group belonging, conflict within himself, and doubts about himself.

2. The child's family may move, and he may therefore find himself with ways of talking, acting, thinking, and feeling that are different from those of his teachers and classmates. Country children move to the city and families move from one section of the country to another. Under such circumstances a child may find himself laughed at in school and may feel embarrassingly different. The resulting tension may find expression in clowning, withdrawing, fantasy fabrications, arguing, fighting, truancy, or vandalism and other de- linquencies.

3. The child who has internalized the customs of a particular ethnic group and feels belonging and loyalty to this group may face prejudice against his group or feel "social distance" from his classmates and teacher. The tension growing out of feeling different and unaccepted may result in any of the de- fensive behaviors described under 2. Then, during adolescence, internal con- flicts of loyalty may arise if the youth observes that the way he has grown up in his ethnic group is more restricting than the way others in his peer group at school have grown up. Second-generation children of recent immigrant families often feel that old ways are no longer desirable, and frequent con- flicts at home may result. Yet these children have no other traditions to help them set moral and social limits as to how they will act, so they may "run wild" for a time. They lack a sure basis for a stable conscience; they are confused about codes of conduct. The more glamorous material aspects of our society create desires that are difficult for them to satisfy, so they are frequently frustrated and may come to feel that school people and others in authority are "against" them. All these experiences produce strong unpleasant emotions.

4. A lower-class child may find that the school and its middle-class staff expect different language and behavior from him than is customary at home. He may be embarrassed by his mistakes and tend to withdraw, or he may feel that the school's expectancies are unreasonable or unfair and so become hostile. Or, as time goes on, he may feel that the school is "right" and begin to reject his own background, to "get uppity" at home. In any case there will

be frequent situations where the child is not at ease and even feels strong emotions of humiliation or hostility. In contrast, the schools can be a place where relatively underprivileged children find themselves greatly enriched by experiences not available to them elsewhere and where they feel genuinely valued by persons who open doors for them into many new and thrilling activities without implying any rejection of their home background.

5. A lower-class child may find that the school with its middle-class values demands that he learn facts and skills that seem meaningless to him and irrelevant to his life. And sometimes the accomplishment of these learnings would tax his capacity to the utmost. When such an unmotivated child (in middle-class terms) does not do his work, he may find himself blamed and "failed." The result is disapproval and humiliation that he feels are not merited. Under such circumstances it is all too easy for a child to become convinced that school is not right for him and that school people are against him. School then becomes an unpleasant experience for the individual, and misbehavior and conflict with authority often result. Curriculum flexibility and the acceptance by school people of the necessity for providing experiences that build readiness for required learnings might change the emotional climate very significantly for a great many of these children. One of the regrettable things is that so many skilled and experienced teachers request and get transfers from schools serving mostly lower-class children, leaving it to relatively inexperienced young people to make their way with these children as best they can.

6. Our times are marked by rapid changes in customs and by much geographic and social-class mobility. Many parents have rejected the rigid codes under which they were brought up and are not sure what they should insist upon with their children. Consequently, large numbers of children come to school without clear-cut ethical codes. They seem to lack certainty both about what they should believe and how they should act. They must test limits pragmatically by finding out through experience what they may or must do. The consequences are often the rejection of school tasks, hostility toward school personnel, and an increase in delinquent behavior among middle-class children. These actions inevitably result in emotion-arousing situations. Sometimes the school aggravates the problem by arbitrary punishments, calling in the police, or suspension, in lieu of analyzing the causes of the behavior and providing the child with much-needed guidance over a period of time. Of course, overcrowded schools are short of personnel who are adequately trained for and specifically assigned to this kind of work.

7. The caste tradition of our society still gives Negro, Oriental, and American Indian children a terrific emotional load to carry. They experience daily feelings of humiliation, frustration, and anxiety.

Obviously, only a few aspects of the socialization process which produce strong emotions in children have been presented here. But the number and vividness of the factors are sufficient to establish the fact that this aspect of development carries many problems which cause difficulties for children. These difficulties will vary from child to child, and no one way of handling them ensures emotional health and maximum self-realization. In our culturally complex, rapidly changing society, there is no substitute for understanding the individual if the school is to ensure healthy development rather than contribute to maladjustment.

Peer-group Factors. The role of peer-group experiences in development was presented in connection with the case of Anne Hart and again earlier in this chapter. From these discussions it must be evident that each child needs and seeks to win belonging in his group. His daily successes and failures in playing the roles he seeks and in attaining the status he desires are factors that influence his feelings and emotions in the classroom. Much pleasure, joy, and self-assurance come to children as they are successful in these activities. But frustration, anger, envy, and hostility are recurring emotions in children who fail and are rejected by their fellows. Anxiety must constantly beset the fringer, alternating perhaps with joy at small successes. Isolates frequently evidence doubt as to their personal worth or feel inferior. Group experience is a daily recurring element in the lives of school children; consequently they must work steadily at the developmental task of winning belonging in the peer groups at their respective maturity levels. If they are rejected or isolated, they have a continuing adjustment problem with which to deal, and their feelings and emotions in the classroom will be strongly flavored by this fact.

Self-developmental Factors. Selfhood was defined earlier as the capacity to perceive meanings related to self in any situation, and the self was defined as the range of meanings which an individual can perceive in the light of his accumulated experience and characteristic mental processes. In addition, we have seen that each of us perceives *himself* as a phenomenon—along with things in the world and other people—and that each of us has concepts of and feelings about himself as well as about others.

Certain of the meanings associated with the self-concept were described as "dynamic," that is, they were thought to shape behavior and even to initiate action. Some of these dynamic meanings were called "values"; others were designated by the terms "goals" and "aspirations." In other words, a person sees himself as believing in or valuing something and consequently sets goals to be achieved by his immediate actions, and aspirations to be realized through long-term, purposive behavior. He uses energy, makes sacrifices, and may even run extreme risks in order to accomplish his goal or to approach nearer to his aspiration. His goal-accomplishment or progress toward an aspiration constitutes self-realization; and joy or happiness are the affective by-products. Failure to attain the goal and inability to progress toward an aspiration, on the other hand, result in frustration and unhappiness.

Feelings about Self. But this is too oversimplified and generalized a statement to have much value for teachers, for the concept of self is many-sided and any aspect of it may be vulnerable to damage or distortion. If we study psychiatric and psychoanalytic literature to find out what has happened to the self-concepts of persons who are mentally ill, we can see quite clearly the essential facets which, together, determine the form of each individual's self-concept. For example, we find such persons variously described as feeling: threatened, insecure, rejected, inferior, inadequate, frustrated, or in conflict with themselves. Logically, *a healthy self-concept should involve* feelings which are the obverse of these, namely, *feelings of safety, security, belonging, adequacy, self-realization, and integrity.* These, then, are the feelings which a child or youth needs to have about himself to maintain full and vigorous mental and emotional health. Perhaps it is worth the space to analyze briefly the factors upon which each of these feelings depends.

Safety. Safety seems to mean that the child or youth is confident of physical survival and health. This feeling results from good nutrition, adequate medical care, the absence of war, and rich opportunities to learn to manage the body effectively in a wide variety of physical activities. But not all children feel safe. Some have been traumatized by illnesses or accidents, others are fearful because of associations with adults who are often afraid or who have restricted the child's activitives to the degree that he cannot gauge the amount of hazard in physical situations and does not feel confidence in managing his own body in many activities.

Security. Security has already been discussed adequately. It is the feeling that one is fundamentally valued as he is, that he is "at home" in the world. This seems to come only when one is loved. In turn it seems to be the necessary basis for learning to love others.

Belonging. Belonging also has been described. It depends upon having the requisite knowledge, skills, and personal characteristics to win roles in peer groups and to function in the social institutions and situations appropriate to one's maturity level.

\ *Adequacy.* Adequacy requires more analysis. It seems to depend not only upon being able to win roles in peer groups, but also upon learning to understand the world about one well enough to deal with it effectively. This implies knowing how to use the physical forces and material things around one. It means meeting successfully the demands and expectancies of parents, teachers, employers, and the public generally. It depends upon being successful in a fair proportion of the things one is asked, or undertakes, to do; but not in everything, of course. Physical handicaps, limited intelligence, meager experience background, traumatizing emotional experiences, or cultural differences all tend to make a person feel inadequate to deal effectively with his world. The repeated experience of failure in school also can go far to convince a child that he is inadequate. An inadequate person always feels that the fault is his, that he lacks the requisite capacities or characteristics for successful living, that he is unlucky or predestined to failure, that he will never amount to anything. Such hostility as he has turns inward in self blame. The antidotes for inadequacy are repeated experience of genuine, not "phony," successes; direct, merited praise from persons important to him; and recognition of successes by peers. *But the tasks set and the demands made must be appropriate to the individual's developmental level, learning capacity, performance ability, and motivation.*

ϰ *Self-realization and Frustration.* Feelings of frustration arise when the individual fails to achieve the goals he has set for himself, when he cannot see real evidence of progress toward the realization of his aspirations, when he feels that he is "not getting anywhere." In contrast, feelings of self-realization and success provide the aura of happiness that goes with objectives accomplished and progress noted. Research has shown that the level of aspiration rises as the individual achieves success after success. With growing self-confidence, the developing individual dares to undertake more difficult tasks. In like manner, level of aspiration is lowered by failure to accomplish one's goals and lack of progress toward self-realization.

There is also a significant qualitative difference between feelings of inadequacy and feelings of frustration. Feelings of inadequacy seem to grow out of failure to meet successfully the expectations of others and the demands of institutional processes, whereas feelings of frustration grow out of failure to achieve goals set by oneself and to feel the inner self-growth and development for which one has the potential. It is natural, therefore, that feelings of inadequacy are accompanied by self-doubt, by a sense of inferiority, by feelings of hopeless inability to meet life's demands.

In contrast, feelings of frustration often are accompanied by hostility toward persons around one, toward authority, "school," or society in general. Clearly the remedy for feelings of frustration lies in giving wise guidance to the individual as he sets his goals and formulates his aspirations so that they are actually realizable and socially appropriate and useful. Further assistance can be given by helping the individual to analyze what he will need to know and what skills and personal char-acteristics he must have in order to succeed. Finally, he can be helped to gain this knowledge and develop the necessary skills through curricular tasks appropriate to his needs and capacities.

ϰ *Integrity and Inner Conflict.* Inner conflicts arise when the child or youth internalizes inconsistent codes of conduct, attitudes, desires, and goals from the individuals with whom he identifies or from the various cultural groups in which he seeks or feels belonging. In contrast, integrity is achieved when all a person's codes of conduct and attitudes are consistent with each other, when the realization of one of his desires or goals does not render impossible the realization of another of his goals.

Inner conflicts and mutually incompatible desires are, indeed, most difficult to avoid in a society as culturally varied and as rapidly changing as ours. The reiterative insistence of advertising, the flaunting of material symbols of status by one's peers, and the publicizing of successful athletes, entertainment stars and winners of give-away programs influence many young people to hope for notoriety or easy successes, without helping them to see that hard, self-developmental study and practice are necessary to long-term self-realization and that a comfortable living must be based on sound economics. On four successive plane flights recently I have sat next to very worried parents whose children, accustomed to every material comfort in the parent's home, were having great difficulties in adjusting themselves to early marriages before their own earning power could approach that of their parents. Somehow these young persons had never learned the economic realities of family life, nor were their desires realistically related to their own developmental levels. Conflicts between loyalties, codes of conduct and ethics, and values can be equally disturbing and give rise to intense emotions.

To summarize, emotions have been shown to be caused by the meanings which situations have for the individual. These meanings are always unique for each person and depend upon the simultaneous interaction of many dynamic components: organic, affectional, cultural, peer-group, and self-mediated goal-seeking components. *All occur together; all interact.* At one time one aspect is more heavily weighted in determining the emotion; at another time, another. But *all are there, and all play their part. The emotion actually experienced depends upon the meanings arising from the interaction of all these processes in any particular situation.* Consequently we have not listed the separate causes of emotion but rather the factors that interact to produce the meanings that are accompanied by emotions. This means that emotions are difficult to understand and that a teacher must have extensive information about a child or youth to understand why he feels and acts as he does.

THE MANAGEMENT OF PERSISTING STRONG EMOTIONS

Adjustment Mechanisms

Most strong emotions last only a short while because the individual involved acts to overcome their causes or because conditions change. On the other hand, the factors that produce strong unpleasant emotions in some children or youth may last for months or even years. When this happens, organic damage to the body and distortion of mental processes can occur. For this reason, every child or youth who shows long-term or frequently recurring active or depressive emotions of strong intensity needs help.

Ordinarily, however, long before a child is referred to a clinic or to the school psychologist for help, he will have worked out, without being conscious of what he is doing, some means of neutralizing his own emotion and finding temporary relief from tension. These means are called adjustment mechanisms. They generally do nothing whatever to remedy the real causes of the emotions. Indeed, they may become habitual and release enough tension to render the individual unwilling to make the effort necessary to work out a real solution to his problem. Since emotions are always appropriate to the meaning which the situation has for the individual, anything which will change the meaning will change the accompanying emotion. This explains how most adjustment mechanisms work.

Distorting Meanings

It is very easy for the child to discover adjustment mechanisms either accidentally or by copying adults. For example, a child may accidentally break something and fear punishment or guilt. Perhaps an adult who has not seen the accident says, "George, did you break this, or did Rover knock over the stand?" The reply, "Rover," is to be expected; but in giving this answer, the child has learned to shift blame and to seek excuses. Many children come to school already quite skilled in distorting the significance of facts in such a way as to fool themselves as well as others. For example, the meaning of a situation can be altered to show that it really is a good situation and not a bad one; this is called rationalization. Or a child who acts harmfully toward another may avoid feeling guilty by telling himself and others that the other child was trying to harm him; this is called projection. There seem to be an almost endless number of ways in which a person can distort the meaning of a situation to make it more favorable to himself. These distortions make the individual temporarily more comfortable, but they do not change the actual situation in any way. So they may become a dangerous habit, accustoming the child to see in a situation only what he wishes to see and not what is really involved.

Fantasy

The use of fantasy is another adjustment mechanism. A child who is physically or mentally handicapped, is unsuccessful in meeting the expectancies of his parents or teacher, or has not won peer-group belonging may spend many hours fancying himself a great athletic hero, a brave soldier, a daring flyer, or a great movie star. This habit may yield considerable mild pleasure and give the body a chance to return to normal functioning instead of continuing the emergency patterns of energy release found in strong active or depressive emotion. This much is good about fantasying. But it has the danger of letting the child get the habit of not thinking about things as they really are, not analyzing the steps necessary to reach a goal, and not actively working at his own development, but instead finding pleasure chiefly in the unreal.

Compensation

Another adjustment mechanism is called compensation. Children who feel insecure, rejected, inadequate, or in conflict may comfort themselves by overeating or by masturbating. Bright children who are not accepted by their fellows may compensate by striving to beat their classmates in academic learning, "getting all A's." Or an incompetent student may put his major effort into developing athletic skills and dominating playground activities. Children who lack game skills may remain glued to the television for hours on end or tease to go to the motion-picture theater when most other children are engaging in active play. None of these compensatory activities is dangerous if indulged in infrequently; in fact they help keep a fair balance between excitement and pleasure on the one hand and drudgery and disappointment on the other. But too frequently indulged in over a long period of time, they are undesirable, for they permit the individual to find a good deal of pleasure while still avoiding coming to grips with his real adjustment problem. And these very pleasures do not really satisfy because the basic problem persists.

In summary, it is clear that most of these adjustment mechanisms, although they give a temporary relief from tension, are undesirable, either because they distort the individual's perception of the realities he faces or because they afford a relief which robs him of motivation to do the work necessary to successful development. The problem is further complicated by the fact that few persons ever catch themselves using these mechanisms or realize that they are fooling themselves rather than others. So the remedy must be found in guiding each child into a series of mentally healthy ways of dealing with situations that produce strong unpleasant emotions. I see this as just as real a curricular task for schools as building reading skills or communicating necessary information.

CONSTRUCTIVE WAYS OF MANAGING EMOTIONAL TENSION

Frequently recurring, strong, unpleasant emotions are bound to occur in a considerable number of children and youth at school. Nor is it possible always to work out quick "solutions" for these emotion-generating situations. Therefore, in order to avoid the risk of physical or mental damage, it is often necessary to find ways of reducing the tensions temporarily.

Catharsis

One way to reduce tension is by developing hobbies. Another is by free participation in active games. A third is by carrying on creative activities.

Given adequate materials, opportunity, and encouragement, many children who are under strain will paint or draw, model clay, play a musical instrument, make things out of wood, metal, or paper, or write poetry or stories. Often this creative activity offers the child or youth the chance to state how he feels, to examine the meaning for him of his adjustment problem, and to explore possible solutions. These expressional and creative activities are cathartic in that they help the individual to use up the energy generated by his emotion in socially acceptable ways. But they also often lead to deeper insights into the causes of unhappiness and to the discovery of ways of coming to terms with them.

Creative activity is effective because it permits the child to deal with his problems at the feeling level rather than intellectually—to express what he feels without putting it into words. Then, too, creative activities have value in themselves. As skill develops, the individual is able to do things that win merited attention and approval from others, and the discovery of his own capacities enhances his feelings of personal adequacy and worth. Far from being a fad or an educational frill, the creative arts are necessities in school, as health-giving emotional cathartics and as constructive avenues by which the child may learn to come to grips with situations that disturb him deeply.

Love

For a long time I believed that the teacher's task is to respect children as human beings and to provide experiences through which they can learn effectively, that love is out of place in the classroom and belongs in the home. But the study of hundreds of case records compiled by teachers and the examination of the roles many effective teachers are playing in the lives of certain children have forced me to change my opinion. The case of Jane was illustrative of what I have seen happen to a great many children.

It was not until I had analyzed the nature of love that I realized that love has a place in the classroom and that genuine love is neither romantic nor instinctive. It is a valuing to the degree that one achieves empathy with the loved one and a willingness to make one's resources

available to promote his self-realization. Many teachers satisfy these
criteria of love for particular children who are insecure and have great
need of it. The analysis of how Mrs. Summers began to give security
to Jane was a good example.

Obviously every teacher cannot love all her pupils every year. Most
children do not need love from their teachers. Also, it is clearly impossible for a given teacher to love every sort of child, and no teacher
should feel guilty or be blamed when he cannot love a particular child.
Nevertheless, there are children who are denied the security that comes
with being loved at home, and there are teachers who can love many
of these children in the way I have described. When this occurs, in-
estimable good comes to the child; it is not too much to say that later
mental illness or delinquency is often prevented. So it becomes most
important to recognize insecure children early in their school life and
to make every effort to put them with teachers who can truly value
them. Furthermore, it is often desirable to make it possible for a given
child to stay with such a teacher for at least two years, because the relationship is genuinely therapeutic.

✗ Participating and Belonging

The current tendency to stress group processes in education and to
organize extracurricular clubs and activities is frequently criticized. Yet
many children with serious adjustment problems first begin to find themselves and to have a sense of personal competence and worth as participants in class groups under the skillful guidance of understanding
teachers. Shy children gradually lose their timidity, and underprivileged
children find that they have significant contributions to make to class
discussions, to the painting of a mural, to the building of a group project,
or to a presentation in assembly. As children play roles in school activities their concepts of self as contributors to the life of the school grow
and they begin to think of themselves as personally significant. Being
chosen as work partners or committee members on class projects, functioning as members of safety patrols, being elected to offices in classes
and clubs, all such experiences help children suffering emotional tensions to find meaning in life and to discover that they are needed and
useful. They encourage children to look ahead, to dare to believe in
themselves, to hope, and to aspire. Too many adults regard these activities as insignificant, whereas actually they are the experience stuff
by which children learn how to function effectively under responsibility,
how to evaluate their own worth, and of what sound character consists.
These activities are not fads, but are being used because school people
are recognizing the processes by which responsible, self-directing personalities develop.

Learning and Facing Facts

Most adjustment mechanisms encourage the individual to avoid facing the facts about the causes of his tension and the effects of his behavior. In repression, one simply refuses to think at all about his problem. In rationalization, projection, and reaction-formation, one distorts either the facts themselves or the way one reacts to the situation and so perceives it falsely. In fantasying, one creates the facts he would like to be true and basks for a time in the aura of this imaginary situation. In compensation, one proves to oneself that it is possible to be happy anyway. So each of the adjustment mechanisms involves distorting one's perception of the situation by repressing, omitting, distorting, or changing the facts that are the basis of his understanding. One changes the meaning of the situation and so fools himself. Many children learn to use some of these mechanisms even before they learn to reason validly, so it is not surprising that these habits are hard to break.

It follows that the school has a major responsibility to help children and youth learn to check on their own thought processes. There are countless opportunities to do this every day, and the manner of doing it is very important. Humiliation, sarcasm, and blame do not motivate the thoughtless child to change. Rather, the teacher needs time alone with the child who has been handling his tension inappropriately. Together they can talk over the factors involved in whatever is bothering the child, with the teacher mostly listening, so as to hear how the child perceives the situation without judging, preaching, or telling the child what he ought to do. At later conferences the child will bring out more and more facts and will order them better and better in relation to each other, thus approaching closer and closer to a genuine understanding of the problem and of himself in relation to the problem. It is often astonishing to discover that, when the child or youth really understands his problem, no matter how difficult it is, he can figure out something constructive to do.

Essentially the task is that of helping the child to become habituated in using the essential steps in reasoning when analyzing his own life situation or behavior. This means taking time to define clearly what is really bothering him, then to marshal all available facts about why the situation is as it is, consider whether there are other facts that he does not have in mind and try to get these facts (from other children or from the teacher perhaps), think of possible ways of solving the problem and evaluate which of these is the best one to try first, work out criteria for judging whether the attempt is successful, and then go into action. In most schools reasoning is taught formally in relation to particular mathematical or scientific material in the curriculum. But this is not very effective. It is better to guide children to reason about problems they face in their life situations, in their daily activities in and around the school, and especially in matters that stir their emotions, for these problems are important to them, and they will value and remember a method of thinking that helps them solve serious personal problems.

Helping children to learn to reason soundly about their adjustment problems should be a recognized part of the school curriculum at all levels, particularly in junior and senior high schools. Facing the truth, the relevant facts, has a curious effectiveness in setting one free from the false thinking characteristic of adjustment mechanisms.

Clarifying Values

Values are more than wishes or desires; they are convictions. They are an individual's deepest and most sincere statement to himself of what his life is about, what he believes, aspires to do, bring about, and become. These assessments of what is ultimately worth striving for are initially internalized from the teaching and example of individuals and groups with which one identifies, but most often these initial values do not remain unchanged. Meanings, distilled out of a person's accumulating experience, alter some of these initial conceptions and reenforce others, with emotional as well as cognitive content. Most mature persons consistently strive to realize no more than a half-dozen major values, and these usually have a hierarchical order, with one value uppermost and the others falling into an ordered sequence.

Values have a number of important functions in relation to perception, behavior, and mental health. Six of these functions are listed below:

1. Values select, shape, and order perceptions. What one is ready to see in a situation, how he interprets what he sees, and what he perceives the significance of the situation to be for himself are determined by what matters most to him as well as by the details of information he has about various factors in the situation. This is why projective tests yield significant leads to understanding a person's motivations.

2. Values help shape goals. One approaches a situation from the viewpoint of the values and derived goals he wishes to achieve and looks at the situation in terms of the possibilities it contains for accomplishing a goal that is a step toward value realization. Or he analyzes a situation in terms of his value hierarchy and discovers its possibilities (goals) for action toward the realization of his values. Clear-cut values help a person to perceive clear-cut goals for behavior in specific situations.

3. When an individual sees a goal that he wishes to accomplish, he must choose a sequence of behaviors that his experience tells him will be effective in achieving the goal. Here values again become a factor, for a person will choose behavior patterns that are consistent with his values even though they may involve more work or less assurance of success than other possible actions.

(I am not using code of conduct and values as synonymous here.) For example, the teacher who genuinely values every child because of his human potentialities will never use humiliating or debasing methods of controlling any child's conduct.

4. Values are the organizing core of a person's cognitive and affective life. Experiences find their meanings in relation to or through this organizing core. In this way integration is achieved. As the individual acts on the basis of the meanings that situations, so interpreted, have for him, his integrity is expressed and maintained. In other words, if a person has developed a hierarchy of values that are compatible with each other, all experiences will have interrelated meanings and all behavior will be consistent. Thus inner conflict is avoided.

5. A person with a strongly established and integrated value hierarchy can withstand privations, make "sacrifies," and run serious risks in order to progress toward the realization of a value. For example, a parent who truly loves (values) a child will deny himself many things enjoyed by his peers in order to give his child a good education. Yet he does not experience this as a privation or sacrifice. A scientist will work endlessly against fatigue and at a low relative salary in order to discover the truth he seeks. So will an artist, to express the beauty or truth he feels the pressing need to externalize. A strong organization of compatible values is therefore the essential basis for what is commonly called "strength of character"; and it is notable that persons whose values are so organized seldom break down and more often become "self-actualizing," to use Maslow's term,[2] or "fully functioning," to use Carl Rogers' term.[3]

6. An individual with a strongly established hierarchy of compatible values remains, of course, susceptible to strong emotions from all the usual causes. He will still feel fear, anger, frustration, and other emotions. But if some of his values relate to things outside himself, if they are social concerns, he still has an excellent basis for managing these strong emotions through sublimation. Sublimation is the use of the energy released in emotion-producing situations to accomplish socially useful goals not related directly to the causes of the emotion. A tense person who deeply values other human beings can always find useful social activities in which to engage—community-chest drives, church work, union activities, youth organizations—and through which he can get relief from discouraging happenings and avoid the loss of the feeling of personal significance. Thus social values can guide an individual into actions that sublimate strong emotions and help maintain mental health.

Reworking Values during Adolescence

Adolescence is the time when values are tested and re-formulated, for at that time organic development and social expectancies both imply

---

[2] Maslow, A. H. Self-actualizing People: A Study of Psychological Health, in Moustakos, Clarke E. (ed.), *The Self*. New York: Harper, 1956. See also Rogers, Carl, What It Means to Become a Person, in Moustakos, *op. cit.*

[3] Rogers, Carl. "The Concept of the Fully Functioning Person." Unpublished manuscript. Library of the Institute for Child Study, University of Maryland.

that the individual will become fully self-directing and socially responsible. But many adolescents find that they have internalized values that
are incompatible with each other at home, at church, in their peer
groups, and through their contacts with events occurring in the wider
society. So they face the task of reworking their central organizing core
of convictions and deciding what they must stand for as they enter into
adult responsibilities. Enough of them come out of this disillusioned, in
conflict, rebellious against authority, cynical, flippant, and superficial in
thinking to indicate to us that we have not yet learned enough about
how to guide youth in the formulation of their value dynamics.

The School's Task in Value Formation

There are clearly two steps that schools can take to help children and
youth in this matter, beyond what we are now doing. First, we can
realize that each individual faces the task of formulating his own values
and that this is something that cannot be done for him and taught to
him as an intellectual concept or by the kinds of controls used in totalitarian societies. Then we can set up machinery that will make it
possible for each young person to get help from a wise adult when and
as he needs it. This means that every secondary school student should
have someone on the staff who knows him well, who is identified as his
friend and sponsor at school, and who is ever ready to talk with him,
listen to him, and facilitate his efforts to think through his problems of
value.

A second necessary step is for the school to be organized and operated
in such a way that it everywhere and always exemplifies the valuing of
every human being. This can be done by student government, student
participation in planning learning activities, flexible curricula, and the
provision of counseling services, testing services, and studios for free
creative activity. The manner in which disciplinary problems are handled also tells students whether or not each human being is deeply
valued.

Acquiring Faith

Another path to stability in times of stress is faith—in God, man, oneself, and, consequently, the future. Faith seems to result from orienting
oneself clearly in the universe and in the stream of evolving life. It is
achieved by identification with persons and groups who have faith and
show it by their actions, and by the study and practice of religion or
philosophy. Faith brings the individual a strong sense of his own personal significance as the latest link in the unending chain of human life.
It brings an appropriate humility as to one's personal power and the
feeling that truth, unchanging and eternal, underlies the organization

and processes of the universe and of human life on the earth. Far from being an opiate, faith is a constant source of reassurance and permits a person to believe in a future that he cannot yet see clearly.[4]

Of course, people disagree violently about statements of faith, and this complicates greatly the task of young people striving to orient themselves in the universe and among living things. Most religions are so heavily loaded with dogma as to obscure the fundamental tasks involved in the human being's relating himself to the organizing force of the universe. But here is one of the fundamental challenges of our time. Shall we struggle endlessly to swallow or to refute some item of dogma, or shall we brush aside nonessential details and seek simply and honestly to know God and His purposes? Shall we forever regard science as unrelated or antithetic to religion and philosophy? Or shall we study it searchingly to discover the grand design of the universe and its operating processes and to understand the dynamic push of life forces which underlie the evolution and emergence of new life forms and the ceaseless strivings of human beings to discover truth, create beauty, and build a superior society? Any individual who succeeds in orienting himself significantly in the universe and in the stream of living things finds direction and meaning in his life. He has then a basis for faith, and he can meet the problems of living because he knows his own significance.

It is not possible to discover a neat formula for schools to use in fostering faith in children and youth. When I ask myself the sources of my own faith, I find them to be identifications with persons who had faith and lived superbly in their humble ways, leaning on faith when they needed it. When I seek the source of the faith of these persons, I find it is the continuing diligent study of religion and philosophy, testing the tenets of their belief in action, and persistent contemplation, alone, of the meaning of life as it unfolds. Hence the best I can do is to urge school people to try to augment their faith, to live in accord with it, and to encourage young people to spend time becoming acquainted with the grand design of the universe, the resistless force of life in process, and the directions man has taken in his search for truth, beauty, and goodness.

Conclusions

In the preceding chapter, the question was raised whether it is necessary for school personnel to understand each child or youth as a unique individual or whether it is possible to understand children and youth in general and to work out satisfactory educative processes that will be effective with all. We have seen that each individual has to be under-

---

[4] Schweitzer, Albert. *The Philosophy of Civilization.* New York: Macmillan, 1950, part II, Civilization and Ethics. Also, Mumford, Lewis. *The Conduct of Life.* New York: Harcourt, Brace, 1951, chap. VII, The Fulfillment of Man.

stood for what he is, a unique and dynamic human being, and have proved this by listing the forces that shape the organic, mental, and emotional characteristics and behavior of human beings and by showing that these forces vary qualitatively and quantitatively in their impacts upon different individuals, thereby creating unique persons. Indeed, this is no new idea, for individual differences have been recognized as long as schools have existed and longer. The purpose of outlining the way these diverse forces interact to shape the development and behavior of the individual and to give rise to values and purposes was to show that it is now possible to understand individual children and to make wise decisions in dealing with them at school.

The magnitude of this task has also been described, for it cannot be accomplished intuitively or as a side issue in education. If teachers are to know their pupils, this understanding must be planned for from the beginning. They must be trained for it, and schools must be organized and operated in such ways that the information they need will be readily available to them. Time must be set aside and used to help them understand the individuals they are teaching each year. A suitable code of ethics must govern the way the information and insights are communicated and used. And the school must be operated in such a way that the implications of what the teacher understands about each child can be put to use in daily interaction between the teacher and the child, without conflict with requirements and institutional procedures. It can be done.

PART FOUR

On Changing
the Educative Process

CHAPTER 12

Education Is Changing

Extensive experience in any area of human endeavor leads a person to make generalizations about it. Naturally such conclusions must be tested objectively before one recommends their acceptance by others. Sixteen years of experience in public school situations, simultaneous with experimentation in the development of our child-study program, has led me to certain conclusions about the educative process. These conclusions are presented in this chapter, not as fully and objectively tested truth, but as preliminary conclusions or hypotheses which should be, and can be, tested objectively. For if these conclusions are true, they imply the need for extensive changes in educational practice.

The experiences that have given rise to these conclusions were of three kinds. More than a thousand times I have sat with a group of a dozen teachers for a period of two hours, have heard them read the records they have compiled about individual children, and have helped them work out interpretations of why these children behaved as they did and learned, or failed to learn, as they did. Then we have tried to figure out practical ways of helping these children. I have had this experience in the schools of fifteen states in all regions of the country, in large cities, in small towns, and in rural areas. In addition, I have had the experience of reading critically more than a thousand case records made by participants throughout a whole school year and interpreted by the teacher with the assistance of the group. A third set of experiences has included long talks with hundreds of school staff members—principals, supervisors, superintendents, teachers, counsellors, and classroom teachers. We have discussed the concrete problems they faced in developing educational policy and in carrying out educational practice in such ways as to give each child his chance for full development and wholesome adjustment.

These experiences have forced me to draw certain conclusions about the effects of present educational practice on *some* children, ways in which education is changing for the better, and ways in which further improvement can be effected. The most cogent of these conclusions are the following:

1. Many children actually become maladjusted as a result of attending school. This is because the demands made upon them at school are inappropriate to their capacities, maturity levels, experience backgrounds, motivations, and developmental tasks.

2. Many children who are maladjusted because of factors outside school are unrecognized as such and not only do not receive the help they need, but become more maladjusted because of the way they are dealt with at school and go on to later breakdowns or delinquency.

3. The capacities of many children for becoming more than average in social usefulness and personal creativity are never recognized and developed because routine tasks, rigid curricula, and standardized teaching techniques kill their curiosity and creativity and no one is close enough to them to realize what is happening to them.

4. Most children have periods in their school life when they face real adjustment difficulties and are greatly in need of help based on genuine understanding. This is particularly true of adolescents.

5. In many communities, schools have improved tremendously in these matters during the past sixteen years, but in others they have stood still, or even regressed, in response to the wave of public criticism of education that has arisen during recent years. For, although schools have often failed to accomplish the educational miracles expected of them, the reasons for this have seldom been those put forward by the most vigorous critics of education. So the effect of criticism has been to make improvement more difficult rather than easier.

6. With adequate in-service training through the necessary period of time, *teachers can learn to understand individual children* well enough to make truly wise decisions in dealing with them in the classroom. Of this I am completely sure because I have seen it happen so many times.

7. When a teacher understands a child or youth he virtually always can figure out ways of helping him even though the causes of the difficulty lie outside the school.

8. Arbitrary regulations and rigid school practices often make it difficult for the teacher to give the child the experiences he needs.

9. Lack of the necessary information about individuals is one of the factors that make it impossible for most teachers to understand most children at present. The necessary information is seldom gathered until the child is already in serious difficulty.

10. In many school systems, an amazing and unwholesome apartness exists between schools and homes. Except for superficial P.T.A. contacts with a minority of the parents, teachers never see a parent unless the child is in trouble of some kind. Yet all that we know of human development indicates that a partnership between school and home is necessary for the best learning

and development in the child. In my judgment the school and the home should be close partners in the education and development of every child.

This chapter will describe what must be done to make it possible for teachers genuinely to understand their pupils as individuals and to act effectively on the basis of this understanding to help the child become all that he potentially can become, given his life situation. Most of the things described are actually being done somewhere, for I have not had the wit to invent them before some practical school person has tried them. Thus in most instances I am merely reporting what I have seen. But no one school system is, as yet, doing all these things.

Practicing a Philosophy of Education

I have repeatedly had the experience of participating in educational meetings where a rather high-sounding philosophy of education was stated in very general terms, and then of visiting schools in the same area where this philosophy was violated in practice in dozens of ways, as a matter of expediency. Invariably I have found that this tends to make teachers cynical and reluctant "to stick their necks out" in the effort to help individual pupils. Yet a philosophy is a series of value assumptions that are supposed to be of real help in decision making when alternatives present a dilemma.

The philosophy of totalitarian societies is clear-cut and decisive. The state and its demands come first, and the individual must be bent in conformity with these authoritarian expectancies. But in a democracy, the individual is the factor of value, for we have faith that institutions, the government, and society as a whole can continue to evolve in ways that will give every individual the chance for full self-realization in a context of social responsibility and usefulness. This assumption of the value of the individual self and of his inherent rights underlies our historical evolution as a society and is buttressed by the religious convictions held by the vast majority of our citizens.

But, unless one consciously makes use of one's philosophical assumptions in decision making, institutional regulations and traditional practices have a way of shaping our decisions. The needs of the individual are readily lost from view and frequently remain unmet as institutional processes grind on. This happens all too often in school. We recognized from the beginning of our child-study program that we were operating on the basis of certain philosophical assumptions when we brought scientific knowledge and skill in the scientific method to teachers. So in our work we have always affirmed our conviction that every human being is valuable and has a right to the conditions, relationships, and experiences that will ensure his best self-realization as a responsible and useful member of society. Indeed, we have kept this value assumption conscious and lively in the thinking of participants in our child-study program as they tried to understand individual children and to figure out ways of helping them.

The results have been most interesting to observe. A teacher asks himself, "How can this child be valuable in the classroom? On the playground? Around the school?" Then he asks the child to do small, helpful things. In a little while the teacher begins "to see something in that kid after all." As this happens the child gradually begins to get a sense of personal worth and to feel valued in a small way by his teacher and often by his peers as well. Sometimes helping teachers to make their philosophy articulate and functional seems to be the most important thing that happens through child study.

Another teacher may question his own value as a person, asking himself what he really accomplishes as a member of the teaching profession. Since he is participating in the child-study program, this question leads him to examine the significance of his daily classroom decisions in relation to the development of individual children. Of course, he finds that the children's happiness or unhappiness is very much a function of what goes on in the classroom, and he finds it possible to enhance the happiness of many individuals.

But he also discovers that he is the only person in the world who understands what really is happening, developmentally, to certain children. This produces both anxiety and a sense of personal significance, for he sees that responsibility comes with understanding. He becomes sincerely concerned when his plans to help do not work out effectively and happy when he sees his efforts actually helping individual children to learn or to adjust. However, we constantly emphasize to participants the fact that they are never to regard themselves as therapists, but only as facilitators of healthy growth. Thus we encourage all participants to refer children to counsellors, school psychologists, clinics, or psychiatrists when their insights tell them that the child's adjustment problem is severe or when their own efforts to facilitate healthy development do not seem to bear fruit. Large numbers of teachers tell us that their own sense of personal worth has been enhanced by learning to see more clearly the parts they play in the development of individual children.

However, child study does increase the tension a teacher feels if, when he glimpses what a child needs and tries to do something constructive about it, he is blocked by the decision of an administrator, arbitrary rules, or discouraging and resistant attitudes from fellow teachers. We try to reassure such participants by pointing out how hopeless a child's situation would be without their understanding help and by citing changes in policy and practice that we know to be occurring in many places. So despite the occasional increase in anxiety, teachers usually feel a great enhancement of their own personal significance as professional persons when they consciously try to act on the assumption that every child is valuable and has potentialities for development still to be realized.

THE PARTNERSHIP OF HOME AND SCHOOL

Most parents value their children highly and are eager to see them grow in knowledge and skills through their school experiences. They are concerned about their children's health and interested in their rates of physical maturing. They want them to be well-liked by their playmates and to be successful in games and sports. Character development, including learning a sound code of ethics, acceptable patterns of courtesy, and social responsibility and diligence at assigned tasks are other great concerns of parents. Most parents also want their children to be happy and become anxious about them when the children show signs of continuing tension or maladjustment. So the concerns of parents about their children are identical with the professional concerns of teachers about these same children.

Children's Experiences at Home

The school day usually is only about six hours long for five days a week during nine months a year. The schools are responsible for the conditions, relationships, and experiences that make up the child's life during this time. But parents are responsible for the conditions, relationships, and experiences that comprise the child's life during the remainder of every twenty-four hours and for two whole days a week even while school is in session. The parent-regulated part of each child's day affords highly significant learning experiences for him and also carries expectancies and demands for certain kinds of actions, attitudes, and deportment. Health habits and medical care, home tasks and chores, religious training, recreational experiences, neighborhood and community contacts, family life, and all vacation experiences are regulated by the parents.

Here, then, are two good reasons why the school and the home should feel themselves partners in the education of every child. They are equally concerned for the full, wholesome development of particular children; and the home regulates so much more of each child's learning and the experiences that shape his development than does the school that the school cannot understand the child's interests, needs, motivations, and view of life without an intimate relationship with the home.

As we have worked through the years in various school systems, we have seen the following activities carried out successfully in different places. No one place does all of them, yet each activity has its particular value in developing mutual understanding between parents and teachers and in promoting the healthy development of children. Each of these activities has been carried out successfully somewhere.

Mothers' Clubs

Mothers' clubs are formed in the first grade, the teacher taking the initiative. Meetings are held monthly at the school, during the school day, and mothers observe their own children engaging in the various activities of the classroom and playground. Then the teacher and the parents sit down together and discuss the goals of these activities and the reasons why they are conducted as they are. At the end of the year these first-grade mothers feel so much a part of the school and are so enthusiastic about their experiences that they organize parties for the children who will enter the first-grade the following September, along with their mothers. The party introduces the new children and their mothers to their prospective teacher and to the classroom and its materials. At the party, play activities are organized, both in the classroom and on the playground, with the first-grade children encouraging and leading the new children to participate. Then come refreshments, and the new mothers are encouraged to organize the first-grade mothers' club for the following year.

This plan has been carried out, with great effectiveness, in the Negro schools in a number of Maryland communities. It is evaluated by school people as contributing greatly to children's adjustment to their first school experiences and to winning support in the home for the educational activities of the school. It works very well in rural communities and with underprivileged parents, as well as in town centers.

Home Visits by First-grade Teachers

Kindergarten or first-grade classes meet for a half-day only during the first month of school. During the free half-day, the teacher visits the home of every child in her class. The first objective of this visit is to establish a friendly rapport with the parents, to explain to them the aims of the school for the year, and to describe how the school will operate. The second purpose is to make the parent feel that the teacher needs to see the child through the parents' eyes, to have the parent give to her such information about the child's earlier development and experiences as will enable her to understand the child's needs and motivation. The third purpose is to obtain needed information for the child's cumulative record. The result usually is a very friendly feeling toward the school on the part of the parents and a willingness, later, to discuss all matters of mutual concern frankly and fully.

Home Visits by Elementary School Teachers

Teachers in every grade in eight-grade elementary schools visit the homes of every one of their pupils at least once during each school year. These first-hand contacts with each child's life space and with some of the persons most closely related to him give the teacher a realistic, meaningful, and vivid appreciation of each child's background and relationships and sometimes of what a particular child is up against in terms of adjustment problems. These insights could never be gained from written records alone. At the same time, parents have an informal social experience with each child's teacher which permits them to interpret more accurately the accounts given by the child of his school experiences. Best of all, perhaps, the parents feel that the school really is sincerely interested in their children's learning and development and is ready to do everything possible to help. Because these visits are made without reference to disciplinary problems or school failures, the parents lose their defensive attitudes in relation to school people and, when problems do arise, tend to cooperate more readily with the school.

Of course, these home visits are recognized as a part of each teacher's regular professional work, and the time required for them is considered in planning other activities. Where administrators and teachers agree on the need for home visits, many different means can be found to free teachers for this work and to provide transportation.

Parent Conferences at School

Two conferences per year between the teacher and a parent of each child are substituted for, or used to supplement, regular report cards. These conferences usually occur in the classroom after school so that the teacher is able to show the parent examples of the child's work, textbooks, and other study materials and to describe the child's part in the group projects that are a part of his work. The purpose of these conferences is to analyze various aspects of the child's development and find ways in which the home and the school can work together consistently to encourage and guide the child. These conferences are most successful where an initial extended home visit by the first-grade teacher and annual visits by other teachers are the custom, and where the teacher prepares carefully for each conference by analyzing the child's cumulative record.

Classroom P.T.A. Meetings

Parent-teacher groups devote a part of most meetings to visits to classrooms; there the teacher explains the work of the class in various subject-matter areas and tells how the children work together to facilitate each other's learning and carry out group projects. In numerous instances groups of children are present to demonstrate certain learning processes and to display their own work materials to the parents. Parents often are amazed at their children's knowledge and at their facility in discussions. Children also frequently lead the devotionals which sometimes open the parents' meetings, or provide part of the program by singing or making dramatic presentations, which they have written themselves, appropriate to certain patriotic or holiday celebrations. Thus in many ways the school experiences of children become real to their parents.

Parent Child-study Groups

Parent-teacher associations organize parent child-study groups. These groups have many diverse activities in the various communities in which we work, and each different process seems to have its appropriateness for particular groups. Some groups begin with monthly meetings at which guest lecturers discuss some aspect of human development. Perhaps a psychiatrist, a physician, a psychologist, an educator, and a minister appear in sequence, or one of these gives a series of lectures followed by discussion. Other groups are organized as discussion groups at the outset. These groups are led by school psychologists, counsellors, or the leaders of teacher child-study groups. Some groups see and discuss motion pictures or mental hygiene skits suggested or outlined by the National Society for Mental Health. Other groups have parent leaders chosen from among themselves, and the discussions center around reports of ideas presented in books or articles selected by the group as of special interest to them. Still other groups choose not only their own leaders but the topics to be discussed at each meeting and employ group processes for developing ideas out of their own experiences through discussion. Some school systems hold regular workshops, with outside consultants, to help the parent leaders get the scientific knowledge they need, to guide them in practicing various group processes, and to assist them in analyzing reports of meetings their groups have held. Most parent groups seem to like some combination of these various methods. Wise and enthusiastic leadership seems to be the key to their success, and training periods for the leaders, with expert help, seem to pay good dividends in continued interest and participation.

A number of values are ascribed to these parent child-study groups. They bring needed scientific knowledge about human development and behavior to the parents and help to dispel popular misconceptions and superstitions. They greatly reassure parents, who learn that all children face problems in the course of growing up and that many other parents face problems similar to their own and are dealing with them successfully. The discussions suggest many alternative ways of handling numerous specific situations, leaving each parent free to choose the pattern which seems most appropriate for him. Many sources of information and of help are brought to the parents' attention through these meetings, including pamphlets, books, school services, community agencies, clinics, and research centers. The parents acquire some skill in being objective about their children and in discussing with others the factors that are shaping their children's development. This prepares them for more fruitful conferences with the teachers of their children.

Parents as "Grade Mothers"

Many schools encourage certain parents to act as "grade mothers." It is the function of these parents to help in many ways in carrying on the educational activities of the class—by arranging transportation and accompanying the children on trips to places of educational value, helping to arrange and hold class parties to celebrate birthdays or patriotic occasions, helping to procure materials needed for class projects, including enlisting the help of fathers in certain scientific or construction projects, and helping to sponsor socially useful class activities. Grade mothers have experiences which permit them to know the daily work of schools intimately, and so they can be spokesmen for the schools to other parents, helping them to understand better the why's and wherefore's of certain activities or happenings.

There are, of course, many other ways in which individual parents and committees of parents help the schools of their communities. The activities we have discussed illustrate the fact that the education of children actually is a partnership between the school and the parents of the children in the school. Anything that can bring understanding of these children to both parties concerned is of great value. For this reason schools can profit greatly by consciously devoting a significant amount of the professional time and activity of school personnel to working closely with parents in the effort to understand each child, sharing insights with each other, and working out joint plans for helping each child and youth become all that he potentially can become.

CUMULATIVE RECORDS

Teachers can learn to understand their pupils as developing individuals only if they have access to the necessary information about each child. And very few school systems have records which contain the needed facts. It follows that training teachers to be able and to want to understand children is futile unless the information they need is systematically recorded from the moment each child enters school. For no teacher has the time or strength to gather this amount of information each year about thirty or more individuals and still to carry on his many other professional tasks.

The Scope of Needed Information

A major reason for outlining the scope of the forces that shape human learning and development and showing that these factors vary from child to child was to call attention to the kinds of information that must be included in cumulative records if they are to be functional. For the content of the personnel records about each child must be sufficient to permit sound initial conclusions to be reached, early in the school year, about how each of these factors operates for each child. This implies a developmental history of the child before entering school, medical and health information, growth information, facts about interpersonal relationships in the home, data about the cultural background and socioeconomic status of the family, information about the child's interaction with his peers, test findings about the child's learning capacities and subject-matter accomplishment, illustrative samples of his work in various subjects, observational information about the way he uses his mental processes, facts giving clues to his attitudes, codes of conduct, values, and goals, information about adjustment problems which he faces and the ways in which he manages himself in emotion-producing situations, and periodic analyses of how he is functioning in the light of the interaction of these factors.

Clearly, no "cumulative-record form" can cover all this. A folder is needed, containing various open forms for different areas, in which successive teachers can record new pertinent facts and evidences of growth. An accompanying manual to guide teachers in recording their observations has been found helpful in several places.[1]

Role of the Child's First Teacher

The heaviest task in building the necessary record falls upon the child's initial teacher, usually the kindergarten or first-grade teacher. Two plans for making it feasible for her to do the job successfully are suggested. The first is to have the kindergarten or first grade meet for a half-day only during the first six weeks of school. This leaves the teacher free during the afternoon—or evening in cases where both parents work— to make a visit of an hour or more to one home per day and still to have time to write up the visit during the same day. Such visits enable a trained teacher to get an adequate developmental history of the child and a good initial picture of the interpersonal relationships within the

---

[1] *Manual to Explain the Use of Cumulative Records in Parker District Schools.* Greenville, S.C.: Greenville County Board of Education, 1947, Mimeographed.

family as well as of the family's cultural background and social functioning in the community. We have seen this plan work out extremely well in certain communities.

A second possibility is to employ the teacher for three weeks or a month before school opens to register all children entering school for the first time, to make the necessary home visits, and to initiate the cumulative record for each child. Few school systems have the money to employ social workers to do this job; at any rate, having the child's teacher do it offers the advantage of permitting the development of a home–school partnership in the education of the child before any untoward happening can prejudice this relationship.

Keeping the Record Up-to-date

For each year after the child's initial year at school, the teacher's responsibility for continuing the development of his cumulative record should be clearly defined, the responsibility should be spaced throughout the school year, an analysis of the time required should be made in each school system, and this time should be taken into consideration when other plans requiring work by individual teachers are developed. There is at present a disturbing tendency to employ additional persons for supervisory and other special services part of whose work is to organize more meetings and additional time-demanding activities from teachers without setting up an adequate coordinating process that prevents the overloading of the most willing teachers and insures that the time load is equitably distributed. There are grounds for anxiety lest these services, good in themselves, shall so overload the classroom teacher that time does not remain to analyze and understand individual children. Indeed, in certain communities overloading has caused a lowering of teacher morale and the beginnings of an undesirable mood of discounting and resisting these services. This is not an argument against adequate supervisory services, for they are most desirable. It is rather a plea for the careful study of how teachers' time is employed and for the careful coordination of the work of supervisors with other special services.

Access to Records

Cumulative records that are filed in the principal's office and never used except in times of trouble or at the end of the year are of little value. In the elementary schools of one school system, an alternative plan is used. The industrial arts department has made a wooden file with a lock for each elementary school classroom, in which the personnel folders for each child are kept and where teachers have ready access to them. The principal's office contains the cumulative public records of enrollment, attendance, subjects studied, and marks. This system works extremely well, and the teachers regularly consult the records prior to periodic conferences with parents and at times when they need help in interpreting puzzling behavior or working out plans for adapting curricular experiences to the backgrounds and motivations of individual children. Under this system teachers make many more entries in the records than formerly when the files were kept in the principals' offices. The system has the added advantage of keeping the records confidential, for outside persons do not have access to these personnel folders as they sometimes do to the public records. This makes teachers willing to enter in these records vital facts which they are often reluctant to place in more public files for fear of damage to the reputation of a child or his family. There should be a law requiring that these personnel folders be considered confidential and privileged, just as a physician's records are; for it does not seem possible for schools to care for the mental health of developing children and youth unless they have information that should be handled confidentially.

Early Interpretation of the Records

No matter how adequate and how accessible the cumulative records are, they are of little value unless they are interpreted by each child's teacher at the beginning of each year and at other times as needed. In recent years I have participated in the activities of many school systems just prior to or early in the school year. Seldom, if ever, have I seen provision made for teachers to have time for and assistance in the analysis of the cumulative records in the attempt to get an early understanding of their new charges. In fact, many teachers have told me that they prefer not to look at the records for some months lest they be prejudiced against a child by the judgments or opinions of other teachers so frequently found in the usual records. This, of course, is a condemnation of the value of the records and a statement about the nature of the training the teacher has received.

School people may look forward to the time when all teachers will be employed for ten full months a year and will start work three or four weeks before schools actually open. Half of each day during this period could be spent studying and interpreting the cumulative records of their new pupils with the help of school psychologists, visiting consultants, helping teachers, supervisors, principals, and counsellors. Certainly both principals and supervisors would make wiser judgments and be of more help to teachers later in the year if they had participated in the analyses of the records of certain children. They would appreciate more fully what these children are and what they are facing in their daily lives. Consequently, they would understand the teacher's task better. As a result of this study of cumulative records, the other half-days during the preschool work period would be more fruitfully used, for curriculum or guidance workshops would then operate in the context of knowledge of and insight into the pupils to be affected by the outcomes of these workshops. The vitalization of subject matter and the development of superior learning operations would be accomplished better with the children more vividly in mind. Philosophical assumptions would not be stated in vague general terms but would be tested in terms of how to deal with specific individuals.

In-service Education of Teachers

It goes without saying that most teachers are not yet adequately trained either to build the sort of cumulative records I have been describing or to interpret them where they may exist. So the suggestions I have made above cannot be put into effect overnight. We carried on a child-study program in one community for seven years before the teachers were ready and able to rebuild their cumulative records; and new teachers coming into that system require considerable supplementary training before they can interpret available records adequately. This is not to say that a like period of training is required in all systems or that our child-study program is the only or even the most effective way of carrying out this training. It means rather that simply revising cumulative record forms will not result either in adequate records or in their effective use. The people who are to make and use the records must be carefully trained in both processes.

CURRICULAR IMPLICATIONS

The Educational Tradition

Despite the uniqueness of every individual, children must have most of their school experiences in groups, and this is highly desirable. It does, however, pose difficult problems for educational administrators, because the educational tradition under which we operate regards each class group as a "grade" rather than as a grouping of children for effective learning. Classes commonly are thought of as first grades, fifth grades, tenth grades, and so on. Each grade suggests to parents and to most teachers, too, a specific body of information and a specific set of skills which each and every child should learn in that particular grade—in other words, a definitive "grade-level standard" to be met. The accomplishment of these particular learnings is required to justify "promotion" to the next higher grade. The lack of a significant proportion of the expected learnings, usually anything over "30 per cent," is supposed to represent a "failure" on the child's part. In such cases, the tradition maintains, the child should be held back to repeat the work of that grade in order to prepare himself adequately to do the work of the next higher grade.

The learnings required in each grade are simply the knowledges and skills that traditionally have been regarded as necessary for effective adult living; in this tradition, they have been split up into a series of "subjects" that were given names such as reading, writing, arithmetic, history, geography, grammar, spelling, English composition, biology, chemistry, drawing, music, etc. Most parents and teachers still feel that children should learn these logically organized subjects bit by bit at appropriate grade levels and that this is the best way to ensure that each child will enter life with a mind well equipped to meet its demands and with thoroughly habituated skills.

Scientific Research Bears Fruit

Each year the Federal government and many state governments spend millions of dollars for scientific research at agricultural experiment stations to find out how to breed and grow superior cattle, poultry, and crops. As rapidly as new knowledge is acquired, it is disseminated to the farmers of the nation through thousands of county agents, with the result that agriculture has increased its productivity enormously during the past half-century and requires many fewer persons to carry on its work. Industry, too, spends many millions of dollars each year for scientific research and for working out the practical application of new knowledge. New machines and manufacturing processes and a great variety of new products have been developed which have raised our standards of living immeasurably during the same period. Medicine also has improved its practice wonderfully in the past half-century by applying what has been learned through scientific research. The life span has been lengthened considerably, and the deadliness of many diseases has been greatly reduced. Great strides also have been made in the prevention of disease.

Human-development Research

During this same period, much less money has been spent for scientific research into how human beings grow and learn and why they behave and develop as they do than has been spent for agricultural and industrial research. Private foundations have contributed the greater part of this money and deserve great applause and gratitude from the public for their recognition of the need and their initiative in encouraging this relatively neglected area of research. Nevertheless, despite the limited resources available, the sciences that study human beings have made great progress during the past three decades and uncovered new knowledge of enormous value and significance to school people. Indeed, the facts uncovered show very clearly and beyond any possibility of objective refutation that the traditional organization and processes for educating children described above are generally quite ineffective and, in numerous cases, actually damaging to the development and adjustment of children.

Public Unawareness of Research Findings

But the dissemination of these findings to the public has been sporadic, piecemeal, and disorganized. Scientists have taken the position that their task is to do the research, and educators have been more concerned with finding ways to improve the educative processes than with telling the public why improvement is necessary. Perhaps educators have not seen the necessity for taking to parents the explicit facts uncovered by scientific research, which show that schools of the old type are unwholesome places for many children. Or perhaps they are not yet sure enough that they have better ways of guiding children's learning and development, since they have usually lacked both funds and human resources for adequate evaluation of their experiments. The most probable reason, however, is that educators simply have not had the money and personnel required to obtain the scientific facts and to test their implications soundly over a period of time, because they are overwhelmed with the tasks of providing physical plants, teachers, materials for learning, transportation, special services, and a thousand other things made necessary by the fact that during the past thirty years all the children of all the people have begun to stay in school until they are sixteen or even eighteen years of age. So the public continues to demand, very widely, a pattern of education that students of the life sciences and leaders of education know is ineffective and often damaging. This is yet another reason why the activities described above as necessary to build a partnership between the home and the school are so important.

Why Traditional Schools Are Undesirable

So many teachers experience serious emotional conflicts about whether to enforce "grade-level standards" or to try to adapt the work in their classes to the capacities and needs of their pupils that it seems wise to provide here a minimum list of reasons why the traditional, piecemeal, lock-step pattern of education simply cannot work, despite the fact that to present such a list means approaching the subject of the traditional schools negatively.

1. Children mature physically at strikingly different rates. Some normal, healthy six-year-olds in the first grade will have the organic maturity usual to children at four-and-a-half years, whereas others will have the physical maturity usually achieved at seven-and-a-half years. Some normal, healthy twelve-year-old children will have the physical maturity usually achieved at nine years of age; others will already be developed to the point usual to fifteen-year-

olds. But children constantly work on developmental tasks appropriate to their organic-maturity levels; therefore, the motivation and needs of children are determined by their organic maturity rather than by their "mental ages." Mental ages and intelligence quotients are not indices of maturity but of brightness, of learning capacity. Hence a twelve-year-old child with an organic-maturity level of ten and a mental age of fourteen is actually a very bright ten-year-old in terms of interests, motivation, and needs, whereas a twelve-year-old with an organic-maturity level of fourteen and a mental age of ten is really a fourteen-year-old with a limited learning capacity but with the interests, motivation, and needs common to fourteen-year-olds.

2. A child's perceptions—what experiences mean to him—are a function of his maturity level, cultural background, accumulated individual experiences, values, goals, and emotional preoccupations. Children vary enormously in these, so a given classroom experience must have a different meaning for each child. Therefore, identical or standardized outcomes cannot be obtained from all children by the same instructional means. Where standardized outcomes are necessary for all, as with number facts, the spelling and meaning of words, and grammatical usage, the teacher must be prepared to vary the learning experiences for a good many children.

3. If what one learns is to be useful to him as a basis for understanding, thinking, and solving his life problems, it must be learned in relation to his total life experience and situation rather than in isolation. Therefore, subject matter has more usable meanings when learned through broad units of work than when learned as separate subjects; and skills are developed more effectively by functional use than by meaningless drills. This is ample justification for the "unit of work" in the elementary school and for the core course at the secondary level.

4. Ideas and attitudes are not learned once and for all at a particular time. They grow gradually and gain richer meaning as they are related to the experiences being accumulated by the child. Thus learning is a continuous process in every area of knowledge and not something that can be completed in a particular grade or through the study of a particular subject.

5. Each child's full and wholesome development requires that he work at many learning tasks not touched by the traditional curriculum. More than half his developmental tasks are not dealt with by these subjects, yet the accomplishment of these tasks is necessary to his development and therefore must become the concern of the school.

6. Difficult, emotion-producing adjustment problems occupy the attention of many children to the exclusion of most unrelated matters, such as the content of many subjects. Therefore, many children are unable to understand and learn particular skills and subject-matter areas until they have made progress toward acquiring feelings of safety, security, belonging, and adequacy. Yet, although they are not capable of much traditional subject-matter learning, they can profit tremendously from classroom experiences and interpersonal relationships at school, which contribute to meeting their emotional needs. And once they make progress toward adjustment they often learn the necessary facts and skills with considerable rapidity.

Imp.
Dev.
Tasks

7. Wherever children are brought together for a considerable period of time, a child society develops, with its own goals, activities, and customs. Most of these activities are developmental, being concerned with the accomplishment of developmental tasks and with physical and social functioning not provided for elsewhere. Winning roles and belonging in this child society is important for every child and occupies a considerable amount of his thought, time, and energy at school. It is therefore a matter of concern for school people; indeed, it is a significant part of the school's actual operating curriculum, from which each child learns much that will be of fundamental value to him throughout life.

8. Research has shown that holding children back to repeat a grade while their friends move ahead has very unwholesome effects upon their behavior and adjustment.[2] Nonpromoted children exhibited more troublesome behavior, were more inattentive, less cooperative, more easily discouraged, and worried about their failure. They choose companions from among their former classmates rather than from among their current classmates. Nonpromotion gives a child a difficult adjustment problem and often leads to truancy and leaving school.

9. A child's concept of himself is altered by nonpromotion in such a way that he tends to lose confidence in himself and has a much lower level of aspiration in relation both to his schoolwork and to what he hopes to become.[3] This means that nonpromoted children are not stimulated to do better work, but on the contrary actually are influenced to set lower goals for themselves and to try less hard.

10. Elsbree and McNally [4] have evaluated the research findings and conclude that nonpromotion does not maintain graded school standards, reduce variation within grades, provide good motivation, enable slow learners to catch up, or bring about better adjustment in pupils. In other words, teachers' tasks are not simplified by the practice of "failing" children, but on the contrary may be made more difficult.

11. Caswell and Foshay [5] cite a number of research findings which show that "failing" children who are promoted actually show greater progress than similar pupils who are held back. Obviously the enforcement of grade-level standards defeats its purpose. Otto compared the work of groups of second- and fifth-grade children who were assured of passing to the next grade with that of equivalent groups who did not have this assurance.[6] The gain in edu-

[2] Sandin, A. A. *Social and Emotional Adjustment of Regularly Promoted and Nonpromoted Pupils.* New York: Bureau of Publications, Teachers College, Columbia University, 1944.

[3] Barker, Roger G. Success and Failure in the Classroom. *Progressive Education,* 1942, **19,** 221–224.

[4] Elsbree, W. S., and McNally, J. H. *Elementary School Administration and Supervision.* New York: American Book Company, 1951, pp. 141–148.

[5] Caswell, H. A., and Foshay, A. W. *Education in the Elementary School.* New York: American Book Company, 1950.

[6] Otto, H. J. *Elementary School Organization and Administration.* New York: Appleton-Century-Crofts, 1944.

cational age was greater in the groups that were assured of promotion. So objective research has demonstrated the superiority in practice of regarding learning as a continuous development for each child regardless of the class group in which he is placed.

This list was presented to show that traditional concepts of what the educative process should be run counter to what we know scientifically about how children develop and learn. It also showed that traditional procedures are not effective in practice and often are detrimental to a child's learning and adjustment. Furthermore, it shows that the traditional curriculum does not touch many of the interests and needs of developing children and youth.

Grouping Children for Learning

Our concept of a school class should be that it is a means of grouping children for most effective learning and not that it is a "grade" at a certain stage on the educational ladder where all children must learn the same things at the same time in the same way. Nor should we think of children as being "promoted" from one grade to another; rather we should see each child as making steady progress, appropriate to his own rate of maturing, intellectual competence, and experience background, toward gaining the knowledge and skills he needs for full self-realization and social usefulness.

Viewed in this way, the concept of "grades" loses its meaning and the concept of a class as a place for developing through learning and action takes its place. Parents and teachers will welcome this concept of a class because it is realistic and frees both the teacher and the parents from the bugaboos of failure and rigidity. Far from "lowering standards," this concept of a school class permits the teacher to accept each child where he is and to use the most effective means of helping him to take his next steps in learning in each area of his development and on the basis of a genuine understanding of him.

Promising Adaptations of the Educative Process

It is the function of the Institute for Child Study to help teachers learn to understand children as developing individuals. It is not our role to promote any particular pattern of education, for we work in all types of schools, from the most traditional to the most modern, and feel that, no matter how the school is organized, its teachers still need to know the forces that shape the development and learning of their pupils. Furthermore, we know that every school system must evolve in its own way, and we believe this evolution is the joint task of school administrators and teachers working together with the school board and the parents.

Consequently, the adaptations of educational arrangements and processes listed below are not "promoted" by our staff in specific communities. They are presented here as possibilities for educators to consider as they try to operate schools in ways that are consistent with the healthy development of children in the light of modern scientific knowledge. Some of these procedures are certainly inappropriate for particular communities at present. Others are at best only transitional measures.

Marking on the Basis of Individual Growth. Because children naturally mature at strikingly different rates, because their perceptions are personal and based on their individual experience backgrounds and emotional preoccupations, and because learning is continuous and unitary rather than piecemeal, many school systems are basing school marks and evaluations on the individual's growth in knowledge and skill. In other words, each pupil is marked on the gain he has made in comparison with what he knew before, instead of in relation to a grade-level standard. The availability of reliable and valid standardized tests of certain skills and areas of knowledge has helped to make this feasible. But test results always have to be supplemented by the analysis of samples of the pupils' day-by-day work and by anecdotal material showing how the child utilizes his mental processes.

Marking on this basis points up with special force to teachers, parents, and pupils the fact that expectancies of accomplishment must be very much higher for gifted children than for pupils with average capacities. It also emphasizes the need of gifted children for opportunities to do independent study and for supplementary experiences beyond the usual subject-matter requirements instead of more of the same thing, for without these enriching experiences and without help in pushing ahead in independent study, the gifted child fails to make the progress he should. Many gifted children "loaf" through traditional schools with rigid grade-level standards and still make high marks. Marking on the basis of individual accomplishment also spares the dull child the social humiliation of "failure" and the consequent lowering of his level of aspiration below what he actually is able to accomplish.

Combination Classes. To make acceleration and enrichment more practical for the gifted, and to make work at their capacity levels more feasible for the dull, many school systems are using "combination classes." That is, fourth and fifth grades or fifth and sixth grades are mixed in the same classrooms, and individual children work in groups within these classes. In this way dull children are stimulated by and learn from the more advanced, who play leadership roles on class committees and report on what they have learned through independent study. At the same time, friendship groups and peer-group learnings appropriate to the organic-maturity level of the children are maintained. Children are reported to learn more in these combination grades because rigid grade lines are deemphasized and teachers are able to make better provision for individual differences.

Grade Classification on the Basis of Chronological Age. Many schools have adopted the policy of classifying children entirely on the basis of chronological age, except in extreme cases. According to this system, which has been called the policy of universal promotion, every child moves ahead to the next grade every year. W. W. Cook[7] reports that controlled research studies have shown that this policy does not result in greater extremes and variations among pupils in upper-grade classes, lower their average achievement, or reduce the incentives of pupils to learn, as had been feared. It has the advantage of eliminating "failure," with its consequent psychological damage, without reducing or limiting the learning accomplishments of the pupils. But it may not provide adequately for accelerating early-maturing children or for placing slow-growers with their maturity-level peers. Nevertheless, this policy is being widely and successfully applied, although exceptions are made when implied by a given child's developmental rate.

The "Primary-unit" Organization. A practice that is being widely adopted and appears to be a common-sense step toward adapting educational practice to the needs of individual children is that of organizing schools into primary and intermediate units. The primary unit carries on the work of the child's first three years of schooling, where children enter at the age of six, and of the first four years where they enter at the age of five. There are no grades and no promotions or failures. Children are grouped in terms of organic and social maturity and learning readiness. Groups progress in their learnings at rates appropriate to their maturity levels, readiness, and capacities; and a child who outstrips or falls behind his group or is socially uncomfortable in it can be moved into another group at any time for the particular learning experiences he needs. The grouping is flexible, and children may function in several different groups during a given period.

Some high-capacity and early-maturing children may complete the three years of work in two years and move into the intermediate unit after that time. Those who grow up organically and socially more slowly than the average may require four years of preparation for work in the intermediate unit, but at no time will they fail or be demoted. The child who needs more than three years in the primary unit will be shifted into a slower learning group whenever the need becomes apparent. Since these adjustments are made in consultation with parents and on the basis

[7] Cook, Walter W. Grouping and Promotion in the Elementary School. Series on the Individualization of Instruction, No. 2. Minneapolis: University of Minnesota, 1941. Also, Individual Differences and Curriculum Practice. *J. Educ. Psych.*, 1948, 39, 141–148.

of joint analyses of the children's learning and developmental rates, there is never the distress, blaming, and pressure at home that damages so many children who "fail" in traditional schools. Furthermore, the flexible organization of the unit requires that every child must be well understood by his teacher or teachers, with the result that better records are developed and decisions are based on a broad analysis of all the different aspects of the child's development.

Cutting across Class Lines. School people are now realizing that important learnings occur in all situations where children of widely different ages work together in a variety of activities. Therefore, many activities that cut across class lines are now planned and carried out on a school-wide basis. One of the best of these activities is student government, in which each class works out its own rules for living together, elects representatives to an all-school legislature and administrative body that develops an over-all code, and reexamines policies from time to time in terms of how well they work. Junior safety patrols also involve children from a number of different classes in many schools. Planning and presenting assembly programs often require the cooperation of pupils from a number of classes. Lunchroom and housekeeping committees for the school as a whole facilitate interaction among children and adults and among children of different maturity levels. Indeed, when the importance of the learning that results from cooperative living together is recognized, endless possibilities for such learning appear at school. A recent book by Howard Lane and Mary Beauchamp is replete with illustrations.[8]

Cooperative Curriculum Planning. In many communities, school curriculums are outlined by committees made up of teachers, administrators, supervisors, parents, and other resource people from the community. Teachers often are supplied with printed resource guides, developed by these committees, which show the great variety of books, pictures, audiovisual aids, experiments, trips, and other resources for learning experiences. Then the children and the teacher of a given class work out the details of these experiences in what is called pupil-teacher planning. Together the children and the teacher define the specific aims they are seeking to accomplish within the larger framework, state the problems they face in working toward these aims, analyze the steps to be taken to solve these problems, organize themselves and allot responsibilities for specific tasks, plan how they will evaluate their progress toward the goals and then go into action to accomplish the necessary learnings.

Utilizing Group Processes. Much progress has been made in recent years in analyzing group processes and using the results of these analyses as guides in the teacher's own planning with children. Needless to say,

[8] Lane, Howard, and Beauchamp, Mary. *Human Relations in Teaching.* New York: Prentice-Hall, 1955.

this planning together makes possible a wide variety of roles for different children and better use of the various experience backgrounds and levels of competence of different children. In fact, individual differences cannot be provided for in the program without this kind of cooperative planning and action. It results in group skills, better thinking habits, and mutual respect among the children, which are important aspects of growing up.

Advantages of Pupil–Teacher Planning. Discipline almost ceases to be a problem under effective pupil–teacher planning, because the learning purposes are those of the children, who frown upon anything that interferes with the carrying out of their plans. It is easy to see how children grow to feel belonging, adequacy, and a sense of developing their potentialities by functioning day after day, month after month, and year after year in classrooms that operate in this manner. Not only are gifted children stimulated to become all that they have the potentiality to become, but less gifted ones are able to make significant contributions and to gain a sense of their value. Thus each child's concept of self is functionally developed, and each comes to see himself as he is and yet as valuable, even as essential to the whole group process. Furthermore, children who are maladjusted from out-of-school causes find a place where they have personal significance that is most supporting and even therapeutic. Uniqueness is recognized, accepted, and enhanced in directions that lead to social responsibility and usefulness.

Moving on with the Group. When one grasps the teacher's roles as those of living and planning with children for the children's learning and development and of making decisions from moment to moment that will facilitate this learning and development, it becomes clear that teachers must know each child intimately and must understand his motivation and needs thoroughly. As this is made possible by more adequate training, by building the necessary cumulative records, and by providing time and help through which to make the necessary evaluation of each child early in the school year, teachers show remarkable growth in capacity to work effectively with children and become much happier in their work. But many of them regret at the end of the year that they cannot continue to work with the same children. Consequently a good many school systems are now making it possible for teachers to stay with the same children over periods of two or three years, to the great advantage of everybody concerned. It is quite likely that this policy will be widely adopted during the next quarter century, for it does not make sense to cut off these understanding relationships annually.

GUIDANCE IN EDUCATION

Secondary School Students Need Understanding

It is generally assumed that high school teachers cannot be expected to understand their pupils as individuals because their work necessarily must be departmental, with the result that each teacher will have from 150 to 200 different students in his classes each semester. Obviously departmental teachers cannot learn to understand such a large number of young people each semester, and the consequence is serious: high school pupils are not understood as individuals by anyone at school until they begin to fail or get into trouble. My conviction is that each high school pupil should have some adult on the faculty of the school who understands him deeply and is a sort of sponsor or "friend at court" for him in the school. I have seen this worked out practically in three different ways.

Personnel Function of the Home Room

Perhaps the easiest way to solve the problem is to organize the school into home rooms for administrative purposes, as is usually done. The home-room teacher will be expected to stay with this group of young people as home-room teacher throughout their school life, be it three or four years. With adequate cumulative records sent up from the elementary school, with adequate time allotments for studying these records and having conferences with the students, and with a modest amount of training for this professional task, high school teachers generally can do an excellent job of understanding and guiding their home-room clients and of interpreting their motivations and needs to their colleagues. This personnel task is an essential part of the professional work of all public school teachers, and many high school teachers in our child-study groups have found a deep significance in this aspect of their work.

Furthermore, the taking on of this responsibility by "academic" teachers through their home rooms gives the school counsellors and deans more time to deal with pupils' adjustment problems. Under the present system, counsellors and deans are "snowed under" and can deal effectively only with the most severe cases because they must guide all the students in routine matters which could be cared for just as well by home-room teachers with adequate information. Again, the academic teachers themselves would profit by understanding a limited number of children deeply, for it would alter their attitudes toward many happenings in their classrooms, the significance of which they do not now grasp. Finally, the morale and mood of the whole school changes when all teachers have personnel functions, consult freely with each other in a professional way about the motivation and needs of individual pupils, and have counsellors and deans available to give prompt help to young people referred to them.

Mixed Home Rooms

A successful variant of this policy is to have home rooms made up in part of students from each grade level with the same teacher staying with the group throughout their time in school. This practice has the advantage of giving the home-room teacher about fifteen new individuals to learn each year instead of the usual forty or more all at once. Also, the older students can accept the responsibility for inducting the new ones into the traditions and ways of functioning of the school. This has been found to be a real advantage, for older students can answer many questions that trouble the freshmen, hazing is diminished, and the home rooms become responsible units in student government. School spirit was very high in one school in which this system operated because there was a feeling of oneness and of common purpose throughout the student body that does not exist in schools where the different grade levels maintain greater apartness.

Personnel Function of Core Teachers

A third way of organizing this vital personnel function at the secondary level is to give "core" teachers the responsibility for understanding the pupils in their classes and to have these teachers continue with the same groups at least for a second year. The core teacher's task already is a heavy one; consequently time would have to be allotted for studying records and having conferences with each pupil. But this system has the advantage of making it possible for the person who understands the individual also to guide his learning experiences for several hours each day, and this is of great importance.

Training Young People for Responsible Self-direction

Obviously guidance should not be an excuse for either the "babying" or the dominating of adolescents by adults. Secondary school teachers who understand the developmental tasks of adolescents, including their need to become responsible and self-directing, are able to offer excellent nondirective counselling to guide the student into effective ways of using his mental processes to clarify values, weigh alternative means for achieving goals, envisage consequences, reach decisions, and act on these decisions. The unhappy results of our present "sink or swim" policies are only too apparent in mental illness and juvenile delinquency. So it is not possible to evade much longer our responsibility for operating sound personnel practices that will provide real help for young people before they fail or get into trouble. And sound procedure requires giving responsibilities to adolescents as rapidly as they can accept them.

The Role of Counsellors

It is not unusual to find only two or three counsellors on the staff of a junior or senior high school serving twelve or fifteen hundred students. Obviously they cannot be expected to understand deeply the motivations and needs of each of these young people. Yet, too often, the subject-matter teachers in these schools take the position that it is their task to teach and the counsellors' task to understand the students, interpret to teachers the special needs of any individuals facing difficulties, and take whatever steps are necessary to help the students choose wisely the subjects they are to study, adjust to the demands of these courses, and function properly throughout their school activities. In other words, these teachers seem to feel relieved of all responsibility to understand individual young people because there are two or three counsellors on the staff of the school.

The counsellor's role is somewhat different from this, and it is tremendously important. Trained to understand young people, he is an ideal leader for groups of teachers making case studies of individuals. A considerable portion of his time can well be used in helping home-room or core teachers to interpret the cumulative records of their students, guiding these teachers as they decide what further information they need about each individual and as they get and record this information, and helping them apply and interpret sociometric tests. In other words, the counsellor's role is to help teachers understand individual young people and the structure and dynamics of the groups of young people with whom they work. It is neither needful nor possible for counsellors to understand each student in the school.

In addition, counsellors have the task of gathering and making available to teachers and to groups of students information about occupations and institutions of higher education that will help them make vocational and educational choices. They also must deal with young people who are not functioning well at school or who give evidence of persisting adjustment problems. This means that they have to confer with teachers, study cumulative records, contact parents, and interview the young people themselves in order to screen out those who need clinical help and refer them to proper agencies. Others can be dealt with effectively by the counsellors themselves through a series of interviews.

As teachers become more and more aware of the factors influencing the learning and adjustment of individual young people, the services of the counsellors are in greater and greater demand, not only to study individuals with adjustment problems, but to help teachers plan ways to enable students to fulfill their potentialities, even though they are causing no trouble at school and are getting passing marks. In this way, counsellors become involved in many of the extracurricular activities of the school, which provide important developmental experiences for many youth.

In general the effect of the child-study program in secondary schools has been to increase the demands on counsellors' time, since more students are referred to them and more teachers request conferences as they try to figure out ways of helping students. The result usually is the demand for more counsellors, as school staffs increasingly appreciate the personnel aspects of secondary school life.

Action Research

After three or four years in our child-study program, many teachers become quite skilled in the scientific method of analyzing and solving problems and therefore are ready for "action research." The teachers in a given school or those concerned with a particular aspect of education select a problem on which they will work together for a year or more. They analyze the factors that seem to account for the problem, gather data in order to define its dimensions and causes more accurately, analyze these data by group processes, consider possible directions in which solutions may be sought, try out alternative plans for solving the problem, keep records of what they do and of the conclusions they reach, evaluate these data, and revise their plans in accordance with what they find. It is a thrilling experience to sit in on some of these groups and see them think about a problem. Discovering their own blind spots and the sensitivities that cause them to resist certain ideas, these teachers gradually train themselves, with the help of a consultant, to find out and take practical steps for remedying many troublesome problems in their schools.

Conserving the Teacher's Time and Energy

There is the danger that presenting the nature of the teacher's task clearly and strongly, as we have here, may frighten teachers away from trying to understand children, and even from teaching itself, because of the genuine complexity of the task. On the other hand, I have seen so many hundreds of teachers actually learn to see deeply into the motivations and needs of their pupils that, in good conscience, I cannot longer refrain from telling the story of what we have learned. There is, however, a word about staff personnel policy that must be added.

Teachers are human beings. There are limits to their time and strength, although, for most, there are almost no limits to their professional conscientiousness. At any rate, this was true sixteen years ago. During the past decade, however, I have noted a serious decline in teacher morale in many sections of the country and, in some areas, the beginning of resistance to professional-improvement activities and a skeptical attitude toward innovations of any sort.

I do not wish to labor the obvious point that, as society has changed, more and more responsibilities and activities have been turned over to the schools until the teachers are so loaded with special duties that they are hard put to it to find time to guide the basic learnings and development of their charges. Furthermore, the responsibility for carrying on and participating in the many extra activities has not always been equally distributed among the teachers in the school systems which I know well. Finally, there are many professional-improvement activities, all good, which constantly compete for the teacher's time and strength.

The time has come to ask the help of teachers themselves in analyzing the demands on their time, in working out more reasonable schedules, and in planning together long-term programs of in-service professional growth. It is necessary to recognize that no group of persons with duties as demanding as those of teachers can learn everything they need in any single period of training. Professional growth cannot be treated as an extracurricular activity much longer. Regarding it as a vital aspect of every teacher's life, we must set aside time for it and then not trespass further on the teacher's private life, time, and resources.

Learning to Understand Children

The next chapter will describe in detail the steps required to help in-service teachers learn to understand their pupils as individuals. Certainly our child-study program is not the only possible method; perhaps it is not even the best method. Only further experimentation will tell. But we do have research data which show that it accomplishes what it aims to accomplish. In a way it is surprising that it accomplishes so much, considering that it takes so little of the participants' time—about four hours a week over a period of three school years, plus a two-week workshop during each of the intervening summers.

Yet there is something in the mood of our times which makes school people reluctant to undertake child study. Some hope that it can be learned effortlessly in "ten easy lessons" or avoided entirely by having an expert describe to teachers exactly what to do to get a child to learn to read skillfully or to behave properly, without troubling to know that child as a person. But we have not found any series of smart tricks during our sixteen years of work with teachers. Furthermore, we have seen numerous instances where improved educational practices—parent conferences, new cumulative record forms, universal promotion, pupil-teacher planning—were initiated by mandate without in-service education to prepare the teachers for it, only to have these desirable practices fail to make the anticipated improvement in the educative process because the teachers did not understand the human material with which they were working.

CHAPTER 13

The Child-study Program

Earlier chapters demonstrated the outcomes of our child-study program in terms of the kinds of case studies participants make and the insights gained by the group in analyzing these case records. It remains to describe in detail how we carry on this program for the in-service professional growth of school people.

Purposes of the Child-study Program

In order to maintain adequate continuity and consistency in the work, as our various consultants serve groups in a given school system, the staff has developed a statement of the purposes of the program and of the minimal procedures that all groups should follow from year to year. Much of the material to follow will be quoted directly from the statements prepared by the staff. The purposes of the program are:

1. To communicate to participants a body of specific scientific knowledge from many of the disciplines that study human beings.

2. To aid participants as they organize this knowledge into an integrated theory of human development, learning, and behavior.

3. To guide participants to discover the kinds of information about individual children that are necessary to understand them, and to develop skill in gathering and objectively recording this information.

4. To acquaint participants with the steps in reasoning that are necessary to arrive at scientifically sound judgments about the motivation, behavior, and needs of individual children; and, by group processes, to guide them in developing skill in this method of analyzing children and arriving at sound judgments about them.

5. To encourage and aid participants in working out, within the scope of the teacher's normal professional functions, specific plans for assisting individual children and groups of children to take their necessary next steps in development, learning, or adjustment; and to aid them in working out the implications of the insights gained through their study of children for planning and practice in the general educative process.

6. To assist participants to recognize children who need expert diagnosis, therapy, or remedial instruction, and to help them locate and refer the child to available agencies for diagnosis, therapy, or remedial instruction.

7. To stimulate participants to develop and to live by a strong code of professional ethics; to encourage them to recognize the worth of every individual and to respect the dignity of all human beings.

Launching the Program

Participation in our child-study program always is, and should be, completely voluntary on the part of teachers and others. Consequently, whenever a school system considers starting a program, a consultant from our staff visits that community, explains the purposes and processes of the program to the school personnel, and answers any questions that may arise. Principals and teachers then are given time to think about it and to talk it over among themselves before making any commitment to participate. Groups usually are made up of from eight to fifteen persons from a particular school or from the school system at large, according to local preference. They meet every other week throughout the school year, and each meeting lasts about two hours. Each group chooses its own leader and co-leader. Agreement to participate implies *full participation,* that is, the individual agrees to gather the necessary information about one child each year, to record this information in writing, to present it to the child-study group for criticism and interpretation, and to participate in the group processes through which all the case records are interpreted and skill in the scientific method of arriving at judgments is developed. Auditors and visitors are not permitted in working groups because they would not feel bound by our code of ethics and could get only an inadequate understanding at best.

The program usually is launched during the springtime so that leaders can be chosen and trained during the summer, prior to beginning work in the groups when school opens in September. The leaders are trained during a local two-week workshop either in June or in August; some prospective leaders attend our six-week workshop at the University of Maryland. The leader-training procedures used in these workshops will be discussed later in this chapter.

Our standard program is a three-year one for each participant, but nobody is expected to commit himself to three years of work when he enters the program. A participant is free to drop out at any time. In fact, illness, family responsibilities, and other factors do cause a considerable number of teachers to quit the program after one or two years of participation. An amazing proportion of these dropouts prove to be only temporary, however, for many teachers reenter and complete the program after a lapse of one or two years. For example, in a school system in which we worked for eight years, 95 per cent of all the persons who entered the program and remained in that school system eventually completed it.

It is highly desirable to include administrators and supervisors in as many groups as possible, in order that they may share in the experience of learning to see school situations through children's eyes. Child-study experiences lead teachers to change in a number of ways that may be disconcerting to their principals and supervisors, unless the latter have shared their experiences. For example, teachers become more permissive toward certain children in some situations, after they understand the meanings of these situations for the child, and send fewer children to the principal's office. At the same time, the teachers refuse to let these children "get away" with certain patterns of behavior and work with them in carefully timed positive ways, giving the children plenty of time to "cool off," but following through by helping them to analyze the significance of their actions and to correct inappropriate behavior. Teachers also tend to become more flexible in the subject-matter demands they make upon certain pupils. They become more aware of the needs of some children to develop readiness for certain learnings, and of the needs of more gifted children for enriching experiences and opportunities to push further their special interests.

Principals and supervisors need to share these experiences so that they can understand and cooperate effectively with teachers who are trying to act on their new insights. Furthermore, our experience has taught us that principals and supervisors must participate actively, that is, they must build case records, often with the help of classroom teachers, and attend group meetings regularly in order to have a part in interpreting the records presented. Auditing in study groups simply does not work. Happily, most principals and supervisors enjoy full participation, and many develop much closer professional relationships with their teachers in the process.

FIRST-YEAR PROCEDURES

First-year groups begin with a discussion and clarification of the goals of the child-study program and the reasons for the procedure they will follow during the year. Special emphasis is then given to the reasons for developing and living by a strong code of professional ethics.

In developing the code of professional ethics it is necessary to be very explicit in first-year groups. The need for intimate information about the child's developmental history and interpersonal relationships within the family becomes clear. But it must be stressed that this information is highly confidential. Because it is written, the record must be kept constantly under lock and key, if it is at school, or in a private place at home, and the information, when it is presented to the group, must be safeguarded by all members of the group. For example, it must not be discussed in the teachers' room in the presence of nonparticipating teachers, at soda fountains, or on busses where the conversation might be overheard. Nor can it be divulged to members of the teacher's family at home. Finally, the complete record must be turned in to the leader at the end of the year and either destroyed or sent for research purposes to the Institute for Child Study at Maryland, where anonymity is guaranteed. Since these are training records, they may not properly be placed in the child's cumulative folder at school, lest some untrained person gain access to it. Of course this code of ethics is primarily for the protection of the child and his family, but it also is an important protection for the teacher and for the school system, too, for indiscreet use of the information could cause trouble for everyone. Groups are urged to write out their code of ethics and to read it at the beginning of each meeting of the group throughout the three years.

Choosing Children for Study

At the first meeting, after the discussion of purposes, processes, and the code of ethics, the group takes up the kind of children to be studied. The chief criterion is that the teacher should be interested in the child about whom he is to gather data. But it is important for the group as a whole that these children should have diverse characteristics, so that the whole gamut of forces influencing learning can be identified. The group is urged to include some children who are very successful with their schoolwork and others who are having difficulties with learning, some who are models of good behavior and others who cause trouble, some who are much liked by their peers and others who are rejected or socially isolated, some who seem completely healthy and others who have physical handicaps, some who are very mature for their ages and others who are slow growers, some who are from prominent families and others who come from underprivileged areas, some who come from the chief ethnic groups served by the schools and others who come from minority groups in the community, some who experience caste discrimination, some who are secure in being loved at home and others who give evidence of being insecure or overprotected, some who are physically very attractive and others who are unattractive in face, figure, or grooming.

Each participant is encouraged to consider two or three children from whom one will be selected after consideration by the group at its second meeting. The object of giving so much thought to the selection of the children for study is to call attention from the outset to the wide range of factors that influence learning and behavior and to ensure that the group will have the opportunity to analyze how each of these factors operates.

There is a tendency for participants to want to choose the child who seems to face the most severe adjustment problems, in the hope of getting help from the group. But this is discouraged because many of these children need therapy that the teacher cannot and should not undertake to give. Furthermore, maladjustments of long standing often have complex backgrounds which cannot be penetrated by first-year child-study participants, and the choice of such children for study would only result in frustration. Despite these warnings, a certain number of teachers always choose children with severe problems, like Jane in Chapter 3; consequently each group is faced with important questions about mental-health and mental-hygiene policies.

In choosing a child it is also important to consider whether the family is likely to move away during the year. This is sure to happen occasionally, but taking thought ahead of time can decrease the probability. In schools serving migrants or shifting populations, the chance has to be taken.

Gathering the Necessary Information

Participants are urged to begin promptly to tap the various sources from which information can be obtained. Emphasis is placed upon recording the information objectively, specifically, descriptively, and completely, and upon avoiding interpretations of behavior and opinions about the child or his family. Participants gather information from the seven sources described in Chapter 6.

At an early meeting of the group the leader describes the characteristics of a good anecdote and reads to the group several which he has obtained at his training workshop. The group then analyzes these samples to see how they illustrate the criteria presented. At later meetings, each participant in turn reads an anecdote and then discusses what it tells about the child. This continues for several months.

The cumulative records of several children also are brought to an early group meeting, and each item of the record is considered for inclusion in the case study. If the item is factual and seems to the group to have significance, it is included; if it is an opinion or an unsupported evaluation of the child, it is not included. In this way, training in objectivity, specificity, and the validity of evidence is continued. Also, teachers' backgrounds of scientific knowledge are reviewed, for growth data are interpreted, test scores are discussed as to their meaning, and often subtest scores or item analyses are made in the attempt to see what significance the total score has. Sometimes the mass of subjective ratings of the child's supposed traits is analyzed, not to get data about the individual himself, but to answer the question, "What is the climate of feeling about him which the child has been experiencing at school?" Teachers change rapidly with regard to what they enter into cumulative records after even one year in child study.

Home visits are discussed early in the year, suggestions are made about how the initial visit can be arranged, and the four purposes of the visit, described in Chapter 6, are discussed. As rapidly as visits are made by participants, their records of these visits are read to the group, who then discuss the significance of the information gathered. Most often all four purposes of the visit have not been fulfilled, so the group discusses how the teacher can get the required information at a conference at school, after a P.T.A. meeting, over the telephone, or at another visit.

Participants are urged to chat with former teachers of the child to learn characteristic ways of behaving, patterns of learning, and significant facts about the child during previous years or in other class situations during the current year. They know that the initial responses of fellow teachers will be subjective and evaluative, and they are told to accept these and then to ask for specific illustrations which they can use as evidence. They also are encouraged to ask other teachers to estimate the frequency of certain occurrences, to give the sources of hearsay data, to describe earlier contacts with parents, and to describe the characteristics and schoolwork of siblings of the child being studied. Participants often are amazed at the amount of information fellow teachers have but have not placed in the cumulative records, and they learn to tap this source of information about other children in their classes as well as about the child being studied by the group. Principals can sometimes supply valuable information about children and their family situations, and many teacher-principal conferences about a number of children may eventuate, for the principal's information seldom is found in the cumulative records. Principals, in turn, learn that they have much pupil-personnel information to share with teachers through conferences and through the cumulative records.

Life-space descriptions are read to the group as rapidly as they are written and are discussed in terms of what the child has had the opportunity to learn in his life space. Teachers gradually become aware of the tremendous fund of out-of-school learnings that each child brings to the classroom with him and begin to write anecdotes about it when it is revealed in class. Participants also discuss whether the child is aware of the same factors in his environment as those the teacher noted and recorded, and this question is sometimes followed up in informal conversations with the child in the effort to learn what the child perceives in his life space and what meanings these things have for him. The intimate way in which children explore their life space is seldom appreciated until the teacher has followed up his own description of the child's life space with these informal conversations or by encouraging the child to talk freely in class discussions.

Samples of the child's written work in arithmetic, spelling, language, social studies, and science are included in the record, brought to the group, and analyzed for the knowledge and skills they display. They also are analyzed as projective material for what they show about the child's experiences, feelings, concepts of society, life, and self, codes of conduct, and goals. Sometimes participants ask their classes to write autobiographies and essays on special topics through which they learn more of the child's background, experiences, and feelings. Samples of the child's creative work—poems, drawings, paintings, and the like—also are included in the record, analyzed in the group as to content, and dealt with as projective material. Caution is exercised lest the participant's own feelings induce conclusions not validated by other evidence. Informal conversations with the child are analyzed in the groups in the same manner as anecdotes.

It requires at least three months of work—a minimum of six or seven meetings—to learn how to gather objective information from each of these sources and to discuss the meaning of this material. During this time participants inevitably show a tendency to jump to conclusions, to infer more from particular data than is justified. Furthermore, because of the policy of taking turns at each meeting in the presentation of material, no participant has had the chance to present all his material to the group. By December most participants are restive about refraining from making interpretations and are eager to begin more systematic attempts to understand each child.

Making Multiple and Tentative Hypotheses

Making multiple and tentative hypotheses about a specific bit of behavior is the first systematic interpretive experience of the group. A participant who wants a particular piece of behavior interpreted reads to the group the anecdote describing it. Then the group finds as many possible causes as they can think of which might lead a child to behave in this manner. This is done without reference to the record, and groups are encouraged to continue making hypotheses until they have twenty or more. From there on, the process is carried out as it was described in Chapter 5.

The staff of the Institute feels that there are at least seven reasons for including this process in the work of our child-study groups. They are:

1. It makes explicit for each participant the steps involved in the scientific method of reaching a conclusion about the causes of a child's behavior.

2. It makes participants aware of the nature of evidence, and that recorded facts are the only valid basis for supporting or refuting a hypothesis.

3. It causes each participant to review his knowledge of the scientific principles that explain behavior and reveals to them gaps in this knowledge, which they need to fill by further reading and study.

4. It reveals to participants that they are in the habit of judging children on the basis of a more limited set of causative factors than actually operates to shape behavior.

5. It convinces participants of the truth of the axioms we have given them— that behavior is caused, that the causes are always many, that the causes are always interrelated, and that each child is unique.

6. It constitutes an inventory of the material already assembled in the record, points out to the participant the gaps in his record, and indicates the kinds of additional information that he needs to seek.

7. It readies participants for their next step in interpretation, the identification and explanation of recurring patterns of behavior and situations in which the child finds himself. In seeking support for particular hypotheses, participants observe recurring factors in the evidence.

Most participants are not accustomed to state hypotheses, and it requires some time for them to learn to do this on the basis of their scientific knowledge. At first almost any hypothesis is accepted by the leader as stated. Then as the record is read, it becomes clear that some of the hypotheses are too crudely stated, so they are refined as the process continues. New hypotheses frequently are added to the initial list as the record is read, and often after the reading of the record the major hypotheses that have been validated are considerably refined.

The whole process is an intriguing one for most groups, having many aspects of solving a mystery. Indeed, this is the spirit in which it must be carried out: "Let's go to the record and find out the real reasons why the child acted in this particular way." The attempt to refine hypotheses too much at the first moment they are made will block many participants from making suggestions. Too strong an insistence that the participants state the scientific principle that underlies their hypotheses likewise prevents many participants from proposing explanations. Furthermore, there is no harm in proposing unscientific explanations, such as "he is lazy" or "he inherited it from his father's side of his family," because these hypotheses will always be refuted by the evidence, or will not be touched by any of the data because they are invalid. In this way many teachers learn that their folk explanations of behavior are invalid without anyone ever telling them so.

The group may require two meetings to complete their making and testing of multiple hypotheses on the first record they process in this way.

Then they practice this method at two or three more meetings, utilizing a different record each time. A good deal of skill develops in managing the process. Then each participant is asked to make and test multiple hypotheses on one anecdote in his own record, outside the group meeting. Or, if a number of participants do not yet feel able to carry out the process alone, the group may decide to split into pairs at the next meeting so that half the records can be processed in this way at a single meeting with the more skilled participants helping the less skilled. It usually takes about two months for a group to learn to hypothesize effectively. Sometimes it requires even longer, because so few teachers seem to have learned the steps in the scientific method of testing judgments in their early training.

Studying Recurring Situations and Patterns

Recognizing and listing recurring situations and patterns of behavior is the next analytical experience of the group. Situations that tend to recur for the individual and ways of acting that characterize him at various times can be found in the anecdotal material, in his written work and paintings, in the cumulative records, in what other teachers say about him in conferences, and in what he reveals in informal conversations.

A participant volunteers to read his record, and whenever a recurrence is noted, a phrase characterizing it is put on the blackboard together with the dates when it occurred. Each time it recurs, the appropriate date is placed beside it, so at the end of the reading the frequency and timing of the situations and patterns are apparent. Then the group discusses these situations and patterns, seeking to find threads of meaning for the child's life running through them. Sometimes the patterns are mere habits that go with his cultural background, peer group, or physical makeup. Others may seem to indicate developmental tasks on which the child is working or continuing adjustment problems that he faces, as in the case of Chester in Chapter 5. The group will then select one of these recurring patterns or situations that is interesting and will use the multiple-hypothesis technique to find out the causes for its recurrence. This is the point at which groups usually begin to penetrate somewhat deeply into the adjustment problems that the child is facing and spend a good deal of time in deliberating about steps that can be taken to help him.

This analysis of recurring patterns usually is repeated in three or four group meetings, using a different record each time. Then participants whose records have not been processed in this way by the whole group are asked to list the recurring patterns and situations in their own records and to make and test multiple hypotheses concerning the causation of one of these patterns outside the group meetings. Or the group again may split into pairs at a subsequent meeting to do this.

The staff feels that recognizing, listing, and testing hypotheses about the causation of recurring situations and patterns of behavior results in an experience of the consistency often found in children's behavior and demonstrates how adjustment problems faced by a child persist and appear in various times and places. It makes participants aware of ways in which children and youth continue to work on developmental tasks. It reveals how a child's concept of himself continues to influence his way of meeting situations. Finally, it is a step which links the making of hypotheses with the organizing of the case material for interpretation at the end of the year.

Interpreting the First-year Record

Toward the end of the school year, participants seek to describe what the year has been like for the child and to assess it in developmental terms. Utilizing all the skills and insights gained through their child-study experiences, they frame answers to the following questions:

1. What was the child working on during this year?
2. What was he up against?
3. What assets did he have?
4. What did the school do to help him accomplish what he was working on and to deal with what he was up against?
5. What can the school do in the future to facilitate his best development?

The questions are phrased in this manner to make participants aware of factors in each child's life which very often are not considered when classroom decisions are being made. For example, every teacher enters his classroom each morning with a series of learning goals to be accomplished by his pupils during that day. As the day progresses, he makes decision after decision, hundreds of them per hour, concerning the realization of his own goals for these children. Under these conditions it is very easy to forget that each child also has his own goals, which he is working very hard to accomplish as the next step for him in living successfully and in growing up. Sometimes the teacher's goals and those of the child are identical or at least consonant. Then everything goes well. But often the child's goals are different from and perhaps even incompatible with those of the teacher. In these cases the child must work at his own goals, for his perceptions are in terms of his own goals, and his goal-directed motivations guide his actions in this direction.

These are the conditions under which teachers and pupils come into conflict. It would be nice if children simply could be obedient, put their own interests, developmental tasks, and adjustment problems out of their minds, and devote their full mental powers to learning what the teacher has decided is good for them. But the natural law that governs human behavior rules otherwise. The child can see, hear, perceive, and understand only those aspects of each situation which bear upon his own interests, goals, developmental tasks, and adjustment problems. So he cannot attend to the goals the teacher has set. This is the primary reason why teachers need to understand children as developing individuals. For the *understanding* teacher has two ways out of the dilemma he faces. If he knows what the child is working on and judges it to be legitimate and developmental, he can help the child learn and work toward realizing his goals, temporarily putting aside those the teacher has set. Or, if he knows that the goals he has for the child that day are compatible with the child's needs and developmental tasks but are not perceived as such by the child, he can build bridges from what the child already knows and perceives to the goals he has for the child. In other words, he can relate the learning tasks he is presenting to the child's experience background and continuing motivations, thus harnessing the child's motivations to his own goals for the child.

Our aim, then, at the end of the first year of child study is to make our participants aware of three factors that shape the child's motivation and determine his learning readiness in the classroom. These three factors are:

1. The developmental tasks and conscious goals that the child is striving to accomplish.
2. The adjustment problems the child faces, which occupy his mind and make it difficult for him to accomplish his developmental tasks and to meet the school's expectancies and demands.
3. The child's assets in terms of experience background, personal relationships, interests, aptitudes, and learning capacities.

With awareness of these three sets of factors, the teacher can understand the child's motivations and see school situations through the child's eyes. He can evaluate his work with the child in terms of the constructive elements that helped the child toward the accomplishment of his developmental tasks or the facing of his adjustment problems. He also can envisage ways in which the school could do even more effective work in facilitating the child's learning, adjustment, and development.

During the first year, each participant gets these insights in relation to one child in his class about whom he has gathered data and for whom he was responsible. But to a lesser degree he gets the same insights into most of the children or youth who were studied by his group, for he has participated in the analysis of each of these children. A sense of the uniqueness of individuals and of the need to understand each child as a developing person usually ensues. Also the participant develops a broad awareness of what is involved in coming to understand a human individual and has acquired many of the skills he must use to do it. Finally, the participant has learned something of the scope of the scientific knowledge about human development and behavior that is available to him and has begun to discipline himself in the scientific method of arriving at judgments.

SECOND-YEAR PROCEDURES

In the second year of the child-study program, groups of from eight to fifteen participants who have completed the work of the first year are formed. Each participant selects one child about whom to gather information, as in the first year, and the seven sources of information are tapped in the same manner as before. The records are built up as swiftly as possible, with full regard for objectivity, specificity, and completeness. The code of professional ethics developed in the first year is reemphasized and further developed.

Developing an Organizing Framework

The six-area framework already presented in Chapter 7 is explained to each group by the leaders at the first or second meeting. The leaders have learned it at the local two-week leader-training workshop that is a regular and necessary part of the program. Participants are told that they will find the following uses for this organizing framework:

1. It will guide them in reading scientific material and the building of scientific concepts to explain human learning, behavior, and development.
2. It will guide them as they organize the facts they are gathering about each child whom the group is studying.
3. It will suggest the scope of the hypotheses that must be formed to account adequately for each child's behavior and development.

Ordinarily we do not mimeograph the complete framework for participants, but simply put its chief elements on the blackboard as we discuss them. This is because we want to avoid mere verbal learning. We encourage each individual to build the details of his own framework, both as he reads to fill in gaps in his knowledge and as he uses the framework to organize his information about the children being studied. A framework that is built gradually, with regard to details, and that is constantly used in analyzing case records will become a genuine tool to guide thought processes.

Synthesizing Scientific Knowledge

We have found it desirable to say very little about reading during the first year of the program and to stress primarily the development of skills in gathering data, recording it objectively, making hypotheses, and using the scientific method in arriving at judgments. But consultants always give a lecture on some aspect of growth, motivation, or behavior at each visit they make to the community; bibliographies are supplied to guide such reading as participants care to do; constant reference is made to explanatory scientific principles; and each school system is urged to begin building a good professional library of materials dealing with growth, learning, and behavior.

During the second and third years of the program, however, a good deal of emphasis is placed upon acquiring scientific knowledge. The participants are supplied with bibliographies that indicate sources dealing with each of the areas in the organizing framework, and they are encouraged to read extensively. It is suggested that participants begin their reading in the areas about which they feel they know least. More detailed lectures are given by the consultants than in the first year. Plenty of time is allowed for discussion in order to clarify concepts, aid participants in seeing relationships between the different aspects of development, and give consultants the opportunity to suggest readings appropriate to the knowledge levels of various participants.

Classifying Data about Individual Children. To conserve the time of participants, they are told simply to record each item of information serially in the record, as they come upon it, being careful to date each entry. Hence there is no order in the recorded material. A few anecdotes will be followed by many entries from the child's cumulative records; then may come more anecdotes followed by the report on a home visit. Examples of the child's written and creative work may then appear, followed by more anecdotes, accounts of informal conversations with the child, and a description of his life space. Participants must be encouraged to get the needed information whenever they have the time and opportunity; hence it cannot be entered in any particular order. It must, therefore, be organized so as to facilitate interpretation.

Our organizing framework and a Dewey-decimal system of notation along the margins of the record, as illustrated in Chapters 7 and 9, provide an easy way of organizing information. The first two meetings of the second year usually are devoted to getting organized, selecting the children for study, learning the organizing framework, and beginning to develop the record.

The next four or five meetings are devoted to learning to classify the material being gathered in the manner described and illustrated in Chapter 7. This usually is done by "going around the circle," giving each participant in turn the opportunity to read an item from his record and to tell how it should be classified. To do this, the participant answers the following questions about the item:

1. What facts about the child are found here?
2. What do these facts tell us about the child?
3. To what area or areas of the framework are these facts relevant?

Another way of phrasing the third question is to ask, "What area or areas of the framework will these facts help us to understand?" When the participant reading the item has indicated to what areas he thinks the item is relevant, other participants may raise objections, if they have any, cite additional areas to which they think the item is relevant, and give their supporting reasons. The group also may discuss explanatory scientific concepts at any time when they come up in connection with classifying material, if some members of the group do not understand them or hold a different view.

Marginal Dewey-decimal classifications are made by placing in the margin beside the item read the number of the area or areas to which the item is relevant. Then a decimal point is placed after each number, and after this is written the number of this item in the series of facts so far assigned to a particular area. So a given item may be numbered 2.06 to signify that it is the sixth fact in the series bearing upon the child's relationships within the family and 6.12 to denote that it is the twelfth item relating to the child's adjustment problems and emotional behavior.

Of course, groups will bog down in the process of classifying data if they are too meticulous in the work and try for too great certainty and scientific validation. It is necessary to warn each group against this, and to suggest that they can classify an item in any area if the answer to the following question is in the affirmative: "Shall I wish to see this item when I am trying to understand the child in this aspect of his life?" If there is any chance that an item will throw light on an area, it should be classified there, for classification simply means that this item will be included when the participant is putting together all the information he has about a particular area to find out how factors in this area are affecting the child's learning and development. It is at the moment of interpretation that all the laws of evidence must be followed most carefully to ensure valid conclusions.

Adequate practice in this process of relating information about the individual child to explanatory scientific concepts is ensured by going around the circle and giving each group member a turn at each successive meeting. But these short practice periods in the group meetings do not suffice to classify all the information each one is gathering. Two ways are used to keep classification up-to-date. As soon as an individual participant has developed fair skill in classifying, he carries on the process outside group meetings. Then in later meetings the group is split up into pairs or trios who help each other with classifying. In this manner, less-skilled participants learn the process from others and there is a general check on the work of all.

As suggested above, this process of classifying information has great value beyond that of simply organizing the facts for interpretation. We are aware of at least the following values from it:

1. It disciplines participants in being objective by giving them practice in discriminating between facts and opinions.

2. It reviews the scientific knowledge possessed by the group, for the question, "What does this fact tell us about the child?" nearly always evokes the scientific principles to which the fact is relevant.

3. As different participants see different significances for the same fact, all are disciplined to consider the possible relationship of each fact to all the different areas in the framework. So the process of classification helps participants observe the interrelationships of the different forces that shape motivation and learning and accomplish an integration or synthesis of discrete items of scientific information. This is, in fact, one of the major reasons for classifying data in this way.

4. Participants may disagree about where an item is to be classified, and this results in discussion of the scientific concepts that are the bases for the differing opinions. In this way concepts are clarified, new scientific information frequently is communicated, and reading for greater depth of understanding is stimulated.

5. The participants learn much about the nature of evidence from the process. For example, in some cases they discover that one fact is relevant to a given area only if a second fact is true, but they have no way of knowing whether the second fact is true and so must not classify the item on the basis of unsupported second-level inference.

So the process of classifying information results in continuing review and ordering of each participant's scientific knowledge and in further training in the scientific method of arriving at a judgment.

Interpreting Individual Areas

One of the major purposes of the second year of the program is to give each participant a systematic, organized picture of the forces that interact to shape each child's motivation, behavior, and development and consequently to influence his learning. School people often are but dimly aware of some of these forces and are therefore unable to see school situations through the eyes of individual pupils. We are fully aware that each child is an indivisible unit and that all the forces that shape his development are interrelated and interactive. Nevertheless, to highlight some of the forces that school people often leave out of consideration and to get an adequate picture of the nature of each of the forces acting upon and within the child, it seems necessary to analyze each dynamic area separately and then, later, to integrate these separate findings into a unified explanation of the individual's behavior and development. Actually, in our analysis of each area we do not seek to find out how that area is affecting learning and development. Rather *we seek to identify and to describe,* both qualitatively and quantitatively, *the forces in that area.* The effects on learning and development of the forces in any particular area depend upon their place in the total constellation of forces influencing the individual pupil.

However, participants in our program deal every day with the individuals they are studying; hence it would be idle to claim that what they learn about these children, area by area, does not influence their classroom decisions. And we are quite sure that the general effect of these partial insights is to improve their decisions. As the year progresses and they gradually acquire more knowledge of what is making Tommy tick, there is a continuing refinement of their judgments along with increased capacity to understand the child as an organized whole.

When most participants have gathered and classified adequate information (usually by mid-December), the group will be eager to begin interpreting the records area by area, usually beginning with physical factors and processes. First the group develops a series of questions to guide them in the analysis of the material in the record pertaining to the area they are studying. The questions usually are similar to those in Chapter 8, which dealt with the case of Timothy Thyme, and concern factors which research has shown to have significant influence on behavior and development. After the questions are phrased, all items classified in the area are read to the group and facts that bear upon each question are noted under that question on the blackboard. When all the material has been read and noted, the group makes hypotheses about how to answer each question and tests the validity of each answer in terms of whether it is supported by the facts. If data are inadequate to validate an answer to any question, the group discusses what further facts are needed and how they may be obtained. This discussion guides the participant in collecting additional material about the child. It frequently happens that the questions reveal almost no facts to support some hypotheses, and this makes participants aware of forces which they had so far ignored in building their records.

There usually is time during the second year to spend only one group meeting in interpreting each area; hence all the group members are expected to interpret at home, between meetings, the area in their own records which was demonstrated at the previous group meeting. It sometimes happens that a considerable number of them will have trouble doing this, so that the group will have to spend a second meeting in working on a particular area. There is time for several of these repeat sessions, but it is highly desirable for second-year groups to interpret each of the six areas during the year. However, to do this creates a very full year of work, and most groups are not satisfied with the depth of the interpretations they achieve in the two areas relating to the development and adjustment of the self, which are the subjects of more intensive study during the third year of the program.

Each participant continues to gather information about his subject throughout the year and periodically considers how the new data tend to support or to refute conclusions already reached. Often the new data not only modify the answers tentatively made to some of the questions but result in wholly new conclusions. Sometimes, also, conditions change for the child while he is being studied, or the child himself changes, and this necessitates new conclusions about him.

Interpreting the Record as a Whole

Toward the end of the year, each participant tries to see the child he is studying as a functioning unit, as a whole person. He is guided in this by seeking answers to the following questions, which require that the forces in all areas be evaluated as a constellation, producing certain effects by their interaction:

1. What developmental tasks was the child working on during the year?
2. What adjustment problems was he facing?
3. What assets did he have in accomplishing these developmental tasks and meeting these adjustment problems?
4. What did the school do to help him with his developmental tasks and adjustment problems?
5. What could the school have done, or what can it still do, to help him with these developmental tasks and adjustment problems?

It is desirable that the last two meetings of the year be given over to reports from several participants dealing with these questions. Such reports help everyone to tie together what he has learned during the year and to get deeper meanings in the interpretation of his own record.

THIRD-YEAR PROCEDURES

In the third year of the child-study program, the groups usually include from six to twelve participants, because some members will have dropped out. Each participant selects one child about whom to gather information, and the same seven sources of information are tapped. The record is built as swiftly as is consistent with full regard for the objectivity, specificity, and completeness of the information obtained. The code of professional ethics is emphasized again.

Objectives

In addition to strengthening the objectives sought during earlier years, the program has the following purposes in the third year:

1. To study the self-developmental and self-adjustive processes of each individual in terms of the impacts of organic, affectional, cultural, and peer-group processes upon the developing personality.

2. To study the influence of already developed aspects of the self upon the behavior and continuing development of the child. The influence of such factors as skills, knowledge, interests, attitudes, values, goals, adjustment mechanisms, and concepts of self in the world are analyzed in terms of how they affect observed behavior and the further development of the child or youth during the year.

3. To study the development of the individual within the context of classroom and playground group processes. This involves studying the structure and dynamics of the class group of which the child is a part, learning the roles played by the individual in group activities, assessing his status in the group, and studying the reciprocal influence of the group upon the individual and of the individual upon the group.

Continuing the Synthesis of Scientific Knowledge

One of the effects of the second-year program is to make participants uncomfortably aware of how limited is their knowledge of the great store of facts about human development and behavior that science already has uncovered. Since most of them are eager to dig deeper into this knowledge during their third year in the program, they are supplied with bibliographies listing works that deal with the dynamics of development and adjustment and with group structure and processes. Group leaders will have completed their third local two-week workshop and will have new information to share with participants. Each time they come to the community, consultants give separate lectures to third-year participants which deal especially with group dynamics, the evolution of concepts of self, and adjustment processes. Extensive reading is encouraged, and many informal conversations about scientific findings occur among participants and between participants and consultants.

Building the Third-year Case Record

Certain aspects of the record-building process are stressed with third-year participants in order that their records will contain material which will yield the necessary insights. Utilizing skills already developed, participants are urged:

1. To note especially and record the details of posture, gesture, facial expression, and voice quality that give clues to the pleasant and unpleasant feelings children are experiencing in observed situations.

2. To quote directly as many conversations as possible between the child and other members of the class group.

3. To write many anecdotes about the interaction between the individual being studied and groups of children, including comments made either by the child or by others about the significance of the happening, and also including later comments by the child or by others about the observed happening.

4. To record many informal conversations with the child about how he feels about happenings in the class, at home, in the community, and in the world at large and about what he hopes to do and become in the world.

5. To collect autobiographical material, compositions about out-of-school experiences, political happenings, friendships, life goals, trips, etc.

In other words, the record should contain anything and everything that can give a hint of how the child sees himself, society, and the world at large, and of what he regards as satisfying day-to-day living.

Classifying Facts about the Individual

The six-area framework developed in the second year is used again in the third year for the classification of data, and the same processes are followed. But classification also becomes the occasion to develop and clarify participants' ideas about how the self emerges and is shaped and about how self-mediated factors, including interests, values, goals, and adjustment mechanisms influence perception, behavior, and further development. While information is being classified, the usual questions are asked:

1. What facts about the child are found here?
2. What do these facts tell us about the child?
3. To what area or areas of the framework are these facts relevant?

Then additional questions are raised, such as:

4. Are there clues to how the child feels about these facts?
5. Are there clues as to how the child sees himself in relation to these facts?
6. Do the facts show anything about how the child sees his world?
7. Do the facts show anything about how the child feels about himself in relation to the world he is experiencing?

Raising these questions makes participants sensitive to many things that children say and do which formerly escaped their notice. As a result they make better records and begin to think soundly about the experiences that shape the child's ideas and feelings concerning himself, his relationships with others, society, and the quality of his own life.

Sociometric Study of the Class Group

Before Christmas, and after a fair number of anecdotes describing the interaction of the children in group situations have been recorded, participants are encouraged to make a sociometric analysis of the structure of their class group. This sociometric study is based either upon a functional situation in which children choose each other as a natural part of some classroom activity, such as seating arrangements or committee work on a group project, or upon simple friendship choices. Sociograms similar to that presented in Chapter 9 give valuable clues to the status of different individuals in the group and to the relationships existing among them. But the sociograms give only clues, and judgments about interpersonal relationships among the children must be based on observations and anecdotal material describing actual interaction among them. Some participants become so interested in studying group structure and processes that they do a second sociogram in the spring in order to observe both persistence and change in the class structure.

Interpreting Areas in Terms of Self

Early in January, third-year groups begin to evaluate each area in terms of how its factors influence the development and adjustment of the self. They phrase a series of questions similar to those used in the second year to serve as a guide in the analysis of each area. To these are added additional questions dealing with the influence of the area factors on the development and adjustment of the self, such as:

1. Are there clues to how the child feels about each factor in the area?
2. Are there clues to how the child thinks of and feels about himself because of each factor in the area?
3. Are there clues to how each factor is influencing the child's ideas and feelings about the world?
4. Are there clues to how each factor is influencing the way the child sees himself in relation to the world he is experiencing?

These questions are added to those used in analyzing the first four areas of our framework in order to focus participants' attention on the way factors in each of these areas are shaping the child's development as a person and determining his adjustment problems. The questions used as a guide in the analysis of areas five and six are those presented in Chapter 8 in the case of Timothy Thyme.

As each area is assessed, the question is always raised whether the facts are adequate to support the tentative answers to each of the questions posed and, if not, what additional facts are needed. The group also takes note of questions that remain unanswered by the material available in order to use them as guides in gathering additional information.

When the interpretation of a given area has been made in the group meeting with regard to one case, each participant then interprets this area in his own record outside the group meeting, going through each of the steps involved and writing down each question and the tentative answers he obtains together with notations (Dewey-decimal numbers) indicating supporting evidence. Each participant continues to gather information throughout the year and periodically considers how the new data support or refute the tentative conclusions already made or suggest modified or substitute answers to the questions posed.

Interpreting the Record as a Whole

Toward the end of the year the motivations that stir the child are compared with the expectancies and demands to which he is being subjected. The whole record is interpreted in writing in terms of answers to the following questions:

1. How does the child see and feel about himself and about the world he is experiencing?
2. How does his world—for example, his parents and teachers—see and feel about him?
3. What are the important differences between the two views of the child functioning in his world?
4. What developmental tasks is the child working on?
5. What continuing adjustment problems does he face?
6. What can the school do to harmonize apparent differences between the child's view of himself and others' views of him?
7. What can the school do to help him accomplish his developmental tasks and deal effectively with his adjustment problems?

THE PROCESSES USED IN CHILD STUDY

Learning through Experience

The child-study program is *not* a course of of instruction which participants receive. Rather, it is *a program of guided experiences* that participants undergo and through which they gradually learn to see school situations through the eyes of individual children.

Teachers must always have goals in mind for their pupils to accomplish—the learning of facts and skills, attitudes and codes of conduct, and ways of using the mind. But, because every child is unique, the teacher must be equally aware of the factors and forces that mold the varied meanings that come to different children out of a given experience. Consequently, we believe it is necessary for teachers to experience the uniqueness of a number of children quite thoroughly in order to convince them of the vital necessity for this dual awareness in the classroom. Our child-study program, then, is a program designed to bring to them, through direct experience, insights into the varied factors and forces that shape the motivations, learning readinesses, and perceptions of individual children.

A Clinical View of the Child

Many of the experiences which yield these insights come to participating teachers as part of the process of gathering the information they need about the children they are studying. These experiences include: observing and writing objective descriptions of the child's behavior in many situations; visiting the child's home; studying the child's cumulative records; observing and describing the child's life space; conferring with former teachers of the child to learn how he behaved earlier in his development; analyzing actual work materials produced by the child both in terms of knowledge and skill and in terms of its "projective" content; listening to what the child has to say in informal conversations; conferring with parents at school; and making a sociogram of the structure of the class group. These experiences help the teacher to get a "clinical view" of the child, a sense of the forces shaping his motivations, to supplement the teacher's customary evaluative perceptions of the child as meeting or not meeting learning and behavioral expectancies appropriate to his grade level.

Group-process Experiences

Participating in group processes within the study group supplies many additional insight-giving experiences. These include submitting recorded material to the group for evaluation of its objectivity, specificity, and scope and participating in the evaluation of material recorded by others and so discovering the pervasive way in which preformed judgments color everyone's perceptions; participating in formulating and testing hypotheses about the causes underlying the specific behavior of a number of children and so discovering the multiple causation of the actions of children; spotting recurring patterns of behavior and recurring situations in the case records of a number of children; and making and testing hypotheses about the causes underlying these recurring patterns and situations and thereby learning that each child constantly is working on certain developmental tasks and adjustment problems even while he is dealing with arithmetic or science or social studies in the classroom.

Through classifying case data into areas defined by an organizing framework and formulating questions to be answered by these data in each area, many participants discover the vagueness of their concepts regarding the causation of behavior and set about building a more adequate comprehension of the scientific explanation of development, learning, and behavior. As they seek answers to the questions formulated in the different areas on the basis of the data supplied by several case records, evaluate the validity and scope of the data available for answering these questions, and consider what further facts are needed, participants become wary of snap judgments, aware of the kinds of information they must have, and sensitive to the influence on children's behavior and learning of factors they had tended to ignore earlier. Participation in the sociometric analyses of the structure and dynamics of several classrooms results in understanding of why a given classroom situation will have different meanings for different children and of why some classes function so much more smoothly than others.

A New Perspective on Education

As they discuss the developmental tasks and adjustment problems on which a number of children are working, as revealed by the case records, participants gain further insights into the meanings classroom situations have for children and raise significant questions about the goals the teacher must have in mind for a given school year for a particular child. Analyzing the assets available to a number of children for dealing with their developmental tasks and adjustment problems and raising the questions of what the school has done and can do to help them with these tasks and problems deepens the participant's understanding of the dual tasks all teachers face—building skills and communicating knowledge, on the one hand, and helping each individual child take his next step in development and adjustment. Furthermore, participants come to see the interdependence of these dual goals and to understand that the traditional mass goals of education cannot be accomplished successfully while the particular needs of the differing individuals are disregarded.

Experiencing Changes in Attitude

Perhaps most meaningful of all for participants is the experience of working from day to day in the classroom with children whom they are coming to understand deeply. Among the more influential experiences of this sort reported by participants are discovering that their attitudes toward given children are changing from dislike to acceptance and from blaming to valuing as they gain insights into what situations mean to the children; having children change from avoiding the teacher to approaching the teacher with questions, comments, or proffers of help, or simply for informal conversation and companionship; and seeing children's behavior change from troublesome to cooperative and thoughtful. Interestingly enough, teachers report that these kinds of changes in the children's actions usually come shortly after the teacher has become aware of his own attitudinal changes toward the children.

Another meaningful classroom experience reported by participants is that of consciously giving children time to come to terms with difficult situations before making necessary demands upon them, helping children to analyze the effects and the causes of their own behavior, and seeing the children respond as desired to these procedures. Other significant new classroom experiences include: sensing when to ignore and when to intervene in interactions between children; seeing the interest of children waken when bridges of relationship are built between the child's experiences and school subject matter; and enjoying the "we" feeling as pupils and teacher plan activities together and subsequently carry them out.

The child-study program, then, is a guided experience of utilizing scientific knowledge and the scientific method, of participating in group processes with professional colleagues, and of utilizing insights gained in day-to-day interaction with children as valued individual personalities and as groups whose particular structure and dynamics the teacher understands.

Requirements for Success

"Child study" by some definitions can be a waste of time and effort; indeed, this has been true of a certain number of the groups with which we have worked. But it also can be tremendously rewarding to its participants. Repeatedly, the staff has analyzed why the program is so successful in certain schools and communities and only mediocre in its effects in others. We have decided that the following factors are crucial to an effective program:

1. Adequate training for group leaders.
2. Three consultant visits per year to each working group.
3. An effective local child-study coordinator.
4. Understanding of and sincere belief in the value of the program on the part of the superintendent, supervisors, and principals.
5. An adequate professional library.

So crucial are these factors that we are unwilling to start programs in any community where they cannot be provided. Each of them will be discussed in turn.

LEADERSHIP TRAINING

Choosing Leaders

In most school systems, the groups themselves choose their leaders and co-leaders; but in some, leaders are selected by the child-study planning committee. All sorts of persons become successful child-study leaders. Most of them are classroom teachers, but supervisors, principals, school psychologists, helping teachers, counsellors, school nurses, research personnel, and librarians have all become excellent leaders of child-study groups.

The Role of Leaders

Group leaders must not think of themselves as instructors, nor must participants regard them as such. Rather, they are the conveners of the group and the facilitators of the processes that the group seeks to carry out. They are people with "know how" rather than with answers. They must know when to "go around the circle," giving each his turn in presenting material or formulating a hypothesis, classifying material presented by someone else, or figuring out the answer to a question posed in an area. They must be skilled in preventing a talkative participant from monopolizing a discussion or deflecting the group with an item of gossip. They must be alert to raise meaningful questions when a group is confused or bogged down.

They must know when to change the direction of the discussion to protect a participant from revealing too much about himself and his work to the group. Most of all, they must sincerely value human beings, including every group member, every child being studied, all family members of children being studied, and the total staff of the school system. The leaders set the professional mood and the ethical standards of the group's activities, and these are crucial factors. These, of course, are some of the "group-process" roles of the leaders and imply a certain amount of child-study-group experience prior to becoming leaders, even of first-year groups.

The Training of Leaders

We have found that adequate training for group leaders for each year of the program can be given in a two-week local workshop, preferably at a camp or resort where participants and consultants will be living together and having recreational experiences together, are free from home duties and other interruptions, and have time for informal conversations. Each day's schedule provides for an hour-and-a-half lecture, a two-hour "laboratory-group" session, two hours of reading, recreational activities, and free discussions. In the ten lectures, an overview of the forces and processes that shape growth, learning, and behavior is given. In the laboratory sessions, the groups actually carry on the child-study-group processes in which they will be leaders during the coming year.

Mimeographed case records obtained from participants in former groups and authorized by them for this use are studied in the laboratory sessions to acquaint the new leaders with such aspects of the program as the characteristics of a good anecdote, how to arrange for a home visit, the objectives of a home visit, how to interact with parents during a home visit, how to confer with other teachers, the significance of information found in cumulative records, what to observe in a child's life

space, the projective content of children's writings and drawings, and
how to carry on informal conversations with children.

Group processes practiced in the laboratory sessions include analyzing
anecdotes for objectivity, specificity, completeness, and significance;
analyzing cumulative records for objectivity and significance; filling out
and interpreting the Wetzel grid; analyzing home-visit reports; role-
playing home visits and conferences with other teachers; analyzing life-
space reports; analyzing children's writings, especially for mood clues;
carrying out the full multiple-hypothesis procedure for analyzing the
causes of specific behavior; and spotting recurring patterns of behavior
and recurring situations.

Consultants to the leader-training workshops have the following roles:
communicating the goals and purposes of child study, presenting the
basic assumptions that underlie child study, communicating scientific information through lectures, demonstrating the roles of leaders in laboratory sessions, describing the bases for selecting children for study, em-
phasizing the code of professional ethics and discussing its implications,
explaining the reasons for each element in the program year by year,
presenting the organizing framework to second-year leaders, helping
second-year leaders frame the questions to be answered in each area,
helping third-year leaders make a sociogram, protecting group leaders
from revealing too much about themselves to their fellows, exemplifying
what it means to value human beings, building group morale, building
confidence in individual leaders, conferring with the local program coordinator, and conferring with local administrators.

Of course, leaders of groups at each of the three levels are trained in
separate lectures and sessions, if all three years of the program are going
on simultaneously. Persons who have led first-year groups ordinarily
move on with their groups and become second-year leaders; hence they
attend a second local workshop to prepare for this. In the same way,
they attend a third-year workshop to prepare for leadership in that year
of the program. Sometimes successful leaders or co-leaders of first-year
groups repeat that year in order to lead newly organized first-year groups,
and so they repeat the first-year leadership workshop. They report that
it is not a boring experience because each case record is new and different and there is so much to learn about human beings that being group
leaders for as long as five years still affords challenging experiences. In
fact, we have consultants who have served working child-study groups
for more than ten years and report that they, too, are still acquiring
deeper insights into human development and behavior and into the potentialities for learning by group processes through workshop experiences. We have had a few successful first-year groups in which the
leaders had no preparatory workshop, but it simply is not possible for

second- and third-year leaders to have successful groups without previous leadership training.

Group-leader Meetings

Beginning about the third or fourth week of school, the child-study groups meet fortnightly until near the end of the school year, usually holding about sixteen meetings a year. As the groups begin to operate, leaders often find themselves puzzled about some detail of procedure or unsure of the answers to some of the questions posed by participants. So leaders' meetings are held on the alternate weeks when the child-study groups are not meeting.

These leaders' meetings usually are chaired by the child-study coordinator of the area and are likely to include the following activities:

1. Practice by the leaders of the processes that the groups are currently employing, with analysis of how each step is taken and why.

2. Analysis and evaluation of factors influencing the morale, or the effectiveness, of the meetings of specific groups, with each leader contributing ideas or anecdotes about how to remedy specific difficulties that have arisen or about how to clarify matters about which a group is confused.

3. Discussion to clarify scientific facts or concepts about which confusion or disagreement has arisen, together with suggestions for reading by the leader or by the group. Sometimes plans are made for reports on reading to be given to the leader group itself, so that all may clarify or deepen concepts about which they are uncertain.

4. Practice by the leaders of the group activity into which the groups will move next, so that things learned at the workshop during the summer will be fresh in the minds of the leaders when they undertake to guide the working groups into the new activity.

5. Discussion of questions of professional ethics that arise in connection with the actions or case records of specific participants.

6. Planning for using consultants in each working group, during meetings just prior to consultant visits, and evaluating the outcomes of consultants' work in the groups during the meeting following the consultant's visit.

7. Refreshments and informal conversations among leaders, during which group morale is fostered and many good ideas are shared.

These leader-group meetings are necessary to a successful program, but it must be noted that as a result of them, leaders attend twice as many meetings as regular participants. For this reason, persons carrying leadership responsibilities should be recognized as playing special roles in the professional in-service training program, and their other extra-teaching duties should be lightened by principals and supervisors. A compensation is that leaders, because of their summer workshops, more frequent meetings, and more careful analysis of group processes, learn more rapidly and acquire deeper insights than other participants. In fact, it has been startling to note over a period of years how many teacher leaders have moved into positions as principals and supervisors. Although this is doubtless due mostly to the selection of capable persons as leaders, they themselves have reported that their child-study experiences were of great help in preparing for work that carried greater responsibility. Of course, leaders keep records about individual children and carry on all the other activities of regular participants.

CONSULTANT SERVICE

Characteristics of Effective Child-study Consultants

Competent child-study consultants are hard to find, and even to develop, because of the capacities and characteristics required. In the first place, the consultant must have a good working knowledge of the research findings in all the major sciences that study human beings. In addition, he must have knit this information into an organized explanatory system or theory which describes the processes of growth, learning, perception, behavior, development, and adjustment. Then he must be able to communicate this information in simple, nontechnical language.

A good consultant likewise has knowledge of and skill in functioning on a "group-process" basis, together with knowledge of and skill in specific child-study processes. He must have been trained in case analysis to the point where he has sound clinical insights into the motivations of individual children, but he must not feel a compulsion to explain to the group all that he sees and understands, for his task is rather to help the group learn how to gain the insights for themselves. This implies that a consultant must be able to accept the pace of the group with which he is working so that he neither discourages them by pressing too hard nor leaps ahead of their insights and so makes them dependent upon him or upon the group leader. Furthermore, the consultant must be able to empathize to the extent of recognizing immediately, or in advance, potential threats to the participants and so refrain from expressing ideas or evaluations which would be too unsettling to them. At the same time he must see that the learning process is continuous. This implies that an effective consultant is deeply interested in human behavior, deeply values all human beings, and is consciously dedicated to a well-defined code of professional ethics.

But a child-study consultant is an educational consultant as well. He therefore needs extensive knowledge of educational policies and practices and considerable direct experience of managing the educative process in school situations. Participants must feel that "he knows what he is talking about." Because regional and area differences in culture are so extensive, he also must be flexible enough to accept and operate in accord with local customs and school policies, and he must not feel a compulsion to challenge them arbitrarily. For people learn by acquiring deeper insights and evolving new convictions, not by being told that they are wrong.

Finally, a consultant needs sound health and good physical stamina. Some communities are eager to have the consultant "accomplish all he can while he is with us" and hence seek to use him morning, afternoon, and evening. For this reason we have had to make it a policy that a consultant may work afternoons and evenings, or mornings and afternoons, but not during all three periods of the day. This is to protect communities receiving the service as well as ourselves, for a consultant's effectiveness decreases rapidly as he becomes fatigued.

Roles and Functions of Consultants

There seems to be a national tradition that consultants are supposed to give lectures and answer questions, but, actually, people get a minimum of usable insights by this method. As we have seen, our child-study participants learn most effectively through their experiences in gathering information about the children they study, through the group processes in which they interact with other participants, and through their interaction with children in their classrooms as they perceive the implications of their deepening insights into these particular children. Of course, participants need to add steadily to their scientific knowledge of human development, behavior, and adjustment, so both lectures and the reading of suggested materials have their place. But these are not the primary sources of learning in the child-study program.

With this background, the chief functions of consultants can be described. They are:

1. The consultant meets with each working group separately, observes their child-study processes in operation and participates in them, thus enriching and focusing them. He meets with each group separately, because the "group feeling" disappears when groups are combined and many individuals do not participate. Often these withdrawing individuals are the very ones to whom the consultant could be of greatest help.

2. In each group, the consultant takes whatever time is necessary to clear up confusion about how to gather information, the importance of certain sources of information, the processes being used by the group to interpret information, or the objectives of the program.

3. The consultant presents briefly to each group, as part of the discussion of a particular child, such scientific facts or explanatory principles as are germane and of which participants seem unaware. He also suggests specific reading material from which more extensive information can be secured.

4. The consultant evokes discussion in the group of the educational implications of the group's insights into children's needs, developmental tasks, and

adjustment problems, in terms of what can be done to help the particular child being studied.

5. Toward the end of the meeting, the consultant sometimes evaluates its processes for the group and makes constructive suggestions for improving their work, using illustrations from the meeting then being concluded.

6. The consultant sometimes takes the role of the leader in demonstrating to the group the next step they will take in the child-study process. Leaders report that such demonstrations are a great help to them and get the group off to a good start on the new process.

7. The consultant always asks to hear the code of professional ethics under which the group is operating. He also exemplifies the code in operation by the manner in which he discusses children, family situations, school situations, and the actions of teachers, principals, and supervisors, as well as by the way in which he deflects comments that would threaten group members.

8. At each visit to a given community, the consultant gives separate lectures on relevant scientific material to the first-year, second-year, and third-year participants as separate groups. These lectures usually are held in some central place, and their content is adjusted to the knowledge and understanding achieved by participants in their particular year of child study.

9. At each visit to a given community the consultant holds a separate meeting with the group leaders of each year of the program, as described above.

10. Each time a consultant visits a given community, immediately upon his arrival he sits down with the local coordinator for an hour or more to be briefed on his schedule, on the most desirable content for his lectures, on the needs of each working group, on how he can be of most help at the leaders' meeting, on questions about the program to which the superintendent of schools or central administrative staff are seeking answers, and on any concerns or problems of the coordinator. This preliminary briefing is necessary to prepare the consultant to serve most effectively and intelligently.

11. Shortly before the end of his visit, the consultant again spends an hour or two with the local coordinator. In this conference he gives his evaluation of the work of the groups and of their leaders and suggests ways in which their work can be strengthened, points which may need emphasis at leaders' meetings before the next consultant arrives, and ways in which his own time could have been used more efficiently, if he feels this is important. In the springtime he discusses the recruitment of new child-study participants and leaders for new groups for the following year and helps the coordinator plan for the local summer workshop.

12. At some time during his visit the consultant usually has a conference with the superintendent of schools, or with other administrators involved in the program, to answer any questions they may have about it and to discuss how it can be strengthened. He may also have a meeting with the child-study planning committee for the same purposes. It is most important that the chief administrators of the system be kept fully informed about the nature of child-study processes and about the accomplishment of groups, since they may have to answer questions or criticisms from the local school board. In fact, it is quite common to have the superintendent ask a consultant to attend a

meeting of the board of education to explain the goals and processes of the program and to answer any questions board members may have. This usually occurs before the program is launched or soon thereafter.

13. Some communities have parent child-study groups which carry on programs of their own, somewhat different from the teachers' program. Consultants sometimes are expected to work with these parent groups, or with their leaders, and parents frequently attend the child-study lectures given by the consultants.

14. On his return to the Institute for Child Study, the consultant files a brief report of his visit to a community. This record evaluates the work of various groups, lists the suggestions the consultant has made for strengthening the program, whether in group meetings, to the local coordinator, or to the administration, and describes the plans made. These records are of great value to the next consultant who visits the community, and they serve to refresh the memory of the consultant if he happens to return to the same community.

15. It is natural that consultants should vary a good deal from each other in what they perceive in group processes, in the factors of human development and motivation they stress, and in their ways of working with groups. For this reason it has proved desirable to rotate the consultants who serve a given community so that the groups can profit from the varying perspectives, stores of information, ways of expressing concepts, and clinical insights of different staff members. Of course, this creates the problem of maintaining consistency, because groups sometimes are confused by apparent contradictions in the methods used by different consultants. Consultants can minimize this confusion by staff meetings at which they analyze their ways of working and iron out differences of opinion amongst themselves. Despite occasional confusion, the plan of rotating consultants seems to enrich the work of most groups.

16. A consultant can usually serve about a dozen working child-study groups and do all of the other tasks outlined above in a five-day week, but this requires careful planning by the local coordinator, willingness of participants to hold group meetings at hours different from their usual meeting time, and sometimes the release of leaders for meetings on school time.

THE LOCAL COORDINATOR

Choosing the Coordinator

It is not too much to say that the success or failure of a child-study program depends upon the functioning of the local coordinator. For child study is a serious, long-term program of professional growth for members of the educational profession. It will not succeed if it is thought of as a mere side line to more important duties by the person who is locally responsible for it. Furthermore, the coordinator, no matter how devoted, can carry on a successful program only if certain conditions obtain which make it possible for him to function efficiently. We have found that coordinators are effective if the following conditions exist and if they have the characteristics described below:

1. The coordinator must have the full confidence and support of the central administration in his work.

2. The coordinator must command sincere professional respect from supervisors, principals, and teachers.

3. The coordinator must be a person who can have a significant proportion of his time assigned to child-study work. Obviously the amount of his time required depends upon the number of groups in the local program. Large school systems require a full-time child-study coordinator.

4. The coordinator must be genuinely convinced of the practical value of the program to members of the educational profession and must feel a sense of personal accomplishment and of self-fulfillment in carrying on the program.

5. The coordinator must be willing to get whatever training is necessary to understand the program thoroughly. This usually means attending at least two six-week summer workshops at the University of Maryland. An alternative is one semester of graduate study at the Institute for Child Study.

6. The coordinator must be skillful in dealing with his administrators, principals and other personnel as he interprets the program to them and makes the necessary arrangements for its work.

7. The coordinator must be alert to numerous essential details in his planning and must meticulously follow through on each of these details to ensure the effective operation of the program.

We regard child-study programs as local programs which we serve, not as separate parts of a national program which we are conducting. It is clear, then, that the administration, the coordinator, and the participants must all regard the local coordinator as the leader of an important in-service program of professional growth.

Many different kinds of persons have functioned effectively as local coordinators. Any of the following types of persons can do the coordinator's job well, given the conditions and characteristics indicated above: a member of the department of research and guidance, a curriculum coordinator or supervisor, a school psychologist, a helping teacher, a counsellor, a member of the department of pupil personnel, a coordinator of in-service teacher education, or an assistant superintendent in charge of teacher personnel.

Functions of the Child-study Coordinator

Many of the duties of the local coordinator already have been described, but it may be valuable to enumerate all of them here to give a clearer picture of the important and essential functions he performs. His chief roles are:

1. To interpret the program to teachers, principals, and supervisors, and to supervise the voluntary enrollment of participants.

2. To plan in detail all consultant visits, and to accompany the consultant as he fulfills his various roles, participating as needed, evaluating his work, and making needed suggestions.

3. To conduct the leaders' meetings between consultant visits and when the consultant is meeting with the leaders.

4. To visit working groups as needed by them, and to assist in clarifying points of confusion either about child-study processes or about explanatory scientific concepts.

5. To supervise the circulation of necessary books among the working groups so that all may have access to the scientific knowledge they need.

6. To spot potential leaders for new groups or co-leaders within new groups, and to recruit them for leadership training.

7. To plan and operate, usually with a steering committee, the local leader-training workshop each summer.

8. To meet with the child-study planning committee, or steering committee, to evaluate the program in progress, to plan for changes, and to develop it further.

9. To confer with the consultant, briefing him on his schedule when he arrives, evaluating the work they have observed together, and planning together how the program can be improved.

10. To keep the administration informed about the operation of the program, its effectiveness, and the plans for its development.

11. To serve as mediator when difficulties arise, to assist leaders individually when they face special problems, to provide information about community facilities for aiding children and communicate it to participants who need to make referrals, to find help for participants facing special problems in their classrooms, and to be a liaison person with curriculum supervisors and guidance personnel so that insights gained through child study can find fruitful expression in the day-to-day work at school.

A review of the functions of the child-study coordinator demonstrates the great professional significance of the position and implies the need for adequate recognition of the role on the part of administrators and colleagues.

THE PROFESSIONAL LIBRARY

A necessary adjunct to a successful child-study program is a good professional library adequately stocked with books containing the scientific information which participants need. The Institute for Child Study supplies each participating community with up-to-date bibliographies each year and encourages the accumulation of the necessary books. Then the local coordinator works out a plan at the leaders' meetings for ensuring the circulation of these books among the various groups on a rotating basis. In this way a minimum number of books will be needed, and yet each participant will have easy access to the needed information.

INFLUENCE OF ADMINISTRATORS

A program is unlikely to be very successful if it is merely authorized by the central administration, provided for in the budget, and then largely forgotten by the persons who run the school system. For child study is not a theoretical study but a way of acquiring insights that affect day-by-day decisions in the classroom and that lead to various kinds of adaptations in the operation of schools. It is important for administrators to share in these insights so that they can see the reasons for the changes that occur or are sought by participants. The local coordinator, the consultants, and the participants, as opportunities arise, all share in the responsibility for communicating these insights to administrators. But administrators are very busy people, carrying terrific responsibilities, and sometimes so preoccupied with other matters that they do not receive the necessary communications.

Recently we have been carrying on a series of five-day workshops for school superintendents that seem to bridge the gap successfully. They include lectures which give an overview of the factors that shape the child's learning, behavior, and development, with adequate discussion to clarify explanatory scientific principles. They include the analysis together of a few case records to emphasize the uniqueness of individual pupils, point up the kinds of practical decisions teachers and school principals must make, and clarify the developmental principles that need to be considered in making these decisions. They provide a series of discussion periods in which the superintendents consider together the implications for educational practice of the scientific knowledge and facts about children and school situations that are communicated. Participating superintendents report these workshops to be very valuable experiences. The result, often, is that the superintendents give special encouragement to supervisors and principals to participate actively in the program and recognize the time required for this participation on the part of key personnel.

Nothing is more discouraging to teachers participating in the program than to work hard at getting the information they need to understand certain pupils, achieve insights, and work out plans for helping these pupils to learn or adjust, only to have the principal or a supervisor throw cold water on their ideas or actually forbid them to carry out their plans. The best remedy for this, of course, is participation by principals and supervisors in the child-study program. Failing this, we sometimes hold one- or two-week workshops for the supervisors and principals of a particular school system. These workshops are similar to those described above for superintendents, and they seem to provide significant experience for the participants.

CRITIQUE OF THE PRESENTATION

Because of the detail in which the program has been described, the reader may feel that the presentation is authoritarian and carries the implication that these are the only ways, or the best ways, in which teachers can come to understand children. This was not the attitude with which the chapter was prepared. Actually, terms like "should" and "must" ought to read, "our experience through the years makes us believe that it is best to . . ." for this is all that is implied. For each process described above, we surely have tried four or five others that failed. The intent here is only to describe limited first steps toward the discovery of more effective ways of providing for the in-service professional growth of teachers. Our hope is to encourage others to collaborate in this work, for we are still baffled at the magnitude of, and humbled by the formidable importance of, the task of making it possible for teachers to reach wise decisions in the classroom. We do feel, however, that this book is a record of progress toward that goal.

Bibliography

The following bibliography has two purposes. It contains basic references which tend to validate the synthesis of concepts set forth in Chapters 10 and 11. Also, it can serve as a reading guide for persons studying children in the manner described in this book. To facilitate this use, numbers precede each item which has special value for one or two of the areas in the six-area framework used in the case records. References that are not preceded by numbers contain significant material for more than two areas of the framework. All material cited is of a reading difficulty appropriate for the average graduate student or public school teacher except those marked T, which are for advanced students, and those marked N, which are appropriate for lay persons. To keep the bibliography within manageable limits many symposia and books of readings have been included and many books with extensive bibliographies. Child-study participants are urged to consult the bibliographies in these books especially for references in periodicals which are available to them.

5,6   Adams, D. K., et al.: *Learning Theory, Personality Theory, and Clinical Research: The Kentucky Symposium.* New York: John Wiley, 1954.

5,6   Adorno, T. W., E. Frenkel-Brunswick, D. J. Levinsen, and R. N. Sanford: *The Authoritarian Personality.* New York: Harper, 1950.

N.2   Aldrich, C. A., and M. M. Aldrich: *Babies Are Human Beings.* New York: Macmillan, 1938.

T.5   Allport, F. H.: *Theories of Perception and the Concept of Structure.* New York: John Wiley, 1955.

5   Allport, G. W.: *Becoming.* New Haven: Yale University Press, 1955.

5   ——: *Personality, A Psychological Interpretation.* New York: Henry Holt, 1937.

5   ——: "The Ego in Contemporary Psychology," *Psychol. Rev.,* **50:**451–478, 1943.

    Almy, Millie: *Child Development.* New York: Henry Holt, 1955.

5   Anderson, C. M.: "The Self-image: A Theory of the Dynamics of Behavior," *Mental Hygiene,* **36:**227–244, 1952.

5,6   Anderson, H. H., J. E. Brewer, and M. F. Reid: "Studies of Teachers' Classroom Personalities: Part III. Follow-up Studies of the Effects of Dominative and Integrative Contacts on Children's Behavior," *Appl. Psych. Monogr.,* no. 11, Stanford University Press, 1946.

2,5   Angyal, A.: *Foundations for a Science of Personality.* New York: Commonwealth Fund, 1941.

5,6   Arbuckle, D. S.: *Teacher Counseling.* Cambridge, Mass.: Addison-Wesley, 1950.

6   Axline, Virginia M.: *Play Therapy*. Boston: Houghton Mifflin, 1947.
2,6   Bakwin, H.: "Emotional Deprivation in Infants," *J. Pediat.*, 35:512, 1949.
      Baldwin, A. L.: *Behavior and Development in Childhood*. New York: Dryden, 1955.
6   Barker, R. G., T. Dembo, and K. Lewin: "Frustration and Regression: An Experiment with Young Children," *University of Iowa Studies in Child Welfare*, 18:1, 1941.
      ——, J. S. Kounin, and H. F. Wright (eds.): *Child Behavior and Development*. New York: McGraw-Hill, 1943.
      —— and H. F. Wright: *Midwest and Its Children*. Evanston, Ill.: Row, Peterson, 1954.
N.6   Baruch, Dorothy: *New Ways in Discipline*. New York: McGraw-Hill, 1949.
N.2   ——: *Parents Can Be People*. New York: Appleton-Century-Crofts, 1944.
1   Bayley, Nancy: "Growth Curves of Height and Weight by Age for Boys and Girls, Scaled According to Physical Maturity," *J. Pediat.*, 48:2, 187–192, February, 1956.
1   ——: "Skeletal Maturing in Adolescence as a Basis for Determining Percentage of Completed Growth," *Child Develop.*, 14:1, 1943.
1   —— and S. R. Pinneau: "Tables for Predicting Adult Height from Skeletal Ages: Revised for Use with the Greulich–Pyle Hand Standards," *J. Pediat.*, 40:423, 1952.
T.1   Beach, F. A.: *Hormones and Behavior*. New York: Paul B. Hoeber, 1948.
3   Benedict, Ruth: *Patterns of Culture*. Boston: Houghton Mifflin, 1934.
4   Berenda, R. W.: *The Influence of the Group on the Judgments of Children*. New York: King's Crown Press, 1950.
2,3   Bernard, Jessie: *American Family Behavior*. New York: Harper, 1942.
      Biber, B., Lois B. Murphy, L. Woodcock, and J. S. Black: *Life and Ways of the Seven- to Eight-year-old*. New York: Basic Books, 1952.
      Blair, A. W., and W. H. Burton: *Growth and Development of the Preadolescent*. New York: Appleton-Century-Crofts, 1951.
5   Blake, R. R., and G. V. Ramsey (eds.): *Perception: An Approach to Personality*. New York: Ronald, 1951.
5,6   Blos, Peter: *Adolescent Personality*. New York: Appleton-Century-Crofts, 1941.
4   Bonney, M. E.: *Popular and Unpopular Children, A Sociometric Study*. New York: Beacon House, 1947.
2,3   Bossard, James H.: *Parent and Child*. Philadelphia: University of Pennsylvania Press, 1953.
      ——: *The Sociology of Child Development*, rev. ed. New York: Harper, 1954.
2   Bowlby, John: *Child Care and the Growth of Love*. Baltimore: Penguin Books, 1955.
2   ——: "Maternal Care and Mental Health," *WHO Technical Monogr.*, Geneva, 1951.
2   ——: "Some Pathological Processes Set in Train by Early Mother–Child Separation," *J. Mental Science*, 159:265–272, 1953.
1   Boyd, W. C.: *Genetics and the Races of Man*. Boston: Little, Brown, 1950.
      Breckenridge, M. E., and E. L. Vincent: *Child Development*, rev. ed. Philadelphia: W. B. Saunders, 1955.
6   Bridges, K. M. B.: *The Social and Emotional Development in the Preschool Child*. London: Kegan Paul, 1931.

5,6   Brown, J. S., et al.: *Current Theory and Research in Motivation.* Lincoln, Neb.: University of Nebraska Press, 1953.

2   Burlingham, Dorothy, and Anna Freud: *Infants without Families.* London: George Allen & Unwin, 1943.

Bush, R. N.: *The Teacher–Pupil Relationship.* Englewood Cliffs, N.J.: Prentice-Hall, 1954.

N.1   Cannon, W. B.: *The Wisdom of the Body,* rev. ed. New York: W. W. Norton, 1939.

5   Cantor, N.: *The Teaching–Learning Process.* New York: Dryden, 1953.

5   Cantril, H.: *The Why of Man's Experience.* New York: Macmillan, 1950.

1   Carlson, A. J., and V. Johnson: *The Machinery of the Body,* 4th ed. Chicago: University of Chicago Press, 1954.

Carmichael, L. (ed.): *Manual of Child Psychology,* 2nd ed. New York: John Wiley, 1954.

T.4,5   Cartwright, D., and A. Zander: *Group Dynamics Research and Theory.* Evanston, Ill.: Row, Peterson, 1953.

5,6   Child, I. L.: "Children's Preference for Goals Easy or Difficult to Obtain," *Psychol. Monogr.,* **60,** 4 (whole no. 280), 1946.

2,6   Clancy, N., and F. Smitter: "A Study of Emotionally Disturbed Children in Santa Barbara County Schools," *Calif. J. Educ. Res.,* 4:209–218, 1953.

Coladarci, A. P.: *Educational Psychology—A Book of Readings.* New York: Dryden, 1955.

Cole, L. E.: *Human Behavior.* Yonkers: World Book, 1953.

—— and W. F. Bruce: *Educational Psychology.* Yonkers: World Book, 1950.

3,4   Cook, L., and E. Cook: *Intergroup Education.* New York: McGraw-Hill, 1954.

Coutu, W.: *Emergent Human Nature.* New York: Alfred A. Knopf, 1949.

N   "Creating a Good Environment for Learning," *1954 Yearbook, Assn. for Superv. and Curric. Devel.* Washington: National Education Association, 1954.

Cronbach, L. J.: *Educational Psychology.* New York: Harcourt, Brace, 1954.

——: *Essentials of Psychological Testing.* New York: Harper, 1949.

N.4   Cunningham, Ruth, et al.: *Understanding Group Behavior of Boys and Girls.* New York: Teachers College, Columbia University, 1951.

3   Davis, A.: *Social-class Influences upon Learning.* Cambridge, Mass.: Harvard University Press, 1948.

3   —— and J. Dollard: *Children of Bondage.* Washington: American Council on Education, 1940.

3   —— and B. Gardner: *Deep South.* Chicago: University of Chicago Press, 1941.

3   —— and R. J. Havighurst: *Father of the Man.* Boston: Houghton Mifflin, 1947.

1   Dearborn, W. F., and J. W. M. Rothney: *Predicting the Child's Development.* Cambridge, Mass.: Sci-art Publishers, 1941.

Dennis, W.: *Readings in Child Psychology.* Englewood Cliffs, N.J.: Prentice-Hall, 1951.

3   ——: *The Hopi Child.* New York: Appleton-Century-Crofts, 1940.

5   Deutsche, J. M.: *The Development of Children's Concepts of Causal Relations.* Minneapolis: University of Minnesota Press, 1937.

N.2   D'Evelyn, K. E.: *Individual Parent–Teacher Conferences.* New York: Teachers College, Columbia University, 1945.

1   Dimock, H. S.: "Research in Adolescence. I. Pubescence and Physical Growth," *Child Develop.,* **6:**177–195, 1935.

6   Dollard, J., L. W. Doob, N. E. Miller, O. H. Mowrer, and R. R. Sears:
     Frustration and Aggression. New Haven: Yale University Press, 1939.

6   Driscoll, Gertrude P.: *Child Guidance in the Classroom.* New York: Teachers
     College, Columbia University, 1955.

N   ———: *How to Study the Behavior of Children.* New York: Teachers College,
     Columbia University, 1941.

1,6 Dunbar, Flanders: *Mind and Body: Psychosomatic Medicine.* New York:
     Random House, 1947.

N.1,6 ———: *Your Child's Mind and Body.* New York: Random House, 1949.

     Erikson, E. H.: *Childhood and Society.* New York: W. W. Norton, 1950.

1   Espenschade, A.: "Motor Performance in Adolescence," *Monogr. Soc. Res.
     Child Develop.,* **5**:1, 1940.

     Forest, Ilse: *Child Development.* New York: McGraw-Hill, 1954.

N.6 "Fostering Mental Health in Our Schools," *Yearbook, Assn. for Superv. and
     Curric. Devel.* Washington: National Education Association, 1950.

5   Frank, L. K.: *Nature and Human Nature.* New Brunswick, N.J.: Rutgers
     University Press, 1951.

N   ——— and Mary Frank: *How to Help Your Child in School.* New York:
     Viking Press, 1950.

T.1,5 Freeman, G. L.: *The Energetics of Human Behavior.* Ithaca, N.Y.: Cornell
     University Press, 1948.

5,6 Frenkel-Brunswick, E.: "Intolerance toward Ambiguity as an Emotional and
     Perceptual Variable," *J. Personality,* **18**:108–143, 1949.

6   Freud, S.: *An Outline of Psychoanalysis.* New York: W. W. Norton, 1949.

5,6 Fromm, E.: *Escape from Freedom.* New York: Farrar & Rinehart, 1941.

5,6 ———: *Man for Himself.* New York: Rinehart, 1947.

2,6 ———: *The Art of Loving.* New York: Harper, 1956.

3,6 ———: *The Sane Society.* New York: Rinehart, 1955.

5   Frondizi, R.: *The Nature of the Self.* New Haven: Yale University Press, 1953.

     Fullagar, W. A., H. G. Lewis, and C. F. Cumbee: *Readings for Educational
     Psychology.* New York: Thomas Y. Crowell, 1956.

1,5 Gardner, I. C., and H. H. Newman: "Mental and Physical Traits of Identical
     Twins Reared Apart," *J. Hered.,* **31**:119–126, 1940.

1   Gerard, Ralph: *Unresting Cells.* New York: Harper, 1940.

     Gesell, A., C. S. Amatruda, B. M. Castner, and H. Thompson: *Biographies of
     Child Development.* New York: Paul B. Hoeber, 1939.

1,5 Gilchrist, F. G.: "The Nature of Organic Wholeness," *The Quarterly Review
     of Biology,* **XII,** September, 1937.

2,6 Goldfarb, W.: "Effects of Psychological Deprivation in Infancy and Subse-
     quent Stimulation," *Am. J. Psychiat.,* **102**:18–33, 1945.

2,6 ———: "Psychological Privation in Infancy and Subsequent Adjustment,"
     Amer. J. Orthopsychiat., **15**:247–255, 1945.

     Goldstein, K.: *The Organism.* New York: American Book, 1939.

     ———: *Human Nature in the Light of Psychopathology.* Cambridge, Mass.:
     Harvard University Press, 1940.

     Goodenough, Florence L.: *Exceptional Children.* New York: Appleton-Cen-
     tury-Crofts, 1956.

1   Greulich, W. W.: "Rationale of Assessing the Developmental Status of Chil-
     dren from Roentgenograms of the Hand and Wrist," *Child Develop.,*
     21:33–44, 1950.

1   ——— et al.: "A Handbook of Methods for the Study of Adolescent Children,"

Monogr. Soc. Res. Child Develop., 3:2. Washington: National Research Council, 1938.

1 Greulich, W. W., and S. I. Pyle: *Radiographic Atlas of Skeletal Development of the Hand and Wrist.* Stanford University Press, 1950.

Group Processes—Transactions of the First Conference. New York: Josiah Macy, Jr., Foundation, 1954.

1 Hanley, C., and A. B. Nicolson: "Indices of Physiological Maturity: Derivation and Interrelationships," *Child Develop.*, 24:3, 1953.

1 Hardin, Garrett: *Biology: Its Human Implications*, 2nd ed. San Francisco: W. H. Freeman, 1954.

4 Hare, A. P., E. F. Borgatta, and R. F. Bales: *Small Groups, Studies in Social Interaction.* New York: Alfred A. Knopf, 1955.

3,4 Hartley, E. L., and R. E. Hartley: *Fundamentals of Social Psychology.* New York: Alfred A. Knopf, 1952.

Havighurst, R. J.: *Developmental Tasks and Education*, 2nd ed. New York: Longmans, Green, 1952.

———: *Human Development and Education.* New York: Longmans, Green, 1953.

5 Hayakawa, S. I.: *Language in Thought and Action.* New York: Harcourt, Brace, 1950.

N Henry, N. B. (ed.): "Adolescence," *43rd Yearbook, Natl. Soc. Stud. Educ.*, part I. Chicago: University of Chicago Press, 1944.

——— (ed.): "Learning and Instruction," *49th Yearbook, Natl. Soc. Stud. Educ.*, part I. Chicago: University of Chicago Press, 1950.

6 ——— (ed.): "Mental Health in Modern Education," *54th Yearbook, Natl. Soc. Stud. Educ.*, part II. Chicago: University of Chicago Press, 1955.

——— (ed.): "The Education of Exceptional Children," *49th Yearbook, Natl. Soc. Stud. Educ.*, part II. Chicago: University of Chicago Press, 1950.

5 Hilgard, E. R.: *Theories of Learning*, 2nd ed. New York: Appleton-Century-Crofts, 1956.

———: *Introduction to Psychology.* New York: Harcourt, Brace, 1953.

3,4 Hollingshead, A. deB.: *Elmtown's Youth.* New York: John Wiley, 1949.

3,5 Honigmann, J. J.: *Culture and Personality.* New York: Harper, 1954.

6 Horney, Karen: *Our Inner Conflicts.* New York: W. W. Norton, 1945.

5,6 ———: *Neurosis and Human Growth.* New York: W. W. Norton, 1950.

5,6 ———: *The Neurotic Personality of Our Time.* New York: W. W. Norton, 1937.

6 Hunt, J. McV. (ed.): *Personality and the Behavior Disorders*, vols. I and II. New York: Ronald, 1944.

Hurlock, Elizabeth: *Child Development.* New York: McGraw-Hill, 1949.

Hymes, J. L., Jr.: *Behavior and Misbehavior.* Englewood Cliffs, N.J.: Prentice-Hall, 1954.

———: *Discipline.* New York: Teachers College, Columbia University, 1949.

N.5 ———: *'Teacher Listen,' The Children Speak.* New York: State Charities Aid Association, 1949.

N.3 ———: *Effective Home–School Relations.* Englewood Cliffs, N.J.: Prentice-Hall, 1953.

5 Ittelson, W. H., and H. Cantril: *Perception: A Transitional Approach.* New York: Doubleday, 1954.

4 Jennings, H. H.: *Leadership and Isolation*, 2nd ed. New York: Longmans, Green, 1950.

4   Jennings, H. H.: *Sociometry in Group Relations*. Washington: American Council on Education, 1948.

     Jersild, A. T.: *Child Psychology*, 4th ed. Englewood Cliffs, N.J.: Prentice-Hall, 1954.

5   ———: *In Search of Self*. New York: Teachers College, Columbia University, 1952.

5,6 —— and K. Helfant: *Education for Self-understanding*. New York: Teachers College, Columbia University, 1953.

5,6 Johnson, W.: *People in Quandaries*. New York: Harper, 1946.

1,5 Jones, M. C., and N. Bayley: "Physical Maturing among Boys as Related to Behavior," *J. Ed. Psych.*, 41:129–148, 1950.

1   Kallmann, F. J.: *Heredity in Health and Mental Disorder*. New York: W. W. Norton, 1953.

6   Kanner, L.: *Child Psychiatry*, 2nd ed. Springfield, Ill.: Charles C Thomas, 1948.

2,6 ———: *In Defense of Mothers*. Springfield, Ill.: Charles C Thomas, 1941.

3,5 Kardiner, A., R. Linton, C. DuBois, and J. West: *The Psychological Frontiers of Society*. New York: Columbia University Press, 1945.

1,5 Keliher, Alice V.: *Life and Growth*. New York: Appleton-Century-Crofts, 1938.

5   Kelley, E. C.: *Education for What Is Real*. New York: Harper, 1947.

     —— and M. I. Rasey: *Education and the Nature of Man*. New York: Harper, 1952.

5,6 Kierkegaard, S.: *The Concept of Dread*, trans. by W. Lowrie. Princeton, N.J.: Princeton University Press.

3,5 Kluckhohn, C.: *Mirror for Man*. New York: McGraw-Hill, 1949.

3,5 ———, H. A. Murray, and D. M. Schneider (eds.): *Personality in Nature, Society, and Culture*, 2nd ed. New York: Alfred A. Knopf, 1953.

3,5 Kroeber, A. L. (ed.): *Anthropology Today*. Chicago: University of Chicago Press, 1953.

1   Krogman, W. M.: "Growth of Man," *Tabulae Biological*, **XX**, The Hague, June, 1941.

3,5 La Barre, W.: *The Human Animal*. Chicago: University of Chicago Press, 1954.

N   Lane, Howard, and Mary Beauchamp: *Human Relations in Teaching*. Englewood Cliffs, N.J.: Prentice-Hall, 1956.

     Langdon, Grace, and I. Stout: *Those Well-adjusted Children*. New York: John Day, 1951.

     —— and ———: *Teacher–Parent Interviews*. Englewood Cliffs, N.J.: Prentice-Hall, 1954.

T   Lashley, K. S. (ed.): *Studies in the Dynamics of Behavior*. Chicago: University of Chicago Press, 1932.

5,6 Lecky, Prescott: *Self-consistency*. New York: Island Press, 1945.

5,6 Leeper, R. W.: "A Motivational Theory of Emotion to Replace Emotion as Disorganized Response," *Psychol. Rev.*, 55:5–21, 1948.

3,6 Lemkau, P. V.: *Mental Hygiene in Public Health*, 2nd ed. New York: McGraw-Hill, 1955.

2,6 Levy, D. M.: "Primary Affect Hunger," *Am. J. Psychiat.*, 94:643–652, 1937.

2,6 ———: *Maternal Overprotection*. New York: Columbia University Press, 1943.

2,6 ———: "Studies in Sibling Rivalry," *Res. Monogr. Amer. Orthopsychiat. Assn.*, no. 2, 1937.

N.2,5   Levy, J., and R. Monroe: *The Happy Family.* New York: Alfred A. Knopf, 1938.

Lindgren, H. C.: *Educational Psychology in the Classroom.* New York: John Wiley, 1956.

3,6   Lindner, R.: *Prescription for Rebellion.* New York: Rinehart, 1952.

Lindzey, G. (ed.): *Handbook of Social Psychology.* Cambridge, Mass.: Addison-Wesley, 1954.

3,6   Lippitt, R.: "An Experimental Study of the Effect of Democratic and Authoritarian Group Atmospheres," *University of Iowa Studies in Child Welfare,* **16** (3): 43–195.

Lorenz, K.: *King Solomon's Ring.* London: Methuen, 1952.

4   Loughlin, Frances: *The Peer Status of Sixth- and Seventh-grade Children.* New York: Teachers College, Columbia University, 1954.

5,6   Lowenfeld, V.: *Creative and Mental Growth.* New York: Macmillan, 1952.

1,6   Macfarlane, J. W., L. Allen, and M. P. Honzik: "A Developmental Study of the Behavior Problems of Normal Children between Twenty-one Months and Fourteen Years," *Univ. Calif. Pubs. Child Develop.,* no. 2, 1954.

4   Malinowski, B.: *The Dynamics of Cultural Change.* New Haven: Yale University Press, 1945.

Martin, W. E., and C. B. Stendler: *Child Development.* New York: Harcourt, Brace, 1953.

――― and ――― (eds.): *Readings in Child Development.* New York: Harcourt, Brace, 1954.

6   May, R.: *The Meaning of Anxiety.* New York: Ronald, 1950.

5,6   ―――: *Man's Search for Himself.* New York: W. W. Norton, 1953.

McClelland, D. C. (ed.): *Studies in Motivation.* New York: Appleton-Century-Crofts, 1955.

1   McGraw, Myrtle B.: *The Neuromuscular Maturation of the Human Infant.* New York: Columbia University Press, 1943.

3,5   Mead, G. H.: *Mind, Self, and Society.* Chicago: University of Chicago Press, 1934.

3   Mead, Margaret: *And Keep Your Powder Dry.* New York: William Morrow, 1942.

3,5   ―――: *From the South Seas.* New York: W. W. Norton, 1939.

3,5   ―――: *Male and Female.* New York: William Morrow, 1949.

1,4   Meek, Lois: *Personal–Social Development of Boys and Girls with Implications for Secondary Education.* Chicago: Committee on Workshops, Progressive Education Association, 1940.

N.5   Miel, Alice, et al.: *Cooperative Procedures in Learning.* New York: Teachers College, Columbia University, 1952.

5   Miller, G. A.: *Language and Communication.* New York: McGraw-Hill, 1951.

Montagu, M. F. Ashley: *The Direction of Human Development.* New York: Harper, 1955.

2,5   ―――: *The Meaning of Love.* New York: Julian Press, 1953.

More, Douglas M.: "Developmental Concordance and Discordance during Puberty and Early Adolescence," *Monogr. Soc. Res. Child Develop.,* **18**:1, serial no. 56. Washington: National Research Council, 1953.

T   Morgan, C. T., and E. Stellar: *Physiological Psychology,* 2nd ed. New York: McGraw-Hill, 1950.

Morse, W. C., and G. M. Wingo: *Psychology and Teaching.* Chicago: Scott, Foresman, 1955.

5,6   Moustakas, C. E.: *Children in Play Therapy.* New York: McGraw-Hill, 1953.
      —— and S. R. Jayaswol (eds.): *The Self: Explorations in Personal Growth.*
          New York: Harper, 1956.
5,6   ——: *The Teacher and the Child.* New York: McGraw-Hill, 1956.
      Mowrer, O. H.: *Learning Theory and Personality Dynamics.* New York:
          Ronald, 1950.
      Mullahy, Patrick (ed.): *A Study of Interpersonal Relations.* New York:
          Hermitage, 1949.
6   ——: *Oedipus, Myth and Complex.* New York: Grove Press, 1955.
6   Munroe, Ruth L.: *Schools of Psychoanalytic Thought.* New York: Dryden,
          1955.
      Murchison, C. (ed.): *Handbook of Child Psychology,* 2nd ed. Worcester,
          Mass.: Clark University Press, 1933.
      Murphy, Gardner: *Personality.* New York: Harper, 1947.
      Murphy, L. B.: *Social Behavior and Child Personality: An Exploratory Study
          of Some Roots of Sympathy.* New York: Columbia University Press, 1937.
5,6   Murray, H. A., et al.: *Explorations in Personality.* New York: Oxford Univer-
          sity Press, 1938.
      Mussen, P. H., and J. J. Conger: *Child Development and Personality.* New
          York: Harper, 1956.
      Newcomb, T. M.: *Social Psychology.* New York: Dryden, 1950.
1,5   Newman, H. H., F. N. Freeman, and K. J. Holzinger: *Twins: A Study of
          Heredity and Environment.* Chicago: University of Chicago Press, 1937.
      Olson, Willard C.: *Child Development.* Boston: D. C. Heath, 1949.
2,5   Orlansky, H.: "Infant Care and Personality," *Psychol. Bull.,* 46:1–48, 1949.
5   Osborn, A. F.: *Applied Imagination: Principles and Procedures of Creative
          Thinking.* New York: Charles Scribners, 1953.
5   Piaget, Jean: *Judgment and Reasoning in the Child.* New York: Harcourt,
          Brace, 1928.
5   ——: *The Child's Conception of Physical Causality.* New York: Harcourt,
          Brace, 1930.
5   ——: *The Child's Conception of the World.* New York: Harcourt, Brace,
          1929.
5   ——: *The Construction of Reality in the Child.* New York: Basic Books,
          1954.
5   ——: *The Language and Thought of the Child.* New York: Harcourt, Brace,
          1926.
5   ——: *The Moral Judgment of the Child.* Glencoe, Ill.: The Free Press, 1948.
3,5   Plant, J.: *Personality and the Cultural Pattern.* New York: Commonwealth
          Fund, 1937.
4,6   Powdermaker, Florence B., and J. D. Frank: *Group Psychotherapy.* New York:
          Commonwealth Fund, 1953.
5   Rapaport, Anatol: *Operational Philosophy.* New York: Harper, 1953.
4   Redl, F.: "Preadolescents—What Makes Them Tick," *Child Study,* 21:2, 1943.
      ——: *Understanding Children's Behavior.* New York: Teachers College,
          Columbia University, 1949.
      —— and W. W. Wattenberg: *Mental Hygiene in Teaching.* New York: Har-
          court, Brace, 1951.
      Remmers, H. H., and N. L. Gage: *Educational Measurement and Evaluation,*
          rev. ed. New York: Harper, 1955.
6   Reymert, M. L. (ed.): *Feelings and Emotions.* New York: McGraw-Hill,
          1950.

BIBLIOGRAPHY

2,6 Ribble, Margaretha A.: *The Rights of Infants.* New York: Columbia University Press, 1943.

3,5 Riesman, David: *The Lonely Crowd.* New Haven: Yale University Press, 1950.

6 Rogers, C. R.: *Client-centered Therapy.* Boston: Houghton Mifflin, 1951.

6 ——— and Rosalind F. Dymond (eds.): *Psychotherapy and Personality Change.* Chicago: University of Chicago Press, 1954.

5,6 Roethlisberger, F. J.: *Management and Morale.* Cambridge, Mass.: Harvard University Press, 1941.

1,5 Russell, E. S.: *The Directiveness of Organic Activity.* New York: Cambridge University Press, 1946.

1 Scheinfeld, A.: *The New You and Heredity.* Philadelphia: J. B. Lippincott, 1950.

Schroedinger, E.: *What Is Life?* New York: Cambridge University Press, 1951.

Schuessler, K., and A. Strauss: "Socialization, Logical Reasoning, and Concept Development in Children," *Am. Sociolog. Rev.,* **16**:514–523, 1951.

6 Sears, R. R., J. W. M. Whiting, V. Nowlis, and Pauline S. Sears: "Some Child-rearing Antecedents of Aggression and Dependency in Young Children," *Genet. Psych. Monogr.,* **47**:135–236, 1953.

6 Selye, H.: *The Physiology and Pathology of Exposure to Stress.* Montreal: Acta, 1950.

6 Shaffer, L. F., and E. J. Shoben, Jr.: *The Psychology of Adjustment.* Boston: Houghton Mifflin, 1956.

3,6 Shaw, F. J., and R. S. Ort: *Personal Adjustment in the American Culture.* New York: Harper, 1953.

5 Sherif, M., and H. Cantril: *The Psychology of Ego-involvements.* New York: John Wiley, 1947.

3,4 ——— and C. W. Sherif: *Groups in Harmony and Tension.* New York: Harper, 1953.

6 Sheviakov, G., and F. Redl: *Discipline for Today's Children and Youth,* rev. ed. Washington: National Education Association, 1944.

1 Shuttleworth, F. K.: "The Adolescent Period: A Graphic and Pictorial Atlas," *Monogr. Soc. Res. Child Develop.,* **3**:3. Washington: National Research Council, 1938.

1,5 ———: "The Physical and Mental Growth of Girls and Boys, Aged Six to Nineteen, in Relation to Age at Maximum Growth," *Monogr. Soc. Res. Child Develop.,* **4**, 3. Washington: National Research Council, 1939.

1,5 Sinnott, E. W.: *Cell and Psyche.* Chapel Hill, N.C.: University of North Carolina Press, 1950.

1,5 ———: *The Biology of the Spirit.* New York: Viking, 1955.

2,5 Skodak, Marie, and H. M. Skeels: "A Final Follow-up Study of One Hundred Adopted Children," *J. Genet. Psych.,* **75**:85–125, 1949.

2,5 ——— and ———: "A Follow-up Study of Children in Adoptive Homes," *J. Genet. Psych.,* **66**:21–58, 1945.

4,6 Slavson, S. R.: *Analytic Group Psychotherapy.* New York: Columbia University Press, 1950.

5 Snygg, D., and A. W. Combs: *Individual Behavior.* New York: Harper, 1949.

2,3 Sorokin, P. A.: *Altruistic Love.* Boston: Beacon, 1950.

2,6 Spitz, R. A.: "Hospitalism: A Follow-up Report," *Psychoanalytic Study of the Child,* **2**:113–117, New York: International Universities Press, 1946.

2.6 ———: "The Influence of Mother–Child Relationships and Its Disturbances."

in K. Soddy (ed.), *Mental Health and Infant Development*. New York: Basic Books, 1956.

2,6   Spitz, R. A.: "The Role of Ecological Factors in Emotional Development in Infancy," *Child Develop.*, **20**:145–162, 1949.

2,6   ————: "Unhappy and Fatal Outcomes of Emotional Deprivations and Stress in Infancy," in I. Goldston (ed.), *Beyond the Germ Theory*, Public Health Council, 1954.

1   Stackpole, Caroline E., and Lutie C. Leavell: *Textbook of Physiology*. New York: Macmillan, 1953.

       Stevens, S. S. (ed.): *Handbook of Experimental Psychology*. New York: John Wiley, 1951.

5   Stoddard, George D.: *The Meaning of Intelligence*. New York: Macmillan, 1943.

1   Stolz, H. R., and Lois M. Stolz: *Somatic Development of Adolescent Boys*. New York: Macmillan, 1951.

6   Stouffer, G. A., Jr.: "Behavior Problems of Children as Viewed by Teachers," *Mental Hygiene*, **36**:271–285, 1952.

       Strang, Ruth: *An Introduction to Child Study*, 3rd ed. New York: Macmillan, 1951.

5,6   Sullivan, H. S.: *The Interpersonal Theory of Psychiatry*. New York: W. W. Norton, 1953.

2,6   Suttie, I. D.: *The Origins of Love and Hate*. New York: Julian Press, 1943.

3,4   Swanson, G. E., et al. (eds.): *Readings in Social Psychology*, rev. ed. New York: Henry Holt, 1952.

6   Symonds, P. M.: *The Dynamics of Human Adjustment*. New York: Appleton-Century-Crofts, 1946.

2,6   ————: *Dynamics of Parent–Child Relationships*. New York: Columbia University Press, 1949.

4   Taba, H.: *With Perspective on Human Relations*. Washington: American Council on Education, 1955.

       Thompson, G. G.: *Child Psychology*. Boston: Houghton Mifflin, 1952.

       Tolman, E. C.: *Purposive Behavior in Animals and Men*. Berkeley: University of California Press, 1949.

3,4   Trager, H. G., and M. R. Yarrow: *They Learn What They Live*. New York: Harper, 1952.

4   Tryon, Caroline M.: "Evaluation of Adolescent Personality by Adolescents," *Monogr. Soc. Res. Child Develop.*, **4**, 4, Washington: National Research Council, 1939.

6   U.S. Department of Health, Education, and Welfare, Public Health Service: *Listing of Outpatient Psychiatric Clinics in the United States and Territories, 1954*. Washington: U.S. Government Printing Office, 1954.

       Vernon, P. E.: *The Structure of Human Abilities*. New York: John Wiley, 1950.

3   Warner, W. L.: *American Life*. Chicago: University of Chicago Press, 1953.

3   ————, R. J. Havighurst, and M. B. Loeb: *Who Shall Be Educated?* New York: Harper, 1941.

3   ———— and P. S. Lunt: *Social Life of a Modern Community*. New Haven: Yale University Press, 1941.

3   ————, Marcia Meeker, and K. Eells: *Social Class in America*. Chicago: Science Research Associates, 1949.

       Watson, E. H., and G. H. Lowrey: *Growth and Development of Children*. Chicago: Yearbook Publishers, 1951.

1   Wetzel, Norman C.: *The Treatment of Growth Failure in Children.* Cleveland: NEA Service, 1948.

1   Wheatley, G. M., and Grace T. Hallock: *Health Observations of School Children.* New York: McGraw-Hill, 1951.

5   White, R. W.: *Lives in Progress.* New York: Dryden, 1952.

6   ————: *The Abnormal Personality.* New York: Ronald, 1948.

3,5   Whiting, J. W. M., and I. L. Child: *Child Training and Personality.* New Haven: Yale University Press, 1953.

3   Whyte, W. F.: *Street-corner Society,* 2nd ed. Chicago: University of Chicago Press, 1955.

6   Wickman, E. K.: *Children's Behavior and Teachers' Attitudes.* New York: Commonwealth Fund, 1928.

    Witkin, H. A., et al.: *Personality through Perception: An Experimental and Clinical Study.* New York: Harper, 1954.

    Witmer, H., and R. Kotinsky: *Personality in the Making.* New York: Harper, 1952.

5   Witty, P. (ed.): "The Gifted Child," *American Association for Gifted Children.* Boston: D. C. Heath, 1951.

    Wolf, Katherine M.: *The Controversial Problem of Discipline.* New York: Child Study Association of America, 1953.

6   Young, Kimball: *Personality and Problems of Adjustment.* New York: Appleton-Century-Crofts, 1940.

6   Young, P. T.: *Emotion in Man and Animal.* New York: John Wiley, 1943.

    Zubek, John P., and P. A. Solberg: *Human Development.* New York: McGraw-Hill, 1954.

Index